TEXTS FROM EXCAVATIONS

EDITED BY T. G. H. JAMES

SEVENTH MEMOIR

SAQQÂRA DEMOTIC PAPYRI

I

(P. DEM. SAQ. I)

BY

H. S. SMITH AND W. J. TAIT

EGYPT EXPLORATION SOCIETY

3 DOUGHTY MEWS, LONDON WC1N 2PG

1983

LONDON

SOLD AT

THE OFFICES OF THE EGYPT EXPLORATION SOCIETY

3 Doughty Mews, London WC1N 2PG

British Library Cataloguing in Publication Data

Saqqâra demotic papyri.—(Texts from Excavations
ISSN 0307–5125; 7th Memoir)
Vol. 1
1. Egyptian language—Papyri, Demotic
I. Smith, H. S. II. Tait, W. J.
III. Series
893'.01 PJ1801
ISBN 0–85698–084–6

Printed in Great Britain
at the University Press, Oxford

SAQQÂRA DEMOTIC PAPYRI
I

EXCAVATIONS AT NORTH SAQQÂRA

DIRECTED BY W. B. EMERY

DOCUMENTARY SERIES

UNDER THE GENERAL DIRECTION OF H. S. SMITH

5. H. S. Smith and W. J. Tait, *Saqqâra Demotic Papyri* I

NOTE. The excavations of the Egypt Exploration Society in the Sacred Animal Necropolis at North Saqqâra, initiated by the late Professor W. B. Emery in 1964, yielded a great many documents written in different scripts and languages. The various groups of documents, prepared for publication by many scholars, will appear in the order in which they are made ready in the series Texts from Excavations. Reports on the excavations and catalogues of special categories of objects, which will include discussions of the inscribed material in its archaeological context, will be published in the Excavation Memoirs of the Egypt Exploration Society.

CONTENTS

LIST OF PLATES *page* vii
LIST OF TEXT FIGURES vii
INTRODUCTION ix
NOTE ON PAPYRUS DESCRIPTION AND NUMBERING xi
NOTE ON TRANSLITERATION xii
ABBREVIATIONS AND SYMBOLS xiii

THE DEMOTIC TEXTS

1. Djedseshep, Nanoufesakhme, and Ḥarmakhroou 1
1a. Djedseshep, Nanoufesakhme, and Ḥarmakhroou 65
2. *Front*: The vengeance of Isis 70
Back: Merib, the High Steward, and the captive Pharaoh 109
3. Tjimoou and the Lord of the East 143
4. The Cat and Falcon of Wax 149
5. A narrative of evil-doing 154
6. A text including appeals to gods 160
7. A narrative mentioning Ḥat-Boinu 163
8. A narrative mentioning Ashsury and Darius 166
9. A narrative concerning Ḥarudj 168
10. A narrative mentioning a meeting 170
11. A narrative mentioning Pharaoh 172
12. A narrative mentioning Petiese 174
13–21. Fragmentary texts in hands bearing similarities to those of Texts **1** and **2** 176
22. A narrative mentioning Djeḥo, son of Nekhtanebof (?) 188
23. A narrative mentioning a journey 190
24. A narrative mentioning the great men of Pharaoh 192
25. A narrative including an oath before Pharaoh 194
26. A narrative mentioning Khaʿḥape 196
27. Copybook, including names of birds, trees, and places 198

THE INDEXES

A. Demotic words 214
B. Demotic titles and epithets 221
C. Demotic personal names 222
D. Demotic divine names 222
E. Demotic place names 222
F. Coptic words quoted 223

CONCORDANCES OF NUMBERS 225

PLATES *at end*

LIST OF PLATES

1. Text **1**, front: fr. 3 (cols. 9–10)
2. Text **1**, back: fr. 3 (cols. 13–14)
3. Text **1**, fr. 1–2, 4–5; Text **1a**
4. Text **2**, front
5. Text **2**, front: details
6. Text **2**, back
7. Text **2**, back: details
8. Text **2**, back: detail
9. Text **2**, back: detail
10. Text **3**
11. Texts **4, 5**
12. Texts **6, 7, 8**
13. Texts **9, 10**
14. Texts **11, 12**
15. Texts **13–21, 22, 23**
16. Texts **24, 25, 26**
17. Text **27**

LIST OF TEXT FIGURES

1. Reconstruction of roll bearing Text **1** — *page* 2
2. Diagram of hypothetical conflation of Texts **1** and **2** on a single roll (rejected on pp. 62–4) — 63
3. Text **27**: a. hypothetical reconstruction of roll bearing original documentary text; — 198
   b. diagram showing relation of extant fragments to roll — 198

INTRODUCTION

In 1966–7 the late Professor W. B. Emery, while directing excavations for the Egypt Exploration Society in the Sacred Animal Necropolis at North Saqqâra, uncovered a large find of torn and crumpled papyrus fragments.[1] They were scattered in a layer of organic debris at the west end of the courtyard north of the Main Temple Enclosure in which was situated the entrance to the Catacomb of the Mothers of Apis.[2] The debris included fragments of ropes, baskets, sandals, matting, and linen as well as papyrus, and had been dumped into the northern courtyard, most probably from the temple terrace. The stratification demonstrated that the papyri must have been dumped after the destruction of the temples, which is likely to have taken place later than 41 BC, the date of the last recorded burial in the Mother of Apis Catacomb.[3] Any closer dating is speculative, though it seems possible that the dumping was contemporary with that of similar organic material to the south of the temple terrace, which cannot have taken place earlier than the fourth century AD, perhaps during clearance of the temple site for Christian occupation.[4] The basic conservation work to prepare the papyri for study was carried out in 1966–7 and 1967–8, mainly by Dr G. T. Martin, and they were photographed by Mrs H. F. Smith. Responsibility for registration and publication of the papyri was assigned to Mr H. S. Smith. Initially, 82 Aramaic, 5 Greek, 4 hieratic Egyptian, and 485 demotic Egyptian fragments were registered. In the years 1968–70 further papyrus fragments were found in unstratified contexts in the Main Temple Enclosure and the adjacent areas (1 Aramaic, 4 Greek, 2 hieratic, and 18 demotic).[5]

At this stage the Society was fortunate to obtain the co-operation of Professor J. B. Segal for the Aramaic papyri, Professor E. G. Turner for the Greek papyri, and Mr J. D. Ray and Mr G. R. Biggs for the demotic documents. After Professor Emery's sudden death in Cairo in March 1971, the Society appointed Professor Smith as over-all director and Dr Martin as site director of the Sacred Animal Necropolis work. The valuable help of Professor R. H. Pierce of the University of Bergen and of Dr W. J. Tait of Christ's College, Cambridge, was enlisted for work on the demotic papyri. During three study seasons from 1971 to 1974 Dr Tait undertook conservation work on further fragmentary papyri (98 Aramaic, 2 Greek, 7 hieratic, and 23 demotic), and established many joins between fragments. The whole series were safely stored between sheets of glass, and many of them were rephotographed. Meanwhile, Dr Martin discovered further large deposits of papyri in his excavations of the Southern Dependencies of the Main Temple Enclosure in 1971–2 (13 Aramaic, 14 Greek, 4 hieratic, and 170 demotic) and in 1972–3 (9 Aramaic, 7 Greek, and 57 demotic). They were found in the South and West Dumps and in surface debris, and had been dumped, as was clear from their situations, at some time after the destruction of the temples.[6] These were conserved by Dr Martin and Dr Tait, photographed by Mrs Smith and Mr van Veen, and placed between sheets of glass. A preliminary transcription of the whole series of papyri had been made by 1974. While all the scholars named contributed to this work, the Society

[1] *JEA* 53 (1967), 141–5; *JEA* 54 (1968), 1–2.

[2] *JEA* 57 (1971), 9–13, with pls. xi–xiv.

[3] *JEA* 56 (1970), 1–2; *JEA* 57 (1971), 11–12; *RdE* 24 (1972), 176 ff.

[4] *JEA* 63 (1977), 24.

[5] *JEA* 56 (1970), 11.

[6] *JEA* 59 (1973), 5–15; *JEA* 60 (1974), 16–18; see G. T. Martin, *The Sacred Animal Necropolis at Saqqâra: The Southern Dependencies* (EES, London, 1981), 57 ff., 101.

acknowledges with deep gratitude the leading role taken by Professor Pierce in the transcription of the demotic papyri. A scheme for publication was then drawn up.[1]

The demotic papyri form the most numerous and varied group among the Saqqâra papyri, and many of the documents are so fragmentary as to defy easy classification.[2] They are therefore to be published in a series of numbered volumes of convenient size under single or joint editorship on the lines of the Society's *Oxyrhynchus Papyri*. The volumes may contain texts of varied character or, as in this volume, concentrate upon a special category. The papyri here edited are principally of literary or didactic content, though some narratives which might belong to either a literary or a documentary genre are included. The editors have concentrated upon elucidating the text itself; the documents are so fragmentary and difficult that the discussion of historical and literary considerations is best omitted from an *editio princeps*. A standard form of presentation has been adopted. In the preparation of this volume, the editors have worked together throughout and accept joint responsibility for the final form and content of the publication. The work was in its final typescript when a discussion was held by demotists at the Second International Congress of Egyptologists at Grenoble in September 1979 upon the transliteration to be used in future for demotic. The system here used differs from that agreed in some respects, mostly minor;[3] the editors felt it unwise to make changes in advance of the publication of the Grenoble agreement. The terminology used in the physical description of the papyri is discussed below.[4]

The texts may be left to speak for themselves, but two comments may be appropriate here. First, they are probably among the earliest manuscripts of demotic literary texts preserved to us. For, although their final dumping was late, internal evidence suggests that the papyri had originally been deposited at a much earlier date. The latest regnally dated document from among those found in the northern courtyard belongs to the reign of either Alexander the Great or his son Alexander IV; among those found in the southern dependencies, one document is dated to an unknown Ptolemy, but otherwise the latest is dated to one or other of the Alexanders. Moreover, a large proportion of the regnally dated documents belong to the fourth century BC, a few to the fifth. It therefore seems probable that they were originally deposited in the third century BC, quite possibly at the beginning of the Ptolemaic reconstruction of the Sacred Animal Necropolis site,[5] and re-dumped where they were found much later.[6] They seem likely, then, even without recourse to speculative palaeographical arguments, to antedate by two centuries or more such great literary manuscripts as Khaʿemwese I, Insinger, ʿOnchsheshonqy, and the main body of the texts of the Petubastis/Inaros cycle. Secondly, the manuscripts demonstrate once more the value of fragmentary

[1] *JEA* 60 (1974), 256–8, subsequently modified owing to the retirement from the scheme of Professor Pierce. See J. D. Ray, *The Archive of Ḥor* (EES, London, 1976); J. B. Segal, *Aramaic Texts from North Saqqâra* (EES, London, 1983). Further volumes by Turner, Smith, Tait, Ray, and Biggs are in active preparation.

[2] Brief accounts of the contents of the papyri are contained in 'The Saqqara Papyri' in *Proceedings of the XIV International Congress of Papyrologists*, Oxford, 24–31 July 1974 (Graeco-Roman memoirs 61, London, EES, 1975), 247–67, and in H. S. Smith, *A Visit to Ancient Egypt; Life at Memphis and Saqqara (c.500–30 B.C.)* (Aris & Phillips, Warminster, 1974), 13–20, 59–61.

[3] See p. xii.

[4] See p. xi.

[5] The building history of the temples will be fully discussed in *The Sacred Animal Necropolis at Saqqâra; the Main Temple Enclosure and the Catacombs*, by †W. B. Emery, H. S. Smith, and K. J. Frazer. Relevant comment has appeared in G. T. Martin, *The Tomb of Ḥetepka* (EES, London, 1979), 125–7; in G. T. Martin, *The Sacred Animal Necropolis at Saqqâra; The Southern Dependencies*, 119 ff., and in H. S. Smith, A Visit to Ancient Egypt, 21 ff.

[6] Possibly in Christian times, see above p. ix. A considerable proportion of the whole papyrus material yields internal evidence of having been of Memphite origin. If the papyri were in part brought from Memphis, whether for safety or perhaps more probably as scrap paper, this may account for the relative sparsity of joins between fragments, and their subsequent re-dumping will no doubt have contributed to the tattered state in which they were found.

material which, however frustrating to work with, can illustrate the existence of works or even whole genres not at present attested in the corpus of demotic literature.

It is a great pleasure to the editors to acknowledge the help given to them by their collaborators, more especially Professor Pierce, Mr Ray, and Professor Turner, and by other colleagues, whose aid with matters of detail is acknowledged in the appropriate places. To the late Professor Emery and his many collaborators, British and Egyptian, the discovery of these priceless documents was due; among them special mention must be made of Dr ʿAly el-Khouli for his care and frequent aid in administrative matters. Dr Tait gratefully acknowledges his indebtedness to the Master and Fellows of Christ's College, Cambridge, for subventions from the Lady Wallis Budge Fund and for leave of absence to allow him to pursue these studies in Egypt, and Professor Smith likewise thanks successive Provosts of University College London for their continuing liberality over leave of absence. To Mr E. Hitchcock and his staff at the Central Photographic Service at University College London we owe the skilled printing of the photographs reproduced in this volume. Our deepest debt is to Mrs Hazel Smith who, without previous experience, laboured over eight seasons under unfavourable field conditions to produce an adequate photographic record of these stained and worm-eaten papyri, without which these documents could neither have been edited nor published. For this and for her constant and successful efforts to provide a comfortable camp at Saqqâra, both editors express their warmest gratitude. To the Society's officers and especially to its *quondam* secretary, Miss Mary Crawford, our sincere thanks are due. Finally, it is to Mr T. G. H. James, the Society's editor, and to the Oxford University Press, that we are indebted for their unfailing courtesy, patient help, and unrivalled skill in making this book.

H. S. SMITH
W. J. TAIT

March 1980

Note on papyrus description and numbering

Recent studies[1] have emphasized the difficulty of applying the traditional terminology of 'recto' and 'verso' correctly to papyri that were originally rolled, especially where documents are so fragmentary that no joins between sheets of papyrus are preserved. As this is true of the majority of the documents published in this volume, we have preferred to use the terms 'front' and 'back' in order not further to confound the issue.

The texts in this volume are numbered consecutively from **1** to **27**. The number **1a** has been used for a papyrus fragment which appears to contain part of the same story as **1**, but is nevertheless part of a different roll in a different hand. Bold figures are used for these numbers, normal figures for column numbers, and figures following the oblique are line numbers. Each text has, in addition, two other numbers, both of which are given in the preliminary descriptions of the pieces. The first is the excavator's number. Those papyri found by Emery between 1964 and 1970 are numbered by the grid square of the excavation in which they were found, followed by the symbol DP (demotic papyrus), followed by a running number (e.g. H5-DP377). Those papyri found by Martin in 1971–3 are numbered by the season in which they were found, followed by DP and a running number (e.g. 71/72-DP79+84, an instance where two fragments have been joined after registration). The second number, given in square brackets after the excavator's number, is that

[1] See E. G. Turner, 'The terms recto and verso: the anatomy of the papyrus roll', in *Actes du XVe Congrès international de papyrologie, 1e partie* (Bruxelles, 1978), (Papyrologica Bruxellensia, 16); W. J. Tait, 'The use of the terms recto and verso', forthcoming.

assigned to the object in the register kept for the Egyptian Antiquities Service; these numbers run consecutively throughout the whole history of the excavation, and include all classes of material found.[1] A concordance of numbers is given on p. 225 below.

Note on Transliteration

The system of transliteration for demotic followed in this volume is historical, and broadly follows the practice of W. Erichsen's *Demotisches Glossar*.[2] Certain minor matters, however, require comment.

a. A double bar is used to separate suffix pronouns (e.g. *sdm=f*): a single bar is used to separate the true object pronoun (e.g. *ḥn=f-s*): a dot is used to separate the pronominal ending *.ṯ*, the feminine singular termination *.t*, the feminine plural termination *.wt*, and the masculine plural termination *.w*. However, this dot is used only where these terminations are written after the determinative. Where they are not so written, they are either omitted as in the script (e.g. *rpy* 'Lady'), or compounded in the writing of the word where a ligature is in question (e.g. *mdt* 'word'). Occasionally for grammatical clarity (*.t*) and (*.w*) are used where the terminations are not written.

b. The symbol *ḫ̭* is used to distinguished demotic  from *ḫ*, demotic .

c. Demotic does not clearly distinguish *t* from *d*: Erichsen used the former everywhere. In those words where there is no clear indication that the demotic scribe intended *t*, we have used the consonant which normally appears in Late Egyptian transliterations (e.g. *drt* 'hand'), even where in classical Egyptian the sound had another origin (e.g. *sdm* 'hear' for ME *sḏm*, LE *sdm*, Coptic ⲥⲱⲧⲙ).

d. Erichsen's use of *j* for non-initial *ỉ* has not been followed. *ỉ* has been used for initial  and , and occasionally in medial and final positions where there seemed an advantage in clarity in doing so (e.g. *sỉ* 'satisfy'). *y* always and only renders demotic , whether initial, medial, or final. *ꜣ* is used to represent both  and ; the symbol ʾ is not used. The group  is transliterated *ỉw* where it clearly derives from LE , but *ỉ* where it derives from LE  (e.g. in the 'Emphatic' auxiliary *ỉ-ỉr*). The symbol *e* is not used.

e. For the division of compounds, we have used the hyphen everywhere.

f. Abbreviated writings of certain words (e.g. (*hrw*), (*pꜣỉ=f*)) are placed between round brackets to distinguish them from fuller writings of the same words.

g. Otherwise, our general practice is to use round brackets to indicate elements which should be present but have been omitted by the scribe (e.g. (*n-*)*drt.ṯ=f* 'in his hand'); full square brackets [. . .] to indicate *lacunae* in the text, together with our restorations where applicable; half square brackets ⌜. . .⌝ to indicate doubtful readings and damaged signs; braces { } to indicate superfluous elements in the text; and the symbol \` ′ to indicate words subsequently inserted above the line by the scribe.

[1] The system is the same as that used in Ray, *Archive of Ḥor* (see p. xv); in G. T. Martin, *The Tomb of Ḥetepka* (p. viii); in G. T. Martin, *The Sacred Animal Necropolis* (pp. 2–3); and in J. B. Segal, *Aramaic Texts from North Saqqâra* (p. xix).

[2] The system used by J. D. Ray in an earlier volume of this series, *The Archive of Ḥor*, is in principle the same, though differing in some details.

ABBREVIATIONS AND SYMBOLS

1. BOOKS AND TEXT PUBLICATIONS

Ägypter und Amazonen	A. Volten, *Ägypter und Amazonen: eine demotische Erzählung des Inaros-Petubastis-Kreises aus zwei Papyri der Österreichischen Nationalbibliothek, Pap. Dem. Vindob. 6165 und 6165A.* (Mitteilungen aus der Papyrussammlung der Österreichischen Nationalbibliothek, Papyrus Erzherzog Rainer, Neue Ser., 6.) Wien, 1962
Canopus	W. Spiegelberg, *Der demotische Text der Priesterdekrete von Kanopus und Memphis, Rosettana, mit den hieroglyphischen und griechischen Fassungen und deutscher Uebersetzung nebst demotischem Glossar.* Heidelberg, 1922
Černý, *CED*	J. Černý, *Coptic etymological dictionary.* Cambridge, 1976
Coffin Texts	A. de Buck, *The Egyptian Coffin texts.* 7 vols. (The University of Chicago, Oriental Institute publications, 34, 49, 64, 67, 73, 81, 87.) Chicago, 1935–61
Copt. Ryl.	W. E. Crum, *Catalogue of the Coptic manuscripts in the collection of the John Rylands Library, Manchester.* Manchester, 1909
Crum, *CD*	W. E. Crum, *A Coptic dictionary.* Oxford, 1939
DG	W. Erichsen, *Demotisches Glossar.* Kopenhagen, 1954
Demotic Chronicle (Orakel)	W. Spiegelberg, *Die sogenannte Demotische Chronik des Pap. 215 der Bibliothèque Nationale zu Paris, nebst den auf der Rückseite des Papyrus stehenden Texten.* (Demotische Studien, 7.) Leipzig, 1914
Erman, *Näg. Gr.*	A. Erman, *Neuaegyptische Grammatik.* 2., völlig umgestaltete Aufl. Leipzig, 1933
Gardiner, *Egyptian Grammar*	A. H. Gardiner, *Egyptian grammar, being an introduction to the study of hieroglyphs.* 3rd edn., rev. Oxford, 1957
Gardiner, *Onomastica*	A. H. Gardiner, *Ancient Egyptian Onomastica.* 3 vols. Oxford, 1947
Gauthier, *DNG*	W. Gauthier, *Dictionnaire des noms géographiques.* 7 vols. Le Caire, 1925–31
Insinger	F. Lexa, *Papyrus Insinger: les enseignements moraux d'un scribe égyptien du premier siècle après J.-C.* 2 vols. Paris, 1926 A. Volten, *Das demotische Weisheitsbuch: Studien und Bearbeitung.* (Analecta aegyptiaca, 2.) Kopenhagen, 1941. *Also issued outside the series*
1. Kh., 2. Kh.	F. Ll. Griffith, *Stories of the High Priests of Memphis: the Sethon of Herodotus and the demotic tales of Khamuas.* 2 vols. Oxford, 1900. *Vol. 2 is plates*
Krugt.	W. Spiegelberg, *Demotische Texte auf Krügen.* 2 vols. (Demotische Studien, 5.) Leipzig, 1912. *Vol. 2 is plates*
Mag. (Pap. Mag.)	F. Ll. Griffith and H. Thompson, *The demotic magical papyrus of London and Leiden.* 3 vols. London, 1904–9. *Also issued Oxford, 1921. Vol. 3 is plates*
Montet, *Géographie*	P. Montet, *Géographie de l'Égypte ancienne.* 2 vols. Paris, 1957–61
Mythus	W. Spiegelberg, *Der ägyptische Mythus vom Sonnenauge, der Papyrus der Tierfabeln — 'Kufi', nach dem Leidener demotischen Papyrus I 384.* Strassburg, 1917
ʿOnchsheshonqy	S. R. K. Glanville, *The instructions of ʿOnchsheshonqy, British Museum papyrus 10508.* 2 vols. (Catalogue of demotic papyri in the British Museum, 2.) London, 1955. *Vol. 2 is plates*

P. Berlin	W. Spiegelberg, *Demotische Papyrus aus den Königlichen Museen zu Berlin.* Leipzig und Berlin, 1902
P. Cairo	W. Spiegelberg, *Die demotischen Papyrus.* 2 vols. (Catalogue géneral des antiquités égyptiennes du Musée du Caire, 30601–31270, 50001–50022: die demotischen Denkmäler, [1.]) Strassburg, 1906–8. *Vol. 2 is plates* W. Spiegelberg, *Demotische Inschriften und Papyri, Fortsetzung.* (Catalogue géneral des antiquités égyptiennes du Musée du Caire, 50023–50165: die demotischen Denkmäler, 3.) Berlin, 1932
P. Carlsberg 7	E. Iversen, *Papyrus Carlsberg nr. VII: fragments of a hieroglyphic dictionary.* (Historisk-filologiske skrifter udgivet af Det Kongelige Danske Videnskabernes Selskab, 3, ii.) København, 1958
P. Carlsberg 12	A. Volten, 'An "alphabetical" dictionary and grammar in demotic, Pap. Carlsberg XII verso', *Archiv orientální,* 20 (1952), pp. 496–508
P. Ebers	W. Wreszinski, *Der Papyrus Ebers: Umschrift, Übersetzung und Kommentar. 1. Teil: Umschrift.* (Die Medizin der alten Ägypter, 3.) Leipzig, 1913. *No more published* H. Grapow, *Die medizinischen Texte in hieroglyphischer Umschreibung autographiert.* (Grundriß der Medizin der alten Ägypter, 5.) Berlin, 1958
P. Krall	see Petub.
P. Lond.–Leiden	see *Mag.*
P. Spiegelberg	see Petub.
P. Tebt. Tait	W. J. Tait, *Papyri from Tebtunis in Egyptian and in Greek, P. Tebt. Tait.* (Texts from excavations, 3.) London, 1977
P. Vindob. D. 6257	E. A. E. Reymond, *A medical book from Crocodilopolis, P. Vindob. D. 6257.* (From the contents of the libraries of the Suchos temples in the Fayyum, 1.) (Mitteilungen aus der Papyrussammlung der Österreichischen Nationalbibliothek, Papyrus Erzherzog Rainer, Neue Ser., 10.) Wien, 1976
P. Westcar	A. Erman, *Die Märchen des Papyrus Westcar.* 2 vols. Berlin, 1890
Petub. (Petubastis)	W. Spiegelberg, *Der Sagenkreis des Königs Petubastis nach dem Strassburger demotischen Papyrus sowie den Wiener und Pariser Bruchstücken.* (Demotische Studien, 3.) Leipzig, 1910
Ranke, *PN*	H. Ranke, *Die ägyptischen Personennamen.* 3 vols. Glückstadt, 1935–77
Ray, *Archive of Ḥor*	J. D. Ray, *The Archive of Ḥor.* (Texts from excavations, 2.) London, 1976
Ryl.	F. Ll. Griffith, *Catalogue of the demotic papyri in the John Rylands Library, Manchester.* 3 vols. Manchester, 1909. *Vol. 1 is plates*
Siut	H. Thompson, *A family archive from Siut from papyri in the British Museum, including an account of a trial before the Laocritae in the year* B.C. *170.* 2 vols. Oxford, 1934. *Vol. 2 is plates*
Spiegelberg, *Dem. Gram.*	W. Spiegelberg, *Demotische Grammatik.* Heidelberg, 1925
Totb.	F. Lexa, *Das demotische Totenbuch der Pariser Nationalbibliothek, Papyrus des Pamonthes.* (Demotische Studien, 4.) Leipzig, 1910
Urk. IV	K. Sethe ([and] W. Helck), *Urkunden der 18. Dynastie.* 22 pts. (Urkunden des ägyptischen Altertums, 4.) Leipzig, 1906–58. *From pt. 18 published Berlin*
Wb.	A. Erman und H. Grapow, *Wörterbuch der aegyptischen Sprache.* 7 vols. in 12. Leipzig, 1926–63. *Vols. 6–7 published Berlin*
Wb. Drog.	H. von Deines und H. Grapow, *Wörterbuch der ägyptischen Drogennamen.* (Grundriß der Medizin der alten Ägypter, 6.) Berlin, 1959
Westendorf, *KH*	W. Westendorf, *Koptisches Handwörterbuch.* Heidelberg, 1965–77

2. PERIODICALS

Ac. Or.	*Acta orientalia.* Lugduni Batavorum [Leiden]. 1923– . *From vol. 21 (1951–3) published Hauniae [Copenhagen]*
BIFAO	*Bulletin de l'Institut français d'archéologie orientale au Caire.* Le Caire. 1901–
BSOAS	*Bulletin of the School of Oriental and African Studies, University of London.* London. 1917– . *Title of vols. 1–8 varies*
JEA	*The Journal of Egyptian Archaeology.* London. 1914–
JNES	*Journal of Near Eastern Studies.* Chicago. 1942–
RdE	*Revue d'égyptologie.* Paris. 1933–
Rec. Trav.	*Recueil de travaux relatifs à la philologie et à l'archéologie égyptiennes et assyriennes.* Paris. 1870–1923
ZÄS	*Zeitschrift für ägyptische Sprache und Altertumskunde.* Leipzig. 1863– . *From vol. 79 (1954) published Berlin*

3. OTHER ABBREVIATIONS

adj.	adjective
advb.	adverb
art.	article
col.	column
conj.	conjunction
def.	definite
det.	determinative
fem.	feminine
fr., frag.	fragment
h.	height
imp.	imperative
indef.	indefinite
masc.	masculine
n.	note
N.	unnamed person
neg.	negative
para.	paragraph
pers.	person
pl., plur.	plural
prep.	preposition
pres.	present
sing.	singular
subst.	substantive
vb.	verb
w.	width

4. SYMBOLS

§	paragraph
↔	horizontal fibres
↕	vertical fibres
⤡	diagonal
[ ]	missing or restored
( )	not written in text: expansion of abbreviated writing
⌜ ⌝	of doubtful reading
{ }	written otiosely in text
ˋ ˊ	inserted above line in text

THE DEMOTIC TEXTS

1. DJEDSESHEP, NANOUFESAKHME, AND ḤARMAKHROOU

Plates 1–3

H5-DP1+2+2A [1598+1599+1600]

Sector 1 (North Courtyard) debris (1966–7)

Fr. 3, the major fragment, is made up of several pieces joined together, and measures over all 37.0 cm. *h.*×29.0 cm. *w.* It preserves parts of four columns, two on the front, and two on the back. A top margin of 2.0 cm. is preserved for all four columns. Very little of the bottom margin survives below col. 10 on the front and col. 13 on the back. Although it is not certain that the actual bottom edge of the roll is preserved below col. 9 on the front and col. 14 on the back, probably each column had a bottom margin of 4.0 cm., the depth now surviving. The margin between the columns naturally varies in width from line to line, but in each case it is as narrow as 1.0 cm. at the top, and as wide as 2.0 cm. at the bottom. The second (left-hand) column on the back is numbered in the bottom margin as the fourteenth: the numeral is set at the normal line-spacing below the last line of text, but 9.0 cm. in from the beginnings of the lines of the column. The first (right-hand) column on the back is thus certainly the thirteenth, although its numeral is lost. The original numbering of the two columns on the front (cols. 9 and 10) can be deduced, but only by taking the numerals preserved on fr. 2 into consideration (see p. 2).

Fr. 2 (H5-DP2A [1600]) measures 10.0 cm. *h.* ×7.5 cm. *w.* The two main pieces of papyrus of which it consists are still joined by a few fibres. Part of the last seven lines of a column, together with a portion of bottom margin, are preserved on both the front and the back. In each case the original numbering of the columns survives in the bottom margin: the column on the front is the seventh, while the numbering of that on the back, although partly damaged, can be read with confidence as the sixteenth. The nature of the hand, of the papyrus, and of the spacing of the lines of text, the presence of bottom margins of 4.0 cm., and the kind of column numeration, all make it probable that fr. 2 belongs to the same papyrus as fr. 3. However, one other very similar papyrus, **2** edited in this volume, was found in the 1966–7 season; but the contents provide two decisive reasons for assigning fr. 2 to **1** rather than to **2**—the name Ḥarmakhroou (col. 16 [=fr. 2, back], l. 4) is that of a character who occurs throughout cols. 13 and 14 of **1**; and the title *Stm* (col. 7 [= fr. 2, front], l. 3) occurs twice in **1**, col. 14, ll. 20–1[1] (although on both occasions in conjunction with the proper-name Ptaḥḥotpe, which does not appear on fr. 2). There is no such link with the contents of **2**.

Fr. 1 measures 3.0 cm. *h.*×1.5 cm. *w.* It consists of two pieces joined. Its general appearance and colour suggest that it belongs to **1**, and near to fr. 2, perhaps close to the top of the fragment. As it is very badly worn, there is no hope of suggesting a precise position for it. The text, both on front and back, is here transcribed before that of fr. 2.

Fr. 4 measures 4.0 cm. *h.*×6.0 cm. *w.*: fr. 5 measures 3.0 cm. *h.*×4.0 cm. *w.* These two fragments are very badly worn and frayed. They are strikingly similar in general appearance to the portion of fr. 3 that preserves part of 10/22–7 on the front, and part of 13/21–6 on the back. The two fragments are opaque, unlike the

[1] Hereinafter throughout the volume such references are quoted in the form **1**, 14/20–1.

rest of **1**, but it is quite possible that this is due to dirt that they have absorbed. No fibre-correspondence has been observed between them and fr. 3, although the papyrus is so badly rubbed that any correspondence may have been obscured. In any case, a sheet-join is to be expected at the extreme left-hand edge (as seen from the front) of fr. 3, so that frs. 4 and 5 may

The loose horizontal fibres at the extreme left-hand edge of fr. 3 may possibly indicate the original width of the left-hand sheet: at any rate they show that it was at least 13.5 cm. wide. The fibres confirm, as is to be expected from the column numbering, that fr. 2 is not part of the sheet of which a mere 1.0 cm. is preserved at the right-hand edge of fr. 3.

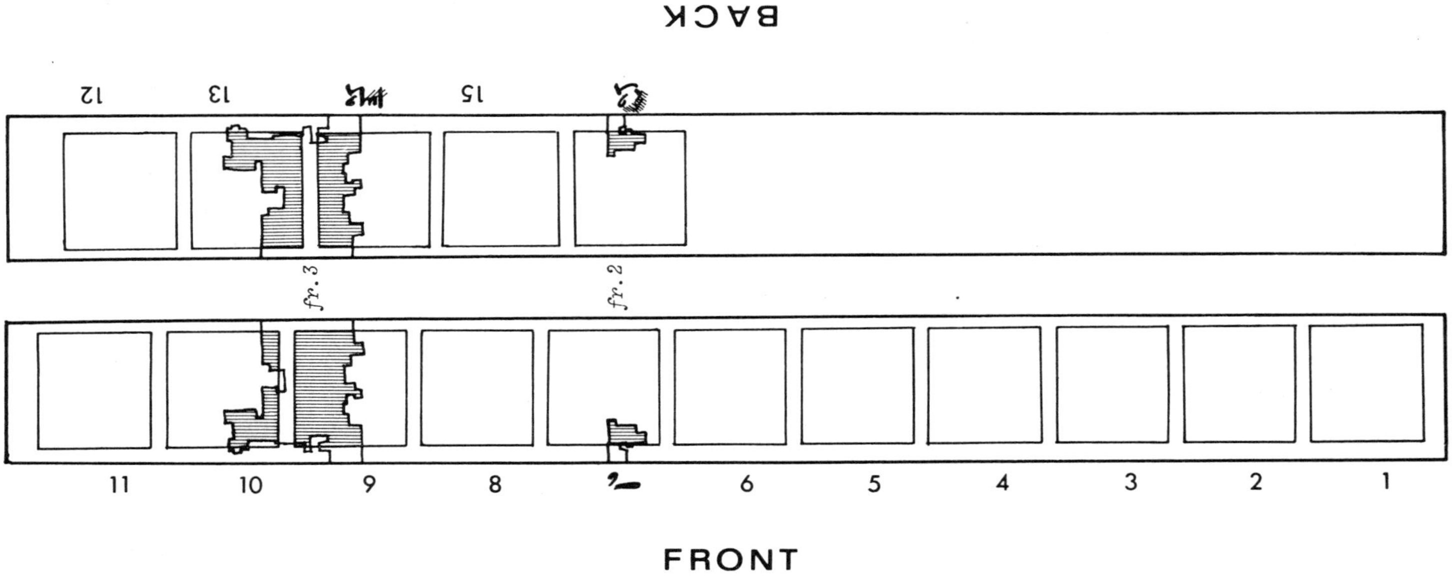

FIG. 1. Reconstruction of roll bearing Text 1. The column numerals that survive on the papyrus are shown as they appear on the papyrus.

well have belonged to a different sheet of papyrus. On balance, it is possible that both fragments are to be placed in the area (as seen from the front) to the left of 10/16–26, and (as seen from the back) to the right of 13/14–24. Such a position receives some support from the contents: see p. 25.

The papyrus is translucent, but not very fine-textured. Its thickness is uneven: this variation is more marked in the vertical strips. As is mentioned above, frs. 4 and 5 are opaque. Fr. 3 is of a light straw shade, and remarkably clean. The other fragments are more darkened, apparently by dirt. Two sheet-joins are preserved. As seen from the front, one is at the right-hand edge of fr. 3, and the other is 14.0–14.5 cm. to its left. They are 1.0–1.3 cm. wide.

At no point is the full width of a column preserved. The maximum line-length that certainly survives is one of 16.0 cm., in col. 9. The position of the column-number belonging to col. 14 is identical with that of the one surviving numeral in **2**. As the two papyri are very similar in all other respects, there is at least a strong possibility that the original column widths of **1** approximated to the 27.5 cm. displayed by **2**. The column-numbers preserved on both sides of fr. 2 and on the back of fr. 3 allow the deduction that the two columns preserved on the front of fr. 3 were the ninth and the tenth. This is best explained by the accompanying figure 1. It will be found that any attempt to disturb the arrangement suggested there leads to highly improbable fluctuations in column-width.

In two places a fresh line has been started, and a space larger than normal left between the lines, to mark the beginning of a new section of the text: 13/13–14 (1.0 cm.) and 14/14–15 (0.5 cm.).

At col. 14, l. 22, it can be seen quite clearly that a phrase was washed out as soon as it had been written, and the correct text was resumed in its place (see p. 33, n. *dr*). Some extensive and problematic traces of erased writing can be made out on the front of fr. 2 (col. 7; see p. 10, n. *e*). See also p. 21, nn. *dq*, *du*. At 14/3, the first sign of a word was omitted, and has been supplied above the line. The correction has every appearance of having been made by the original scribe, although this cannot be judged with certainty from the appearance of a single sign. (The word as first written is senseless, and the restoration is an obvious one.) In sum, the text resembles a number of other demotic literary papyri in showing signs of having been checked as it was written, but no trace of any subsequent revision.

The **hand** is rapidly and skilfully written with a fairly thick, soft brush, which allows considerable variation in the thickness of the strokes. The ⤢-strokes are generally thin, and are made more freely than strokes in other directions. Therefore, although the hand is upright, it is not at all rounded in appearance. The hand of **2** in this volume is very similar (see the discussion on p. 71 f.), and various small fragments in similar hands are included here as **13–21** (see the introduction to each fragment, pp. 176 ff.). A comparison between the hand of the present papyrus, **1**, and that of **1a** is made on p. 65 f. Some aspects of the orthography of **1** are mentioned on pp. 61, 71.

One feature of the orthography of this text requires separate discussion here. Throughout the papyrus, many examples can be seen of small dots (or occasionally very short strokes) of ink between the lines of the text. These are clearly different from the usual array of dots and strokes found in demotic texts, some of which are often referred to as 'space fillers', that are in fact an integral part of the writing: the present hand uses these as freely as any other, but they are more boldly drawn than the marks being discussed here, are much more consistently used, and serve more obvious purposes in the script. The small marks in the present text, although it is impossible in all cases to be sure to which line of text they belong, generally stand above the writing (a possible case of a dot of this kind below a sign is in *ḫꜣ* in 14/5: this might better be understood as a space-filler, although a dot is not usually found under a *ḫ*). Their commonest use is immediately before a simple vertical stroke. They do not seem to occur before initial vertical strokes (perhaps because they are initial, or possibly because they happen all to derive from 𓇋; e.g. *ỉnk*, *ỉw=y*, *ỉrp*, etc.—but see p. 28, n. *av*). There are many places without a dot that are apparently exactly parallel to others where a dot is to be found. No strict rules for the use or omission of the dots have yet been discovered, and probably none exists. It may be noted that all the instances of *wn*, 'pastophoros' in col. 9 (ll. 20, 26, 31, and 33) have a dot above the first sign, although this seems, no doubt without any particular significance, not to be the case with the instance of the plural in 10/25 (the example of the singular in 10/12 is damaged). Dots seem to occur or not to occur at random above the various plant determinatives in 9/34–5 and 10/20.

It cannot, of course, be assumed that every dot was made for exactly the same purpose, or even at the same time. Although their use is not consistent, they do seem to relate to the writing of individual words, rather than to the physical arrangement of the text, or to its division into phrases or sentences. They are thus most likely to have been made as the text was written, together with the signs they accompany—the more or less unconscious habit of an individual scribe. The only other serious possibility is that they were made by someone, perhaps the original scribe, checking the text for mistakes, pen in hand; however, their use in certain words and positions seems too consistent for this to be probable. It is undoubtedly difficult to make sense of them as marks made after the text was written, in counting the lines, or as punctuation. Nor could they all have been made beforehand, as guides for the spacing of the lines of the text. One of these explanations might, however, be correct for the three dots occurring close together in 14/33–5 (above *r-ḫr=w*, *rdwỉ.ṱ=f*, and *gm.ṱ=w*).

The same feature is occasionally visible in **2**, although, as far as can be judged in the damaged state of the papyrus, it is not as common as in **1**. One or two marks in **1a** may conceivably be of the same kind.

Transliteration

FRONT (↔) — Plate 3

Fr. 1 (col. 7?)

— — — — — —

x+1. - - -] . . . . . [- - -
x+2. - - -] . . . . . [- - -
x+3. - - -] *ỉr n-ỉm=s* . [- - -

— — — — — —

Fr. 2 (col. 7)

— — — — — — — — — — — —

x+1. - - -. . . . .] . [. .] . . . . [. . .] . .[a] [- - -
x+2. - - - . . . .] . . . .[b] *ỉw=y r dỉt ỉr=w-s n=k ỉw=f ḫpr* . .[c] [- - -
x+3. - - - . . . .] ⌜*ẖd*⌝*b r-ỉr=f ḏd Stm*[d] *m-ỉr* . .[e] [- - -
x+4. - - -]⌜*pꜣỉ(=y) sn*⌝[f] *ỉ-ỉr-ḥr=y r bn(-pw)=y ỉr ꜥwỉ-drt.ṱ=y*[g] *ỉrm=f* ⌜*ḏd*⌝ [- - -
x+5. - - -] *ꜥnḫ n* ⌜. . -*Rꜥ*⌝ *ꜥnḫ pꜣ-Rꜥ*[h] *mtw=f pꜣ ntỉ* ⌜*ỉw=f*⌝[j][- - -
x+6. - - - . . .] . .⌜*ḳdy*⌝ . .[k][. . . .] ⌜*m-sꜣ nꜣy*⌝.[l] [- - -
x+7. - - -. . . . .] ⌜*ntỉ ỉw*⌝ [. . . .]⌜*=f*⌝[. .] . ⌜*hy*⌝[m][- - -
x+8. vacat]*mḥ* 7[n] vac. [

Bottom margin (disregarding the column-number in l. 8) of 4.0 cm.

Fr. 3 — Plate 1

col. 9

top margin of 2.0 cm.

1. - - - . . . . .] ⌜*ḥms*⌝ *n=k dꜣỉ ỉrm=n*[a] *ỉ(w)=k ỉr rnpt* 100 *ỉ(w)=k ꜥnḫ.ṱ*[b] *bn-ỉw=n dỉt ỉr=k* . . . . .[c]
2. - - - . . . . .]⌜*r*⌝*y*[d] *r-ḥr=n bn-ỉw=y swr ḥnḳt ỉrp r-šw my dỉ=w n(=y) wꜥ ṯꜣỉ-ḥbs*[e] *ṯꜣỉ=tn nꜣ ḥbs.w n šs-nsw*
3. - - - . . . .] . . .*=f*[f] *ỉr=w ꜥwỉ.w-drt.ṱ=w ḏd mdt nbt ntỉ ỉw=w r-rḫ ỉr=w r tm dỉt šm=f r-bnr* ⌜*bn(-pw)*⌝*=f sdm*[g] *n=w*
4. - - - . . .] . . ⌜*tꜣ*⌝ *h̭m-ẖr(t) ḫpr=f ỉw=w ḏd*[h] *pꜣ hrw*[j] *n ḫpr r-ỉr mdt bỉn.t n pꜣ*[k] *rmt ꜥꜣ pꜣỉ*[l] *ḫpr=f ỉ-ỉr*
5. - - -] *ḏd*[m] *bn-ỉw=f ḫpr ỉn n-ḥꜣt.ṱ=f*[n] *ḫpr pꜣ nw n šm r pꜣ ꜥwỉ n nꜣ sdm(-ꜥš).w*[o] *m-dr Pr-ꜥꜣ*

6. - - - nꜣ] sꜣwtỉ.w nꜣ mr-mšꜥ.w[p] nꜣ rmt.w ꜥꜣ.w n Pr-ꜥꜣ dr=[w] ⸢ntỉ⸣ ḥn[q] ỉwꜣy[r] ꜥꜣ m-šs ḏd[s] bw-ỉr rḫ=n pꜣ ntỉ ḫpr

7. - - -] . . . .[t] tꜣ ḥ̭m-ẖr(t) pḥ=f r pꜣ ꜥ(wỉ) (n) mꜣy[u] ⸢m⸣šꜥ=f r wꜥt hyꜣ(t)[v] dỉ=f ḥḏ ḳdt 1 n tꜣ ḥmt

8. - - -] . .[w] ḫpr=f i-ỉr=s md ỉrm=f r ẖ(t)[x] pꜣỉ=s ḥrỉ dỉ=s ỉr=w n=f wꜥt rỉt ỉw=s ḥp.⸢ṱ⸣[y] n šbw[z]

9. - - - - . . tꜣ ḥ̭]m-ẖr(t) ḏḳm=s[aa] mtw=s tꜣ ntỉ n yꜥby[ab] ṱꜣỉ=s tꜣ ḥ̭m-ẖr(t) dỉ=s ḏḳm=s[ac]

10. - - - . . . . . .] . . .[ad] i-ỉr=f sdm[ae] pꜣ ḫrw n hyn.w rmt Wn-ḫm ỉw=w swr ḥnḳt ẖn

11. - - - . . . . . Ḏd(t)]-sšp[af] pꜣ ḥm-ntr n Ḥr-nb-Sḫm pꜣỉ ḫpr ḏꜣ[ag] n-ỉm=f mn mtw=f ⸢šr⸣ [n] ⸢pꜣ tꜣ⸣ m-sꜣ[ah]

12. - - - . . . .] . . ⸢pꜣ mr⸣-sẖ Mꜣ-wr[aj] ỉr=w-s n ḥm-ntr Ḥr-nb-Sḫm nꜣ wꜥb.w r-wn-nꜣ-w ⸢pꜣỉ=f⸣ ỉrỉ n[ak]

13. - - - . . . .] . =y ⸢n ḥm-ntr⸣[al] n Ḥr-nb-Sḫm r Ḏd(t)-sšp[am] [.] . . . [. . .] . . . [. .] . . r pꜣ tꜣ rsỉ[an]

14. - - - . . . .] . =f[ao] bn(-pw) nꜣ wꜥb.w ḫꜣꜥ=f dỉ=w ỉw=n ⸢r-bnr⸣ . . . . . .=f[ap] tꜣ wnwt[aq]

15. - - -] ⸢ỉr=f⸣[ar] [. . .] nꜣỉ=f ḥbs.w pgy[as] rmy=f ỉw=f ḏd i-ỉr=y r šm r-tn

16. - - -] ⸢n=s⸣[at] pꜣ ꜥš-sḥn dỉt ⸢šm⸣=n r Wn-ḫm bn-ỉw=w nḥy-ṱ=s[au] ḏd tw=n n-ỉm[av]

17. - - -] ⸢Wn⸣-ḫm[aw] n grḥ mšꜥ=f r wꜥ km ỉw=f pꜣ bnr n pꜣ dmỉ ỉw=f ḫf[ax]

18. - - - . . .] ⸢ꜥš r⸣ ḥwt-ntr ḫpr[ay] ỉw=y r ỉỉ r-ẖry . .[az] [. .] . . . ỉw=y[ba] r dỉt pḥ=⸢t⸣ r ⸢Wn⸣-ḫm[bb] ỉw=y r ḫꜣꜥ=t

19. - - -] ⸢ỉrm⸣=f[bc] rmy=f r-ḥr=s rmy=s r-ḥr=f[bd] ḫpr pꜣ nw n ꜥš r ḥwt-ntr ỉw=f ỉw r-bnr[be]

20. - - -] . .[bf] pꜣ ꜥwỉ n wꜥ wn n Ḥr-nb-Sḫm ḏd=f n=s r nꜣ ntr.w r-pḥ=t r pꜣỉ=w dmỉ r ỉr n=t[bg]

21. - - -] r-dbꜣ ỉḥ̭ ⸢ḏd⸣=s n=f i-ỉr=y rmy ḫpr ⸢bn(-pw)⸣=y[bh] wꜣy mtw=k ꜥn (sp-sn) tw=k dỉt-wꜣy n-ỉm=y n pꜣ (hrw)[bj]

22. - - - . . . .] .⸢rmt⸣ ꜥn.t[bk] bn-ỉw=w msty=t[bl] n pꜣ(ỉ) ꜥwỉ[bm] ntỉ i-ỉr=t r šm[bn] r-r=f i-ỉr pꜣ ntr

23. - - - . . . . .] . . n šn r-ḥr=y[bo] m-ỉr dỉt ỉr=s n=t yꜥby[bp] ỉn-nꜣ-w rhy ḫpr ỉw=y r ỉỉ

24. - - - . . . .] ⸢k⸣m[bq] ỉw=y ꜣby[br] ỉw=y r ỉr pꜣỉ=s smt m-mnt šꜥ-tw=y

25. - - - . . . .] . . .[bs] m-ỉr rmy bw-ỉr mdt ḫpr m-sꜣ mdt mtw pꜣ ntr sḥn-ṱ=s

26. - - - . . . .] pꜣ wn n pꜣỉ=s ꜥwỉ dwy[bt] i-ỉr=s gm[bu] tꜣ ẖr.t ỉw=s ḥms

27. - - - . . . . . .] ⸢nw⸣ r ⸢tꜣ ntỉ⸣ ḥms n-bnr[bv] snd pꜣỉ-ỉr=y[bw] n-drt nw=y r-r=s r šm r-bnr[bx]

28. - - - . . . . . .] ⸢f⸣. . .=f-s[by] m-sꜣ ⸢ꜣt⸣.ṱ=f[bz] nw=s r-r=f n pꜣ gy n stꜣ.ṱ=f ḥꜣ=f[ca]

29. - - -] ⸢ntr.t⸣[cb] ḏd=s n=f bn-ỉw-tw=k [. . .] . . .[cc] ⸢ỉn tꜣ⸣ rmt ỉw=s ỉỉ.ṱ r wḫꜣ ꜥwỉ n ꜥnḫ[cd] ḏd=f n=s

30. - - -] .[ce] r-ẖn ḏd pꜣ wn n tꜣỉ=f ḥm.t ḥrḥ=t r-ḥr=t[cf] ỉrm tꜣ rmt.t gy n rmt ꜥꜣ tꜣỉ

31. - - -] pꜣ wn nw=s r ẖ(t)[cg] pꜣ ꜥwỉ ỉw=f ḏḫm ḫꜣꜥ=s nꜣỉ=s ḥbs.w r-ẖry mr=s[ch] n wꜥ

32. - - - r]⸢ẖ⸣=s[cj] mḥ=s[ck] wꜥ ḥn n mw ḫꜣꜥ-s ḥr tꜣ wꜥbt[cl] ꜥḫy=s[cm] nꜣ ḥmt.w[cn] ḫꜣꜥ-st

33. - - -] ⸢ẖ⸣m mw[co] ḏd=s n tꜣ ḥm.t n pꜣ wn skr [. . . . .] . . . . ḏḳm=s[cp]

34. - - - ḫn]ty grr[cq] ỉn=w wꜥ gy[cr] ỉrm hy⸢n.w⸣. [. . . . .] . . hyn.w ꜥ⸢r⸣y.w[cs]

35. - - -] . bny[ct] ỉpy n rmt[cu] ỉw r-bnr ḥr drt . .[cv] . .[cw] [. . . .] ⸢tꜣ wnw⸣[.t[cx] . . . .

up to 4.0 cm. of bottom margin

col. 10

top margin of 2.0 cm.

1. ꜥḥꜥ=w n=w ỉw=w ⸢ẖ⸣.[cy] [- - -

2. ỉw=f (ỉr)[cz] n šb⸢w⸣[da] [- - -

3. ꜥš=f r tꜣ ẖr.t[db] [- - -

4. n šbw[dc] ḏd=s [- - -

5. i-ỉr-ḥr=k[dd] my ⸢dỉ⸣[de] [- - -

6. nꜣ šyš.w[df] . [- - -
7. -sšp[dg] n-ỉm=. [- - -
8. ỉrm=s[dh] gm=⌜f⌝ [- - -
9. n yꜥby šꜥ-⌜tw⌝ [- - -
10. stꜣ.ṱ=f-s r pꜣ mkṱ⌜r⌝[dj] [- - -
11. ỉw=t ỉr n pꜣ(ỉ) ꜥwỉ[dk] [- - -
12. tꜣ ḥm.t[dl] n pꜣ ⌜wn⌝ [- - -
13. n[dm] nw r ⌜tꜣ/nꜣ⌝ [- - -
14. . . . . . [[dn]- - -
15. no trace[do]
16. no trace
17. ⌜ntỉ⌝ bn-ỉw=⌜n⌝[dp] . [- - -
18. n ⌜hrw⌝ r (pꜣỉ=f) ỉrỉ[dq] . [- - -
19. n Wn-ḫm[dr] ⌜ỉrm⌝ [- - -
20. ḫnt grr[ds] . [- - -
21. . . . . . n-ỉm=w[dt] [- - -
22. . . . . ⌜md(t)⌝ . [du][- - -
23. . . . . .⌜mḳy⌝[dv] [. .] . ḏd=w n=f[dw] wḏꜣ pꜣỉ=k ṯꜣw[dx] bn-ỉw-tw=⌜n⌝ . . . . [dy][- - -
24. mtw=y šr ỉw=f r⌜my wbꜣ⌝=y[dz] ḏd=f n(=y) ỉw=y r dỉt ỉn=w n=k wꜥt ẖr(t)
mtw=y . . . .[ea][- - -
25. wn-nꜣ-w ỉw=y n-ỉm=f ⌜ỉwt[eb] nꜣ wn.w n Ḥr⌝-nb-Sḫm ⌜dr=w⌝. . . . .[ec][- - -
26. r pꜣỉ=s dmỉ r pꜣỉ(=y) .[ed] [. . . . .] . . . . . .ꜥnḫ=⌜n⌝ . . .[ee][- - -
27. rḫ ḏd n=s mdt n-ỉm=w [.] . . [. . . . .] . . . . ẖr ỉn . .[ef][- - -
28. r ḫpr n-ỉm=s n pꜣỉ (=y) ꜥwỉ bn-⌜ỉw=f ḫpr⌝ . . . . .[eg] ⌜pꜣ⌝ wn . . . .[eh][- - -
29. ỉw=k šn[ej] n ḥwt-ntr r tꜣỉ=k mdt ꜥꜣy[ek] n Wn-ḫm [- - -
30. šw[el] pꜣ ntỉ nꜣ-nfr=f [. .] ⌜pꜣ⌝ ntỉ ỉw=y ḏd n-ỉm=f[em] šꜥ-tw . .[en] [- - -
31. šꜥ pꜣ (hrw)[eo] md ⌜ỉrm=⌝[. . .] =y[ep] ỉr n=s mdt šw ḏd=w[eq] . . . [- - -
32. ỉw=n r md ỉrm=s ⌜ỉw=n⌝[er] r dỉt ỉr=s n=s šw ḏd=f . . . .[es][- - -
33. dỉ[et] n=n pꜣ ntr r hyn.w ẖ(r)yr[eu] n Ḥr-wr nḥm=f[ev] n-drt.ṱ=n . [- - -
34. ỉw=w[ew] m-sꜣ=n ỉw=f ḏd n=n ỉꜣw[ex] hyn.w ḥḏ n hbr . . .[ey] [- - -
35. ⌜r⌝k[ez] [. . .] s̭ḫy[fa] n ḥꜣt.ṱ=w ỉw ꜥwỉ-n-drt[fb] dỉ=s s⌜wr⌝ [fc][- - -
36. . .] . [. . . .] . . .[fd][. . . .] ḏd=f n=k my ỉn=w tꜣ(ỉ)[fe] ẖ⌜r⌝[.t - - -
37. . . . .] ⌜ḫpr⌝ r bn(-pw)=tn dỉt ỉn=w tꜣ(ỉ)[ff] ẖr.t [- - -

up to 1.5 cm. of bottom margin

Fr. 4 (col. 10?) Plate 3

— — — — — — — — — — — —

x+1. - - - . . . . . .] . . [. . .] ⌜t/nꜣỉ=s⌝ [- - -
x+2. - - - . . . . . .] . . [. . .] n=s ⌜mdt⌝[a] [- - -
x+3. - - -] . . . . r-bnr ⌜n ḳns⌝ mtw=y dỉt ỉr=w[b] [- - -
x+4. - - - my ỉr]=w n=n ⌜tꜣ(ỉ)⌝ mdt nfr.t ỉ-ỉr-ḥr[c] [- - -
x+5. - - - . . . .] ⌜ḥr⌝[d] [- - -

— — — — — — — — — — — —

Fr. 5 (col. 10?) Plate 3

x+1. - - - - .] . . . . [- - -
x+2. - - - .] . . . . . [- - -
x+3. - - -] ⸢*r-dbꜣ*⸣*.ṯ=s* . . . . [- - -
x+4. - - - .] . . *mtw=* . . . . .[a][- - -

BACK (↕)

Fr. 4 (col. 13?) Plate 3

x+1. - - - - .] .[a] [- - -
x+2. - - - .] . . . [. . .] . .[b] [- - -
x+3. - - -] . . *=w* . . . .[c][- - -
x+4. - - -] *pꜣ mr-pr-nsw*[d] *r tm ꜥḥꜥ* . [- - -
x+5. - - -] . . . . .[e] [. . . .] . . . [- - -
x+6. - - - .] . . [- - -

Fr. 5 (col. 13?) Plate 3

x+1. - - - .] . . . . [- - -
x+2. - - -] . . . . . [- - -
x+3. - - -] ⸢*rmt.w*⸣ *ꜥy.w* . [- - -
x+4. - - -] . . ⸢*drt*⸣ .[a][- - -

Fr. 3
col. 13 Plate 2

top margin of 2.0 cm.

1. about 23.0 cm.] *ḫr.t r-ḫṯ*[a] *pꜣ ḥm-ntr n Ḥr-nb-Sḫm*
2. „] . .[b] *bn(-pw)=y ḫdb rmt mtw=k n pꜣi(=y) ꜥḥꜥ*
3. „] .[c] *ir=s n=k ḥm.t swr=s wnm=s irm=k*
4. „] *ḥn iwꜣy ꜥꜣ m-šs*[d] *bn(-pw)=s ḫꜣꜥ ḥt.ṯ=s*[e]
5. „] . *irm=y ir=y pꜣ (hrw)*[f] *irm=k i-ir=k*
6. „] ⸢*r*⸣*my nꜣ gr-šr.w*[g] *r-wn-nꜣ-w ꜥḥꜥ*
7. „] ⸢*ḫr.t*⸣[h] *ḏd=w n pꜣ ḥm-ntr n Ḥr-nb-Sḫm pꜣ* ⸢*ꜥḳr*⸣[j]
8. „] . . *-s/=s ḫdb=w-s*[k] *n tꜣi ḥṯy*
9. „] . . *ṯ=s r-ḥr=w in*[l] *ṯꜣi rnpt 6 r tꜣi*[m]
10. „] . *r-ḥꜣt mwt=w/Mwt(?)*[n] *n tꜣ hyꜣ(t)*[o] *nꜣi=s sn.w* ⸢*ꜥn*⸣[p]
11. „] ⸢*mdt*⸣*-bin.w*[q] *n-im=f tw* . ⸢*mḥṯ*⸣ . . *tꜣi(=y) šrt*[r]
12. „] ⸢*mdwt*⸣[s] *nti iw=k ḏd n-im=w bn(-pw)=f sḥn.ṯ=w r ir=w*[t]
13. „ . .] . *m-šs*[u] vacat

larger space between lines

14. about 26.0 cm.] ⸢nw⸣=y r wꜥ mk⸢ṱr⸣[v]
15. ,,] ⸢nw⸣ r pꜣ rmt ꜥꜣ ⸢ỉrm⸣
16. about 23.0 cm.] ⸢pꜣỉ(=y)⸣ nb ꜥꜣ[w] . . .[x] [.] . ⸢mdwt⸣[y] ntỉ ỉw bn(-pw) pꜣ . . .[z]
17. ,,] ⸢wnwt⸣ 11 Pr-ꜥꜣ ỉw r-bnr n-rꜣ
18. ,,] . .[aa] n tꜣ yꜥby n pꜣ tꜣ[ab] ḫpr[ac] sny pꜣ ⸢nw⸣
19. ,,] . =w-s[ad] r nꜣ ꜥwỉ.w n ḥrr[ae] dỉ Pr-ꜥꜣ
20. ,,] . =f r ḏd.⸢ṱ=w⸣ . . ⸢ỉ-ỉr⸣-st dr=w[af] ḏd Pr-ꜥꜣ
21. about 15.0 cm.] . . ⸢wꜥ tgs⸣ . . . ⸢dỉ⸣ [. .] . [.] . [. .] ⸢b⸣yry[ag] . . [.] . . . . . wꜣy=w sh̭ r-r=f[ah]
22. ,, Ḥr-nb] -⸢Sẖm⸣ ỉrm tꜣỉ=f mhwꜣ šꜥ h̭⸢m-ẖ⸣r[aj] . . . . ⸢=f⸣ . . ⸢ỉrm⸣[ak] (nꜣỉ=f) ỉrỉ.w n wꜥb[al]
23. ,,] . . . . ⸢bn(-pw)⸣=w ḫpr m-sꜣ=s[am] m-ỉr ⸢ḥrr⸣[an] r Mn-nfr ỉrm nꜣ(ỉ) lwl.w[ao]
bn-ỉw=y šm
24. ,, dỉ] ⸢Pr-ꜥꜣ⸣[ap] ꜥr=w r-⸢mr.t ꜥn⸣ bn(-pw)=w ⸢ḥrr⸣[aq] [r] ⸢Wn⸣-ẖm šm Pr-ꜥꜣ r pr-Pr-ꜥꜣ
25. ,,] . . mdt nbt ỉ-ỉr . . . .[ar] [. . . . . . .] . . .[as] ỉrm H̱rd pꜣ ntr ỉ-ỉr-ṯꜣỉ-ṱ=w[at] gmꜥ=f[au]
26. ,,] . . . . ⸢ỉ-wn⸣-nꜣ-w[av] . . . . . =⸢f⸣ rẖ šn[aw] r nꜣỉ=f ẖrd.⸢ṱ.⸣w bn(-pw)=f[ax] hb n mdỉ
mtw=⸢w⸣ ꜥn[ay]
27. about 17.0 cm.] ⸢m⸣-bꜣḥ Pr-ꜥꜣ my ḥn=w-s n pꜣ mr-pr-ỉpy-nsw r dỉt šm=y r-bnr[az]
28. ,, ỉ]⸢p⸣y-[nsw][ba] r-bnr ỉrm=s ⸢ḫpr⸣ wꜥt nẖy ꜥꜣ ẖ(t) n Mn-nfr[bb] bn(-pw) rmt ỉr sp[bc]
29. about 16.0 cm.] ⸢Ḥr-nb⸣-Sẖm ỉw . [. . .] . wꜥb.w[bd] ꜥḥꜥ=w ỉrm=w[be] ỉr=w nꜣ sm.w n[bf]
30. about 15.0 cm.] ⸢ỉrm tꜣỉ⸣=k[bg] mhwꜣ nꜣỉ=k ⸢ỉrỉ⸣.w n wꜥb n tꜣ gm[bh] n pꜣ mr-sẖ Mꜣ-wr my
31. ,, (nꜣỉ]⸢=f)⸣[bj] ỉrỉ.w n wꜥb dr=w dỉ Ḥr-mꜣꜥ-ẖrw ỉr=f ꜥnẖ[bk] ḏd mn rmt ḥw ẖn=w[bl]
32. ,,] . (pꜣỉ=f)[bm] ỉrỉ n-ỉm=w dỉ=f ꜥr pꜣ mšꜥ n[bn] nꜣ byry.w r-ḥrỉ dỉ=f ỉn=w nꜣ-w-ꜥwỉ.w[bo]
33. ,,] mšꜥ Ḥr-mꜣꜥ-ẖrw r pꜣ mkṱr dỉ[=f] rk=w pꜣ h̭mꜥ tꜣ rỉt-ḥrỉ.t[bp]
34. ,,] . . .[bq] šḳy[br] ḫpr . [[bs]. . . .] . . [. . . .] . . [. .] . . . . . . [. . .] . .[bt]

up to 2.0 cm. of bottom margin

col. 14

top margin of 2.0 cm.

1. mnẖy[bu] n nꜣ rmt.w ꜥꜣ.w r nꜣy km[bv] pꜣ mr-⸢mšꜥ⸣[bw] ỉrm pꜣ mšꜥ [- - -
2. dỉ=w ḥtp=w ẖn (nꜣỉ=w)[bx] ḥnw.wt[by] ḏd Ḥr-mꜣꜥ-ẖrw sdm pꜣ mšꜥ[bz] [- - -
3. ḥn-s Pr-ꜥꜣ r dỉt-s[ca] r pꜣ ꜥẖ ỉrm (tꜣỉ=f)[cb] ˋmˊhwꜣ[cc] nꜣỉ=f ỉrỉ.⸢w⸣[cd][- - -
4. dỉt rmt ỉs[ce] pꜣ ḥm-ntr n Ḥr-nb-Sẖm r pꜣ ꜥẖ bn-ỉw=f ꜥnẖ ỉn[cf] . [. .] .[cg][- - -
5. my ṯꜣw m-sꜣ pꜣỉ ẖ(r)yr[ch] ṯꜣỉ=f ẖꜣ ỉn=w[cj] pꜣ tgs . ṯꜣỉ nb[ck] . .[cl] [- - -
6. ỉrp ỉr=w grr w⸢tn i⸣-ỉr-ḥr nꜣ rmt.w ꜥꜣy.w bn(-pw)=w ḥrr r Mn-nfr [- - -
7. ꜥn-smy n-ỉm=⸢s m-bꜣḥ⸣ Pr-ꜥꜣ ḏd pḥ nꜣ rmt.w ꜥꜣy r Mn-nfr [- - -
8. rmy=f ḏd ỉ pꜣỉ(=y) ỉt ỉ pꜣỉ(=y) sn ỉ pꜣỉ(=y) ỉrỉ[cm] tw=y rw⸢š⸣[cn] [- - -
9. tꜣ ḥm.t-nsw ỉw r-rꜣ[co] tꜣ ḥwt[cp] ỉr=s pꜣỉ=s smt ⸢ꜥn⸣[cq][- - -
10. tꜣ ḥwt ỉr=f grr ỉw=w m-šs[cr] šm Pr-ꜥꜣ r pr-[Pr-ꜥꜣ[cs] - - -
11. Pr-ꜥꜣ m-šs šm Pr-ꜥꜣ r pꜣ ꜥwỉ n nꜣ ⸢sdm⸣[(-ꜥš).w[ct] - - -
12. n tꜣ šb(t) n pꜣỉ=k ỉt.ṱ ntỉ šm my wꜣy=w r pꜣ ⸢ḥrỉ-ỉb⸣[cu] [- - -
13. ⸢mḥ.ṱ=f⸣ [.] ẖꜣꜥ=s[cv] r (pꜣỉ=f) ꜥwỉ ḥn-s Pr-ꜥꜣ ⸢ḏd⸣ [- - -
14. ḫpr=f ỉw mn rmt n pꜣ tꜣ mỉ[cw] tꜣ mdt n Ḥr-⸢mꜣꜥ⸣-[ẖrw - - -

larger space between lines

15. ḫpr wꜥ hrw šm Ḥr-mꜣꜥ-ḫrw r tꜣ ḫꜣst Mn-nfr[cx] [- - -
16. n-drt.ṱ=w ỉw=w dỉt r-ḥꜣt.ṱ=w n-ỉm=w[cy] šrf⸢=s⸣[cz] mtw=f . . .[da] [- - -
17. i-ỉr=tn ỉr n-⸢ỉm=w r-dbꜣ⸣ nm n-ỉm=w[db] ḏd n=f wꜥt n-ỉm=w ỉw=s ḫpr . . .[dc] [- - -
18. ⸢pꜣ(ỉ)⸣ km[dd] ⸢pt⸣=y r-bnr[de] ỉrm tꜣ(ỉ) ḫr(t) ntỉ i-ỉr-ḥr=k i-ỉr=y . . . [.] .[df] [- - -
19. dỉt n=n[dg] tꜣỉ ḫrỉ[dh] m-mnt ṯꜣỉ rnpt 6 r tꜣỉ[dj] ỉw=n n tꜣ hyꜣ(t)[dk] [- - -
20. ḏd šm Pr-ꜥꜣ r nhpy[dl] n Ptḥ-ḥtp Stm[dm] ỉrm nꜣ s-ḥm.wt n ⸢pr⸣-[ỉpy]-⸢nsw⸣[dn] [- - -
21. i-ỉr=y rḫ=s[do] ṯꜣỉ-ṱ=y Ptḥ-ḥtp Stm[dp] r-r=s ỉw . . . .[dq] [- - -
22. ḫpr n-ỉm=s ḏd=s n-drt pt=y r-bnr[dr] i-ỉr=y dỉt ḥr . . .[ds] [- - -
23. r tn ḏd=f n(=y) i-ỉr=y mḥṱ=y[dt] šꜥ pr-ḥtp[du] [- - -
24. nꜣ ḥbs.w r-wn-nꜣ-w tḫb n sšn ḥr-ꜣt[dv][- - -
25. ỉrm=f ḏd bw-ỉr=f dỉt gm=w-ṱ(=y)[dw] ḫpr=y . . . .[dx] [- - -
26. tꜣ sndyt i-ỉr-ḫpr n Mn-nfr n sf ḏd=f . . .[dy] [- - -
27. r nhpy[dz] n wꜥ rmt ꜥꜣ Ḏd(t)-sšp[ea] ⸢rn⸣=f ḏd .[eb] [- - -
28. my wḏꜣ=f[ec] ỉnk tꜣ ḥmt Ḏ⸢d(t)-sš⸣p[ed] . . . .[ee] [- - -
29. n sšn ḥr-ꜣt.[ṱ=.[ef]] . . . ḫpr[eg] r šn . . . .[eh] [- - -
30. ḥr tꜣ ḫꜣst ḏd=f n(=y) wꜥ wꜥb ⸢pꜣ i⸣-ỉr dỉt gm=w mdt nbt i-ỉr ḫpr n-ỉm=[- - -
31. pḥ=y r-bw-nꜣy i-ỉr=y ỉỉ r-bw-nꜣy ỉrm Nꜣ-nfr-Sḫm.t[ej] ỉw=s [- - -
32. n pgy ꜥš=f dny[ek] r-ḥr=w ḏd=w n=f my ỉr=w n=n tꜣỉ mdt ⸢nfrt⸣[el] [- - -
33. . [. .] . . . . . .=w n-rdwỉ.ṱ=f[em] n tꜣỉ ḥṱy ḏd=w n=f .[en][- - -
34. . . . .] . pꜣ gm.ṱ=w r-ỉr=k n pꜣ (hrw)[eo] ḏd=f n=w skr[ep] [- - -
35. . . . .] sḏy=f i-ỉr-ḥr=w n mdt nbt i-ỉr-ḫpr n-ỉm=f ṯꜣỉ[eq] [- - -
36. . . .] (nꜣỉ=f)[er] sn.w r pꜣ ꜥḫ r-ỉr=w ḥr-rꜣ[es] tꜣ ḥwt[et] tꜣ wnwt[eu] [- - -
37. . . . . . .] vacat mḥ 14 [vacat

bottom margin (disregarding the column-number) of 4.0 cm.

Fr. 1 (col. 16?) — Plate 3

— — — — —

x+1. - - -] . . [- - -
x+2. - - -] ⸢md.wt⸣ . . [- - -
x+3. - - -] ⸢s⸣ḳ=f[a] [- - -
x+4. - - -] dỉ . . . [- - -

— — — — —

Fr. 2 (col. 16) — Plate 3

— — — — — — — — — — —

x+1. - - - .] . . . [. .]=y ỉr pꜣỉ=s smt n .[a] [- - -
x+2. - - -] . . ⸢y⸣=w[b] r ṯꜣỉ-ṱ=f r rsỉ ỉrm=f dỉ . .[c] [- - -
x+3. - - -] ⸢pꜣ ḥm-ntr⸣ 4-nw[d] r Nỉwt sḏy=f n mdt ⸢nbt⸣ [- - -
x+4. - - -] . . . Ḥr-mꜣꜥ-ḫrw pšn n swr ḥnḳt n . . .[e] [- - -
x+5. - - -] . . r bw-ỉr pꜣ ḥm-ntr 4-nw ỉr wš n dỉt ỉn=w nkt n Ḥr-⸢mꜣꜥ⸣-[ḫrw - - -
x+6. - - -] . ỉw ỉn=w ⸢nꜣ⸣ mr-mšꜥ.w[f] nꜣ⸣ rmt.w ⸢ꜥꜣ.w⸣ . . . . [- - -
x+7. - - -] . . ḥ. [. . . . .] . . . [- - -
x+8. - - -] vacat mḥ 1⸢6⸣ [vacat

bottom margin (disregarding the column-number) of 4.0 cm.

Notes on transliteration

FRONT

Fr. 2

col. 7(?)

a. Several tiny traces survive of l. (x+)1. The first trace is clearly in shape, and, in the middle of the fragment, one trace is presumably of the tail of an *=f*; apart from this, however, nothing can be read.

b. The first traces in l. 2 are , and a reading *pꜣ rmt* seems possible.

c. The trace immediately after *ḫpr* would suit an *r*, either introducing the nominal subject of a circumstantial clause, or belonging to an *r*/*ỉw sdm=f* verb form (cf. p. 34, n. *eh*).

d. The title *Stm* is here written , and stands alone, without any accompanying personal name. It recurs at 14/20, 21 in similar writings, but in each case preceded by the personal name *Ptḥ-ḥtp*. See the discussion on p. 46; cf. p. 62.

e. The traces at the end of l. 3 are . The edges of these traces are badly damaged, and it is difficult to judge the shape of the strokes to which they belong. *m-ỉr ẖdb* is perhaps a probable reading, especially as *ẖdb* occurs earlier in this line (compare the writing preserved at 13/2), although the upward curl at the end of the *d* might seem exaggerated. A reading *m-ỉr* ⌜*ẖ*⌝[is not impossible, but does not seem so likely.

Here in l. 3, just beneath l. 4 below, and perhaps also between ll. 1 and 2, extensive traces can be identified of writing that has been imperfectly washed away. The hand seems to be similar to, and is very probably the same as, that of the present text. No words can be read for certain, and it does not seem possible to recognize any words that are also preserved in the present text. The whole of the written portion of the front of this fragment has a slight greyish tinge (although the same might be said of the whole of the back surface). It is possible that a very extensive passage of the present text was erased, perhaps because a substantial omission had been made, and the correct text resumed in its place. Otherwise it must be assumed that just a part of the roll bore a previous text, which was imperfectly erased in preparation for the present text. Compare p. 33, n. *dr*, concerning an example of a short passage that has been erased and rewritten.

f. The first traces in l. 4, preceding *ỉ-ỉr-ḫr=y* are . The final, high traces might be explained as belonging to the preceding line, but their shape and the distance between the lines at this point does not make this very likely. If so, the only plausible restoration is of *sn*, 'brother', (cf. 13/10 and 14/8, 36). The sole objection to this reading is that the top of the vertical stroke seems to curve to the right more than in the other examples. Certainly, if *sn* is read, the preceding traces would suit *pꜣỉ(=y)* perfectly. Other possible readings, such as *ṯ=w*, (*ntỉ*) *ỉw=w*, or a plural noun, are all open to objection.

g. For the writings of *ꜥwi-drt* in this papyrus, see p. 24, n. *fb*.

h. Apart from one small problem, the forms of the writings are clear enough. At the beginning of the line stands a writing of *ꜥnḫ*, without any det., . The preceding slight trace would not suit an well, and presumably none was written. A preposition *n* follows and then , which is discussed below. Finally, before the certain writing of *pꜣ-Rꜥ*, there is a writing of *ꜥnḫ*, with det., , the kind of writing that is generally used for the noun 'oath' (*DG*, 63. 7) rather than the oath-formula 'As . . . lives' (*DG*, 64. 1): the small trace of ink at the foot of the first stroke seems certainly to belong to it, and not, for example, to a preposition *r*.

The reading of the signs is problematic. Taken together, they may be a writing of a god's name. Although in the Roman period the det. is sometimes used in the name of any major deity, for example Ptaḥ, in this text it might be expected to indicate a solar god. Either *Šw* or *Ỉn-ḥr* might be suggested as readings. Alternatively, the writing may be of a word compounded with *Rꜥ*, perhaps a personal name intended to be of an Old Kingdom type. The reading *Ḫꜥ-Rꜥ* might be suggested, cf. *Ḫꜥ=f-Rꜥ* in **15**/7 and *ḫꜥ* in **2** back, x+1/33, where the upper stroke has a simple cross-bar (this difference may not exclude the reading). The writing, without any cartouche, seems to indicate that a king's name cannot be in question. However, if the name appears in an oath-formula, this might suggest an invented royal name, possibly a reminiscence of *Ḫꜥ=f-Rꜥ*. If the first two signs are to be analysed separately, the upper sign is indistinguishable from the large bolt-*s* in, for example, *sšn* in 14/24, 29; and the lower sign must either be *h* or represent .

Whether a human or divine name is read in the first phrase, there seems little alternative to understanding the following *ꜥnḫ pꜣ-Rꜥ* as the oath-formula 'As Parēꜥ lives'; the det. of *ꜥnḫ* is unusual, but, considered by itself, acceptable. The scribe of **1** is in general a careful writer. It is possible that the first *ꜥnḫ* is therefore to be understood as the noun meaning 'life', rather than that meaning 'oath'. The sense would in this case be that someone takes an oath involving the life of a character . .-*Rꜥ*(?): in view of the mention of a killing in l. 3 above, this does not seem implausible. However, it is also possible that the distinction between *ꜥnḫ* with and without det. is a distinction between the oath-formula, and the noun 'oath'. The sense might, for example, be that an oath is sworn to or for a character . .-*Rꜥ*(?). In that case, the orthography must almost certainly be inconsistent with that at 13/31.

j. The reading *nti iw=f* is virtually certain. The last trace is apparently of a curved, horizontal stroke, positioned rather high, , and it closely resembles the head of a suffix *=f* (cf., for example, *rmy=f iw=f* in 9/15).

k. The traces make the reading *m-ḳdy* possible, although there is very little room before the following traces ; these seem to resemble *wn*, but the papyrus is badly torn here, and they may be quite misleading: perhaps read all these traces as *in-ḳdy.k* . Apparently one stroke, beginning rather high, is preserved after this, ; it is somewhat puzzling. The surface of the papyrus is almost completely lost at several points here.

l. m-sꜣ seems quite clear. The following traces are . The reading *m-sꜣ=s* . . . might be considered, but *m-sꜣ nꜣy* seems more probable, with *nꜣy* written in the form , which is otherwise attested in this papyrus only in *r-bw-nꜣy*, 'hither' (see, for example, 14/31; cf. the form of *nꜣ* in *r-wn-nꜣ-w* at 14/24). This common phrase, 'After these things', might well begin a fresh section of the narrative, and it is possible that a blank space was left before it, rather than that the papyrus has been rubbed completely clean of ink.

m. The traces here are . The final signs certainly represent *hy*[. . . Several restorations are possible, including *hy*, 'expense', and *hyn.w*, 'some'. The preceding group could well be the masc. def. article *pꜣ*, or the final sign of *irm*. The tail of a sign, probably from *ir=f*, is preserved below.

Although these signs appear to be written rather close to the writing in l. 6, the fragment upon which both they and the column number are preserved is still attached by a few fibres to the main fragment; there is no possible doubt as to its location.

n. The page numbers in this papyrus are not located centrally beneath the column, but about 9.0 cm. from the right-hand edge of the column; see p. 1.

Fr. 3
col. 9

a. ḥms is probably imperative. For writings of *ḥms*, see 9/26, 27 and 13/27. The reading *n=k* seems inescapable for . Usually in **1**, *n=k* has the form , with neither the large dot below, nor the small stroke above (see, for example, front, 10/24, 36). Similarly, *r-bnr* is sometimes written , although more usually . The faint stroke above *n=k* here is perhaps one of the light marks, usually dots, but sometimes short strokes, that the scribe has frequently placed above the text (see p. 3 f.). For the form *dꜣi*, see *DG*, 604. 1; this form is also found in the letters from Saqqâra.

b. iw=k ir rnpt 100, using the infinitive, must be Circumstantial (or Continuative), and *iw=k ꜥnḫ.ṯ*, using the Stative, must be Circumstantial; Positive Third Future forms in the present text always include a written *r*.

c. The traces present a problem, although the det. and the context make it clear what kinds of phrase might be restored. After *ir=k* there must stand a noun or a verb of more than three consonants. There is a tiny dot of ink above the first sign, which presumably may be disregarded; it might be one of the dots discussed on p. 3 f. The small strokes immediately before the final det. are not as evenly spaced as the usual form of final *y*, and might alternatively be seen as a det. Possible restorations are (i) *mḏꜥ* (or, less probably, *mḏꜥy*), , 'We shall not let you grieve' (see *DG*, 680. 3 under *ḏmꜥj*: for a similar form of *ꜥ*, see *mšꜥ* at 9/17 and 13/33). (ii) *ꜣkm*, , which is attested as a noun, 'We shall not let you be sorrowful' (see *DG*, 12. 3, *ꜣkm*). (iii) *ꜣyṯy* or *ꜣyṯ*, , 'We shall not let you be in want' (see *DG*, 13. 1, *ꜣt*).

d.]⌈*r*⌉*y*, : the word *ḫ(r)ꜥry*, 'wrath', 'to be wrathful', might be restored here. See the discussion of the word on p. 24, n. *eu*.

e. ṯꜣi-ḥbs, written , is plainly to be understood as a 'garment', 'suit of clothing'; cf. Coptic (Bohairic) ϭιϩⲃⲟⲥ, Crum, *CD*, 660a.

f. The traces are . The reading *n-im=f* is not convincing, and the traces certainly do not suit *irm=f*. Perhaps read]. . . *ṯ=f*, although the preceding traces then present a problem; possibly restore *ḥꜣt.ṯ=f*, with an abbreviated form of the flesh-det.

g. sdm is here written , instead of the more usual ; this is the only such writing in this papyrus.

Compare **2** back, x+1/2 (note *am*); and in this papyrus see 9/26, 14/25, 30 for a similar variation in the writing of *gm*. See also **4**/3, 5 for two forms of *gm*.

h. It is uncertain whether *iw=w ḏd* has a personal antecedent (presumably the group of people last mentioned in l. 3), or should be taken as the passive periphrasis, 'it was said'.

j. *hrw*, in the expression *pꜣ hrw*, 'the particular day' (not in the sense 'today'), here has a full writing, 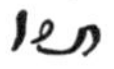 (contrast, p. 16 n. *bj*).

k. Below and slightly to the left of *pꜣ*, there is a dot of ink. Conceivably *pꜣ(i) rmt ꜥꜣ*, 'this great man', should be read. However, no other writing of *pꜣi* has merely a dot, rather than a stroke, and the dot here may be of the kind discussed on p. 3 f., and belong with the vertical stroke in the line below (cf. p. 16, n. *bm*, and the dot just beneath *pꜣ nṯr* in the same line, 9/22). This argument, and perhaps also the context, suggest that *pꜣ rmt ꜥꜣ* should certainly be read.

l. Literally 'This is the day of happening that an evil thing did to the great man'. It is impossible to be sure if the actual evil event referred to has happened, is happening, or is about to happen. The *r-ir* is certainly the relative form, which normally in demotic has past sense. Here, however, it may simply be the day of disaster that is thought of as having already been brought about, rather than the disaster itself, and thus the particular event may yet lie in the future.

m. The reading *ḏd* at the beginning of l. 5 is certain.

n. *bn-iw=f ḫpr in* must be Neg. First Pres., and therefore is certainly direct speech. It is uncertain whether the sense is 'saying in his heart "It is not happening"', or 'saying (*or* because) "It does not occur in his heart (i.e. He does not realize it *or* has not thought of it)"'.

o. This abbreviated writing, 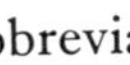, represents *sdm-ꜥš*, and not just *sdm* (cf. p. 118, n. *br*).

p. *mr-mšꜥ.w*: the traces are . Plainly 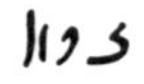 (or conceivably 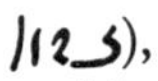), and not 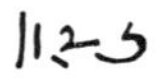 was written. This title is presumably the same as that in 14/1, written  (see p. 30, n. *bw*). The reading *mr-ꜣḥ.w*, 'overseers of field(s)', would well suit the signs, but this title would be most unexpected. Although *mšꜥ*, 'army', is written quite differently (see 13/32 and 14/1), *mr-mšꜥ(.w)*, 'generals', is the obvious reading in both contexts, and is confirmed by the very similar phrase *nꜣ sꜣwti.w nꜣ mr-mšꜥ.w nꜣ rmt.w-ꜥꜣy.w pr-pr-ꜥꜣ* at ꜥOnchsheshonqy 2/14–15, where the reading is indisputable.

q. *nti ḥn*: between *dr=w* and *ḥn* there is room to restore only a single sign or small group. To judge by the traces, the only possibilities are *r* and *nti*. The shape and position of the traces slightly favour *nti* (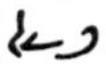 rather than 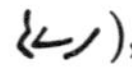), and this reading might give good sense. A relative form, *r-ḥn*, would plainly be nonsense in the context, and it is most unlikely that *r-ḥn* could be written for *i-ir-ḥn*, the active participial form consistently used in this papyrus.

r. *iwꜣy* is written 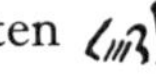. The initial sign might conceivably be read in a number of ways. However, it is plainly not the regular practice of this scribe to employ  for initial *š*, nor for *m* (except in *m-sꜣ*, *my*, *m-šs*, and once in *mk̭ṭr*; see p. 27, n. *v*), nor for *ẖ* (except before *r*); and plausible readings beginning with these letters are not forthcoming. The word might be read *ḥwꜣy*, and connected with Coptic ⲡⲉⲑⲟⲟⲩ 'wickedness' (Crum, *CD*, 731b), although there is no parallel for such a nominal form from *ḥw*, ϩⲟⲟⲩ (see *DG* 295. 1; Crum, *CD*, 731a; Černý, *CED*, 304. 2), and all the other initial *ḥ*s in this papyrus have the precise shape  (*ḥw*, *ḥp*, *ḥrḥ*, *ḥty*). The most probable reading is *iwꜣy* (*DG*, 22. 9, *iw(j).t*, cf. Crum, *CD*, 306a; Černý, *CED*, 141. 7, ⲣⲁⲟⲩⲱ), giving the sense 'who ordered a very great evil (*or* harm)'.

s. The main verb of this sentence is lost in the lacuna at the beginning of the line. Normal usage suggests that *ḏd* should be taken with the missing main verb, and not with the relative clause *nti ḥn iwꜣy ꜥꜣ m-šs*; see n. *q* above.

t. The traces are . No satisfactory reading suggests itself. Although some of these traces resemble a suffix *=f*, and this would suit the context, it is an impossible reading, chiefly because the tail of the sign does not descend far enough. A reading 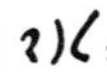, det.+*ṯ=s* is difficult to reconcile with the context, and with the few immediately following traces, and the same is true of a reading , det.+*=y*.

u. It is difficult to know if the common curved stroke above the first sign of *mꜣy*, 'new' (*DG*, 148. 1), should be transcribed as an *n*; the fact that it is often found in writings of *mꜣy*, 'island' (perhaps originally a cognate word), suggests it was not felt to be a written *n*. However, *mꜣy*, 'new', is plainly always treated as a noun in demotic (cf. Černý, *CED*, 79. 5, [F]ⲙⲉⲟⲩⲓ).

v. This fem. word, *tꜣ hyꜣ(t)*, is almost certainly to be identified with  (Wb. ii. 476. 4 ff.), cf. *DG*, 266. 1, 268. 2, and appears also in **1**, 13/10 and 14/19. A masc. word of similar meaning written *ẖyṯ* appears in

27/16, cf. *DG*, 377. 7 (masc. or fem.), equated with Coptic ϩⲁⲉⲓⲧ (Černý, *CED*, 298. 4). Fem. writings *ḫyṯꜣ.t* occur in ꜥOnchsheshonqy 2/18, 19. The meaning is discussed by Glanville in *Catalogue of the Demotic Papyri in the British Museum*, i (London, 1939), xxxiii. Černý derived from *ḥꜣty* (*Wb.* iii. 222. 5). Possibly, therefore, *hyꜣ*(*.t*) and *ḫyṯ* are etymologically distinct words. However, by demotic times there is confusion over gender and apparently little distinction in meaning, while by Coptic times only one word survives. Dr P. A. Spencer has studied the earlier history of *hꜣy.t* in her London University thesis upon the lexicography of Egyptian terms for certain buildings and their parts; we are grateful to her for allowing us to consult her treatment of the term.

w. The traces are . The verb *sdr*, 'to sleep', 'to lie down' (*DG*, 480. 5), is the obvious restoration. The word is entirely differently written in **2** back, x+1/15, 36, 38, . Although the det. here has a longer tail than in most other occurrences, it is presumably not a distinct sign from that used, for example, in *ḥbs* and in *šs-nsw* in l. 2 above.

x. *r ḫ*(*t*) here is written ; it plainly has the basic sense 'in the manner (of)' (*DG*, 375. 2). The fact that the natural translation is 'She spoke with him as (with) her master', or even 'as (if with) her master' need not suggest that there is an unnatural ellipse in the demotic.

y. *ỉw=s ḥp.ṯ*: clearly *ḥp* is here written with a Stative ending, but it is difficult to decide from the traces between *.w* and *.ṯ*. The sign begins as a vertical stroke, and bends round to the left at the base. Although the papyrus is torn at this point, the curve seems sufficient to suggest that *ḥp.ṯ* is the more likely reading. The only other written Stative endings preserved in **1** are in *ꜥnh.ṯ*, 9/1 and *ỉỉ.ṯ*, 9/29; possibly *ỉn-ḳdy.k* is to be restored at front, 7/6 (see p. 11, n. *k*).

z. *šbw* is here written , and the reading is certain. It is probable that the same word occurs in 10/2, where the det. is lost, , and in 10/4, with a house-det., . The word has every appearance of being masc. Its identification is problematic.

The word *šbn*, 'to join' (*DG*, 499. 1; Crum, *CD*, 573b, ϣⲱⲛϥ), might yield reasonable sense in the context here in col. 9, 'a room that was hidden from company'. However, in demotic and in Coptic this word seems to be distinguished from *šb*, 'to (ex)change', etc. (*DG*, 497. 1; Crum, *CD*, 551a), the former always, the latter never, containing an *n*. It is most improbable that *n šbw* could be understood as a phrase 'in exchange for'; the regular expression for this in demotic is *n tꜣ šbt* (cf. in Coptic the Bohairic ⲛⲧϣⲉⲃⲓⲱ etc.), and the normal writing of this fem. noun is ; the phrase appears in this form and writing at 14/12. A cognate masc. noun ϣⲓⲃⲉ is found in Coptic (Crum, *CD*, 552a), and this might justify the phonetic writing of *šbw*. Conceivably *n šbw* (masc.) might be a phrase with a meaning different from that of *n tꜣ šb*(*t*); but, even if this were acceptable in this context in col. 9, it seems that another different, and equally unparalleled, explanation would have to be found for the occurrences in col. 10. Thus this kind of interpretation is unlikely to be correct.

In view of the context here in col. 9, and the variation in the dets. of the word, it is tempting to suggest a connection with *ḫyb.t* (fem.), 'shade', 'awning' (*DG*, 377. 1; Crum, *CD*, 657b ϩⲁ(ⲉ)ⲓⲃⲉⲥ, Bohairic ϧⲏⲓⲃⲓ, etc.). The *š* and the *w* present problems, and the *w* implies that the scribe thought of the word as masc. Apart from the question of the *š*, the word might be explained as an otherwise unattested masc. cognate of *ḫyb.t*.

Perhaps the least difficulties, certainly as far as orthography is concerned, are posed by connecting *šbw* with the loan-word ϣⲏⲃⲉ, masc. (and ϣⲃⲉ), Crum, *CD*, 551a; Černý, *CED*, 237. 3, which might bear the sense 'filth'. If the context in 10/4 is similar to that here, the house det., although unexpected, might not be inappropriate.

aa. *ḏkm=s*: the signs written after *ḏkm*, , occur elsewhere in this papyrus, at 9/32 (after a damaged writing of a verb), 10/8 (*ỉrm=s*), and 10/32 (*ỉrm=s*); they are also found in **2** expressing a suffix. A similar, but not identically formed group is listed by Erichsen as an early writing of the suffix pronoun *=s* (*DG*, 399. 1), and a comparable group, found in Memphite documents, and certainly reading *=s*, is mentioned by P. W. Pestman, *Receuil de textes démotiques*, vol. 3, p. 110. It should perhaps not be taken for granted that the sign here is to be read *-s*/*=s* (the one plausible alternative is the suffix *=w*). However, the context in 10/32 seems to demand the reading *-s*/*=s* (see p. 23, n. *ep*), and this is here adopted for each occurrence. Certainly, unless the group is used inconsistently, the examples after *ỉrm* indicate that a suffix, not an object pronoun, is in question.

No special significance has been suggested for the use of this form of the pronoun. Normal writings of both *ỉrm=s* (13/28) and *ỉrm=w* (13/29) are found elsewhere in **1**. Examples of *=s* and of *=w* alone expressing the object after the infinitive are naturally very rare; see *ỉr=w* (9/3) and possibly *ẖꜣꜥ=s* (14/13), and see also p. 31, n. *ca* on *r dỉt-s* (14/3). Here, however, in 9/9, the writing must be contrasted with *dỉ=s ḏkm=s* at the end of the line, where the final *=s* is clearly a suffix pronoun expressing the subject of *ḏkm*. It may well be that the use of the rarer form at the beginning of the line was prompted by the fact that it represents the object.

In the context here, the antecedent of the pronoun might be *wꜥt rỉt*, 'a room', which occurs in l. 8 (see n. *z* above, and compare the girl's reaction to the pastophoros's house in ll. 31 ff. below), or might be connected with *nꜣ ḥbs.w*, 'the clothing', which occurs in l. 2 above, and conceivably plays a part later in the story (see 14/24 ff.). However, it might also be a reflexive pronoun.

ab. Presumably the sense of this construction is '*She* is in trouble', 'She is the one who is in trouble (and not I)', rather than 'She is the person (already mentioned) who is in trouble'.

ac. *ḏkm=s*: this *=s* suffix is in the normal writing ; see n. *aa* above. The verb *ḏkm* may be used intransitively, 'She caused her to get washed', or the object of the verb may have stood at the beginning of the next line. As it is virtually impossible to understand *ḏkm=s* earlier in this line as intransitive, the latter possibility is much the more likely here.

ad. The traces at the beginning of l. 10 are . The det. shows that an expression of time must be restored here.

ae. It is difficult to say if the phrase 'emphasized' by the Second Tense *ỉ-ỉr=f sḏm* is to be looked for in this line, or in the lacuna at the beginning of l. 11, where there perhaps stood a phrase introduced by *ỉw=w ḏd*.

af. The following writings of this personal name occur in **1**:

9/11
9/13
10/7
14/27
14/28

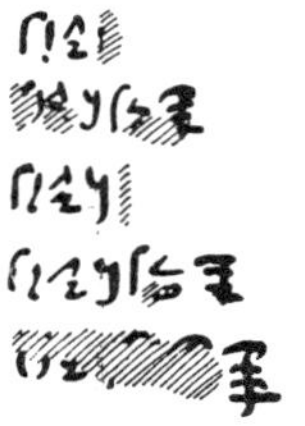

The variant in 14/28 leaves no doubt that the first element is to be read *Ḏd(t)*. The second element is written phonetically *sšp*, although the dets. suggest that *šps* (*DG*, 503. 5) was the word intended. See further on this name, p. 43 ff.

ag. The word following *ḫpr*, although it might at first sight be read *bỉn*, is not written in the same way as *bỉn* in *mdt bỉn.t* in l. 4 above. In particular, the first sign specifically resembles the *ḏ* found in this papyrus, and not the *b*. Further, the word here must be a noun, and no appropriate nominal form of *bỉn* is cited by *DG*, 112. 3; the usual phrase is *mdt bỉn.t* as in l. 4 above. (A fem. noun ⲃⲟⲟⲛⲉ, 'evil', 'misfortune', is found in Coptic: Crum, *CD*, 39b.) Thus there is good reason to reject the reading *bỉn* here. A plausible alternative is *ḏꜣ* (*DG*, 672. 5), with the sense 'evil' or perhaps 'loss' (cf. *Wb*. v. 518. 3 ff.).

ah. The torn condition of the papyrus has inevitably resulted in slight distortion of the traces in the photograph. The descending stroke visible above *ỉrỉ* in l. 12 belongs to *tꜣ*, 'land' (cf. 9/13, end); before this, *pꜣ* is certain, and leaves only one group following *mtw=f*. Judging from the trace of its base, this must be , presumably to be read *šr*. At the end, *m-sꜣ* is certain.

The grammar does not provide any indication whether the clause beginning *mn mtw=f* itself states the nature of the *ḏꜣ* just mentioned, or begins a longer explanation.

aj. The title *pꜣ mr-šn Mꜣ-wr* may be restored here with certainty by comparing the well-preserved writing at 13/30. The group that is used in this text in *Mꜣ-wr* (*DG*, 147. 7) presumably represents the dets. .

ak. The traces at the end of the line are . Here *ỉrỉ* is plainly a sing. form, written , as in 13/32, 14/8, and, probably, 10/18, in contrast to the plur. writings preserved at 13/22, 31 and 14/3, in the common phrase *nꜣỉ=f ỉrỉ.w n wꜥb*. The sense is presumably 'the priests, who (i.e. each one of whom) was/is his fellow . . .'. It is impossible to tell if the obvious 'who (each) was his fellow priest' should be restored, or, for example, *ỉrỉ n swr wnm*, 'who were his drinking and eating companions'.

The portion of papyrus that bears *ỉrỉ n* is positioned some 7 mm. too low relative to the area of margin to its left. Thus, although there are slight traces of a vertical stroke visible after *ỉrỉ n*, they in fact belong to the line below (see n. *an* below).

al. At the beginning of l. 13 the traces are . The 1st pers. sing. suffix *=y* and *n ḥm-nṯr* following are certain, although obscured in the photograph by the distortion of the papyrus. Probably either *ṯ=y* or *ỉw=y* should be read, and *ṯ=y* might suit the context very well (cf. *ỉr=w-s* in the preceding line).

am. r Dd(t)-sšp could be understood as the beginning of a circumstantial clause, or a future clause. The following traces are not legible, and the evidence they provide is too slight to form the basis of a restoration.

an. The traces at the end of l. 13 are . The fragments are badly displaced at this point, and some of the traces of *rsi* are completely obscured in the photograph. Contrast the writing of *rmt n pꜣ tꜣ* at 14/14, and compare the writing of *rsi* in 16/2. The reading *r pꜣ tꜣ rsi* here seems clear. It is difficult to escape the reading *rmt* for the preceding sign. As the context here is uncertain, the phrase *rmt n pꜣ tꜣ rsi*, 'inhabitant of Upper Egypt', might seem an obvious reading, but *n* in this papyrus usually has a horizontal form, and certainly cannot be read in the present case.

ao. At the beginning of l. 14 the traces are . The reading *=f* is certain, but the preceding trace cannot be identified.

ap. The traces between *iw=w* and *tꜣ wnwt* are . The first traces strongly suggest *r-bnr*. The last sign is *=f*, the preceding trace might be of a  det. (the fragments of papyrus are twisted and distorted at this point). It is possible that we should restore the text to mean that the men of Wenkhem say they have been sent out 'to fetch him' (or, perhaps, 'to warn him'). However, this would require a preposition *r* introducing an infinitive, and there is no sign of this after *r-bnr*. Possibly *m-sꜣ=f*, 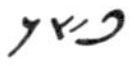 might be read. This would suit the traces and the context, but no reading has yet suggested itself for the three signs that would still stand between *r-bnr* and *m-sꜣ=f*.

aq. Probably a phrase beginning a new section of the narrative should be restored here, such as the common *tꜣ wnwt n sdm . . . r-ir=f*.

ar. The long tail beneath the beginning of l. 15 plainly belongs to a writing of *ir=f*. The form is wrong for the tail of *ḫpr*, and a numeral in the hundreds is not to be expected here. The angle of the tail suggests that little or nothing can have stood between *ir=f* and *nꜣi=f ḥbs.w*. It is hardly possible to read a Second Tense, e.g. *i-ir=f ṯꜣi nꜣi=f ḥbs.w pgy*, as there is no adverbial expression following. It is possible to read *r-ir-f*, which would form the end of the preceding clause. It is debatable whether or not this could belong to the phrase *n sdm . . . r-ir=f* that is expected after *tꜣ wnwt* at the end of l. 14.

as. pgy occurs in demotic only as a noun (*DG*, 141.5, *pk.t*). Presumably *ḥbs.w pgy* is a compound expression, in which, as is usual in such phrases, *pgy* more closely defines *ḥbs.w*: 'his mourning-clothes'.

at. The reading of *n=s* at the beginning of l. 16 is virtually certain (the traces are 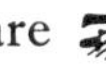), and it therefore seems likely that, despite his exclamation of dismay at the end of l. 15, it is the male character and not the girl who puts forward the plan of proceeding to Wenkhem. Plainly he plays the dominant role throughout col. 9, until he leaves her in l. 25.

au. nḫy-ṯ=s is commonly in demotic written with a  det., but this papyrus, with one exception (see p. 18, n. *cf*), appears to avoid its use. The sign here seems to have the form , although the way it is drawn is not certain.

av. The reading *n-im* is certain, although the writing is a little cramped as the scribe came to the end of his column-space. If any suffix was written in the margin at the end of l. 16, it is surprising that no trace is visible, as it would surely be written close to *n-im*. Conceivably a pronoun was carried over into l. 17. There are examples of this in the demotic letters from Saqqâra (and see also in this vol. **23**/6, with the discussion on p. 191), but in those cases the short line-lengths give a stronger motive for the practice. It is here most likely that is a complete writing of *n-im(=w)* in the sense 'there', Coptic ⲙⲙⲁⲩ. Cf. **2** front, 6/30.

aw. The traces here are ; this might be seen as the end either of *Mꜣ-wr* (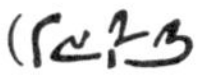 : cf. 9/12 and 13/30) or of *Wn-ḫm* (written  in 9/10 and 13/24, but  in 9/16, 18; the det. is doubtful in 10/29, and for the writing in 10/19, see p. 21, n. *dr*). In fact, the events recounted in 14/15 ff. show that the garden (*km*) mentioned in 9/17 must be in the Memphite area; *Wn-ḫm* is therefore to be restored here, and this would suit the apparent course of the story here very well.

ax. The writing of *ḥf* here is . Clearly this is the Coptic ϣⲱϥ (Crum, *CD*, 609b; cf. *DG*, 358. 1). The precise sense here is more likely to be 'deserted', 'unwatered' than 'destroyed' (by violence).

ay. ꜥš r ḥwt-ntr: the traces of *ꜥš* are very slight, , but suit the word very well. The preposition *r* is quite plain. The phrase *ḫpr pꜣ nw n ꜥš r ḥwt-ntr* in the following line strongly suggests here the restoration of *in-nꜣ-w pꜣ nw n ꜥš r ḥwt-ntr ḫpr*; compare *in-nꜣ-w rhy ḫpr* in 9/23. Contrast the phrase *i(w)=k šn n ḥwt-ntr* in

10/29. The expression here evidently signifies the hour of summoning to the temple, and indicates a recognized time of day, just as do *dwꜣy*, *rhy*, and *wnwt 6* elsewhere in these papyri.

az. *r-ẖry* . .[: the photograph is slightly misleading here, as the fibres are distorted. The traces after *r-ẖry* have the shape , and so seem to be of *pꜣ*, or possibly of *ḥr*, which would suit the context well, but elsewhere seems to be written rather larger.

ba. Although the papyrus is torn horizontally at this point, *iw=y* is certainly written ; this form of *iw*, common in early demotic papyri, does not occur elsewhere in this papyrus. Another example in this volume is at **1a**/20 (*iw=y*). Its use seems to be occasional and without special significance.

bb. The reading *Wn-ḥm* here is certain; for the variations in the writing of the name, see p. 15, n. *aw*.

bc. The traces at the beginning of l. 19, , would suit *irm=f*, but this is not a certain reading.

bd. In both *r-ḥr=s* and *r-ḥr=f* here, *ḥr* is written with the flesh det. (cf. 13/9 and 14/22, 32), in contrast to writings of *i-ir-ḥr* and *r-ḥr=* (the writing of the preposition *r*+suffix). Plainly *r-ḥr=* in this papyrus corresponds to Coptic ⲉϩⲣⲛ-, ⲉϩⲣⲁ=, whereas ⲛⲁϩⲣⲛ-, ⲛⲁϩⲣⲁ=, derives from *n-i-ir-ḥr*, the form that replaces *i-ir-ḥr* in Roman texts. A different view has been taken in Černý, *CED*, 272–3, under ϩⲟ, 272. 3.

be. Owing to a horizontal break in the papyrus, the photograph distorts some of the signs towards the end of l. 19; the readings are certain.

bf.]. . *pꜣ ꜥwi*: the signs before *pꜣ ꜥwi* are the house det. The most obvious restoration is *ḥn pꜣ ꜥwi*. However, the context strongly suggests that the first half of what is preserved of l. 20 is narrative, and not speech, and yet it is apparent from the following lines that the girl was deliberately left *outside* the pastophoros's house. Thus any reconstruction of this passage would have to be somewhat complex if it had to take account of a phrase 'in the house' here. Various nouns might be restored (e.g. *hyꜣ(t)*; see p. 12, n. *v*), although in this text an *n* in a phrase such as *hyꜣ(t) n pꜣ ꜥwi* would probably be written out. A number of verbs can be determined by the house det. However, perhaps the most plausible restoration would be of the compound preposition *r-rꜣ*, 'at' (*DG*, 240. 1; Černý, *CED*, 135 under ⲣⲟ 134. 6); cf. 14/9, where the phrase is not followed by an *n*.

bg. This Third Future with nom. subj., *r nꜣ ntrw* . . . *r ir n=t*, is introduced by *r*, not *iw*.

bh. *bn(-pw)=y* is certainly to be restored here, rather than *tw=y*. A negative is to be expected before *ꜥn* (*sp-sn*), and the traces would not quite suit a normal writing of the First Present (cf. 14/8), chiefly because the horizontal stroke is too long; compare the writing of *tw=k* later in this line.

bj. *n pꜣ* (*hrw*): as elsewhere in this papyrus where *pꜣ hrw* occurs with the meaning 'today', (*hrw*) is written in an abbreviated form, . The traces here are . The occurrences of the two uses of *hrw* are distinguished in the index.

bk.]. *rmt ꜥn.t*: the traces at the beginning of l. 22 are . The sign before *ꜥn.t* is almost certainly *rmt*. Conceivably the sense is 'You are a beautiful woman' (and therefore you will be well received). However, there are several more natural ways of expressing this in demotic than by *rmt ꜥn.t*. More probably, the sense is that the wife of the pastophoros is 'a decent (sort of) person'. The subsequent change to passive periphrasis ('they will not hate you') is quite natural in demotic. The small trace before *rmt* would permit the restoration *mtw=s rmt ꜥn.t*, but there are numerous other possibilities.

bl. *msty* is written .

bm. *n pꜣi ꜥwi*: the reading is certainly *pꜣi*, with the usual short vertical stroke below and to the left of the *pꜣ* sign (cf. p. 12, n. *k*). However, directly below this there is a short, light, diagonal stroke which it appears impossible to connect with the writing in either this or the following line. Presumably it is an unusually prominent example of the ink-marks discussed on p. 3 f. The very abbreviated form is used here for *ꜥwi* (cf. p. 145, n. *j*, p. 150, n. *k*).

bn. The form *nti i-ir=t r šm* is probably not to be explained as a Second Tense, but just as a 2nd pers. fem. sing. form of the Third Future+Relative Adjective.

bo. The first two signs in l. 23 are , clearly to be restored , and represent the speaking-man det., probably preceded by *m* (possibly by *ꜣ*, *n*, *ḥ*, or *š*). One plausible restoration would be *wḥm* (cf. **1a**/12 and **2**, 6/28 *bis*). The following signs are . From its shape and position, the first stroke should almost certainly be read as *n*, not *r*, although this is one of the very few cases where some doubt between the two readings is possible. The reading *šn* seems quite inescapable for the following word, although elsewhere in **1** it is always written . The writing *r-ḥr=y* here is plainly of the preposition *r*+1st pers. sing. suffix (ⲉⲣⲟⲓ); contrast the writings of *r-ḥr* mentioned on p. 16, n. *bd*. Presumably *šn r-ḥr=y* means 'enquire after/about me' (cf. the uses given in Crum, *CD*, 569a for ϣⲓⲛⲉ ⲉ-).

bp. The suffix *=s* might be interpreted either as 'Do not let her annoy you', or 'Do not let it worry you'.

bq. *km*, 'garden': the reading is certain; cf. 9/17 and 14/18.

br. The reading of *ꜣby*, 'to be thirsty' (*DG*, 3. 9), with the water-dets., rather than *ꜣbyn*, 'to be poor', etc. (*DG*, 3. 14), which might require *ỉr ꜣbyn*, is certain.

bs. Nothing can be made of the slight traces here.

bt. Plainly [*tꜣ ḥm.t n*] *pꜣ wn* must be restored because of the following fem. suffix in *pꜣỉ=s ꜥwỉ*: 'the wife of the pastophoros came out(?) of her (own) house'.

bu. *gm* is here written , as opposed to the more usual ; cf. p. 11, n. *g*.

bv. The traces here are . The only plausible interpretation of the traces seems to be *nw r tꜣ ntỉ ḥms*, although there are a number of small difficulties. The *r* is written rather high, and the space available for it is not so small as to explain its short, straight form. Below it there is a hole in the papyrus (this is not clear in the photograph). At the top of this hole are two minute traces of ink, which may very well be disregarded. The trace of the top of the *tꜣ* is convincing, although perhaps a trace of the bottom of the sign bending back to the right might be expected; but it appears impossible to read *tꜣỉ*. The tail of *ntỉ* is quite distinctive. The reading of *ḥms* is surely certain, although it is necessary to suppose that the cross stroke of the was drawn with a very exaggerated bend, ; the closest parallel is in *ḥms* in the preceding line, where the *ḥm* sign is not made in exactly the same way (). Compare **2** front, 6/19, **2** back, x+1/35 for writings of *ḥms* within **2**. At the very beginning of the line, the imperative *ỉ-nw* might be restored, or perhaps *ỉn tw=k nw*. . . .

bw. *pꜣỉ-ỉr=y*: clearly this phrase grammatically should contain a relative form, *r-ỉr=y*. However, as a point of orthography, it is very difficult to say whether the scribe intended to write *pꜣ r-ỉr=y* or *pꜣỉ-ỉr=y* (with *pꜣỉ* in the form used in this text for the copula). Although *r* frequently sweeps round under the following sign, no other example in this text seems to start so low, and probably the scribe deliberately employed *pꜣỉ*. For a clear example of the relative form *r-ỉr=w*, see 14/36. See, for this question in general, R. A. Parker, 'The orthography of article plus prothetic *r* in Demotic', *JNES* 33 (1974), 371–6.

bx. The only satisfactory explanation of *r šm* here is as depending on *snd*, 'fearing . . . to go out'. The word-order is by no means perverse. The expression *snd pꜣỉ-ỉr=y* has been kept intact, and the time clause *n-drt nw=y r-r=s* has been directly appended to clarify the past reference of the relative form. It is also probable that at the beginning of the next line a further phrase should be restored, explaining what the pastophoros's wife was afraid might happen if she went out, or something similar, and this naturally follows on after *r šm r-bnr*.

by. Plainly a verb must be read before *=f-s*. The traces are : the final det. can hardly be a form of , and it is not very likely to be the book-roll det. of, for example, *gm*, , even though this is often carelessly formed. The distinctive det. of *nḥm* (see 10/33), presumably a form of the striking-man det., is a possibility, or the group found in *mḫ̱t* at 14/23. However, none of these particular readings would well suit the preceding traces. The first trace is probably of the tail of an *=f*, which might belong to this verb, or, if the verb were a short one, might be the last sign of the preceding sentence; alternatively, this trace might be of an *l*, which is otherwise preserved in this papyrus only in *lwl.w* at 13/23 (see p. 28, n. *ao*), where the sign, unlike a normal *r*, plainly comes well below the line (see also p. 20, n. *cw*): this might suggest the restoration of *lg*, 'to hide' (*DG*, 264. 7; Černý, *CED*, 77. 2), which might have a det. that compromised between and . A verb meaning 'to hide' would suit the context (cf. n. *ca* below); *ḫp* in 9/8 above is written with a normal legs det., and can hardly be restored here.

bz. *m-sꜣ ꜣt.ṯ=f* may be restored with certainty; cf. *ḥr-ꜣt.ṯ=f* in 14/23, 29. There seems to be no parallel for this expression in demotic or in Coptic, and no warrant for understanding it as a compound preposition with some unspecific meaning such as 'behind him'. Presumably it means literally 'behind his back'. See next note.

ca. The final signs in l. 28, , are certainly to be interpreted as , and this might conceivably be a writing of *tp=f*, although it does not correspond to either of the standard writings recorded in *DG*, 626. 2. The immediately preceding sign, , might be understood as an object pronoun after *stꜣ.ṯ*. However, it has the wrong shape for *-s* (see for example 7/2); an example of *stꜣ.ṯ=f-s*, in which *-s* is presumably a reflexive pronoun, can be compared in 10/10. The sign here would perfectly suit initial *ḫ*, although *tꜣ*, *nꜣ*, and even *dit* cannot definitely be ruled out on palaeographic grounds alone. A writing occurs in **2** front, 6/4, and it is reasonable to understand both this and as writings of *ḥꜣ=f*, 'behind him', in which the elaborate dets. serve to distinguish the word from *ḥꜣ=f*, 'before him' (cf. p. 80, n. *cg*). Thus *stꜣ.ṯ=f* is plainly infinitive, as is to be expected after *pꜣ gy n*, and its object is expressed by a suffix pronoun. The phrase *r-ir=f* might be expected in l. 29, or something similar, completing the sense of *pꜣ gy n stꜣ.ṯ=f*.

Perhaps the sense in this line as a whole is that the pastophoros came out, bearing some object (masc.) on his back, or hiding it behind his back. From the following words, the girl is plainly aware of what he is doing; if he was in fact trying to hide something, perhaps she recognized this by magical or supernatural means. In view of what follows, and the 'fear' already mentioned by the pastophoros's wife in the preceding line, the pastophoros may well have armed himself with a weapon, or perhaps with an amulet. It is necessary to explain why the two different expressions *m-sꜣ ꜣt.ṯ=f* and *ḥꜣ=f* are used, presumably of the same object, and if a verb meaning 'to hide' is to be restored at the beginning of this line, the contrast might be a natural one.

cb. The first traces in l. 29 are . Although at first sight it might seem plausible to read *rmy*, 'to weep' (see, for example, the writings in l. 19 above), and this word might easily fit the context, it certainly cannot be read here. The final sign is at the wrong angle and in the wrong position for , the preceding sign can certainly be identified as , not , and the form of the *y* is not convincing. Another possibility would be to read *rpy.t*, 'lady', but the form of the *y* is again not convincing, and *y* and *.t* are not generally both written in fem. words in this text; in fact *rpy* occurs without any *.t* in **2** front, 6/10, 27, 28. The traces here would match precisely the writing of *ntr.t* found in **2** back, x+1/14, . This restoration therefore seems virtually certain here, and it strongly suggests that in response to the behaviour of the pastophoros the girl revealed herself, or acted, as or like a goddess.

cc. The traces following the short lacuna after *bn-iw-tw=k* and before *i(w)=s* are . The papyrus is torn at this point, and the edges at the break do not correspond correctly in the photograph. It is probable that *=k* must be read immediately preceding *in*. The traces of *in* seem convincing (although the writing would be less broad than often), and it is certainly to be expected after *bn-iw-tw=k*. If this is accepted, then *tꜣ rmt* seems the only possible reading of the last traces. The *=k* would not be one placed below the line, and *ṯ=k*, , is a possible reading. Probably the best solution is to assume that a reflexive verb stood in the lacuna, and governed, later in the line, either [*n*] *tꜣ rmt* or [*r*] *tꜣ rmt*, although there is certainly very little room for the preposition.

cd. For the expression *ꜥwi n ꜥnḫ*, no precise parallel seems to be forthcoming. The context suggests the translation 'a place to live', although *ꜥnḫ* will not simply have the sense 'to dwell'.

ce. The initial trace, , might be of the object pronoun *-s* or of the suffix pronoun *=s*; either might suit a restoration to the effect that the pastophoros took her (the girl) within.

cf. The det. of *ḥrḥ* is damaged. The traces are ; it seems likely that they should be restored to read *ḥrḥ* to include a writing of the det. , and, if so, this would be the only occurrence of this det. that is preserved in the papyrus, although other signs of similar shape are common (cf. *wn*, *ḥmt*, *km*). However, an expression probably to be read *ḥrṯ=k r-r=k* occurs in Saq. DP 71/2–130, perhaps suggesting *ḥrṯ=t r-ḥr=t* here. For the expression, 'be wary of', see *DG*, 322. 5, cf. *ḥrḥ*, 326. 2; Černý, *CED*, ϩⲱⲣ, 291. 3; cf. ϩⲁⲣⲉϩ, 296. 2.

cg. For the writings of the *ḫ(t)*, *ḫt.ṯ* words in this text, see p. 25, col. 13, n. *a*. The phrase virtually means 'She saw how dirty the house was', 'She saw the state of the house, which was dirty'; *iw=f ḏhm* must have *pꜣ ꜥwi* as its antecedent, not the fem. *ḫ(t)*. The next two lines make it clear that the pronoun in this sentence refers to the girl, and not to the wife of the pastophoros.

It may be noted that *nw=s* here is not a Second Tense.

ch. *mr* is written ; although the curve at its top is very small, the first sign is plainly made as an *m*, and the whole shape is not quite correct for a *ḫ*; the det. suits *mr* (*DG*, 166. 2). The sense will be that she bound (herself) with [some piece of clothing].

cj. The traces at the beginning of l. 32 are . The first sign strongly resembles *ḫ*, and probably the water det. follows, although the backward bend at the foot of the second sign is surprising. It seems quite impossible to restore a writing of *ṯḫb*, even if the signs were differently arranged from those in the example at 14/24. Possibly a phonetic writing of *rḫ*, 'to wash', might be restored (Černý, *CED*, 143. 3, ⲣⲱϩⲉ; Crum, *CD*, 310b; cf. *DG*, 253. 2, *rḫ.t*), although no precise parallel is forthcoming. After this there follows an example of an *-s*/*=s* suffix in the form discussed on p. 13, n. *aa*. In the context (quite apart from the form employed), the pronoun here could hardly be understood as the subject (unless a relative form were in question). The verb *rḫ* might be an imperative with object pronoun, but there is no particular reason to suppose this, and it does not provide an argument for understanding the following verbs as imperatives.

ck. The writing of *mḫ=s* is ; the form of the signs that follow *mḫ* and *ꜥḫy* in this line would suit the suffix pronoun *=s* or the object pronoun *-s*. Clearly the two verbs begin parallel sentences. If both are understood as narrative *sdm=f* forms, then the two following phrases, *ḫꜣꜥ-s*/*=s ḥr tꜣ wꜥbt* and *ḫꜣꜥ-st* | [- - -], seem unintelligible. All the four verbs *mḫ*, *ḫꜣꜥ*, *ꜥḫy*, and *ḫꜣꜥ* might be understood as imperatives, but this would demand either that a redundant object pronoun be read after both *mḫ* and *ꜥḫy*, or that these signs be read *n*(*=y*), which does not suit their form, and is not very appropriate in the context. It thus seems preferable to read *mḫ=s* and *ꜥḫy=s* as narrative *sdm=f* forms. To do this, it is necessary to suppose that the scribe has deliberately or accidentally omitted a pronoun after both instances of *ḫꜣꜥ*, presumably the subject *=s* in each case. This might have been done because of the assonance of *ḫꜣꜥ=s-s* and *ḫꜣꜥ=s-st*.

cl. *wꜥbt* is written ; this precisely suits the word for 'embalming-place' (*DG*, 83. 4), but the context demands a reference to a simple domestic fixture or implement, probably something called 'a (place of) purification', rather than an object resembling an embalming table.

cm. *ꜥḫy* is written , and there can be little doubt that it is *ꜥḫy*, 'to hang' (*DG*, 70. 1; Crum, *CD*, 88b, ⲉⲓϣⲉ; Černý, *CED*, 50. 1). At first sight, it is not clear how the vessels are first 'hung' and then 'placed'. It is not very probable, judging from the Coptic evidence, that *ꜥḫy* could simply mean 'to raise up', 'to lift' here. As it seems likely from the following line that the vessels are used to heat water, the setting up of some simple device to suspend them over a fire may be involved, or *ḫꜣꜥ* may mean 'left' here.

cn. *ḥmt.w* is written , and this is precisely the form to be expected of the plural of *ḥmt*, 'copper'; although there seems to be no parallel, presumably 'copper (vessels)' are meant.

co. *mw* can be read with certainty. The preceding traces are , and *ḫm*, 'to be hot', seems a highly probable restoration (*DG*, 380. 6, *ḫmm*).

cp. The traces before *ḏkm* are . The det. of a verb of motion may be read with certainty, and the preceding group might resemble the (derived from *nw*) of which a clear example can be seen in *ꜥn.t* in l.22 above. Possible readings are *tkr*, 'to hasten', and *twn*, 'to raise', 'to arise'.

cq. A number of plant names seem to be mentioned in this line, all with the det. . The reading *grr* is certain for although the word could hardly be identified with *grr*, 'burnt offering', which occurs in this text at 14/6, 10 with the det. , unless the scribe has simply written the plant det. by mistake. The plant name *grr* recurs at 10/20, where it is preceded by another plant name , *ḫnt*. Despite the slightly different writing, the same name should probably be restored before *grr* here in 9/34 in the form *ḫnty*; the traces are . This name may perhaps be identified with *šnt.t*, 'thorn-tree' (*DG*, 516. 7; Černý, *CED*, 247. 3 ϣⲟⲛⲧⲉ); there seems to be no parallel for the writing with a *ḫ*, but it does not seem impossible. Perhaps compare *grr* with the Coptic word of unknown meaning appearing in *Copt. Ryl.* 348 ⲛⲉⲥⲓⲡⲡⲉ ⲛϭⲓⲗⲗ 'the tow/fibres of . . .' (cf. σίππιον = στυππεῖον, Crum, *CD*, 811a).

cr. For the signs , the reading *gy* seems inescapable. Perhaps compare Coptic ϭⲏⲟⲩ, 'coriander' Crum, *CD*, 835a), or ᴮϭⲏ, 'quince' (Crum, *CD*, 803a), which the orthography perhaps suits better.

cs. The reading *ꜥry.w* seems highly probable for the signs ; compare Coptic ⲁⲣⲟⲟⲩⲉ, 'burr', 'thistle' (Crum, *CD*, 16a, cf. ⲁⲣⲉ, 15a; Černý, *CED*, 12. 2), and ⲁⲗⲓ, 'fenugreek' (Crum, *CD*, 4b).

ct. The first sign in l. 35 is another plant-name det. The plant name that follows is perhaps *bny*, 'date palm' (*DG*, 117. 1, *bn.t*).

cu. *ỉpy n rmt*; the signs are quite clear: 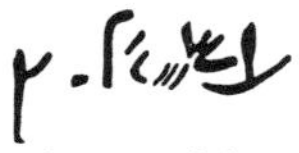

The first word, *ỉpy*, is undoubtedly by its writing cognate with *ỉp*, 'to count', 'to think' (*DG*, 28. 8; Crum, *CD*, 526a ff., ⲱⲡ), and the small final *y* probably identifies it as the fem. noun (Saʿidic Coptic ⲏⲡⲉ, Bohairic and Faiyûmic ⲏⲡⲓ, Crum, *CD*, 527b), used in the senses 'number', 'quantity', 'multitude'. A divine det. is not to be read: for the group , compare the two writings of *wḥꜣ* in **2**, 6/29, 30.

The sign 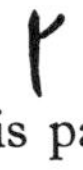 resembles equally well two signs that occur in this papyrus, the det. of the names of plants (see several examples in the preceding line), and *rmt* (see ll. 29–30 above). An abbreviated writing  of *s*(*y*)*m*, 'plant' (*DG*, 430. 2) is attested in Mag., as well as fuller writings with the same sign as det. (see Mag. Index no. 720), but such a writing is perhaps not to be expected in this papyrus, and the reading *rmt* seems inescapable.

cv. *ḥr drt* is certain, but it is possible to read either *ḥr drt.ṯ=s* or *ḥr drt pꜣ*. The former reading has the disadvantage that it is very difficult to suggest how the sentence might continue, or a new sentence begin with the traces that follow.

Coptic usage suggests for *iw r-bnr ḥr-drt* the sense 'came forth from', or perhaps 'were produced by': compare Crum, *CD*, 71a ff. for ⲉⲓ ⲉⲃⲟⲗ, and 428b ff. for ϩⲓⲧⲛ.

cw. The traces before the break are ; the first sign may plausibly be read as an *l* (compare the cramped writing of *lwl.w* at 13/23, where perhaps the signs may be restored as 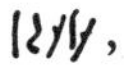, although the *l*s there clearly do not exactly resemble the sign here). The first sign clearly cannot be seen as an initial *ỉ*. It seems most unlikely that *lwl* could be restored here, as a *w* with a very large, rounded top is not to be expected in this hand. A reading of *lhb*, 'vapour', etc., might be considered (*DG*, 263. 5); the *h* seems to be situated rather high, but this might be explained by the shape of the *l*.

cx. The traces are , and the reading *tꜣ wnwt* seems certain; compare the writing in l. 14 above. The phrase *n tꜣ wnwt*, 'immediately', seems possible here, ending a sentence, as a new sentence may well start at the beginning of 10/1.

col. 10

cy. The traces of the verb following *ỉw=w* are . The first sign appears to be an *h*, although the bottom of the first stroke has been made, or perhaps reinforced, with a second movement of the pen. It seems unlikely that *hb*, 'to send', can be read, as in all the Saqqâra hands the *b* is written rather small, and above the second curve of the *h* (cf. **1**, 13/26. Possible restorations include *hm*(*hm*), 'to tread', *hmhm*, 'to shout', *hn*, 'to pay attention', 'to agree', and perhaps *hn* = *ẖn*, 'to approach'.

cz. The signs here transliterated (*ỉr*) represent the usual writing of the Stative of *ỉr* (*DG*, 36. 3); this appears to be the only example in this volume.

da. *šbw*: words written *šbw*, presumably the same word, occur in 9/8 and in 10/4 below; see p. 13, n. *z*.

db. The sense of *ʿš r* here is presumably 'to cry to' or 'for' someone. The sense might have been completed by an adverb later in the sentence, e.g. *r-bnr* (compare the Coptic usages in Crum, *CD*, 533a ff.).

dc. See n. *da* above.

dd. Although there appears to be a separate stroke in the margin before l. 5, an obvious unevenness in the papyrus has interrupted the long stroke of the *=k* of *ỉ-ỉr-ḥr=k*, and neither the typical Roman writing *n-ỉ-ỉr-ḥr=k* nor any kind of check mark before the line is to be read.

de. The final traces in l. 5, including those preserved on a single horizontal fibre, , strongly suggest the reading *my dỉ*.

df. The writing of the noun here is ; the precise shape of the signs favours the reading *šyš.w* rather than *šym.w*. The existence of such a masc. noun is set beyond doubt by a fragmentary unpublished Ptolemaic document housed in the Institute of Classics of the University of Copenhagen,[1] which includes an unambiguous writing of *pꜣ šyš*, 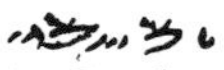 (apparently referring to a bird-rearing farm). It therefore seems preferable not to read the word here *šym.w*, and not to try to associate it with the still problematic word(s) *šym*, *šymꜣ.t*, etc. listed at *DG*, 486, 3–4 (cf. 510, 7), explained by Černý, *CED*, 242, 6, as masc. and fem. cognates of *šm*, 'to go', in the senses 'row', 'street', etc., and discussed with careful regard to their orthography by M. A. A. Nur el-Din in *The Demotic Ostraca in the National Museum of Antiquities at Leiden* (Leiden, 1974), 52–3. Any connection between *šyš* and *šsꜣ*, *DG*, 523. 4 (see Černý, *CED*, 259. 4 for a dubious Coptic derivative) is highly questionable.[2]

[1] P. Haun. inv. no. Dem. 2: we thank Professor J. Christensen for permission to quote from this document, and to Dr A. Bülow-Jacobsen for an excellent photograph.

[2] See also Hermopolis Legal Code, 3/18.

dg. Plainly the name *Ḏd(t)-sšp* (see p. 14, n. *af*) is to be restored here. This, together with other indications below, show that the events in col. 10 are closely linked to those in col. 9, and that no separate episode or interlude has begun.

dh. *ỉrm=s*: the suffix *=s* here has the form discussed on p. 13, n. *aa*.

dj. *mkṯr*, 'tower', recurs at 13/14, and 33; the def. article precedes in both cases. It is likely that the same tower is referred to in each passage.

dk. *ỉw=t ỉr n pꜣ(ỉ) ꜥwỉ*: it does not seem possible to restore any kind of relative expression here, nor is it likely that *n pꜣ(ỉ) ꜥwỉ* represents the object of *ỉr*. It is perhaps best to suppose that *ỉr* is here used intransitively, with some adverbial phrase following: for example, the sense might be 'as/while you are acting (*or* have acted) in this house [as though you were its mistress]'. 'This house' presumably refers to the house of the pastophoros, which plays a large part in col. 9, and this is strongly supported by the mention of the pastophoros's wife in the following line.

dl. The split in the papyrus here requires closing, as ll. 10–11 and l. 13 show, and the reading *tꜣ ḥm.t* is certain.

dm. The first sign in l. 13 is certainly to be read *n*, not *r*, and the restoration of a phrase such as *tꜣ wnwt n nw r . . . r-ỉr . . .*, 'the moment that (someone) saw (these things *or* what had happened)', might be suggested: *gy n nw* is another possibility.

dn. The traces at the beginning of l. 14 are . The first trace, by its shape and position, precisely resembles only , as in *ỉỉ.ṯ* at 9/29, among the signs preserved in this text. The reading here cannot be *ỉỉ*, or any other word requiring a tall stroke after this sign. The name of the goddess Isis, 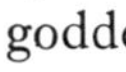, might be read; it is impossible to say if this is likely in the context. Another sign in a distorted form, e.g. *bnr*, might be read.

do. The apparent trace of ink in the margin before the beginning of l. 15 is preserved upon a few twisted fibres, and belongs to the text upon the back.

dp. A clear trace of ink stands before *bn-ỉw=n*, which is positioned too far to the left to form the beginning of the line: . There is insufficient room to read *ḫpr*. The stroke appears to be rather thick, and not to be at a steep enough angle to read *r*, although this is not impossible. The most probable reading is *ntỉ*; plainly the scribe dipped his pen between *ntỉ* and *bn-ỉw=n*. Many restorations might be possible for the final trace, for example *ỉn*, 'to bring'.

dq. At the beginning of l. 18, the papyrus is split and the surface fibres disturbed, but the signs are certainly 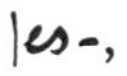, and *n hrw* rather than *n hb* should be read; *hrw* appears here in a full writing: cf. p. 12, n. *j*. The writing of (*pꜣỉ=f*) is the abbreviated form . The following *ỉrỉ* is almost certainly singular; if it had been followed by a plural stroke, this would surely have been set closer to the word, and would now be clearly visible. The final trace cannot be read.

The phrase *n hrw* might mean 'by day', as opposed to *n grḥ*, 'by night' (cf. 9/17), but, in this case, *n hrw* would have to end a clause, and *r (pꜣỉ=f) ỉrỉ* begin a new clause, and this is not very likely. Probably *n hrw r (pꜣỉ=f) ỉrỉ* is to be understood together as 'from one day to another'.

Immediately before the beginning of l. 18, there may be some very faint traces of erased writing..

dr. *Wn-ḫm*: the writing here is 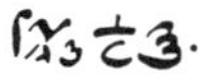. This appears to be a conflation of the place-names *Sḫm* (e.g. 9/11–13) and *Wn-ḫm* (see p. 15, n. *aw*), which are in part similar both in orthography and pronunciation. The writing here might be taken at its face value as reading *Wn-sḫm*, and this might perhaps be understood as a personal name. However, it seems obvious that a writing of *Wn-ḫm* is intended, and the variations in the other writings of the name in the text support this.

ds. For these two plant-names, written 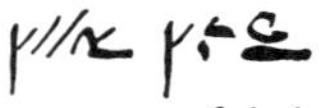 see 9/34, with p. 19, n. *cq*; the following traces of ink cannot be read.

dt. The last traces in l. 21 are ; the reading *n-ỉm=w* is certain, and the preceding sign is almost certainly *=s* or *-s*. Before that, the surface of the papyrus is largely lost, and only some shredded and twisted vertical fibres survive. Most of the ink visible here belongs to the text on the back, and it is impossible to offer any reading or copy of the signs, although one low trace of ink makes the reading *=f-s n-ỉm=w* probable.

du. At the beginning of l. 22, only a few vertical fibres survive, and the few minute traces of ink may belong to the text on the back. Thereafter the traces are ; *md(t)* is a probable reading. At this point the papyrus has a greyish tinge, and a faint diagonal stroke can be made out, as though of the tail of an *ỉr=f* from the line above; but it is impossible to be certain if this is a case of erased writing.

dv. The traces at the beginning of l. 23 are . After the first four traces, an *m* is almost certain, and]*mky*[seems a plausible reading; perhaps understand *mky*, 'to protect' (cf. p. 30 n. *br*). The apparent trace immediately below *mky*, that suggests that *=f mḳy* might be read, is to be disregarded, as it stands upon a few displaced fibres.

dw. The traces are ; the precise shape of the signs and the slight trace of the foot of a vertical stroke make the reading *ḏd=w n=f*, rather than *ḏd=f* or *ḏd n=f*, very probable.

dx. Careful investigation of the twisted fibres here shows that the traces are , and the reading *wḏꜣ pꜣi=k ṯꜣw* is virtually certain. See *DG*, 669. 9, and contrast 14/28, [*pꜣi=k ṯꜣw*] *my wḏꜣ=f*.

dy. The signs and traces are ; the reading *tw=n* is certain, and *tw=y* cannot be read. It is difficult to be sure if any of the following traces are merely stray marks: *bn-iw-tw=n ḥꜣꜥ* is a possible reading (cf. 9/14).

dz. The first signs of *rmy* may be identified for certain, . After a space of 7 mm., in which only a few fibres and slight traces survive, the traces occur. The intervening fibres are a little distorted; if they are stretched to lie straight, there is just the correct room to restore , *iw=f rmy wbꜣ=y*, 'weeping by my side'. It is tempting to restore *mn* at the end of the preceding line, and to understand 'I have no son to weep by my side (when I come (*or* now that I have come) to die)'. However, it is difficult to see how this could be followed immediately by *ḏd=f n*(*=y*), 'He said to me'. If the sense were 'I no longer have a son; for he said to me', this would surely have been differently expressed. It is conceivable that a quotation within a quotation ended with *wbꜣ=y*. An alternative is to understand 'I have/had a son, who wept by my side; he said to me . . .'.

ea. The traces of the *=y* of *mtw=y* are clear. The following traces are preserved on shredded horizontal fibres, and may be misleading; together with *mtw=y* they appear to be . It does not seem possible to decide if *mtw=y* is likely to mean '(a girl) belonging to me', or to begin a Conjunctive form, 'and I shall . . .'.

eb. The traces of *nꜣ wn.w n Ḥr-nb-sḫm* are clear. Before this, only the one sign immediately following *n-im=f* is legible. The pronouns *-s* and *=s* cannot be read in the context, and almost certainly *iwt*, 'between', 'among', should be read. For a writing of *iwt*, see **2** back, x+1/18, 35, 37. Presumably the kind of restoration required is 'the humiliation that I was in (that I suffered) among the pastophoroi'.

ec. *dr=w* appears a certain restoration of the traces immediately after *Ḥr-nb-Sḫm*: ; restore ; the writing in 13/31, rather than that in 13/20 should be compared. The final traces in l. 25 cannot be identified; immediately after *dr=w*, *iw*+suffix or *irm* are possibilities.

ed. *r pꜣi*(*=y*).[: the traces are . The position of the final trace favours the restoration of *ꜥwi*, rather than the other obvious possibilities, *r pꜣi=n* or *r pꜣi=k*. Compare the same phrase in 10/28 below, although that example does not show as broad an end to the horizontal stroke of *ꜥwi* as some others in this text.

ee. Although nothing can be made of the preceding traces, *ꜥnḫ=n* appears certain. The following traces are . They do not suit *ꜥnḫ=n irm*. A reading of *iw*, *i-ir*, or *i-ir-ḥr* seems inevitable; *iw*, 'come', does not seem probable in the context.

ef. After *in*, the sign is quite clear, and *in-nꜣ-w* cannot be read. Immediately after this the fibres are badly disturbed, and, although many tiny traces of ink are visible, it is impossible to tell if they belong to the text on the front or the back, or to identify them. Of the two readings *tm* and *ḥbs* that suggest themselves, *tm* seems to be excluded by context and grammar. The other slight traces earlier in this line cannot be made out.

eg. A little after *bn*, the tail of an *=f* is apparent, , although it is perhaps not possible completely to exclude the reading *=s*. Immediately after the top of the *bn*, a single horizontal fibre survives in place, and preserves two separate traces of ink, which strongly support the reading *bn-iw=f*, rather than *bn*(*-pw*)*=f*. After this, the distinctive shape of the base of *ḫpr*, , is quite clear, but the next few traces cannot be identified, and it is impossible to say if the post-negative *in* is to be read here.

eh. At the end of l. 28, the traces are . At the beginning of this, *wn*, 'pastophoros', appears a certain reading, and the preceding trace might well be of *pꜣ*, written as in 9/30 with a small tail. The large sign at the end of the line has the same shape as the first sign of *wn*, and this seems, at least in 9/30, to be indistinguishable from the first sign of *ḥmt*, 'wife'. Conceivably the phrase *ḏd pꜣ wn n* (*tꜣi=f*) *ḥm.t* should be restored here, as in 9/30. The abbreviated form of *tꜣỉ=f*, , would have to be assumed, and this does occur at 14/3. There would still, however, be very little room between *wn* and *ḥmt* for *n* (*tꜣỉ=f*). Perhaps another verb might be restored, with (*tꜣỉ=f*) *ḥm.t* as its object.

ej. *šn* is here written ; cf. p. 16, n. *bo*.

ek. *ꜥꜣy* appears in the form . The phrase can hardly be taken as a variant of *mdt ꜥꜣt*, nor is it likely that *nꜣỉ=k mdt ꜥꜣy* should be read, with no plur. stroke written with *mdt* or *ꜥꜣy*. Perhaps a circumstantial clause should be understood, 'your affair (*or* story *or* speech) being great at Wenkhem', or the expression may be future, for example, 'your affair will become famous at Wenkhem'.

el. *šw* is here written with the older and more elaborate form of *š*, , and this is not found elsewhere in this papyrus. Otherwise, the word is written just as in ll. 31 and 32 below, and this does not differ from the writing of the common phrase *r-šw*, 'ever' (apart from the initial *r*), which occurs at 9/2. It seems unlikely that the scribe of this text would write *šw* for *r-šw*, and do so inconsistently. There is presumably some connection between all these three occurrences of *šw*. The examples in ll. 31 and 32 may easily be interpreted as occurring in parallel phrases, and the difference between *mdt šw* in l. 31 and simply *šw* in l. 32 may well be due to the fact that the first clause is negative and the second positive. In both cases the word *šw* is the last word of a speech. This is evidently not the case in l. 30, but *šw* is certainly best interpreted here as the last word of a sentence. See further, n. *en* below. Possibly the position of *šw* at the beginning of a line might explain the elaborate form of the *š*, although this papyrus shows very little tendency to exaggerate the signs at the beginnings of lines.

em. The trace of the head of the suffix *=f* after *nfr* is fairly distinctive. Most probably *pꜣỉ* is to be restored in the lacuna, which is of just the right length. The alternative restoration *n=s* might be considered. After the lacuna, the trace suits *pꜣ* perfectly.

en. The reading *šꜥ-tw* is certain, although nothing can be made of the tiny traces that follow. Possibly the sense might be 'What I am saying is the right course, until . . .' or 'in order that . . .'.

eo. The reading is clearly *šꜥ pꜣ* (*hrw*), and not *šꜥ-tw*. The abbreviated form of *hrw* is used here, the sense being 'up to today'. This phrase plainly ends a sentence.

ep. The reading *md ỉrm* is certain, and therefore *md* must be imperative. The parallel phrase in the response to this request in the following line indicates that *md ỉrm=s* is to be restored. The suffix *=y* before *ỉr n=s* is certain. Comparison with the following line (cf. n. *er* below) suggests that the most plausible restoration is *r bn(-pw)=y* (there is perhaps insufficient room for *r bn-ỉw=y*, or even *bn-ỉw=y*, which are in themselves less probable restorations). The sense is presumably 'Speak with her, as I have not been able to do anything useful for her'; cf. n. *el* above. For *šw*, 'use', etc., see *DG*, 493. 1; Crum, *CD*, 599a ff.; Černý, *CED*, 257. 1: note the instances of *šw* in the Hermopolis Legal Code, esp. 6/9.

eq. The reading *ḏd=w* is virtually certain, but nothing can be made of the following traces. Plainly the reply to the request just made begins here, and continues into the next line.

er. The traces of *ỉw=n* are ; only very slight and entirely inconclusive traces remain of the suffix *=n*. In the context, *ỉw=n* seems the only possible restoration (both *ỉ*(*w*)*=k* and *ỉ*(*w*)*=s* are ruled out by the clear first trace). The parallelism with the preceding line demands the interpretation here 'We shall cause her to do something useful for herself', possibly in the sense 'to fend for herself': the clearly preserved *=y* suffix in the preceding line shows that the subject of this phrase cannot be impersonal. From the context, there is no reason to suppose that two different women are referred to by the pronouns in *ỉr=s n=s*, and, if this were the case, then the parallelism with the preceding line would be destroyed (because in this line the woman to be spoken to would not be the same woman as the one who is to be helped).

es. The traces after *ḏd=f* are very slight: . It might be possible to read *ḏd=f my* . . , with *my* written rather large; the sense might be 'Let this favour be done for me'. However, other restorations are no doubt possible.

et. The phrase *dỉ n=n pꜣ nṯr* is plainly grammatically incomplete, and in the following *r hyn.w ḫ*(*r*)*yr n Ḥr-wr nḥm=f n-drt.ṯ=n*, the *=f* suffix needs to be found an antecedent in the preceding clause. Neither the context nor grammar will allow *pꜣ nṯr* to be the object of *dỉ*, and the only plausible restoration is of a relative form; *r-dỉ* is extremely unlikely to be divided across a line-break, but *pꜣỉ* as a writing of *pꜣ r-* might perhaps be restored at the end of l. 32. The sense would be '. . . the one whom the god gave to us, some fits of wrath of Ḥar-wer will seize from us'. The relative form would come at the end of the preceding clause, for example, as the object of the verb.

eu. ḫ(r)yr: this word is the same root as *ḫ(r)yr* at **1**, 14/5 and, for example, *ḫ(r)ʿry* at **2** front, 6/31, with the sense 'to smite', 'to be angry' (*DG*, 351. 5, 352. 1; Crum, *CD*, 583b; Černý, *CED*, 251. 3). The group , derived perhaps from the particle *ḫr*, is that used to write the sound *ša*. The writings in this text with no written ʿ are both nouns, but they may indicate Bohairic forms such as the ϣⲁⲣⲓ and ϣⲁⲓⲣⲉ given by Crum. Cf. p. 11, n. *d* for the restoration of the verb *ḫrʿry* in 9/2.

ev. The det. of *nḥm* here, , is a little different from the common book-roll det. that occurs, for example, in *gm* and in *n-ỉm=*, even though the form of this sign varies. Presumably this det. of *nḥm* represents the striking man.

ew. The writing here certainly includes a suffix *=w*, and hence this will be a prospective *sdm=f* form. Thus *di=f* or something similar may be restored in the preceding line, and this will provide the antecedent for the suffix pronoun in the following *ỉw=f ḏd*.

ex. The writing of *ỉꜣw* is ; this may be interpreted as the imperative 'give', 'bring here', for which see Černý, *CED*, 14. 1 ⲁⲩ. The writing is unlike any of those listed at *DG*, 57. 1, but seems plausible: it consists of *ỉ*, *ꜣ*, perhaps a form of the legs det., and a speaking-man det., unless the last sign is intended as a *w* ending.

ey. The reading of *hbr* is plain enough, and it must be the word *hbr*, 'to be cast down', *DG*, 273. 4, which might perhaps be found in an active sense, 'to cast down', although this is not attested (cf. Černý, *CED*, 275. 5). It is only possible to speculate on the meaning here: conceivably 'money of casting down', 'largesse'. Note, however, the use of *hbr* with *ꜣyt*, 'misfortune', and *ḏdḥ*, 'imprisonment', in ʿOnchsheshonqy 4/19. The final traces are probably of *ỉw*.

ez. In the margin in front of l. 35 there is a clear trace of ink, perhaps the top of a vertical stroke; it is impossible to tell if it is a mark or a trace of writing.

The first traces in the line are . Plainly is to be restored, and this is more likely to be the common *rk*, 'to end', 'to cease', than *rḳ*, 'to turn'; cf. 13/33 with p. 30, n. *bp*. A plausible restoration would be [*bn (-pw)=s*] *rk* [*ỉ(w)=s ỉr*]-*sḫy n-ḥꜣt.ṱ=w*, 'She did not cease to have power in/over their hearts'.

fa. The traces are ; this should almost certainly be interpreted as forming part of the compound verb *ỉr-sḫy*, 'to have power over' (*DG*, 452. 1), rather than as *sḫy*, 'to beat' (*DG*, 451. 1), since the noun *sḫ* from this root is written at 13/21.

fb. ỉw ʿwỉ-n-drt: the writing is . As the scribe of this text is elsewhere consistent in distinguishing *drt* and *n-drt*, clearly the latter should be read here. A reading *ỉw bn n-drt* yields no sense. The phrase must be connected with the expressions listed at *DG*, 52. 2 and 57. 2; and Černý, *CED*, 193. 2. Compare the phrases *ỉr=w ʿ.wỉ.w-drt.ṱ=w*, at 9/3, and *r-bn(-pw)=y ỉr ʿw-drt.ṱ=y ỉrm=f* at 7/4. Probably the scribe has correctly distinguished the phrases 'to act as those who extend their hand', etc. from the phrase here 'extent of hand'. The sense here is presumably 'as far as possible', or perhaps 'as (it) is possible'.

fc. The traces of *swr* here are ; this corresponds to the form in 9/10, 13/3, and 16/4, but not to in 9/2. Probably *di=s swr=w* is to be restored, the *=w* suffix having the same antecedent as that of *ḥꜣt.ṱ=w* earlier in the line. This phrase makes it virtually certain that the subject of the preceding sentence is fem. sing., and, further, that it is a personal subject, and not a thing.

fd. Nothing can be read of any of the traces before *ḏd=f*.

fe. The phrase here is clearly closely connected with that in l. 24 above, *ỉw=y r dit ỉn=w n=k wʿt ḫrt* (cf. also l. 37). Here *tꜣ(ỉ)* is read in preference to *n(=y)*, as the writings in this text seem to be distinguished as and respectively. The presence of *n=k* in l. 24 might suggest that *n(=y)* should be read here; but *wʿt* in l. 24 might equally suggest the need of an article of some kind before *ḫrt*. However, the difference in the phrases is probably a natural one: in l. 24 the sense is 'I shall have a girl brought for you' (or 'a girl . . . who is . . .'), whereas in l. 36 it is 'Let this girl (of whom you have spoken) be brought before me'.

ff. For the reading *tꜣ(ỉ)* and the whole phrase, cf. n. *fe* above. The first trace, a thick horizontal stroke below the line, can be identified with virtual certainty as *ḫpr*; see, for example, 9/18. It may or may not be the case that the speaker of this sentence is the person who wishes to have the girl brought before him. The sense might, for example, be 'I am surprised at the fact that you have not had this girl brought before me (*or* before N.) previously'. Alternatively, *ỉw=f ḫpr* might be restored: . . . if you have not/shall not have caused this girl to be brought . . .'.

Fr. 4
col. 10 (?)

a. On p. 2 above it was suggested that frs. 4 and 5, viewed from the front, might conceivably belong in col. 10 of the text, to the left of ll. 16–26: however, it is not possible to establish a precise location, and it should be borne in mind that the fragments may belong elsewhere in the story. For *n=s mdt*, cf. 10/30–2.

b. Cf. 10/24. Fr. 4 front, x+3 belongs to a speech in the 1st pers. sing., as do 10/24–5.

c. For plural speakers in col. 10, see ll. 17, 23, 26, and 31–4. Perhaps then fr. 4 front, x+3 corresponded with 10/25 and fr. 4 front, x+4 with 10/26 (see n. *b* above).

d. *ḥr*, 'face', written with det.: cf. p. 16, n. *bd*.

Fr. 5
col. 10 (?)

a. See n. *a* above. In l. 4, conceivably read *mtw=y*, and cf. fr. 4, l. 3 above, and 10/24.

BACK

Fr. 4
col. 13 (?)

a. For the possible location of this fragment and fr. 5, see nn. *b–c* above, according to which fr. 4 back, x+4 = either 13/21 or 22. Nothing can be made of the tiny trace in l. 1.

b. The traces are  [ ] ; after the tall plur. or suffix *=w* stroke, *m-bꜣḥ Pr-ꜥꜣ* might be restored (cf., for example, 14/7).

c. The traces are ; at the beginning, *ẖdb=w* might well be restored, as *ẖdb* occurs elsewhere in this text (with the  dets. at 13/8, although not at 13/2); however, other words may have these dets. The immediately following traces might suggest *Pr-ꜥꜣ*: the final trace of the *ꜥnḫ wḏꜣ snb* group is perhaps a little tall. Almost immediately thereafter the tail of an *=f* might be read.

d. Cf. *mr-pr-ỉpy-nsw* at 13/27, 28.

e. The traces are : perhaps restore *Wn-ḥm*, . Cf. 13/24.

Fr. 5
col. 13 (?)

a. See n. *a* on fr. 4 back, above.

Fr. 3
col. 13

a. *r-ẖṯ* is written . This is not any well-known demotic or Coptic expression. The preposition and conjunction *r-ẖ*, 'in accordance with', etc., occurs at 9/8, and is written with neither the *ṯ* nor the flesh det. Two occurrences of , *ẖ(t)*, are mentioned on p. 18, n. *cg*, and p. 29, n. *bb*. The writing 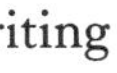, *ẖt.ṯ=*, before a suffix occurs at 13/4 below, where it may have the sense 'emotion'. Here *ẖṯ* is not followed by a suffix, and hence might be a form of the same word as that in l. 4 below. Probably the word here has the literal sense of 'belly' or 'body', and the whole phrase may mean 'at (*or* to *or* from) the presence of'. It seems unlikely that the curved stroke, here conventionally transcribed as *ṯ*, can correspond to a pronounced *t*. For the use of the det., compare p. 16, n. *bd* on *r-ḥr*. Note also the usage *sdr=w n=w r-ẖt.ṯ=w*, 'they prostrated themselves on their bellies', in **2** front, 6/20, cf. **2** back, x+1/36, 38.

b. The traces at the beginning of l. 2 are . Because *pꜣ ḥm-nṯr n Ḥr-nb-Sḫm* occurs in the preceding line, *Ḥr-nb-sḫm* might be restored here, although other names and words (e.g. *ḥwt-nṯr*) might equally suit the traces.

c. The traces at the beginning of l. 3 are , and might suit a fem. *.t* ending, as in *ẖr.t* in l. 1 above.

d. For this phrase see 9/6 above, with p. 12, n. *r*.

e. *ẖt.ṯ=s* is written . For the words written *ẖ(t)*, *ẖt* in this papyrus, see this col., n. *a*. The available examples are too few to be certain if and how this papyrus distinguished the equivalents of ϩⲉ, 'manner', and ϩⲏ, 'belly', and the present instance is the only writing with a suffix pronoun. A plausible interpretation of *bn-pw=s ẖꜣꜥ ẖt.ṯ=s* is 'she did not cease from her emotion'.

f. (*hrw*) here occurs in the abbreviated writing mentioned in p. 16, n. *bj*. The phrase here *ỉr=y pꜣ* (*hrw*) cannot mean 'I spent a day', but it is not certain whether the sense is 'I have spent today' or 'I spent the day (in question)'; however, the abbreviated writing suggests the former.

g. The traces are : cf. p. 12, n. *p*, on writings of *mšꜥ*.

h. The traces make the reading *ḫr.t* virtually certain; compare the writing in l. 1 above.

j. The traces of *ꜥḳr* are ; the reading of the uniconsonantal signs is almost certain. The word has an elaborate det., which may recur at **2** back, x+1/28; see p. 124, n. *ec.*

Here the reading of *ꜥḳr*, 'reed(s)', 'clump', etc. seems inescapable. It is not obvious how this would belong in the context; possibly it begins a proverbial statement.

k. The first traces in l. 8 are ; in the context, the last sign here is probably *=s* or *-s*. The shape is not correct for *dỉt*. The surface immediately before this pronoun has flaked away, and it would be possible to restore parallel *sḏm=f* forms,] . . ⌜*=w*⌝*-s* *ḫdb=w-s*; this, however, is not the only kind of restoration possible in the context. The antecedent of the object pronoun after *ḫdb=w*, and the preceding *-s*, if it is read as an object pronoun, might be either male or female.

l. The *ỉn* indicates that a Neg. First Pres. must be restored, expressing what has not happened 'for the last six years'. The first traces in l. 9 are , and these clearly suggest the reading] . . *ṯ=s*. The writing of *ḥr* in *r-ḥr=w* includes a flesh det.; cf. p. 16, n. *bd.*

m. The same phrase, *ṯꜣỉ rnpt 6 r tꜣỉ*, recurs, in a different context, but presumably referring to the same lapse of time, in 14/19. The writing of *r tꜣỉ* is . For the common adverbial phrases meaning 'onwards', 'up to now' used after *ṯꜣỉ* see *DG*, 667. 1 and Crum, *CD*, 773a; plainly *r-ḥrỉ* cannot be read here, and *r-bnr* has a quite different and consistent writing in this papyrus. The form here may plausibly be taken as the fem. sing. absolute demonstrative pronoun, Coptic ⲧⲁⲓ, of which there is no other example in these texts.

n. The traces and signs at the beginning of l. 10 are . The sign virtually guarantees a reading *mwt*. The following stroke by its shape is most probably the divine det., indicating that the name of the goddess Mut might be read. The possibility should also be considered of reading *mwt=w*, 'their mother' (*mwt.w*, 'mothers', seems unlikely); *mwt=f* and *mwt=s* are common in filiations (*DG*, 156 under 155. 2): *mwt=w* does not seem to be attested except in the Ptolemaic royal epithet *mr-mwt=w*, and *tꜣỉ=w mwt* might well be expected. The preceding signs might be read *r-ḥꜣt*, 'before'. A reading *m-ḥꜣt* might suit the form a little better; this might be expected in a proper name. At the beginning of the line there seems to be a divine det., perhaps at the end of a divine or personal name.

Thus the interpretation of these signs is uncertain. To understand] . . *r-ḥꜣt Mwt*, '. . . before Mut' (perhaps 'N. stood before Mut') is open to the objections that the preposition *r-ḥꜣt* is unexpected in this context, and that it is very difficult to see how this could fit in with the words that follow. To understand] . . *r-ḥꜣt mwt=w*, 'before their mother', might make sense in the context. A single personal name, [*god's name*] *m-ḥꜣt mwt*, would easily fit the context, but it is very doubtful if such a formation of a proper name is possible, the usual form of such names being, for example, *Ỉmn-m-ḥꜣt*, with the sense 'Amun is foremost'.

o. The word *hyꜣ(t)* occurs at 9/7 (see p. 12, n. *v*), where it is unlikely that the context has any connection with that here, and in 14/19, which is plainly closely related to the present passage (in particular, the phrase *ṯꜣỉ rnpt 6 r tꜣỉ* recurs there).

Presumably the sense is 'in the hall/porch of her brothers', but no *n* is written before *nꜣỉ=s*, although this text does not usually omit such an *n*. The reason may be that the following phrase begins with the sound *n*. Cf. p. 32, n. *cx*, and p. 34, n. *ed.*

p. The traces are sufficient to make the reading *ꜥn*, 'again', certain; cf. 9/21; 13/26; and *ꜥn-smy* in 14/7.

q. Despite some disturbed fibres, the reading of *mdt-bỉn.w* is certain; *mdt* is not written as a plural. The following *n-ỉm=f* suggests that *ḫpr* in some form may have been the verb of this sentence.

r. The traces at the end of l. 11 are , and the reading *tꜣỉ(=y) šr.t*, 'my daughter', if not certain, is highly probable. The signs before this are very badly distorted in the photograph, as the papyrus is torn horizontally, and it is impossible to make the edges correspond correctly for photography. The analogous problem on the front surface is mentioned in p. 14, n. *ah.* The traces here might be reconstructed as . The first sign is large and set rather high, and is apparently complete and self-contained. An obvious reading for such a sign is *mḥ* (*DG*, 171 ff.), and *mḥ*, 'to seize', might obviously suit the context. For writings of *mḥ*, 'to seize', see 14/23 and cf. **2** back, x+1/30–1 (*mḥ*, 'to fill', which is often distinguished from 'to seize', occurs at 9/32). Another possibility is *šd*, 'to demand', 'to take', etc., which does not occur elsewhere in this text; cf. **2** front, 6/20, *sdr*, **2** back, x+1/14, *šdy*.

The signs might be read as *tw-s*, 'behold' (cf. **2** front, 6/23). However, the might be taken as part of *mḥ*, and *tw(=t)*, 2nd pers. sing. fem. First Pres., might be read (possibly *tw(=t) mḥ.ṯ=w*).

s. The first traces in l. 12 are ; the fibres are considerably disturbed here, and, although the first sign seems a little low and broad, the obvious restoration in the context is *nꜣ mdwt*.

t. The fragments of papyrus are out of alignment here, but the traces can be reconstructed as , and the only possible reading seems to be *bn(-pw)=f sḫn.ṯ=w r ỉr=w*, 'he did not order them to be done'. Compare 14/36 for a writing of *r-ỉr=w* (there a relative form).

u. The reading *m-šs* is certain; a vertical split in the papyrus has opened widely, and the writing is simply , as in 9/6; cf. the writings in 13/4 and 14/10.

It is impossible to tell if l. 13 contained speech or narrative. It is notable that the fresh paragraph begun in l. 14 already contains speech in its first line.

v. *mkṯr* is here written with the form of *m*, unlike the examples in 10/10 and 13/33.

w. *pꜣỉ(=y) nb ʿꜣ* seems a certain restoration of the traces . The phrase indicates that Pharaoh is being addressed.

x. An obvious reading of the traces is *tw=* forming a First Pres. Therefore *tw=y* or *tw=n* seem probable; there is very little room for the restoration of the following words, and *tw=y* might take up the smaller space. Alternatively *tw-s*, 'behold', is plausible. The traces might be read *ṯꜣỉ=w*, but this does not seem likely in the context.

y. The traces are ; the restoration *mdwt* is very probable, written as *mdt* in 14/14 or 30. If *ntỉ* is read to follow, then *mdwt* must be defined; *tw=y rḫ nꜣ mdwt* might just fit the space available. The restoration *tw-s nꜣy mdwt* would certainly fit the space.

z. The reading *ntỉ ỉw bn(-pw)* seems certain. The form of the *ntỉ* is not clear in the photograph, but it certainly has a decidedly curved shape, which makes the reading *ntỉ* rather than *r* certain, and its position also favours this. At the end of the line the traces are clear, and other more damaged traces suggest a further sign or signs might conceivably be restored after this. The papyrus before what seems to be the last sign is not badly damaged, and it is very unlikely that further strokes or signs can be restored here. Neither *pꜣỉ* nor *pꜣỉ(=y)* seem possible readings. Conceivably the *pꜣ* sign is not to be read *pꜣ*; but *bn(-pw)*, with the dot below, is difficult to read in any other way. Possibly *ntỉ-ỉw bn(-pw) pꜣ* ⌜*ỉt*⌝ might be read, with the second sign of *ỉt* made even more carelessly than in the example at 14/12: for *ỉt* written without the *ṯ*, see 14/8.

aa. The traces at the beginning of l. 18 are . One possibility is that *Ḥr-nb-Sḫm* should be read here.

ab. No parallel seems to be forthcoming for taking *tꜣ yʿby n pꜣ tꜣ* as a phrase 'all the anxiety in the world' (cf. 2. Kh. 7/6, *myh n pꜣ tꜣ*), and presumably *n pꜣ tꜣ* must literally mean 'in (*or* of) the land'.

ac. *ḫpr* might belong with the preceding or following sentence; the latter seems the more probable.

ad. The traces would suit *ṯꜣỉ=w-s* perfectly, and this restoration is very probable in the context.

ae. For the *ʿwỉ.w n ḥrr*, 'houses of delay', 'prison', see p. 145, n. *j*, p. 147, n. δ.

af. The traces in l. 20 before *dr=w* are . The shape of the *=f* does not seem correct for *n=f* (cf. *n=f* at 14/32 and 33, and the *=f* at 14/33). Either *ṯ=f* or *ỉw=f* seem the most probable readings. Thereafter, *r-ḏd* seems certain, and the only natural explanation of the last two well-preserved signs before *dr=w* is as the 3rd pers. plur. object pronoun *st*. The fibres in the middle of this section of text are loose, and the photograph is misleading. A reading *ỉ-ỉr-st dr=w* seems very probable, and this suggests the restoration *mdt nb ntỉ-ỉw=f r ḏd.ṯ=w n=k ỉ-ỉr-st dr=w*, 'Everything that he shall say to you, do them all'. The form of *ḏd.ṯ=w n=k* would be (for the tapering vertical stroke of *ṯ=w*, cf. *gm.ṯ=w* at 14/34; for *n=k* see 9/1 with p. 11, n. *a* and the writing at 13/3, which has a small loop below, like the example here).

ag. The traces in the first part of l. 21 are

Towards the end of this piece of text, the signs *yry* are quite plain. As *nꜣ byry.w*, 'the ships', occurs at 13/32 below, the restoration of the same word here, in sing. or plur., seems very probable, and the other slight traces would suit this. In the middle, , *di*, may be restored with confidence. A little before this, the traces are clearly an *s* followed by a long descending stroke and, in the context, the reading *tgs*, 'boat', seems probable; the word recurs at 14/5. If this reading is accepted, then the immediately preceding signs might well be read as *wꜥ*. After *tgs*, the reading *ẖt.ṯ=f* might be considered (cf. p. 25, col. 13, n. *a*). Possibly the first traces in the line represent an *=w* suffix pronoun, with traces of a preceding det.

ah. Only a very slight trace survives of the sign preceding *w(ꜣ)y* , and this gives no help in deciding between the readings *wꜣy*, *dỉt-wꜣy*, and *ḥwy*. The meaning of *sḫ* might be 'blow' or 'scorn', 'reproach'. Of all the possibilities it is likely that the common phrase, paralleled in Coptic, *dỉt-wꜣy=w sḫ r-r=f* 'they uttered reproaches against him', 'they scorned him', should be restored. For the writing of *dỉt-wꜣy* in this papyrus, and for its use as a compound verb (cf. ⲧⲟⲩ(ⲉ)ⲓⲟ, Crum, *CD*, 444a f.), see 9/21, where the context places the reading beyond doubt.

aj. The reading *šꜥ ḥ⌈m-ḫ⌉r* seems certain; compare the writing at 9/4.

ak. The traces after *ḥm-ḫr* are . The first two traces are the tops of two vertical strokes, and they survive to a greater length than is apparent in the photograph. It is probable that a short circumstantial clause beginning *ỉw=f*, qualifying *ḥm-ḫr* should be restored. The final traces would suit the *ỉrm* that is to be expected before *nꜣỉ=f ỉrỉ.w n wꜥb*. Before this, the tail of an *=f* can be identified, which runs precisely into the top of an *l* in the line below; however, the *=f* cannot have stood immediately before *ỉrm*.

al. This whole phrase, without the expression *šꜥ ḥm-ḫr* . . . . *=f* . . , occurs also at 13/30 and 14/3.

am. The traces at the beginning of l. 23 are As *ḫpr m-sꜣ=s* makes no sense by itself, and the traces as a whole do not suggest any other explanation, *bn (-pw)=w* is a probable reading of the preceding signs; although the sense of *m-sꜣ=s* ('after it', 'without her') is obscure. Before this, an *y* might be read, followed by a speaking-man det.: perhaps restore [*ꜥn*]-*smy=s* ⌈*n=s*⌉.

an. The traces after *m-ỉr* are ; these, and the space available, would precisely suit *ḥrr*, 'to delay'; compare the writings at 13/19 and 14/6; cf. **2** back, x+1/21, 28 (see p. 124, n. *eb*).

ao. The traces are ; the reading *lwl.w*, 'youths', seems certain, although the signs are cramped.

ap. The first two traces in l. 24 suggest the *ꜥnḫ wḏꜣ snb* group at the end of *Pr-ꜥꜣ*, and the restoration *dỉ Pr-ꜥꜣ ꜥr=w r-mrt* seems probable. However, other restorations are no doubt possible, and *ꜥr=w* might be a narrative *sdm=f* beginning a new sentence.

aq. Apart from a portion of the first vertical stroke, only minute scattered traces of ink survive of *ḥrr*, but the restoration seems obvious, and would fit the available space exactly.

ar. The fibres before *mdt nb* are badly rubbed; the traces are , and a preposition *n* might be restored before *mdt*. Despite the appearance of the photograph, *ỉ-ỉr* and not *bw-ỉr* should be read. The shape is quite wrong for *bw*; the horizontal stroke here is perhaps more likely to be an accidental mark than part of *nb*. Nothing can be made of the small traces of ink on the disturbed fibres after *ỉ-ỉr*. A plausible restoration would be *sḏy=w ỉ-ỉr-ḥr*]*=y n mdt nbt ỉ-ỉr ḫpr*.

as. The traces are . It is most likely that this is the end of the same fem. personal name, *Nꜣ-nfr-Sḫmt*, that occurs at 14/31 (see p. 34, n. *ej*) and in **1a**. The present writing, like those in **1a**, and like the writing of the name of the goddess Sakhmet at **2** front, 6/31, does not have the final divine det. that is found at 14/31, but this variation is perhaps acceptable.

at. The second half of l. 25, considered as a whole, seems to make sense only if the phrase *ỉ-ỉr-ṯꜣỉ.ṯ=w* is taken as an active participial construction, 'who took them'. It seems impossible to understand *Nꜣ-nfr-Sḫmt ỉrm ḫrd* as 'Nanoufesakhme and a/the child', whether a divine or human child. A personal name *Ḫrd* is attested (Ranke, *PN*, i. 277. 13), and *Ḫrd-pꜣ-ntr*, although not attested, seems a plausible formation. Thus the phrase might mean 'Nanoufesakhme and Khered, the god who took them', or (more plausibly) 'Nanoufesakhme and Khratipnoute, who have taken them'. If the kind of restoration suggested in n. *ar* above is correct, there would be little room for restorations before *Nꜣ-nfr-Sḫm.t*.

au. Presumably *gmꜥ=f* begins a new sentence. This might explain the previous statement, 'For he had wronged . . .'. However, it is possible that a speech closes with *ṯꜣỉ.ṯ=w*, and that *gmꜥ=f* resumes the narrative. Thus the antecedent of the *=f* suffix of *gmꜥ=f* is not clear; certainly the word *gmꜥ*, 'to wrong', would hardly be applied to a god.

av. The traces at the beginning of l. 26 are . The sign *wn* is clear, and before this an initial *ỉ* seems inescapable. A small, high dot precedes the *ỉ* (see p. 3). The apparent high trace that follows does not support either of the obvious restorations, *ỉ-wn*, 'open!' or *ỉwn*, 'colour', 'condition', and *ỉ-wn-nꜣ-w*, as a writing of *r-wn-nꜣ-w* is perhaps more likely. A little before this there stand the signs . Possibly *ntr.w* should be restored (cf. 9/20). Another possibility is the det. found in *ỉpy* at 9/35, which might be expected in both verb and noun from this root; it would also be natural to find it in words from the roots *wḫꜣ*, *mr*(*i*), and *ḥs*(*i*); and there may be other possibilities. Between this det. and *ỉwn* an *n* or an *r* might be restored.

aw. Nothing can be made of the slight traces of ink in the 3.5 cm. before *=f rḫ šn*. However, this kind of phrase is common in the negative, and *bn*(*-pw*)*=f rḫ šn* is the obvious restoration here; the past tense is consistent with the following *bn-pw=f hb*. Nevertheless, other restorations are possible.

ax. The traces are . The reading *bn*(*-pw*)*=f* seems inevitable. Before this the traces do not support *ỉw-bn*(*-pw*)*=f*, and clearly *ẖrd.ṱ=w* was written, as often, .

ay. The reading *hb n mdt mtw=w* seems certain, and in particular *mtw=w* must be read rather than *mtw=s*. Conceivably at the beginning of the next line *sp-sn* should be restored; however, it would be surprising for the expression *ꜥn sp-sn* to be divided in this way, and *ꜥn* more probably stands here alone, in the sense 'either'. Thus the meaning of this whole passage may be 'He has not been able to inquire after his children, nor has he written a word about them, either'.

az. From the context it is natural to assume that a woman is speaking here, and the fem. sing. pronoun in *ỉrm=s* in l. 28 below would support this.

ba. The traces are , and make the restoration of *ỉpy* certain (cf. l. 27 above). The most probable restoration is *mšꜥ* (or another verb of motion) *pꜣ mr-pr-ỉpy-nsw r-bnr ỉrm=s*, but . . . *n pr-ỉpy-nsw r-bnr* is perhaps possible. Cf. *mr-pr-nsw* at back, fr. 4, l. 4.

bb. *ẖ*(*t*) *n Mn-nfr* is written . See p. 25, col. 13, n. *a* on various *ẖt* words in this papyrus. Here the context suggests the sense 'in, within Memphis'; the meaning may almost be 'throughout'. Conceivably, *ẖt* here might represent the old preposition 'through' (*Wb*. iii. 343. 9–22), though its use in demotic is not attested by *DG*.

bc. *ỉr sp* is here written with the abbreviated writing of *sp* familiar in documentary texts. Writings of the verb *spy* are rare (*DG*, 426. 4); all seem to be full writings, and the abbreviated writing appears to be proper to the noun. Perhaps the sense here is 'No one was left behind . . .'; the place thus deserted may have been specified at the beginning of the next line, and need not necessarily have been Memphis.

bd. Presumably the restoration to be made here is simply [*pꜣ ḥm-ntr n*] *Ḥr-nb-Sḫm ỉw ỉrm nꜣ wꜥb.w*, 'The prophet of Horus, Lord of Letopolis came with the priests'. As *wꜥb.w* is a plural form, *dỉ pꜣ ḥm-ntr n Ḥr-nb.Sḫm ỉw nꜣỉ=f ỉrỉ.w n wꜥb* is impossible.

be. *ꜥḥꜥ=w ỉrm=w* probably means 'they met with them', in which case an antecedent for the suffix pronoun of *ỉrm=w* must be restored. Cf. ꜥOnchsheshonqy, 1/17.

bf. This passage strongly suggests the expression common in narratives *ỉr=w nꜣ sm.w n Pr-ꜥꜣ*, 'they greeted Pharaoh', 'performed the greetings appropriate to Pharaoh'. However, there is no reason to suppose this phrase could *only* be used of Pharaoh.

bg. The traces at the beginning of l. 30 are , and in the context *ỉrm tꜣỉ=k* may be restored with certainty.

bh. *n tꜣ gm* is written . A restoration such as '[Let them deliver you], and your family and your fellow priests into the power of the Chief Scribe of Moeris, and let . . .' seems likely to make sense of this passage. The reading of *gm*, 'power', 'strength' seems plausible; the det. is generally in demotic (cf. *DG*, 580. 1), but the scribe of **1** is very reluctant to employ this det. (cf. p. 18, n. *cf*), and the speaking-man det. seems a natural alternative. The sign read as *tꜣ* has a form that could be taken as that of *dỉt*, but this reading does not impose itself, and *dỉt* would make no sense in the context; *r dỉt* certainly cannot be read, as the preposition before *tꜣ gm* is plainly *n* and not *r* in form. No word *ḥgm* seems possible here.

The phrase *n tꜣ gm* here bears some resemblance to the words read *r nꜣy km* at 14/1: , but on p. 30, n. *bv*, a quite different explanation is offered of that passage.

bj. Despite its curved shape, the trace at the beginning of the line will be a trace of the abbreviated form of *nꜣỉ=f*; cf. l. 22 above.

bk. The noun *ꜥnḫ*, 'oath', is here written in the normal form ; cf. p. 10, n. *h*.

bl. *mn rmt ḥw ḥn=w* is written . In the Ptolemaic period, *ḥw* seems always to be written with a det. of some kind, but a few early writings are more similar to the form here (see *DG*, 294. 3). The initial *ḥ* is precisely of the shape to be expected, and there is no plausible alternative reading. The writing of *ỉwt*, 'between', is quite different in **2** (see p. 22, n. *eb*).

The signs might be read *mn rmt-'Imn ḫn=w*, 'There is no man of Amun among them', but this is implausible in the context.

bm. Certainly an abbreviated writing of *pꜣi=f* should be read here. The preceding traces are too slight for certainty, but *r* is a possible reading, and a phrase such as the common *nw rmt r (pꜣi=f) ỉrỉ n-ỉm=w*, expressing a reaction of surprise or dismay, might be considered.

bn. The reading of the preposition *n* rather than *r* before *nꜣ byry.w* is certain. The phrase *ꜥr r mrt*, 'to go up on board ship', is common (cf. l. 24 above). It would be surprising if the preposition *n* were used in a similar expression, 'to go on board the fleet', and the sense is presumably 'to disembark *from* the fleet'. Another less likely possibility is that *pꜣ mšꜥ n nꜣ byry.w* is to be taken together as 'the crews of the boats' or 'the marines'.

bo. In the context, here might be understood as the plural possessive article. The writing is indistinguishable from that of the abbreviated form of *nꜣi=w* (cf. 14/2). If *nꜣ-w* is read, no article precedes *ꜥwi.w* here: *ꜥwi.w* may form part of a compound noun. The phrase *ꜥwi.w n ḫrr* occurred at l. 19 above.

bp. There is no doubt of the readings here, *di=f rk=w pꜣ ḫmꜥ tꜣ rỉt-ḥrỉt*, but the identification of the words is uncertain. The word written *rk* might be the verb 'to stop' or 'to hide' or 'to turn' (see p. 24, n. *ez*). The word *pꜣ ḫmꜥ*, , might be a substantive or an infinitive or similar verbal noun. Coptic ϣω(ω)ⲙⲉ, 'cliff' (Crum, *CD*, 564b; Černý, *CED*, 243. 4), might seem plausible, but it is a fem. word. A noun from the Egyptian root *ḫm*, *ḫmꜥ*, 'to overturn', 'to demolish' (of buildings), seems more probable (cf. *Wb.* iii. 281. 1–4; 282. 7). The sense of *tꜣ rỉt-ḥrỉt* is also not certain. Its common use is as a prepositional phrase, 'above'; however, it might also be used here adverbially, 'above', or in the sense 'the upper chamber', 'upper part'.

Thus the meaning might, for example, be 'He caused them to cease the destruction of the upper part', or 'He caused them to turn (*or* remove) the rubble (from) above'.

bq. The first traces in l. 34 are . A reading *di=w* might seem plausible, but other writings of *di=w* in this text have a substantial dot below (see 9/2 and 14/2). As this is absent here, other readings should be considered; perhaps a det. or followed by *.w* or *=w* is possible.

br. The writing of *šky* is . The first sign does not favour *m* as well as *š*. The word *šky*, 'to dig', etc., might be appropriate after the passage mentioned in n. *bp* above. See *DG*, 524. 3 and 528. 1; Crum, *CD*, 555b; and Černý, *CED*, 238. 6.

bs. The trace immediately following *ḫpr* may well be of *pꜣ*. After a space of 1.5 cm., there survives the thick top of a tall vertical stroke, and, after a further 2 cm., the traces ; these might suit the dets. found in words of time, although no doubt there are many other possibilities. Thus it is conceivable that a lengthy time expression was introduced by the *ḫpr* here.

bt. The final trace in l. 34, which seems to have been the last sign in the line, may well have been a 3rd pers. plur. suffix pronoun *=w*. Plainly col. 14 does not start with the beginning of a sentence. Possibly *di=w* should be restored here.

col. 14

bu. *mnḫy* is used equally of 'clothing' and of the 'wrapping' of a mummy.

bv. *r nꜣy km* is written . These signs bear some resemblance to the words read *n tꜣ gm* at 13/30: see p. 29, n. *bh*. Here it is impossible to read a word *ḥygm*, as no such word seems to exist, and, even if it suited the context to read *ygm* or *ykm* (presumably = *ỉkm*, 'shield': see *DG*, 12. 9, *ꜣkjm*), it is apparently not the practice of the scribe of this text to begin a word with the sloping form of *y*, . It thus seems inescapable that must be taken as a word, and presumably *km* is to be read, as a verb beginning a new sentence. See *DG*, 563. 1–2; no doubt *km*, 'to finish', rather than *km*, 'to become black', is in question. If this reading is accepted, then the only plausible explanation of is as the absolute demonstrative pronouns *tꜣy* or *nꜣy* after the preposition *r*. A writing has already tentatively been identified for the fem. form of this pronoun, (see p. 26, n. *m*), but no example of the plural form has been identified, and perhaps *r nꜣy* may be read here.

bw. The writing of the title read *pꜣ mr-mšꜥ* here is quite clear: . For the reading, see p. 12, n. *p*.

bx. *nꜣi=w* is here written in the abbreviated form , which is apparently indistinguishable from the writing of *nꜣ-w*, 'those belonging to', at 13/32.

by. *ḥnw.wt*, 'coffins', is written , and is thus distinguished by the (rather cramped) wood det. from , *ḥn*, 'pot', which occurs at 9/32.

bz. sdm pꜣ mšꜥ is probably to be understood as an imperative followed by a vocative expression, 'Listen, o army . . .'.

ca. From the masc. pronoun in *nꜣỉ=f* later in this line, it is quite clear that this pronoun is masc. Plainly the object pronoun has here been employed after the infinitive of *dỉt*.

cb. tꜣỉ=f is written in the abbreviated form .

cc. The initial *m* of *mhwꜣ*, 'family', has been omitted by mistake, and then supplied above the line, midway between (*tꜣỉ=f*) and *-hwꜣ*. The writing of the *m* is in every way indistinguishable from that of the adjacent signs in l. 3, including the shade of the ink. The text as at first written, (*tꜣỉ=f*) *hwꜣ*, makes no sense. This whole phrase has already occurred at 13/22 (with some expansion), 30.

cd. The form in which Pharaoh's order is presented in l. 3, in a kind of *oratio obliqua*, 'Pharaoh gave orders for him to be put on the brazier', suggests that someone is here reporting a previous order of Pharaoh, rather than that Pharaoh is present at this point in the narrative, and actually gives the order.

ce.  here is certainly a writing of the old *ns*, 'belonging to' (see *DG*, 227. 3), here preceding the masc. def. article *pꜣ*.

cf. The reading of a Neg. First Pres. here is certain, and the sense must be 'he is not (now) alive'. The antecedent of the suffix pronoun is not certain. 'The prophet of Horus, Lord of Letopolis' stands closest. The expression *rmt ỉs pꜣ ḥm-nṯr* at the beginning of l. 4, which has no def. or indef. article, is likely to belong in a negative or similar sentence: 'We cannot place/How are we to place anyone (at all) belonging to the prophet . . .'. If this kind of restoration is correct, then an obvious way to continue is '(for) he is not alive', that is, 'No such person is alive'. This would explain the use of the expression *bn-iw=f ꜥnḫ ỉn*, rather than some phrase including *mwt*. However, there are other possibilities.

cg. Little can be made of the two separate traces at the end of l. 4. The first is probably part of a low, thick, horizontal stroke, as of *bn* or *ṯꜣỉ*, and the second is probably part of a vertical stroke.

ch. ḫ(r)yr is here written . The exact form of the det. cannot be made out, but it is probably . The word also occurs in exactly this writing at 10/33: see p. 24, n. *eu*.

The beginning of l. 5 is presumably to be read *my ṯꜣw*, 'Grant breath after this (divine) blow/wrath'. It should perhaps be noted that a word for wind is attested in a phonetic writing *my* at Mythus 3/30.

cj. ḫꜣ is here written 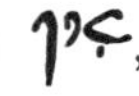, and the reading seems certain. The det. is the same as that of *grr* (see 14/6, 10) and differs from that of *ꜥḫ*, 'brazier': (e.g. 14/3, 4). Probably the word is to be identified with the word *ḫ.t*, 'fire' (*DG*, 345. 3; *Wb.* iii. 217. 10 ff.), and to be distinguished from *ꜥḫ*, 'brazier'.

The sense of the expression *ṯꜣỉ=f ḫꜣ* is less clear. A phrase *ṯꜣỉ ḫ* is listed by *DG* on p. 666 under *ṯꜣỉ*, 663. 5, clearly from Mag. 4/24, where the sense 'to cook' is suggested. Possibly 'He kindled a flame' might be understood here. Alternatively *ḫꜣ* might be identified with *ḫꜣ(y).t*, *ḫꜣ(w).t*, 'altar', *Wb.* iii. 224. 13 f., 226. 11 ff.; Coptic ϣⲏⲩⲉ, cf. *DG*, 345. 4; 353. 1.

ck. tgs has probably already occurred at 13/21. Although *ṯꜣỉ-nb* stands upon a detached fragment of papyrus, it seems likely that there is room for a sign between *tgs* and *ṯꜣỉ*, and that the small trace immediately after *tgs* probably does not belong to the end of a very large writing of *ṯꜣỉ*. A possible restoration is *pꜣ tgs n ṯꜣỉ-nb*, and this might mean 'treasure-ship', or perhaps a 'gilded barque' (e.g. for the funeral).

nb, 'gold', is here written in a typical writing , but after this there is a rather faint curved stroke: . This can hardly be part of *nb*, even though it might suit some Roman-period writings of the word, and it cannot well be a sign in its own right. It might perhaps be the tail of a sign in the line above, although no sign with this shape appears elsewhere. It might be a stray mark, or signal a cancellation, but there is no other indication that this is likely.

cl. The traces at the very end of l. 5 are , and this strongly suggests the reading *dỉ*: despite the appearance of the photograph, *r-dỉ* does not seem possible. The normal form of *sdm* would not suit the traces so well.

cm. The antecedent of the suffix *=f* pronoun of *rmy=f* is uncertain. It may be that this is the reaction of Pharaoh himself to the news brought in l. 7. On the other hand, there is plenty of room for these to be taken as someone else's words. If the words are Pharaoh's, then *ỉt* and *sn* may be used here, as often, as a formal way of addressing an elder and a contemporary, not necessarily related; it remains, however, questionable in what sense Pharaoh might use the term *ỉrỉ*, 'fellow'. The series 'father, brother, fellow' here recalls the phrase 'with his family and his fellow priests' applied in this text to the prophet of Horus, Lord of Letopolis.

cn. The signs at the end of l. 8 are : *tw=y rw*. . . is obviously to be read, and in the context *rwš* seems a probable restoration.

co. *r-rꜣ* will perhaps have the sense here of Coptic ⲉⲣⲛ- (Crum, *CD*, 289b; see Černý, *CED*, 135. l. 7 ff.; *DG*, 240. 1), 'to', 'at', after verbs of motion, and does not mean literally 'to the door of': cf. 13/17 and 14/36.

cp. *tꜣ ḥwt* is here written , which may be compared with the writing  in *ḥwt-ntr*. The same writing occurs in l. 10 and in l. 36 below. Here and in l. 10, *ḥwt* might have the sense 'palace' or 'tomb', but the meaning in l. 36 below is probably 'palace', see p. 35, n. *et*; it is reasonable to assume the same sense here.

cq. In 9/24, the phrase *iw=y r ir pꜣi=s smt m-mnt šꜥ* . . . was understood in the common sense, 'I shall do likewise daily, until . . .', and the phrase that occurs here *pꜣi=s smt ꜥn* is frequently used in the sense 'likewise'.

cr. *m-šs* is here written merely in the form , although elsewhere it appears as  or 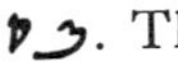. This is in fact the only case in these texts where it is used alone in a circumstantial phrase ('they being very copious'), although such phrases are common.

cs. The traces at the end of l. 10 are . The restoration seems virtually certain: see 13/24.

ct. Cf. 9/5.

cu. The traces at the end of l. 12 are , and *r pꜣ ḥri-ib* seems the only plausible reading. It is not difficult to provide a translation of this line, but how it fits into the context is obscure. In particular, it is uncertain whether *nti šm* means simply 'who has gone', or is used as a euphemism for 'who has died'.

cv. The traces at the beginning of l. 13 are . At the end of this, *ḥꜣꜥ=s* (or *-s*) is a certain reading. The preceding sign or signs have possibly been redrawn or corrected. Perhaps *mḥ.ṯ=f* [*r*] *ḥꜣꜥ=s* should be read.

cw. The writing of this word is plainly 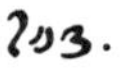. The first sign should be *m*. Some writings of *šꜥ* have a sign resembling an *m*, but *šꜥ* does not seem possible here. Presumably the word is (*ꜥ*)*mi*, 'to know', etc. (*DG*, 60. 6; Coptic ⲉⲓⲙⲉ etc., Crum, *CD*, 77b; Černý, *CED*, 46. 7: cf. *ꜣmj.t*, *DG*, 5. 1). No other writing without an initial *ꜥ* (or *ꜣ* or *i*) seems to be attested. (A word written  at **2**, 6/15 is taken to be this same word.) But some Coptic spellings suggest that such a reading is possible. It is not clear whether *mꜥ* or *mi* should be read here.

The word *mi* here must presumably be understood as a participle: it is difficult to think of another reading that would remove this problem.

cx. *tꜣ ḥꜣst Mn-nfr* is a clear case where an *n* might be expected to be written before *Mn-nfr* (cf. 1. Kh. 3/9), but certainly there is none. It may be significant that the following word begins with an *m*. Cf. p. 26, n. *o*.

cy. *iw=w dit r ḥꜣt.ṯ=w n-im=w*: although the papyrus is torn and distorted here, it seems certain that *r ḥꜣt.ṯ=w* is written 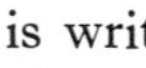, and does not unambiguously contain the expected det. . This sign varies in this papyrus, from the large and elaborate form usually found with *ḥr*, to the small sign that occurs in *ḥꜣt* in 9/5, while *ꜣt*, 'back' seems to favour a slightly differently shaped sign. Probably, rigid distinctions should not be drawn among all these forms, and, certainly, intermediate shapes do occur.

However, this leaves an uncertainty as to whether *r-ḥꜣt.ṯ=w* here represents the 'heart' word, or is a writing of one of the other similar words, perhaps 'front'. The phrase might mean 'as they put (them) in front of them'. However, an intransitive use of *dit* might be in question, although no precise parallel is forthcoming. For the position of *n-im=w*, see n. *cz* below.

cz. The signs 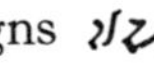 here present several problems. The phonetic signs seem to give the certain reading *šrf*, and therefore the word here cannot well be other than *šlf*, 'shame', 'shameful' (*DG*, 518. 12; Crum, *CD*, 561b, ϣⲗⲟϥ). However, this word is attested as a noun, and is also employed adjectively, but should not occur as a verb. It is also surprising that it does not here have a det. : presumably  would have to be understood as a speaking-man det. The last of these signs seems to be a suffix *=s* pronoun (or possibly an *-s* object pronoun). However, even if it were thought possible to understand *šrf=s mtw=f* as 'She was ashamed of/for him', the difficulty remains that this makes little sense in the context. Indeed, there is no indication that any singular fem. character is concerned in these lines until *ḏd n=f wꜥt n-im=w* in l. 17, and this phrase suggests that she had not been mentioned individually before. Possibly  may form some kind of det. A reading *n pꜣi=w šrf* might remove some of the difficulties; this would seem to demand that the preceding phrase be understood in an elliptic or intransitive sense. Another possibility is to read *iw=w dit r ḥꜣt.ṯ=w n-im=w* (*n*) *šrf mtw=f*, 'they setting (them) in front of them there in shame at him'. The most difficult feature of this puzzling passage is the position of *n-im=w*; no other reading of this group seems feasible, however.

Possibly the best solution is to regard it as the adverb 'there' rather than as the object of *dỉt*, despite the different writing of the adverb in 9/16 (p. 15, n. *av*).

da. The traces after *mtw=f* are : *r-dbꜣ* is perhaps a possible restoration.

db. The signs in the first half of l. 17 are , and there is little doubt that this is to be restored . It should be noted that the two different writings of *n-ỉm=w* occur here in close proximity.

dc. *ỉw=s ḫpr* is presumably not to be understood as equivalent to Coptic ⲉϥϣⲱⲡⲉ, as *ỉw=f ḫpr* is consistently used in this sense in this papyrus and in demotic of this period. Presumably the sense is 'One of them, who happened to be . . .' or 'One of them who lived . . .' The traces following *ḫpr* are .

dd. The traces of *pꜣ(i) km* are clear, : see 9/17, 24.

de. The traces are : *pt=y r-bnr* recurs in a better preserved writing at 14/22 below.

df. The traces at the end of l. 18 are : *i-ỉr=y dỉt* seems a very plausible restoration. It is conceivable that the phrase *i-ỉr=y dỉt ḥr*, which occurs in a similar context in l. 22 below, should be restored here. The traces make a reading *ḥr* possible, but are too slight to confirm it. The traces might also, for example, suit *i-ỉr=y dỉt r-ḥꜣt.ṱ=y*. . .: see l. 16 above.

dg. The reading *dỉt n=n* seems certain for .

dh. *tꜣỉ ḫrỉ* is written , in which *tꜣỉ* is written differently from the form of the demonstrative article commonly found in this text, . It is indistinguishable from the fem. 1st pers. possessive article *tꜣỉ(=y)*, but it seems highly improbable that this can be read here, because it would be difficult to explain a sentence '. . .[have] given *us my* food daily for the last six years, while *we* have been . . .'. No other example of this form of the article can be identified in this text, although it is conceivable that the two examples of *pꜣỉ(=y) ꜥwỉ* at 10/26(?), 28 (cf. l. 11) could be interpreted in this way.

dj. The same phrase occurs at 13/9 (see p. 26, n. *m*), and this or a similar phrase at 14/35.

dk. For *tꜣ hyꜣ(t)*, see 9/7 (p. 12, n. *v*) and 13/10 (p. 26, n. *o*).

dl. The traces of *nhpy* are . The papyrus is badly worn here, and this may explain the straight-sided appearance of the *h*. Plainly the writing is identical to that in 14/27 below, except that the latter writing appears to lack the dot after the *p*. Coptic ⲛⲉϩⲡⲉ (Crum, *CD*, 245a) is attested both as verb and noun. It is perhaps more likely that the sense here is 'Pharaoh went to mourn for Ptaḥḥotpe'.

dm. *Ptḥ-ḥtp Stm* is written . The same name and title recur at 14/21 below. The title *Stm* also occurs alone, without any proper name at 7/3: see p. 10, n. *d*. There seems no way of understanding the words here except as a proper name with title in apposition. 1. Kh. and 2. Kh. have title and name in the reverse order.

dn. The traces at the end of l. 20 are . In many papyri *pr*, alone, or, more commonly, in compounds, is written with a horizontal stroke above. However, the traces here would suit the reading *pr-ỉpy-nsw* perfectly, and this would be appropriate after *s-ḥm.wt*: the trace above *pr* would be of the horizontal stroke of the *nsw*-sign. This phrase has already occurred at 13/27 and (incompletely preserved) 28. Compare the writing of *mr-pr-nsw* at fr. 4, back, l. 4.

do. The reading *i-ỉr=y rḫ=s* is certain. The fem. suffix pronoun *=s* after *rḫ* might have a person or a thing as an antecedent, or it might be a pleonastic object. The form *i-ỉr=y rḫ=s* at first sight appears to be a Second Tense. However, this would demand a following adverbial adjunct, and this cannot necessarily be found. Therefore *i-ỉr=y rḫ* may be a writing of *ỉr-rḫ*, 'to know', in a 1st pers. sing. *sḏm=f* form, introduced by Circumstantial *ỉw*, or this may simply be the form of Circumstantial *ỉr-rh*.

A conceivable restoration is *ḫpr(=f) i-ỉr=y rḫ=s* . . ., 'It happened that I knew it, as Ptaḥḥotpe the Setm priest had taken me to it.'

dp. see n. *dm* above.

dq. The traces at the end of this line are . The first traces might be restored *ỉw=y* or *ỉw=f*, followed most probably by *ṯꜣỉ n pꜣ*.

dr. The scribe has here made a mistake which he has incompletely corrected. He began by writing *ḏd=s n-drt pt=y r-bnr n-drt pt=y*. At about this point, realizing he was writing words twice, he erased the superfluous signs, but did not do so very thoroughly; the first two strokes of the second *n-drt* survived, and the rest of the erasure can to a varying extent be made out. He then wrote *in i-ỉr=y dỉt ḥr* after *r-bnr*, but the first two strokes of the erased *n-drt* still stood between them.

ds. The traces after *i-ir=y dit ḥr* are . It is likely that the expected preposition *r* can be restored here: immediately thereafter *pꜣ* is a possibility, but no more.

dt. The reading *i-ir=y mḥṯ=y* seems to be certain. It is unlikely that *mḥ*, 'to fill', could make good sense in this context. The obvious sense for *mḥ*, 'to grasp', would be 'I betook myself', but it does not seem to be attested in this kind of sense. Coptic ⲁⲙⲁϩⲧⲉ (Crum, *CD*, 9a ff.) might suggest the sense 'I restrained myself', although precisely such a phrase is not attested.

du. The reading *šʿ pr-ḥtp* is certain: the writings are . The first sign of *šʿ* resembles an *m* rather than an *š*, but this is also the case with *šʿ pꜣ* (*hrw*) at 10/31.

dv. This or a similar phrase recurs in l. 29 below. In each case the suffix pronoun after *ḥr-ꜣt* is lost. It is uncertain whether *ḥr-ꜣt.ṯ=w* should be restored, in a reflexive sense, 'the clothes which were sprinkled upon themselves with lotus', or a restoration should be made such as 'he put on (himself) the clothes that were sprinkled with lotus'.

dw. The context and the writing make it clear that *gm=w-ṯ(=y)* should be read, with the 1st pers. sing 'suffix' not written out after the *ṯ*. There is at least one example in this text of the suffix written out in the usual way, *ṯꜣi-ṯ=y* in 14/21, but this does not follow another suffix.

dx. The traces after *ḫpr=y* are , and a reading *irm* seems very probable. Presumably *ḫpr* here has the sense virtually of 'to stay', 'to live'. The last traces are too small to make out.

dy. The signs at the end of l. 26 are . The shape of the sign does not allow a decision between the readings *ḏd=f n(=y)* and *ḏd=f tꜣ/nꜣ*. On close inspection *ḏd=f n=w* does not seem possible.

dz. Compare the same phrase at 14/20 above: see p. 33, n. *dl*.

ea. For the name *Ḏd(t)-sšp*, see p. 14, n. *af*.

eb. A reading *ḏd=w*, although suggested by the state of preservation of the papyrus, is no more than one of several possibilities here.

ec. Possibly restore the common phrase *pꜣi=k ṯꜣw my wḏꜣ=f*: cf. p. 22, n. *dx*; or *pꜣi=f ṯꜣw*, see p. 50.

ed. For the name *Ḏd(t)-sšp*, see p. 14, n. *af*. The sense here is plainly 'I am the wife of Djedseshep', and yet there appears to be no genitival *n* written before *Ḏd(t)-sšp*. The only other two occasions where an expected *n* is omitted in this papyrus might be explained on phonetic grounds (see p. 26; n. *o* and p. 32, n. *cx*), but no such explanation is possible here. Conceivably an *n* was written here, but runs into the lowest cross-stroke of the initial sign of *Ḏd(t)*; however, this is not a convincing explanation, especially as the writing of the name at 9/13 shows just as long a lowest cross-stroke as that in the writing here.

ee. The papyrus is distorted at this point. As two fragments overlap slightly, the photograph is misleading. It seems almost certain that *in* should be read, but *in-nꜣ-w* is impossible.

ef. This phrase, or one very similar, has already occurred in l. 24 above: see n. *dv* above.

eg. *iw=f ḫpr* might seem an attractive restoration here. The traces before *ḫpr* are , and evidently could not be the usual form of *iw=f*, , with a distinctive head to the *=f* (cf. the other occurrence of *iw=f ḫpr* at 7/2). Thus the reading *iw=f* here is very dubious, and the sign immediately before *ḫpr* could clearly be read as an *r*. However, it is difficult to think of any alternative restorations for this line if *iw=f ḫpr* is rejected.

eh. The traces at the end of the line are , and the reading *Pr-ʿꜣ* seems probable. This is the only example of the *r sḏm=f* verb form preserved in this text, although another instance might be restored after *iw=f ḫpr* in 7/2 (see p. 10, n. *c*).

ej. *Nꜣ-nfr-Sḫmt* is here written : see p. 28, n. *as*.

ek. *tny* is here written . The obvious reading in the context here is *tny*(*t*), 'cry', 'lamentation' (*DG*, 640. 1), regardless of the problems of the precise relation of this word to Coptic ⲧⲟⲉⲓⲧ etc. (*DG*, 608. 12; Crum, *CD*, 437b; Černý, *CED*, 198. 1). The one doubt is whether or not *šny*, 'to be sick', 'sickness', could be read here. This word does not occur in this papyrus.

el. This phrase also occurs at fr. 4, front, l. 4. It seems likely from the context here that it is being used as a conventional phrase meaning 'Please . . .'.

em. To judge by the normal practice of this scribe, *n*, not *r*, is certain before *rdwi.ṯ=f*, but this is not one of the well-known expressions found compounded with *rdwi*. The traces at the beginning of l. 33 are . It is tempting to assume that the sense is 'They threw themselves down at his feet' (see, for example, **2**, x+1/36, 38; 2. Kh. 3/1; and *DG*, 379. 3 for a phrase from an unpublished text); but no restoration that suggests itself seems satisfactorily to account for the traces, and possibly the context is quite different.

en. After *ḏd=w n=f*, only the minutest of traces of ink survive, set rather high: .

eo. The reading of *pꜣ gm.ṯ=w r-ỉr=k n pꜣ* (*hrw*), 'the finding them that you have done today', is quite certain. The preceding trace is .

ep. *skr*, written , appears certain here: cf. 9/33.

eq. Perhaps restore here *ṯꜣỉ rnpt 6 r tꜣỉ*: cf. 13/9 and 14/19.

er. The traces are , and the restoration of the abbreviated form of *nꜣỉ.f* appears certain: cf. for the writing 13/22. For *sn*, *sn.w*, see 14/8 and 13/10.

es. It is not strictly possible to decide if *ḥr rꜣ* here means 'at the door of' or simply 'before' (cf. p. 32, n. *co*, and see *DG*, 240. 1; Crum, *CD*, 289b; and Spiegelberg, *Dem. Gram.*, 150, § 332), but there will be little practical difference between these meanings in the present context.

et. It is probable that *ḥwt* here means 'palace' and not 'shrine' or 'tomb': cf. ꜥOnchsheshonqy 4/4, where *pr-Pr-ꜥꜣ* is used.

eu. Perhaps *tꜣ wnwt* begins a new sentence, e.g. *tꜣ wnwt* [*n sḏm* . . . . . *r-ỉr=w*], 'The moment that they heard . . .'.

Fr. 1

Col. 16 (?)

a. Despite the speaking-man det., *sk*, 'to collect' (*DG*, 466. 2) seems the most probable reading.

Fr. 2

Col. 16

a. The reading seems certain: cf. 9/24 and 14/9. A possible restoration at the end of the line is *n sf*, 'yesterday' (cf. 14/26).

b. The traces are , and *w*(*ꜣ*)*y* can certainly be read, but it is not clear if *wꜣy=w* or *ḥwy=w* should be restored, or possibly some other word.

c. *dỉ* here lacks a dot beneath, and *dỉ=w* should not be read: it is impossible to identify the following traces, but they do not seem to resemble any suffix pronoun.

d. The reading of *pꜣ ḥm-ntr 4-nw* is assured by the example in l. x+5 below.

e. The traces are . The first sign resembles *g* (or *gr*) more than *w*. The writing does not sufficiently resemble that of *grḥ*, 'night', at 9/17.

f. See p. 12, n. *p*.

Translation

FRONT (↔)

Fr. 1 (col. 7?)

— — — —

x+1. *only traces*
x+2. *only traces*
x+3. - - -] do it . . . [- - -

— — — —

Fr. 2 (col. 7)

— —

x+1. *only traces*
x+2. - - -] the man; I shall cause it to be done for you. If it happens that . . . [- - -
x+3. - - - the] killing which he had done. The Setm priest said 'Do not kill (?) [- - -
x+4. - - -] my brother[a] before me, when I have not done my utmost with him, . . . [- - -
x+5. - - -] an oath . . . . . . -Reꜥ (?) 'As Preꜥ lives, he is the one who is [- - -
x+6. - - -] . . . sleep . . . . *space* (?) After this, . . . [- - -
x+7. - - -] which [. . . . . .] he [. . .] . . . . . [- - -
x+8. 7th (column)

Fr. 3
col. 9

1. - - -] Stay here with us, and live to be a hundred years old; we shall not let you be in want
2. - - -] wrath against us. I shall never drink beer or wine again. Let me be given a suit of clothing, since you took the clothes of royal-linen[β]
3. - - -] . . . . . They did their utmost, everything they could do to prevent him from going out, but he did not listen to them
4. - - -] . . . the girl. It happened that they said 'This is the day on which a disaster happened to the great man'.[γ] It happened that
5. - - -] because he does not realise it'. The time arrived for Pharaoh to go to the House of the Attendants[δ]
6. - - - all . . . the] guards, the generals, and the great men of Pharaoh, who (?) ordered a very great evil,[ε] saying 'We do not know what has happened
7. - - -] . . . . . the girl. He reached the new house, and he walked to a gatehouse. He gave one *kite* of silver to the wife
8. - - -] . . . . It happened that she spoke with him as (with) her master. She had a chamber made for him, which was hidden in . . . . .[ζ]
9. - - - the] girl wash it. She is the one who is anxious'. She took the girl, and she made her wash
10. - - -] . . . . . he heard the voices of some men of Wenkhem[η] who were drinking beer in
11. - - - Djed]-seshep, the prophet of Horus, Lord of Letopolis. A misfortune has happened to him. He has no son on earth, except
12. - - -] . . . the chief scribe of Moeris. He has been made prophet of Horus, Lord of Letopolis, and the priests who were his fellow
13. - - -] . . . me as prophet of Horus, Lord of Letopolis; Djed-seshep . . . . to (?) Upper Egypt[θ]
14. - - -] . . . him. The priests did not abandon him. They caused us to come out . . . . him.' The hour
15. - - -] he . . . [. . . . .] his mourning-clothes. He wept, saying 'Where shall I go?'
16. - - -] to her 'The circumstances cause us to go to Wenkhem, for they will not believe[ι] that we are there.
17. - - -] Wenkhem by night. He walked to a ruined garden[κ] which was outside the town,
18. - - - When the time of] summoning to the temple arrives, I shall come down . . . [. . .] . . . . I shall cause you to reach Wenkhem, and I shall leave you
19. - - -] with him. He wept before her, and she wept before him. The time of summoning to the temple arrived, and he came out.
20. - - -] at (?) the house of a pastophoros of Horus, Lord of Letopolis. He said to her 'The gods whose town you have reached will make for you
21. - - -] 'Why [are you weeping?'] She said to him 'I am weeping because I have never once been apart from you, and today you are parting from me
22. - - -] . . . a fair person. You will not be hated in this house, to which you are about to go. For the god
23. - - -] . . . . . of enquiring for me,[λ] do not let her/it cause you trouble/anxiety. When evening arrives, I shall come
24. - - -] garden, suffering thirst, and I shall do the same daily until I

25. - - -] . . . . . Do not weep. Nothing happens except that which the god orders[μ]
26. - - - The wife of] the pastophoros [. . . . .] of her house in the morning. She found the girl sitting
27. - - -] 'Look at her who is sitting outside. When I saw her, I was afraid to go out
28. - - -] He . . . . it behind his back. She saw him and the way in which he was drawing it behind him
29. - - -] goddess. She said to him 'You are not [. . .] . . . the woman who has come to request a place to live'. He said to her
30. - - -] her (?) within. The pastophoros said to his wife 'Be wary of the woman, for she is some kind of great person'.
31. - - -] the pastophoros. She saw how dirty the house was. She laid aside her clothes, and she bound on a
32. - - -] wash it. She filled a pot with water, and placed it on the wash-place. She hung up the copper (vessels), and she placed them
33. - - -] heat water. She said to the wife of the pastophoros 'Go [. . . . .] . . . she arose, and she washed
34. - - -] a thorn tree, ... They brought a quince/coriander and some . . . [. . . . . .] . . . and some thistles/fenugreek
35. - - -] . . . date-palm.[ν] A number of men came forth from . . . . .[ξ] [. . . . .] the hour [. . . . . . .

col. 10

1. They stood up and they . . . [- - -
2. which was in/of . . . . [- - -
3. He cried to the girl [- - -
4. in/of . . . . She said [- - -
5. before you (masc.) Let [- - -] grant [- - -
6. the . . . . [- - - Djed-]
7. -seshep was in [- - -
8. with her. He found [- - -
9. in anxiety, until [- - -
10. He withdrew/returned to the tower[ο] [- - -
11. you are acting in this house [- - -
12. the wife of the pastophoros [- - -
13. of seeing the [- - -
14. *only traces*
15. *no trace*
16. *no trace*
17. which we shall not . . . [- - -
18. from one day to another . . . [- - -
19. of/in Wenkhem with [- - -
20. thorn-tree . . . .[π] [- - -
21. . . . . [- - -
22. . . . . thing/speak . . . [- - -
23. . . . . . . protect (?) [. . .] . . . They said to him 'May your breath be safe, we are not . . . . . [- - -

24. I had a /have [no] son, to weep by my side. He said to me 'I shall have a girl brought to you, ...[ρ] [- - -
25. that I was in among all the pastophoroi of Horus, Lord of Letopolis . . . . [- - -
26. . . . her town . . . . my . . . . . .[σ] [. . .] . . . . . we live(d) . . . . . [- - - without being (?)]
27. able to say anything about them to her [. . .] . . . [. . . . . . .] . . . . . girl . . . [- - -
28. will happen to her in my house; it will not happen . . . . . the pastophoros . . . his wife (?) [- - -
29. When/if you ask at the temple, your affair will be/being important (?) at Wenkhem [- - -
30. useful. What I am saying is what is best [. . .] until . . . [- - -
31. until today. Speak with [her, as I have not] done anything useful for her'. They said . . . . . [- - -
32. We shall speak with her, and we shall make her do something useful for herself.' He said . . . . [- - -
33. whom the god gave to us, some ragings of Ḥarwer[τ] will seize from us. . . . [- - -
34. that they should come after us, and he said to us 'Give some money . . . . [- - -
35. cease [from having] power over (?) their hearts as far as possible. She caused [them (?)] to drink [- - -
36. . . .] . . . [. . . . .] . . . [. . . . .] He said to you 'Let this girl be brought [- - -
37. . . . .] . . . . you have not had this girl brought [- - - -

Fr. 4 (col. 10?)[υ]

x+1. - - -] her [- - -
x+2. - - -] . . . [. . .] to her a matter/word [- - -
x+3. - - -] . . . . . out by force, and I shall cause them to do/make [- - -
x+4. - - -'May] this favour be done for us before [- - -
x+5. - - -] face [- - -
— — — — — — — — — — — — — — — — — —

Fr. 5 (col. 10?)

— — — — — — — — — — — —
x+1. *only traces*
x+2. *only traces*
x+3. - - -] because of her/it . . . . [- - -
x+4. - - -] and I shall (?) [- - -
— — — — — — — — — — — —

BACK

Fr. 4 (col. 13?)[φ]

— — — — — — — — — — — — — — — — — — — —
x+1. *only traces*
x+2. *only traces*
x+3. *only traces*
x+4. - - -] the Overseer of the Royal Household, not to stand/meet . . . [- - -
x+5. *only traces*
x+6. *only traces*
— — — — — — — — — — — — — — — — — — — —

Fr. 5 (col. 13?)

— — — — — —

x+1. *only traces*
x+2. *only traces*
x+3. - - -] great men . . . [- - -
x+4. - - -] . . . hand . . . [- - -

— — — — — —

Fr. 3
col. 13

1. - - - the] girl into the presence (?) of the prophet of Horus, Lord of Letopolis
2. - - -] . . . I have not killed any man of yours in my life
3. - - -] . . . She was your wife; she drank and ate with you
4. - - -] ordered a very great evil.[χ] She did not cease from her love (?)
5. - - -] . . . with me, and I spent the day with you. You
6. - - -] The soldiers who were in attendance wept
7. - - -] girl. They said to the prophet of Horus, Lord of Letopolis 'The reed[ψ]
8. - - -] . . . him/her (?); they slew him/her instantly[ω]
9. - - - not - - -] . . . it/her in their presence, for six years up to now.[αα]
10. - - -] . . . before their mother (?) in the gatehouse of her brothers again.
11. - - -] evil to him. . . . . taken (?) my daughter
12. - - - the] things that you are saying, he did not order them to be done
13. - - -] . . . exceedingly. *space*

larger space between lines

14. - - -] I saw a tower[αβ]
15. - - -] saw the great man with
16. - - -] 'My great Lord, ... the things that the . . . . . did not
17. - - -] eleventh hour, Pharaoh came out of (the door of)
18. - - -] . . . in/of the distress in/of the land. It happened that the time passed
19. - - -] they took him/her to the Houses of Delay,[αγ] and Pharaoh caused
20. - - -] that he shall say to you, do them all!' Pharaoh said
21. - - -] . . . a boat . . . . . cause . . . . the fleet . . . . . they hurled blows/reproaches at him
22. - - - the prophet of Horus, Lord] of Letopolis, with his family down to any child who shall come after him (?) and with his fellow priests
23. - - -] . . . . they did not happen without (?) her. Do not delay to go to Memphis with these children. I shall not go
24. - - -] Pharaoh [made] them mount on board again. They did not delay to go [to] Wenkhem. Pharaoh went to the House of Pharaoh.[αδ]
25. - - -] . . . everything that had . . . . . [. . . . . Nanoufe]sakhme (?) and Khratipnoute who had taken them. He wronged
26. - - -] the gods, who were (?) . . . . . he had not been able to ask after his children, and he had not written any matter of theirs, either
27. - - -] before Pharaoh. 'May it be ordered to the Overseer of the Royal Harem that I should be allowed to come out

28. - - - Royal] Harem [came] out with her. There was a great lamentation throughout Memphis, and no one was left behind
29. - - - the Prophet of] Horus, Lord of Letopolis came with the priests. They met with them, and they performed the greetings of
30. - - -] with your family and your fellow priests in(to) the power of the Chief Scribe of Moeris. Let
31. - - -] his fellow priests, all of them. Ḥarmakhroou made him take an oath, namely, 'There is no man in excess among them
32. - - -] . . . his fellow among them. He made the army mount up from the ships, and he made them bring those of the houses
33. - - -] Ḥarmakhroou walked to the tower.[αε] He made them cease/remove the destruction/rubble above
34. - - -] . . . . . . digging . . . . . . There happened . . . *only traces*

col. 14

1. clothing/wrapping of the great men upon (?) these. The general and the army finished [- - -
2. They laid them to rest in their coffins. Ḥarmakhroou said 'Listen, o army, [- - -
3. Pharaoh ordered that he should be placed upon the brazier with his family and his fellow [- - -
4. to place a man belonging to the prophet of Horus, Lord of Letopolis upon the brazier, for he is not alive . . . . . [- - -
5. Grant breath (of life) after this wrath!' He kindled (?) a flame. They brought the boat . . . . gold . . .[αζ] [- - -
6. wine. They made a burnt-offering and a libation before the great men. They did not delay (to go) to Memphis [- - -
7. reported about it before Pharaoh, saying, 'The great men have arrived at Memphis [- - -
8. He wept, saying, 'O my father, O my brother, O my companion, I grieve [- - -
9. The Queen came to the door of the Palace, and she also did the like thereof. [- - -
10. the Palace. He made very great burnt-offerings. Pharaoh went into the House [of Pharaoh - - -
11. Pharaoh exceedingly. Pharaoh went to the House of the Attendants[αη] [- - -
12. in exchange for your father, who is departed. Let them be far from the midst [- - -
13. seize him to place him at his house. Pharaoh ordered, saying [- - -
14. It happened that no man on earth knew about the matter of Ḥarma[khroou - - -

larger space between lines

15. It happened one day that Ḥarmakhroou went to the necropolis of Memphis [- - -
16. from/in their hands, as they put . . . . shame . . . . [- - -
17. on behalf of which of them are you doing them?' One (fem.) of them, who happened . . . said to him [- - -
18. this garden.[αθ] I fled out with this girl who is in front of you. I gave . . . [- - -
19. giving to us this food daily for six years up to now,[αι] we being in the gatehouse [- - -
20. saying/because Pharaoh went to mourn for Ptaḥḥotpe, the Setm priest, with the women of the Royal Harem [- - -
21. I know . . . . . Ptaḥḥotpe, the Setm priest, took me to her/it, while . . . . [- - -

22. had happened to her. She said 'When I fled out, I paid attention to . . . . . [- - -
23. whither [are you going?'] He said to me 'It is to the place of the setting [of the sun (?)] that I am taking myself [- - -
24. the clothes that were dipped in lotus upon[ακ] [- - -
25. with him, because he would not let them find me. And I dwelt (?) . . . . . [- - -
26. the terror which happened in Memphis yesterday. He said . . . . [- - -
27. to mourn for a great man, whose name is Djedseshep . . . . . [- - -
28. may he/it be saved, I am the wife of Djedseshep . . . . . [- - -
29. in/of lotus upon [. . .] . . . . . If it should (?) happen that Pharaoh (?) ask [- - -
30. upon the necropolis. He said to me 'It is a priest who has caused to be discovered everything that has happened to [- - -
31. I reached this place. It was with Nanoufesakhme that I came to this place when she was [- - -
32. in mourning linen. He uttered a cry of distress to them. They said to him 'May this favour be done for us [- - -
33. . . . . at his feet instantly. They said to him . . . [- - -
34. [. . . . .] . . . the discovery of them which you have made today. He said to them 'Travel
35. [. . . .] He related before them everything which had happened to him since [- - -
36. [. . .] his brothers upon the brazier which had been done at the door of the palace. The moment [- - -
37. 14th (column)

Fr. 1 (col. 16?)

x+1. *only traces*
x+2. - - -] matter . . . [- - -
x+3. - - -] he collected [- - -
x+4. - - -] give . . . [- - -

Fr. 2 (col. 16)

x+1. - - -] . . . . [. . .] I do the like thereof . . . . [- - -
x+2. - - -] . . . . to take him to the South with him . . . . . caused . . . [- - -
x+3. - - -] the Fourth Prophet to Thebes. He related everything [- - -
x+4. - - -] . . . Ḥarmakhroou was taking part in drinking beer . . . . [- - -
x+5. - - -] . . . without the Fourth Prophet's failing to have things brought to Ḥarma[khroou - - -
x+6. - - -] . . . they having brought the generals and the great men . . . . [- - -
x+7. *only traces*
x+8. 16th (column)

Notes on translation

α. In demotic literary texts the term 'brother' can be used of contemporaries who are not in any way related, and 'father' and 'son' are similarly used of seniors and juniors; it is therefore often difficult to tell if such terms are being used literally (see p. 31, n. *cm*, and p. 52).

β. Apart from mentions of mourning-linen, and, probably, of wrappings for mummies, distinctive clothing is mentioned again at 14/24 (cf. l. 29): it is not clear if the passages are connected.

γ. It is impossible to be sure from the grammar (see p. 12, n. *l*) if this 'disaster' lies in the future or the past, and it is also uncertain if it relates directly to the character who insists on 'going out' in the preceding line (l. 3), or concerns another character (see, for example, ll. 6 and 11–15 below).

δ. Cf. 14/11.

ε. Cf. 13/4.

ζ. Perhaps 'which was hidden in filth', which would suit the references to 'washing' in the following line (l. 9): if so, it is not certain what exactly is meant by 'she had a chamber *made* for him' in this line. See p. 13, n. *z*, for the problems of reading. Despite the word 'hidden' here, it is not certain if the male character here is already acting secretively, before he hears disastrous news in ll. 10 ff. below.

η. Wenkhem: a town near Memphis. See pp. 55–6.

θ. Despite the damaged state of the papyrus this isolated reference to Upper Egypt is certain. The only other mentions of the South are in fr. 2 back (col. 16).

ι. Although 'they' here could have a precise antecedent in the preceding lines, probably the pronoun is used indefinitely, as often, 'no one will believe'.

κ. Cf. l. 24 below and 14/18.

λ. A plausible restoration here might give the sense 'repetition of inquiring', perhaps 'If people are continually inquiring for me . . .'.

μ. For this proverbial phrase see ʿOnchsheshonqy, 22/25, and Mythus 14/29–30 (cf. *Acta Orientalia*, 36 (1974), 36–7; 37 (1976), 31).

ν. Despite problems in identifying the precise words here, probably various plants and herbs are brought. It is tempting to suppose they are brought either for the fire to heat the water (l. 33 above) or as ingredients of a brew prepared for practical or magical purposes. See n. *π* below.

ξ. The interpretation seems inescapable that 'a (particular) number of men came forth', possibly 'upon the vapour (of the fire or cauldron?)'. Presumably it must be these 'men' who 'stood up' in 10/1 immediately following. It is very difficult to understand these words as anything but a description of the working of some piece of magic. See pp. 48, 60.

ο. A 'tower ' is also mentioned in 13/14, '*a* tower', and 13/33, '*the* tower'.

π. The two plants (?) mentioned here seem to be same as those at the beginning of 9/34, but the readings are problematic, and it is not therefore certain how closely the passages are related.

ρ. It is difficult to restore this passage, and to know where speeches begin and end: it is an especial problem to identify the antecedents of the various pronouns.

σ. Possibly restore 'my house': cf. l. 28 below.

τ. The god Ḥarwer does not occur elsewhere in what is preserved of this text: see p. 45.

υ. The fragments 4 and 5 possibly belong fairly close to fr. 3. See pp. 1–2 and also p. 25 for conceivable links with the contents of col. 10.

φ. Cf. n. *υ* above, and see p. 25 for conceivable links with the contents of col. 13.

χ. Cf. 9/6.

ψ. Possibly this is a proverbial phrase.

ω. Apart from the uncertainty of the antecedent(s) of the pronouns here, it is impossible to be sure if the 'slaying' mentioned here is narrated or reported as a fact, or is referred to more obliquely.

αα. Cf. 14/19, and possibly 14/35.

αβ. Cf. n. *ο* above.

αγ. A prison where prisoners await trial or are detained at Pharaoh's pleasure: see pp. 145, n. *j*, 147, n. *δ*.

αδ. This phrase is used to translate *pr-Pr-ʿꜣ* rather than 'palace', simply because a different word for the palace (*ḥwt*) also occurs in the text: see p. 32, n. *cp*, and p. 35, n. *et*.

αε. Cf. n. above.

αζ. The expressions in the second half of this line are problematic, but the sense may be 'He (presumably Ḥarmakhroou) kindled a flame (for the burnt offerings: as a ritual act he might well do this himself), and they brought the treasure-ship (to the bank, in order to unload provisions for the offerings)'; alternatively, perhaps, 'they brought the gilded barque', see p. 31, n. *ck*.

αη. Cf. 9/5.

αθ. Cf. 9/17, 24.

αι. Cf. 13/9, 14/35 (?).

ακ. Cf. p. 41, n. *β* on 9/2.

DISCUSSION

1. The Characters

The story is mainly told through conversations. In the incomplete state of the text it is often uncertain who is speaking, where speech begins and ends, and whether one speech is contained within another. The identity and relationship of characters are thus difficult to judge, for in part they determine, in part they depend upon the reconstruction adopted for the story. Circular argument is therefore not easy to avoid; in the paragraphs below a preliminary attempt is made to present and analyse the evidence.

a. *Nanoufesakhme*

Nanoufesakhme first appears in **1a** (referred to as col. x), 11 ff., in which she is taken somewhere. In the following lines there is a discussion involving the royal herald, the master of the treasury, and Pharaoh; there is something she is not to hear (x/13), and someone threatens to have someone killed (x/19). In x/15 a 'beautiful young (girl)' is referred to, who may be Nanoufesakhme, as her name is mentioned in x/16. Probably she was brought to the court and questioned by Pharaoh (x/21), for in answer to the remark '. . . I slept. Who [was it that] found him?' Pharaoh answered 'to *her*' (x/22); but this is uncertain, for two female characters may be present. In x/23 Nanoufesakhme is again named; the following words 'it is in a tomb that she has died/is dying/will die' may refer to her but do not necessarily do so. As suggested on p. 68, nn. *aa*, *ab*, x/24–5 could perhaps be reconstructed to mean that Nanoufesakhme became pregnant and had a son by Pharaoh.

The other certain reference to Nanoufesakhme occurs in 14/31 in a speech: '. . . I arrived at this place; it was with Nanoufesakhme that I arrived at this place . . .'. The speaker's identity is uncertain. If this speech is part of that which begins in 14/30, then it is quoted within a speech of a woman, probably the same woman ('girl E', see pp. 49–50) who claims to be the wife of Djedseshep in 14/28. It does not, however, necessarily follow that this woman is identical with Nanoufesakhme, for the reference is to a past event. If the speech is not part of that which begins in 14/30, then it may be part of an answer to the woman's speech by her interlocutor, who is quite likely on the general tenor of 14/15–36 to be Ḥarmakhroou (see p. 46). In either case 'this place' seems likely to be the 'garden' mentioned in 14/18, which seems from 14/15 to have been in the necropolis of Memphis. This 'garden' may or may not be the same as the 'ruined garden which was outside the town' (9/17, 24). There are thus at least two possibilities, perhaps three, about the identity of the man who claims in 14/31 that 'It was with Nanoufesakhme that I came to this place [. . . .': i. he may be Ḥarmakhroou; ii. he may be a character who flees with 'girl E', cf. 14/15 ff.; iii. he may be some other male character.

In 13/25 a determinative preserved after a lacuna suggests (see p. 28, n. *as*) that the name Nanoufesakhme is perhaps to be restored in the passage: '. . . . .] me (?) everything that had [happened to Nanoufe]sakhme (?) and Khratipnoute who had taken them'. If this is correct, then Khratipnoute may (under iii above) be the character associated with Nanoufesakhme in 14/31 (see p. 45).

Nanoufesakhme is not named in cols. 9–10, where the female protagonist is called 'the girl' (see pp. 47–50).

b. *Djedseshep, the prophet of Horus, Lord of Letopolis*

In 9/10–14, a male character 'A' (see pp. 46–7) overhears some men of Wenkhem saying: '. . . . Djed]-seshep, the prophet of Horus, Lord of Letopolis. A misfortune has happened to him. He has no son on earth, except [. . . . .] the chief scribe of Moeris. He has been made prophet of Horus, Lord of Letopolis, and the priests who were his fellow [. . . . .] me as prophet of Horus, Lord of Letopolis; Djedseshep [. . . . .] to (?) Upper Egypt [. . . . .] . . . him. The priests did not abandon him. They caused us to come out [. . . . .] him'. The 'misfortune' (*ḏꜣ*) is unlikely to be Djedseshep's death, as mourning for him is not reported until 14/27. More probably, Djedseshep has been disgraced and deprived of his prophetship, since a new prophet has been appointed. The fact that 'the priests did not abandon him' would fit with this, particularly if the deprivation was undeserved. But possibly the 'misfortune' is described in the following words: 'he has no son on earth, except [. . . . .]'. This would mean that something untoward had happened to this son. Whichever suggestion is right, the words 'a misfortune has happened to him' in 9/11 seem likely to refer to the same event as is mentioned in 9/4: 'this is the day on which a disaster has happened to the great man'; compare 14/27, 'a great man whose name is Djedseshep'. This speech in 9/4 immediately follows the departure of a character from the place where he was staying, although his hosts wished him to remain. Possibly it is this disappearance that 'the guards, the generals, and the great men of Pharaoh, who had ordained a very great evil', lied about, saying 'We do not know what has happened to [. . . . . . .]' (9/6), after Pharaoh's visit to the House of Attendants. Conceivably, the character who disappears here might be the 'son' of Djedseshep mentioned in 9/11.

It is not clear in 9/12 who is appointed to succeed Djedseshep as prophet of Horus, Lord of Letopolis. It may be 'the chief scribe of Moeris', the immediate antecedent grammatically; but it may also be the son of Djedseshep, since the text may have read 'he has no son on earth, except N, who is [in such-and-such a relation to] the chief scribe of Moeris'. In 13/30 somebody says to the prophet of Horus, Lord of Letopolis (cf. 13/29) '. . . you with your family and fellow priests in(to) the power of the Chief Scribe of Moeris.' This prophet may well be the man appointed in 9/12, so that it is at least possible that 'who is in the power of the Chief Scribe of Moeris' should be restored there, in which case Djedseshep's successor was almost certainly his son. In 9/13, it seems to be the successor who is speaking (see p. 14, n. *al*); probably this is a quotation of his words on being appointed by the men of Wenkhem, though it could conceivably be an interpolation by character A, who overhears them (in which case character A would be the successor of Djedseshep, see p. 46 f.). The important point to notice in 9/13 is that the speaker says: '. . . me as prophet of Horus, Lord of Letopolis; Djedseshep will [. . . . .] to Upper Egypt', the order of words quite clearly distinguishing the prophet of Horus from Djedseshep. And indeed in the rest of the text, the title 'prophet of Horus, Lord of Letopolis' and the name Djedseshep always appear in separate contexts, a possible indication that from 9/13 onwards, the title may refer to Djedseshep's successor. For this reason he is treated in a separate section below (p. 50 f.).

In 10/7 the place (?) 'in which [Djed]seshep was' is mentioned in a broken context. It must remain uncertain whether Djedseshep played a role in the action in this column, though the statement 'I had a/have no son to weep by my side', when compared with 9/11, suggests that he may have done so.

In 14/26–8 at the garden in the necropolis of Memphis a woman is telling her story, probably to Ḥarmakhroou: 'the terror which happened in Memphis yesterday. He said ". . . . [. . . . .] to mourn for a great man, whose name is Djedseshep . . . . ." [. . . . . .] ". . . may he/it be saved, I am the wife of Djedseshep [. . . . .]" '. Unfortunately, it is unclear whether 'He said' refers to her interlocutor (Ḥarmakhroou?) or is a quotation within her speech. Nevertheless, probable inferences from the passage are: i. Djedseshep has died and been mourned; ii. the woman has been unaware of this until told; iii. she is the wife of Djedseshep; iv. the person she is speaking to is unaware of this fact.

c. *Ḥarwer*

In a broken context in 10/33 someone says: 'whom the god gave to us, some ragings of Ḥarwer will seize from us . . .' (see p. 23 f., nn. *et*, *eu*, *ev*). This passage makes it clear that there is a god-given character in the story, who has been doomed to die by the god Haroeris. As in the story Djedseshep and perhaps also his successor as 'prophet of Horus, Lord of Letopolis' die, it is possible that the reference is to one or other of them. While the passage certainly seems to deal with one of these prophets and with 'girl C' (see p. 48 f.), the identity of the doomed character remains uncertain. In the text Ḥarwer is clearly distinguished from Horus, Lord of Letopolis, though historically the god of Letopolis was often referred to as Haroeris.[1]

d. *Khratipnoute*

In 13/25 at the House of Pharaoh, somebody perhaps recounts before Pharaoh '. . .] . . . everything that had [happened to Nanoufe]-sakhme (?) and Khratipnoute who had taken them' (see p. 28, nn. *ar*, *as*, *at* for restorations). The name or epithet *Ḫrd pꜣ nṯr*, 'Child (of) the god', is suggestive, and could perhaps be taken to indicate the identity of this character with the god-given person mentioned in 10/33 (see section c above). On the other hand, if x/24–5 are rightly interpreted to mean that Nanoufe-sakhme had a child by Pharaoh (p. 68, nn. *aa*, *ab*), *Ḫrd pꜣ nṯr* would be a suitable name for, or description of, such a child. It is uncertain in the broken context what 'them' refers to, though, as the text in 13/26 reads: 'he had not been able to ask after his children', it conceivably refers to these children (see below, section j).

Khratipnoute is not mentioned by this name or epithet elsewhere in the text; for the possibility that he might be identified with Nanoufe-sakhme's companion who speaks in 14/31, see pp. 43, 50, and for the possibility that he might be a son of hers by Pharaoh, see p. 59.

e. *Ḥarmakhroou*

The first certain appearance of Ḥarmakhroou in the story is in 13/31, where he administers an oath, almost certainly to 'the prophet of Horus, Lord of Letopolis', in which the latter swears 'There is no man in excess among them', referring probably to his family and fellow priests. In 13/33 Ḥarmakhroou 'walked to the tower. He made them cease/remove the destruction/rubble above . . .'; it is therefore probable that it was he who gave orders to disembark to the army in 13/32. This activity at the 'tower' suggests indeed that it may have been Ḥarmakhroou who reported what he had seen at the 'tower' in 13/14–15 and that he may have played a role throughout col. 13; but this is by no means a certain inference. When the general and the army have completed the laying to rest of 'the great men' in their coffins (14/1–2; see p. 30, nn. *bu–by*), Ḥarmakhroou addresses the army with an order or a plea that no other man belonging to the prophet of Horus, Lord of Letopolis, should be put to death, since none such are any longer alive (14/2–5; see p. 31, nn. *cd–cf*). Clearly, Ḥarmakhroou's anxiety throughout these events is to save the lives of any innocent surviving members of the prophet's family in the future—a point which is possibly, but not necessarily, significant for his own relationship with the prophet. Possibly it is Ḥarmakhroou who kindled (?) the flame for the burnt offering in 14/5, but it is uncertain whether he returned

[1] H. Junker, 'Der sehende und blinde Gott', *Sitzungsberichte der Bayerischen Akademie der Wissenschaften*, Phil.-hist. Abteilung, 1942, 7.

with the army and its general to Memphis and took part in the mourning for 'the great men' and subsequent events. On the whole it appears more likely that he did not; at all events, it is stated in 14/14 that 'it happened that no man on earth knew about the matter/story of Ḥarma[khroou'.

In 14/15 Ḥarmakhroou goes to the necropolis of Memphis and meets a group of people. Probably he asks the question in 14/17 which is answered by a female member of the party, who says: 'I fled out with this girl who is in front of you'. If, as seems probable, it is 'this girl' who begins her story in 14/22 with the words 'When I fled out', then it seems probable that this is in response to a request from Ḥarmakhroou to tell '[everything that] had happened to her'. If this is so, Ḥarmakhroou should respond at the end of 'this girl's' story. As indicated above (p. 43), this may have ended in 14/30, in which case the speech in 14/31 might be attributed to Ḥarmakhroou; this would prove that he had come to the garden with Nanoufesakhme on a previous occasion. More probably, however, it ended in 14/31, and Ḥarmakhroou's response was to utter a cry of distress to them (14/32). 14/32–4 would then most plausibly contain pleas from the group to Ḥarmakhroou (notice 14/34 'the discovery of them which you have made today') and his responses. This would suggest that it was Ḥarmakhroou who 'related before them everything which had happened to him since [. . . . .] his brothers upon the brazier which had been done at the door of the palace' (14/35–6) (with the important reservation that in view of the substantial lacuna this does not imply that 'his brothers' are brothers of Ḥarmakhroou). Thus a plausible case may be made out for Ḥarmakhroou being present from 14/15–36, but it is at best very uncertain.

In 16/4–6 'Ḥarmakhroou was taking part in drinking beer [. . . . .] without the Fourth Prophet's failing to have things brought to Ḥarmakhroou [. . . . .], they having brought the generals and the great men . . .'. The scene is probably Thebes (see p. 58), where conceivably Ḥarmakhroou is consorting with the Fourth Prophet in order finally to reveal the duplicity of the generals and the great men.

At the beginning of the story in x/6 and x/27 a broken name *Ḥr*-[. . . . .] appears, which might be restored as Ḥarmakhroou (p. 67, n. *e*, p. 68, n. *ac*); if so, he seems to have gone off by himself (x/7–8) and to have made a journey (x/27 *mšꜥ*). These incidents occur before and after the incident of Nanoufesakhme's introduction to Pharaoh.

Ḥarmakhroou's titles and position are nowhere explicitly revealed by the extant text. The only clue may be in 14/30, where a male character is quoted by the woman who is telling her story as saying: 'It is a priest (*wꜥb*) who has caused to be discovered everything that has happened to . . .'; in the context, this could be a reference to Ḥarmakhroou.

f. *Ptaḥḥotpe, the Setm priest*

This character is referred to only in 14/20–1: 'saying/because Pharaoh went to mourn for Ptaḥḥotpe, the Setm priest, with the women of the Royal Harem [. . . . .] I know . . . Ptaḥḥotpe, the Setm priest, took me to her/it, while [. . . . .]'. The identity of the speaker is uncertain; it seems likely that the incident is one recalled from the past to explain the speaker's knowledge of something or somebody.

A Setm priest also appears in 7/3 '". . . the killing which he did." Setm said: "Do not kill . . ."'. Evidently this character plays an important role at this point in the story, but is not named, so there is no firm reason for identifying him with the Setm priest Ptaḥḥotpe.

g. *Male character 'A'*

This designation is used for the male protagonist in the events of col. 9 and probably col. 10; he is always referred to by the third singular masculine personal pronoun, and neither his name nor title is preserved in the extant text. Clearly it is because of his continuous presence and the incomplete state of the text that this is so, not because of any deliberate suppression of his identity (see on 'girl B' below). It is therefore *a priori* probable that as a principal character in the story he was named, though it does not necessarily follow that he is identical with one of those whose names are preserved.

His first certain entry into the story is in 9/7, where in company with 'the girl' B he arrives at 'the new house', and arranges inconspicuous accommodation for them both. While lodging there, he hears the men of Wenkhem talking of the misfortune which has happened to Djedseshep (9/10–14: see p. 43 f.). As a result, he puts on mourning clothes and weeps, saying 'Where shall I go?' (9/15). He flees to Wenkhem with the girl by night; next morning at dawn he lodges her with a pastophoros of Horus, Lord of Letopolis, in Wenkhem, while he himself returns to a ruined garden outside the town to spend the day, promising to visit her in the evening to comfort her in her distress at their parting (9/16–25).

In 9/1–3, some persons are trying to persuade a male character to stay with them permanently, and promise that he shall not be in want, but he refuses and goes forth despite their efforts. In view of the fact that he apparently uses a plural pronoun (9/2 'wrath against us') and that 'the girl' is mentioned at the beginning of 9/4, he may be 'A'; his subsequent flight with 'the girl' would fit well with this, and with the events of 9/4–6, but the identity is not certain.

The most significant clue to the identification of 'A' is his reaction of grief, despair, and flight on overhearing the men of Wenkhem speak of the 'misfortune' to Djedseshep, the prophet of Horus, Lord of Letopolis. He must be implicated in the consequences, and in fear of his life. He is likely therefore to be *either* Djedseshep himself *or* his successor as prophet of Horus, Lord of Letopolis; it is probably significant that these two men are both killed later in the story. This would fit with 9/16: '[he said] to her "The circumstances cause us to go to Wenkhem, for they will not believe we are there" '. The fact that 'A' probably refuses safe accommodation in 9/3 but decides to flee in 9/16 is no doubt explained by 9/4–5, where it is likely that it is 'A' who does not realize that 'This is the day on which a disaster happened to the great man'. The crime committed by the guards, the generals and the great men of Pharaoh in 9/6 is apparently compounded by their denial of any knowledge of what has happened to somebody; the context suggests that this might either be 'the great man' of 9/4 (who is probably Djedseshep, see b, p. 43 f.) or 'A' and 'the girl'.

The decision whether 'A' should be identified with Djedseshep or his successor must depend in part on whether 'the girl' in col. 9 is to be considered the same as other 'girls' who appear elsewhere in the story.

h. *'The girl'*

In order not to prejudge the issues, it seems wise initially to label the 'girls' who appear in different portions of the text as B, C, D, and E.

'Girl B' first appears in 9/7 as *tꜣ ḥm-ẖr*, 'the servant-girl', in a broken context. 'A' hires a room, which is hidden by filth (?) (see p. 13, n. *z*); in 9/9 he says 'Let the servant-girl wash it. She is the one who is anxious', and the landlady takes the servant girl and makes her wash it. Here 'B' is clearly posing as 'A''s servant. After 'A' learns of Djedseshep's disaster, however, he discusses with her whither he should flee (9/16), tells her how he will provide for her, and weeps with her before the parting (9/18–19); and, when he leaves her at the house of the pastophoros, he does his best to reassure her despite her weeping and expostulation at his departure (9/20–5). It is clear then that their true relationship is not that of master and servant, but is one of affection, consonant with their being husband and wife, lover and mistress, or very close relatives, e.g. brother and sister, mother and son, or father and daughter. In the following passage, the fear that 'B' causes in the pastophoros's wife and her perception of the pastophoros's hidden weapon (?) lead up to his observation to his wife 'Be wary of the woman for she is some kind of great person (*gy n rmt-ꜥꜣ*)', an expression used of people of high rank, but also of ghosts and of divine persons (9/26–30). In this light the occurrence of the word 'goddess' (*ntr.t*) in a broken context in 9/29 is significant (p. 18, n. *cb*); the probability is that 'B' is a divine or august personage in disguise. This supposition is reinforced by 9/31–5, where she sets out to clean up the house (cf. 9/9), giving instructions to the pastophoros's wife, apparently makes a fire or brew, and out of the fumes produces a number of persons—almost certainly an act of magic (see p. 20, nn. *cu*, *cv*, *cw*). Clearly 'B' is deliberately not named, and is referred to as *tꜣ ḫm-ẖl(t)* (9/7, 9) and *tꜣ ẖrt*, because she is in disguise. The fact that she is perhaps a goddess or a magician is, however, rather against her identification with human females appearing in the story.

In the much damaged col. 10, all inferences are speculative. As the text is consecutive, 10/3 'he cried to the girl (*tꜣ ẖr.t*)' is likely to refer to 'girl B', though it is uncertain whether 'he' refers to 'A' or someone else. Likewise, 10/11–12 mentioning the pastophoros's wife should refer to 'girl B' (see p. 21, n. *dk*). But it is not clear whether the text was continuous throughout this column, since a new section may have started after an interval in the missing lines 10/14–16 (cf. intervals after 13/13 and 14/14. Thus the term 'girl C' is used for 10/17–37.

'Girl C' first appears in 10/24, in which a male character is reporting a conversation with another male: ' ". . . I have a/[no] son to weep for me." He said to me "I shall have a girl brought to you, . . ." ' (see p. 22, nn. *dz*, *ea* for the uncertainties of translation). The use of the indefinite article *wꜥt ẖr(t)* should show that the 'girl' concerned is first introduced here. But as the conversation may be a past conversation reported back, this does not rule out identification of 'girl C' with 'girl B'. The speaker in 10/24 is uncertain; but if, as seems best, 'I have [no] son to weep for me' is restored and the passage is compared with 9/11 'he is Djedseshep, the prophet of Horus, Lord of Letopolis; a misfortune has happened to him; he has no son on earth except . . .', then the speaker may well be Djedseshep. If this were so, Djedseshep (who is mentioned in 10/7) would be telling how the bringing of a 'girl' had been promised to him by a male (10/24 *ḏd=f n(=y)*) to a plural group. If 'They said to him "May your breath be safe! we are not leaving (?) you . . ." ' be restored in 10/23 (see p. 22, n. *dy*), and the passage compared with 9/14 'the *wꜥb*-priests did not leave him', then this group could be Djedseshep's priestly companions.

In 10/26–7 the feminine pronouns should refer to 'girl C' because the conversation is clearly continuing, and so should that in 10/28 '[. . . anything bad (?)] to happen to her in my house, it will not happen'. As the pastophoros and his wife are almost certainly mentioned later in this line (see p. 22, n. *eh*), 'girl C' may well be the same as 'girl B', who was lodged in the pastophoros' house by 'A' (9/20 ff.).

It is uncertain whether the same conversation is continued in 10/30 ff., but since the parties are still a male and a plural group it is quite probable. If so, it is of 'girl C' that the male speaker (Djedseshep ?) says 'Speak with her, as I have not done anything useful for her', which the others promise to do (10/31–2). Fairly evidently 10/36–7, 'He said to you "Let this girl be brought [. . . . .]"; [. . . . .] "you (pl.) have not had this girl brought" ', must refer back to the promise to bring 'girl C' in 10/24 (see p. 24, nn. *fe*, *ff*). Whether 10/35 'She caused [them?] to drink [. . . . . . .]' also refers to her is less certain, but the probable magical activities of 'girl B' in 9/35 and the words 'I shall never drink beer or wine again' in 9/2 (probably to be attributed to 'A') are to be noted.

At the beginning of 13/1 'a/the girl into the presence(?) of the prophet of Horus, Lord of Letopolis' introduces 'girl D', unfortunately in a broken context in which the words may be narrative or speech and may refer to past, present, or future. In 13/2–4 a speech is being made, probably though not certainly continuous, in which a female, quite probably but not necessarily 'girl D', is referred to: ' "[. . . . .] I have not killed any man of yours in my life" [. . . . .] "She was your wife; she drank and ate with you [. . . . .] ordered a very great evil. She did not cease from her love(?) [. . . . .]" ' (see p. 25, n. *e*). As the words in 13/4 *ḥn iwꜣy ꜥꜣ m-šs* repeat those in 9/6, there is a strong presumption that those events are being recalled here; 'girl D' should probably then be the 'girl B' who refused to desert 'A' despite the evil done by the guards, generals, and great men of Pharaoh and the disaster to Djedseshep, and the character addressed should be 'A'. This inference is reinforced by 13/5, if it is the 'girl D' speaking, since '[. . . . .] with me, and I spent the day/to-day with you (m.)' seems clearly to recall the relationship of 'girl B' with 'A' inferred from 9/18 ff., especially if '[you (masc.) spent the night] with me' is to be restored. It would then seem that it is the pathos of this relationship that causes the soldiers to weep (13/6), and may have incited them to demand or carry out the killing of the presumed culprit (13/8; see p. 26, n. *k* and p. 42, n. *ω*); note that 'the girl' (*ẖr.t*) appears in a broken context in 13/7.

In the following lines, 13/9–13, female characters are mentioned (13/9 'her/it'(?); 13/10 'their mother'(?); 'her brothers'; 13/11 'you (fem.)(?) are seizing my daughter'(?)), but none is specifically called *tꜣ ẖr(.t)*. While one of them might be identical with 'girl D', they are best treated separately (see p. 50).

In 14/15 ff., Ḥarmakhroou meets a group of people on the Memphite necropolis, and asks for whom they are doing something (most probably supplying food), and 'one (fem.) of them, who happened [. . . . . .] said to him [. . . . .]'. The identity of this group is partly settled by her reply to Ḥarmakhroou: '[. . . . .] this garden. I fled out with this girl ('E') who is in front of you. I gave [. . . . .] giving to us this food daily for six years up to now, we being in the gatehouse [. . . . .]' (14/18–19); for *tꜣi rnpt 6 r tꜣi* echoes 13/9, and *tꜣ hyꜣ(t)* should therefore be 'the gatehouse of her brothers' in 13/10. The group is then 'the family' of 13/9–13 (discussed below, under j, p. 50); 'girl E' is presumably the most important among them. If it is 'girl E' who is speaking in 14/20–1, then the implication is that she had been an acquaintance of Ptaḥḥotpe the Setm priest, and a member of the Royal Harem; but this is uncertain. Probably it is she who in reply to a request from Ḥarmakhroou begins her story in 14/22 with the words 'When I fled out' (cf. 14/18). As far as it can be reconstructed, this story is that she asked a male to whom she paid attention whither he was going; he replied that he was going to the west, with a reference to '(wearing?) clothes dipped in lotus' (14/22–4), i.e. probably to the necropolis. She decided to go with him 'because he would not let them find me' (14/25), and dwelt with (him?). When there occurred 'the terror which happened in Memphis yesterday' (14/26), he told her that '[everyone had gone(?)] to mourn for a great man, whose name is Djedseshep', in reply to which she cries out: '[His (?) breath,] may it be saved! I am the wife of Djedseshep.' 'Girl E' is thus identified with high probability as a wife of Djedseshep (see also p. 44 f.).

Thus 'girl C' (10/17–37) and 'girl D' (13/1–8) both seem likely to be identical with 'girl B' (col. 9). 'Girl E' (14/18 ff.) is almost certain to be one of the females mentioned in 13/9–13, and a wife of Djedseshep. If 'girl D' (13/1–8) also appears in 13/9–13, then 'girl E' might be identified with her, and so also probably with 'girls B and C'. In that case, if 'A' is Djedseshep, the girl who flees in his company in col. 9 and is spoken of as his wife in 13/1–8 proclaims herself actually to be his wife in 14/28. At first sight this might seem to confirm the identity of all the 'girls', but there are in fact grave difficulties. Firstly, the circumstances of the flight of 'girl E' (14/22–5, see above) appear not to correspond in detail with those of the flight of 'girl B' with 'A' (9/15–25). Secondly, 'girl E' has been hidden for six years and is clearly unaware in 14/26–8 of Djedseshep's death and the events leading up to it, whereas 'girl D' appears to have been present at them (13/1–8).

j. *The family of Djedseshep*

'Girl E' (14/18) is firmly connected by the words of her female companion in 14/19 'giving to us this food daily for six years up to now, we being in the gatehouse' with the persons mentioned in 13/9 '[. . . not . . .] . . . it/her in their presence for six years up to now'. As 'girl E' is probably the wife of Djedseshep, these persons are of the family of Djedseshep. In 13/10 the translation is insecure (see p. 26, n. *n*); if 'before their mother (?)' is correct, it seems that children are involved, and it might well be in their presence that someone (e.g. Djedseshep?) had not been for six years. If so, 'their mother' is likely to have been a wife of Djedseshep (cf. 14/28). In 13/11, the reading is again uncertain; if 'they have seized my daughter' is correct, someone other than Djedseshep is presumably speaking or being quoted. The great importance of the passage (13/9–13) is that it shows that Djedseshep must have been involved in the events narrated or reported in 13/1–8; the concern with his wife and children may well indicate that it is Djedseshep whose death was spoken of in 13/8.

It is possible that this passage is to be connected with 13/23, where someone says 'they did not happen without (?) her. Do not delay to go to Memphis with these children (*lwl.w*). I shall not go [. . . . .]'; this passage follows immediately upon what appears to be Pharaoh's sentence on the prophet of Horus, Lord of Letopolis and his family. Again, in 13/25 '[. . . .] told (?) everything that had [happened to Nanoufe]sakhme (?) and Khratipnoute, who had taken them', 'them' could refer to these children; for they appear in 13/26: 'he had not been able to ask after his children, and he had not written about any matter of theirs, either'. If these are indeed the children of Djedseshep, then Nanoufesakhme (?) and Khratipnoute seem likely to be identical with the wife of Djedseshep and her male companion in 14/22–31 (see p. 43). It is notable that in 13/27, quite possibly because of the question of the children, a lady of the Royal Harem requests permission from Pharaoh to leave the harem, and the overseer comes out with her. Her connection, if any, with the family of Djedseshep is uncertain, but it should be noted that the speaker in 14/20, who may be Djedseshep's wife or a member of his family, had probably once been a member of the Royal Harem (see p. 53).

k. *The prophet of Horus, Lord of Letopolis*

These considerations raise again the question whether in cols. 13–14 the title 'prophet of Horus, Lord of Letopolis' refers to Djedseshep or to the person appointed in his stead (9/11–14; see pp. 43–5. The title appears in 13/1, 7, 22, 29–30 and 14/3–4). If Djedseshep's family is discussed in 13/9–13 and it is therefore inferred that his murder is narrated or spoken of in 13/8, it could be argued that he is referred to in 13/1, 7 as 'the prophet of Horus', especially as in 13/7 the soldiers make some proverbial (?) utterance to him (see p. 26, n. *j*).

But after the events at the tower (see p. 56) have been reported to Pharaoh (13/14–16), somebody is taken to the prison called 'The Houses of Delay' (13/19), and in 13/22, after intervening dialogue, the prophet of Horus with his family and fellow priests is almost certainly sentenced to death (cf. 14/3). This person can hardly be Djedseshep if his death is recounted in 13/8; only if the reading *dỉt ẖtb=w-s*, 'cause him (or her) to be killed', rejected on p. 26, n. *k*, is adopted, can Djedseshep still be alive. Pharaoh sends the army to Wenkhem in 13/24, and, after the conversations about the children discussed above, a great lamentation (*nẖy*) occurred throughout Memphis (13/28). If this refers to a funeral, it cannot well be that of the prophet of Horus, since he is clearly alive in 13/29–31 and swears an oath; probably then it is the mourning for Djedseshep, later referred to in 14/27 (*nhpy*). In 13/31–2 in all probability the execution of the prophet and his family and fellow priests took place (see discussion below, pp. 56–8); and it is absolutely clear from 14/36 that this took place on the brazier at the door of Pharaoh's palace in Memphis (see p. 57). Yet in 13/32 the army is disembarked (?) (see p. 30, n. *bn*) and Ḥarmakhroou goes to the tower, which is near Wenkhem (see p. 55 f.), and by removing the rubble (13/33, see p. 30, n. *bp* and p. 56) and digging apparently discovers corpses which are placed in their coffins (14/2) and taken back to Memphis (14/7) (see pp. 54, 57). These corpses cannot then well be those of the prophet of Horus who was executed at Memphis, but could be those of Djedseshep and his companions. It may be objected to this conclusion that in 14/2–5 Ḥarmakhroou tells the army that, although Pharaoh has ordered the prophet with his family and his fellow priests to be put on the brazier, there is no need to put any further person belonging to the prophet on the brazier because he (the prophet) does not survive (see p. 31, nn. *ca–cf*, and p. 57); and that therefore the persons placed in coffins in 14/2 must have been the prophet and his companions. But this does not follow; for, even if Djedseshep and 'the prophet' are separate individuals in this part of the text, they were probably closely related (as father and son? see pp. 43–5).

Thus it seems best on balance to refer the mentions of 'the prophet of Horus, Lord of Letopolis' in cols. 13–14 not to Djedseshep but to the prophet appointed in his stead (9/11–14).

l. *The Chief Scribe of Moeris*

The Chief Scribe of Moeris, who may or may not have been named, appears first in the words of the carousing men of Wenkhem overheard by 'A' (9/12). As shown above, he may have been the person appointed in place of Djedseshep to be prophet of Horus, Lord of Letopolis, or he may not (p. 43). In 13/30 somebody, probably Ḥarmakhroou (see p. 45), says to the prophet of Horus, Lord of Letopolis, probably just before his execution: '[. . . . . . . you] and your family and your fellow priests in/into the power of the Chief Scribe of Moeris. Let [. . . . .]'. If, as argued above in section k, 'the prophet of Horus' here must refer to the person whom the men of Wenkhem say was appointed to succeed Djedseshep, and if also that person was the Chief Scribe of Moeris mentioned in 9/12, then the Chief Scribe of Moeris in 13/30 cannot be the same man as in 9/12 but must be his successor. On the basis of economy of assumptions it seems considerably better to assume that they are the same man, and that it was not the Chief Scribe of Moeris who was appointed to the prophetship of Horus, Lord of Letopolis. If, perhaps overdaringly, the phrase *n tꜣ gm n* from 13/30 is restored before *pꜣ mr-sẖ Mꜣ-wr* in 9/12 and rendered 'in the power of the Chief Scribe of Moeris', then it would clearly not have been the Chief Scribe who was appointed as prophet of Horus.

Whichever view is correct, the Chief Scribe of Moeris is clearly opposed to the interests of Djedseshep and his family, and is presumably one of the villains of the piece. There is no evidence for identifying him with any of the characters named in the extant portion of the text.

m. *Pharaoh and his Queen*

Pharaoh plays a role throughout the story, but is not named in the extant portions. He first appears in x/16, where he is perhaps told about Nanoufesakhme (see p. 67, n. *r*), and replies in x/17. In x/21–2 he questions her (or possibly some other female); she says 'I was sleeping. Who found him?' In x/24–5 the words 'before Pharaoh in her month' and 'son to/of Pharaoh' might perhaps suggest that she bore a child to Pharaoh (p. 68, nn. *aa*, *ab*).

In 9/5 'The time arrived for Pharaoh to go to the House of Attendants' (cf. 14/11), but it is not certain that he actually went, or whom he intended to visit. There follows immediately the denial by the guards, generals, and great men of Pharaoh 'who (?) (had) ordered a very great evil' of knowledge of what had happened; possibly these events are connected.

Pharaoh is addressed in 13/16, and the events of 13/14 ff. therefore probably take place at court. Pharaoh's exit from the door (of the palace) at the eleventh hour (13/17) may have been in order to pronounce judgement, for, as a result perhaps of a speech blaming (?) the prophet of Horus, Lord of Letopolis (see p. 27, n. *aa*), for the troubles of the land, the twelfth (?) hour is allowed to pass by, and someone (presumably the prophet) is then taken to the Houses of Delay (13/18–19). Pharaoh then takes some other action, and, after being advised to do whatever someone (Ḥarmakhroou?) shall tell him, gives instructions which perhaps concern preparation of the fleet (13/19–21). These cause some persons, presumably the prophet and his companions, to hurl blows or abuse at 'him' (i.e. Pharaoh?); Pharaoh then probably pronounces sentence on the prophet, his family, and fellow priests (13/21–2). After somebody has spoken about the children (13/23), Pharaoh sends the army by boat to Wenkhem, and retires into his palace (13/24). During the incidents which follow he is therefore no doubt absent, though he is asked in 13/27 to order the Overseer of the Royal Harem to allow an inmate to come out, which he does (13/28); just possibly this might be the Queen, but it seems unlikely.

Pharaoh re-enters the story in 14/7, when the arrival of the 'great men' (i.e. the corpses, see below, p. 54) is reported. Probably it is Pharaoh who 'wept, saying "O my father, O my brother, O my companion, I grieve [. . . . .]"' (14/8), since the Queen comes out of the palace and does likewise in 14/9. As pointed out (p. 31, n. *cm*) these expressions do not necessarily imply physical relationship with the speaker, though they must at least show that the dead were part of the intimate court circle, and probably that one of them belonged to Pharaoh's father's generation. Probably Pharaoh made a great holocaust and then went back into the Palace (14/10). Perhaps as a result of being exceedingly troubled, Pharaoh went to the House of Attendants again (cf. 9/5); if 'your father' (14/12) is interpreted in the same way as in 14/8 above, then Pharaoh probably receives advice there rather than gives it (14/12). Conceivably, this advice concerns Djedseshep's children (cf. p. 50); Pharaoh then gives some instructions.

Pharaoh plays no part in the events of 14/15 ff., though the past incident of his having gone with the women of the Royal Harem to mourn for Ptaḥḥotpe the Setm priest is quoted in 14/20. Possibly 'at his feet instantly' in 14/33 might refer to a message to Pharaoh, but there is no certain indication of this.

Pharaoh is thus concerned and apparently emotionally involved in the incidents of the story, but gives the impression of acting rather more under the constraint of events beyond his personal control or upon the advice of others than from his own will. The Pharaoh of cols. 9–14 appears to be the same individual; but there is at least the possibility that the Pharaoh of col. x was his predecessor. If 'the father [of Pharaoh]' (*pꜣ* ⌜*it*⌝ [*n Pr-ꜥꜣ*]) were a correct restoration in 13/16, as seems conceivable, this possibility would be confirmed. If so, the youthfulness of Pharaoh might be the explanation of his using the expression 'O my father' in 14/8 and of his perhaps asking advice at the House of Attendants (14/11–13).

n. *The character at the House of Attendants*

As seen above in section m, this person gives advice to (or possibly is advised by) Pharaoh in 14/11–13, and it was no doubt he or she whom Pharaoh intended to visit in 9/5. Probably this person played a role of some importance in the story, but there is no clue to his or her sex or identity; presumably he or she worked in some capacity in the palace. As females might be expected to have resided in the Royal Harem, a male is perhaps more probable. As Ḥarmakhroou is mentioned in 14/14, he is a possible candidate, but nothing appears to confirm such an inference.

o. *The lady of the Royal Harem*

This character appears in 13/27–8; after asking for an order from Pharaoh, she comes out of the Royal Harem under the surveillance of the overseer. As this may have to do either with the matter of Djedseshep's children (13/26) or with the events concerning the prophet of Horus, Lord of Letopolis, which follow, she may be an important character. She is not identifiable. The mention of the women of the Royal Harem in 14/20 is such as to suggest that the female speaker may in the past have been one of them, but as she has apparently been secluded for six years, she can hardly be identical with the woman in 13/27–8.

p. *The Fourth Prophet*

The Fourth Prophet appears in 16/3–6. Either he himself comes to Thebes, or, more probably, someone comes to him at Thebes, and past events are related. He assiduously entertains Ḥarmakhroou with beer and other desirables, and the generals and the great men are brought. Probably this is the denouement of the story, in which the role of the generals and the great men is exposed at Thebes before the Fourth Prophet. He is for historical reasons likely to be the Fourth Prophet of Amun of Karnak (see p. 61).

q. *The guards, the generals, and the great men of Pharaoh*

This group of courtiers appears in 9/6; if *nti* is correctly read (see p. 12, n. *q*) they are qualified by the phrase 'who (?) ordered a very great evil'. This action seems likely to have been in the past, and their role in 9/6 is to deny knowledge of what has happened. This may refer to 'the disaster which has happened to the great man' (9/4), and doubtless their denial is due to complicity. They are almost certainly mentioned in 13/4, where '[. . . . .] ordered a very great evil' occurs in a speech reporting the loyal conduct of 'girl B' (see p. 49). 'The generals and the great men' appear in 16/6, where probably they are brought before the Fourth Prophet and Ḥarmakhroou at Thebes (see above); the omission of 'the guards' here does not seem significant. They appear to be, as in the story prefixed to ꜥOnchsheshonqy, among the villains of the piece.

In 14/1, and presumably in what precedes and follows, a general is present with the army;

but as he appears here to be loyally carrying out the instructions of Pharaoh and, moreover, acting in concert with Ḥarmakhroou, he is presumably unconnected with the criminals.

r. *The great man, the great men*

The term 'a great man' is used of Djedseshep in 14/27, where the context shows that he is dead. In 13/14–15 a character (possibly Ḥarmakhroou, see section e above) says: 'I saw a tower . . . saw the great man with . . .'. If, as argued below (pp. 56–8) from 13/32–4 and 14/1–11, Djedseshep and his companions met their death at the tower, it seems likely that it is Djedseshep and his companions who were mentioned in 13/14–15. This is particularly likely if Djedseshep is the subject of 13/1–13, as suggested in section j, p. 50.

In 14/1–2: 'clothing/wrapping (*mnḫy*) of the great men upon these. The general and the army finished [. . . . .]. They laid them to rest in their coffins', it is probable that 'the great men' (*nꜣ rmt.w ꜥꜣ.w*) are the antecedent of *ḥtp=w*. If so, they are dead, in which case *mnḫy* here may mean grave-clothes, as often (*DG*, 163. 3). In 14/2–5 Ḥarmakhroou makes his speech to the army, telling them that it is not necessary to place any further man belonging to the prophet of Horus, Lord of Letopolis, on the brazier, 'for he is not alive [. . . . .] Grant breath (of life) after this wrath!' In 14/5–6 'He (Ḥarmakhroou?) kindled a flame. They brought the barge for carrying gold . . . wine. They made a burnt-offering and a libation before the great men.' This passage clearly confirms that 'the great men' are dead; the offerings are funerary and the barge is clearly either the funerary vessel or one for bringing the funerary equipment (p. 31, n. *ck*). Finally, in 14/7, a report is made to Pharaoh, saying 'The great men have arrived at Memphis', upon which Pharaoh and his Queen immediately weep, mourn, and make burnt-offerings (14/8–9; see p. 52). There are clear parallels for this usage of *nꜣ rmt.w ꜥꜣ.w* or *pꜣ rmt ꜥꜣ* in the famous passages 1. Kh. 4/10–11, 16, cf. 21–2. The only doubt about the passage can be whether 'the great men' referred to represent Djedseshep and his adherents or his successor as prophet of Horus, Lord of Letopolis, and his family and fellow priests (see pp. 56–8).

s. *Other characters*

Other characters appear to play only minor or incidental roles in the story. The references are as follows.

The magician/doctor (?)	x/7
The prophet of Thoth (?)	x/9
The Royal Herald	x/12
The Master of the Treasury	x/13
The Setm priest (see on Ptaḥhotpe, p. 46)	7/x+3
. . . -Reꜥ (?)	7/x+5
The wife [. . . . .]	9/7
The men of Wenkhem	9/10
The pastophoros of Horus, Lord of Letopolis, and his wife	9/20; 9/26–31; 10/12; 10/28
The pastophoroi of Horus, Lord of Letopolis	10/25
The Overseer of the Royal Household	13/frag. 4, x+4
The Overseer of the Royal Harem	13/27, 28
The soldiers	13/6
The army	13/32; 14/1, 2
Those of the houses [. . . . .]	13/32
The women of the royal harem	14/20

2. The Story

a. *Problems of time and place*

The events of col. x evidently belong early in the story, but there is no clue to their temporal relationship with events recorded on the later pages. The appearance of Pharaoh and of court officials like the Royal Herald and the Master of the Treasury shows that the events from x/12 on are taking place in Memphis, as this is the location of the Court later in the story; this need not necessarily apply to x/1–11. There is no means of fixing the events of col. 7 either in time or in space; the fact that the oath in 7/5 is taken by Preʿ, not by Ptah, may suggest that the scene is somewhere other than Memphis, e.g. Heliopolis, but this indication is too slight to rely on.

The events of col. 9 evidently form a direct chronological sequence throughout, with the exception of the events reported by the men of Wenkhem (9/10–14), and even these plainly constitute the latest news. The locale of the place where 'A' and 'the girl' refuse to stay in 9/1–4 is not strictly deducible. Pharaoh's visit to the House of the Attendants should take place in Memphis (9/5–6), as the Court are present. The location of 'the new house' to which 'A' and 'the girl' move (9/7) is not stated; as, however, it is there that 'A' overhears the carousing men of Wenkhem and, as a consequence, decides to go to Wenkhem, it seems quite likely to be Memphis. The garden to which he first goes is said to be 'outside the town' (*dmỉ*) (9/17); as Wenkhem is the last place mentioned, the garden should be outside Wenkhem. Certainly, the house of the pastophoros of Horus, Lord of Letopolis, where he leaves 'the girl' is in the town of Wenkhem (9/18, 20), and there the remainder of the action in this column takes place. This raises an interesting point about the location of the temple of Horus, Lord of Letopolis, at which Djedseshep held his prophetship; if a pastophoros of the temple lived at Wenkhem, was the temple there also? In 9/20 'A' says to 'the girl': 'the gods whose town you have reached will do (something good/of value?) for you', and again in 9/22 and 9/25 emphasizes that matters are in the hands of 'the god'. If 'A' is a member of the family of Djedseshep, the prophet of Horus, Lord of Letopolis, then the god he invokes, if not simply vague, is likely to be Horus, Lord of Letopolis, and his words suggest that at Wenkhem the girl is in the god's protection. In 10/29 some persons (perhaps his fellow priests) say, most probably to Djedseshep: '(If) you inquire at the temple, your affair will be important (?) at Wenkhem'; though this does not itself show with certainty that the temple is at Wenkhem, it does make it likely. None of the action of the extant portion of the story takes place at Letopolis (*Sḫm*), so there is no clear reason for presuming that the temple is there; as Wenkhem lay in the area between Memphis and Letopolis,[1] there is no reason why there might not have been a cult of the god of Letopolis there.

The action of 10/1–13 probably continues to be at Wenkhem, since the 'wife of the pastophoros' is mentioned in 10/12; if so, at 10/10, 'he withdrew himself/returned to the tower' suggests that this fortified building was somewhere in the neighbourhood of Wenkhem. The time sequence is not deducible in the state of the text. In 10/17–37, if the conversation is between Djedseshep and his fellow priests, it may well have taken place at Wenkhem, as probably did some of the episodes mentioned (10/19 and 10/25), but, in view of the structure of the passage and the way in which 'a/this girl' is mentioned, there is at least a strong possibility that past events are being recounted.

In 13/1 ff., the time referred to depends upon whether the narrative verbs (13/6 *rmy*, 13/7 *ḏd=w*) belong to the main narrative of the story, or whether the whole passage down to 13/8 or possibly 13/11 is part of a speech reporting past events. The evidence for the latter view is 13/12 '[. . . . . the things] which you have said, he did not order that they should be done'; if, as suggested above, this refers to the killing of Djedseshep by order of the

[1] J. Yoyotte, 'La localisation de Ouenkhem', in *BIFAO* 71 (1972), 1–10.

prophet of Horus, Lord of Letopolis, then 13/1–8 (or –11) must relate in the past the events leading up to this killing. If, however, the verbs are part of the main narrative, then the speeches are part of the current action of the story and the speakers are alive; this, though in itself perfectly possible, leads to real difficulties over the identities of the prophet of Horus, Lord of Letopolis, 'the girl' and character 'A', when 13/3–5 are compared with 9/6 ff. and 14/26 ff., and 13/9–11 with 14/17 ff. As to the place where the events of 13/1–13 take place, there is no direct or certain clue. However, in 13/14 at the beginning of the next paragraph, someone says: 'I saw a tower 13/15 [. . . . . . .] saw the great man with 13/16 [. . . . . . .] O my great lord, [. . . . . . .] things which the father (?) [. . . . . .] did not [. . . . .]'.[1] If this is a report to Pharaoh by someone present at the events retailed above, e.g. the speaker of 13/12, then those events presumably took place at the tower, which is most likely to have been in the neighbourhood of Wenkhem.

That the events of 13/14 ff. take place at the court in Memphis is shown by 13/19 'at the eleventh hour Pharaoh came out of the door (of the palace?)' and 13/24 'Pharaoh went to the House of Pharaoh'. This is consonant with the sending of somebody to the Houses of Delay in 13/19 and with the passing of sentence on the prophet in 13/22. In 13/23 somebody says 'report it to her (?), for they did not happen without her (?); and do not delay (to come) to Memphis with these children', a request apparently to someone to go to fetch the children to Memphis. In 13/24 (possibly but perhaps not necessarily as a result of this), Pharaoh causes some people, most probably the army, to re-embark, and they go to Wenkhem. The narrative, however, continues with events at court, and the request of an inmate of the Royal Harem to go out, which is granted. In 13/28 'a great mourning happened before/within (*ḫ(t) n*) Memphis' may refer to the mourning for Djedseshep; but the following words 'No man remained over . . .' may perhaps indicate that this event is quoted here merely to show why no one observed the events, the description of which follows. Thus it is not certain, though possible, that the prophet of Horus, Lord of Letopolis, arrives in Memphis. After greetings, Ḥarmakhroou tells the prophet that he is in the power of the Chief Scribe of Moeris, and administers the oath to him in which he swears there are no extra men among his fellow priests; then something happens which ends '. . . his fellow among them'. Then he (presumably Ḥarmakhroou) causes the army to mount up out of the boats and to have those of the houses of . . . (?) brought (13/32); then Ḥarmakhroou walks to the tower, and there follows the sequence of events leading to the placing in coffins of 'the great men'. There are two mysteries in this passage: i. Was the execution of the prophet of Horus, Lord of Letopolis, which we know from 14/36 happened on the brazier at the door of the palace, and therefore inferentially at Memphis, recounted here? ii. If the scene continues to be Memphis in 13/32 ff., how can the army, who apparently went to Wenkhem in 13/24, be embarked or disembarked at Memphis, and how can Ḥarmakhroou (who is clearly where the prophet is in 13/31) walk to the tower in 13/33, if the tower is indeed located near Wenkhem?

Though the lacunae preclude certainty, there can be little doubt that the events of 13/34–14/6 form a continuity. On arrival at the tower, Harmakhroou causes the debris (?) of its upper chamber to be turned over (?) and some digging (?) to be done, perhaps to discover the corpses buried by the ruin of the tower; the

[1] If this passage is compared with 13/12 'the things which you are speaking of, he did not order them to be done', it is possible that 13/16 should be restored 'things which the father of Pharaoh (?) did not order'. If so, the speaker here is likely to have been present in 13/9–13.

(grave)-clothes of 'the great men' are placed (?) upon these, the general and the army complete (the wrapping and treatment of the corpses?), and they are caused to rest in their coffins: Ḥarmakhroou then makes his appeal to the army, following which a funerary boat or a treasure-ship (?) with funerary goods and provisions (?) is brought and burnt offerings and libations are made before 'the great men' (i.e. the dead); and 'they did not delay (to return) to Memphis' (14/6), the arrival of 'the great men' at Memphis being announced to Pharaoh in 14/7. Thus the events of 13/34–14/6 happened away from Memphis in the neighbourhood of the tower. So the answer to question ii above is *either* that Ḥarmakhroou moved from Memphis to the neighbourhood of the tower between 13/32 and 13/34 *or* that, notwithstanding the mention of 'the great mourning' which 'happened *ẖ(t) n* Memphis' in 13/28, the meeting of Ḥarmakhroou and the prophet of Horus, Lord of Letopolis, itself happened in the neighbourhood of the tower and not in Memphis. The choice involves the answer to question i, whether the execution of the prophet and his fellow priests was recounted in 13/32. That the execution had taken place before Ḥarmakhroou's conversation with Djedseshep's wife and family in the necropolis (14/15 ff.) seems to be proved by 14/35–6, where the speaker, inferentially Ḥarmakhroou, tells them 'everything which had happened to him since [. . . . . and about the placing of the prophet of Horus, Lord of Letopolis,] and his brethren upon the brazier which they had done at the door of the palace'; for though it is perhaps theoretically possible to restore 'the order for the placing of the prophet' etc., thus implying that the execution though ordered had not yet taken place, one would then expect the relative form *r-ḥn Pr-ʿꜣ*, 'which Pharaoh had ordered', or the like in place of *r-ỉr=w*, 'which they did'. Granted that the execution has in fact taken place, there is no point in col. 14 where it can be fitted into the events of the story. Ḥarmakhroou's words in his appeal to the army in 14/2–5 are, as preserved, ambiguous: 14/3 'Pharaoh ordered him to be placed upon the brazier with his family and his fellow (priests)' refers to the order, not the execution itself, while in 14/4, '(do not/not to?) place any man belonging to the prophet of Horus, Lord of Letopolis, upon the altar, for he is not alive', it is uncertain whether 'he' refers back to *rmt*, 'man', or to *pꜣ ḥm-nṯr*, 'prophet'; if the latter, the prophet himself is dead, if the former, it is certain only that his companions are dead. Nevertheless, as they were ordered to die together, the implication that the execution has taken place is strong. Yet the prophet of Horus, Lord of Letopolis, is certainly alive in 13/29–31, and, as the execution is shown by 14/36 to have taken place at the palace (*ḥwt*) at Memphis (cf. 14/9), it must occur before the scene shifts to the neighbourhood of the tower, i.e. in the lacuna at the beginning of 13/32 or of 13/33. If it was recounted in 13/32, the restoration would presumably have to be along these lines: 'Ḥarmakhroou caused him to make an oath saying: "There is no excess man among them". [And immediately he caused him together with his family and his fellow priests to be placed upon the brazier at the door of the palace, each man embracing?] his fellow among them.' Then the incident of the embarkation or disembarkation of the army[1] and the bringing of those-of-the houses (perhaps to be restored *nꜣ-w-ʿwỉ.w-ḫrr*, 'those of the prisons', but perhaps *nꜣ-w-ʿwỉ.w pr-Pr-ʿꜣ*, 'those of the domain of Pharaoh's house' (or the like)), must have taken place at Memphis (despite 13/24), and presumably led up to the journey of Ḥarmakhroou and the army to the neighbourhood of the tower in the lacuna at the beginning of 13/33. If the execution is described at the beginning of 13/33, then the

[1] *dỉ=f ʿr pꜣ mšʿ n nꜣ byry.w r-ḥrỉ*: either 'he caused the army of the boats to rise up' or 'he caused the army to rise up from the boats'. The latter must mean 'disembark' but the former might mean 'embark', though this is *ʿr r-mr.t* in 13/24.

embarkation or more likely disembarkation of the army and bringing of the prison-officers (?) must be preparations for the execution; but in this case there cannot have been room both for the execution and a description of Ḥarmakhroou and the army's journey to the neighbourhood of the tower. The former alternative is thus preferable; but in either case the restorations required are quite substantial.

The incidents following the arrival of 'the great men' at Memphis (14/7) concern the mourning of Pharaoh and his Queen 'at the door of the palace' (14/9), Pharaoh's return to his own house (14/10), and his second visit to the 'House of the Attendants'. These events evidently occurred consecutively within a short space of time at Memphis. The rest of column 14 retails a single incident, Ḥarmakhroou's discovery of Djedseshep's wife and children in the Memphite necropolis, though in the conversation past events are recalled. In the speech of the first woman (14/17 ff.) her flight is recalled and her residence for six years in the gatehouse, while the mention of Ptaḥḥotpe, the Setm priest (14/20–1), whether part of her speech or a reply by Ḥarmakhroou, probably refers to a time even before that. The wife of Djedseshep's speech (14/22 ff.) also recalls her flight, presumably six years back, and then shifts to her conversation with her male companion about 'the terror which happened at Memphis yesterday', which causes her to learn of Djedseshep's funeral and reveal herself as wife of Djedseshep. As she is reporting a previous conversation, 'yesterday' refers to the day before that conversation, and not necessarily to the day before Ḥarmakhroou's meeting with her, but the event is likely to have been in the recent past (cf. 14/15 'It happened one day' which indicates no long lapse of time). Her speech probably ends in 14/30 and is followed by one by her male companion in 14/31 (see p. 43) in which he recalls his arrival at the necropolis with Nanoufesakhme, in the distant past—six years ago if Nanoufesakhme is to be identified with the wife of Djedseshep. The final lines (14/32–7) retail Ḥarmakhroou's grief and conversation with the relatives of Djedseshep whom he has discovered, concluding with his account to them of 'everything that had happened to him since [. . .]' (in which context it is reasonable to restore 'since six years ago up to now') down to the execution of the prophet of Horus, Lord of Letopolis (see pp. 50–1).

The location of the events recorded in col. 16 is probably Thebes, though this inference is not quite inescapable. In 16/2 '(beat them/caused them to be far off (?)) in order to bring him south with him' may be narrative or part of a speech; probably, but not certainly, it shows the subject to be in the south. 16/3 'the Fourth Prophet to Thebes (*Nı̓wt*). He related everything . . .' could possibly refer to a past event, in which case the subject of *sḏy=f* might be somewhere other than Thebes. However, the facts that 'the Fourth Prophet' is likely to refer to the temple of Amun at Karnak, and that in 16/5 'the Fourth Prophet' is evidently entertaining Ḥarmakhroou, and that in 16/6 the generals and the great men (of Pharaoh) are brought, do suggest that the action is at Thebes. Temporally, these events cannot be related with those of other columns by internal evidence, though there is no reason to suspect that they are not posterior to them.

b. *Summary*

Even after the foregoing analyses, there are clearly several different ways in which the story could speculatively be reconstructed, and no absolutely decisive criteria for choosing between them. To retail all such possibilities would be unhelpful. The editors feel, however, that a summary of what, in their subjective view, may tentatively be regarded as probable may stimulate further work by others.

Ḥarmakhroou is likely to be the hero of the

story, in that it appears to be he who puts the wrongs that have occurred to rights. In 13/28 ff. he is apparently responsible for the execution of the wicked prophet of Horus, Lord of Letopolis (the ex-Chief Scribe of Moeris), and in 13/31 ff. for the recovery from the tower of the bodies of 'the great men', i.e. Djedseshep and his companions, their proper obsequies, and their transport back to Memphis. In view of this it may well be he who discovered the secrets of the killing of Djedseshep and his colleagues at the tower, and of the survival of his wife and children, by obtaining a confession from the wicked prophet of Horus, Lord of Letopolis, in 13/1–13 and the lost text before it. If so, it is probably he who reports these circumstances to Pharaoh in 13/14 ff. Certainly, Ḥarmakhroou is the man who discovers Djedseshep's wife and children in their hide-out in the Memphite necropolis, hears their story, tells them his own, and advises them how to proceed. He it is too who appears at Thebes, where perhaps with the aid of the Fourth Prophet of Amun he may have secured the final downfall of the generals and the great men, whose crime seems to have sealed Djedseshep's fate. If it is Ḥarmakhroou who appears apparently in association with Nanoufesakhme at the beginning of the story, it would be proper that he should rescue her and her children at the end.

Nanoufesakhme appears to be the virtuous heroine of the story, who, through the misfortunes of Djedseshep but through no fault of her own, suffers separation from her husband, six years of hiding with her children in lowly circumstances, followed by the news of his death; and this may not have been the end of her tribulations, as Ḥarmakhroou apparently advises her to travel to somewhere else after he has discovered her in the Memphite necropolis. With her in the necropolis is her male companion in flight, probably Khratipnoute. What his relationship with her is is uncertain, but it seems unlikely to be that of lover; son is more probable but, if so, perhaps not the son of Djedseshep, but just possibly a son of hers by Pharaoh, whose conception might have been related in col. x. It may be that the existence of this son of Pharaoh's and Nanoufesakhme's and his disappearance are at the base of Djedseshep's misfortunes. At all events, it seems probable that at the end of the story Nanoufesakhme and Khratipnoute were vindicated and restored to their rightful positions.

Djedseshep, the original prophet of Horus, Lord of Letopolis, is, as it were, the fulcrum of the story. Perhaps he was fated (by Haroeris?) to die from the start; perhaps it was a threat of murder made by him or a wrongful accusation of murder against him (e.g. by the Chief Scribe of Moeris, abetted by the guards and generals and great men), that led to his downfall. At all events his disaster, the appointment of someone in the power of the Chief Scribe of Moeris to his prophetship, his probable flight and retreat to the tower at Wenkhem, his probable murder there with his family and fellow priests and the subsequent discovery of their corpses and their return in coffins to Memphis by Ḥarmakhroou form the nucleus of the extant part of the story, upon which the activities of the other characters hang. How Djedseshep is regarded depends upon whether 'the prophet of Horus, Lord of Letopolis' in cols. 13–14 represents him or not. The probability seems to be, however, that he is the doomed or unlucky or half-innocent victim of the machinations of others, on the human plane perhaps of the Chief Scribe of Moeris and of the guards, generals, and great men of Pharaoh, on the divine plane perhaps of Haroeris. Were he morally an evil character, it seems unlikely that Pharaoh and the Queen would publicly lament for him, and that his wife and children should survive to be vindicated.

The nature of Djedseshep's alleged wrongdoing is unclear; but it is the Chief Scribe of

Moeris, who gains power over the prophet of Horus, Lord of Letopolis, who profits by it, and it is the crime of the guards, the generals, and the great men of Pharaoh which leads directly to his disaster. Their disavowal of knowledge of what has happened to someone occurs during a visit of Pharaoh to the House of Attendants, and it is notable that after Pharaoh has mourned the death of Djedseshep he goes to the House of Attendants, where apparently he receives advice to look to the children 'in exchange for your father who has departed'. Perhaps Khratipnoute was originally lodged in the House of Attendants, and his disappearance thence caused Djedseshep's disaster, and it was of Khratipnoute's fate that the guards, generals, and great men disclaimed knowledge. However this may be, it seems possible that it was Khratipnoute's disappearance that gave the Chief Scribe of Moeris the chance to gain control over the prophetship of Horus, Lord of Letopolis, after Djedseshep's disaster.

The history of the Chief Scribe of Moeris depends upon whether he is identified with the prophet of Horus, Lord of Letopolis, after Djedseshep's disaster reported by the men of Wenkhem in 9/10–14. If he is, then he eventually suffers execution on the brazier with his family and fellow priests, apparently for the crime of killing Djedseshep and his companions without Pharaoh's order. The difficulties of the story of his execution (discussed above) are compounded by the fact that someone, probably Ḥarmakhroou, tells him just beforehand that he and his family and fellow priests are in the power of the scribe of Moeris; this is presumably the new scribe of Moeris, but his identity is unclear.

If 'the girl' of cols. 9, 10, and 13/1–8 is to be differentiated from Djedseshep's wife Nanoufesakhme (see pp. 43, 47–50), then it seems that she is a goddess or high-born human with magical powers in the disguise of a servant-girl, whom Djedseshep acquires from an acquaintance in his anxiety to have a son. Though she has accompanied him throughout his flight, whether deliberately or not, it seems likely that it is she who, when left with the pastophoros of Wenkhem, perhaps partly through magic, reveals the place of retreat of Djedseshep at the tower to his enemies, and she who in 13/1–8 may be partly responsible—by rousing the sympathy of the soldiers—for his death. Her conduct towards Djedseshep is therefore perhaps equivocal, and she may, if genuinely a separate character, form an element of his fated doom.

Finally, it should be recollected that less than half the text of four columns (plus a few fragments) from a story of over sixteen columns survives. It is not surprising that residual problems abound; nor will it be surprising if a future fortunate discovery of a more complete text of the story proves these suggestions to be wide of the mark.

3. The composition, nature, and date of the text

While the plot of the story as a whole cannot be reconstructed, it is evident that its elements were most skilfully woven into a consistent pattern, and are themselves remarkably varied, even within the fragments preserved. They appear to comprise intrigue at court and probably murder; a public execution at Pharaoh's behest; escape, disguise, and concealment; faithfulness on the part of a wife, probably contrasted with desertion on the part of her husband; discovery and probably rescue of the innocent who have suffered injustice; and no doubt final vindication of the good with restitution of their rights, and exposure and punishment of the wrong-doers. It thus combines morality, adventure, crime, romance, and probably love in a manner and to an extent not fully paralleled among other extant demotic or, indeed, earlier Egyptian stories. Though this may be due to accidents of survival, the tale widens our present knowledge of the range of Egyptian story-telling.

The narrative technique resembles that of other demotic stories, showing perhaps particular ingenuity in the manner in which much of the action of the story is conveyed through speeches, with minimal connecting narrative. Past events are often reported (e.g. the speech of 'the girl' in 14/22 ff.); these reports may indeed sometimes include events which have already been retailed in their chronological place, but it is not clear that this is always so. There may therefore be a partial analogy with the use of 'the messenger' in Greek drama. The device by which character 'A' gains knowledge of the disgrace of Djedseshep through overhearing by chance the casual conversation of the men of Wenkhem is also noteworthy. The use of 'speeches within speeches' is ubiquitous. Nevertheless, there is nothing in the means of telling the story which goes beyond normal Egyptian techniques or suggests any outside influence.

The date of the manuscript must for the present depend upon the dating of the group of papyri found in the Mother of Apis Courtyard to which it belongs. This group is not dated by its archaeological context, but seems to comprise no dated document later than one or other of the Alexanders; on this ground it has been suggested (p. x) that individual texts within it are unlikely to post-date the third century BC. Study of the palaeography of Memphite demotic, especially of literary hands, is not yet at the stage to provide valuable confirmation of such a dating, though there seems to be no clear contradictory evidence. That the text was written in the Memphite area is of course an assumption, though a probable one; the closeness of the hand to that of **2** and of other fragments (see **3**–**5** and **13**–**21**) suggests that its scribe may have belonged to a school based upon the capital. The orthography, though it shows occasional variations in writing the same word (more especially in the determinatives used), is remarkably accurate, and shows a number of fine orthographical distinctions in writing phonetically similar but grammatically disjunct forms that are not always observed in later demotic literary hands. The pagination (also present in the Khaʿemwese texts) and the division into paragraphs by leaving blanks strengthen the impression that the scribe was trained in a highly educated literary school, perhaps at or close to a time when there was still a native Pharaonic court to be catered for.

The date of composition cannot be argued directly from that of the manuscript, and there are few internal clues. The most interesting is the mention of 'the Fourth Prophet' in connection with Thebes in col. 16, frag. 2/3, 5. The selection for a role in such a tale of the fourth prophet in preference to the first, second, or third prophets inevitably suggests that the writer intended the scene of the story to be set during or immediately after the Napatan Twenty-fifth Dynasty, when a pre-eminent political role was played at Thebes by the fourth prophet of Amun, Montuemḥat. If so, the chronological setting is little later than that of the Petubastis–Inaros cycle of stories, which this text does not in other ways resemble. The titles used in the text are not otherwise indicative of any one particular period (except possibly the unread title in col. x/7). Certain of the personal names could perhaps be thought to convey an archaizing flavour (*Ḏd-sšp*, *Ptḥ-ḥtp*), but others (*Nꜣ-nfr-Sḫm.t*, *Ḥr-mꜣʿ-ḫrw*) belong within the onomastic repertoire of the Late Period. The geographical milieu of the text, apart from the Theban incident in col. 16, is Memphis and its environs (Letopolis, Wenkhem, Moeris), and it is clear that Pharaoh's residence is Memphis for the purposes of the story. Taken together, these factors suggest a chronological setting early in the Saïte Twenty-sixth Dynasty (seventh century BC) for the story.

Thus the probable *termini* for the composition of the story are the late seventh–late third centuries BC. Given the preference in Egyptian stories (especially in demotic literature) for using settings in the past, it may perhaps be suggested that the fourth century BC is the most likely date of composition.

In its general character, the story does not suggest that it formed part of one of the known demotic story cycles. The only detailed evidence which might be used is the presence of an unnamed Setm priest in col. 7, frag. 2/3, who could be speculatively identified with the Setm priest Khaᶜemwese in the Stories of the High Priests. In 14/20–1, however, a Setm priest Ptaḥḥotpe appears, and, though he is not necessarily identical with the Setm priest of 7/3, his presence warns that an identification with Khaᶜemwese should not be lightly assumed. Indeed, if the date attributed to the milieu of the story above is correct, then the presence of Khaᶜemwese, who was the son of Ramesses II of the Nineteenth Dynasty, might be considered an anachronism. Until further evidence is published, then, it seems best to assume that the story of Nanufesakhme and the prophet of Horus, Lord of Letopolis, is an independent text, belonging well within the general tradition of demotic story-telling but of a slightly different genre from any extant text.

4. The relationship between texts 1 and 2

The papyri containing **1** and **2** are closely similar in appearance, and it is reasonable to ask if they might not belong to the same papyrus roll. In this volume the papyri (and also the texts) are regarded as distinct; the reasons are set out here.

The physical details, hands, and layout of each papyrus have been discussed separately; see especially pp. 1–4 and 70–2. The only significant difference between them is that the greater part of **2** is badly discoloured, whereas **1** is, as a whole, quite clean. This is no reason for concluding that they could not have belonged to the same roll. The two papyri were found in the same deposit, but not together: evidently both **1** (apart from fr. 2) and **2** were large, roughly square pieces torn or cut from a discarded roll for use as scrap; see p. x. Various differences between the orthography of **1** and **2** have been noted; although they suggest the papyri are different, their interpretation is problematic (see p. 71 f.).

The columns of both **1** and **2** were numbered in the bottom margin, and some of these figures are preserved. The numbering of the columns of **1** has been discussed on p. 1 f., and the probable arrangement of the columns on both sides of the papyrus, together with the relative positions of the surviving fragments, are illustrated by a figure (fig. 1, p. 2). One column number is also preserved in **2** (see p. 70), and it can be seen that, with an acceptable degree of latitude, **2** could be made to occupy the appropriate place among the columns of **1**: this possibility is illustrated in the accompanying figure (fig. 2, p. 63), which shows only the relevant portion of the roll.

Unfortunately, it is quite impossible to test this hypothetical relationship between **1**, fr. 2 and **2** by a search for fibre correspondences. In the case of the vertical fibres (viewing the papyrus from the back), it is debatable whether or not any overlap at all is to be expected between the top right-hand corner of **2** and the left-hand edge of **1**, fr. 2; but in any case it would be minimal, and the intervening vertical space of some 20 cm. makes it unlikely that any conclusive fibre correspondences could be observed. In the case of the horizontal fibres (viewing the papyrus from the front), a join between two sheets of papyrus occurs at the left-hand edge of the lower portions of **2**, and only a few damaged fibres surviving from the next sheet can be compared with the fibres of **1**, fr. 2. Examination of both these possibilities has yielded no conclusive results.

Thus the various physical details of the two papyri make it possible that **1** and **2** might come from the same roll, but provide no positive evidence that they do so. In a papyrus find of this kind, it is, of course, surprising if two substantial and closely similar fragments do *not* belong together. It is therefore necessary to consider the texts themselves, and these pose a more difficult problem.

The contents of the various fragments are discussed elsewhere; see pp. 58–60, 107–9, and 139–42. All the surviving portions of text preserve passages of continuous narrative. The text on the front of **2** in col. 6 is more frequently divided into fresh paragraphs than seems to be the case elsewhere. These appear to mark successive stages or episodes in the narrative, just as in other columns, and do not suggest that the organization of the text is different.

The most important point is that no personal name occurs both in **1** and in **2**; and there is no hint at all that any character referred to by title or in any other way in either text should be identified with a character appearing in the other. Of course, a Pharaoh is mentioned frequently in both texts (a Pharaoh is referred to by name in **2** back, x+1/1, 2, 4), but this is true of virtually every demotic narrative, and is of no significance for the present problem. Apart from the characters, there are no place-names, nor any other distinctive detail of the plot that the two texts have in common. It must be pointed out that it is similarly impossible to find any name or detail that clearly links the texts on the front and on the back surfaces of **2** itself; see pp. 141–2.

By contrast, there are obvious links between the front and the back surfaces of **1**, fr. 3. The problems of reconstructing the story of **1** are discussed on pp. 43–60. However, sufficiently clear indications are provided by the characters mentioned on both sides: Djedseshep, the priesthood of Horus of Letopolis, and the Chief Scribe of Moeris. The character Ḥarmakhroou plays an important part on the back of **1**, but does not appear upon the front;

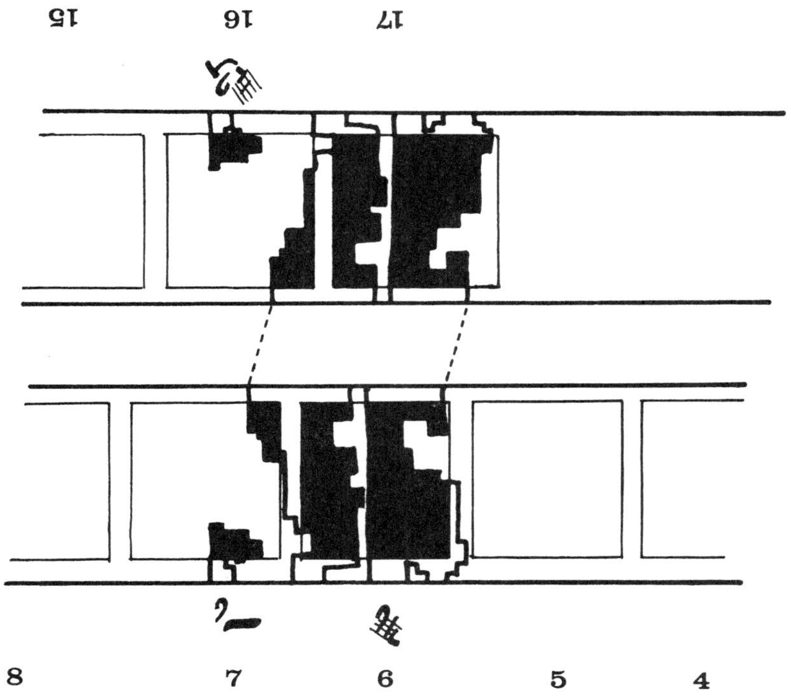

FIG. 2. Diagram of hypothetical conflation of Texts **1** (fr. 2) and **2** on a single roll (rejected on pp. 62–4)

he also appears upon the back of **1**, fr. 2 (col. 16); see pp. 45–6. A possible, but not certain, connection between the front of **1**, fr. 2 (col. 7) and the rest of **1** is provided by the reference to an unnamed Setm priest in **1**, fr. 2 (col. 7), l. 3; see p. 46 (cf. p. 62). A clear continuity can also be seen in the general character of the story upon the front and upon the back of **1**. It is difficult to see any connection with the material upon either the front or the back of **2**.

It might be argued that **1** and **2** belong to the same roll, which bore two or three completely separate stories; or alternatively that it consisted of loosely linked stories or episodes, or contained stories narrated within a story. Although all these suggestions are in themselves quite plausible, the surviving columns give no positive indication that any of them is correct, and in fact the story of **1** appears to be remarkably close-knit, despite its obvious complexity.

However, **1**, fr. 2 provides decisive evidence on this point. If **1** and **2** are combined in the manner shown in fig. 2, then the text preserved upon the back of **1**, fr. 2 (col. 16) belongs within **2** back, col. x, and it must be read after **2** back, x/1–15, and immediately before the whole of **2** back, col. x+1. However, ll. 1–15 (and also what little can be understood in the following lines) of **2** back, col. x can be seen to be closely related to the contents of col. x+1, whereas **1**, fr. 2, back (col. 16), with its mention of Ḥarmakhroou, is connected with the story on the back of **1**. It is impossible to explain how the contents of **1**, fr. 2, back might belong at this point in the course of **2**.

The difficulty might be avoided by suggesting that, contrary to all the indications, **1**, fr. 2 does not belong to the same roll as **1**, fr. 3. However, although it is a small fragment, **1**, fr. 2 is quite sufficient to indicate the existence of another text in the same kind of hand and format. Thus the chief argument for trying to combine **1** and **2** (that it is surprising if two fragments happened to be preserved from two separate papyri) would apply equally to **1**+**2** and **1**, fr. 2. If a choice is to be made between combining **1** with **2**, or with **1** fr. 2, then the latter is clearly preferable.

In sum, the text of **1** is a consistent story, which clearly affects the same characters throughout, and this becomes even more evident when **1a**, which preserves another portion (probably the opening) of the same text as **1**, is taken into account. To insert any columns of the text of **2** into the fabric of this story is to interrupt its course in a way which may be theoretically possible, but is highly improbable.

TEXT 1A

1a. DJEDSESHEP, NANOUFESAKHME, AND ḤARMAKHROOU — Plate 3c

H5-DP523 [5983]

Overall: 27.5 cm. *h.*× 11.5 cm. *w.*

Sector 1 (North Courtyard) debris (1966–7)

The papyrus is thin, even-textured, and translucent. It is discoloured to a uniform light-brown shade. The front (↔) surface bears part of 28 lines of continuous demotic text. Although the bottom portion of the lowest fragment (fr. 3) is badly rubbed, and traces of further lines of text may have been lost, it is probable that up to 1.5 cm. of the bottom margin are preserved. In that case the maximum column height preserved is 26.0 cm.: the three fragments are torn on all sides, and no other margins are preserved.

A considerable proportion of the papyrus is of a double thickness. This feature apparently extends no further than 5.5 cm. from the right-hand (as seen from the front) edge of the fragments taken together. The sheet of papyrus upon which the text is written is quite normal, but it is backed by another ordinary sheet of papyrus of precisely similar appearance. The fibres of the back surface of the entire double-thickness sheet run vertically, and thus it outwardly presents the usual inside and outside surfaces of a normal papyrus roll, with horizontal and vertical fibres respectively. Although in many places the backing sheet has become detached, in others it still adheres very firmly. All the indications suggest it has been glued on deliberately. The back surface of the top sheet and both surfaces of the backing sheet are entirely blank. A number of loose, blank fragments were found together with the rest of **1a**, and they obviously belong to the backing sheet: the largest of these appears from its shape to be the lost backing of fr. 3, and it helps to establish the position of the fragment. The natural explanation of this backing is that it was a sheet of blank papyrus pasted on to the very beginning of a roll as reinforcement. However, it is conceivable that any portion of an already written roll that became damaged might be repaired in this way. Thus it is probable that the present fragments belonged to the *first* column of the text, but this is not certain.

Fr. 1 measures 22.5 cm. *h.*× 11.5 cm. *w.* Fr. 2 measures 6.0 cm. *h.*× 3.5 cm. *w.*: its vertical position is fixed by fibre-correspondences with fr. 1, and the horizontal position assigned to it here is made probable by the general appearance of the papyrus and by various plausible restorations of the text in ll. 7–10. Fr. 3 measures 9.5 cm. *h.*× 4.5 cm. *w.*: its vertical position is also fixed by fibre-correspondences with fr. 1, and the horizontal position assigned to it here is supported by the general appearance of the papyrus, by probable, although not quite certain, fibre-correspondences between the backing sheets of frs. 2 and 3, and by the possibility, although no more, of restoring the text in ll. 21–4. The suggested locations of both the small fragments receive some confirmation from a consideration of the pattern in which the scribe's pen has run dry and been recharged.

The **hand** of **1a** is of the same general type as that of **1**, but, apart from matters of orthography and the layout of the text, consistent differences can be observed in the way the writer's pen moves (differences far greater than any between the hands of **1** and **2**, possibly written by a single scribe), which make it certain that the hands of **1** and **1a** cannot be identified. The hand of **1a** is more rounded, and the strokes are more carefully and deliberately formed. The hand is a little smaller, and the spacing of the lines is wider in proportion than that in **1**. The orthography of a few words can be seen to differ in the two texts: see *ỉrm*, **1a**/14 , **1**, front, 9/1 ; *wnwt*, **1a**/18 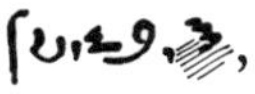, **1**, front, 9/14 ; *n=s*, **1a**/9 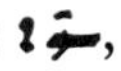, **1**, front, 9/29 ; *grḥ*, **1a**/18 , **1**, front, 9/17 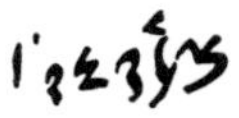: the form  of *ỉw=y* in **1a**/20 (the form  is consistently used in **1**, e.g. front, 9/24) may be an isolated variant.

However, the contents of the two papyri appear to be closely connected: see p. 69.

Transliteration

1. --- ....]..[---
2.]...[........]...[
3.]... *ỉw=w* . [.....] ⌜*st šm*⌝[a] [......] .... [
4.]....[.....]....[b] *=s/nꜣ* . *ḥr*.[c][. .].⌜*=f*⌝ *ỉn-ḳd*⌜*y*⌝.*k* [
5. ...].[....]⌜*=f*⌝......... [...].... [
6. .] *ỉḫ* . . [.....].*=f ỉr=w yꜥby* .....[d] *ḏd=w* ⌜*Ḥr*⌝-[e][
7.]*=f šm=*⌜*f*⌝ *n=f ỉw=f ꜥš* . [. .] *ỉw=f ḫtm nꜣ(ỉ) rꜣ.w m-sꜣ=f ḏd pꜣ* . . . .[f][
8.] . .[g]*=w-tn ḏd mtw=tn* ⌜*nꜣ*⌝ *ntỉ dỉt šm=*⌜*f*⌝ *n=f pꜣ* ⌜*ntỉ*⌝ *ỉw=tn dỉt ḏd st* [
9. ..]......... *hwš* .....*=s*[h] *ḏd=w n=s* . [
10. .....] . ⌜*ḫpr*⌝ [*n*]-*ỉm=f* ⌜*dỉ=w*⌝[j] *ḳdy n=s wꜥ* . [
11. ....] *n=s* ⌜*dỉ=f*⌝[k] *ṯꜣỉ=w Nꜣ-nfr-Sḫmt* . .[l] [
12. ....] *wḥm-nsw*[m] *ỉrm pꜣ ḥrỉ n pꜣ* ⌜*pr*⌝-*ḥḏ*[n] . [
13. ....]...[o] [.] *ꜥn m-ỉr dỉt sdm=s* [
14. ....] *ỉrm=y* ....[p] [
15. ---]*=f*[---] ⌜*ḥmt nfrt*⌝[q] *ỉn wn* . [
16. ....] *ꜥꜣ*[r] *Nꜣ-nfr-Sḫmt* .[s][
17. ....] . *ḏd Pr-ꜥꜣ* ⌜*my*⌝...... [
18. ....] . . *wnwt* ⌜*6 n grḥ*⌝[t] [
19. ....] ⌜*ỉn n(=y)*⌝ *ḏd* . . [.] .[u] *ỉw=y dỉt* ⌜*ḥdb=w*⌝ . [
20. ....] . *ꜥꜣy.ṯ n ms ỉw=y dỉt šn*[v] [
21. .] ..... ⌜*ỉn=w*⌝ . [......] *šn-s Pr-ꜥꜣ ḏd* ....[w] [
22.]⌜*ỉrm=f ỉr*⌝*=y ỉn-ḳdy.k* ⌜*nm*⌝ [*pꜣ ỉ-ỉr*]-⌜*gm*⌝-*ṯ=f*[x] *ḏd n=s Pr-ꜥꜣ* ⌜*m-ỉr*⌝ . . [
23. ...] . . ⌜*Nꜣ-nfr*⌝-*Sḫmt* [....] . ⌜*ỉ-ỉr=s*⌝ *mwt n mḥw* . .[y] [
24. ...] ....[z] [.....] .... ⌜*r-ḥr*⌝-*n Pr-ꜥꜣ n pꜣỉ=s* ⌜*ꜣbd*⌝ .[aa] [
25. .] . . ⌜*šr*⌝[ab] *n Pr-ꜥꜣ* ... [.......] . [
26. ...] .... [
27. . .] ⌜*rỉt*⌝-*ḥrỉt* ⌜*m*⌝*šꜥ* ⌜*Ḥr*⌝-[ac][
28. ......] ... ⌜*ỉrm*⌝[

up to 1.5 cm. of blank papyrus

Notes on transliteration

a. st here will be the object pronoun: for a completely preserved writing, see l. 8 below.

b. The traces are 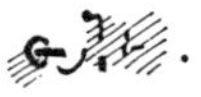. The central signs, where the papyrus is badly rubbed, might suggest *mwt*, but this is not a convincing reading. The last traces might be read *r-bnr* or *r-r=k*. The final sign does not have the same form as *šm* in ll. 7–8. It can hardly be read as *pḥ*.

c. The *ḥr* is written , as, for example, in *ḥrḥ*.

d. The traces after *ỉr=w yꜥby* are . Although they cannot be read, they seem consistent with a new sentence's beginning at *ḏd=w*.

e. The reading *Ḥr* is virtually certain. Possibly the name *Ḥr-mꜣꜥ-ḫrw* that occurs in **1**, cols. 13–14 should be restored. See also l. 27 below.

f. The traces after *ḏd pꜣ* are . They are too damaged for any reading firmly to be suggested in such a fragmentary text. No title etc. occurring in **1** seems plausible here. The readings *ḥrỉ-tp*, 'magician', which sometimes has a sign resembling a above (*DG*, 321. 4) and *swnw*, 'doctor' (*DG*, 415. 3), are possibilities, but other titles derived from hieroglyphic writings might be considered.

g. Probably the verb to be restored here ends with the det.

h. The word *hwš*, 'to abuse', etc. is quite certain here, but the other signs cannot be made out with confidence. Possibly *r-ḥr=tn n-ỉm=s* follows *hwš*. At the beginning of the line, *ḥm-nṯr Ḏḥwt* might be read, although the form of the *Ḏḥwt*-sign does not have any precise parallel. Another possibility here is *fꜣy=w* or *fꜣy.w* (a similarly upright form of non-initial *y* can be seen in *ꜥꜣy.ṯ* in l. 20 below). Immediately before *hwš*, the traces might suggest *ntỉ*, but it is difficult to tell if signs are lost before or after this: [*pꜣ*] *ntỉ* is a possibility.

j. *dỉ* is probably here written very large, as often in these hands: cf. the restoration *dỉ=f* in l. 11 below. There seems too little room to read *dỉ*+a god's name (*'Imn* or *Ḏḥwt* ?). For a good example of such a writing, see **1**, 13/32.

k. For the large writing of *dỉ* assumed here, compare the example, also damaged, in l. 10 above.

l. For the writing of the name *Nꜣ-nfr-Sḫmt*, cf. l. 16 and l. 23 below; and **1**, 14/31. Possibly restore *n/r pꜣ* after the name. Perhaps Nanoufesakhme was taken 'to' a person.

m. For the title *wḥm-nsw*, see *Wb*. i. 344. 8. For the semi-hieratic writing of *wḥm*, see the early writings given in *DG*, 97. 5.

n. The two supralinear dots strongly support the reading *pr-ḥḏ*.

o. The traces at the beginning of the line are . They do not suit the dets. of a time word (cf. l. 18); possibly a place-name is in question, or a word with the same dets.

p. The traces are in part quite clear, , but no reading imposes itself. The final traces are surely too large to be read *Pr-ꜥꜣ* (cf. ll. 17, 21–2, 25). Perhaps read *rpꜥịt*.

q. *ḥmt*, rather than *wrt*, is the natural reading of the signs. Presumably the reference is to *Nꜣ-nfr-Sḫmt*.

r. In view of the fact that Pharaoh speaks in l. 17 immediately following, the restoration of a vocative expression, *pꜣỉ(=y) nb ꜥꜣ*, 'my great Lord', addressed to Pharaoh, is more than a mere possibility.

s. Probably read *tꜣ* after *Nꜣ-nfr-Sḫmt*.

t. Probably *nb*(*t*), 'all', is to be read before *wnwt*. Little remains of the numeral 6, but the reading is almost certain; in any case, the sixth hour either of night or day, as round figures, 'midnight' and 'midday', are rather to be expected in Egyptian narratives, although 'the eleventh hour' at **1**, 13/17 is a striking exception.

u. A name or title seems likely to stand after *ḏd*, but nothing that occurs elsewhere in this text suits the traces. Conceivably *ỉn n*(=*y*) might be followed directly by the proper name *Ḏd-ḥr*, 'Teos', but neither the traces, nor any other indication in the text, suggest this is very likely.

v. The reading *šn* is almost certain, but it is impossible to tell whether *šn*, 'to inquire', or *šny*, 'to be ill', should be restored. However, the sense may be resumed by *šn-s Pr-ꜥꜣ* in the next line (l. 21).

w. Possibly read *tꜣ šrt pꜣ* . [, 'the daughter (of) the . . .'.

x. The restoration of *gm.ṯ=f* here is almost certain: for the variations in the det. of *gm* found in the Saqqâra texts see, for example, pp. 17, n. *bu*, 150, n. *l*.

y. It is possible to read either *bw-ỉr=s mwt* or *ỉ-ỉr=s mwt* (the latter reading would assume that a horizontal stroke from a preceding sign ran into the *ỉ*-). However, *ỉ-ỉr* is almost certainly the correct reading. All the indications from other Saqqâra texts suggest that *bw* might be expected to have the form , not . The habitual sense of *bw-ỉr* seems inappropriate to *mwt*, unless it could be understood in the sense 'she cannot die'. The det. of *mḥw* clearly indicates *mḥw*, 'tomb', rather than *Mḥw*, 'Lower Egypt' (see *DG*, 174. 6–7). The final signs are uncertain, but might read *ḥꜣt*.

z. The traces are . The last sign might be *šr* or *wꜥt*: for *šr*, cf. n. *ab* below, on l. 25. The preceding traces as a whole cannot read *wnwt* or *grḥ* (cf. l. 18 above), and it is difficult to make all the traces fit *mtr*, 'midday'. Near the beginning of the line, *ꜣbd*, 'month', might be read (cf. *ꜣbd* at the end of this line).

aa. The reading *n pꜣỉ=s* is certain, and *ꜣbd* is very probable; the following traces cannot be made out. The phrase suggests expressions such as *pꜣỉ=s ꜣbd n ms*, 'her month of giving birth' (see P. Tebt. Tait 1. 29 with n., with reference to 2. Kh. 1/8–9), and the possibility of a mention of pregnancy or birth here might be strengthened by *šr n Pr-ꜥꜣ* in the following line (see n. *ab* below). However, it is possible that *ꜣbd* here might be used in different contexts as, for example, 'her month (of carrying out some task or duty)'.

ab. The exact form of the sign here tentatively read *šr* cannot be made out (see n. *z* above for a sign that might be read *šr* in l. 24, although the context there does little to decide the reading). However, the *n Pr-ꜥꜣ* that follows is clear enough, making *wꜥt* (*1.t*) a highly improbable, although not impossible reading, and the spacing of the previous trace suggests the sign is unlikely to be a det. of a preceding word. The reading *šr n Pr-ꜥꜣ* is therefore very plausible: see p. 43 and p. 59 for possible references to pregnancy or birth in these lines.

ac. The reading *Ḥr* here is not certain: cf. the clearer writing in l. 6 above. No other reading that comes to mind seems defensible, certainly not *ḏd* or *ỉrm*. As in l. 6 (see p. 67, n. *e*), it is tempting to read the name *Ḥr-mꜣꜥ-ḫrw*.

Translation

— —

ll. 1–2, *only traces*

3.] . . . they . . . . them. [. . . . .] went . . . . . [
4.] . . . . he (?) slept [
5.] . . . . he . . . . [
6.] What . . . . him?' They were troubled . . . . They said 'Ḥar-[makhrouou (?)
7.] him. He went off by himself, crying . . . . . , and he shut the doors behind him. The . . . . .[α] said [
8.] they . . . . .[β] you, because you are the ones who made him go off by himself. Anyone whom you cause to say them [
9.] . . . .[γ] abuse . . . . . her/it.'[δ] They said to her [
10.] that happened to him. They caused a [. . . . . .] to turn to her [
11.] to her. He made them take Nanoufesakhme to [
12.] Royal Herald together with the Master of the Treasury [
13.] . . . . . again. Do not let her hear [
14.] with me . . . . [
15.] he [. . . . . .] beautiful little (girl). Does there exist [- - - ?
16.] great.[ε] Nanoufesakhme [
17.] Pharaoh said 'May . . . . [
18.] the sixth hour of the night [
19.] bring . . . . said 'I shall make them kill [
20.] older. I shall cause [. . . . . . .] to ask/to be ill [
21.] . . . . they brought [. . . . . . .] Pharaoh asked, saying . . . .[ζ] [
22.] with him. I slept. Who [was it that] found him?' Pharaoh said to her 'Do not [
23.] Nanoufesakhme [. . . . . . .] she dies/cannot die in a tomb[η] [
24.] . . . . [. . . . .] . . . . . before Pharaoh in her month . . .[θ] [
25.] a son to/of Pharaoh . . . . [

26. *only traces*
27.] upper chamber/above. Ḥar-[makhroou (?)] walked [
28.] . . . with [

Notes on translation

α. 'The magician' or perhaps 'the doctor' are among possible readings here.

β. The det. of this word indicates a verb implying violence or more vaguely a pejorative action: for example, 'they blame you' is a possibility.

γ. The reading is uncertain: there may be a reference to 'carrying' (or 'porters'), or a 'prophet of Thoth' may be mentioned.

δ. Possibly read 'who abuse you (plur.) because of it'.

ϵ. The beginning of a speech addressing Pharaoh 'O my great Lord, Nanoufesakhme is . . .' might be restored here.

ζ. Perhaps read 'saying, "The daughter of the [" '.

η. Although the precise syntax of this sentence is uncertain, a reference to a female character's dying in a tomb seems inescapable.

θ. For the possibility that a birth is related in these lines, see p. 68, nn. *z–ab*.

DISCUSSION

This text three times (ll. 11, 16, 23) mentions the name Nanoufesakhme, the name of a female character who plays a major role in **1**, and a name that is not attested in any other extant literary text. It also appears to mention, possibly twice, a character Ḥar . . . . . . (ll. 6, 27): this name might be restored Ḥarmakhroou, the name of a male character who plays a major role in **1**, also a name not otherwise attested in literary material. These indications are perhaps sufficient in themselves to make it highly probable that the fragments of **1a** belong to another manuscript of the same text as that preserved in **1**, and the contents of **1a**, together with more detailed aspects of the links between **1** and **1a**, are dealt with in the Discussion appended to **1** (see pp. 43–64).

TEXT 2

2. FRONT: Plates 4–9

THE VENGEANCE OF ISIS

BACK: MERIB, THE HIGH STEWARD, AND THE CAPTIVE PHARAOH

H5-DP153(A+B)+357+376 [1751(A+B)+2278+2297]

Sector 1 (North Courtyard) debris (1966–7)

The text consists of a considerable number of fragments joined together, or linked by fibre and textual correspondences. The majority of these are registered as H5-DP153, and measurements and other details are not given for each of them individually. The piece measures over all 36.5 cm. *h.*×35.5 cm. *w.* It is divided vertically down the middle by a complete break, which occurs at a join between two sheets of papyrus. These two sections of the text were for convenience registered as A and B. The left-hand portion, as seen from the front (recto), is 153A [1751A], and the right-hand portion is 153B [1751B]. Two further fragments were relaxed and registered separately. The fragment in the upper central portion of the text (which preserves in l. 1 on the front surface the words *]mḥ-ṯ=y n=w ḏd bn-pw=n rḫ . . . . di=s ỉr=w wꜥt ḳnḥy* [and which extends as far as l. 5) is registered as H5-DP 357 [2278], and measures 7.0 cm. *h.*×10.5 cm. *w.* The fragment lying at the extreme upper right-hand corner, as seen from the front, is H5–DP376 [2297], and measures 7.5 cm. *h.*×8.5 cm. *w.* The provenance given above applies to all the fragments, and they were in fact all found in the same large deposit of papyrus material.

The front (↔) surface preserves most of one column (labelled as the sixth) and a little of the beginnings of the first nine lines of the following (seventh) column. There are also slight traces of the very ends of two lines of the preceding (fifth) column. The back (↕) surface preserves most of one column (its original numbering is not preserved), together with portions, varying from a few words to merely a few signs, of the ends of some of the lines of the preceding column. The column substantially preserved on the front (col. 6) has a width of 27.5 cm., while the width of the column substantially preserved on the back (col. x+1) varies between 27.0 and 27.5 cm. On the front, a top margin of 3.0 cm. is preserved above the columns, while, on the back, the top margin varies between 1.5 and 2.0 cm. A bottom margin of 4.0 cm. is preserved on both surfaces. The margin between columns varies between 1.0 and 1.5 cm.

Col. 6 upon the front is numbered in the bottom margin. The numeral is set at the normal line-spacing below the last line of text, but 9.0 cm. in from the beginnings of the lines of the column. The numbering of col. x+1 on the back was no doubt in a similar position, and is lost. A small vertical ink mark is preserved immediately before the beginning of l. 26 of col. 6. This may have been used by the scribe as a guide in laying out the columns. A large sign stands in the middle of the top margin of col. x+1 on the back, but its reading and purpose have not been determined (see p. 113, n. *ah*: this mark is for convenience disregarded in the numbering of the lines in this edition). In three places on the front, and once on the back, a fresh line has been started, and a space larger than normal left between the lines, to mark the beginning of a new section of the text: front, 6/8–9, 14–15, 25–6; and back, x+1/19–20—in each case, a space of about 1.0 cm. has been left.

The papyrus is translucent, and is fairly fine

and even-textured. It was manufactured with many of the vertical strips of papyrus overlapping slightly, forming thin opaque bands: this is not the case with the horizontal strips. A few portions of the text are of a straw colour, and only a little darkened, but the greater part is badly stained to a shade that varies from light- to dark-brown. As usual, it is impossible to be sure what has caused this discoloration; but most probably, as the sheet's torn and crumpled condition would suggest, the chief damage was done when it was finally used up as scrap paper. At all events, the result is that much of the papyrus is extremely brittle, and the staining also appears to have exaggerated the fineness of the papyrus.

Three joins between sheets are preserved (right over left, as is to be expected). As seen from the front, at the extreme right-hand edge and towards the bottom, a small portion of a join is preserved. The next join is 14.5 cm. to the left of the first, and measures up to 1.6 cm. in width. The third join is 14.0 cm. to the left again, and is about 1.4 cm. wide. A further 5.5 cm. of papyrus remains from this join to the extreme left-hand edge of the piece. On both the front and the back surfaces, the first and third joins roughly coincide with the line-ends of the columns. Demotic scribes often place their columns within single sheets of papyrus, or within pairs of sheets, when writing continuous texts that are not laid out in a framework of ruled borders (although many papyri show no trace of any such tendency). Presumably this practice arose simply because the joins provide a convenient guide for the line-ends. Other demotic papyri that clearly show this feature include P. Spiegelberg (Petub.) and the Demotic Chronicle (Orakel)—in both cases, the columns are confined to a single sheet, and not to a pair of sheets, as in the present papyrus.

The **hand** is in every way similar in appearance to that of **1** in this volume, and the brief remarks concerning its general style on pp. 3–4 above should be consulted.

It cannot be said, however, that the two hands are indistinguishable. The hand of **2** might be described as a little more precise and less rounded than that of **1**, and it seems to have been written with a slightly stiffer brush. These differences are well within the variation that might be expected in one man's writing over a moderate period of time. Certainly the hands are so alike when compared with the range of material that survives from the Memphite area that they must be close in date and scribal training.

Detailed comparison, while in general confirming the similarity in the formation of most of the individual signs, and in the writing of many common words, also reveals numerous differences in orthography between the two texts. It further emerges that some of the orthographic distinctions observed in **1** that reflect matters of grammar, for example the differentiation of two writings of *n-ỉm=*, cannot be seen to operate in the same consistent fashion in **2**.

One possible explanation of these differences is that the two texts were written by different scribes. This might seem a simple explanation, but it would be hard to demonstrate that personal preferences could play such a large part in shaping a scribe's orthographic practice. It is more probable that the differences (whether or not the two hands are the same) chiefly arise from differences in the orthography of the papyri from which these two manuscripts were copied, which might well have been of different dates, or even have been written in different places. It is of course being assumed here that both these texts were copied from other written texts, although this can hardly be proved rigorously. Certainly a few differences *within* **1** and perhaps also within **2** might be explained as deriving from sometimes more and sometimes less faithful copying of the orthography of an older hand. It thus seems likely that the texts were copied visually, not from dictation (as has been argued was the case with some demotic literary texts), and the same tentative conclusion might be drawn from the various mistakes (no doubt made in copying) mentioned in (Text **1**) p. 31, n. *cc*, p. 33, n. *dr* (cf. p. 10, n. *e*, p. 21, n. *du*) and (Text **2**) p. 80 n. *cd*.

In view of the problems of comparing the hands of these two texts, it is interesting to note R. A. Parker's brief remarks on the orthography of the two parts of *A Vienna Demotic Papyrus on Eclipse- and Lunar-omina* (pp. 3–4): similar problems have arisen with *Ägypter und Amazonen* and P. Carlsberg 1 and 1a.

The Vengeance of Isis

Plates 4, 5

Transliteration

FRONT (↔)

col. 5

x+1 - - - . . .[a]

x+2 no surviving trace

x+3 - - - . . .[b]

col. 6

top margin of 3.0 cm.

1. *⸢ntỉ⸣ bw-ỉr=f*[c] *ỉr pꜣỉ⸢=f⸣*[d] *ḳmꜣ*[e] *i-ỉr-ḥr pꜣ mšꜥ ⸢ỉ⸣[.] . . . . [. .].*[f] *ỉn-ỉw=w r . . . .*[g] *[. . . . .] ⸢pr-ꜥnḫ⸣*[h] *[. . .] mḥ.ṱ=y*[j] *⸢n=w⸣*[k] *ḏd bn-pw=n rẖ . . . .*[l] *dỉ=s ỉr=w wꜥt ḳnḥy [. . .] . . . .*[m]
2. *[. .] . . . . [. .]*[n] *⸢ỉw⸣=s sẖn n ỉny ỉw=s . . . . .*[o] *[. . . .] nꜣỉ=s sbꜣ.w*[p] *. . [. . . . .] . . nꜣỉ=s ḳry.w n ḥmt ꜣkm*[q] *r nꜣỉ=s ššt.w n . .*[r] *[. . . . . . .]*
3. *[. .] . . ⸢ṱp⸣ ỉynm*[s] *ḏd ršꜣ r . . [.] . . . [. . .] . . Yb*[t] *. . . [. . . . .]y*[u] *ỉw=s . . .*[v] *n nꜥm(.w) ỉw=w sḳrḳr.⸢w⸣*[w] *[. . . . .] . . .*
4. *[.] . wrs n ḥr . . .*[x] *[. . . .] . . [. . .] . . [. . .] . . i-ỉr-ḏꜣḏꜣ*[y]*[. . . . .] . . ḥꜣ=f*[z] *n nkt ẖnṱ n ḥm*[aa] *[. . . . . . .] . . .*
5. *. . ⸢ꜥr⸣ r-ḥrỉ*[ab] *[. . . . .] ⸢ḥr⸣-ꜣt.ṱ*[ac] *[. . . . .] . . .*[ad] *m-bꜣḥ=f n pꜣ stꜣ.ṱ hn⸢y⸣ . [. . . . .] . . . .*[ae]
6. *. [.] . . . .*[af] *[. . . . .] . [. .] ỉr=s . . . .*[ag] *[. . . . .] . . tꜣỉ=s mwt . . . . ⸢dw.w⸣*[ah] *ꜥš=s n=f ⸢ḥs.w⸣*[aj] *[. .] . . . .*[ak]
7. [about 8.5 cm. lost . . . .] *. . . . ỉn*[al] *pꜣ i-ỉr-dỉt wꜣ[y]⸢=k⸣*[am] *[. . . . . . .] . ⸢r⸣ ntr nb ḳn*[an] *m-ỉr . . . . . .*[ao] *[. . .] ⸢šr šrt⸣ dỉt rẖ=t . . . ꜥn*[ap]
8. [about 8.0 cm. lost . . . . *ḳ]⸢n⸣ḥy pꜣỉ(=y) ⸢pr⸣ ẖn ⸢wꜥb⸣*[aq] *[. . . . . . .] . . .*[ar] *[. .] ⸢pꜣ⸣ ḥmꜣr ỉw=f nby ỉw=f r šm n=f*[as] vacat

slightly larger space between lines

9. [about 6.5 cm. lost . . . . . .] *. . . . [.] ⸢ꜥꜣy⸣ tꜣ ⸢ꞽImnt.t⸣ i-ỉr-n(=ỉ)*[at] *pꜣ bỉk . . . .*[au] *rk=s wbꜣ=s*[av] *ꜥḏb=s ḏd ꞽIst ẖꜣꜥ.ṱ n=s*[aw] *ỉrm=f ḏd pꜣ mwt.ṱ*[ax] *ntỉ ỉw=s r dỉt . .*[ay] *[. . .] . .*
10. *[. . . .] ⸢tꜣ byry⸣*[az] *. . . =s n nꜣ . . . .w*[ba] *ỉw=s ỉỉ.ṱ ⸢r⸣ tꜣỉ=s rỉt ỉw=s rmy [.] . . .*[bb] *šm=s r pꜣ ⸢kꜣ⸣*[bc] *md=s r-ḥr n tꜣ rpy ꞽIst ntỉ ỉw=s dỉt šm=s r dỉt ⸢ms⸣*[bd] *ꜥḥꜥ ⸢sdm⸣ [. .]*[be]
11. *[.] tꜣ nbt ⸢tꜣ.wy⸣*[bf] *ỉnk . . n tꜣỉ . .*[bg] *. . . .*[bh] *n pꜣỉ . . . . .*[bj] *ntỉ ḥs r pꜣ .*[bk] *[. . .] ⸢r⸣ bw-ỉr=s swr ntỉ ꜥr nwy . .*[bl] *r bw-ỉr=s wnm ntỉ ḥwy mnš.w ‵r . . . . .′ ỉw . . . .*[bm]
12. *⸢ꜥs⸣ i-ỉr-bw-ỉr=w*[bn] *⸢krp⸣ nꜣ ntr.w r nꜣ rmt.w ⸢. . .⸣ wbn*[bo] *ỉw bw-ỉr=w ẖd[b*[bp] *. .] rẖ .*[bq] *⸢i⸣-ỉr-ḏd r wꜥ rmt ẖm*[br] *ỉw=y r t̠ꜣỉ n=f ḳbꜥ*[bs] *⸢ꞽIst⸣*[bt] *m-ỉr šlf=f r-dbꜣ . . [. .]*[bu]

13. [.] . . . sỉ . . [. .] twt[bv] ḳ(n)s=⸢f⸣[bw] . . tꜣ šfꜣ n nꜣỉ=f ỉwỉw.w[bx] . . . .[by] [. . . . .] . . . . . tꜣỉ=w ḥny[bz]
n sgn n ḳn r ẖdb nb[ca] pꜣ wdb ḫꜥ . [. .][cb]

14. . . . . . . ḥrỉ . . . pꜣ nhr n sn-th.ṱ[cc] {.} ḥḳ=f ỉn=f[cd] vacat . . . =f ⸢tꜣ⸣ pt pꜣ ⸢tꜣ⸣ tꜣ dwꜣt[ce] vacat

slightly larger space between lines

15. [.] . ṯꜣw ntỉ mtw=y[cf] tw=y ḥꜣ.ṱ=s[cg] tꜣỉ(=y) mwt ꞽIst[ch] ḏd ỉw=y r mwt ỉw=y r dỉt ꜥm=s[cj] n nꜣỉ sꜥḥꜥ.w r
bw-ỉr-tw . . [. . . .] .[ck] nꜣỉ=t sṱny⟨.w⟩[cl] mn rḫ n-ỉm=w[cm] nꜣỉ=t sḏy.w sr.w[cn] bn-pw=w ḫpr n . . [. .][co]

16. tꜣỉ-ḏd=w n=s pꜣ 5 ⸢ntr.w⸣[cp] bn-pw=s ỉr-wpy ḏd bn-pw=w wpy⸢.ṱ⸣=s[cq] ỉr=s ỉrỉ n sḏy [.] . . . [. . .][cr]
dỉ=s gm=w tꜣ/nꜣ i-ỉr-ḫpr n pꜣ nb sšm[cs] ꜥḥꜥ tꜣ ntỉ n sšm n ꞽIst[ct]

17. ẖyṱ[cu] n ꞽIst[cv] n-ỉm=t ỉn=t n(=ỉ) ꞽIst n nꜣỉ=s ỉwf.w . . . . wꜥt wnwt[cw] [. . . . .] ⸢pꜣ⸣ mwt ⸢ỉw=⸣f
ḫpr n-ỉm=n pꜣ myt n ḥr nb pꜣỉ[cx] ẖꜣꜥ`=s´ pꜣ sšm ꞽIst[cy] . . . . . . [. .][cz]

18. [. . k]ꜣ[da] wšd=s ꜣs⸢ḳ=w ỉw⸣=w ỉr n nꜣy[db] bn(-pw)=w nw [.] . [.][dc] ⸢ḫpr wꜥ⸣ [. . . . .] . . . .[dd]
⸢nw=w⸣ r wꜥ ꜥꜣpy ꜥꜣ r ỉw=f ỉw r-ẖry[de] n tꜣ pt wꜣḥ=f i-ỉr-ḥr=w[df]

19. [. .] . . . . nw.w[dg] nhs=f nw ỉrt.ṱ=w[dh] nw=w r ꞽIỉ-⸢m-ḥ⸣tp ⸢stꜣ.ṱ⸣[dj] [. .] . [.] . . rk=f-s . . . [. .] .[dk]
mtw=f ỉr pꜣỉ=f smt[dl] ḥms=f ḥr wꜥ ifd n ỉny r nꜣ ỉwf.w

20. . . . . ⸢.ṱ⸣=f . . . .[dm] sdr=w n=w r-ẖt.⸢ṱ=w⸣[dn] ẖr=s n(=ỉ)[do] ḏd n=f tꜣ ntỉ šny[dp] [. . ꞽIỉ]⸢-m-ḥtp⸣[dq]
pꜣỉ(=y) ḥrỉ ỉn . [. . .] . ⸢ḥr⸣ n . . . . . nḥm.⸢ṱ⸣=.[dr] ỉn dỉ=k drt.ṱ=k r ꞽIst ntỉ ⸢m⸣nḳ[ds]

21. nꜣỉ mdwt n ḏd[dt] r-dbꜣ ẖdb ḫpr n pꜣỉ(=y) ⸢smt⸣[du] ỉmnṱ[dv] dỉ=y-s n ⸢ḥꜣt⸣[dw] [. . . . .] . [. .] . [.] . [. . .]
. .[dx] pꜣỉ(=y) nkt ḫpr n k.t pꜣỉ(=y) smt dỉ=y . . . . =y[dy]

22. bn(-pw)=w rḫ tw=k ỉỉ.ṱ n=n n Nfr-ḥr[dz] ỉw=k n nꜣ rḫ.w n Ḏḥwt ỉw=k ⸢n-drt⸣ . . [. . .] . .[ea] ỉn-ỉw=k
. . . . .ṱ=k[eb] ḏd bn(-pw)=k nꜥš r ꞽIst i-ỉr nꜥš Ḥr r ntr nb ḳn[ec]

23. ⸢šn⸣ [. .] .⸢i-ỉr pꜣ⸣ ntr[ed] dỉt ḫpr=f n pꜣ ntỉ ỉỉ r mwt r ⸢tm⸣ dỉt ỉr=f ḥꜣt.ṱ=f m-sꜣ[ee] .[. . . .] ⸢ꜥs⸣[ef] my
ỉꜣw[.][eg] tw-s tꜣỉ(=y) dbḥy mtw=k ⸢šꜥ-r⸣[eh] ṯꜣỉ.ṱ⸢=f⸣[ej] pꜣ ḥmꜣr [.] ⸢m⸣n

24. ỉn-⸢mwt⸣[ek] m-ỉr ⸢dỉt⸣ ꜣsḳ=f ꜥḥꜥ[el] ẖn st-dbꜣ bn(-pw) . . . .[em] [. . . . . .] . . . m-sꜣ tꜣỉ ⸢ẖr.t⸣[en] [. .] . dwꜣ=s
(-ntr) n=k[eo] my n=s pꜣ myt n ꜥnḫ i-ḏdy-s n(=ỉ) [. . . .][ep]

25. . . . . [. . . .] . .[eq] wnwt n sḏy mnḳ=s nꜣ mdwt n ḏd ⸢ỉ⸣[. . . . .[er]] . . =f nw r pꜣ ỉtn[es] vacat

slightly larger space between lines

26. wpy ⸢tꜣ ẖr.t rꜣ⸣=s[et] md=s ỉrm pꜣ ntr ỉḫ pꜣỉ ḥr ntỉ ỉw=k n-ỉm[=. . .]⸢dbꜣ⸣ ⸢tꜣỉ=k⸣ bꜣk.t[eu] ntỉ ỉw bn-pw
⸢pꜣ dwꜣ⸣ ṯꜣỉ tꜣ ẖm.t r-r=s[ev] ỉw=s dỉt ⸢ys pꜣ ꜣp⸣wṱ [. .] .[ew]

27. r ỉỉ m-sꜣ=k ẖr ⸢ḥty⸣[ex] hmy mtw=s dỉt ỉr=w n=f ḥb Skr mtw=s dỉt ỉr=w n=f ⸢nꜣ ḥ⸣s.w n tꜣ ẖr.t ntỉ n
ꞽIst[ey] vacat ḏd pꜣ ntr n-drt gr=s n=t ⸢(n-)ḥꜣ(t)⸣ nꜣ wꜥ.w r-ḏd[=.] r tꜣỉ=t rp⸢y⸣ [. .][ez]

28. ỉn i-ỉr=t r ḏd wꜥ wḥm n pꜣ sp mḥ-2[fa] nꜣ ẖrw.w n wsṱn r-ḏd=s . [.] ⸢rp⸣y ꞽIst ⸢(n-)ḥꜣ(t)⸣ nꜣy pꜣ ḏd wḥm[fb]
ḫpr ḏd=s hmy mtw=s dỉt ỉr=w ⸢ḥb Skr⸣ . . . [. .] . . [. .][fc]

29. r-ḏd=s bw-ỉr=s rḫ ỉr=s ỉḫ ỉn-ỉw=s r rḫ ỉr=s gr m-sꜣ ṯꜣỉ ⸢pꜣ ṯꜣw⸣[fd] ỉn bw-ỉr=y wḫꜣ=f m-sꜣ tꜣỉ(=y) mwt
⸢ẖꜣꜥ⸣ st[fe] ⸢šꜥ-r⸣ . .[ff] [.] . [. . .] . [. . .]

30. i-⸢ỉr⸣=k ⸢tn⸣ wn-nꜣ-w ỉrt.t(=y) wḫꜣ=k[fg] ḏd pꜣ ntr wn-nꜣ-w i-ỉr=y n pr ⸢ỉꜣb⸣[ṱ][fh] . .=y Wsỉr[fj] r-dbꜣ ꞽIst
r-wn-nꜣ-w n-ỉm[fk] ỉw pꜣỉ ḥm⸢ꜣr⸣[fl] [. . . . .] . [. .]

31. sšm[fm] bn-pw=f dỉt hwš ms ⸢ꜣ(w)ỉ ḥsy⸣[fn] m-ḳdy ẖr r-ꜥš=f . . . ḥwt(-. .)[fo] ẖrꜥry ḳy Sḫmt[fp] dỉ=t nb.t
. . . .[fq] [. . . . .] . . [. . .]

32. vacat mḥ 6 vacat

col. 7

1. nw r . . . . . .[fr] [- - -
2. hb=t m-sꜣ=y ỉw=y r ⸢ỉỉ⸣[fs] . .[- - -
3. wn nꜣ⸢i=k fꜣ⸣y.w[ft] ỉw=y [- - -

4. *r-bn(-pw)=y mwt sny=f* [- - -
5. *twt pr-nfr*[fu] [- - -
6. *r tꜣ/nꜣ wsẖy*[fv] [- - -
7. *mn* . . . . .[fw] [- - -
8. *nw r-r=w r-ẖ(t)*[fx] [- - -
9. . .] . *pꜣ mwt*[fy] [- - -

All subsequent lines lost, except for possible traces of beginnings of lines opposite ll. 9, 19, 21, and 23 of col. 6

Notes on transliteration

FRONT

col. 5

a. : *šny* is possible, cf. 6/20.

b. : *mwt*, 'death' is possible, cf. 6/17, 7/9.

col. 6

c. : *bw-ỉr=f*, not *ỉ-ỉr=f*, should be read. The preceding sign is disfigured by a large black blot, which is not ink. Although the precise shape of the upper trace is debatable, the position of the traces renders any other restoration than *ntỉ* implausible. These will have been the first signs in the line.

d. : while *pꜣỉ=f* and *pꜣỉ=s* are almost equally plausible readings, *pꜣỉ(=y)* (cf. 6/8) is excluded. *pꜣỉ=f* is preferred on the grounds of the straightness of the final diagonal descender and the context.

e. : *ḳmꜣ* secure. Cf. *Wb.* v. 36. 9–15.

f. : interpretation of the traces is uncertain. i. The relative positions of the upright stroke following *mšꜥ* and the two following traces suggest *ỉw=w*; ii. *ỉr* or *ꜥš* (cf. 6/6) are perhaps possible; iii. of the following group, only two upright strokes are clear; if *ỉr* is read, *pꜣỉ=n* (?) might be considered; iv. the final word is determined with ; the previous high trace might perhaps suggest *rn* (?).

g. : *in-ỉw=w*, despite slight flaking of the ink, is hardly doubtful, and should presumably be interrogative. A clear trace of *r* follows. Very careful examination has convinced us that the next word is written exactly like normal Memphite writings of the word *ꜥꜥn*, 'baboon' (*DG*, 56. 12), and what is preserved of the det. supports this. But after the construction *in-ỉw=w r* the infinitive of a verb is required; we have no convincing reading to suggest.

h. : *pr-ꜥnḫ* seems a better reading than *pr-ḥd*, as the latter is mostly written (*DG*, 133. 7), and *ḥd*, when written, is more usually made (*DG*, 335. 1). The apparent traces on the photograph of a divine det. are not ink, and are illusory, though a further det. may of course have been present.

j. : the curious arrangement of signs seems to be paralleled only by *mḥṭ=y* in **1**, 14/23. Although the *mḥ*-sign is less fully written here, it is similarly formed, and the clear initial *m* restricts other possibilities. There is room in the preceding lacuna for 2–3 small signs.

k. : *n=w* (cf. 6/20) is highly plausible, *n=k* being quite differently formed in this text (cf. 6/24); *bnr* is also possible.

l. : *ḏd bn-pw=n rẖ* virtually certain, despite the slightly unusual form for the 1st pers. plur. suffix *=n* (cf. 6/17). Careful tracing shows that the tall sign followed *rẖ* directly and is most likely to be *w*. A verb in the infinitive is required following *rẖ*; *wꜣy* fits the traces, though unfortunately all the instances of this verb in this text are damaged (cf. 6/7, 13).

m. : *ỉw=s* seems fairly secure, while the final group, which perhaps begins with *m*, presents a variety of possibilities. The papyrus is warped here, and it is uncertain whether there was room for a short word between *knḥy* and *ỉw=s*.

n. : *ḳd* fits the traces better than, for example, *ꜥwỉ*, and probably filled the lacuna before *ỉw=s*.

o. : the very uncertain traces following *ỉw=s* hardly favour the restoration here of the phrase common in documents: *ỉw=s* ⌜*mḥ n nꜣỉ=s*⌝ [*sy.w*] *nꜣỉ=s sbꜣ.w* (*DG*, 407. 4).

p. : *nꜣỉ=s sbꜣ.w* secure.

q. : *ḥmt ꜣkm* secure. A trace high up before *nꜣỉ=s ḳry.w* on a joined fragment may perhaps (in the context) suggest *nbw*, 'gold'.

r. : *ḥḏ*, 'silver', possible but uncertain.

s. : [*pꜣỉ*]*=s ṯp* seems palaeographically acceptable. For a parallel see perhaps the word (Insinger 22/17, 24/15) interpreted by *DG*, 627. 2 as 'etwas am Mast (Rahe?)'; the writing here would suggest that the scribe, perhaps correctly, connected the word etymologically with *tp*, 'head'. Prothetic *ỉ* coupled with following *y* gives the following word a bizarre appearance, but is perhaps due to the scribe's desire to separate *ỉnm*, 'skin' (*Wb.* i. 96. 14 ff.; Crum, *CD*, 12a ⲁⲛⲟⲙ), from *nm*, 'who?' (Crum, *CD*, 225a ⲛⲓⲙ), though he appears to have borrowed the det. from the latter word.

t. : *ḏd ršꜣ r* probable, the det. leaving a doubt whether *ršꜣ* is ⲣⲁϣⲉ, 'rejoice' (Crum, *CD*, 308b). The following sign might in theory be read *nsw*, 'king', *rsỉ*, 'south', or *smꜣ*, 'unite', depending upon its complements. The next certain word begins *gr* . . , and in view of the following mentions of *nꜥm*(*.w*) *ỉw=w skrkr*, 'rolled sheets', and *wrs*, 'head-rest', the restoration *r pꜣỉ=s grg* seems sound. In this case, stands alone. If these words give, as we surmise, the text upon the *ṯp*, *nsw* seems preferable. *yb* is certain, and it is tempting to take it as the material of the bed, 'ivory' (*DG*, 49. 7), but the det. shows that Elephantine is intended (*DG*, 49. 8). The preceding traces may represent . . *ny* with wood det., read perhaps [*hb*]*ny*, a wood imported from the south.

u. : the det. is that of stone, cf. *ỉny* (6/2); a high trace suggests *mfky*, 'turquoise' (*DG*, 157. 9), often combined with *ḫsbd*, 'lapis lazuli', in decorative inlays.

v. : though only slightly damaged, this verb is of doubtful reading, since the upper sign is uncertain, and the lower may be *n*, *s*, or just possibly *k*; it must mean something like 'be covered, be adorned'. Perhaps *tn* (*DG*, 635. 2) is best.

w. For a comment upon the etymology of these words, see *JEA*, 61 (1975), 197–8.

x. : ⸢*r*⸣ *wrs n ḥr* virtually certain. The traces that follow are problematic; if is here the divine det. (and not *ḥ*(*ꜣ*)), then perhaps the most likely god to figure on a head-rest might be *Bs* (e.g. the fine head-rest BM 63783),[1] but this would only fit the traces if, exceptionally, *b* were written above *s*.

y. : *ỉ-ỉr-ḏꜣḏꜣ* probably represents the preposition quoted by *DG*, 673. 3, from which Coptic ⲉϫⲛ- derives (Černý, *CED*, 310–11). The preceding det. is that for 'hair', cf., for example, *fꜥỉ* (*DG*, 144. 4), *šn*(*y*) (*DG*, 513. 1).

z. : we take the whole group as a writing of *ḥꜣ=f*, 'behind', determined somewhat elaborately with head, hair, and flesh dets., cf. **1**, 9/28. The preceding det., though perhaps part of that for 'wood', is unclear.

aa. nkt ḫnṯ n ḥm: we take *ḫnṯ* as an example of the old *nisbe* adjective *ḫnty* in it meaning 'outstanding, pre-eminent', rare in demotic. *ḥm* may well have formed part of one of the compound expressions *ḥm-ḫt*, *ḥm-wsy*, etc.

ab. : *ꜥr r-ḥrỉ* probable, perhaps here of the god ascending into the shrine rather than of embarkation, though there is perhaps room for a reference to the divine barque. The preceding trace is puzzling; perhaps read *ỉw=k*.

ac. ḥr-ꜣt.ṯ[*=f*]: perhaps used here, as often, of vestments 'upon the back of' the image.

ad. : *m-bꜣḥ=f* implies that something was done before the god, and the following words show that it was an offering of incense. The traces before *m-bꜣḥ=f* may fit *ḫwy*, 'altar' (*DG*, 353. 1), cf. **2** back, x+1/14.

ae. ; uncertain, though final group could perhaps be *ỉỉ* 'come'.

af. : *nꜣỉ=s sn.w*, 'her brothers', or *nꜣỉ=s šn.w*, 'her pleas', seem possible readings. The spacing of the traces seems wrong for the phrase *tꜣ ntỉ šny*, 'she who is sick', present in 6/20, unless the first trace belongs to a previous word.

ag. : *ỉr=s* alone secure. The following word may begin with *h*. Speculatively, *hnw*, 'dances, jubilation' (*Wb.* ii. 493. 17 ff.), might be suggested as a typical temple celebration.

ah. : *n tꜣỉ=s mwt* certain. The following group is a crux. While the lower sign is not of a form very usual in the fem. attributive adjective *ꜥꜣ.t*, neither the cross-bar on the upper sign, nor the way it turns downward fits *nmḥ* or *nḏm* well. *ꜥꜣ.t* is adopted with some reserve. The final word is identical with that which appears in **2**, back, x/2, in the note to which we argue for reading *dw.w*, 'mountains', despite the rather different writing used for the singular (p. 112, n. *d*).

[1] We are indebted for this reference to Miss R. M. Hall of University College London.

aj. : *ꜥš=s n=f ḥs.w*; the reading *ḥs.w* is open to the objection that the verb *ḥs* is written in 6/11. This scribe does, however, allow himself some variation over the dets. of different parts of speech from the same root (cf. *mwt* 'die'), and *ḥs.w* seems best here.

ak. : strictly, nothing is assured here, but *bn(-pw)=f sdm n-ỉm=w* fits the traces well.

al. : ⸢*nbỉ*⸣ *ỉn*. In 6/8 the verb *nby* is written , but with this scribe this is hardly a fatal objection to reading the root here. *sbꜣ* (*DG*, 420. 3) is a plausible alternative, which removes the difficulty.

am. : the sublinear *=k* makes the reading *dỉt wꜣy=k* almost mandatory.

an. : the phrase recurs in 6/22 *i-ỉr nꜥš Ḥr r nṯr nb ḳn*. Doubtless a similar phrase should be restored here, though whether the subject was Horus depends upon the reconstruction of the story. The traces are possibly compatible with ⸢*Ḥr*⸣.

ao. : the traces here do not correspond exactly with the writings of *ỉr wpy* and *wpy* in 6/16; though *ỉr ḳnb.t* is perhaps possible, the reading remains uncertain.

ap. : the reading *šr šr.t* is subject to some reserve, since the final group resembles the papyrus-roll det. rather than the fem. *.t* as written by this scribe. However, the difference is no more than a slight flourish, and there seems to be no plausible alternative reading. Comparison with the forms in 6/9, 19 leaves little doubt that the same word *rk* stood here; there seems good reason for equating it with Coptic ⲗⲁϭⲉ, 'cease' (Crum, *CD*, 151b), rather than with ⲣⲓⲕⲉ, 'turn' (Crum, *CD*, 291b), cf. *DG*, 256.3, 264.6, though the other instances are less clear. In view of the length of the lacuna and a trace before *šr*, *bw-ỉr* is a plausible restoration. The contrast between *rḫ=t* here and *dỉt wꜣi=k* earlier in the line shows that the speaker changed in the central lacuna.

aq. : for *ḳnḥy* cf. 6/1. Though *pr* is damaged, writings with the superlinear stroke are especially common in Memphite and Lower Egyptian hands. Whether *wꜥb* or *wꜥb.t* should be read here is uncertain, but since a temple was within it, it must refer to a whole sacred precinct here rather than a single feature such as an embalming-place.

ar. : indecipherable traces.

as. A suggestion concerning the identity and etymology of *pꜣ ḥmꜣr* was made in *JEA* 61 (1975), 198–200. The word appears again in 6/23, 30, and also occurs in the demotic self-dedication texts in the British Museum six times, see Sir Herbert Thompson, in *JEA* 26 (1940), 68–78.

at. : the first groups are indecipherable, though the final group may be *ṯ*, e.g. a Stative ending or *mwt.ṯ* (p. 77, n. *ax*). The next traces are probably to be read *my ꜥꜣy*, 'cause to be great' (cf. 6/24 for *my* and ʿOnkhsheshonqy, 5/9, 8/2, 14/10, etc. for the writing of the dependent *sdm=f* of *ꜥꜣ*, 'be great'). Comparison of the next group with the less damaged writing of *ỉmnṯ*, 'west', in 6/21 suggests that after the def. article *tꜣ* the first sign is the same; the complements may perhaps be restored as follows to read *ʾImnt.t*, 'the west, the necropolis' (*DG*, 31. 4). After the following *i-ỉr* the form of is rather upright for *dỉt* (cf. 6/10); *tꜣ* is ruled out by the following *pꜣ*. *i-ỉr=s* would have to be either the emphatic form, in which case there is no clear adverbial phrase for it to emphasize (see n. *au* below), or the relative form, in which case *ỉmnt.t* (?) must be the antecedent; 'cause to be great the west which she has made' is poor sense. *i-ỉr-n=ỉ*, 'to me', seems a better reading: 'May the West be great to me!', perhaps meaning 'May the necropolis greet me!'; possibly *my ꜥꜣy* here is the ancestor of the Coptic expression of welcome ⲙⲁⲓⲟ=, 'be hale; hail!' (Crum, *CD*, 158b; Černý, *CED*, 78. 4, where the expression is given a somewhat unsatisfactory etymology from *ỉꜣwy*, 'old age', see *BSOAS* 41 (1978), 360), or means 'honour, adorn', cf. ⲧⲁⲉⲓⲟ (Crum, *CD*, 390b; Černý, *CED*, 177. 4).

au. : *pꜣ bỉk* 'the falcon', is certain (*DG*, 123. 7 under *bk*). In view of the presence of the def. article and the Imperative *my ꜥꜣy*, this may well be a Vocative, but it could equally be in apposition to the 1st pers. suffix pronoun of *i-ỉr-n=ỉ* (see n. *at* above for reading). Comparison of the following word with *tn*, 'where?' (6/30), suggests that it is not this word, as there is no trace of the det.; also neither *i-ỉr=s pꜣ bỉk tn*, 'Where did she make the falcon?', nor *i-ỉr-n=ỉ pꜣ bỉk tn* seems satisfactory, nor do they account for the final group before *rk=s*. If *ꜥn*, 'beautiful' (*DG*, 62. 4), is read in preference to *tn*, 'exalted' (*DG*, 635. 2; cf. also 637. 4), the final group, distinct from *ḥꜣt*, 'heart' (6/23), and *ỉrt* 'eye' (6/19), should be *ḥꜣt*, 'forepart'

(*DG*, 287.1; *Wb.* iii. 19.2 ff.); the phrase may then be an epithet of the falcon.

av. : *rk=s wbꜣ=s*: if we are right in concluding that the speaker of the preceding words is the doomed male, the fem. suffix in *wbꜣ=s* must refer to a fem. noun lost in the lacuna at the beginning of the sentence, perhaps *Ỉst* or the place where she was. seems usually to represent ⲗⲁϭⲉ rather than ⲣⲓⲕⲉ in **1** and **2** (see p. 76, n. *ap*).

aw. : *ḥꜣꜥ.ṯ* must certainly be interpreted here as the 3rd pers. fem. sing. of the Stative, in view of the 3rd pers. fem. sing. reflexive dative *n=s*. More difficult to decide is whether the first *ḏd* genuinely introduces direct speech, or simply marks the explanation of the woman's actions; to an Egyptian, doubtless, the difference was academic.

ax. : *pꜣ mwt.ṯ*. In this text there are examples of three nouns from the root *mwt*, 'to die', which are differentiated in the writing: i. (here, and just possibly earlier in this line, see p. 76, n. *at*); ii. *pꜣ mw(t)* (in 6/17, 7/9, compare perhaps the traces in 5/x+3); iii. *in-mwt* (in 6/24, just possibly to be restored at the end of 6/12). The apophthegm in 6/17 makes it quite clear that ii must represent the Coptic ⲙⲟⲩ, 'death' (Crum, *CD*, 159b). iii. *in-mwt* appears among the various malignant external influences which the demotic self-dedication texts and the earlier amuletic decrees were intended to protect children against (*JEA* 26 (1940), 76; I. E. S. Edwards, *Oracular Amuletic Decrees of the Late New Kingdom*, *passim*). Its meaning there is doubtless 'dead man' in the sense of 'ghost', which fits the context in 6/24 well. Though in 2. Kh. 5/36 and 6/28 it is used to mean 'death', and in Insinger 23/14 may be verbal, it may be that these writings by late scribes were based on misunderstanding of the writing. Griffith's treatment of the prefix *in* as phonetic in his note on Mag. 9/22 hardly convinces, and it is at least possible that the original significance of the term was 'death-bringer'. i. *pꜣ mwt.ṯ* was evidently distinguished from these by the fact that the final *t* of the root was pronounced in speech. Coptic yields two distinct nouns formed with the prefix ⲣⲉϥ showing this feature: ⲣⲉϥⲙⲟⲟⲩⲧ, 'dead person or thing' (Crum, *CD*, 160a), and ⲣⲉϥⲙⲟⲩⲟⲩⲧ, 'killer' (Crum, *CD*, 201a). While it is possible to argue for the latter translation for *pꜣ mwt.ṯ* in this text, examples of the transitive verb ⲙⲟⲩⲟⲩⲧ, 'kill', do not seem to be identifiable in demotic. We prefer to take the term to mean 'the dying man, the man fit to/about to die'. Note that the verb *mwt* in this text is written with the same det. as i, cf. 6/15, 23 and 7/4.

ay. : the traces are consistent with reading *mwt=f*, as the context suggests.

az. : *tꜣ byry* probable.

ba. : *stꜣ.[ṯ]=s* very probable. The following preposition is certainly *n*, not *r*, while the following noun is clearly plural. Comparison with the writing of *st*, 'place', in 6/24, and with the forms used in *sỉ* in 6/13 and in *Ỉst* perhaps suggests that *swt* is to be preferred to *ꜥwỉ.w* or *ḳd.w* for the broken word, but this remains uncertain.

bb.] : *ỉw=s ỉỉ.ṯ r tꜣỉ=s rỉt ỉw=s rmy* very probable. After room for the det. of *rmy*, the group is perhaps to be restored *m-šs*.

bc. : in this text the det. for fire is written either (*nb.t* 6/31) or (*ḥwt-[tkꜣ?]* 6/31); that for 'wood' either (*kry.w* 6/2; *šst.w* 6/2; *wrs* 6/4) or (*sbꜣ.w* 6/2; *ḫwy*? 6/5; *ḏꜣ*? 7/7). The scribe thus seems to have used the forms interchangeably, but no intermediate form is attested. *kḥt*, 'flame', is therefore not an acceptable reading of this group. The meaning 'chapel, shrine' seems to emerge from the context; a reading *kꜣ* provides a possible etymology from *kꜣr* (*Wb.* v. 107. 12 ff.), a word regularly used of portable or stationary shrines for images. While, however, the original gender of *kꜣr* might be expected to be masc., in demotic it is regularly represented by the fem. *gꜣ.t* (*DG*, 570. 4), with the same range of usage. A probable Coptic derivative ⲕⲱ (Crum, *CD*, 98b) is unfortunately attested only in the plural. The late hieroglyphic form (*Wb.* v. 150. 1 ff.) and the demotic *gꜣ.t* are subject to the suspicion that the fem. ending in the writing was used originally to mark a final weak vowel caused by the desinence of post-vocalic *r*, and that the use of the fem. article followed through misunderstanding, because the noun sounded like a fem. formation. It is possible that the scribe of this text was better informed. No better suggestion for the identity of the word presents itself.

bd. : *r dỉt* ⌜*ms*⌝. The first sign of *ms* is slightly damaged, and the base of the determinative is overwritten by the insertion in the line below, but the reading seems secure: the form bends over less than that in *ntỉ ỉw=s dỉt šm=s*, but *dỉt* seems a preferable reading to *tꜣ*. But the absence of a suffix, e.g. *ms=s*, does cause some grammatical difficulty.

be. : *ꜥḥꜥ sḏm* virtually certain; there is room for *n(=i)*, and just possibly an extant trace of it.

bf. : *tꜣ nb.t tꜣ.wy* seems assured, the first det. belonging to *tꜣ.wy*, the second to the whole expression. A trace before *tꜣ* demands the presence of *ỉ* or a similar interjection.

bg. : this passage is a crux, in that the traces preserved give no means of deciding whether *ỉnk s-ḥm.t* or *ỉnk tꜣ šrt* was written. The latter reading, however, involves the complication that *tꜣỉ* . . . must then presumably represent a description of the mother of *tꜣ šrt*, e.g. *s-ḥm.t*, which the spacing of the traces renders somewhat dubious: 'I am the daughter of the woman who . . .'. If *ỉnk s-ḥm.t* is read, there is the grammatical objection that the *ntỉ* to be assumed before *spr* would have an undefined noun as its antecedent.

bh. : the initial sign is a rarity in demotic. It resembles some forms of in the word *sꜣwty*, 'guard', but a markedly different group is used on the back of **2**, e.g. x+1/22. A closer parallel is the hieratic form of (Möller, *Hier. Pal.* iii. 2), used in demotic writings of the verb *spr*, 'petition' (*DG*, 427. 2), which we read here. The parallel relative clauses which follow suggest that the preceding trace should be read *ntỉ*.

bj. : the word also occurs in an insertion near the end of the line without a def. article , where the final *ṯ* is clear. The final dot of appears to leave no alternative to reading *n pꜣỉ*, so that the following word must be masc. The reading is a crux. The striking resemblance of the word, with the exception of the det. and final *ṯ*, to normal writings of *ntr.t*, 'goddess' (*DG*, 233. 1), convinces us that the root *ntr* enters into the reading of the word. The det. is that used with words for 'child' (e.g. *šr*, 6/7, *ẖr* 6/31, *ẖr.t* 6/24, 26), and occasionally with words for 'image' (e.g. *twt*, 6/13). The sign *ṯ* is regularly used to express elements suffixed to a root (e.g. *ỉỉ.ṯ*, Stative, *ỉrt.ṯ=f*, pronominal), or to show that the final *t* of a root is to be pronounced (e.g. *mwt.ṯ*, see p. 77, n. *ax*). A reading *ẖrd-ntr(ỉ)*, with *ṯ* representing the final *d/t* of *ẖrd* is possible; against it tell the facts that the regular demotic writing is (*DG*, 392. 8), and that an explicit writing *ẖrd pꜣ ntr* appears in **1**, 13/25 (perhaps as a proper name). A compound word meaning 'divine image' would fit both contexts even better, but a suitable reading is not apparent to us. Conceivably, the word is simply a masc. deverbal noun from the stem *ntrỉ*, indicating sacral objects in general, the final *ṯ* showing that the last radical *r* was not pronounced. But precise parallels are not easy to find from *Wb.* ii. 363–4.

bk. : *ntỉ ḥs r pꜣ* certain; the final trace resembles *ẖ* more than *ntỉ*.

bl. : the writing of the first word exactly corresponds to that of *nwy*, 'lance', except for the preference for over , as det. (*DG*, 210. 2). The upright stroke which follows is unlike the majority of this scribe's forms for *ṯ* (cf., however, 6/1 *mḥ.ṯ=y*) and may rather be the plural stroke. In this case, the final sign should not be interpreted as the flesh det. (from some examples of which it differs slightly, cf. *r-ḥr* in 6/10), but read as *ḥb* (cf. 6/27, 6/28) or possibly *sp-sn* (contrast, however, *n pꜣ sp mḥ-2*, 6/28). The word must mean something that was ascended or raised (if *DG*, 67. 5 is right in attributing transitive meanings to this verb) in the course of temple ritual. If the word *nwy* could be used of military standards (cf. Petub. quoted by *DG*, 210. 2, *pꜣ wš n pꜣ nw*), conceivably it could be used also of 'festival standards' in temples, where the bone/ivory det. might be appropriate.

bm. : palaeographically the writings for *ḥwy* and *dỉt wꜣy* are virtually indistinguishable, except that the rather upright form of here favours *ḥ* rather than *dỉt* (see p. 76, nn. *am*, *at*, p. 77, n. *bd*). Semantically also *ḥwy* seems preferable. In the final phrase *ỉw ꜥ(.wỉ)=s* . . . . ., 'her hands . . . . .', seems a possible reading; the phrase *ỉw ꜥ drt.ṯ=s*, 'to her utmost' (cf. **1**, 10/35: *DG*, 52. 2), is not compatible with the traces. An alternative reading is *ỉw bn(-pw)=s ḏd* . . . . ., 'without her having said . . . . .'; this assumes an unusually small and cramped form of *ḏd*.

bn. : reading secure. *ꜥs* also occurs in 6/23, followed by an imperative, while *tw-s* in 6/23 is followed by a noun. The use of these two forms by the same scribe is of interest as both have been claimed as ancestors of Coptic 'behold' (Crum, *CD*, 85a).

bo. : reading secure; perhaps read [*n*] *pꜣỉ=w wbn* which seems required by the orthography in preference to *n pꜣ*.

bp. : for this writing of *ḥdb*, cf. 6/13, and contrast the abbreviated form of the first sign in 6/21.

bq. : a crux. The sign following *rẖ* has either been written with an overfull brush, or has been altered, rather clumsily. In the first case it must be taken as , of which all the elements are present, and read *šr*, (*wꜥ.t* being grammatically untenable). In the second case, it is not clear whether it has been altered to or from *šr*, or whether the sign to or from which it was altered was intended as a plain upright stroke (plural suffixed pronoun) or , the fem. sing. or plur. def. article. Our own conclusion is that the scribe most probably intended *šr* to be read, though the lack of the def. article before the participial form *i-ir-ḏd* is puzzling. See p. 95, n. λ.

br. *rmt ḫm* is a regular phrase in demotic, contrasted with *rmt ꜥꜣ* (*DG*, 360, under *ḫm*, 359. 3), while *rmt wr*, a technically possible reading, seems not to be attested in demotic.

bs. For *ṯꜣi n=f ḳbꜥ* Coptic ϫⲓⲕⲃⲁ ⲛ̄, 'take vengeance upon' (Crum, *CD*, 99b), probably indicates the correct meaning. Should it, however, mean 'take vengeance for him', the roles of the persons have to be changed accordingly. *r ṯꜣi=f ḳbꜥ* seems grammatically unsound.

bt. : clear examples of *ꞽst* in this text are written (6/9, 10, 15, 16, 17 (end), 22 (end), 27, 28, 30). A certain example of *Wsir* written occurs in 6/30 *šn=y Wsir r-dbꜣ ꞽst*, and a probable broken example in 6/22, where, however, [*ꞽmn-*]*Rꜥ* might perhaps be read. The intermediate form written here occurs also in 6/16–17 *ꜥḥꜥ tꜣ nti n sšm n* *ḥyṯ n* *n-im=t in=t n(=i)* *n nꜣi=s iwf.w*. In that context, there might at first sight appear to be good reason for reading two different deity names, but analysis of the story leads us to think that *ꞽst* should be read in all three instances. In the present context, where Isis is being addressed, there is valid justification for reading *ꞽst* and treating it as a vocative. However, a direct genitive may also be read: 'I will take the vengeance of . . . upon him'; in which case, while Isis might still seem the most probable reading, it is less certain. This latter reading has consequences for the story, see p. 104, d. A textual reason for our preference for the vocative rendering, which may or may not be well founded, is that the scribe has clearly dipped his pen anew before writing *ꞽst*, suggesting that he considered it to belong with what followed.

bu. : the traces might represent *in*, cf. 6/14, 17, so conceivably the compound *in-mwt* (6/24) might be restored in the lacuna. Alternatively, *ṯꜣi* may perhaps be read, there being just room to restore *ṯꜣi ḳbꜥ*, written as earlier in the line.

bv. : this short passage raises several problems: i. There is room for one large or two small groups at the beginning of the line; to read simply *n pꜣ* is thus inadequate, while the form of the traces render *irm* or *iw=t* palaeographically untenable. A second *r-dbꜣ* is conceivable (cf. 6/12), but there are other possibilities. ii. The following group seems clearly to represent the root *si*, 'be sated' (*DG*, 407. 5), but whether the final stroke preserved should be read as part of *i* or as *ṯ* is unclear. The latter would be very awkward grammatically after the def. article. iii. If *si* is read and a det. (?) has been lost in the lacuna, then there is probably room for no more than *n* before *twt*. iv. The reading *twt*, 'statue', is itself in some doubt, since when compared with that in 7/5 it exhibits an extra curved upright stroke before the det. (e.g. .*ṯ*?). The det., however, seems to guarantee the reading of the root, and attempts to parse *twt* as a part of a verb 'be like: collect' (*DG*, 616. 2) seem not to yield tolerable sense. v. If *ḳns=f* is correctly read (n. *bw* below), the sentence should end at *twt*. Tentatively, we suggest [*r-dbꜣ*(?)] *pꜣ si* [*n*] *twt*, 'for the satisfaction of an image'.

bw. : prolonged examination of the papyrus has tended to convince us that the short diagonal stroke above the det. of *nhr* in 6/14 is indeed the tail of an *=f* following *ḳs*. If so, it should be the *sdm=f* form of a verb. The lack of the clothing det. makes it improbable, though perhaps not impossible, that *ḳs* here represents *ḳ(r)s*, 'bury, place in a coffin' (*DG*, 548. 4); granted that the broken det. is , the writing may well represent the root *ḳ(n)s*, 'force, violence' (*DG*, 541. 5) as a noun, 'pierce, slay' as a verb (*DG*, 541. 4; Coptic ⲕⲱⲛⲥ, Crum, *CD*, 112a). The question whether the sentence beginning *ḳ(n)s=f* represents a continuation of the woman's speech or a resumption of the narrative is discussed below, p. 96, n. μ.

bx. : the first sign is problematic, the rest may be read with some assurance *tꜣ šfꜣ n nꜣi=f iwiw.w*, but the interpretation of these two lines is very difficult. The sign perhaps most resembles *nw*, used in ordinal numbers, which is clearly not appropriate here; otherwise, though rather low, it may well be the masc. possessive article *pꜣ.n* (Coptic ⲡⲁ-). *šfꜣ* may represent either *šfyt*, 'might, awe, splendour' (*Wb*. iv. 457. 2 ff.) or *šfꜣ*, 'tale, story' (Coptic ϣϥⲱ Crum, *CD*, 610b), and the det. , though slightly favouring the latter (see *DG*, 504. 6–7), is hardly decisive. Thus the expression might mean 'he who belongs to splendour' or 'he who belongs to fable'. Whether these expressions should be taken as the proper name or epithet of one of 'his dogs' (e.g. 'the most renowned of his dogs'), or whether it should be taken as the name of a human person depends upon whether the following *n* is construed as the genitive adjective or as the preposition *n* (old *m*) of instrument, see p. 96, n. μ. Comparison with 6/19 rules out *ḥr* as a possible reading of the initial group.

by. : there are sound reasons for reading the final group *ym*, 'sea', or *ym.w*, 'waters', for the traces of the dets. fit those for water exactly, and the word perhaps connects with *ḥny*, 'canal', beyond the next *lacuna*. The preceding group is, however, puzzling; the initial traces might perhaps be explained as *ḥr* (6/19), but then neither *pꜣ* or *nꜣ* easily fit the final trace unless written very large; nor does *pꜣỉ=w* (cf. p. 78, n. *bo*) fit well.

bz. : *n tꜣỉ=w ḥny* appears certain. The previous group can hardly be *ỉnk*, as this is differently written in 6/11; it displays all the traits of the Stative of *wꜣy*, written simply .

ca. While the reading and sense of this phrase is clear, it is difficult in the broken and uncertain context to know whether *n sgn* should be understood as genitive after *ḥny* or be taken as adverbial. The det. of *ḥny* seems decisive for the rendering 'canal, channel' (*DG*, 311. 9).

cb. *pꜣ wdb ḥʿ . . . .*: *wdb* as a verb is used both of the rise or return of the Inundation and of the rise or return of the star Sothis (*Wb.* i. 408. 5, 8). With the stative *ḥʿ* following, *pꜣ wdb* seems most likely here to be a name for the Inundation or an appellation of Sothis. Perhaps restore *r-ḥrỉ* or the like at the end of the line.

cc. : *pꜣ nhr n sn-th.ṯ* (?) fits well what is written on the papyrus (cf. *DG*, 222. 2 *nhr*; *DG*, 650 under 649. 9 *sn-th.ṯ* (?)), though the true reading and etymology of the latter fairly common expression for 'misfortune, danger, doom' remains obscure.

At the beginning of the line one group may perhaps be missing. Comparison with **2** back, x+1/11 suggests *snḥ*, 'bind' (*DG*, 439. 1), as a better restoration than *snt*, 'fear' (*DG*, 440. 1), for the initial verb. The intervening group is difficult; in view of the presence of *ḥrỉ* a title seems probable. If *sʿ* is read, this might be interpreted as a writing of *sꜣ* and compared either with the word for 'amulet' (*DG*, 403. 1) or with that for 'phyle' (*DG*, 404. 1), while we admit that the majority of writings given there are ideogrammatic and do not resemble this one. Nor can we quote other instances of either *ḥrỉ sꜣ*, 'Master of the Amulet (?)', or of *ḥrỉ sꜣ*, 'Master of the Phyle (?)'. On the other hand, the word does not closely resemble the mysterious group read doubtfully *Ḥʿ-Rʿ* in **1**, 7/x+5, though *s* is perhaps a misreading in both instances (see p. 10, n. *h*).

cd. : the photographs show fairly clearly the fact that the scribe here erased an earlier version, and has written *ḥk=f ỉn=f* over it. He has then left a gap in his final text, whether simply to avoid the rest of the erased area, or because he felt an interval to be required is unclear. While it is tempting to connect *ḥk=f* in this context with *ḥkꜣ*, 'magic' (*Wb.* iii. 175, 176. 1 ff.; *DG*, 333. 5; Coptic ϩⲓⲕ, Crum, *CD*, 661a), the word should rather represent *ḥꜣk*, 'capture' (*Wb.* iii. 32. 14 ff.; *DG*, 333. 4) or *ḥk(r)*, 'hunger' (*Wb.* iii, 174. 23 ff.; *DG* 334. 2; Coptic ϩⲕⲟ, Crum, *CD*, 663b), the former perhaps being preferable in the context, though a quite different writing of the word appears in **2** back, x+1/38. Whether the diagonal stroke low down before *ḥk=f*, which almost certainly belonged to the earlier version, was intended by the scribe to be read in the final version as *r* is problematical (see p. 96, n. μ).

ce. : *tꜣ pt pꜣ tꜣ tꜣ dwꜣt* is certain. In view of the possible parallels with 6/25, 7/1, *nw=f r* might be expected to precede, but the traces rule this out. As somebody is speaking at the beginning of 6/15 (see p. 97, n. ν) and the preserved det. may be , some verb of saying would suit best, but neither *ʿš=f* nor *sḏy=f* fit the traces convincingly; *sm=f*, 'he greeted, he supplicated' (*DG*, 430. 3), fits little better.

cf. : the beginnings of ll. 20–5 are preserved, and show that at most one group can have been present in the *lacuna* at the beginning of the line, and *my wḏꜣ=f* cannot therefore be restored. *pꜣ*, or better *pꜣỉ*, seems the best restoration before *ṯꜣw ntỉ mtw=y*. *ṯꜣw* is very probable.

cg. : *tw=y ḥꜣ.t=s* appears much the best reading. As *ḥꜣt(.ṯ)*, 'heart' (*DG*, 289. 2) is always written with the flesh det. in this hand (cf. 6/23,) this writing should presumably represent the pronominal form of the preposition (*n*-)*ḥꜣ*(*t*), 'before, in front of' (*DG*, 287. 1), of which the absolute form appears in 6/27, 28. (While in the context it may be tempting to connect with *ḥʿ.t*, 'end' (*DG*, 378. 1; Coptic ϩⲁⲉ, Crum, *CD*, 635a), there seems to be no parallel for so abbreviated a writing of this word.) The fem. suffix *=s* cannot well refer back to the masc. *ṯꜣw*, and there is no other specific antecedent available for it; probably, then, it refers forward to the following *tꜣỉ(=y) mwt ꜣIst*, though one might then perhaps expect simply *(n-)ḥꜣ(t) tꜣỉ(=y) mwt*.

ch. : *ꜣIst*, though faint, is certain. Given the reading advocated in n. *cg* above, *ꜣIst* should be in apposition to *tꜣỉ(=y) mwt* and the whole phrase to the suffix pronoun of *ḥꜣ.ṱ=s* (see p. 97, n. *ξ*). If *ḥꜣ.ṱ=s* is rejected, *tꜣỉ(=y) mwt ꜣIst* could be interpreted as a vocative; this, however, makes it difficult to know to whom to refer the suffix pronoun of *ʿm=s* later in the line (see n. *cl* below).

cj. : we take the first group as an unusual ligature of + , which occur both in the Ptolemaic and Roman periods in *ʿm*, 'swallow, know', perhaps more especially in Lower Egyptian hands.

ck. : the det. after the lacuna is clearly the form of the dying-man sign used with *mwt* earlier in the line. The occurrence of the phrase *pꜣ ntỉ ỉỉ r mwt* in 6/23, with the presence of a trace which might be part of *ỉỉ* suggests a speculative restoration *r bw-ỉr-tw=[y ỉỉ r mwt]*.

cl. : *nꜣỉ=t sṱny(.w)* (with no plural det.) certain. Here begins a series of disturbing alternations between the 2nd and the 3rd pers. sing. suffix pronoun. Comparison of the form of the suffix here with *nꜣỉ=t sḏy.w* in 6/15, *n-ỉm=t* and *ỉn=t* in 6/17, and contrast with *ḥꜣṱ=s* and *ʿm=s* in 6/15, *n=s*, *bn-pw=s*, *ỉr=s*, and *dỉ=s* in 6/16, and *nꜣỉ=s ỉwf.w*, *ḫꜣʿ=s* and ⸢*šm*⸣*=s* (?) in 6/17, will leave no doubt of the correctness of the readings. Three explanations seem possible: i. that the speaker is talking of Isis in the third person to another female, whom he is addressing directly in the second person: ii. that the speech is in the nature of a soliloquy, and the speaker passes from discussing Isis's conduct in the third person to addressing the goddess directly (a view which does not explain the utterance in 6/16–17 well): iii. the utterances in the second person may be quotations. The decision between these rests upon the interpretation of the story; we think the simplest explanation (i) is also the best. We do not think it realistic to dismiss the alternations as error on the part of the scribe, because this particular writer has been singularly careful in amending his omissions and errors.

cm. : *mn*, 'there is not' seems certain. *rẖ* is presumably the Infinitive used as a noun.

cn. : *nꜣỉ=t sḏy.w sr.w*. Whether *sr.w* has adjectival or nominal function here is perhaps uncertain. Note that the plural dets. are written here, though omitted with *sṱny*.

co. : after *n tꜣ*/*nꜣ* there appears to be a single fleck of ink high up. Possibly restore *n tꜣỉ* [*ḥṱy*].

cp. : careful examination has convinced us that the reading *pꜣ 5 nṯr.w* (*DG*, 234. 1–235; source not named) alone satisfies all the requirements of the traces. Who the Five Gods were the text does not tell us; for the probability that they are the Five Gods of the Osirid cycle, see H. De Meulenaere's remarks on Osiris and Thoth in *JEA* 68 (1982), 142 ff. *tꜣỉ* at the beginning of the line is certain; what is less so is whether it should be constructed with the previous sentence (e.g. 'your prophetic statements have not come to pass in (the manner) which the Five Gods told her'), or taken as an anticipatory subject of *bn-pw=s ỉr wpy*, as we have tentatively done in translation. The lacuna at the end of l. 15 inhibits a clear decision.

cq. : *wpy* was written in almost the same manner in each instance, though in the second the final det. is less upright and is followed by the pronominal object *ṱ=s*. Presumably the second is the verb *wpy*, 'open, decide, judge' (*DG*, 86. 2), while the first may either be the noun *wpy(.t)*, 'judgement', or *wpy(.t)*, 'message, business, work' (*DG*, 86. 1); *ỉr wpy(.t)* is attested with the meaning 'to work'. Whether the 3rd pers. sing. fem. subject suffix of *bn(-pw)=s ỉr-wpy* and the similar object suffix of *bn(-pw)=w wpy.ṱ=s* should be referred back to *tꜣỉ-ḏd=w n=s*, or taken as personal, referring presumably to Isis, remains uncertain; we prefer the former.

cr. : though strictly nothing is certain after *ỉry n sḏy*, the traces, though slight, conform well enough with the writing of *pꜣ 5 nṯr.w* earlier in the line for it to be tempting to restore it here with a preceding *n*. (The following lacuna might perhaps have been filled by a short space between sentences and a long initial *dỉ*.) The force of these sentences would then be that the female subject (probably Isis) had not obtained any decision or revelation from the five gods, but had talked with them and thereby caused them to find out what had happened to the Lord of the Image. The use of past narrative forms in this line leaves open the possibility that there was a resumption of the narrative here, but as the speech to a woman resumed with *ʿḥʿ* (see p. 82, n. *ct*) without introduction, it seems best to treat ll. 15–17 as part of a single speech.

cs. : *pꜣ nb sšm*; the ink is faint but the reading is certain (cf. 6/16 end, 17 end, 31 beginning). Who is meant by the phrase is a difficulty encountered in attempting to reconstruct the story, see pp. 102 f.

ct. : while on grammatical grounds the independent pronoun *mtw=s* would be required as subject of a non-verbal sentence with nominal predicate, *st* would be an acceptable reading for the first group on palaeographical grounds alone, provided that it is accepted that a scribe might use differentiated writings for the 3rd pers. sing. subj. pronoun and for the 3rd pers. plur. obj. pronoun (cf. *ḥꜣꜥ st*, 6/29) (see Spiegelberg, *Dem. Gram.* § 135, p. 67: § 258, p. 119). But the fact that there is a direct address to a female at the beginning of l. 17 strongly favours the rendering of *tꜣ ntỉ n sšm n Ỉst* as a vocative—in which case what precedes must almost certainly be an imperative, cf. the similar use of the imperative *ꜥḥꜥ* in 6/10. One palaeographical detail should induce caution, however: in 6/10 *ꜥḥꜥ* shows a final dot, whereas in 6/16 this is missing. If the passage is narrative, not speech, *ꜥḥꜥ* may of course be a *sdm=f* past narrative form, but then there is nothing to introduce the speech at the beginning of l. 17. *Ỉst* is written larger than usual, with superscript *n*, but despite the unusual clumsiness of the form, it is made in the same way as the standard examples; the expression *ḥꜣꜥ=s pꜣ sšm n Ỉst* (6/17) affords strong inferential evidence that Isis was mentioned in this phrase.

cu. : *ḫyṯ* (*DG*, 350. 2) is certain. The word can have both good and bad meanings, its fundamental significance being apparently the spell a deity may wield over a human being: 'doom' seems appropriate here. In view of the large initial *ḫ*, it is unlikely that *pꜣ* was written before *ḫyṯ*.

cv. : for the problem of the reading, see n. *bt.*, p. 79. As the bringing of Isis to the man about to die proclaims his fate (6/15), it should surely be the spell of Isis, not that of any other deity, under which the woman is said to have fallen here.

cw. : comparison suggests that the first groups are likely to be the preposition *ḥꜣ*, 'behind', written as in 6/4, but here in a temporal sense. The phrase seems parallel to *m-sꜣ wꜥt wnwt n sdy* in 6/25, and it seems plausible that one should restore here *ḥꜣ wꜥt wnwt* [*n sdy ỉw=y r ỉỉ r mwt*]. Cf. 6/23.

cx. : the only doubt in the reading of this adage is whether to read *ỉw=f ḫpr* or *ỉ-ỉr-ḫpr*, but the former seems preferable on palaeographic, syntactic, and semantic grounds alike. Probably it is better to regard it as the climax of the speech of the doomed individual which started in l. 15, rather than as a reply to it. On the spelling of *pꜣ mwt* see n. *ax*, p. 77 above.

cy. : the suffix pronoun in *ḥꜣꜥ=s* has been inserted above the line as a correction. In *pꜣ sšm (n) Ỉst* the *n*, written superscript in this phrase in 6/16, is apparently omitted, though a slight thickening observable at the right-hand end of the horizontal of may mean that the scribe originally wrote it. The precise meaning of *sšm* is crucial to the interpretation of the passage. *Wb.* iv. 291. 6–16 clearly supports the interpretation 'cult-image' in the sense of the statue of the god in naos or divine barque, and *DG*, 463. 10 gives this sense for the demotic word. If *sšm* could also mean 'form, appearance' like *ḳy* and *ḫprw*, then the passage might mean 'she abandoned the form of Isis', in which case *tꜣ ntỉ n sšm n Ỉst* in 6/16 should be translated 'you who are in the guise of Isis'; there seems, however, to be no clear attestation of this meaning for *sšm*.

cz. : *šm* seems very probable; but careful comparison with the two writings of ⌜*šm*⌝*=s r* in 6/10 throws doubt on whether that phrase may be restored here; for i. the downward diagonal with up-curve does not correspond with this scribe's forms of *=s*; and ii. the final stroke seems far too straight for *r*. Nor can the group be reconciled with the Stative *šm.ṯ*, even if followed by a dative of advantage *n=f*. Perhaps *ḥꜣꜥ=s pꜣ sšm (n) Ỉst (n-)bnr n pꜣỉ kꜣ*, 'she left the image of Isis outside this chapel', is just tenable as a reading, though the final diagonal stroke looks long for *pꜣỉ*; it most resembles some short, straight forms of *=f*, which seems virtually impossible to fit into the sense of the text here.

da. : comparison with the writing in 6/10 leaves little doubt that the word *kꜣ* stood here, despite the fact that a divine det. has been added (see p. 77, n. *bc*).

db. : *ꜣsḳ=w* is secure, *ỉw=w* highly probable; *n* introduces the indirect object required by the Circumstantial. Who the plural subject of *ꜣsḳ=w* and the past narrative forms in the following sentences (down to *sdr=w n=w* in 6/20) is intended to be is unclear. The last plural substantival expression in the text was *pꜣ 5 ntr.w*; possibly these entities are referred to, more especially if *swt* is preferred to *ꜥwỉ.w* in 6/18. But the role of the plural entity, while sufficiently active to negative any suggestion that the plural periphrasis for the passive is being used, is still that of onlookers or bystanders. Perhaps their identity is deliberately left vague.

dc.  : the shape of the trace after *nw*, the length of the lacuna, and the possibility that a slight space may have been left before *ḫpr* (cf. 6/28) suggest *r-ḥrỉ* as being superior to other possible restorations, though *r-bnr*, *r-r=s* can certainly not be ruled out.

dd.  : only *ḫpr wʿ* is certain. The traces are inadequate to decide between *nꜣỉ=w ʿwỉ.w* and *nꜣỉ=w swt*; the preceding *ẖn* seems probable. The point may be that while they were busy inside they had not looked out, but now something caused them to do so; perhaps this was the shadow, darkness, or noise caused by the imminence of the great scarabaeus.

de. 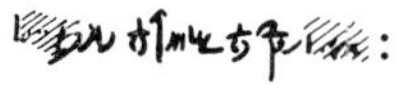: though only the first and last strokes of *ỉw*, 'come' are preserved, the reading is hardly doubtful. Note that *ʿ(ꜣ)py* is here written with its initial group borrowed from *ʿꜣ*, 'great', a writing not attested by *DG*, 59. 6. Possibly the scribe was subconsciously influenced by the following *ʿꜣ*, or possibly the reason was phonetic.

df. 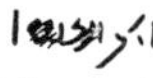 : *wꜣḥ=f ỉ-ỉr-ḥr=w*, reading certain. Note that this scribe writes the preposition *ḥr*  (e.g. 6/19), the noun *ḥr*  (e.g. 6/4, 6/20; so also in the compound preposition *r-ḥr n* in 6/10), the verb *wꜣḥ* (here only), and uses the same form  for *ḥr* in the compound preposition *ỉ-ỉr-ḥr* here, but not in 6/1. While therefore there is variety in this scribe's practice, his writings are so ordered as to distinguish immediately for the native demotic reader the word intended.

dg.  : the position of *nw.w* at the end of a clause here shows that it must be rendered as a plural noun and not a 3rd pers. plur. *sḏm=f* form. Thus *n pꜣ* is ruled out as a reading of the preceding group; it must in the context be read *nꜣỉ=w*, despite being rather differently formed from *tꜣỉ=w* in 6/13. The preceding word, though damaged, displays sufficient of the root consonants for *ḳp*, 'hide, cover, conceal' to be highly plausible. Whether, however, the text read (*ỉw*) *ḳp nꜣỉ=w nw.w*, 'their sight was veiled', or (*ỉw=f*) *ḳp* (*n*) *nꜣỉ=w nw.w*, 'he being hidden from their sight', must remain uncertain.

dh.  : *nhs=f nw irt.ṯ=w*; the text is faded in places, but the reading is secure.

dj.  : despite the damage, *Ỉỉ-m-ḥtp* appears absolutely certain. The final trace is typical for *stꜣ* (cf. 6/5), but whether the intermediate trace is simply the dot which in some hands (though not apparently in this one) accompanies the divine det., or whether it should be read *r* is uncertain.

dk. 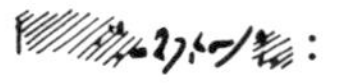 : whatever the traces before *rk=f-s* formed part of, it cannot have been *r dỉt*, which is made with a more pronounced down stroke to the left. The sign is perhaps more like the det. of *md*, 'speak', in 6/10 than it is like the articles *tꜣ*/*nꜣ* or the suffix- or object-pronoun *=s*; certainly there is room for more than just *stꜣ.ṯ=f-s*, but restoration is not easy. *rk=f-s* should be reflexive; the verb is perhaps here 'to turn' (*DG*, 256. 3 under *rk*; Coptic ⲣⲓⲕⲉ, Crum, *CD*, 291b), rather than 'to cease' (*DG*, 264. 6 under *lg*; Coptic ⲗⲁϭⲉ, *Crum*, *CD*, 151b). Of the final phrase too little is preserved for any reading to be more than guesswork. The form and position of the initial traces is, however, strikingly reminiscent of the verb *ḳp* at the beginning of the line, of the verb *ḳ(n)s* in 6/13 and of the verb in 6/20 discussed in note *dm* below. The latter two, however, show the dets.  and , of which one might expect to see a trace here at the top. It is therefore tempting speculatively to restore *ḳp nꜣỉ=w nw.w* as at the beginning of the line; though in the photograph (Pl. 4) there does not seem enough room for this, comparison of the writing of *nw=w* which is certainly to be restored in 6/18 at the end of this fragment with that of *nw=w* earlier in 6/19 demonstrates that the detached fragment has been misplaced slightly too far to the left in the photograph.

dl. mtw=f ỉr pꜣỉ=f smt: our understanding of the passage is founded on the belief that this phrase means that he changed his form from that of a winged beetle to that of Imḥotep. The idiom has parallels in Mythus 13/14 and especially in 2. Kh. 6/28 (cf. ibid. 6/23, 27 and 7/4).

dm.  : the nature of this very broken passage can only be guessed at. The final verb is not *ḳn*, 'be valiant' cf. 6/7; nor is it very likely to be *ḳnm* = *gnm*, 'blind' (*DG*, 581. 5), since it lacks the eye det. and probably the *m*; nor is it written exactly like *ḳ(n)s* in 6/13, though it shares features with it. *ḳnṯ*, 'be angry' (*DG*, 565. 6 under *knṯ*), is perhaps a possible reading. Careful comparison with *ỉrt.ṯ=w*, 'their eyes' (6/19), and *ḥꜣt.ṯ=f*, 'his heart' (6/23), does not favour either reading for the previous word. The form of *ḥꜣt*, 'front, brow', in 6/9 (if correctly read) and in the compound preposition (*n-*)*ḥꜣ.ṯ=s* in 6/15 suggests that *ḥꜣ.ṯ=f*, 'his brow', is more probable. For the initial groups in this line *ỉwn*, 'colour' (*DG*, 24. 2), may fit both the traces and the context, but the next word is unreadable.

dn. : *sdr=w n=w r-ḫt.*⸢*ṯ=w*⸣. This writing of *sdr* derives from the early demotic form (*DG*, 480. 5), which itself derives from the hieroglyphic writing , attested from the Nineteenth Dynasty onwards (*Wb.* iv. 390. 9 ff.); the omission of the clothing det. is, however, surprising.

do. : *ḫr=s n(=ỉ)*. This old parenthetic form 'so said she' (Gardiner, *Egyptian Grammar*, § 436) appears rather infrequently in demotic and mainly in early texts (e.g. Ryl. iii. 9, 4/9) or in archaizing ones (Totb. ii. 35; Mag. 21/35, vo. 33/3). Its appearance here is of great importance, for it implies that what has gone before has been narrated by a female to somebody. How far back in the text its force should be carried is a difficult problem. It can hardly refer simply to *sdr=w n=w r-ḫt.ṯ=w* since this is a single sentence in a connected narrative; indeed, to be logical, its force must be carried back at least to *ꜣsḳ=w ỉw=w ỉr n nꜣy* in 6/18. If it started at that point, or perhaps even at *ḫꜣꜥ=s pꜣ sšm ꜣIst* in 6/17, it is at least possible to conceive that these events are thought of as told by the woman to the doomed man. In this case, through the whole paragraph from 6/15 down at least to this point, and possibly on to the beginning of its last sentence (6/25 *ỉ-ỉr=f nw*), the doomed man might be the first person and the true narrator. Otherwise (a more daring but in some ways easier assumption), it may be thought that the whole text as preserved to us is a first person narrative, with the possible exception of the rather mysterious final sentences of paragraph 2 (6/14 [. .]=*f tꜣ pt pꜣ tꜣ tꜣ dwꜣt*), paragraph 3 (6/25 *ỉ-ỉr=f nw r pꜣ ỉtn*), and 6/31–7/1 ([*ỉ-ỉr=f*] *nw r* . . . . .). These are discussed below, p. 106.

dp. : *ḏd n=f tꜣ ntỉ šny*. Reading secure. *šny*, in addition to being used of physical sickness, seems often to have the sense of being mentally anxious or distraught. This is hardly surprising in a culture which believed in possession; indeed, the original meaning of *šny* derives from the root *šn*, 'be encircled, enclosed', by magical forces. The real difficulty here is to decide whom the phrase *tꜣ ntỉ šny* describes. The most natural candidate is the woman who left the *sšm ꜣIst* in 6/17, because i. she is the only female known to be present at the landing of Imḥotep; ii. she is known to be distraught at the doomed man's imminent death (see p. 101 f.).

dq. : though relatively few traces remain, comparison with the writing in 6/19 shows that the reading *ꜣIi-m-ḥtp* is amply justifiable on palaeographical grounds alone. The interjection *ỉ* would adequately fill the remainder of the lacuna, bearing in mind the slight displacement of this loose fragment (see p. 83, n. *dk*).

dr. : the trace after *ỉn* would fit *pꜣ*, and a nominal subject is required for the verb *nḥm*. *ḥr* is virtually certain. The group following *nḥm* is clearly the pronominal *.ṯ* plus a suffix pronoun, the tail of which is sufficiently long and straight for it to be identified with probability as *=f*; but it might perhaps be the final stroke of *=y*. The meaning of the sentence is then: 'has the . . . with the face of a . . . seized him/me?', clearly with reference to some fiend who carried off the dead. The word after *ḥr n* may end with an animal det., and the preceding signs may be read *dp* or *tp* or *ḳp*, which usually has a more pronounced vertical top in this hand. The first sign is made nearly as this scribe makes the clothing det. (cf. 6/3 *nꜥm.w*), but with a pronounced and intentional backward and forward motion on the upper left element. Purely on appearance it ought to represent hieroglyphic or . If the fiend is in fact the Eater of the Dead (*ꜥm-mwt*) then the head should be that of a crocodile; *dpy* is a fairly common word for crocodile (*Wb.* v. 447. 13–16). Or possibly the word should be taken as a descriptive epithet rather than the normal name of the beast. Since is used in hieroglyphs alphabetically for *g*, conceivably the reading might be *g(ꜣ)-tp*, 'Ugly-head', suitable to a crocodile. Otherwise, *ḥr n šs tp(y)* might be read, comparing *šs tpy*, 'fine linen' (*Wb.* iv. 539. 12–13). Palaeographically this is perhaps an easier solution. What 'a . . . with a face of fine linen' might be is less obvious; could there be a possible reference to the funerary practice of modelling the faces of mummified animals in linen?

ds. : for the reading *mnḳ*, cf. 6/25.

dt. : *nꜣỉ mdwt n ḏd*, for the reading cf. 6/25, where, however, the *n* is not superscript, but clearly written. The construction is infinitival.

du. : for the reading *smt*, cf. 6/19. Much more difficult to decide is whether *pꜣỉ(=y)* should be read or *pꜣỉ*[*=f*] restored in the lacuna. In favour of *pꜣỉ(=y)* are the following observations: i. no trace of the tail of *=f* is visible; ii. there is minimal space available; iii. the writing resembles *pꜣỉ(=y)* later in this line and elsewhere on this page closely; iv. in *pꜣỉ=f smt* in 6/19, the *=f* is written bold and large; v. in l. 25 it is a female character who 'fulfils the words spoken' (*mnḳ=s nꜣi mdwt n ḏd*), presumably by dying, so that it would be appropriate for the distressed female to be speaking of herself here. Against these arguments may be set the fact that we know from 9/15 that a male character is doomed to die, whereas we do not as yet know that a female one is so, and that it seems that in 6/23–4 below the distressed female is speaking of the male who is to die (see p. 102 f., b). But she may have changed topics, and the arguments for *pꜣi*(*=y*) seem much superior.

dv. : the reading *ỉmnṯ* is not in doubt (cf. *DG*, 31. 3–4, and the contrast with the group in 6/30); for the writing in 6/9 with a different det., see note *at* above where the reading *ỉmnt.t* was suggested for that group. It seems clear that there is no dot written before *ỉmnṯ*; this leaves open the question whether *n* should be supplied: 'who has fulfilled these words spoken concerning a killing happening to one of my sort (in) the west', or whether *ỉmnṯ* should be taken as the anticipatory object of the following *dỉ=y-s*. The latter seems preferable, both because this scribe usually writes *n* out, and because otherwise there is no clear antecedent for *-s*.

dw. : *dỉ=y-s* is certain. In the following group there seems to be a trace high up of the flesh det., which would favour the common phrase *dỉ=y-s n-ḥꜣt.ṯ=y*, 'I have set it in my mind', over *dỉ=y-s n-ḥꜣ.ṯ=y*, 'I have placed it before me'. But certainty is not possible.

dx. : in view of the following *pꜣi=*(*y*) *nkt*, *pꜣi*(*=y*) *ḥd* is perhaps a plausible interpretation of the trace.

dy. : *dỉ=y-s* virtually certain, cf. writing earlier in the line. The following group is almost certainly not *m-sꜣ=y*, cf. the clear writing in 6/29; yet a preposition seems required. We suggest with considerable reservations *ḥr-dw=y* (*DG*, 612. 1; Coptic ϩιτοτω=, Crum, *CD*, 444b) 'beside me'. There is clearly a further trace of ink at the extreme edge of the torn papyrus opposite this line, but whether it belongs to this column or to the next (as does a trace opposite l. 19 above) is very uncertain.

dz. : *tw=k ỉỉ.ṯ n=n n Nfr-ḥr* all assured. *n* is presumably written for old *m* in its 'predicative' function here. The epithet *Nfr-ḥr* is attested for many different deities (*Wb.* ii. 255. 7–9).

ea. : *ỉw=k* ⌜*n-drt*⌝ seems unexceptionable palaeographically, and fits the context well enough. If it is right, then the passage broken by the lacuna seems likely to have held the epithet and name of a god, or conceivably the names of two gods. Unfortunately, there are several possibilities. *Nsw* [*nṯr.w Ỉmn-*]*Rꜥ* is perhaps relatively implausible, because the space seems short, because the normal order is Ἀμονρασωνθηρ and because the gods preserved in the tale all belong to the Osirid cycle or have Memphite rather than Theban associations. *Nsw* [*tꜣ.wy Ws*]*ỉr* is a possible combination, though *nsw tꜣ.wy* is commoner as an epithet of *Ptḥ* (*Wb.* ii. 327. 11–12). *Smꜣ*[*-tꜣ.wy Ws*]*ỉr* would fit traces and space equally well, but *smꜣ-tꜣ.wy* would presumably be, as commonly, an epithet of Horus, and it hardly seems likely that Imhotep would be said to be 'in the hand of Somtous (Horus) (and) Osiris' here, in view of the context in which Horus is mentioned later in the line (p. 103, c). We think that perhaps the most plausible restoration may be *nsw* [*nḥḥ Ws*]*ỉr*, for which there seems to be just adequate room. It has the advantage of allowing the comparison with the writing of *Wsỉr* in 6/30, and assuming a normal and appropriate epithet of Osiris.

eb. : *ỉn-ỉw=k* ⌜*md*⌝ [*n*] ⌜*ḥꜣt.ṯ=k*⌝: though this reading is not completely secure, comparisons with *md* in 6/26 and *ḥꜣt.ṯ* in 6/23 render it probable.

ec. : : while these two writings of *nꜥš* differ considerably from one another, they comprise the same basic elements, and, in the context, there can be no real doubt that they represent the same word. For *r nṯr nb ḳn* cf. 6/7.

ed. : *i-ỉr pꜣ nṯr* is certain. The first group in the line seems more likely to represent *šn* than other possibilities because of the angle of the second stroke. There is hardly room for *šny*, 'be ill, in distress', if the sentence is to parse correctly; it seems best to restore the simple imperative *šn* with following ethic dative *n*(*=i*) and to take the trace after the lacuna as the tail of *pꜣ*, 'Seek out for me that which the god has caused to happen to him who has come to die'. The masc. article is required by *ḫpr=f*.

ee. r tm dỉt ỉr=f ḥꜣt.ṯ=f m-sꜣ . . . . . : though *tm* and *m-sꜣ* are slightly damaged, the reading is not in doubt. Whether, however, *ỉr=f ḥꜣt.ṯ=f* is to be taken in the sense of the common Late-Egyptian expression *ỉr n ḥꜣty* (*n*) *N*, 'act according to N's will' (*Wb.* iii. 27. 19), or be taken to represent *ỉr ḥꜣt*, 'to regret, repent' (*DG*, 290, under 289. 2, cf. Copt. ⲣ̄ϩⲏⲧ=, Crum, *CD*, 715b), is a moot point; the latter seems rather more probable since *n* is omitted. Either the god or the doomed man may be the subject of *ỉr=f*; the latter is the last mentioned male person, and clearly more probable in the context.

ef. : for a similar writing of the exclamation *ꜥs* see 6/12 and n. *bn*. Note the use of *ꜥs* and *tw-s* in the same sentence, the former before the imperative, the latter before a noun.

eg. : *my ỉꜣw* . . . . ; that the root *ỉꜣw* appears here can hardly be doubted (*DG*, 16. 6). If *ꜣsḳ=f* is correctly read in 6/24 and *ṯꜣỉ.ṯ=f* later in this line, then a 3rd pers. sing. masc. pronoun must certainly be restored in the lacuna here. Whether the verb (*my ỉꜣw=f*) or the noun (*my ỉꜣwt n=f*) should be preferred is doubtful.

eh. : for the reading *pꜣ ḥmꜣr*, cf. 6/8, n. *as*. Comparison of the first group with *my* earlier in the line and elsewhere in the text rules this reading out. The only obvious and simple alternative is *šꜥ*. Then, however, one might expect the normal demotic auxiliary *šꜥ-tw=f*, since a verb follows. That this is not present (e.g. written *šꜥ.ṯ*) is virtually proved by the scribe's regulation writing of the negative auxiliary *bw-ỉr-tw*, formed on the same pattern as *šꜥ-tw*, in 6/15. We suggest, rather tentatively, that what the scribe has written is *šꜥ-r ṯꜣỉ.ṯ=⌜f⌝ pꜣ ḥmꜣr*, and that we should interpret this as an archaistic use of the late Egyptian construction *šꜣꜥ-r sḏmt.f* without use of the auxiliary *ỉr* shown in such examples as Erman, *Näg. Gr.* § 443. In this case *tw-s tꜣỉ=y dbḥ mtw=k* would be virtually parenthetical, and the sense 'grant unto him old age—that is my request to you—until the *ḥmꜣr* takes ⌜him⌝'. See p. 88, n. *ff.* for a further possible instance of this construction in 6/29.

ej. Strictly the reading *ṯꜣỉ.ṯ=⌜f⌝* adopted in n. *eh* above is not certain palaeographically, though the length of the tail of the final group and the way the ligature with *ṯ* is made render it more probable than the only apparent alternative *ṯꜣỉ.ṯ=y*. The clinching argument is that the scribe appears to have inserted a 3rd pers. sing. masc. suffix pronoun after the verb *ꜣsḳ* in 6/24, so that *=f* is certainly also required by the sense here.

ek. : the reading *ỉn-mwt* can hardly be avoided in view of the upper diagonal stroke of the death det. *mn* is also almost certain at the end of 6/23, leaving only a slight space before it. *ỉw* seems the obvious restoration 'without their being a ghost/corpse'. On *ỉn-mwt* and other nouns from this root, see p. 77, n. *ax*.

el. : the suffix pronoun *=f* in *ꜣsḳ=f* is written very small, as if inserted as an afterthought, but is certain. After *m-ỉr dỉt* a subject for *ꜣsḳ* is required by the construction. *ꜥḥꜥ* may be taken as a Stative or, much less probably, as a writing of the noun *ꜥḥꜥ* 'period of time' (*DG*, 69. 1), without the characteristic time det.

em. : the traces of the word following *bn(-pw)* fit neither *ỉrt*, 'eye' (cf. 6/19) nor *ḥꜣt*, 'brow, front' (cf. 6/15, 27, 28), nor *ẖt* 'belly' (cf. 7/8). *ḥꜣt.ṯ=f*, 'his heart', followed by a verb of bad meaning, e.g. *tḫr*, 'because his intentions were not evil', might fit the context and traces best.

en. : *m-sꜣ tꜣ ẖr(.t)* seems reasonably well assured, cf. 6/27, 29. The group before *m-sꜣ* might be the child det. or the suffix pronoun *=k* with a short stroke above it; if the latter, perhaps restore *hb=k m-sꜣ* or the like?

eo. : the suffix pronoun *=s* before the dative *n=k* seems to require a preceding verb. The divine det. suggests a religious significance, and the initial upright sign conforms well with those used for *nṯr* in this text (cf., for example, 6/27). *dwꜣ-nṯr* seems a probable reading, since *nṯr* is regularly written honorifically at the beginning of this compound (*DG*, 613. 5). Whether the preceding trace should be restored *ḫpr*, *my*, or something else must remain uncertain.

ep. About 1 cm. of text could have stood at the end of the line.

eq. : these traces are uncertain, but ⌜*(n-)ḥꜣt pꜣ*⌝ *h*[*rw*] seems plausible, cf. 6/15; if so, perhaps restore [*n pꜣỉ(=y) mwt*], 'before the day of my death'(?). The traces further on are not inconsistent with *m-sꜣ* (see n. *er* below).

er. : the relative form *ỉ*[*-ỉr*] is suggested by the traces following *mnḳ=s nꜣ mdwt n ḏd*. If *ỉ-ỉr=s* were restored this might mean simply 'she finished the words of speaking which she did', a known demotic means of expressing 'she ended her speech'. But these words must surely be related to those in 6/20–1, *ỉn dỉ=k drt.ṯ=k r ꜣIst ntỉ mnḳ nꜣ mdwt n ḏd r-dbꜣ ẖdb ḫpr n pꜣỉ*[(*=y*)?] *smt*. If so, *mnḳ=s nꜣ mdwt n ḏd ỉ-ỉr* . . . . is likely to mean 'She fulfilled the words of speech/prophecy which . . . made', and this fulfilment would presumably be effected by the woman's death. It is then tempting to restore ⌜*m-sꜣ*⌝ [*wꜥt*] *wnwt n sḏy*, 'after an hour of conversation', and connect this with 6/17 'You have brought me Isis in her own flesh, and after an hour [of conversation, I will die (?)]'. If these interpretations were correct, then the speaker of the prophecy should presumably be restored as Isis.

es. : *r pꜣ ỉtn* certain; [*i*-]*ỉr*=*f nw* seems a more plausible restoration from the traces than *ỉw*=*f nw*, and a second tense seems inherently probable, with emphasis upon *r pꜣ ỉtn*. In the present context, it would seem natural that the masc. suffix pronoun of [*i*-]*ỉr*=*f* should refer back to the god Imḥotep with whom the woman has been conversing. If so, 'the god' with whom the girl speaks in 6/26 may also be Imḥotep. Neither of these inferences, however, is assured.

et. : despite the damage, the reading is hardly in doubt, cf. 6/27 for *tꜣ ẖr.t*, and *DG*, 239–40, under 239. 12 for writings of *rꜣ*, 'mouth', with det. borrowed from *rꜣ* 'door'.

eu. : very careful study of the badly stained papyrus here has convinced us that only the reading [*r*]-*dbꜣ tꜣi*=*k bꜣk.t* will fit what is visible. If the placing of the two halves of col. 6 of the papyrus as close as possible together (on the basis of strong textual evidence from 6/27–31 as well as fibre evidence) is correct, then the lacuna will have been long enough only for *ntỉ ỉw*=*k n-ỉm*[=*f r*]-*dbꜣ tꜣi*=*k bꜣk.t*.

ev. despite some difficulties of translation, the reading *ntỉ bn-pw pꜣ dwꜣ ṯꜣi tꜣ ḥm.t r-r*=*s* seems soundest. For *ṯꜣi*, cf. 6/29; though *r-r*=*s* does not occur elsewhere in this text, it is regularly written not in these Memphite hands (e.g. **1**, 14/21). *nꜣi*=*k*/*tꜣi*=*k* seems an impossible reading before *r-r*=*s*, since even if it were rendered as the absolute possessive adjective (Coptic ⲛⲟⲩⲕ/ⲧⲱⲕ), there would be no clear substantival antecedent for it to refer to; *tꜣ ḥm.t* appears superior. *dwꜣ*, though damaged, appears clear; the final det. suits the word for 'morning' (*DG*, 614. 1), although the preceding house det. must have been borrowed (e.g. from *dwꜣ.t*, underworld, *DG*, 613. 6).

ew. : *pꜣ*(*i*) *ꜣpwṯ*, 'the/this messenger', appears certain from the traces (see *DG*, 85. 8 under *wp.ṯ* for this writing). *ỉw*=*s dỉt* is certain; the following word begins with *y* and must be a verb, which limits the choice; *ys*, 'hurry' (*DG*, 50. 7), written , might fit traces and context well. The final trace of the line might suit a short =*f*, the det. of 'death' or other groups.

ex. : *ḥr ḥty*, 'in fear', certain.

ey. : it seems certain that simply *nꜣ ḥsw* should be read, as no intervening word is easily intelligible grammatically within the limits allowed by subsequent lines. The two halves of the page must therefore be placed as close as possible. *tꜣ ẖr.t ntỉ n Ỉst* is a somewhat curious phrase, most easily explicable on the assumption that *n* stands for the old *m* of equivalence; 'who belongs to Isis' would surely be rendered by *mtw* or *ntỉ n-drt*. As the 'festival of Sokar' had funerary associations, the 'songs' mentioned here are presumably the funeral lamentations, which were uttered by mourners impersonating 'the two kites', Isis and Nephthys. This probably adequately explains the phrase; cf., however, *ntỉ n sšm n Ỉst* in 6/16.

ez. : *nꜣ wꜥ.w*, 'the curses' (*DG*, 82. 3), may be read with assurance, cf. *wꜥ* in 6/28. The preceding tall sign then corresponds closely with *ḥꜣ*(*t*), 'front' (*DG*, 287. 1), probably in the temporal adverb corresponding to preposition (*n*)-*ḥꜣ.ṯ*, 'before, in front of', the pronominal form of which has been read in 6/15; it also appears as a temporal adverb contrasted with *wḥm* in 6/28. The passage there *nꜣ ḫrw.w n wsṯn r-ḏd*=*s* ⌜*r*⌝ [*tꜣ*] *rpy*(*t*) *Ỉst* appears to justify the restoration *r-ḏd*=[*s*] *r tꜣi*=*t rpy*(*t*) [*Ỉst*] here, there being just room for *Ỉst* at the end of the line. A slight cross tick on the *n* of *n*=*t* is perhaps unintentional: .

fa. ỉn i-ỉr=*t r ḏd wꜥ wḥm n pꜣ sp mḥ-2*: *wḥm*, used adverbially, is certain from the writing later in this line (*DG*, 97. 5 under *wḥm*). The reading *mḥ-2* appears to be required to explain the flourish above the second vertical, see *DG*, 172. 1; *wḥm n pꜣ sp mḥ-2* is the adverbial extension emphasized by the Future Second Tense.

fb. ; the first sign is to be read as the adverb (*n*-)*ḥꜣ*(*t*), see above n. *ez*. The most convincing reading of the following group is the plur. demonstrative adjective *nꜣy*, 'these'; *nꜣ ḫrw.w n wsṯn* with the following relative clause will then be the subject placed in anticipatory emphasis because of its length, picked up by the demonstrative *nꜣy*, which introduces the predicate: 'The flaunting words which she spoke against the princess Isis before, this (is) the speaking (of them) again'. The absence of the copula in a nonverbal sentence with substantive predicate is unusual in demotic, but may be influenced, we think, by the use of the demonstrative *nꜣy*. On the analogy of 6/27 *r* rather than *n* should be restored after *r-ḏd*=*s*, following which there is probably not room for *tꜣi*=*t* or *tꜣi*=*s*, but only for *tꜣ*, in the lacuna (cf. 6/10).

fc. : the suffix of *ḏd*=*s* has

been inserted as an afterthought below the line. Comparison with the instance in 6/27 assures, we think, the reading *dỉt ỉr=w ḥb Skr*, there clearly being no space for the dative *n=f* which figures there. At the end of the line the horizontal *s* may again be seen in the same position as in *Skr*. As the relative form *r-ḏd=s* at the beginning of 6/29 clearly needs a noun antecedent which must signify something which 'she' has spoken of, the restoration [*pꜣ ḥb*] *S*[*kr*] is logical, fits the traces, and fills the space. The context makes it clear that the speech in 6/29 is a reply to that of the god, so that a second *ḏd=s*, 'she said', is required; the traces after *Skr* fit this well. The normal construction after *hmy*, 'would that', is *hmy ỉw* (e.g. ʿOnchsheshonqy, 10/11–11/4); *mtw=s dỉt ỉr=w* must surely be explained as the Conjunctive, for which we cannot quote an instance after *hmy*; it presumably has a strong future consecutive force. We take the 3rd pers. fem. suffix to refer back to *tꜣỉ=k bꜣk.t* in 6/26, that is, to the speaker herself.

fd. : the two sides of the page come very close together here and there is room only for a very short word in the lacuna; the reading *ṯꜣỉ pꜣ ṯꜣw* (cf. 6/15) fits traces and space admirably. A difficulty presents itself in the translation of these sentences. In the second, *rḫ* can only well mean 'be able' (Coptic ϣ̄, Crum, *CD*, 541a): 'will she be able to do it even after the breath (of life) has been taken away?'; whereas in the first, following the interrogative word *ỉḫ*, 'be able' makes poor sense even if *ỉr n*(*=ỉ*) is read: 'what is she not able to do for me?'. It seems better to read *ỉr=s* and translate *rḫ*, 'know': '⌜As to the festival of Sokar⌝ she spoke of, she does not know what she is doing', taking *ỉr=s ỉḫ* as an indirect question.

fe. 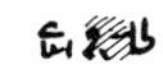: *ḥꜣꜥ st* is certain, cf. *ḥꜣꜥ* in 6/9. What *st* refers to is more problematical. If the plurality of its form may be relied upon, it should not refer to the preceding *tꜣỉ*(*=y*) *mwt*. Perhaps it has a more general reference to the Sokar festival and the songs of the girl who is in the role of Isis (cf. 6/27). The words *m-sꜣ tꜣỉ*(*=y*) *mwt* are important in that they establish that the woman who blasphemed against Isis earlier was mother of the girl (*tꜣ ẖr.t*) who is the speaker here. Whether the sentence should be translated 'Can I not seek/search for him after my mother?', meaning after my mother's death, or 'Can I not seek him except for/without my mother?' is doubtful. If the words *mnḳ=s nꜣ mdwt n ḏd* in 6/25 have been correctly interpreted as referring to death, then the former seems more probable.

ff. ; the first group here is palaeographically very close to that in 6/23, interpreted on p. 86, n. *eh* as *šꜥ-r*. Comparison of the following group with the writings of words from the stem *mwt* (see p. 77, n. *ax*) suggests the reading *šꜥ-r mwt* . . . . . . 'Leave her/it alone until N dies'. This seems to fit well, though it cannot be certain whether the subject of *mwt* should be restored *=s* or perhaps *tꜣỉ*(*=y*) *mwt*, referring to the female whose death may be referred to in the foregoing sentence (p. 99, n. *αι*), or to the male for whom the 'festival of Sokar' is requested, whose death is probably to be inferred from 6/30–1 (see p. 102 f., b). The former seems probable—but the inference would then be that the speaker was unaware of her mother's death.

fg. 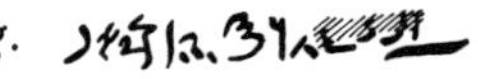: *ỉ-ỉr=k tn* is quite certain palaeographically, *ỉ-ỉr=k* being the auxiliary of the second tense required by oblique question word at the end of the clause. *wn-nꜣ-w* must be restored before *ỉ-ỉr=k*, as this imperfect auxiliary appears both in the reply, and in the explanatory clause *wn-nꜣ-w ỉrt.ṯ*(*=y*) *wḫꜣ=k. ỉrt.ṯ*(*=y*) is certain (cf. 6/19); note that *wḫꜣ* is spelt with two dets., both of which are omitted in the same verb in 6/29, a clear and welcome proof that this scribe, despite his very evident high degree of literacy and skill, is not absolutely consistent in his writings.

fh. : as this is the answer to the question 'Where were you?', these words must name a location, and the use of *pr* in place of the article *pꜣ* before points of the compass is so usual in demotic as to suggest the presence of one here. The sign preserved here contrasts with that used for *ỉmnṯ* in 6/21 (and probably also in 6/9) in its lack of a lateral stroke at the top; unless this is a scribal oversight, another reading must be sought. Though unlike that used in *ỉꜣbṯ* 'east' (*DG*, 17. 5), it does correspond to that used in demotic writings of the related word *ỉꜣby*, 'left' (*DG*, 17. 4). By transference, one might suggest that it was used to write *ỉꜣbṯ*, 'east', here, if it is wished to avoid the assumption of a scribal error. To this reading it might reasonably be objected that the west, not the east, is the proper place in terms of Egyptian mythology for the god to be seeking Osiris, and that *ỉmn*[*ṯ*] should be read. But we cannot fully reconstruct the movements of the gods in this story; and it should be observed that, if the reading *pꜣ dwꜣ* in 6/26 is accepted, the time of these events is dawn or morning, when even Osiris can perhaps properly be thought of as at the eastern horizon. A doubt persists.

fj. : ⸢. . . . .⸣=*y Wsỉr* certain; the preceding verb is strictly not restorable from the meagre traces; but allowing for a det. for the preceding *ỉꜣbṯ*, both space available and what remains fit ⸢*šn*⸣=*y* well (cf. 6/23, beginning).

fk. ; comparison with, for instance, *n-ỉm*[=*f*] in 6/26 shows that the same stem is written here, but careful examination seems to prove that no suffix pronoun ever stood after it. We suggest that this exceptional device was used by this scribe for distinguishing the Coptic ⲙⲙⲁⲩ, 'there' (Crum, *CD*, 196b), from the Coptic ⲙⲙⲟⲟⲩ, 'in them' (Crum, *CD*, 215a ff.), though both are normally written *n-ỉm=w* in demotic literary hands. Cf. p. 15, n. *av* on **1**, 9/16.

fl. ỉw pꜣỉ ḥmꜣr: for the reading *ḥmꜣr* compare 6/8, 6/23, where *pꜣ ḥmꜣr* is written; the form of demonstrative with the oblique dot used here is distinguished by this scribe both from the definite article and from the copula *pꜣỉ* (6/17).

fm. sšm: the word is written the same way as in the phrases *pꜣ nb sšm* and *tꜣ ntỉ n sšm* in 6/16, and also as in *pꜣ sšm ꜣIst* in 6/17. As in 6/23–4 it is certainly a male character whom the *ḥmꜣr* is to seize (*šꜥ-r ṯꜣỉ.ṯ=f pꜣ ḥmꜣr* in 6/23 supported by *m-ỉr dỉt ꜣsk=f ꜥḥꜥ* in 6/24), it seems that [*pꜣ nb*] *sšm* is the most likely of these entities for the *ḥmꜣr* to have arrived to seize in 6/30–1. This is perhaps substantiated by the probable masc. gender of *ẖr* later in the line, since this word must presumably refer to the same person. Simply [*ṯꜣỉ=f pꜣ nb*] *sšm*, 'he seized the lord-of-the-image', would certainly not have filled the gap at the end of 6/30 after *ḥmꜣr* (*c.* 3.5 cm.), but there is no reason why an adjectival phrase or indeed another verbal action should not have preceded *ṯꜣỉ*. Unfortunately the slight surviving traces are too minimal to be helpful, though they could perhaps represent *pꜣ*.

fn. : originally this group was read *ꜣspy*, with the det. of an animal. Though palaeographically plausible, there seems no lexicographical parallel for such an animal name in Egyptian. Careful observation suggests that what at first was taken as the third member of *s* may well have been intended as another animal det., though rather differently made from that at the end of the whole expression. If so, *ꜣwỉ ḥsy*, 'wild bull', may be read (*DG*, 1. 6, quoting Ryl. iii. 9. 25/7; Cairo 50138. 11; Mythus 11/18. 16/2; *Wb.* i. 49. 9 ff.). Apart from its use as *p* in *ꜣIỉ-m-ḥtp* (6/19, 20), elsewhere in this hand reads *ḥs* (6/6, 11). As the traditional sacrificial animal in Egypt was apparently always a male *ỉwꜣ*, it seems best to reject *wꜥt* for the preceding sign in favour of *ms*, 'calf' (*DG*, 179. 1). A male bull calf would seem an appropriate offering at the 'great wrath of Sakhmis'.

fo. : only *ḥwt* is certain. The following det. can in this text denote either wood or fire (examples given on p. 77, n. *bc*). In view of *ḫrꜥry ḳy Sḫmt* (n. *fp* below) and *dỉ=t nb.t* (n. *fq* below) the notion of fire appears appropriate here. While the sign might perhaps be regarded as simply a second det. of *ḥwt*, it seems more likely that it represents a compound 'temple of the fire-altar' or the like, though it must remain uncertain how the second element was read in Egyptian. The broken signs before *ḥwt* should almost certainly be read *tꜣỉ=f* referring back to the subject of the sentence.

fp. : *ḫrꜥry ḳy* (*n*?) *Sḫmt* appears certain. For the word *ḫrꜥry* see p. 24, n. *eu* and Canopus Decree 4:15 *ḫrꜥy.w* 'disasters' (the sole reference quoted by *DG*, 365. 6). Here the word was evidently determined both with the death and the divine dets., appropriately enough, since the reference is evidently to the holocaust made of mankind by the ravening lioness Sakhmet when sent upon her mission of destruction by her father Reꜥ; also to be compared is the legend of the lioness Hathor/Tefnut as the Eye of the Sun-god ravaging Nubia (Junker, *Onurislegende*; Spiegelberg, *Mythus*). For *ḳy* see *DG*, 531. 7; it seems better to supply the genitival *n* after it than to assume a direct genitive at this date.

fq. : *dỉ=t nb.t* is certain. It has been shown (p. 77, n. *bc*) that this scribe uses this det. both for wood and flame; here it seems best to connect with *nbỉ.t*, 'flame' (*Wb.* ii. 244. 7 ff.), for which *DG*, 214. 5 quotes a solitary writing from Mythus 16. 5. The traces following *nb.t* are very uncertain; while they appear reconcilable with the reading *n pꜣ ẖr*, 'to the youth', other possibilities certainly exist.

col. 7

fr. : perhaps *ỉ-ỉr=f* should be restored at the end of 6/31 immediately before *nw*. The subject of this verb seems most likely to be the youth (*ẖr*), mentioned in 6/31, but this is uncertain. The name of the being, presumably divine from the det., following *nw r* is written with a sign which clearly represents a large quadruped with lowered head and probably some form of horns. Its identity remains for us problematic;

lion and bull, at first sight the most obvious choices, would surely have been represented by more familiar demotic groups (see *DG*, 243. 4 under *rw*, 555. 12 under *kꜣ*). Of other large quadrupeds, it perhaps most resembles a hippopotamus, though in this case it is unclear what the adjunct to the head, similar to that used in hieratic to represent horns, may be. Presumably a deity of the other world is involved, which allows of many possibilities. The following sign is probably *w*; on the analogy of 6/26 *wpy N rꜣ=f/=s* might be speculatively suggested.

fs. : *hb=t m-sꜣ=y ỉw=y r ỉỉ* is certain; an indecipherable trace follows. Note that this could possibly refer back to 6/26–7 *ỉw=s dỉt ys pꜣ ꜣpwṯ . . . . . r ỉỉ m-sꜣ=k ḫr ḥty*.

ft. : *wn nꜣi=k* ⌜*f*⌝*ꜣy.w* seems palaeographically the most satisfactory reading; if *r-r=s* is read at the beginning of the line, it becomes difficult to find a reading that will satisfy the requirements both of orthography and grammar.

fu. : *twt pr-nfr* seems probable; there is a parallel for this writing of *pr-nfr* in an unpublished demotic document from Saqqâra (Saq. H5-DP12 [1610] front 1/5). The context is discussed on p. 101, n. *ασ*.

fv. : *r tꜣ wsḫy*, 'to the hall', is certain.

fw. : the word following *mn*, 'there is not', is determined with a det. used of wood and fire in this text, see p. 77, n. *bc*; with great diffidence we suggest *ḏꜣ*, 'fire-drill, fire-stick' (*Wb.* v. 511. 10). The reading *ḥmt ḫt*, 'copper and wood', seems unlikely since *ḥmt* is differently written in 6/2.

fx. : *r-ḫ(t)* is probable; perhaps render the whole phrase 'look at them as if (they were . . .)', see p. 18, n. *cg* on **1**, 9/31.

fy. : *mwt*, 'die, death', seems certain; the previous traces might represent the article *pꜣ* and the end of a lost initial word.

Translation

FRONT (↔)

col. 5

— — — — — — — — — — — — — — — — — — —

x+1. --- sick(?)

x+2. *no surviving trace*

x+3. --- die(?)

— — — — — — — — — — — — — — — — — — —

col. 6

1. ---] 'who cannot make his form in front of the multitude, ... [. . . .] Will they . . . . [. . . . . .] House of Life [. . .] take me to them(?) because we have not been able to . . . . . ?'[α] She caused a sanctuary to be made, [. . . .] . . . .
2. ---] . . . . [. . .] being clad in stone (and) being . . . . [. . .], its doors being of [. . . . .] . ., its bolts being of darkened copper, its windows being of . . [. . . . .]
3. ---] . . . . of hide(?) saying 'Rejoice(?) . . . .' . . . .[. .]. . . of Elephantine, . . . [. . . . . . .] . . ., it being . . . . . with rolled cloths [. . . . . . .] . . .
4. ---] a head-rest with the face of . . . . [. . . . . .] . . [. . . .] . . . [. . . . . . .] being at (its?) head, [. . . . .] being behind him of the finest products of the craftsman [. . . . . . .][β] . .
5. ---] mount up [. . . . .] upon [. . . . .] . . . in front of him for the withdrawing(?) of incense . . [. . . . .] . . . . .
6. ---] . . . . . [. . . . .] . . [. . .], she made . . . . [. . . . . . .] her . . . . mother of/in the mountains. She called out to him praises/songs [. . . .] . . . . .[γ]

7. - - -] [. . . . . '. . . . .] the one who caused you (masc.) to be far off is not [. . . . . .' . . . . '. . . . .] any valiant god. Do not make . . . . . [. . . .] a son or daughter cause you (fem.) to know . . . . . again[δ]

8. - - -] [. . . . .] sanctuary of my temple in (the) precinct(?) [. . . . . .] . . . [. . .] the death-bird(?) who is evil, he shall go away'.[ε] *space*

larger space between the lines

9. - - -] [. . . . .] . . 'Cause (?) the West to be great for me(?), the falcon/O falcon . . . .'. She turned towards her/stopped opposite her, she went cold[ζ] because Isis was left to herself with him, namely the dying man whom she would cause to . . . .[η]

10. - - -] the boat, she returned(?) from(?) the . . . . . , she came(?) to her chamber weeping [. .] . . . She went to the chapel(?), she spoke before the Lady Isis who caused her to go to give birth(?):[θ] 'Stay, listen [. .]

11. [o] Lady of the Two Lands(?), I am [. .] . . . . of this . . [. . .], who(?) prays(?) to this . . . . . ., who sings/praises at the . [. . . . .] without drinking, who ascends . . . . without eating, who casts clothes upon . . . ., ... [. . . .][ι]

12. See, gods are not revealed to men in their glory without their . . . [. . . . . . .][κ] know . . . . . who(?) has said concerning a poor man: "I will take vengeance upon/for(?) him". Isis, do not disgrace him[λ] because of . . [. . .]

13. [.] . . the satisfaction(?) [. .] statue.' . . . . of/with his dogs . . . . [. . . . .] . . . . their canals of(?) balm of potency against any killing/killer. The Turner(?) arose . [. . .]

14. [. .] . . . . . the Master . . . . . . the monster of doom(?). He captured(?), he brought.[μ] *space* He [. .] . . . the heaven, the earth, the underworld.[ν] *space*

larger space between lines

15. '[. .] breath (of life) which is mine, I am before(?) her, my mother Isis; that is to say, I am about to die, (and) I am going to let her know(?) of these accusations while [. .] have not yet [. . . . . . .]. Your (fem.) counsels, there is no wisdom in them; your (fem.) prophetic statements have not come to pass at this [. . . .]'.[ξ]

16. That which the Five Gods said to her, it did not work(?), that is to say, they did not decide/reveal it. She made a confidante . . . . . [. . . . .], she caused them to find out what had happened to the lord of the image.[ο] 'Stand up, you (fem.) who are at(?) the the image of Isis,[π]

17. (a) spell of Isis is upon you (fem.); you (fem.) have brought to me Isis in her own flesh. . . . . . . an hour [. . . . .]. Death, when it happens to us, is the way of everybody.' She left the image of Isis . . . .

18. [.] chapel(?), she worshipped.[ρ] They tarried while they were doing these (things); they did not look [. .] . . [.] A [. . . . .] occurred . . . . their . . . . . [.] They saw(?) a great winged-scarab coming down from the sky.[σ] He landed before them,

19. [. .] . . . their(?) sight. He awoke, (and) their eyes saw; they saw Imḥotep. . . [. . . .] . . . ; he turned/stopped himself; . . . . [. . . .]; and so he made his form. He sat upon a block of stone, the flesh being

20. . . . . ;[τ] they prostrated themselves on their bellies—so she told me.[υ] The one who was sick said to him:[φ] '[. . Im]ḥotep my master, has the [. . . . . .] the face of a . . . . seized him(?)?[χ] Have you set your hand against Isis who is fulfilling

21. these words spoken concerning a killing happening to one of my(?) sort?[ψ] The West, I have set it in . . . . [. . . . . .] . . . . my property has passed to another of my sort; I have placed/given . . [. . .] . . . me.[ω]

22. They do not know that you are come to us as(?) Fair-of-Face, (and that) you are among the learned ones(?) of Thoth, (and that) you are in the hand of . . . [. . . . .] . . . Are you . . [. .] . . your . . . . because you have not been victorious against Isis?[αα] Horus is victorious against any valiant god.

23. . . . . [. . . .] . . . the god has caused to happen to the one who has come to die, so as not to allow him to grieve over/after [. . . . . .].[αβ] See, let [. . .] grow old—behold, that is my request of you—until the death-bird(?) seizes him(?), [. .] not being

24. a ghost(?).[αγ] Do not cause him to tarry waiting(?) in the place of punishment(?), [. . .] heart(?) has not [. . . . . .] . . . after this girl [. . . .] her give worship/thanks to you; grant to her the way of life. Tell it to me(?) [. . . . .]'

25. . . . . . . [. . . . .][αδ] . . [. .] an hour of conversation, she fulfilled the words spoken . . [. . . . .] . He looked at the ground.[αε] *space*

larger space between lines

26. The girl(?) opened her mouth, she spoke with the god:[αζ] 'What is this mood/countenance that you are in because of your maid servant, to whom the morning(?) has not brought the girl-child,[αη] she causing the messenger(?) . . . . . [. . . .].

27. to come after you (masc.) in fear?[αθ] O that she may cause there to be performed for him a Sokar-festival, (and) that she may cause there to be performed for him the praises/songs of the girl who is in (the role of?) Isis!'[αι] The god said: 'When she has desisted/been silent for your (fem.) sake before(?) from the blasphemies which [she(?)] spoke against(?) your (fem.) Lady [. .],

28. are you now about to speak blasphemy again the second time? The overweening utterances which she spoke [against(?) the] Lady Isis before(?), this is speaking a repetition (of them).' It happened that she had said: 'O that she may cause to be performed a Sokar-festival(?).'[ακ] Said . . '[. . .] . . . [. . .]

29. of which she spoke, she does/did not know what she is/was doing. Will she be able to do it after the taking away of . . [.] . . . ? Can I not search for him after/without my mother? Leave them until . . [. . . . .]

30. Where are you (masc.)? My eyes were searching for you.' The god said: 'I was in the west/east(?);[αλ] I [. .] . . . Osiris about Isis who was there(?). The death-bird(?) came [. . . . .] . [. . . . .]

31. image. He never humiliated (even) a wild bull calf(?) as (he did) (the) youth whom he called (to) his temple-of- . . . . . .(?) (at(?) the) high fury(?) of Sakhmis.[αμ] You (fem.) have set a flame(?) . . . .[αν] [. . . . .' . . . .][αξ]

32. 6th (column)

col. 7

1. looked at/saw . . . . . .[αο] . . [- - -
2. 'you (fem.) send/sent after me,[απ] I will come . .' [- - -
3. 'list/sum of your (masc.) dues, I [- - -

4. I not having died'.[αρ] He passed [- - -
5. statue (of the) embalming-house(?)[ασ] . . . . [- - -
6. to the hall[ατ] [- - -
7. there is/was no . . . . [- - -
8. looked at them in the manner(?) [- - -
9. [. .] . . . die/death [- - - [αυ]

remainder lost except for possible traces at the beginnings of lines

Notes on Translation

α. The uncertainties of reading in the first line are too great for a connected translation to be offered. The initial relative clause may belong either to narrative or speech. *ḳmꜣ* is quoted by *DG*, 537. 1 as a noun meaning 'Schöpfung' without references: 'who cannot make his creation before the people' would suggest that the person referred to was a demiurge. Alternatively, *ḳmꜣ* may represent hieroglyphic , 'Gestalt, Wesen' (*Wb*. v. 36. 9–15), which may be used like *irw*, *ḫprw*, or *ḳd* of assuming a different 'form'; 'who cannot make/change his form before the people' would suggest that a divine being or magician was referred to, and it is notable that in 6/18–19 a scarab-beetle lands and changes form into Imḥotep. The following phrase has not been deciphered (p. 74, n. *f*), and it is uncertain whether it belonged to this clause or the next. The question *in-iw=w r* . . . . . must necessarily belong to a speech. If the doubtful word is really to be read *ꜥꜥn.w*, 'baboons', then 'Shall they become baboons'(?), would presumably refer back to the 'making of forms', and some such reconstruction of the previous phrase as *iw=w ir pꜣi=n* [*ḳmꜣ*], 'When our forms are made'(?), might be very tentatively suggested. But, apart from the fantastic aspect of such a translation, a noun following *in-iw=w r* is grammatically a dubious construction, and the doubtful group may conceal a verb (p. 74, n. *g*). The gap between this word and *pr-ꜥnḫ* (p. 74, n. *h*) is sufficient for from three to five groups; the 1st pers. sing. and plur. pronouns in *mḥ.ṭ=y* and *bn(-pw)=n*(?) indicate a speech in which the speaker probably thinks of himself as one of a pair or group. While there may just have been room in the lacuna for such a restoration as [*ḏd pꜣ sḫ*] *pr-ꜥnḫ*, '[Said the scribe of] the House of Life', in which case this speech would have been a reply to the previous question, it seems more probable that the whole is part of a single utterance. Granted the readings proposed on p. 74, nn. *j–l*, it appears best to take *ḏd* as a conjunction and translate '[. . . . the scribe?] of the House of Life [to] take me to them because we have not been able to be far off', i.e. to escape. In sum it seems possible that the speaker is complaining that he and his companion(s) will not be able to escape some dire event because of his inability to change his form in front of the multitude. The response to this is that a female character has a chapel built, presumably to protect him from public gaze; this emphasizes the fact that the male speaker must be divine. The presence of the phrase 'House of Life'[1] is perhaps evidence that magic is involved; how exactly it should be fitted in to the context is unclear, though the phrase *sḫ pr-ꜥnḫ*, 'magician' (Coptic [B]ⲥⲫⲣⲁⲛϣ Crum, *CD*, 374a), may have been involved. The connection of both baboons and the 'House of Life' with the god Thoth might conceivably be relevant.

β. The word *knḥy* is used of the *naos* or statue-shrine of a temple sanctuary (e.g. Rosetta Decree D. 20) and of the vaults in which sacred bulls or cows were buried (e.g. *ZÄS* 51 (1913), 137; *Rev. d'Ég*. 24 (1972), 177). The detailed description fits a particularly sumptuous temple naos, conceivably portable in character. So far as may be guessed from the preserved text, it was constructed of some lighter material (e.g. mud-brick or wood?) lined with stone, its doors perhaps of *ꜥš*-wood covered with gold with bolts of niello, the window grilles perhaps of silver. The difficult passage at the beginning of 6/3 must be an integral part of the description which continues into 6/4, though whether it refers to the exterior or interior of the naos is uncertain. If so, *ḏd* can hardly introduce a speech, yet the words *ršꜣ r nsw*(?) (or however they should be read) are clearly not in themselves a description. With extreme diffidence we suggest that, if *pꜣi=s tp iynm*(?) might mean the streamer of leather or hide placed at the head of the flagpoles to be expected on

[1] A. H. Gardiner, 'The House of Life', *JEA* 24 (1938), 157 ff.

either side of the façade of an Egyptian temple sanctuary (p. 75, n. *s*), then the words following *ḏd*, 'rejoice(?) for the king(?)' or otherwise, might represent a text emblazoned upon it. To the best of our knowledge, no example of such a streamer has survived, so that it is not known whether they were inscribed or not. However, this suggestion may be very wide of the mark. There follows what may be a description of the god's couch within the shrine (restoring *grg*, p. 75, n. *t*), probably constructed of a southern wood (ebony?) or ivory imported through Elephantine, perhaps inlaid with lapis and turquoise; it was covered with rolled draperies, possibly embroidered, with a head-rest adorned with the face of Bes(?) at its head with perhaps a cushion(?) stuffed with hair(?) upon it, and behind it a headboard(?) of the finest craftsman's work, presumably carved in relief and perhaps gilded—a bed highly reminiscent in its detail of those found in the burial of Tutʿankhamūn. (see p. 75, nn. *u*–*aa*).

γ. The lacunae in 6/5 are so large that attempts at reconstruction are perilous. It seems possible that the female here invites the god to ascend into the naos or the divine barque within it (conceivably restore [*in*]⌜-*iw=k*⌝ *ʿr r-ḥri*, 'will you ascend?', see p. 75, n. *ab*), puts vestments or regalia upon him (p. 75, n. *ac*), and places an altar(?) before him for the 'drawing of incense' (p. 75, n. *ad*; the use of the word *sṯꜣ*, 'drag, withdraw' seems here to be a technical one). Probably the end of 6/5 and most of 6/6 continued to describe the woman's cajoling of the god (*ii*(?), 'came'; *ir=s*, 'she did . . .'), since at the end 'she uttered unto him praises/songs'. If so, the puzzling words *n tꜣi=s mwt ʿꜣ.t*(?) *n nꜣ*(?) *dw.w* must form part of this description (p. 75, n. *ah*); possibly the woman repeated for the god some service (e.g. *hnw*, 'jubilation', p. 75, n. *ag*) formerly performed by 'her great(?) mother in the mountains', or reminded him of it, as likely to help her cause. The woman who addresses Isis in 6/10 below may refer to herself (if the text is correctly so interpreted, see p. 78, n. *bg*) in the words 'I am the daughter of the one who' performed various temple duties; if her mother is the same as the woman in 6/5–6 (as suggested below, p. 101 f.), then her mother had done service to the god which might explain her being mentioned here. For this reason, it seems preferable not to render *mwt ʿꜣ.t*(?) as 'grandmother' here, even if *ʿꜣ.t* is correctly read. This mention of her mother is perhaps paralleled by a mention of 'her brothers' at the beginning of 6/6, but this might also refer to 'her pleas' (see p. 75, n. *af* and also p. 102 for another possibility). If *bn*(-*pw*)=*f sdm n-im=w* is correctly restored at the end of the line, despite all this the god 'did not listen to them', that is, the paeans of praise.

δ. A change of speaker must have occurred in 6/7 between *pꜣ i-ir-dit-wꜣy=k* and *šr šr.t dit rẖ=t*, because of the change from the 2nd pers. masc. sing. to the 2nd pers. fem. sing.; the new speech must have been introduced in the lacuna after the former phrase, as there is not room in that before the latter. Thus *pꜣ i-ir-dit-wꜣy=k* should be the subject of the preceding verb, presumably to be restored as a First Pres.: 'the one (masc.) who has caused you to be far off is not evil/hostile(?)', the difficulty being to know the sense in which the verbs are used. On the analogy of 6/22, the lacuna may be restored [*ḏd pꜣ nṯr*(?) *nʿš* . . . .] *r nṯr nb ḳn*, 'the god said: "N is victorious against any valiant god" ', but it would be imprudent to assume that N must here be Horus as in 6/22; Isis, for instance, might fit the surviving trace as well as Horus. The nature of the god's prohibition to her is unfortunately obscured by a lacuna; if *bw-ir* is correctly restored before *šr* (p. 76, n. *ap*) and *rk* correctly read at the end of 6/7, then he warns her against this action 'lest any male or female child cause you (fem.) to know extinction'. It is perhaps significant that in 6/25 a woman (probably the same, see p. 101) dies, and directly afterwards we are told that her daughter is persisting in a blasphemy against Isis which she herself initiated. Unfortunately, neither *wʿy*, 'curse', nor *wpy*, 'judge', fit the traces after *m-ir* (*ir ḳnb.t r*, 'do not take legal action against', is very hesitantly suggested on p. 76, n. *ao*); but this connection may increase the possibility that Isis's name should be restored before *r nṯr nb ḳn*.

ε. Probably 6/8 represents a continuation of the god's speech in which he promises, probably as a reward for the woman's construction of the naos of his temple in the sacred precinct, that the *ḥmꜣr* will go away. If the identification of the *ḥmꜣr* as the ghoulish bird (probably an owl) which carries off the dead (see *JEA* 61 (1975), 198–200) be correct, then this passage shows that some character in the story is threatened with immediate death; this character, described as *pꜣ mwt.ṯ*, appears in 6/9.

ζ. The poor preservation of 6/9 leads to many uncertainties of reading (pp. 76–7, nn. *at*–*az*) and of translation, it being especially difficult to know to whom the personal pronouns refer. The words *rk=s wbꜣ=s*, whether they mean 'she turned towards her' (**ⲣⲓⲕⲉ**), or 'she stopped opposite her' (ⲗⲁϭⲉ; see p. 77, n. *av*) show that two females are involved, for the suffix after *wbꜣ* cannot easily be interpreted as reflexive. This is confirmed by the following words: 'She froze' (presumably with terror) 'because (*ḏd*) Isis was left alone with him, namely the dying man whom she was going to cause [to die]', for here the subject of *ꜥḏb=s* must be different from Isis; she is presumably the same woman to whom the god has promised in 6/8 that 'the evil death-bird shall go away'. (The alternative translation 'She froze, saying (*ḏd*) "Isis is left to herself with him, etc."' does not affect this argument). It therefore seems probable that it was Isis towards whom the woman turned (or opposite whom she stopped). If so, Isis seems likely to have appeared in the early part of 6/9; this would mean either that she was the speaker of the speech there, which might then be translated 'Honour the West for me, O falcon, who is beautiful of front(?)', or she was mentioned in it by another speaker: 'Adorn/honour the west for me, the falcon, who is beautiful of front(?)' (see p. 76, nn. *at*, *au*). The only possible clue to a decision between these versions is the possible trace of a *ṯ* after the initial lacuna, since if this was a Stative ending it might refer to a female within the speech, thus favouring the latter possibility. The whole passage is, however, too dubious in rendering for large conclusions to be built upon it. All that does seem certain, whatever rendering is adopted, is that a male character in the story is identified with 'the falcon' (see further below, p. 103 f.).

η. In *ḏd ꞽIst ḫꜣꜥ.ṯ n=s irm=f ḏd pꜣ mwt.ṯ nti iw=s r dit* ⌜*mwt*⌝[*=f*] the first *ḏd* may introduce either direct speech or a causal clause, the second can only serve to link the suffix of *irm=f* with the noun phrase in apposition: '. . . with him, namely, the dying man'. On the probable meaning of *pꜣ mwt.ṯ*, see p. 77, n. *ax*. *ḫꜣꜥ.ṯ*, being Stative, should have passive meaning and *n=s* is probably an ethic dative. The restoration *mwt=f* 'to die' suggested by the traces might be thought to make the relative clause tautological, but it serves to express Isis's agency in the man's future death.

θ. In 6/9–10 one might restore: '[She arose, she embarked on] the boat, she returned from the ⌜shrines⌝, and she came to her chamber weeping ⌜exceedingly⌝'. The *n*, not *r*, written after *stꜣ.ṯ=s* should imply motion from, not to. The relative clause *nti iw=s dit šm=s* lacks the *r* of futurity written in 6/9 *nti iw=s r dit* ⌜*mwt*⌝[*=f*], and should probably be translated as past (cf. the past negative relative clause in 6/26).

ι. After the initial plea to Isis to listen, the first portion of the woman's speech is clearly intended to establish her worthiness as a petitioner by drawing attention to her own or her mother's faithfulness and abnegation in temple service, though the details are often obscure. The alternative reading *ink* [*tꜣ*] ⌜*šr.t*⌝ *n tꜣi* ⌜*s-ḥm.t*⌝, 'I am the daughter of this woman', is equally tenable with 'I am a woman of this . . .' (see p. 78, n. *bg*). The version of the text underlying the very tentative translation that follows is: ⌜*nti*⌝ *spr*(?) *n pꜣi ntr*⌜*.ṯ*⌝ *nti ḥs r pꜣ* . [. . . . .] *r-bw-ir=s swr nti ꜥr nwy.w n* ⌜*ḥb*(?)⌝ *r-bw-ir=s wnm nti ḥwy mnš.w r ntr.ṯ iw* ⌜*ꜥ.wy=s*⌝ [. . . .] (the grave uncertainties over the readings and meanings of *spr*, *ntr.t*, *nwy.w* and the final groups are discussed on p. 78, nn. *bh–bm*): 'who prays/prayed to this divinity, who sings/sang at the [day of festival?] without drinking, who raises/raised the festival standards without eating, who casts/cast clothes on the divinity, her arms being [weary]'. The tense is presumably present or present perfect if she is speaking of herself, past if she is speaking of her mother.

κ. The gnomic opening words of the woman's appeal on behalf of 'the dying man' should serve to excuse the conduct for which he is doomed. The negative Second Tense of Habitude *i-ir-bw-ir=w krp* places emphasis on the circumstantial *iw bw-ir=w ẖtb*[*=w*] (the space available before *rẖ* hardly allows a longer restoration); it is probably therefore for a killing that she wishes to excuse *pꜣ mwt.ṯ*. Though strictly the passage is ambiguous, it seems more probable that *iw bw-ir=w ẖdb*[*=w*] should mean 'without their (sc. the gods) killing them (sc. men)' than vice versa: in that case, it is probably such a divine killing of a human in which 'the dying man' has been involved, a view perhaps strengthened by what follows.

λ. Apart from its superiority palaeographically, the reading *šr* fits the context better than the alternative *tꜣ* (p. 78, n. *bq*), because it may be taken as the antecedent for the masc. object pronoun in *m-ir šlf=f*. If this is accepted, then Isis is asked not to disgrace 'a youth who has said concerning a poor man "I will take vengeance (or "the vengeance of Isis", see p. 79, n. *bt*) upon him"'. As the woman's plea is for 'the dying man', 'the youth' must surely be identified with him. The taking vengeance is clearly the crime for which he is to suffer death, and in view of what has been said above (n. *κ* above) of the probability of this being a divine killing of a mortal, *rmt ḫm* here may perhaps mean 'mortal man' rather than 'little/poor man'; likewise, 'the youth', if he is divine, might conceivably be Horus (note that in 6/9 a character has been described as 'the falcon'). It is uncertain whether there is room in the lacuna after *ḫtb*[*=w*] to read *iw=t rḫ* rather than simply the imperative *rḫ*; it improves the sense if the woman says to Isis 'you know the youth, etc.'—which certainly she would, were he Horus. Probably there is room.

μ. The following passage is the most obscure in the text, abounding in uncertainties of reading (see pp. 79–80 nn. *bu–cd*) and problems of translation and interpretation, of which the principal are as follows:

i. The doubt concerning the reading at the end of 6/12 (p. 79, n. *bu*) and at the beginning of 6/13 (p. 79, n. *bv*) leaves it uncertain whether these passages belong together, but as there can hardly be space for a main verb in the lacuna, they probably do so. If so, whatever the correct restoration, the words *pꜣ si* . [. .] *twt* suggest that it is to satisfy a (divine?) image that Isis intends to kill and disgrace 'the dying man'; our suggested reading *m-ir šlf=f r-dbꜣ* ⌜*tꜣi*⌝ [*kbꜥ*] ⌜*r-dbꜣ*⌝ *si* [*n*] *twt*, 'Do not disgrace him because of vengeance on behalf of a statue', is in line with this.

ii. The slight doubt whether *ḳ*(*n*)*s=f* is correctly read (p. 79, n. *bw*) makes it uncertain whether a new sentence begins here; if, for instance, (*n*) *ḳ*(*n*)*s*, 'by violence', is read, it must be attached to the previous sentence. If *ḳ*(*n*)*s=f* is accepted, there remains an uncertainty whether this *sdm=f* form marks the resumption of the main narrative and therefore the end of the woman's speech to Isis, or whether it introduces an explanatory narrative passage within her plea to Isis. It is also not certain to whom the subject of *ḳ*(*n*)*s=f* should refer, though the fact that 'the dying man's' death is still in the future while the crime for which he is to die is in the past favours the idea that he is the subject of *ḳ*(*n*)*s=f*, more especially if this is correctly interpreted to mean 'he slew'.

iii. *ḳ*(*n*)*s=f* ⌜*Pꜣ*(*-n*)(?)⌝ *tꜣ šfꜣ n nꜣi=f iwiw.w*: even if the dubious reading *Pꜣ*(*-n*) is accepted (p. 79, n. *bx*), there are two sets of alternatives here. *n* may be a partitive genitive; then ⌜*Pꜣ*(*-n*)⌝ *tꜣ šfꜣ* is either a proper name or the description of one of 'his dogs'. Or *n* may stand for the old preposition *m* in its instrumental use: 'He slew(?) ⌜*Pꜣ*(*-n*)⌝ *tꜣ šfꜣ* by means of his dogs'; then *Pꜣ*(*-n*) *tꜣ šfꜣ* is presumably the proper name of the man whom he slew. Evidently, the decision between them is bound up with the identity of the subject of *ḳ*(*n*)*s=f* and the way in which the story is reconstructed (see p. 104, d).

iv. The uncertainty of reading before *ym* or *ym.w* (p. 80, n. *by*) and the following lacuna of 3–4 groups break the connection with what precedes; the simplest approach seems to be to regard *ḥr pꜣ*/*nꜣ ym*(*.w*), 'upon the lake(s)', as giving the scene of the crime, to restore a place-name in the lacuna, and reading *nti wꜣy* to translate 'upon the lake(s) of . . . which are far from their channels of balm of potency against any killing'. If the trace before *wꜣy* is interpreted as *r* rather than *nti*, there is a somewhat awkward future tense to be accounted for: 'he/they(?) will be far from, etc.'. *tꜣi=w ḥny* 'their channel' ('their vessel' seems to be ruled out by the det.) should strictly refer back to *nꜣi=f iwiw.w*, 'his dogs', but might perhaps have a vaguer reference. There is again a doubt whether the *n* after *ḥny* should be taken as a genitive or as a preposition of instrument; the latter, however, only seems possible if *ḳs=f* is differently interpreted, e.g. as *ḳ*(*r*)*s=f*: 'he embalmed the most renowned of his dogs . . . with balm of potency against any killing'. Aside from the inappropriate determinatives of *ḳs*, this appears to leave the clause '[which] are far from their channels' with little point, and we would reject it, though with some hesitation.

v. *pꜣ wdb ḥꜥ r-ḥri*(?): *ḥꜥ* must be Stative continuing the narrative, though whether within the woman's speech or not remains doubtful. The mention of *ḥny*, 'channel', perhaps favours the interpretation of *pꜣ wdb*, 'The Turner' as the inundation (p. 80, n. *cb*).

vi. The simplest way of translating the damaged and uncertain words at the beginning of 6/14 *snḥ*(?) *ḥri-sꜥ*(?) *pꜣ nhr sn-th.ṯ* is as a verbal sentence introduced by a *sdm=f* form continuing the past narrative: 'The Master of the Amulet(?) bound the monster of doom'. *nhr* seems to be used as a description of Seth himself or his creatures; whether there is here a reference to *pꜣ ḥmꜣr*, 'the death-bird', or to some other creature is doubtful.

vi. *r*(?) *ḥḳ=f in=f*: 'to capture him and bring him' would surely require the writing *in.ṯ=f*. It is preferable to disregard the palimpsest *r* (p. 80, n. *cd*) and to interpret as two *sdm=f* forms with suppressed objects: 'He captured, he brought back' (though *r-ḥḳ=f* might be a relative form, *in=f* without prefixed *r* cannot be so). Unfortunately, this leaves it uncertain whether it is the *ḥri-sꜥ* who captured and brought back 'the monster of doom', or whether it is the 'monster of doom' who captured and brought back 'the dying man'. The fact that it is presumably 'the dying man' who is speaking in 6/15, and may therefore be the subject of the next phrase (n. *ν* below) seems to us to favour the latter. For further discussion of the whole context, see pp. 101–6.

ν. As the speech in 6/15 begins without any introduction, it is possible that the verb in this sentence provided it; 'he called out to' or 'he greeted', for instance (p. 80, n. *ce*). If, however, this sentence belongs to an 'external story' (see p. 106), some other restoration may be required.

ξ. The phrase 'I am going to die' shows that 'the dying man' is speaking here. The decision whether to take *tꜣi͗(=y) mwt ꞽIst*, 'my mother Isis', as a vocative or in apposition to *ḥꜣ.ṯ=s* (p. 81, n. *ch*) is necessarily bound up with the explanation adopted for the alternation of 2nd and 3rd pers. sing. fem. pronouns in this passage (p. 81, n. *cl*). If *tꜣi͗(=y) mwt ꞽIst* is vocative, then the pronouns in *nꜣi͗=t sṯny(.w)* and *nꜣi͗=t sḏy.w sr.w* must refer to Isis in the second person, while the 3rd pers. pronouns in *ḥꜣ.ṯ=s* and *ꜥm=s* must refer to someone else. Yet in 6/16–17 'O you (fem.) who are at the image of Isis, the spell of Isis is upon you (fem.); you (fem.) have brought to me Isis in her own flesh', the speaker is clearly addressing some woman other than Isis in the second person, most probably the same woman who pleaded at the shrine of Isis in 6/9–14. It is thus clearly better to take *tꜣi͗(=y) mwt ꞽIst*, 'my mother Isis', as in apposition to the suffix pronoun of *tw=y ḥꜣ.ṯ=s*, 'I am before her', and to refer back the 3rd pers. fem. sing. pronouns to her, and the 2nd pers. sing. fem. pronouns to the woman. This is in consonance with 6/9, where it is the presence of Isis that is regarded by the woman as fatal to *pꜣ mwt.ṯ*, 'the dying man'. Whether the words 'your counsels, there is no wisdom in them; your prophetic utterances they have not come to pass yet' (perhaps restore *n tꜣi͗ [ḥṯy]* 'at this time', p. 81, n. *co*) form the burden of 'these complaints' of which he will inform Isis is not certain, but seems probable. It is this passage that makes it clear that 'the dying man' regards Isis as his mother, and constitutes the principal evidence that he might be 'Horus' in some guise; though the term *mwt* is not necessarily to be taken in such a context as implying physical kinship. On the advantages and difficulties of this view, see pp. 103 f., 107 f.

ο. For the difficulties of reading see p. 81, nn. *cp*–*cs*. The principal dilemma in interpreting the passage is to know whether it constitutes a continuation of 'the dying man's' speech or whether it is an interpolated piece of narrative inserted in explanation of his words. If it is the former, then the 3rd pers. sing. fem. pronouns in *n=s*, *i͗r=s*, and *di͗=s gm=w* should refer to Isis (p. 81, n. *cl*; n. *ξ* above). This would mean that what the Five Gods had told Isis had been of no avail, because they had not decided (or revealed) it; but that by consulting with them (adopting the restoration *n pꜣ 5 ntr.w* proposed on p. 81, n. *cr*) she had allowed them to discover what had happened to the lord of the image. It appears unlikely that Isis, the great magician, should find it necessary to consult the Five Gods, or had given them information. The passage seems to have much more point if it is parenthetical narrative explaining why the woman's counsels are foolish and her prophecies have not come to pass; not only has what they told her not been decided (or revealed), but in consulting them she has betrayed the whereabouts of the lord of the image (doubts about the precise meaning of *i͗r-wpy* and *wpy* in the context do not affect this much). If this manner of understanding the passage is correct, the phrase *pꜣ nb sšm*, which might equally well mean 'the owner of the image' in the sense of its possessor or 'the lord of the image' in the sense of the being portrayed by it, could well refer to 'the dying man' himself. This would be consonant with 6/30–1 if, as suspected, *pꜣ nb sšm* is to be restored there (see p. 103).

π. The reasons for preferring the reading *ꜥḥꜥ* to *st* are given on p. 82, n. *ct*, and for preferring 'you (fem.) who are at the image of Isis' to 'you (fem.) who are in the form(?) of Isis' on p. 82, n. *cy*. It is to be noted that in 6/10 ff. the woman was at the chapel (*kꜣ*) addressing the image of Isis.

ρ. If the restoration suggested on p. 82, n. *cw* and p. 86, n. *er* is accepted, translate 'After(?) an hour of conversation, I shall come to die'. This is consonant with 6/9, and seems a suitable introduction to the aphorism concerning death. The unfortunate uncertainty of reading at the end of 6/17 leaves doubt whether the woman physically 'left the image of Isis and went out of the chapel (*kꜣ*) and worshipped', as one might expect from the fact that she had gone to the chapel (*kꜣ*) to address Isis (6/10). However, even if *šm=s r* is thought a tenable reading (p. 82, n. *cz*), it could hardly mean 'went out of' but only 'went into', the reverse of what is required in view of 6/10. The alternative reading 'she placed the image outside this chapel, she worshipped' is perhaps preferable, especially as it explains how the image could be worshipped outside the chapel; granted this translation, the image was a portable one.

σ. The difficulty of deciding the identity of the

persons represented by the plural suffix pronouns in 6/17–19 has been discussed on p. 82, n. *db*. These persons are present throughout the account of the arrival of the scarab-beetle and his transformation into Imḥotep, immediately following which comes *ḫr=s n(=i)*, 'so she told me'; as suggested on p. 84, n. *do*, the whole of the narrative section as far back as *ꜣsḳ=w*, 'they tarried', should logically be included in what 'she told me'. Yet this narrative *sdm=f* form *ꜣsḳ=w* carries on from *ḫꜣꜥ=s*, which must surely recommence the narrative after 'the dying man's' speech. So this should also be included, and the 'me' to whom she told it should either be 'the dying man' who has just finished speaking, or a character in an 'external story' to whom all the events on this page are being told. This could conceivably be the significant factor in the paragraphing of the text: see further below, p. 106. These considerations may suggest that the 3rd pers. plur. suffixes refer to persons mentioned earlier in the text, but not on this page. If the restorations on p. 83, nn. *dc–df*, are accepted, 'they tarried while doing these things', and did not look up or out, but when a noise or shadow or other manifestation occurred within their shrines they saw the winged beetle descending. This suggests that 'they' are denizens of the shrines, perhaps priests or temple-servants, and that the things they are doing relate to the execution of the goddess's instructions or the carrying-out of her cult.

τ. If the readings and restorations tentatively suggested on p. 83, nn. *dg–dm*, are correct, then when the beetle landed the onlookers' gaze was veiled; it was only when he awoke that their eyes saw and they recognized Imḥotep; and even then he withdrew and turned himself away, their sight being once more veiled, so that he could change into his normal form of a man. This behaviour certainly recalls the character, probably divine, in 6/1, of whom it is said that 'he is unable to make/change his form before the multitude', and the two may be identical (see p. 105). Evidently, the cube of stone upon which Imḥotep sat represents the block-throne upon which he is regularly shown in statues and bronze statuettes. Possibly his flesh was said to have been of a fair colour; the reason for 'his brow being angry' (if correctly read, see p. 83, n. *dm*) is perhaps Isis's apparent victory, see 6/22.

υ. For the problems raised by the presence of *ḫr=s n(=i)* 'so she said to me', here, see p. 84, n. *do*, n. *σ* above, and p. 106.

φ. 'The one who was sick' (fem.) has not been mentioned before (unless indeed the broken signs at the beginning of 6/6 be thus restored, see p. 75, n. *af*). However, the fact that the only woman we know to have been present when the beetle landed is the woman addressed 6/15–17, whom we have identified with the female supplicant at the chapel in 6/9–14, tells strongly in favour of her being 'the one who was sick'. Perhaps slightly awkward is the fact that the immediately preceding suffix of *ḫr=s n(=i)* presumably refers to the same woman; but the use of that phrase is often more or less parenthetical.

χ. The very slight uncertainty as to whether *=f* should be read after *nḥm.ṯ* in 6/20 on palaeographical grounds (p. 84, n. *dr*), should perhaps be resolved by the consideration that it is 'the dying man' who is to be carried off by a monster, *pꜣ ḥmꜣr*; the woman's own death, apparently presaged in 6/21 ff., presumably comes about through her sickness and Isis's words (see p. 86, n. *er*). Nevertheless, the monster described by the woman can hardly be a *ḥmꜣr*, if that creature has been correctly identified as an owl (*JEA* 61 (1975), 198), which is by no means certain; it may perhaps correspond with *pꜣ nhr n sn-th.ṯ* in 6/14 (p. 80, n. *cc*). The description '⸢the⸣ [. . . . .] with the face of . . . .' may describe a composite creature such as a gryphon or sphinx, or perhaps a creature of the underworld (p. 84, n. *dr*), but this leaves open too many possibilities in face of the uncertainty in reading.

ψ. Granted that the reading *pꜣi(=y) smt* is preferred to *pꜣi=f smt* (argued on p. 84, n. *du*), then the woman turns to her own fate here; having first asked Imḥotep about the fate of 'the dying man', she then asks him whether he has set his hand against Isis, who has sealed her own fate. This has the advantage of explaining the reference to the disposition of her property later in 6/21, and of making it possible for *nti mnḳ nꜣi mdwt n ḏd* in 6/20–1 to refer to the same event as *mnḳ=s nꜣ mdwt n ḏd i-[ir . . . . .]* in 6/25 (see p. 86, n. *er*).

ω. The words 'The West, I have set it in [my] heart' confirm that the woman is talking of her own desire for death; the restoration seems certain in view of 'my property' and 'another of my sort'. The latter character seems likely to be 'the girl' (*tꜣ ḫr.t*) mentioned in 6/26–31, since she is in all probability this woman's daughter (see p. 101 f.). It is this which justifies the tentative reading 'I have placed her beside me(?)', suggested on p. 85, *n. dy* for the broken phrase at the end of 6/22.

αα. For the restorations, see p. 85, nn. *dz–eb*. The reference to 'Osiris, ⸢King of Eternity⸣' gains point if he is in fact 'the god' (*pꜣ nṯr*) mentioned in 6/23 who has decreed what is to happen to 'the one who has come to die'. ⌜*mdw*⌝ [*n*] ⌜*ḥꜣt.ṱ=k*⌝, if correctly restored, is probably to be compared with the phrase *md ỉrm ḥꜣt.ṱ=k*, which means 'to speak with your heart' in the sense of 'to worry' (*DG*, 290 under 289. 2). Whether *nꜣ rḫ.w n Ḏḥwt* means 'the knowledgeable/learned ones of Thoth' or 'the ones who are acquainted with Thoth' is perhaps doubtful, though either would apply to Imḥotep.

αβ. Restore probably 'Seek out [for me] what the god has caused to happen to him who has come to death/to die': presumably 'the god' must be one concerned with the judgement of the dead, i.e. quite probably Osiris, see n. *αα* above. As Coptic constructs ⲣ̄ϩⲏⲧϥ with ⲛⲥⲁ (Crum, *CD*, 715b) 'to repent after', it is probable that *m-sꜣ* is so used rather than temporally here: though theoretically the subject of *ỉr=f ḥꜣt.ṱ=f* might be *nṯr*, it seems better to construe 'so as not to let him pine after . . .', referring to 'the dying man'.

αγ. For examples of *ỉn-mwt* referring to a dead man as a ghost or malignant influence, see Sir H. Thompson in *JEA* 26 (1940), 76. This meaning seems to fit better with what follows than 'corpse'.

αδ. For the restorations suggested, see p. 86, nn. *el-eq*. 'The place of punishment' is presumably where the dead stay between death and justification before Osiris. *tꜣỉ ẖr.t* should presumably refer to the same girl as *tꜣ ẖr.t* in 6/26, in all probability the daughter of the woman who is speaking (see p. 101 f.). Though textually far from secure, the restoration *hb=k m-sꜣ tꜣỉ ẖr.t*, 'May you send for this girl', seems to fit the context well (cf. 7/2). For the speculative restoration 'before the day of my death', see p. 86, n. *eq*.

αε. If *mnḳ=s nꜣ mdwt n ḏd ỉ*[*-ỉr* . . . . .] refers back to 6/20–1 (see p. 86, n. *er*), then 'she completed the words of prophecy which (Isis?) spoke' should mean that the woman dies. The 3rd pers. masc. subject of [*ỉ-*]*ỉr=f nw* is not certainly identifiable. If he is to be identified with the male addressed in the woman's speech, then he is Imḥotep, but this is far from certain. He might be 'the dying man'; and, if he is presumed to be the same as the subject of the last sentence in the previous paragraph 'He . . . the heaven, the earth and the underworld' (6/14), probably is so. On the other hand, he could conceivably be a character in an 'external story' (see p. 106). The meaning of *r pꜣ ỉtn* is also not altogether clear, but as 'the girl' in the next paragraph is presumably on earth 'looked at the earth' seems best.

αζ. For the reading, see p. 87, n. *et*. If the passage is connected with what precedes, 'the girl' (*tꜣ ẖr.t*; restoration highly probable) should be the same as *tꜣỉ ẖr.t* in 6/24 above. 'The god' with whom she speaks cannot be certainly identified. However, the last god to take part in the action was Imḥotep, and there are two passages which may suggest that he is 'the god'. The first is the girl's question 'What is this mood which you are in?', which recalls the woman's words in 6/22, 'Are you communing with your own heart because you have not been victorious against Isis?', and also the doubtful phrase 'his brow was angry' in 6/20. The second is the fact that 'the god' claims in 6/30 to have visited Osiris about Isis; this looks as though he may have reacted to the taunt of the woman that he has not acted against Isis (6/20), suggesting that he is the same god.

αη. The girl asks whether the god's mood is about 'your maidservant' (*tꜣỉ=k bꜣk.t*); in Egyptian, this would be a normal enough way for her to refer to herself in speaking to a god. This may well be so here, though there is at least the possibility that it refers to 'the woman who is sick' of 6/20–6. If this were so, the rather obscure clause 'to whom the morning has not brought the girl-child' (*tꜣ ḥm.t*) (p. 87, n. *ev*) might perhaps be connected with 6/10 *tꜣ rpy ꜣs.t ntỉ ỉw=s dỉt šm=s r dỉt ms*, 'the Lady Isis who caused her (sc. the woman) to go to give birth', for then *tꜣ ḥm.t* might refer to this unborn(?) progeny. However, the girl then asks 'that she may cause there to be made a Sokar-festival for him' etc., and is rebuked for repeating a blasphemy against Isis uttered previously by the woman (6/27–9). So the girl should be speaking of herself here, and *mtw=s* in 6/26 must refer back to *tꜣỉ=k bꜣk.t*, meaning herself. The following relative clause concerning *tꜣ ḥm.t* may have received its explanation elsewhere in the text.

αθ. 'The messenger' (*pꜣ ꜣpwṱ*) is clear, but to whom it refers is uncertain; possibly the short unread group at the end of 6/26 made this clear. It seems quite likely that this passage should be associated with 7/2 '(whom) you (fem.) sent after me'; if, as seems possible (p. 100, n. *αρ*), that passage is spoken by 'the dying man', it may be that here we should restore *pꜣ ꜣpwṱ* [*mtw=f*], 'the messenger belonging to him', referring to 'the dying man', as does *n=f* in the next clause.

αι. The Sokar festival in the Late Period, at least if celebrated for an individual, is a funerary rite (for a recent treatment of the festival as a whole, see G. A.

Gaballa and K. A. Kitchen in *Orientalia*, 38 (1969), 1 ff.). Thus 'the songs of the girl who is in (the role of) Isis' should be a reference to 'the festival songs of Isis and Nephthys', regularly recited by the 'Two Kites' at funerals. This means that there is probably no direct relationship between the phrase *tꜣ nti n ꞽst* in 6/27 and *tꜣ nti n sšm n ꞽst* in 6/16 (see p. 82, n. *ct*).

ακ. For readings and interpretation see p. 87, nn. *ez–fc*. The god warns that in asking that she may perform funerary obsequies for the 'dying one', the girl is repeating a blasphemy against Isis made by the woman and renounced for her sake; the sentence beginning *ḫpr ḏd=s* is a parenthetical narrative explanation giving the woman's words. When these were originally spoken is unclear.

αλ. The girl's reply to the god (for readings and restorations see p. 88, nn. *fe–ff*) appears to repeat the blasphemy, for it is to the effect that the woman is unlikely to be able to carry out the funerary rites because she will be dead, and suggests that there is nothing to prevent her herself seeking the 'dying one' after her mother's death. This identifies 'the girl' with virtual certainty as daughter of 'the woman' (see p. 101 f.), and also reveals that she is unaware that the 'dying one' (and probably also her mother, see p. 86, n. *er*) are already dead.

In spite of the case for the reading *pr-iꜣb*(*ṯ*) (p. 88, n. *fh*), it is difficult to believe that the god was in the east and not the west, for this was, presumably, where the death-bird brought the 'dying one'. The presence of *sšm* at the beginning of 6/31 may suggest (p. 89, n. *fm*) the restoration of [*pꜣ nb*] *sšm* from 6/16, but unfortunately the lacuna at the end of 6/30 renders it obscure whether the death-bird actually carried off the Lord of the Image (in which case this expression must be identified with the 'dying one'), or whether it was acting under his instructions or otherwise in connection with him.

αμ. On the readings and interpretations adopted see pp. 88–9, notes *fh–fj*. The gist of the passage appears to be that the youth who has died has been more ferociously treated than any normal sacrificial bull-calf. The reason is perhaps given in the words 'the youth whom he has called to the chapel of the fire-altar(?) (see p. 89, n. *fo*) at the high wrath of Sakhmis', if this is the doom to which the youth has been fated. In strict grammar the subject of *ꜥš=f* should refer back to *pꜣ ḥmꜣr*. But the role of the death-bird seems to be that of agent rather than initiator, and it is possible that, if *pꜣ nb sšm* is to be restored in 6/30–1 and is not to be identified with the victim, the reference is to that phrase.

αν. For the conceivable, but very uncertain, restoration *n pꜣ ḫr*, 'to the youth', see p. 89, n. *fq*. If correct, it would imply that 'the girl' was directly responsible for the youth's being burnt on the altar(?)—perhaps because of her repetition of the blasphemy against Isis of which the god warned her (6/27–8).

αξ. Col. 7 of the text cannot begin a new paragraph, since an auxiliary verb is required at the end of 6/31, but a space may have preceded that verb.

αο. If (*i-ir=f*) *nw r* ..... is parallel with similar phrases in 6/14, 25 there may have been a gap in the text before it, and the subject of the sentence may perhaps belong to an 'exterior story' (see p. 106). Otherwise it seems logical to assume that the dead 'youth' is the subject. The deity may perhaps be an underworld or night-sky god, for in 6/14, 25 it is respectively 'the heaven, the earth and the underworld' and 'the ground' that are looked at, not a deity, so, if these parallels are in point, he may be the deity of some part of the universe. If the dead 'youth' is the subject, an underworld deity seems probable. For the difficulties of reading, see p. 89, n. *fr*.

απ. If the words 'you (fem.) have sent after me' refer back to 6/26–7, as seems plausible, then whoever is speaking is talking to 'the girl' (or, less probably, 'the woman', see p. 99, n. *αη*). It would further follow that the speaker in 7/2 was the same god as appears in 6/26, since there 'the girl' says of herself 'she is causing the messenger . . . to hasten to come after you', i.e. the god. It is also interesting, though not directly relevant, that if *hb=k m-sꜣ tꜣi ḫrt* has been correctly restored in 6/24 (see p. 86, n. *en*), then the woman is there urging Imhotep (probably identical with 'the god' in 6/26) with the words 'May you send after the girl'. However, these connections are not assured, and may be contradicted by what follows (n. *αρ* below).

αρ. If *nꜣi=k fꜣi.w* is correctly read in 7/3 (see p. 90, n. *ft*), then the speaker has changed and 'the girl' (or 'the woman', see n. *απ*) is now speaking. If the words 'when I had not (yet) died' in 7/4 are part of the same speech, then it should presumably be the woman (*contra* p. 99, n. *αη*). However, it is perfectly possible that the speaker has changed again between 7/3 and 7/4, and the male is now speaking. If so, he is likely to be the dead 'youth', and the inference suggested in n. *απ* above, that 'the girl' is speaking with 'the god' of 6/26, becomes suspect.

aσ. It is tempting to connect the 'statue at *pr-nfr*' in 7/5 with 'the statue' mentioned in connection with Isis's vengeance in 6/13 (p. 79, n. *bv*), but this is pure speculation in the state of the text. While Pernefer was the name of the port of Memphis (see Glanville in *ZÄS* 68 (1932), 28 ff.), in the context of the youth's death, it is more likely to have its funerary meaning 'embalming-place' here (*DG*, 133. 6). If so, 'the statue of the embalming-place' is likely to be the funerary statue upon which the rite of 'Opening the Mouth' was performed during the embalming ceremonies.

aτ. The 'Hall' mentioned here may conceivably be the 'Hall of Two Truths', where the judgement of the dead before Osiris took place.

aυ. It seems possible that the narrative resumed with the *sdm=f* form *sny=f* in 7/4 referring to the dead 'youth'. Perhaps he passed the gate of the underworld, the proper rites were performed in the embalming-place on his funerary statue, he reached the judgement-hall, and looked at the assessors; but any such reconstruction is purely speculative.

DISCUSSION

1. The Characters

a. '*She who is sick*' and '*the girl*'

'She who is sick' (*tꜣ nti šny*) is first specified in this way in 6/20 where she speaks to Imḥotep immediately after he has landed as a winged-beetle. After asking if a monster has carried off 'the dying man', she says: 'Have you set your hand against Isis, who is fulfilling/has fulfilled these words spoken concerning a killing happening to one of my sort? The West, I have set it in (my) heart [. . . . .]. My money(?) and my property has passed on to one of my sort and I have placed her(?) ⸢by my side⸣.' These words show clearly that she expects immediate death, and has made provision by passing on property to her successor, whose identity is given by the final words of her speech (6/24) '[May you send] for this girl, and let her give thanks to you, and grant to her the way of life. Say it to me now before the day of my death(?)' Then after an hour of conversation with Imḥotep she fulfils the words 'concerning death happening to one of my sort', spoken by someone who on the evidence of 6/20 should be Isis, and presumably dies.

In the next paragraph (6/26 ff.) 'the girl' speaks with 'the god' (probably Imḥotep again) and asks to be allowed to have a funerary Sokar-festival and lamentations provided for 'the dying man', now dead. The god tells her that in saying this she is uttering the same blasphemy against Isis which her predecessor had spoken and desisted from for her sake. But the girl replies (6/28–9): 'As to the Sokar-festival of which she spoke, she does not know what she is doing; will she be able to do it even after the loss of (her) life? Can I not search after him after/without my mother?' This passage makes it quite clear that 'the girl' is not only the heiress but also the daughter of 'the woman who is sick'.

There is unfortunately only inferential evidence to show which of these women is concerned in the passages 6/1–8, 9–14, 15–20. If the words *tꜣ nti n sšm n ꜣIst* in 6/16 are correctly translated 'you (fem.) who are at the image of Isis' (p. 82, n. *ct*), then the woman there addressed should be the same as the woman who went to the chapel (*kꜣ*) in 6/10 to supplicate Isis on behalf of 'the dying man'. She does this because the words spoken early in 6/9 cause her to turn(?) and chill with terror, because Isis has been left with 'the dying man'. She then [boards] the boat, returns from the shrines (? restoring *swt*, p. 77, n. *ba*), and comes to her chamber weeping exceedingly. This suggests that she is the same woman who has been building a sanctuary (*knḥy*) for a god in 6/1–8. This is also convenient because it allows consecution between the events of 6/1–8 and 6/9–14; there is probably little room for the introduction of a new character at the beginning of 6/9, and the woman who has been promised by the god in 6/8 that 'the evil death-bird(?)

(*ḥmꜣr*) will go away' is quite likely to be the same who figures there. A clue to the identity of this woman seems to be held in the god's words in 6/7: '[. . . . . . is more victorious] than any valiant god. Do not ⌜. . . . . .⌝ [lest] a son or daughter cause you to know extinction again'; for this might well be a forewarning of the woman's death in 6/25, caused by the blasphemy against Isis referred to in 6/28. If these inferences are correct, then it is the mother who is present throughout 6/1–20; and she must be identified with *tꜣ nti̓ šny* in 6/20. This is a view also argued on p. 84, n. *dp*, on the grounds that she is the only woman, present, so far as we know, when Imḥotep lands. Just possibly *tꜣ nti̓ šny* was written in 6/6, but the traces may be read otherwise.

Unfortunately, another possible chain of inferences may conflict with this. In 6/10 the text reads: 'she spoke with the Lady Isis who had caused her to go to give birth'; in 6/26 'the girl' says to the god: 'What is this mood which you are in because of your maidservant, to whom the morning has not yet brought the girl-child (*tꜣ ẖm.t*)?' These references to a prospective birth might suggest that the same woman is involved in both instances. In 6/26 it is highly probable that 'the girl' refers to herself by the not uncommon locution *tꜣi̓=k bꜣk.t*, 'your maidservant', because it seems clear that she is referring to herself in the third person (*mtw=s*) when she expresses the wish to carry out funerary rites for 'the dying man' (p. 87, n. *fc*). If then the woman in 6/10, 26 were the same, then 'the girl' would be the one who beseeches Isis, and by implication built the sanctuary in 6/1–8; this might be held to explain the otherwise obscure reference to 'her ⌜great?⌝ mother of/in the mountains' in 6/6.

If the opposing views are balanced against one another, the evidence for the mother's being present in 6/1–15 appears stronger, and the countervailing evidence easier to explain away. In speaking of 'the Lady Isis who caused her to go to give birth', she might be talking of the birth of her daughter 'the girl' in the past, and the reference to 'her great? mother' in 6/6 is in lacuna and insufficient to build on. On this view, 'I am a woman of this [. . . .]' should probably be read in 6/11; but if the daughter is present, read 'I am the daughter of this ⌜woman⌝', see see p. 78, n. *bg*).

b. '*The dying man*', '*the youth*', *and* '*the lord of the image*'

In 6/8 a god promises the woman that 'the death-bird (*ḥmꜣr*) who is evil will go away'. In 6/9 she discovers that Isis has been left alone with 'the dying man' whom she will cause to die, and goes to supplicate the goddess on his behalf. (Whether *pꜣ mwt.ṯ* should be translated 'the man doomed to die', 'the dying man', or 'the (virtually) dead man' is not certain, but 6/15 shows that he is not yet dead). In her appeal she says: 'Isis, do not shame him because of . . .', evidently referring to 'the dying man'. But the immediate antecedent of 'him' must be found in the preceding sentence: '[you?] know the youth (*šr*, reading not quite certain, see p. 78, n. *bq*) who has said concerning a poor man: "I will take vengeance upon him"' (6/12). So 'the dying man' must be identified, it seems, either with 'the youth' or 'the poor man'. In 6/30–1, after 'the girl' has been warned by the god for repeating the woman's blasphemy against Isis by asking for a ritual funeral for 'the dying man', she asks the god where he has been. The god replies that he has been in the west (or east, see p. 88, n. *fh*, p. 100, n. *αλ*) seeing Osiris about Isis, and says that 'the death-bird came . . . *ššm*; he never humiliated (even) a wild bull calf like the youth (*ẖr*) whom he called to his temple-of-flame(?) at the high wrath of Sakhmis'. Clearly, it should be 'the dying man' whom the 'death-bird' brings (cf. also 6/23–4), and he should logically also be the youth who is humiliated. This suggests that he should also be identified with the youth (*šr*) mentioned in 6/12 above.

In the passage just quoted from 6/30–1, the word *sšm*, 'image' seems somewhat out of place on its own, and it has been suggested that it should be restored *pꜣ nb sšm* 'the lord of the image' (p. 89, n. *fm*). If so, a simple way of restoring the passage would be: 'the death-bird came, [having . . . (and) carried off/brought the lord of the] image'. Were this correct, the 'lord of the image' would be identical with the 'youth' (*ẖr*) in the next clause and consequently with 'the dying man'. In 6/16, a narrative passage probably explains why 'the dying man' has said to the woman (6/15): 'your counsels, there is no wisdom in them; your prophetic utterances, they have not come to pass . . .'. The text reads: 'What the Five Gods said to her did not work(?), that is, they did not decide/judge it; she became a confidante of the Five Gods(?) and caused/allowed them to find out what had happened to the lord of the image'. This makes good sense if the gravamen of 'the dying man's' accusation against the woman is that in consulting the Five Gods she foolishly allowed them to discover what had happened to him. If so, 'the dying man' is identical with 'the lord of the image', as suggested on the basis of the restoration of 6/30–1. This is, of course, at best a somewhat speculative inference; and the phrase *pꜣ nb sšm* is itself ambiguous, since it might mean either the human owner of a divine image or perhaps the divine owner represented by the image itself.

c. '*The dying man*', *Horus and the falcon*

Horus is mentioned specifically by name only once in the text as it is preserved. 'She who is sick' is trying to persuade Imḥotep to protect 'the dying man' from the indignities Isis intends him to suffer after death, and flatters and rallies him as he is in a bad mood (p. 83, n. *dm*) (6/22): 'They do not know that you have come to us as Fair-of-face, being among the learned ones of Thoth and being in the hand of the King of Eternity Osiris(?). Are you communing with your heart because you have not been victorious against Isis? Horus is victorious against every valiant god.' This passage should mean that Horus is on the side of Imḥotep and of 'she who is sick' in trying to defeat Isis's intentions. [It could, just possibly, mean that Imḥotep is himself Horus in disguise, since he is capable of changing form (6/18–20; possibly also 6/1)]. The phrase '[. . . . . .] against every valiant god' occurs also in 6/7 where 'Horus is victorious' could be restored.

In 6/15 a character says: 'As to the breath (of life) which is mine, I am before her, my mother Isis, that is to say, I am going to die'. This must be 'the dying man' speaking, since it is already known from 6/9 that his confrontation with Isis will mean his death; and the natural interpretation of the passage is that he regards Isis as his 'mother'. If 'mother' is used of a physical relationship here, then 'the dying man' must presumably be Horus in some form, since no other son of Isis is known to mythology. (It should be noted that to reject the reading *ḥꜣ.ṯ=s* and the apposition with *tꜣi͗=y mwt ꞽst* (pp. 80–1, nn. *cg-ch*) and to take *tꜣi͗=y mwt ꞽst* as a vocative does not change this inference.)

In 6/9 the speech which alerts the woman to the fact that Isis has been left with 'the dying man' may perhaps read either 'May the West honour(?) me, O falcon ⸢beautiful of brow⸣' or 'May the West honour me, the falcon ⸢beautiful of brow⸣' (see p. 76, nn. *at*, *au*). In either case it seems most probable that 'the dying man' is the speaker, since he is the one who is threatened by Isis with death and dishonour after death. If 'the falcon' is in the vocative, then presumably 'the dying man' is a human being who enlists the aid of the falcon; if it is in apposition, he is himself 'the falcon'. It is difficult against the background of Egyptian myths to conceive of the falcon referring to any being other than some form of Horus, and it is accordingly the latter interpretation which accords best with 6/15, where 'the dying man' speaks of Isis as 'my mother'.

Obviously, there are difficulties of a mythological order in regarding 'the dying man' as Horus, notably Isis's enmity to him and the fact that he dies, is carried off by the 'death-bird' and is savaged by it at 'the high wrath of Sakhmis'. The inferences above, or the readings on which they are based, may therefore be wrong, and 'the dying man' a human being; but it will remain probable that Horus is invoked on his behalf against Isis.

d. *Patshefo*(?)

In 6/13, after the woman has appealed to Isis saying: 'you know the youth who has said concerning a poor man: "I will take vengeance upon him". O, Isis, do not disgrace him because of vengeance(?) for the satisfaction of a statue(?)', the text perhaps continues: 'He slew Patshefo(?) of/with his dogs'. The great difficulties of this passage are discussed on pp. 79–80, nn. *bw-cd*, and remain unresolved. But if *ḳ(n)s=f*, 'he slew' is correct, then either its subject or its object should be 'the dying man'. We know from 6/12 that the killing results from gods' being revealed to humans, so one of the parties should be divine. These conditions are most easily met if the subject is 'the dying man', that is, the youth Horus, and Patshefo(?), the object, is 'the poor man'. The dogs will then probably have been Horus's agency in accomplishing the killing (note the common proper name 'The dog of Horus': *pꜣ-ỉwỉw-n-Ḥr*).

e. *Isis*

Isis is first named in 6/9, where the woman 'turned towards her(?) and went cold because Isis was left alone with him, namely the dying man whom she would cause to die' (see p. 77, nn. *av-ay*). From this point onwards her role is entirely consistent, as has been seen. She intends that 'the dying man' should be killed or die, that he should be carried off by the death-bird, and that he should be disgraced in the afterworld; and she eventually succeeds in this. Her motive is apparently revenge (6/12–13). The attempts of the woman to rescue 'the dying man' by obtaining the promise of the god in 6/8 that the death-bird will go away, by direct appeal to Isis herself in 6/10–13, and by asking Imḥotep to intervene in the afterworld in 6/23–4, are disregarded by Isis; and, as we learn from 6/27–9, attempts made by the woman and subsequently by her daughter to arrange a Sokar-festival and even the funerary 'Lamentations of Isis' are considered blasphemous by the goddess. Indeed, it is probably words spoken by Isis which have doomed 'the woman who is sick' to death (6/20–1, 25, see p. 84, n. *dt*, p. 86, n. *er*), and (according to our interpretation of the pronouns, see p. 81, n. *cl*) she has been placed under the spell (*ẖyṭ*) of Isis (6/17). This may well be the reason that she is sick.

'The girl's' repetition of her mother's blasphemy against the goddess (6/27–8) is apparently stated by the god with whom she is speaking to be the reason for the death-bird's maltreatment of 'the youth' (i.e. 'the dying man'), when he says 'you (fem.) have set a flame ⌜to the youth⌝(?)' (see p. 89, n. *fq*). So Isis is opposed throughout to the interests of the woman, her daughter, and 'the dying man', the latter despite the fact that he speaks of her as 'my mother Isis' (6/15). As suggested above, it may be her own son Horus whom she pursues so implacably. Even if it is not, the opposition between Isis and Horus may be implied by the woman's remark to Imḥotep (6/22) 'Are you communing with your own heart because you have not been victorious over Isis? Horus is victorious over any valiant god' (cf. 6/7 '[N is victorious] over any valiant god', p. 76, n. *an*, but see pp. 105, 108). And that Imḥotep himself is potentially opposed to Isis is evident from the woman's remark, 'Have you set your hand against Isis?' (6/20).

Thus, at any rate in the column preserved, Isis is the motive force of the drama, though no speech of hers is in fact preserved. She is addressed by the woman 'O Lady of the Two Lands' (6/11), and in the introduction to that speech (6/10) as 'the Lady Isis' (*tȝ rpy ꞽIst*), which is also the form used in speaking of her by the god in 6/27, 28. Elsewhere (6/9, 12, 15 *tȝꞽ=y mwt ꞽIst*, 17 (twice), 20, 22, 27) she is referred to without a title, though the only examples among these which may be vocatives are 6/12, 15 (see p. 79 n. *bt*, and pp. 81, n. *ch*, 97, n. *ξ*).

f. *Imḥotep and 'the god'*

Imḥotep lands as a winged-scarab beetle (*wʿ ʿȝpy*) in 6/18, changes into his normal human form seated on a block, probably out of the sight of the onlookers who have recognized him, in 6/19, and is done obeisance to in 6/20. He is then addressed by 'the woman who is sick' with the words 'O Imḥotep, my lord', which she follows with her plea to him to intervene on behalf of 'the dying man', and to allow her daughter to preserve her life. He is still present in 6/25 when 'she fulfils the words spoken by [Isis(?)]' (p. 86, n. *er*).

In 6/23 'the woman who is sick' puts her request to Imḥotep: 'Ask [what] the god (*pȝ nṯr*) has caused to happen to the one who has come to die/death'. Here 'the god' cannot refer to Imḥotep, and probably refers to Osiris as judge of the dead. But in 6/26 'the girl' speaks with 'the god' (*pȝ nṯr*). As we have seen, Imḥotep is present conversing with the woman until 6/25 (whether he is the subject of the sentence 'he looked at the ground' is discussed below, p. 106). He is therefore the most likely candidate for *pȝ nṯr* in 6/26, especially as the content of his speech (6/27–8) shows that he is familiar with what 'the woman who is sick' has said. Moreover, *pȝ nṯr*, 'the god' cannot be Osiris here as in 6/23, because he tells 'the girl' in 6/30 that 'I have been in the west/east(?), I have [besought (?)] Osiris about Isis, who was there'. As Imḥotep is quite likely to have visited Osiris to find out his decision concerning 'the dying man' in response to the woman's request, it seems best to accept that *pȝ nṯr* may refer to Imḥotep in 6/26, and to Osiris in 6/23.

In 6/1 there is mention of a being 'who cannot make his form before the multitude'. In view of the circumstances under which the winged-scarab beetle changes form into Imḥotep, with the gaze of the onlookers probably veiled (p. 83, nn. *dg*, *dk*), it seems quite probable that 6/1 refers to the same god. (It may also give rise to speculation that if this god could change form, Imḥotep may not be his true identity, despite the woman's so addressing him in 6/20. However, in the absence of other evidence, the fact that the woman says 'you are among the learned ones/acquaintances of Thoth' is perhaps an indication that Imḥotep is his true identity.) If it is Imḥotep who is mentioned in the speech in 6/1, he may be the god for whom the woman builds the sanctuary (*ḳnḥy*), though this inference is not completely assured. If so, it is he who promises her (6/8) that 'the death-bird will go away'. Her rallying remark to Imḥotep in 6/22: 'Are you communing with your own heart because you have not been victorious against Isis? Horus is victorious over any valiant god!' certainly gains point if it is Imḥotep himself who has said to her in 6/7 '[N is victorious] over any valiant god' (see p. 76, n. *an*, and p. 103). In this phrase the god N is almost certainly hostile to the woman's interests; if Horus is restored as in 6/22, rather than Isis, this alters conclusions about the story (see p. 108).

g. *Osiris*

Osiris is mentioned by name in 6/30, where 'the god' tells 'the girl' that he has been to see him in the west/east about Isis. Probably his name also occurs in 6/22, where the woman says to

Imḥotep: 'you are in the hand of the ⸢King of Eternity⸣, Osiris'; but other reconstructions are possible (p. 85, n. *ea*). It has been suggested in the preceding section that 'the god' whom the woman asks Imḥotep to petition about the fate of 'the dying man' in 6/23 is Osiris. If so, his role is probably his normal one of judge of the dead, and it is in this capacity that 'the god' (i.e. Imḥotep) consults him in 6/30.

h. *Who tells the story and to whom is it told?*

There are possible indications in the text that the events are related within the framework of an 'external story', a device common in Egyptian literature (e.g. Pap. Westcar, 1 Kh., and the majority of didactic and wisdom texts). The most direct of these is the phrase *ḫr=s n(=i)*, 'so she told me', in 6/20. It comes at the end of the narrative of Imḥotep's landing as a winged-beetle, and what is narrated should go back at least to the *sdm=f* form *ḫ3ʿ=s* in 6/17, where the woman leaves the image of Isis after hearing 'the dying man's' final speech (p. 84, n. *do*). Almost certainly therefore the woman is speaking, and telling the narrator of events he or she did not witness. Who this narrator is is a problem; the only person who speaks in the first person earlier in this paragraph is 'the dying man' and his speech definitely ends at *ḫ3ʿ=s* in 6/17. While it is possible (see p. 84, n. *do*) that he acted in the 'external story' as narrator of events leading up to and including his own death, it is equally possible that the narrator is some other person, perhaps not named or mentioned in this column at all.

The second type of indication of an 'external story' arises from the phrases 'he . . . the sky, the earth, the underworld' in 6/14 at the end of the second paragraph of the column, and 'he looked at the ground' in 6/25 at the end of the third paragraph. These phrases seem to be somewhat divorced from the immediately preceding and following action; in 6/14 this is emphasized by there being a perceptible space deliberately left before the phrase, and the same may well have been true in 6/25, where there is a lacuna (see p. 86, n. *er*). In 6/14, if normal rules of syntax apply, the subject of the phrase should refer back to one of the entities in the obscure passage which precedes, most probably 'the dying man' himself or the 'Master of the Amulet(?)', less probably 'the monster of doom' (see p. 80, nn. *cc-ce*). In 6/25, the phrase immediately follows the conversation between 'the woman who is sick' and Imḥotep, and in strict syntax the only available antecedent for the subject of the phrase 'he looked at the ground' is Imḥotep. Thus it is not possible for the subject of these two phrases to be the same, as their content and position rather suggests they should be, unless they are considered to be bracketed off from the rest of the narrative, and to refer to a character in an 'external story', who is witnessing the events described. If so, there is of course no certain indication of who this is; the otherwise mysterious 'Master of the Amulet(?)' (*ḥri sʿ*?) in 6/14 is perhaps one candidate, but it should be noted that it is 'the dying man' (almost certainly) who is speaking, without any introduction, at the beginning of 6/15, so that he may be a better choice. In this connection it should be noted that a third phrase at the bottom of col. 6 and the top of col. 7: 'he looked at ⸢. . . . . .⸣' (see p. 89, n. *fr* for the unread divine name) is similar in form, and, though this may be coincidence, it is possible that there too there was a short space before it. Here again the probable subject is 'the dying man'; however, this phrase could well form part of the main 'internal story'.

j. *Other beings mentioned*

For convenience reference is given here to mentions of other beings who do not require further discussion:

The death-bird (*p3 ḥm3r*) 6/8, 23, 30[1]

[1] See *JEA* 61 (1975), 198 f.

The Five Gods (*pꜣ 5 nṯr.w*)	6/16 (twice?)
His dogs (*nꜣi͗=f i͗wi͗w.w*)	6/13
The monster of doom (*pꜣ nhr n sn*(?)-*th.ṯ*)	6/14
The Master of the Amulet(?) (*ḥri͗ sꜥ?*)	6/14
Neferḥer, 'Fair-of-Face' (*Nfr-ḥr*)	6/22
Sakhmis (*ẖrꜥry ḳy Sḫmt*)	6/31
Sokar (*ḥb Skr*)	6/27, 28 (twice?)
Thoth (*Ḏḥwt*)	6/22
Winged-beetle (*ꜥꜣpy*)	6/18

2. Nature and associations of the story

This fascinating and tantalizing story is of special interest for a variety of reasons.

i. *Form and structure*

It exhibits a division into paragraphs, each retailing a separate scene of the story, apparently taking place in a different milieu. This device is relatively rare in demotic stories, though it does occur.[1] Perhaps also the story exhibits the technique of a 'story within a story', of which 1. Khaꜥemwese is the most famous demotic example. It exhibits in a marked degree the Egyptian story-teller's predilection for dialogue over narrative, incidents in the action of the story often being retailed in speech. This feature is no doubt due to the story being designed for oral recitation, so as to give scope for the teller's histrionic skills. It adds considerably, in a fragmentary text like this one, to the uncertainties involved in reconstructing the course of the action.

ii. *Relationship with extant demotic literature*

The story almost certainly does not belong to any of the known demotic story cycles. With the Petubastis and Inaros cycle, it has nothing in common. With the Khaꜥemwese cycle, it shares some general features: events take place both on earth and in the underworld: men and gods are both involved: and magical powers on the part of some of the characters are no doubt assumed. Thus it may, like the story of Merib on the back of this papyrus, belong to approximately the same category of stories as the Khaꜥemwese cycle. But it certainly appears to have no direct relationship with any of the characters or events related in either Khaꜥemwese story. So far as the editors are aware, it is not related to any of the other fragmentary stories preserved in demotic.

iii. *Mythological associations*

Osiris, Isis, and Horus figure in the story: if one interpretation is correct, the youth Horus is doomed to die on account of the vengeance of Isis against him, and he is carried off by the death-bird and maltreated. Subsequently, perhaps, his adventures continue in the underworld on the fragmentary page: at all events, the words 'Horus is victorious against every valiant god' suggest that he eventually triumphs. It is being left with Isis that brings about his death; her wrath against him has apparently been caused by his killing a human being. Two human beings, a sick woman who dies and her daughter, plead for him, and both apparently incur the wrath of Isis for doing so. The demi-god Imḥotep is invoked by the woman to take Horus's part, and it is apparent from her words that he is in opposition to Isis. The role of Osiris is more shadowy, but may be the normal one of judge of the dead. Seth does not appear in the extant portion of the story, though the death-bird and another monstrous being who carried off Horus may have some Sethian connotations.

This story is principally extraordinary for the apparent opposition between Horus and Isis. Apart from the incident of Horus's decapitation

[1] Text **1** in this volume provides an example, as does the story on the back of **2**. The device is used in Mag. to divide sections of text.

of Isis for cutting Seth's bonds or wresting the diadem from her,[1] there is little sign of such opposition between the mother and her son in mythological sources. This casts doubt on identification of the youth with Horus, for which reasons have been given above (pp. 102–4). If it be wrong, then the story turns rather on the intervention of gods in human affairs, a familiar theme in Egyptian literature. Yet, even if the youth is human, it seems probable from the woman's words to Imḥotep: 6/22 'Are you communing with your own heart because you have not been victorious against Isis? Horus is victorious against any valiant god' that Horus is expected ultimately to prevail against Isis on the youth's behalf, so that the opposition between Isis and her son remains latent. The only way of understanding this passage which avoids the assumption of this conflict seems to us to be to regard the woman's words to Imḥotep not as a promise of eventual victory over Isis through Horus, but as comfort for his inevitable defeat, because Horus is invincible and has acted on Isis's side. Then Horus could be restored in the similar but damaged phrase in 6/7 (see p. 105). This involves translating part of the woman's speech to Isis in 6/12: '[you] know the youth who has said concerning a poor man: "I will take the vengeance of Isis upon him"; do not disgrace him ⸢. . . . .⸣', which is in itself grammatically acceptable, and means that the object of 'disgrace' (*šlf=f*) must refer to 'the poor man' (*rmt ḫm*) not to 'the youth' (*šr*). Whether, however, this understanding of the text is compatible with the apparent identity of 'the dying man' with 'the youth' (*ḫr*) in 6/31, and the fact that 'the dying man' says in 6/15 'I am before her, namely my mother Isis, that is to say, I am about to die' seems to us very doubtful.

This apparent opposition between Isis and Horus rules out the possibility that this text is part of 'The Contendings of Horus and Seth', the only mythological story to be partially preserved in demotic manuscripts.[2] It also differs from that text in that human beings take a part in the action; while the style is that of a normal demotic romance, not the archaic and traditional one in which the demotic version of Horus and Seth was framed. Nor does it appear to be a story like 'The Tale of Two Brothers', where characters represented as human take on roles which have their parallels in myth. Rather, it seems to be a story in which humans, by becoming implicated in divine conflicts, innocently bring about their own doom at the hands of Isis, the great magician, and are perhaps only finally restored to their rights by the superior power, perhaps, of Horus and Osiris. It is here that the story perhaps has its closest relationship with the stories of the Khaʿemwese cycle. But the context and character of the events recorded remain strictly within the context of Egyptian mythological and funerary beliefs, even if the opposition of Isis and Horus refers to a part of the myth not known to us.

iv. *Date and Language*

If the date for the whole group of papyri found in the North Courtyard of the Mother of Apis precinct has been correctly defined, this text was most probably written in the fourth century BC, and is unlikely to be later than the third. If so, it is one of the earlier surviving manuscripts of a demotic story. The careful setting-out of the text with paragraphs conforming to the incidents of the story, the correctness of the orthography and language, and the range of the vocabulary all seem to be in conformity with this. They suggest a court scribe of high education and literary competence; for

[1] Plutarch, *De Iside et Osiride* 358 B 19–359 B 20; also *Book of the Dead*, Spell 113; cf. J. Gwyn Griffiths, *The Conflict of Horus and Seth*, (Liverpool, 1960), 103–7.

[2] A fragment on papyrus in the Berlin Museum is to be published by K. Th. Zauzich; a fragment from Saqqâra (H5-DP79) will be published in a future volume of this series.

it is to the complexity and unfamiliarity of the story and to the lacunae in the text, not to scribal error, that its obscurity is due.

These and other aspects of this remarkable story deserve broader and more detailed discussion than is possible in the confines of an *editio princeps*. The editors are very conscious of the many problems raised by the text which they have left unsolved, and hope that its understanding may be improved by the criticisms that their initial attempt may provoke.

Merib, the High Steward, and the captive Pharaoh

Transliteration

Plates 6–9

BACK

col. x

top margin of 2.0 cm.

1. - - -]=f wnm=f[a] ỉ ⸢tꜣ⸣[b] ntỉ wḫꜣ=w ꜥnḫ mtw=s[c] tꜣ ḥrỉ.t [. .]
2. - - -] ⸢pꜣ⸣ tꜣ dr=f tw=y ẖn nꜣ dw.w[d] . . h̭y[e]
3. - - -] mn ṱwy[f] r rdwỉ⸢.ṱ=y⸣ . . [. .]=y[g]
4. - - -]=f ⸢m⸣y gm=y tꜣ mỉ.t . . . [. . . . .][h]
5. - - -] ⸢m⸣dwt n ḏd wꜥ [. .] . ỉw r-ẖr[y[j] . . . . .]
6. - - -] . . =f nꜣ-n⸢fr nꜣ⸣ỉ=f ỉwf.w[k] ẖr . . . . [. .][l]
7. - - -] . ⸢n-ỉm=f⸣[m] ⸢n tꜣ⸣ šb n ꜥḳ ỉ-ỉr=f ỉn . [. . .] . . [. .][n]
8. - - - s]ṱy psy=f pꜣ d . . [. . .] . [. .][o]
9. - - -] . dỉ=f mdw pꜣ dw [.] ẖrw . [. . .] . . . .[p]
10. - - - m]⸢ꜣỉ⸣ ẖt n pꜣ mꜣỉ wꜣḏ (n-)drt.ṱ=f rk [. .] . .[q]
11. - - -] ꜥw n ḥꜣt⸢.ṱ⸣ [. . .] . ⸢.ṱ=f⸣ m-šs[r]
12. - - -] . ỉwf . [. . . . .] . . . [. .] . .[s]
13. - - -] no trace[t]
14. - - - . . . .] . . .y [. .] . .[u]
15. - - - . . . .] . ⸢rswy⸣ . . . .[v]
16. - - - . . . .] . n=n ⸢ỉ⸣-ỉr= . [. . .] .
17. - - - . . . .] . .
18. - - - . . . .] . .
19. - - - . . . .] . .
20. - - - . . . .] . . [.] . .
21. - - - . . . .] . . ḏd [. .] . .
22. - - - . . . .] . . . .[w]
23. - - - . . . . [. .] . ..w
24. - - - . . . .] . . . . ḏd[x]
25. - - - . . . .] . . wẖꜣ[y]
26. - - - . . . .] . ỉr=f ꜥn-⸢smy⸣[z]
27. - - - . . . .] . [. .] . . . [. . .] .[aa]
28. - - - . . . .] . . nb(.t) . . . . [. .[ab]
29. - - - . . . .] ỉw=y sdm [.]
30. - - - . . . .] . . . . [. .[ac]
31. - - - . . . .] . . . . .[ad]

32. - - - ....] ....[ae]
33. - - - ....].
34. - - - ....]........[af]
35. - - - ....]........[ag]
36. - - - ....] ..[.....
37. - - - ....].[......

no surviving trace of last four(?) lines
bottom margin lost

col. x+1

top margin of 2.0 cm

1. ....] . wr.t nb.t ⸢Tp-nꜣ-ỉḥ(.w)⸣ ...... tꜣỉ(=y) ḥnwt[ah] ỉn ẖr [........] ... [. .] .... [. .][aj] ... ⸢rẖ⸣ Pr-ꜥꜣ[ak] Bꜣ-[. . .] ....[al] [- - -
2. .... sḏm ẖrw .. [. .] ..... ỉw ⸢mn⸣ kk[y] n-ḥꜣt.ṱ=f[am] ⸢my⸣ [....] .... ⸢ẖpr⸣ n Pr-ꜥꜣ Bꜣ-... ẖꜣꜥ=y tꜣỉ=t s⸢ndyt⸣ [n]-⸢ḥꜣt⸣[.ṱ f] ...[an] [- - -
3. gm=y tꜣ/nꜣ i-ỉr-ẖpr ⸢n-ỉm⸣=f ...... pꜣ mšꜥ gm.ṱ⸢=f⸣[ao] ... [. .] . [. . .] . [.....] .... ⸢mšꜥ⸣ [. .] .... [. . .][ap] .. r sḏm pꜣ ntỉ ỉw=y r [. . .] ...[aq] [- - -
4. .... ꜥꜣ.w n Pr-ꜥꜣ ⸢dr=w[ar] ỉn i⸣-ỉr=t r rẖ ..[as] [............] .. ⸢ẖrꜥry⸣ .. [. . .] .. ⸢Bꜣ⸣- ... n-ỉm=f[at] my rẖ=y [. .] ..[au] [- - -
5. .... n]-ỉm=w i-ỉr-ḥr pꜣ mšꜥ ẖꜣꜥ⸢=y⸣ tꜣỉ=t sndyt [..............] . ⸢n wꜥ ẖrw⸣ .. [....][av] .. ⸢dr=w[aw] ḏd Mr⸣-ỉb pꜣ i-ỉr-dỉt ⸢ꜣḳ⸣ ..[ax][- - -
6. ......] nꜣ md.wt [.] ḏd[ay] ỉw=f ⸢rmy⸣ ỉw=f šrr[az] [............] .. tꜣ ⸢pt⸣[ba] . [.......] . [.....] .....[bb] bw-ỉr-rẖ [- - -
7. .....] . ỉw=w ꜥš ⸢n=s ẖr⸣ sḏm=s n-ỉm=w[bc] ⸢dr⸣[=w[bd] ....] ... sḏm[be] ... [.............] md.wt ....[bf] [- - -
8. ... [....] .. ỉrf= ỉn-ḳdy[bg] i-ỉr=f ⸢pry⸣ n rswy[bh] [...........] ....[bj] [..............].t nb(.t) ..[bk] [- - -
9. ỉw=s [.....] ⸢sbt⸣ n šꜥ[bl] r wꜥ mw ꜣṱ⸢ḥ⸣[bm] [............] ... ḥr spṱ pꜣ ⸢yr⸣[bn] [- - -
10. ḏd .... [. .] ...[bo] ỉn tw=k nw r pꜣỉ mꜣỉ .....[bp] [. .] ... [. .] ... [.][bq] ... ỉr=f ⸢sḏm(-ꜥš) sfy n⸣[br] ..[bs][- - -
11. ⸢ntỉ⸣ snḥ drt.ṱ=y[bt] n-drt sḏm=f (n-)ḥꜣ(.t) Pr-ꜥꜣ r bn(-pw)=y ⸢sḥn⸣[.ṱ]=⸢s⸣ n=f[bu] i-ỉr ⸢Pr-ꜥꜣ ꜥš⸣ [. .] .... ⸢tꜣ ḥꜣ.t⸣ [n pꜣ] ⸢wtn n⸣ pꜣ- ..[bv] . [- - -
12. sꜣb r-r=f ḏd ỉw=y r ḥwrꜥ pꜣi-ỉr=t sḥn.ṱ=f[bw] ꜥšꜣ ḥꜣt.ṱ=f r ṱkn r-r=f ⸢ỉr⸣=y [. .] .... ⸢r-r=f⸣[bx] dỉ=y .... pꜣ ..[by] [- - -
13. bn(-pw)=f gm mw r swr ỉn=y n=f mw nfr ḥr pꜣ dw ḥḳr Pr-ꜥꜣ ...=f .. [. .] ... r ⸢wnm⸣[bz] dbḥ=f mtw=y dỉ=⸢y-s⸣ n=f ... [.] ..[ca] [. . .] .. [- - -
14. ⸢n⸣ sṱy dmy r-r=f i-ỉr=s ⸢šdy⸣=f[cb] ḥr tꜣ ḥ̭wy n Bꜣstt tꜣ ntr.t ꜥꜣ.t .. [....] pꜣ [. .] ....[cc] dỉ=y .. [. .] pꜣ ⸢mꜣỉ⸣ wbꜣ ...[cd] [- - -
15. dỉ=y ỉn=f n=f ⸢ḥmꜣ⸣[ce] ỉr=f n=f ⸢sḏm(-ꜥš) sfy⸣ ỉw=f sdr ḥr pꜣ dw[cf] ⸢n tꜣ/nꜣ⸣ .. [....] .... ⸢sṱy⸣ i-ỉr-ḥr=f[cg] tw=y .. [. . t]ꜣỉ=f rỉt ⸢ḥrỉt⸣ pꜣ mꜣỉ ...[ch] [- - -
16. ⸢ẖrẖr⸣ ḥr pꜣ dw[cj] ỉr=w tꜣỉ=f rỉt ḥrỉt ḥr pꜣ dw st ḳdy .... [.....] .. [. . .][ck] gm=w-s n ..... ⸢ntỉ⸣ ỉw=f ... =s[cl] ḏd⸢=w⸣ .. ḏd=n . ẖrw[cm] . [- - -
17. nḥm=k ỉw=n ỉn.ṱ=k[cn] r Kmy [.] .... dr=w[co] i-ỉr=y ỉr=w n=f r-dbꜣ ⸢tꜣ⸣ mdt ......[cp] [. .] . [. .] . ⸢tꜣỉ=t sndyt⸣ (n-)ḥꜣt.ṱ=f[cq] ẖꜣꜥ=y-s ỉw bn-ỉw=f ḏd ⸢bn-ỉw⸣=y sḏm ... [- - -

TEXT 2 BACK, COL. X+1

18. *pꜣ ỉ-ỉr-dbḥ⸢=k⸣ mtw=y*[cr] *m-šm ⸢ỉwt⸣ pꜣỉ=k ⸢mšꜥ⸣ .ḏd. n=f*[cs] *pꜣỉ=tn ḥrỉ* [. .] . *⸢wḏꜣ⸣ mtw=k* . . [. . . .] *ẖr nꜣ ⸢sꜣwtỉ.w⸣*[ct] *n nꜣy r-ḏd=y n=k mtw=k ḏd* . . *ỉw=y r šm r pꜣ ⸢dw⸣ m-sꜣ* .[cu] [- - -

19. *⸢r stꜣ⸣.ṱ=f ⸢r⸣ Kmy mtw=k ꜥr r wꜥ [ḥtrỉ] ⸢m-ỉr⸣ dỉt ḫrr ⸢mt⸣ꜥṱ n-ḥr=f m-ỉr mḫy.ṱ=f m-ỉr dỉt mšꜥ rmt* *[(n-)ḥꜣ].ṱ=f*[cv] *ẖꜣꜥ-s ⸢ỉrm⸣* . . .[cw] [- - -

larger space between lines

20. *nhs Mr-ỉb šn=f r pꜣ nw ntỉ ẖpr ḏd=w n=f mḥ-I.t* . . [. . . . .][cx] . . . . *=f*[cy] *bn-ỉw=y šm ⸢r ḫfṱ-ḥ(r)⸣*[cz] *n Ḥwt-Ḥr n pꜣỉ nw ỉn*[da] *ỉw=y r ḏd.ṱ=s ⸢r-ḥr-n⸣* .[db] [- - -

21. *n Pr-ꜥꜣ ỉw bn-ỉw=s ẖn pꜣỉ=s pr ỉn bn-ỉw=y ⸢ḥrry⸣ r* . . [[dc]. . . . .] *⸢dỉ Mr⸣-ỉb* . . . *=w wꜥ ⸢ḥtrỉ⸣ ꜥr=f r-r=f bn(-pw)=f dỉt ḫrr mtꜥṱ n-ḥr=f bn-*[dd]. [- - -

22. *bn(-pw)=f dỉt mšꜥ rmt (n-)ḥꜣ.ṱ=f mšꜥ pꜣ ḥtrỉ ỉrm* . . [. . . .] . . . .[de] [. . . . .] . . [. .] . . . *⸢wnwt 6⸣ n grḥ ẖpr*[df] *gm=f nꜣ sꜣwtỉ.w* . [.] .[dg] [- - -

23. *Pr-ꜥꜣ bn(-pw)=w ⸢swr⸣ wnm md=w dr=w* [.] . . *⸢rꜣ⸣*[dh] *ḏd Pr-ꜥꜣ* . . [. . . .] . . . . [. .] . *⸢sḥn.w⸣ bn(-pw)=⸢n⸣ gm.ṱ=f n ⸢ꜥwỉ⸣ n pꜣ tꜣ*[dj] *ḏd=f m-ỉr* .[dk][- - -

24. *šn=tn nꜣ sꜣwtỉ.w*[dl] *ẖr sdm Ḥwt-Ḥr* [. . .] *dỉt ⸢mwy⸣ ḥr* . . . [. . .] . . *⸢sdm=s⸣ pꜣ ⸢ẖrw⸣ n nꜣ* . . . . . *w n ỉrt.ṱ=w ỉw=w ⸢ẖnm⸣.w*[dm] *mtw=⸢s⸣* . .[dn] [- - -

25. *nꜣ mšꜥ.w n Pr-ꜥꜣ m[tw]=s dỉt n(=y) ꜥmy nb.t*[do] . . . [. . .] . [. .] *mn* . . . [. . . *m]šꜥ.w n Pr-ꜥꜣ n-ỉm* . .[dp] *bn st ḥp r-ḥr=y ỉn ỉw=y* . . . [.] . [. .][dq] . [- - -

26. *Mr-* . . . *pꜣ sẖ n pꜣ wẖꜣ*[dr] *ḏd my rẖ⸢=n⸣* . [. .] . . [. . .] . . [. . . . . .][ds] *ḏd=k ⸢sdm⸣=n tꜣ/nꜣ* . . . *.=k* . . *.ṱ=w*[dt] *nm pꜣ ỉ-ỉr sḥn.ṱ=f (n) Pr-ꜥꜣ m-sꜣ pꜣ mr-⸢ꜥwỉ⸣* [[du]- - -

27. *ỉr ḥrỉ n pꜣ rd.ṱy*[dv] *r dỉ=k n=n Pr-ꜥꜣ ⸢mtw=k⸣ ỉ* [. .] . . *.ṱ=f mtw=k ỉ-*[. . . . .] . . *=f*[dw] *ỉ-⸢ỉr=n wšd nm m-sꜣ⸣ pꜣ mr-ꜥwỉ*[dx] *ỉ-⸢ỉr=n⸣ wšd Pr-ꜥꜣ m-sꜣ=k ḏd ⸢n=w⸣*[dy] [- - -

28. *mdt nb.t r-ḏd=w n=f m-⸢bꜣḥ⸣ ʾIst dr=w*[dz] *ḏd=f tw-s tꜣ/nꜣ ỉ*[. . . . .] *n Pr-ꜥꜣ*[ea] *ỉw=y* . . [. . . . .] . . . *=s* . . . .[eb] *ỉw=y r ⸢gm⸣ Pr-ꜥꜣ n tꜣỉ=s wty* . . [. .] . *tꜣ ỉw=s*[ec] [- - -

29. *ỉw=y r ⸢ỉn⸣ (n=)tn pꜣỉ=tn ḥrỉ ỉw=f wḏꜣ mdt nb.t r-ḏd pꜣ* . . . . . *⸢sẖ⸣ st Mr-⸢. . .⸣* [. . . . .] . . *dr=w*[ed] *ỉ-ỉr=s ẖpr wn-nꜣ-w wn m-dr nb(.t) ꜥnẖ* [. .] . . . . .[ee] [- - -

30. *tꜣ khy n Pr-ꜥꜣ*[ef] *ḏd pꜣ sẖ n pꜣ wẖꜣ ⸢pꜣ⸣* . . . . *⸢mḥ⸣=w n nꜣ ẖrd.w*[eg] *n* . [. . . . .] . *ḏ(d)tḥ=w*[eh] *šꜥ-tw Pr-ꜥꜣ pḥ r-ẖ(t) n tꜣ/nꜣ ⸢mdt/mdwt⸣* [. .] . . [. . . . .] *pꜣ mr-ꜥwỉ ḏd* . .[ej] [- - -

31. *ḏd pꜣ mr-ꜥwỉ nꜣ-nfr nꜣ-w-ḏd=k dỉ pꜣ sẖ n ⸢pꜣ wẖꜣ⸣ mḥ=w n ⸢nꜣ ẖr.w⸣*[ek] [. . . . . . .] . *nw rmt r pꜣỉ=f ỉrỉ n-ỉm=w bn(-pw)=w dỉt rẖ* . . . . . *⸢ẖpr⸣ n-ỉm=w*[el] *ẖꜣꜥ=w st n* .[em] [- - -

32. *n tꜣ ⸢shrꜣ⸣*[en] *m-sꜣ nꜣy ꜥr Mr-ỉb r pꜣ ḥtrỉ bn(-pw)=f dỉt ḫrr mtꜥṱ [n-]⸢ḥr⸣=f bn(-pw)=f mḫy.ṱ=f bn(-pw)=f dỉt mšꜥ rmt [n-ḥ(ꜣ).ṱ=f]*[eo] *pt pꜣ ḥtrỉ r pꜣ d[w*[ep] - - -

33. . [. . . . .] . . . *⸢mn⸣ pꜣ ỉ-ỉr-ḏd n-ỉm=w ỉw=y r šm m-sꜣ=f*[eq] *ỉw-bw-ỉr-rẖ=w mꜣꜥ (n) pꜣ tꜣ* . . [. .] . . *=y r-r=f*[er] *ẖꜥ pꜣ-Rꜥ r pꜣ ḥtrỉ ỉw=f ḏḏy r ⸢bn(-pw)=f ẖꜣꜥ⸣ pꜣỉ=f gy n ⸢ḏḏy⸣*[es] [- - -

34. [. . . . . .] . . . . *⸢ẖpr⸣*[et] *nw pꜣ mr-ꜥwỉ r hyn.w tp-n-ỉꜣwt dw ỉw=w ꜥšꜣ* [. . . .] . *r ẖm*[eu] *mm kḥs ḥyṱy ⸢w. .⸣ ꜣyr ẖ(t) tp-n-ỉꜣ[wt*[ev] - - -

35. . [. . . . . . .] . . . *n-ỉm=w*[ew] *ỉw Pr-ꜥꜣ ḥms ỉwt nꜣ tp-n-[ỉꜣ]wt r bw-ỉr=w ⸢nw⸣ r-r=f n-drt.ṱ=w*[ex] *mdw n=f Pr-ꜥꜣ ỉw=f ỉw ỉr=f swn Pr-ꜥꜣ ỉw=f*[ey] [- - -

36. . [. . . . .] . . . *⸢pꜣ⸣ mꜣỉ*[ez] *sdr=f n=f r-ẖ.ṱ=f wšd=f r* . . [.] . [. .] . [.] . . . *n-ḥꜣt.ṱ=f*[fa] *r-dbꜣ ẖpr ỉ-ỉr=f nw r tꜣ ḥrỉt n rswy ỉw=s*[fb] [- - -

37. *⸢pḥ⸣* [. . . . .] *tp-n-[ỉꜣ]wt*[fc] *mšꜥ=f ⸢ỉwt=w⸣ bn(pw)=w pt (n-)ḥꜣ.⸢ṱ=f⸣ ⸢bn(-pw)=w ẖꜣꜥ tꜣ⸣ mỉt*[fd] *r šm r pꜣ mꜣꜥ ntỉ ỉw Pr-ꜥꜣ n-ỉm=f ỉr pꜣ mꜣỉ wꜥ ⸢ẖrw⸣*[fe] [- - -

38. . . [. .] . . [. .] . [. . .] . . *r Pr-ꜥꜣ*[ff] *ẖꜣꜥ=w pꜣ ⸢myt⸣ r pꜣ mr-⸢ꜥwỉ⸣*[fg] *sdr=f n=f r-ẖ.ṱ=f*[fh] *ḏd n=f Pr-ꜥꜣ pꜣ mr-ꜥwỉ mtw=k ỉ-ỉr-ḥk=y* . . . .[fj] [- - -

bottom margin of 4.0 cm.[fk]

Notes on transliteration

BACK

col. x

a. Cf. x+1/13, 23 for the suggested restoration [*swr*]=*f wnm=f*; perhaps originally the text may have read [*mn-mtw=y pꜣ nti iw=y rḫ swr*]=*f wnm=f*, see p. 130 n. *a*. The passage is certainly part of a speech because a vocative follows with no intervening *ḏd*.

b. The scribe has apparently corrected what he originally wrote here. If he intended *pꜣi šr* to be read, then the following damaged sign is not easily explicable, and its masc. gender accords ill with *mtw=s tꜣ ḥri.t* (n. *c* below). It seems better to read the group as *i tꜣ* with following vocative.

c. : the papyrus is badly stained here and the signs obscured, but *mtw=s tꜣ ḥri.t* is certain. The translation 'She is the mistress . . .' must be rejected in view of the preceding vocative; *mtw=s* must be taken as a preposition with resumptive suffix pronoun referring back to the preceding relative phrase. The whole will then form part of an address: *i tꜣ nti wḫꜣ=w ꜥnḫ mtw=s tꜣ ḥri.t* 'O you from whom life is requested, the mistress [of . . . .]'.

d. : the reading *nꜣ dw.w*, 'the mountains' is adopted here on the grounds that: i. the word sign resembles hieroglyphic and early demotic examples given by *DG*, 611. 3 under *tw*; ii. the *w* is repeated as in certain examples given there, cf. the various multisyllabic plurals of ⲧⲟⲟⲩ in Coptic (Crum, *CD*, 441a); iii. the det. is appropriate; iv. a singular form written similarly occurs in x/9 below; v. no plausible alternative presents itself. Against this, a more normal writing of the singular appears in x+1/13, 15, 16 (twice), 18, 32. Perhaps it should be accepted in this instance that the scribe used two different writings for the same word.

e. : *.ḥy* is almost certain. Perhaps restore *mḥy*, 'fight' (*DG*, 176. 3), or better *nti ḥy*[*.w*], 'which are high' (*DG*, 349. 1).

f. : the doubled det. evidently represents sandals (cf. *Wb.* v. 247. 5 ff.); the final det. is not made like the flesh det. ( ), but does resemble the sign of uncertain reading following *nwy.w*, 'lances(?)', in **2**, front, 6/11. A rather similar det. for 'sandals' is quoted by *DG*, 611. 4 under *tw* from the Canopus Decree, , and elsewhere; this sign, however, is hardly distinguishable from the flesh det., and it is at least possible that it is borrowed from *tw*(*n*), 'bosom' (*DG*, 612. 1).

g. : *r rdwi.ṯ=y* is certain. It seems probable that the *=y* at the end of the line represents the 1st pers. sing. suffix pronoun, but the preceding traces allow several possibilities.

h. : possibly restore *tꜣ mi.t n ꜥ*[*nḫ*], cf. **2**, front, 6/24 (where the masc. noun *myt* is used); but the trace preserved perhaps curls over too much for *ꜥ*. Perhaps the dot should rather be treated as part of the det. of *mi.t*, in which case possibly interpret the following traces as a second imperative *my*.

j. For the expression *mdwt n ḏd*, cf. **2**, front 6/20–1, 25, where the verb *mnḳ*, 'complete, fulfil', is used with it. The det. of the short word in lacuna is not that of a bird, but might be that of an animal ( ). The passage is strongly reminiscent of **2**, front 6/18, *nw=w r wꜥ ꜥꜣpy ꜥꜣ r iw=f iw r-ḫry n tꜣ pt*, 'they saw a great winged beetle coming down from the sky'; possibly *n tꜣ pt* is to be restored after *iw r-ḫry*. The creature, however, cannot have been an *ꜥꜣpy* here, and there is no good reason to think that this resemblance proves a connection between the stories.

k. *nꜣ-nfr nꜣi=f iwf.w* presumably refers to the being or creature that has descended, cf. **2**, front, 6/19–20 *r nꜣ iwf.w n iwn*(?) [. . . .] referring to the winged beetle. The det. of the word lost at the beginning of x/6 resembles that used for linen (e.g. in **1**, 9/2 *ṯꜣi-ḥbs*, *nꜣ ḥbs.w*, *šs-nsw*); but also in *swr*, 'drink' (e.g. in **1**, 9/2, 13/3 and **2**, front, 6/11). The same det. appears in lacuna in x+1/8, and, in view of the context there and in x/6, it is tempting to restore both as *sdr=f*, 'he lay down', the restoration suggested for a similar broken group at the beginning of **1**, 9/8. The awkwardness of this, however, is that undoubted examples of *sdr* appear in x+1/15, 36, 38 and in **2**, front, 6/20 written without the det. Whether this is to be regarded as another instance where the scribe may have used two writings of one word (see n. *d* above on *dw*, 'mountain'), or whether another reading should be sought here and in x+1/8, we feel uncertain.

l. : *ḫr* seems certain, but whether the following traces represent a verb in the *ḫr sḏm=f* form ('tense of habitude'), or a noun with the definite article *pꜣ* or the suffix pronoun *=y* following the enclitic *ḫr*, 'said . . .' (as in **2**, front, 6/20), is quite uncertain.

m. : *n-im=f* seems palaeographically more probable than *r-ḥr=f*.

n. : *n tꜣ šb n ꜥḳ ỉ-ỉr=f ỉn* . . . . . is certain; *ỉn* is normally written in this papyrus, but not exclusively so, see, for example, x+1/17 for the form , also present in x+1/8 in *ỉn-ḳdy*, which might conceivably be restored here.

o. : *sṱy psy=f pꜣ d.* . . .; for *sṱy* cf. x+1/14. The final group might be expected to represent a foodstuff; *dgy*, 'fruit', might fit, but is usually written with a different arrangement of signs (*DG*, 662. 1), and would, perhaps, have been relatively unlikely to have been cooked. But it may be that some apparently unsuitable material was brought in place of bread (x/7) and magically(?) transformed into food on being cooked. Were this so, such words as *ddỉ* (*Wb.* v. 421. 9 ff., a mineral substance, cf. *DG*, 663. 2 under *tt*) or *ḏdꜣ*, 'fat' (*Wb.* v. 632. 4 ff.), might be considered.

p. : *dỉ=f mdw pꜣ* is certain, [*r*] *ḫrw=f* probable. The apparent stroke through *dỉ* may be an accidental mark. The group contains the same word-sign and det. as that read *dw.w* in x/2 (see p. 112, n. *d*), and is taken to be *dw*, 'mountain' despite the different writing in x+1/13, 15, 16 (twice), 18, 32. The final groups in x/9 might perhaps represent *ỉ-ỉr=f*.

q. : the dets. of the broken initial word fit *mꜣỉ*, 'lion', as written in this story with a divine det. (e.g. x+1/10). The group following the second instance of *mꜣỉ* is probably an ideogrammatic writing of *wꜣḏ*, 'green' (*DG*, 104. 4 under *wt*), or *wꜣḏ*, 'papyrus' (*DG*, 105. 1), though whether the meaning is 'a green lion', 'a lion (made) of papyrus', or 'a lion of the papyrus(-thicket)' is uncertain (see pp. 138 f.). The reading *(n-)drt.ṱ=f*, though slightly crowded, seems correct; *rk* is certain, but as usual it is not clear whether *rk*, 'turn' (*DG*, 256, 3 under *rḳ*, Coptic ⲣⲓⲕⲉ), or *rk*, 'cease' (*DG*, 264. 6 under *lg*, Coptic ⲗⲁϭⲉ), is intended (cf. **2** front, 6/9, 19).

r. : *ꜥw n ḥꜣt*⸢*.ṱ*⸣ and *m-šs* are certain. The group before *m-šs* comprises the flesh det., followed by the pronominal *ṱ* and the suffix *=f*; just possibly read *rdwỉ.ṱ=f* as in x/3. A short verb must presumably be restored in the lacuna. *ꜥw n ḥꜣt.ṱ* means 'patient' in Insinger, M. Lichtheim in *Studien zu altägyptischen Lebenslehren* (Fribourg/Göttingen, 1979), 292.

s. ỉwf certain; the following traces are perhaps to be read *dỉt wꜣy*.

t. The only trace in the space under x/12 is a diagonal tick, possibly the tail from an *=f* in x/12. If so, it is conceivable that there was a larger space between lines here, marking the beginning of a new paragraph in x/14.

u. : the reading is uncertain, perhaps *r fꜣy* . . . .

v. : *rswy*, 'dream', seems virtually certain (*DG*, 255. 3), cf. x+1/8 *ỉ-ỉr=f pry n rswy*. The following traces might represent *r wꜥ.t* or the interjection *ỉ* 'o'.

w. : *mdt ḫpr n tꜣ pt* seems a doubtful but plausible restoration; for *pt* cf. **2**, front, 6/18.

x. The traces before *ḏd* should probably be restored *nhs*, 'awake', cf. x+1/20, thus probably confirming that a dream has been recounted (see n. *v* above).

y. : *wḫꜣ* is certain; if this is the noun *wḫꜣ*, 'letter', perhaps read the preceding group as *pꜣỉ*, 'this', but cf. p. 125, n. *er*.

z. ỉr=f ꜥn-smy is virtually certain; a divine det. precedes.

aa. : very uncertain traces, perhaps read . . . .*ṱ=k ỉn=w-s* . . . .

ab. : *t*]*ꜣỉ*(*=y*) *nb.t tꜣỉ*, 'she is my Lady', is perhaps possible; what follows is illegible.

ac. : the traces are ambiguous.

ad. : the final trace may be the child det. The surviving group earlier in the line could be the beginning of the name *Mr-ỉb* (x+1/5, 10, 20, 21, 32) or of the name *Mr* . . . (x+1/26, 29).

ae. : *wḫꜣ* is probable, cf. x/25, x+1/26, 30.

af. : *tꜣỉ šr.t*, 'this girl', seems plausible. The final group may be incomplete, and is uncertain.

ag. : the first group resembles the dets. of *nꜣ sꜣwtỉ.w* (x+1/22). Were this guess right, *nꜣ rmt.w ꜥꜣ.w* might be the best reading of the ambiguous group which follows: 'the Guards and the Great Men [of Pharaoh . . .]'.

col. x+1

ah. : . . . . . . *wr.t nb.t Tp-nꜣ-ỉḥ*(*.w*) fits the traces well (*DG*, 627 under 626. 3 *tp*); the only problem is the presence of the article *nꜣ* in the cult name, normally written *nb.t Tp-ỉḥ.w*; for *Tp-ỉḥ.w* = *Pr-nb.t-Tp-ỉḥw* (Coptic ⲡⲉⲧⲡⲏϩ, ⲧⲡⲏϩ,

Greek Ἀφροδίτης πόλις, modern Aṭfiḥ) see Gardiner, *Onomastica*, ii. 119* f., Montet, *Géographie*, ii. 203. The article is certainly present; possibly the scribe, aware of the cult of the sacred cow Ḥesat (Greek ʽΕσις) at Aṭfiḥ, intended to write (unetymologically) *nb.t Tp-tꜣ-iḥ.t*; at all events, the version with the article seems an acceptable variant. The broken det. preceding *wr.t* is certainly , used in names and epithets of goddesses. As Hathor was the goddess of Aṭfiḥ, and as her name appears below in x+1/19, 24 in the account of the action resulting from this appeal, *Ḥwt-ḥr* should almost certainly be restored here.

Strictly, the following traces are uncertain; however, the epithet *tꜣ ntr.t ʽꜣ.t* is so common in such addresses that it is perhaps permissible to reconstitute the text thus: , cf. x+1/14, which takes account of the surviving traces. The alternative appears to be to take the final group as the interjection *ỉ* as in x/1, with an epithet before it; *tꜣ ntr.t* alone seems less common and we have no alternative suggestion.

Above *nb.t* in the top margin is the sign referred to in the physical description of the papyrus (p. 70). If this belongs to the class of true *marginalia*, it cannot well be a column number because: a. its form does not correspond to that of any demotic figure; b. column numbers are placed in this papyrus (and in **1**) at the bottom of columns. The story clearly continues from the previous column, so the sign could not well mark the beginning of a new text, unless indeed it applied to the whole of the back of the papyrus rather than just to col. x+1, in which case it appears to be oddly placed, near to the top line of writing and probably some distance from the centre of the roll. An alternative approach is to regard it as an insertion of a passage omitted by the scribe from the top line. Admittedly, if our readings are correct, no insertion is possible in the titulary of the goddess above which the sign occurs. But if the insertion were of more than one word, the scribe might have started it to the right of its intended position, and it might form the initial words of the appeal. The sign itself is perhaps closest in form to *sdm* (x+1/7); if, for example, the insertion had been *sdm* [*n*(=*y*)], 'listen to me', or *sdm* [*n*(=*y*) *wḥm n pꜣ sp mḥ-2*], 'listen to me again a second time', this might have been intended for insertion before *tꜣỉ*(=*y*) *ḥnwt*, '(O) my mistress'. Other restorations are clearly possible; but a solution on these lines seems somewhat preferable to assuming an unattested type of *marginalia*.

aj. [ ] : *ỉn ḥr* and *dbḥ* are certain; the interval might fit the restoration *ỉn ḥr* [*sdm=t n pꜣỉ*(=*y*)] ⌜*d*⌝*bḥ* ⌜*m-bꜣḥ=t*⌝, upon which the translation offered on p. 131, n. *v* is based. The papyrus is slightly twisted and misaligned where DP376 and DP153 adjoin, so that *m-bꜣḥ=t* fits the traces better than the photograph suggests.

ak. : . . . . *rḫ Pr-ʽꜣ* is certain, *my rḫ* highly probable. If the preceding restorations (n. *aj* above) be accepted the trace before *my* may well represent *ḏd*.

al. The cartouche appears in three contexts as follows, all unfortunately damaged:

x+1/1

x+1/2

x+1/4

From the combined evidence of these writings, it is clear that: i. the divine det. appears both before and after the sign which closes the cartouche, suggesting that the name may be theophoric: ii. the first sign of the name is certainly , representing hieroglyphic *bꜣ*, commonly used in demotic phonetically for *b*, but also more rarely ideographically in *bꜣy*, 'soul' and related words (*DG*, 111. 4, 5), where sometimes it is followed by a short upright or oblique stroke: iii. the shape of the second group is uncertain; it may have been made either in one or two strokes, though the latter seems slightly less probable; its form is close to those of *ḏꜣ*: *nfr* (normally determined with): *mn* (as in *Mn-nfr*), but could represent, perhaps, certain ideograms, notably *sꜣ* as written in *sꜣ.t*, 'daughter' (*DG*, 402. 6); or it could be broken down into a stroke (e.g. as *n* or as complement to *b*(*ꜣ*)) followed by a sign of the form , which might represent a variety of phonetic or ideographic groups, including perhaps the bird det.

Bꜣ-ḏꜣ, *Bꜣ-mn*, and *Bꜣ-nfr* are readings which might be regarded as archaizing attempts to produce a Pharaonic name of early Old Kingdom type; of these, only *Bꜣ-ḏꜣ* is attractive, as resembling the name attributed to the first king of the Second Dynasty (*ZÄS* 48 (1911), 113; Abydos list 9). *Bꜣ-n-Ỉmn* or *Bꜣ-n-Rʽ* are perhaps just thinkable readings, though palaeographically the final stroke of the pen accords ill with normal demotic writings of the names of these deities. *Bꜣ-Dḥwt* might be considered superior to these, were it not for the larger, clear form for *Dḥwt* in **2**, front, 6/22. If the second sign may be regarded as *sꜣ*, then the name may be read either *Sꜣ-bꜣ* (with honorific transposition) or simply *Bꜣ*, taking as a bird det. Unfortunately, the signs do not seem reconcilable with such historic early Pharaonic names as *Ḥꜥ-bꜣ* (Dyn. III) or *Bꜣw·f-Rꜥ* (Dyn. IV, prince), though an archaizing name like *Bꜣ-ḏꜣ* seems likely. The problem is unsolved: henceforward for convenience we read *Bꜣ-. . . .* in the transliteration, Badja in the translation.

The final traces of x+1/1 after the closing cartouche and *ꜥnḫ wḏꜣ snb* probably represent *tꜣ/nꜣ . . iw*; *nꜣ* [*nti*] *iw*[*=w ḫpr*], 'the things that are happening/will happen', seems the most likely restoration; *nꜣ i-*⌜*ir*⌝ [*-ḫpr*] seems to be ruled out by the traces, but this cannot be certain.

am. : the reading *sdm* assumes that this verb was normally written by this scribe, but also (here and x+1/7, cf. **1**, 9/3). The previous word is doubtless *nm*, 'who?' ( ), though *gr* ( ) is also perhaps possible. The first group is uncertain, though it bears some resemblance to *ḥr* in x+1/1. What should be read after *ḫrw* remains uncertain; the traces immediately following could represent some part of the def. article *pꜣ* or the possessive adjective *pꜣi=*[ ], and the fact that the circumstantial clause *iw mn kky n-ḥꜣt.ṯ f* ends with a 3rd pers. suffix suggests that this cannot be *pꜣi(=y)*. What the context perhaps requires is that the speaker should use some such phrase as 'your servant', 'your priest', or 'your petitioner' of himself, or otherwise describe his relation to the goddess. Careful examination of the following traces suggests that the same group for *tp* is present as in x+1/1, that the final group is most likely to be the place det. , and that the surviving traces between them might (among other possibilities) represent *iḥ*. With great reserve we suggest that the restoration *ḥr nm sdm ḫrw pꜣ* [*ḥm-nṯr*(?) *nb.t*] *Tp-iḥ*(*.w*) *iw mn kk*[*y*] *n-ḥꜣt.ṯ=f*, 'Who is accustomed to hearken to the voice of the prophet of the Lady of Aphroditopolis in whose heart there is no darkness?', may represent the sense of the passage. For *kky*, see *DG*, 568. 11.

an. : *my* and *ḫpr n Pr-ꜥꜣ Bꜣ-. . . .* are virtually certain; some restoration like *my* [*ḏd n*(*=y*)]/*my* [*dit rḫ=y*] *tꜣ/nꜣ* ⌜*i*⌝[*-ir*]*-ḫpr n Pr-ꜥꜣ Bꜣ-. . . .*, 'Please tell me/please let me know what has happened to Pharaoh Ba-. . . .', seems called for, though *tꜣ nti* ⌜*iw*⌝*=*[*s r*] *ḫpr*, 'what shall happen', is also possible. *ḥꜣꜥ-y tꜣi=t sndyt n ḥꜣt.ṯ=f* is partly restored on the analogy of x+1/5, 17, the evidence for *=f* being confined to a trace of the tail.

ao. : *gm=y tꜣ i-ir-ḫpr n-im=f r bw-ir-tw pꜣ mšꜥ gm.ṯ=f* with the negative of unfulfilled action fits traces and sense well.

ap. : the initial group may be the interjection *i*, 'O' with following vocative, or *r wꜥ.t*, in which case *r* might be the circumstantial auxiliary rather than the preposition. The two large signs further on may, but do not necessarily, belong to some part of the verb *mšꜥ*, 'go'; the next traces seem to belong to a word ending with fem. *.t* or suffix *=t* (e.g. *pꜣi=t/tꜣi=t/nꜣi=t*, 'your' (fem.)) rather than with the bad det. ; the final group resembles the initial signs of *ḏ*(*d*)*tḫ*, 'restrain, imprison' in x+1/30.

aq. : . . . *iw=w r sdm pꜣ nti iw=y r* [*ḏd.ṯ=f*] seems the most probable restoration; if the tentative suggestion *ḏ*(*d*)*tḫ* (n. *ap* above) is correct, then there is no room for anything else before *iw=w*, but if it is wrong [*bn*]*-iw=w* might conceivably be restored. The final group of the line is badly damaged but may perhaps resemble the initial group of *sꜣwti.w* (x+1/22) with the plural article *nꜣ* before it.

ar. : [*nꜣ*] ⌜*rmt.w*⌝ *ꜥꜣ.w n Pr-ꜥꜣ dr=w* appears certain, with probably nothing preceding it. As the following *in i-ir=t r rḫ* (highly probable) must begin a new clause or sentence, it seems that *nꜣ rmt.w ꜥꜣ.w* must be taken with the preceding *nꜣ sꜣwti.w* (?) as the postponed subjects of *iw=w r sdm* in x+1/3. *in i-ir=t* is here written for *in iw iw=t*, cf. p. 87, n. *fa*.

as. : *in i-ir=t r rḫ dit* probable, despite appearances in the photograph; the superlinear diagonal strokes belong to *rḫ* and to the tail of *gm.ṯ=f* in x+1/3.

at. : *ḫrꜥry* 'doom, (divine) wrath', is certain, cf. **2**, front, 6/31 and **1**, 10/33. Of the two signs which follow, the second must be the opening of the cartouche of *Pr-ꜥꜣ* because of the preservation of the following *ꜥws* and royal name (see p. 114, n. *al*); the first by its form is *r* rather than *nti*, that is, the circumstantial introducing a relative clause after an undefined antecedent. The traces before *ḫrꜥry* should thus probably not be construed as a def. article.

au. : *my rḫ=y* [*tꜣ/nꜣ*] ⌜*i-ir-*⌝[*ḫpr n-im=f*] seems the most probable restoration. This suggests that *ḏd=y n-im=w i-ir-ḥr pꜣ mšꜥ* might be restored to follow this directly: 'let me know that which has happened to him that I may tell it to the army/people', in which case *nꜣ i-ir-ḫpr* must be read in x+1/4. Note that, if correct, this restoration would fix the amount of space lost at the end of the lines of this column. The restoration *ḥꜣꜥ=y tꜣi=t sndy[t n-ḥꜣt.ṭ=f]* is based upon the occurrences of the same phrase in x+1/2, 17, where the resumptive suffix *=f* refers to Pharaoh. Probably it does so here also, though technically it might refer to *pꜣ mšꜥ*.

av. : *n wꜥ ḫrw* is certain. The preceding traces are slight, but might fit *ꜥꜣ.w* written as in x+1/4. The form of the group following *ḫrw* is uncertain.

aw. : *dr=w* and *Mr-ib* are certain (cf. x+1/20, 21, 32 for *Mr-ib*), the intervening group most probably *ḏd*. As a plural subject is logically to be expected with the phrase *n wꜥ ḫrw*, *dr=w* should agree with this, and it must be represented by the lost words with plural det. before *n wꜥ ḫrw*. As *ḏd* in this position should introduce a speech enclitically, a verb of utterance or the like is required at the beginning of the sentence. A conjectural restoration might be: [*ꜥš nꜣ sꜣwti.w nꜣ rmt.w ꜥꜣ.*]*w n wꜥ ḫrw* . [. . . . .]. *ḏd*, 'All the Guards and the Great Men of Pharaoh cried out with one . . . voice, saying: "Merib . . ." '. For the lost adjectival phrase after *ḫrw*, various possibilities exist; *wstn*, 'strident, loud, overweening' (*DG*, 101. 4), might perhaps be suggested on the basis of the initial trace, cf. **2** front, 6/28.

ax. : *pꜣ i-ir-dit ꜣk* certain; in view of the later events of the story, *Pr-ꜥꜣ* must almost certainly be restored as the subject of *ꜣk*, but will not fit the traces following it; these suggest the reading *ḫf*, 'destroy' (*DG*, 358. 1).

ay. : *nꜣ md.wt* ⌜*n*⌝ [*ḏd*] seems highly probable, cf. x/5, with the subscript tail of an *=f* strongly suggesting *ir=f* or *i-ir=f* at the beginning of the line. Probably restore [*ir=f mnk*] *nꜣ md.wt n ḏd* ,'he completed the words of speaking', after the model of **2** front, 6/25 (see, however, p. 86, n. *er*).

az. : *iw=f rmy iw=f šrr* is certain; for the second det. of *rmy*, cf. **1**, 9/19.

ba. : . . . . . *=f tꜣ pt* is highly probable, see x/22 and **2**, front, 6/14 for writings of *pt* determined as here. There is no certain trace of a preposition before *tꜣ pt*, though *n* (not *r*) is possible; the traces preceding *=f* are undistinctive.

bb. : the traces preceding *bw-ir-rḫ* should on the basis of the det. yield an expression of time; *rsṭ*, 'tomorrow' (*DG*, 255. 7), might fit.

bc. : owing to the join between DP153 and DP357 the early part of x+1/7 is partially obscured in the photograph, but the reading . . . . .*w iw=w ꜥš n=s ḫr sdm=s n-im=w* is quite secure. Presumably the lost plural word at the beginning (e.g. *nꜣ rmt.w*(?)) was the antecedent of both *iw=w* and *n-im=w*.

bd. : *dr=w* very probable.

be. : *sdm*, written as in x+1/2 is certain; the preceding traces are very uncertain, though they are not incompatible with *rmt.w ꜥꜣ.w*, written as in x+1/4.

bf. : *md.wt n* ⌜*sdm*⌝ probable; whether this would suffice to complete the line (see p. 115, n. *au*) is doubtful.

bg. ; the first group is formed like the article *tꜣ*/*nꜣ*, the next like *i*/*iw*; *tꜣi=*/*nꜣi=*, the possessive adjective is certainly possible, but it is difficult to restore convincingly. If *md.wt n* ⌜*sdm*⌝ ended x+1/7, then perhaps read [*mnk=f nꜣ*] *md.wt n* ⌜*sdm*⌝ *nꜣ-i*[*-ir=f*, 'he completed the words of hearing which he did', i.e. he finished listening. It would then be possible to restore [*sdr*]*=f ir=f in-ḳdy*, 'he lay down, he slept', with good sense; however, there is no certain trace of the first *=f*, though there is room for it, and there is a doubt whether *sdr* is a legitimate reading in view of the writings without the det. in x+1/15, 36, 38 (see p. 112, n. *k*). Another conceivable reading is [*swr*]*=f*, 'he drank'.

bh. : *i-ir=f pry n rswy*, cf. *DG*, 136. 2 and Coptic ⲡⲱⲱⲣⲉ (Crum, *CD*, 268a) for this usage, the main doubtful point being whether or not an *n* should be read before *rswy* introducing an indirect rather than a direct object; note that the Second Tense *i-ir=f pry* is used, but this might emphasize an adverbial or circumstantial phrase in the following lacuna (e.g. *iw=w ḏd n=f* regularly used in accounts of dreams, cf. Ray, *Archive of Ḥor*, 10, n. *ff*) rather than *n*(?) *rswy*.

bj. : a very broken and uncertain passage for which we have no convincing reading to suggest; the last sign might well represent the beginning of *mꜣi*, 'lion', the appearance of which here is by no means improbable in view of the question concerning it in x+1/10. The first sign seems to resemble *=s* or the end of *ꜥws* after a cartouche rather than the definite article *tꜣ*/*nꜣ*; it is certainly not *dit*.

bk. : *nb*(*.t*) alone is certain. The sign preceding *nb*(*.t*) is almost certainly either *.t* or *=t*. As these words must almost certainly be picked up by the 3rd pers. fem. suffix of *ỉw=s* at the beginning of x+1/9, the conclusion that a feminine entity is involved is almost irresistible; and, as *ỉw=s* should refer to the goddess who speaks to Merib in his dream in x+1/10–19 and is most probably Hathor (see x+1/20 and p. 137), it is logical to seek a name or epithet of Hathor in these words. Clearly, however, the same epithets are not present as in x+1/1. The final *.t* cannot represent *wr.t* unless the divine det. present in x+1/1 has been omitted, nor does the preceding trace suit. Nor is this likely to represent the name *Ḥwt-Ḥr*, written without final *.t* in x+1/20. Speculatively, the only common female divine epithets which it seems to us may fit the traces are *tꜣ ntr.t* (best fit), *tꜣ ntrt ꜥꜣ.t* (cf. x+1/14) and *wr.t mw.t-ntr*. written . The sign which follows *nb*(*.t*) is made in two strokes and has no final loop; *ꜥ* or *k* are thus preferable as a reading to *pꜣ*. Indeed, comparison with x+1/29 *m-dr nb.t ꜥnḫ* . . . . suggests that the same combination stood here. Presumably a cult-name is required; *nb.t ꜥnḫ-tꜣ.wy* springs to mind, but this is usual only with Bastis and Sakhmis, demotic writings of whose names the traces will not fit (cf. x+1/14 for *Bꜣstt*; **2** front, 6/31 for *Sḫmt*). On the other hand, if the restoration *wr.t mw.t-ntr* is retained, *Bꜣstt* may have preceded this; there is perhaps something to be said for this suggestion, see discussion on pp. 132, n. *aη*, 138 but the arguments in favour of Hathor seem much superior.

bl. : *sbt n šꜥ*, 'mound of sand' (*DG*, 423. 3, 489. 3), seems virtually certain; restore perhaps *ỉw=s* [*ḥms.ṯ ḥr*] *sbt n šꜥ*, 'she being seated upon a mound of sand'(?).

bm. : *r wꜥ mw ꜣṯḥ* certain, though the loss of the det. of *ꜣṯḥ* is unfortunate in view of the unusual forms recorded by *DG*, 14. 2. According to Černý, *CED*, 220. 1, 230. 4 *wdḥ*, 'pour' (*Wb.* i. 393. 6 ff.; Coptic ⲟⲩⲱⲧϩ Crum, *CD*, 498b), is confused with *ỉtḥ*, 'draw, drag' (*Wb.* i. 148. 12 ff., Coptic ⲱⲧϩ), *DG*, 14. 2 *ꜣtḥ*, 'ziehen', representing the latter, *DG*, 14. 4, *ꜣtḥ*, 'schöpfen, giessen', representing both. In the present broken context, the meaning is uncertain, though *r* is doubtless circumstantial; perhaps some such phrase as 'a wave lapping her feet' might suit (see n. *bn* below). The expression *ꜣtḥ n mw*, 'drawings of water' (R. A. Parker, 'A late demotic gardening agreement', *JEA* 26 (1940), 85), should perhaps be noted, though it seems not quite apposite here.

bn. : the vertical break in the papyrus has disturbed the relationship of the first signs in the photograph; *pꜣ ym* is a quite probable reading. *ḥr spṯ*, 'on the bank of' (*DG*, 428. 2; Coptic ⲥⲡⲟⲧⲟⲩ, Crum, *CD*, 353a; Černý, *CED*, 160. 2), is certain; the group cannot be read *n tꜣ/nꜣ* as *pꜣ* follows, but must be regarded as the determinative of *spṯ*, of the same form as that used with *mw* and *ym* earlier in this line (hieroglyphic ?). The previous sign should then perhaps be regarded as phonetic, reflecting the original dual termination of hieroglyphic *spty*, 'lips', retained in Coptic ⲥⲡⲟⲧⲟⲩ. The final groups should doubtless be restored *pꜣ yr* [*ꜥꜣ*(?)], 'the (great?) river' on grounds of traces and sense. It is, however, not easy to picture a lake or sea on the banks of the Nile, unless indeed the inundation is referred to, and the reading *ym* may be questioned on this ground.

bo. : the photograph shows two wormholes at the beginning of this line deceptively dark, which obscures the text. The initial groups read simply *ḏd tꜣ/nꜣ* or *ḏd=s*, while comparison of the traces after the lacuna with the writing of the name *Mr-ỉb* in x+1/20 suggest that it stood here; if so, it must presumably have been a vocative. If this vocative was prefixed by the interjection *ỉ*, 'O', then this would have filled the lacuna (the traces would probably though not certainly fit, cf. the writings in x/1, x+1/3 (?)) and *ḏd=s* must be read; if not, a fem. noun defined by *tꜣ* should probably be restored (e.g. possibly *tꜣ s-ḥm.t*, 'the woman', which might imply that the goddess appeared to Merib in an assumed form).

bp. : *mꜣỉ* is written with the divine det. (cf. x/10; x+1/14, 15, 36, 37). The following group, written with a very full brush, seems on comparison with the names *Mr-ỉb* and *Mr-* . . . . (x+1/26, 29) certainly to be *mr*; yet both the following traces and the context exclude its being identified with either of those names. *mr* might be a *sdm=f* form with nominal subject beginning a new sentence, though compared with most writings the det. is very abbreviated (*DG*, 167. 1). Another possibility is that it qualifies *mꜣỉ* adjectivally, governing a noun or noun phrase (cf. the perfect active participle and the Coptic *participium conjunctum* in such phrases as ⲙⲁⲓ̈ⲣⲱⲙⲉ, Crum, *CD*, 156b). We have, however, no satisfactory reading to offer for the following traces, where the fibres are much distorted.

bq. : *dỉ=y ỉr=f* is probable after the break. The traces before it, though much damaged, may well represent *ỉ-ỉr=y*, or perhaps better *pꜣỉ-ỉr=y*; whichever is correct, a relative form is present, since *dỉ=y ỉr=f* should begin a new sentence. While its antecedent is uncertain because of the preceding lacuna, the simplest solution seems to be to refer it back to *mꜣi*: 'Are you looking at this [. . . . .]-loving lion whom I have made?'

br. : the signs are clear (cf. x+1/15), but the reading of the title is uncertain. *sdm sfy*, 'servant of the sword', i.e. perhaps 'sword-bearer', is clearly a defensible reading. But *sfy*, 'sword' is normally determined with , , not often with as here (*DG*, 429. 3). is a common abbreviated writing for *sdm-ꜥš*, 'servant' (cf. **1**, 9/5 written); a reading *sdm-ꜥš fꜣy*, 'the servant (and) bearer', may thus be possible. Though *fꜣy* is admittedly normally determined with (hieroglyphic), yet the copper det. might be appropriate if the title approximated to 'cup-bearer' (cf. *fꜣy tn nb* κανηφόρος, *fꜣy ḳn nꜥš* ἀθλοφόρος). As *sdm-(ꜥš) sfy* is attested elsewhere (see J. K. Winnicki, 'Die Kalasirier der Spätdynastischen und der Ptolemäischen Zeit', in *Historia*, 26 (1977), 257–68, see p. 264; and K.-T. Zauzich, *Die ägyptische Schreibertradition*, (Wiesbaden, 1968), Band II, p. 254, Anm. 125) this is perhaps the reading to be preferred.

bs. : *n* highly probable. In view of x+1/15 *di=y ir=f n=f sdm-(ꜥš) sfy*(?), where *n=f* must refer to Pharaoh, the trace following *n* should perhaps be interpreted as the opening cartouche of *Pr-ꜥꜣ*.

bt. : *nti snḥ drt.ṱ=y* is certain. As no *n* is written before *drt.ṱ=y*, the straightforward translation is 'who has bound my hand'. However, Crum, *CD*, 348b lists ⲛ̄ⲧⲏⲛ, ⲛ̄ⲧⲟⲟⲧ= as being used with the Stative of ⲥⲱⲛϩ̄, so that, granted omission of *n*, 'who is bound in my hand' is another possibility.

bu. : *n-drt* followed by *sdm=f* can only well be a conjunction (cf. the Coptic past temporal auxiliary ⲛ̄ⲧⲉⲣⲉϥⲥⲱⲧⲙ̄), while *r-bn(-pw)=y* should be negative past circumstantial. In **2** front, 6/27, 28 occurs as the absolute form of the adverb *(n-)hꜣ(t)* used temporally to mean 'before, earlier' (*DG*, 287. 1, where, however, only *(n) tꜣ ḥꜣ.t* is quoted with this meaning); for the present passage it is significant that it is used in **2** front, 6/27 with *n-drt*. It seems better therefore to translate: 'when he heard Pharaoh earlier, when I had not ordered it/him to him', rather than 'when he heard before Pharaoh', i.e. 'obeyed Pharaoh'; the latter would more probably have been expressed by *i-ir-ḥr* or *m-bꜣḥ*. *sḫn.ṱ=s n=f* seems clear from the traces, see also n. *bw* below.

bv. : despite considerable damage, *i-ir Pr-ꜥꜣ ꜥš* [. .] . . . . ⌜*tꜣ ḥꜣ.t n*⌝ [*pꜣ*] ⌜*wtn n pꜣ-Rꜥ*⌝ seems reasonably well assured; the intervening traces are illegible, it being notably uncertain whether a diagonal visible in x+1/12 (before *di=y*) is really the descender of an *=f* from x+1/11; if so perhaps simply *ꜥš r-r=f n tꜣ ḥꜣ.t* might fill the lacuna. On general grounds, however, it seems more likely that the goddess who is speaking was on the prow of the barque of Reꜥ than the lion; if the putative *=f* can be ignored, some such restoration as *ꜥš* [*n(=y) iw=y*] *n tꜣ ḥꜣ.t* might perhaps be considered.

bw. The readings in the first half of the line are clear. *sꜣb* seems most likely to be a metathetical writing of *sbꜣ*, 'enemy' (*DG*, 420. 3, where similar metatheses are recorded). In Insinger the word means 'impiety', M. Lichtheim in *Studien zu altägyptischen Lebenslehren*, (Fribourg/Göttingen, 1979), 291. The words following *ḏd* must be a speech made to the goddess since it contains the 2nd pers. sing. fem. rel. construction *pꜣi-ir=t sḫn.ṱ=f* (cf. p. 17, n. *bw* on **1**, 9/27), quoted within the goddess's speech to Merib in his dream, which continues to the end of the paragraph in x+1/19. Whether the speaker is the lion, as seems most natural, is discussed below, p. 132, n. *aδ*, for this is bound up with the problem of the meaning of *sḫn.ṱ=f*, which appears in similar contexts below in x+1/26, 27.

bx. : *ir=y* and *r-r=f* are certain. The diagonal stroke preceding *r-r=f* is certainly the bad det. , and the traces strongly support the reading *ḫrꜥry*, 'rage', cf. x+1/4 and **2** front, 6/31, here taken as a verb.

by. : *di=y* is certain. Comparison with writings in **2** front, 6/9, 17, 7/9 makes it certain that the final word is a noun from the stem *mwt*, though whether it represents *pꜣ mwt*, 'death' or *pꜣ mwt.ṱ*, 'dying/dead man', may be less certain (see p. 77, n. *ax* on **2** front, 6/9). The traces of the intervening verb seem best to fit *šn*, 'be sick', written (*DG*, 514. 1), though in **2** front, 6/20, this verb is more fully written . If this reading is accepted, the most natural translation would be: 'I caused death/the dying man to be sick'; this seems rather unsatisfactory since neither 'death' nor a 'dying man' have so far appeared in this passage. Perhaps *šn pꜣ mwt* here is the forerunner of Coptic ϣⲱⲛⲉ ⲙ̄ⲡⲙⲟⲩ, 'mortal sickness' (Crum, *CD*, 571a). The text might then have run: 'I raged against him, I placed a mortal sickness [in his heart]', restoring *n-ḥꜣt.ṱ=f* at the end of the phrase.

bz. : *bn(-pw)=f gm ꜥḳ r wnm*; *gm ꜥḳ* is badly damaged, but the traces and the parallelism with *bn(-pw)=f gm mw r swr* virtually assure the reading. For *ꜥḳ*, cf. x/7.

ca. : *di=y-s n=f* highly probable; the following sign is probably the def. article *tꜣ/nꜣ*, whereafter all is uncertain, though *tꜣ wnw.t* is a plausible guess.

cb. : *i-ỉr=s šdy=f* (*DG*, 528. 2) seems the best reading, the top member of the first group being of the form , somewhat obscured by the *y* being started over it, producing a fortuitous resemblance to *fty=f* (*DG*, 145. 6). The form of ensures the reading *i-ỉr=s*, not *i-ỉr(=y) dỉt*; note that the 1st pers. suffix *=y* seems always to be written on the back (though not the front) of **2**. It is uncertain whether this suffix *=s*, introduced at the end of x+1/13, refers forward to Bastet, back to a person, or to *sṯy*, 'flame'; an *n* almost certainly precedes *sṯy* at the beginning of x+1/14, so that it probably forms part of a compound expression '[. . . . .] of flame', not necessarily feminine in gender. The preceding expression *dmy r-r=f* means 'touch, join, reach' (*DG*, 631. 2; Coptic ⲧⲱⲱⲙⲉ ⲉ-, Crum, *CD*, 414b; cf. *Wb.* v. 453. 6 ff.); presumably the masc. suffix should refer to the same person as the object of *šdy=f* and refer back to the last male person mentioned, namely Pharaoh (x+1/13), but this is not certain (see p. 132, n. *αη*).

cc. : nothing is certain. The long initial stroke might represent (among other possibilities) *in*, 'bring', *ṯꜣi*, 'take', or *di*, 'give, place, cause'. After the lacuna *pꜣ* seems probable, followed by a word ending in the divine det.; the exiguous traces and spacing might suggest *pꜣ mꜣi* as a possibility. The last word presents difficulties; the animal det. is preceded by *ṯ* and by a tall sign resembling *sn*, *šn*, or perhaps *ḥḏ*; the first sign seems to be *m* rather than *š*. We suggest a writing of *mꜣ-ḥḏ*, 'oryx' (*Wb.* ii. 11. 4 ff., cf. Late Period *mḥ*, *Wb.* ii. 121. 11 f.), written *my-ḥṯ*; we have not found a demotic example of the word.

cd. : *di=y ḥms pꜣ mꜣi wbꜣ tꜣ/nꜣ* . . . . . seems certain; for *ḥms* cf. x+1/35. The final word begins with an upright stroke, possibly but not necessarily *w* or *ntr*; alternatively, read *tꜣi*[*=f*]/*nꜣi*[*=f*], or, less probably, *wbꜣ=s*.

ce. : *ḥmꜣ*, 'salt' (*DG*, 307. 1) is clearly a superior reading here to *ỉr.ty*, 'eyes', which is written in **2** front, 6/19, 30. The goddess presumably causes the lion to bring salt to Pharaoh to season the oryx meat he has brought him, if the reading suggested in n. *cc* above is correct.

cf. *iw=f sdr ḥr pꜣ dw*: as this is circumstantial, the subject must refer back either to the subject (the lion) or the dative (Pharaoh) in the previous clause; as the goddess has made the lion sit, it seems more likely to be Pharaoh who is lying, especially as he is probably sick (see p. 118, n. *by*).

cg. : the initial group is to be read *n tꜣ wnw.t*, 'at the moment of, immediately' (Coptic ⲛ̄ⲧⲉⲩⲛⲟⲩ Crum, *CD*, 484b). *sṯy i-ỉr-ḥr=f* is certain, but the sign may have been part either of *Bꜣstt* (x+1/14) or of *mw* (x+1/13), among other, remoter, possibilities. The adjacent traces are too exiguous to resolve the problem.

ch. : though damaged, *tꜣi=f rỉt ḫrỉt* is certain through comparison with x+1/16. The curious form after *tw=y* may perhaps be resolved as the 1st pers. Stative of *ꜥḥꜥ*, 'stand' (*DG*, 68. 10) *tw=y ꜥḥꜥ.k(wi)*, though we cannot quote an exact parallel. If *n* is restored before *tꜣi=f*, there being no room for more, then some such restoration as *pꜣ mꜣi* [(*ḥms*/*ꜥḥꜥ*) *n tꜣi=f rỉt ḫrỉt*] is doubtless required at the end of the line, though the verb might have been omited there.

cj. : *ḫrḫr*, 'quaking, destruction' (*DG*, 367. 2; Coptic ϣⲟⲣϣⲣ Crum, *CD*, 589a; Černý, *CED*, 252. 7), appears a better reading than an unattested word *ḫnḫn*, for which the only plausible root would be *ḫnn*, 'confuse, perturb' (*Wb.* iii. 383. 3 ff.), despite the unusual form of *r* . The group seems to be reserved in **1** and **2** for words showing ϣⲁ in Coptic; this would account for its not being used here.

ck. [ ] : *st ḳdy* is certain. Though the dot of the det. is somewhat separated from the 'legs', it is regularly written in this papyrus. The following traces seem therefore most likely to represent *n pꜣ*. The large group which follows may have been amended from something else, though it seems more probable that the scribe has simply filled his reed abnormally full. Much the most probable reading seems to be the numeral 4, cf. the writing in **1**, 16/x+5 of *4.nw*. The restoration is speculative; perhaps *st ḳdy* ⌜*n pꜣ 4.nw*⌝ [*n ḳḥ*], 'they went round on the fourth side' (cf. *DG*, 547.6 *ḳḥ 4*) might give an appropriate sense. The trace after the lacuna is of unclear form; it appears to be followed by an area of blank papyrus, possibly marking the beginning of a new sentence.

cl. : only *gm=w-s* and *nti̓ ỉw=f* can be considered entirely certain. A reading perfectly consistent with what remains is *gm=w-s n tꜣ mrṯ nti̓ ỉw=f n-ỉm=s*. This gives excellent sense, and has been adopted here. Objections which may be raised against it are: i. that *mrṯ* (*DG*, 170. 2) seems to be a rare word of dubious etymology, perhaps unlikely to be preferred in such a context to *smt* or *gy*; ii. that the final traces do not quite suit *n-ỉm=* written as in x+1/4, and would perhaps fit *ẖn* better: this preposition seems relatively unlikely if *mrṯ* is correct. An alternative reading is *gm=w-s n ꞽImrṯ/ꞽIšrṯ nti̓ ỉw=f ẖn=s*; *ꞽImrṯ* would represent hieroglyphic *ꞽImr* (Gardiner, *Onomastica*, i. 187* ff.; Biblical Emor; Cuneiform Amurru) in the northern Levant, *ꞽIšrṯ* hieroglyphic *ꞽIsr*, *ꞽIssr* (Gardiner, op. cit. i. 191* ff.; Biblical Ashur; Assyrian Aššur), used in demotic of both Assyria and Syria (*DG*, 45. 2). This is attractive in that the characters concerned here promise in x+1/17 '[we are] rescuing you, we are bringing you back to Egypt', which implies that Pharaoh is out of Egypt (cf. x+1/33 f., which may imply that the region is mountainous and probably cold). However, objections to this reading are: i. the initial trace perhaps resembles *tꜣ/nꜣ* more than the upright stroke required by *ꞽImrṯ/ꞽIšrṯ*; ii. the reason for the presence of *ṯ* (if correctly read) is not clear: for further comment, see p. 140.

cm. : *ḏd* . . . *ḏd=n r ẖrw* is virtually certain. The traces and spacing suggest that the likeliest restoration is simply *ḏd*⸢*=w n=f*⸣ *ḏd=n r ẖrw*, 'they said to him: "we are speaking at the behest of . . ." '. At the end of this line *ỉw=n* must be restored as the auxiliary for *nḥm=k* in x+1/17, so whatever is restored after *ẖrw* must be relatively brief (probably the name or epithet of a goddess, see p. 132, n. *αθ*).

cn. : *nḥm=k* is certain (*DG*, 223. 2); the short vertical strokes above belong to *ẖrẖr* in x+1/16 (p. 119, n. *cj*). Note that *nḥm* here governs the suffix without interposition of the pronominal *.ṯ*, which appears in *ỉw=n ỉn.ṯ=k* (a weak verb). Whether these forms should be translated as present, or whether *r* should be supplied to produce a future rendering is uncertain; in general it seems that the scribe of **2** normally wrote the *r* of futurity.

co. : only *r Kmy* and *dr=w* are certain. What may be restored between depends rather on whether *Kmy* was here determined with  only or with  (*DG*, 564. 1). If the latter, then *dr=w* should perhaps be referred back to *ỉw=n*, 'we are all bringing you back to Egypt . . .', but this leaves brief but awkward traces after *Kmy* unexplained. The object suffix in *ỉ-ỉr=y ỉr=w* in the next sentence seems to require an antecedent: it is tempting to read *n*[*ꜣy*] *dr=w* and translate: 'All these things, it was because of the words which you spoke that I did them'; the space would fit the single det. for *Kmy*, but the reading *n*[*ꜣy*] is dubious.

cp. : *ỉ-ỉr=y ỉr=w n=f r-dbꜣ tꜣ md.t* is certain, with the following *r-ḏd=k* virtually so; the following traces are, however, much obscured, and though *n(=y)* seems probable on grounds of sense, it is less than certain (see n. *cq* below).

cq. : comparison with x+1/2, 5 shows that some part of the verb *ẖꜣꜥ* should be read before *tꜣỉ=t sndyt* (*n-*)*ḥꜣt.ṯ=f*, and the traces confirm that it preceded *tꜣỉ=t* directly without suffix. As the past *sdm=f* form *ẖꜣꜥ=y* is used in x+1/2, 5, a past auxiliary is required here; the Second Tense *ỉ-ỉr=y ẖꜣꜥ* with emphasis on (*n-*)*ḥꜣt.ṯ=f* seems most probable, and is not irreconcilable with the traces and space available (reading *n*(*=y*), n. *cp* above), but must remain in doubt.

cr. : *ẖꜣꜥ=y-s* ⸢*ỉw*⸣ *bn-ỉw=f* ⸢*ḏd bn*⸣[*-ỉw*]*=y sdm* . . . [. . . . . .]  *pꜣ-ỉ-ỉr-dbḥ=k mtw=y*: despite the damage, the readings *ỉw bn-ỉw=f* and *bn-ỉw=y* seem almost inevitable, and *dbḥ=k* is secure. It is interpretation and what to restore at the end of x+1/17 that is the problem. It appears clear that the goddess's quotation of Merib's words end at (*n-*)*ḥꜣt.ṯ=f* (n. *cq* above); thus the subject of *ẖꜣꜥ=y-s* should be herself and the object presumably Pharaoh, who must then be the subject of the future circumstantial *ỉw bn-ỉw=f ḏd*. Thus *bn-ỉw=y sdm* . . . . . are the words which the goddess promises Merib in his dream that Pharaoh will not say: a following dative, 'I will not hearken to/obey you', seems required, and *n=t* (fem.) seems to fit the traces well. On the other hand, the words *pꜣ-ỉ-ỉr-dbḥ=k mtw=y* must certainly, in view of the following imperatives, be addressed to Merib by the goddess, so some such restoration as 'I will grant to you that which you have required of me' might be put forward; *ỉw=y* (*r*) *dỉt n=k* might reasonably fill the space probably available at the end of x+1/17 (see p. 121, n. *dd*), but not perhaps the slight trace after the postulated *n=t*, so perhaps a short word (e.g. *ꜥn*, 'again') would need to be supplied here. Note, however, that the form used here should, if the scribe is consistent, be the def. article plus the past participle *i-ir-dbḥ* (cf. *pꜣi-ir-dit ꜣḳ* in x+1/5) and not the relative form, differently written in *pꜣi-ir=t sḫn.t=f* in x+1/12. A superior version is therefore probably 'Pharaoh is the one who has required you of me', restoring *Pr-ꜥꜣ pꜣi* at the end of x+1/17.

cs. : *m-šm* ⌜*iwt*⌝ *pꜣi=k mšꜥ i-ḏd[y] n=f*: *iwt* is highly probable, cf. the writing in x+1/35; for the imperative *m-šm*, cf. *DG*, 506 under 505. 7. There are traces of a group between *mšꜥ* and *ḏd*, which may be interpreted as the imperative form written (*DG*, 690 under 689. 1; Coptic ⲁϫⲱ).

ct. : *pꜣi=tn ḥri* [*iw=f*] *wḏꜣ mtw=k* ⌜*smy*⌝ [*i-ir*]*-ḥr nꜣ sꜣwṯi.w*; *wḏꜣ* is certain, but only the merest traces remain of the *iw=f* required by the sense. Sufficient remains of *smy* to render it probable, but the first element of *i-ir-ḥr* is supplied. For *sꜣwṯi.w* cf. x+1/22.

cu. : *n=w* is slightly uncertain, but probable; for *pꜣ dw*, cf. x+1/13; *m-sꜣ* is certain, and the trace at the end of the line might fit the initial cartouche of *Pr-ꜥꜣ*, which seems the most probable restoration.

cv.

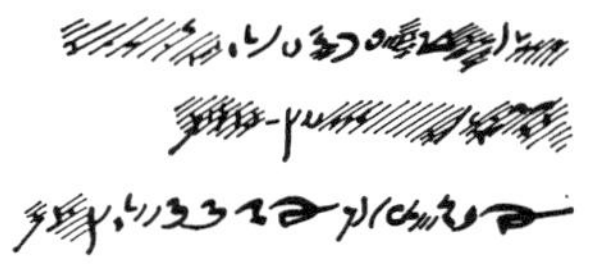

r stꜣ.t=f r Kmy is certain (cf. p. 120, n. *cl* on Pharaoh's whereabouts). Thereafter, though badly damaged, the whole passage is restorable from the parallels in x+1/21–2 and x+1/32 below, with the exception of the final phrase. *mtꜥṯ* was compared with Coptic ⲙⲧⲁⲧ, 'bridle, bit' (Crum, *CD*, 196a), in *JEA* 61 (1975), 197; there, however, *ḫ(r)r* was mistaken for part of the verb *ḫr*, 'fall'. The det. in x+1/21, 32, which the word shares with *ṯwy*, 'sandals', in x/3 excludes this and shows that the word must mean something made of leather or hide (cf. hieroglyphic). It should represent the hieroglyphic word *ḫnr*, not attested in *Wb.*, but exemplified in *Urk.* iv. 1282. 16–17, *sḫpr·n·f ssmwt nn mitwt·sn n wrd·n·sn ḫft ṯꜣ·f ḫnr*, 'he brought up horses which had no equal, which never could weary when he seized the rein'; cf. also *Urk.* iv. 1311. 17.

cw. : The final phrase is not restorable with certainty; unfortunately the parallel in x+1/22 *mšꜥ pꜣ ḥtri irm* . . . . breaks down at the same point and the phrase does not occur in x+1/32; some sense such as 'leave him with/by himself' seems required.

cx. : *mḥ 1.t* is clear. The following traces do not correspond with the expected *grḥ* as written in l. 22; perhaps therefore read *mḥ 1.t* ⌜*gs*⌝ [*n grḥ*] which the traces will fit admirably, though we cannot quote a parallel for this method of expressing the half hour in Egyptian.

cy. : only the final *=f* is certain here. *ḏd=f* seems probable in view of the following soliloquy.

cz. : *ḫft-ḥ(r)*, 'dromos, front court' (*DG*, 359. 1), used regularly of temples and sacred hypogea like the Serapeum; it was the part of the temple accessible to the public for making offerings, giving thanks, supplicating the god, requesting oracles, and other purposes (cf. *Wb.* iii. 275. 8 ff., 276. 10).

da. in is certain, but could be either the post-negation or the interrogative particle. With *n pꜣi nw*, 'at this hour', the Neg. First Pres. *bn-iw=y šm* . . . . *in* is presumably as appropriate as the Future Neg. *bn-iw=y šm*, while a rhetorical question seems less suitable than a statement of intent in the following phrase, as Merib immediately fulfils this.

db. : *iw=y r ḏd.t=s* is certain; what follows is problematic. As it is clear from x+1/18 taken with x+1/22 that it is the Guards and the Great Men of Pharaoh to whom Merib is going to speak, it is tempting to reconstruct the text thus: *iw=y r ḏd.t=s* ⌜*r-ḥr-n*⌝ [*nꜣ sꜣwṯi.w nꜣ rmt.w ꜥꜣ.w*] *n Pr-ꜥꜣ*. However, the traces do not entirely favour *r-ḥr-n*, especially the initial sign, and it is just possible that *m-mitt* , 'likewise' (*DG*, 152. 1), should be read, meaning that he will speak as the goddess has instructed him in his dream. See also n. *dd* below.

dc. : *ḥrry r* (*DG*, 325. 9) is certain; it is regularly used in the negative with a following noun of place without a verb of motion to mean 'not to delay to (go to)'. Thus while the final trace might be part of *ii*, 'come', it might equally form part of a designation of a place (e.g. *Mn-nfr*).

dd. : *di Mr-ib* ⌜*in*⌝*=w wꜥ ḥtri* seems reasonably certain despite the damage. The remainder of x+1/21–2 to *mšꜥ pꜣ ḥtri irm*[*=f*] can be restored with certainty on the basis of the parallels in x+1/19, 32 (see above n. *cv* and *JEA* 61 (1975), 197 for discussion). Note that the mandatory restoration *bn(-pw)* *=f mḥy.t=f* at the end of x+1/21 fixes the width of the column at six groups above the extant length of this line. This poses some problems; the restoration proposed in n. *db* for the end of x+1/20 *nꜣ sꜣwti.w nꜣ rmt.w ꜥꜣ.w* seems a little too long: while the obvious restoration in x+1/22 *nꜣ rmt.w ꜥꜣ.w* is certainly too short on its own. As *nꜣ sꜣwti.w* appears on its own in x+1/18 there seems to be no reason why simply *nꜣ rmt.w ꜥꜣ.w n Pr-ꜥꜣ* may not have stood in x+1/20–1, while an additional element may be present in x+1/22 (n. *dg* below).

de. : the traces are indecipherable.

df. : despite the damage, the restoration [*ỉn-nꜣ-w tꜣ*] ⌜*wnwt 6*⌝ *n grḥ* ⌜*ḫpr*⌝ seems highly probable.

dg. : *gm=f nꜣ sꜣwti.w* virtually certain; for the writing of *sꜣwti.w*, cf. *DG*, 403. 2; ꜥOnchsheshonqy 2/14. While *nꜣ rmt.w ꜥꜣ.w n Pr-ꜥꜣ* seems an obvious restoration, there is too much space for it (n. *dd* above), and it is a suspicious circumstance that no *n* is present before *Pr-ꜥꜣ* at the beginning of x+1/23, for it would probably not have been placed at the end of x+1/22. In fact, the trace after *sꜣwti.w* favours neither *nꜣ* nor *ỉrm*, and suggests perhaps rather *nti*; a short relative clause 'the Guards who looked after Pharaoh' or the like seems conceivable.

dh. : *md=w dr=w* ⌜*n wꜥ rꜣ*⌝ appears highly probable, *rꜣ*, 'mouth' being written with the det. appropriate to *rꜣ*, 'door' (*DG*, 240 under 239. 12), and a trace of *wꜥ* being preserved.

dj. : *Pr-ꜥꜣ* is followed by a very indistinct trace, just possibly *tn*. Comparison suggests that the large group after the lacuna is that read *dw* in x/2, 9; the trace thereafter does not, however (in the present state of the fibres), much resemble *w*, and there is clearly insufficient room for the plural *nꜣ dw.w*; perhaps here *pꜣ dw* was written in contrast with in x/9 and in x+1/13, 15, 16, 32, 34. After the following lacuna [*n*]⌜*ꜣi=k*⌝ *sḥn.w* appears to fit the traces best, but if this is right there is room at most for the preposition *n* before it. *bn(-pw)=n gm.ṯ=f* is clearly preferable to *bn(-pw)=s gm.ṯ=f*, and *n ꜥwi*, though damaged, seems certain. In view of the meaning of the second clause, we would suggest, very tentatively, that the speech might have read something like: 'They all spoke with one voice, saying; "Where is Pharaoh? We have sought him in the mountain according to your orders, but we have not found him in any place on earth" '. This would involve restoring *Pr-ꜥꜣ* ⌜*tn*⌝ *wḫꜣ=n-s n/ḥr pꜣ dw r nꜣi=k sḥn.w*, for which there would only just be room at best; *tn* 'where?' is perhaps to be rejected.

dk. : if the high traces after *m-ỉr* represent *r*, possibly restore *rmy* or *rwš*?

dl. As Merib is addressing the Guards, *šn=tn* must be the optative used as a polite imperative, and *nꜣ sꜣwti.w* must be vocative.

dm. [. . .]

the clauses beginning *ḥr sdm Ḥwt-Ḥr* and ⌜*ḥr*⌝ *sdm=s* are likely to be parallel in meaning. Following *Ḥwt-Ḥr*, *tꜣ/nꜣ nti* is possible. *dit mwy* seems preferable to *dit šwy*, the curious det. perhaps representing (cf. *DG*, 156. 3 for comparable forms, also *Wb.* ii. 34. 17 ff. under *mꜣṯ*; Černý, *CED*, 95. 6 under ⲙⲉⲉⲩⲉ). *ḥr* is then certain, the following badly damaged word conceivably being from the root *ꜥb*, 'offer, libate' (*DG*, 58. 10–13). *ḥr sdm=s pꜣ ḫrw n nꜣ . . . . n ỉrt.ṯ=w ỉw=w ḫnm.w* seems tolerably certain despite the damage (contrast the writing of *n ỉrt.ṯ=w* with *ḥꜣt.ṯ=f* in x+1/12). The unread word certainly begins with *k* and probably ends with the bad det. and a plural stroke; *knm.w*, 'blind', is a plausible reading, but the eye det. is lacking (cf. *DG*, 581. 5 under *gnm*), while *ksn.w*, 'weak', might also be possible, though this verb is usually written with *ḳ* (*DG*, 550. 3). *kp.w* 'covered, hidden', is perhaps also worth consideration, cf. **2** front, 6/19, though there written *kp*. *ḫnm.w* may be the Stative of the verb *ḫnm*, 'smell, cense' (*DG*, 362. 8), despite the inappropriate det. ; *ḫtm.w* sealed, shut' (*DG*, 372. 2), is perhaps possible, though the *t* is not convincing. As a conjectural restoration perhaps 'Hathor has been accustomed to listen to those who give thought to the offerings [of her temple?, she has been accustomed to] listen to the voice of the blind(?) of eye when they are perfumed', perhaps a reference to the Guards' failure to find Pharaoh.

dn. : *mtw=s wn* or *mtw=s wnḥ*, 'she will open/reveal', seem possible restorations.

do. : the word written is perhaps best read *ꜥmy*, taking as the sign present in *mꜣi*, 'new', and several words beginning *ꜥm* (*DG*, 60–1). Given the flesh det., the word is perhaps best identified with the similarly determined word *ꜣmy.t* used in Insinger and ꜥOnchsheshonqy to mean 'character, will, spirit, ability' (*DG*, 5.1). In view of the following *nb.t*, the preceding sign cannot be read as the definite article *tꜣ*; best seems to be to read *m*[*tw*]*=s dỉt n*(*=y*) *ꜥmy*(*t*) *nb.t*, 'and she will give to me every ability' that is necessary for finding Pharaoh. The traces following *nb.t* perhaps begin with *ỉw*.

dp. : *mn* and *mšꜥ.w n Pr-ꜥꜣ n-ỉm=*[. . . are certain, with a high trace rendering *n-ỉm=tn* probable. *pꜣ ntỉ ỉw* fits the traces after *mn*; perhaps restore *mn* [*pꜣ ntỉ ỉw=f rḫ nꜣ*] *mšꜥ.w n Pr-ꜥꜣ n-ỉm=*⌜*tn*⌝.

dq. bn st ḥp r-ḥr=y ỉn certain; for *ḥp*, 'hide', with this det. , cf. **1** front 9/8. The group following *ỉn* may be *ỉw=y*, and the passage should perhaps correspond to x+1/18 *ỉw=y šm r pꜣ dw*; the final traces are, however, uncertain.

dr. : the letter-scribe is named only here and in x+1/29, though he appears also in x+1/30–1 and perhaps in x/25, 32. In this instance, the scribe evidently started to write *Mr-ib* in error and then corrected it to , whereas in x+1/29 it is written . The group perhaps fits the det. of *mr*, 'love' (*DG*, 167. 1), better than a god's name such as *Ỉmn* or *Rꜥ*, though the divine det. should favour a theophorous name; *Mr-* . . . is used here as a conventional transliteration.

ds. : all is uncertain after *my rḫ=n*, though the penultimate traces suggest the group *ꜥws*. which follows *Pr-ꜥꜣ*. Note that there is a considerable space of blank papyrus before *ḏd=k*, filled only by the abnormally large flourish for *=k*, sure signs that *ḏd=k* began a new sentence.

dt. : *ḏd=k sdm=n nꜣ ntỉ i-ỉr=k* [*dd*].*ṯ=w*, though not certain, seems well founded.

du. : *nm pꜣ i.ỉr sḥn.ṯ=f Pr-ꜥꜣ m-sꜣ pꜣ mr-ꜥ*[*wi*] is certain, the broken *mr-ꜥwi* being assured by the writings in x+1/27, 30, 31, 34, 38. There is certainly no *n* extant between *sḥn.ṯ=f* and *Pr-ꜥꜣ*; it is just possible, but unlikely, that one has been lost in a small wormhole. If, however, *sḥn* here means 'appoint' on the model of *pꜣi-ỉr=t sḥn.ṯ=f* in x+1/12 above, *n* must presumably be supplied. While it is technically possible that *=f* is reflexive and refers to the *mr-ꜥwi*, common sense suggests that it refers forward to *Pr-ꜥꜣ*—or perhaps to a reference to him earlier in the line (n. *ds* above).

dv. : *ỉr-ḥrỉ n pꜣ rd.ṯy*. The signs are quite clear; the group written is exactly that which would be used for *rd*(*wi*).*ṯ=y*, 'my (two) feet', and would have stood in x/3 when complete. But a personal suffix cannot follow a defined noun and 'feet' bears no sense in the context; the scribe has evidently used this writing to distinguish Coptic ⲣⲏⲧⲉ, 'manner' (Crum, *CD*, 304b), phonetically from Coptic ⲣⲁⲧ, 'foot' (Crum, *CD*, 302b), compare a Roman writing quoted by Erichsen, *DG*, 258. 2. The writing is the more intelligible if Černý, *CED*, 141.2, is right in ultimately deriving ⲣⲏⲧⲉ from *rd*, 'foot'. The Coptic ⲙ̅ⲡⲣⲏⲧⲉ means 'like as' (cf. Greek ὡσεί, Crum, *CD*, 305a).

dw. : *r dỉ=k n=n Pr-ꜥꜣ* is certain. *r dỉ=k* might theoretically be construed as the past relative form or the past circumstantial. But if it were the former, *pꜣ rd.ṯy* must have been the antecedent, and a resumptive pronoun supported by a preposition would seem to have been needed (e.g. *n.ỉm=f*) to express 'the manner in which you have given us a Pharaoh'. The past circumstantial is thus the better choice, but the argument is somewhat academic, for it is clear that the words are part of an ironic question beginning in l. 26, probably with the words *ỉn i.ỉr=k* '[Are you] acting the master in this manner, having given to us a Pharaoh', i.e. 'as if you had given us a Pharaoh'; thus in thought if not in syntax *r dỉ=k* connects with *pꜣi rd.ṯy*. It follows that the two independent pronoun-plus-participle constructions *mtw=k i-*[*ỉr*] ⌜*sḥn*⌝.*ṯ.f mtw=k i-*⌜*ỉr*⌝ . . . . . *=f* must also be treated as sarcastic rhetorical questions 'Are you the one who appointed him? Are you the one who . . .?'. See n. *dx* below; the traces do not suffice to suggest a restoration of the second of these clauses. Note that in the photograph too little space is shown between *mtw=k* and *sḥn.ṯ=f* owing to warping of the papyrus.

dx. : though badly rubbed, the readings throughout are certain. The presence of the question *i-ỉr=n wšd nm m-sꜣ pꜣ mr-ꜥwi* confirms the interrogative interpretation of the previous clauses, while the positive statement *i-ỉr=n wšd* (*sic*, not *bw-ỉr=n wšd*) *Pr-ꜥꜣ m-sꜣ=k*, 'A Pharaoh other than you it is whom we honour', sums up the letter-scribe's whole onslaught on Merib's credentials.

dy. : *ḏd n=w* certain. No evidence is preserved at the end of the line of the identity of the speaker, but see n. *dz* below, and p. 124, n. *ed*.

dz. : *r-ḏd=w n=f m-bꜣḥ Ỉst dr=w* is certain; for the form of *m-bꜣḥ* cf. x+1/1 above (also damaged), **2** front, 6/5. The fact that Isis, not Hathor, is mentioned here is one argument for believing that the speaker here is not Merib. For Merib's appeal in x+1/1 ff. was to Hathor, and it was to the *dromos* of Hathor that he thought of going when he woke up (x+1/20); thus the goddess he saw in the dream was almost certainly Hathor.

ea. : *ḏd=f tw-s tꜣ/nꜣ* and *Pr-ꜥꜣ* are certain; the obvious restoration is *tꜣ/nꜣ ỉ-ỉr-ḫpr n Pr-ꜥꜣ*, with which the final trace before *Pr-ꜥꜣ* fits. Presumably this noun clause forms the preposed object of the sentence beginning *ỉw=y*; *ỉw=y rḫ.k(wỉ)* [*st*] might fit the surviving traces.

eb. : *ḥrry*, 'delay' (*DG*, 325. 9 under *ḥrr*), appears probable from the traces; the sign before it is certainly *=s*, not *dỉt*, and the preceding traces render *bn(-pw)=s* very probable. The subject of this sentence is thus a female, quite possibly the goddess Isis, the last female mentioned, whose name may have appeared in the lacuna. A high trace in this lacuna might perhaps suggest *ḏd* or *rḫ*; possibly the sense of the passage was that Isis has told the speaker what he knows of what has happened to Pharaoh and 'she has not delayed', but this is speculative.

ec. : *ỉw=y r gm Pr-ꜥꜣ n tꜣỉ=s wty* and *pꜣ tꜣ* are certain; *n ꜥwỉ n pꜣ tꜣ*, if restored from x+1/23, would fit the exiguous traces. The word *wty* with the phallus det. (cf. Möller, *Hieratische Paläographie*, iii, no. 96) appears also in a fragment of the Contendings of Horus and Seth from Saqqâra (H5-DP79/6, 7) with the same det. In that passage it appears to mean 'heritage, realm', and Dr K.-Th. Zauzich has kindly informed us that a word of similar appearance occurs in a fragment of *Horus and Seth* in demotic in a Berlin Museum papyrus which he is editing. This meaning, derived from the root *wt*, 'engender' (*DG*, 103. 4), would fit well here. Perhaps restore at the end of the line something like 'in any place on earth in which she is keeping/hiding him'.

ed. [ ] [ ] : *mdt nbt r-ḏd pꜣ* and *sẖ Mr . . .* (?) certain: on the reading of the name see p. 123, n. *dr*. The trace after the lacuna before *pr=w* exactly suits the det. of *wḥꜣ* in Mer . . .'s title *pꜣ sẖ n pꜣ wḥꜣ* (cf. x+1/26) which must accordingly be restored here. The certain reading *pꜣ* after *ḏd* shows decisively that *Mr-ỉb* cannot have been the person who has just finished speaking; measurement of the various writings of *pꜣ mr-ꜥwỉ* (cf. p. 123, n. *du*) shows that it would have fitted the lacuna exactly, and is thus to be preferred.

ee. : *ỉ-ỉr=s ḫpr wn-nꜣ.w wn m-dr Nb(.t)-ꜥnḫ*, 'it happened that there was in the possession of Neb(et)-ꜥonkh . . .', is certain. A following indefinite article is to be expected and the traces support *wꜥ*. The following word is determined with the det. , the first sign is completely missing, the last two suggest *.tm* (the vertical stroke is the descender of *tꜣ*, 'land', in x+1/28). The correct reading must remain uncertain, though tentatively we suggest *ḫtm*, 'seal-ring' (*DG*, 371. 1, 372. 4, determined differently), as a possibility. Neb(et)-ꜥonkh must clearly here be a personal name or epithet, either male or female; on his or her identity and possible relationship with the personage mentioned at the end of x+1/8, see p. 137.

ef. *tꜣ khy n Pr-ꜥꜣ*: despite the unusual *khy* for *kḥ* and the use of the house det., this must be the word for 'land' (*DG*, 547. 7 under *kḥ*; Coptic ⲕⲁϩ, Crum, *CD*, 131b). The whole phrase is presumably dependent upon the subject of *wn m-dr* in x+1/29.

eg. : *mḥ=w n nꜣ ẖrd.w* may be read with confidence on comparison with the similar phrase in x+1/31. One might expect here *my mḥ=w n nꜣ ẖrd.w*, but *my* fits the traces imperfectly. Moreover, the broken group after the initial *pꜣ* (certain) is perhaps similar to *mr-ꜥwỉ* (cf. x+1/31 for an intact writing), which would make good sense as a vocative here. But, if it is present it seems that there is insufficient room for *my* as well; *mḥ=w* should then be taken as optative *sdm=f*. Better, perhaps, is *pꜣỉ(=y)* [*ḥrỉ*] *my mḥ=w*. *n* is certain after *nꜣ ẖrd.w*, but the following trace is too slight to support any particular reading; see p. 134, n. *aψ* for discussion.

eh. : *ḏ(d)tḥ=w* certain; probably *mtw=w* rather than *my* should be restored before it.

ej. : *r-ḫ(t) n tꜣ mdt/nꜣ mdwt* and *pꜣ mr-ꜥwỉ ḏd* are certain. The trace between fits neither *Mr* nor *sẖ*, but might perhaps represent ; some such reading as *r-ḫt nꜣ mdwt* ⌜*wr.wt*⌝ [*ntỉ ỉw pꜣỉ=n ḥrỉ*] *pꜣ mr-ꜥwỉ ḏd n*[*-ỉm=w*] might then fit the space, with a further phrase to complete the line. There are, however, many other possibilities.

ek. : *dỉ pꜣ sẖ n pꜣ wḥꜣ mḥ=w n nꜣ ẖr.w* is certain; note *ẖr.w* in place of *ẖrd.w* in x+1/30, without apparent distinction in meaning. The traces after *ẖr.w* are minimal, and that following the lacuna uncertain, though (*n-*)*drt* (temporal conjunction) is just possible.

el. : *bn(-pw)=w dỉt rḫ* and *ḫpr n-ỉm=w* are certain. The long descender after *rḫ* may indicate *rmt*; to fill the lacuna adequately perhaps restore *bn(-pw)=w dỉt rḫ* [*rmt n pꜣ tꜣ*] *tꜣ*/*nꜣ i-ỉr-ḫpr n-ỉm=w*.

em. After *ḫꜣꜥ=w st n*, 'they cast them into', some part of the boat (see n. *en* below) is presumably required; the hold, the rowing pits, the cabin, or the like. The trace at the end of the line may represent *pꜣ*.

en. : *n tꜣ shrꜣ* is certain (cf. *DG*, 445. 1); the phrase *shr.t Pr-ꜥꜣ* in 1. Kh. 3/23 makes it clear that the *shr.t* was a royal pleasure-barge (cf. the possible etymology from *shr*, 'make content'). The nature of the temporary prison provided for the children may have implications for their status (see p. 134, nn. *αψ*, *βα*).

eo. For the restoration of this sentence, see p. 121, n. *cv* and n. *dd*.

ep. 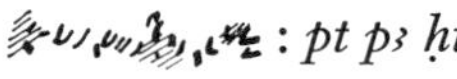: *pt pꜣ ḥtri r pꜣ dw* is certain.

eq. : only *mn pꜣ i-ỉr ḏd n-ỉm=w* is certain, but this with the following *ỉw=y r šm m-sꜣ=f*, 'there is no one who has spoken it: I will go after him' shows clearly that someone is speaking. In view of the events which follow, this must be the Chamberlain, so *ḏd pꜣ mr-ꜥwi* must be restored after *pꜣ dw* at the end of x+1/32. The initial traces in x+1/33 are difficult to resolve; the group may perhaps be read *r tꜣ*/*nꜣ*, though several other readings are possible, and the traces suggest the circumstantial *ỉw* before *mn*. Just conceivably the first group might be a broken  *pḥ*, in which case possibly restore *i-ỉr=f pḥ r tꜣ* . . . .; but quite different solutions are doubtless available.

er. 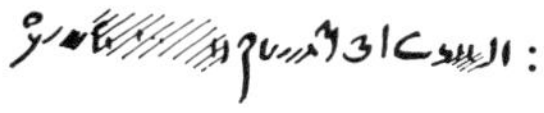: *ỉw bw-ỉr-rḫ=w mꜣꜥ n pꜣ tꜣ* and *=y r-r=f* are certain; the det. of the verb before *=y* would suit *wḫꜣ*, 'seek', if it were written like *wḫꜣ*, 'letter' (e.g. x+1/26, cf. *DG*, 98. 8 for this det. with the verb). Possibly therefore restore *mꜣꜥ n pꜣ tꜣ* ⸢*ỉw=w*⸣ [*rḫ*] ⸢*wḫꜣ*⸣*=y r-r=f*, 'without their knowing any place on earth where they might be able to seek me' (in **2** front, 6/29 *wḫꜣ* is used with the suffix object of the person sought, though the det. is there omitted). The 3rd pers. plur. here might refer to the Guards and the Great Men, or be an example of the passive periphrasis.

es. : *r bn(-pw)=f ḫꜣꜥ pꜣi=f gy (n) ḏdy* appears certain; a short phrase must be restored at the end of the line, just possibly *ṯꜣi tꜣ wnwt 6 n grḥ*, 'since the sixth hour of night', cf. x+1/22.

et. : despite the rather exiguous traces, [*ỉn-nꜣ-w tꜣ wn*]*wt 6 ḫpr* seems a very probable restoration. This would mean that the horse had been running twelve hours (see x+1/22 above).

eu. : *ỉw=w ꜥšꜣ* and *r ẖm* are certain; there is no doubt in view of the det. and the damaged but clear writing in **1**, 9/33 that *ẖm* must be the verb 'to be hot, to heat' (*DG*, 380. 6 under *ẖmm*). How to restore the passage is unclear. The use of the phrase *ꜥšꜣ ḥꜣt.ṯ=f r tkn r-r=f*, 'his heart swelled so as to attack him', of the lion in x+1/12 suggests *ỉw=w ꜥšꜣ* [*ḥꜣt.ṯ=w*] *r ẖm*, 'their hearts being swelled to anger/fever'. Apart from the slightly awkward syntax, the behaviour of the mountain animals in x+1/37, 38 does not suggest anger. Another highly speculative approach is to suggest *ỉw=w ꜥšꜣ* [*n ḥd*] *r ẖm*, 'they being more numerous [in cold] than heat', perhaps an appropriate description of mountain animals applicable to the species named with the exception of *mm*, 'the giraffe' (for *ḥd*, 'be cold', cf. *DG*, 344. 8; the writing here would have had to be briefer to fit the lacuna).

ev. : *mm*, 'giraffe' (*Wb.* ii. 58. 14 under *mmj*), *ḥyty*, 'hyena' (*Wb.* iii. 203. 16 under *ḥṯt*; *DG*, 282. 3 under *ḥṯ.t*; Coptic ϩⲟ(ⲉ)ⲓⲧⲉ Crum, *CD*, 720b, Černý, *CED*, 299. 6), and *ꜣyr*, 'hart' (*Wb.* i. 38. 16 under *ỉjr*; *DG*, 1. 7 under *ꜣiwr*; Coptic ⲉⲓⲉⲟⲩⲗ Crum, *CD*, 77a, Černý, *CED*, 46. 4), are certain; *kḥs* for *gḥs*, 'gazelle' (*Wb.* v. 191. 1 ff.; *DG*, 591. 8 (fem.); Coptic ϭϩⲟⲥ, ϭⲁϩⲥⲉ Crum, *CD*, 839b, Černý, *CED*, 340. 1) is probable, while *wnš*, 'wolf' (*Wb.* i. 324. 16; *DG*, 92. 3; Coptic ⲟⲩⲱⲛϣ Crum, *CD*, 485b, Černý, *CED*, 214. 2), is a guess based on the initial *w* which alone is preserved. *ḫt tp-n-ỉꜣwt* is certain from the writing earlier in the line; restore perhaps *ḫ(t) tp-n-ỉꜣwt* [*dw dr=w*], 'and every species of mountain beast'.

ew. 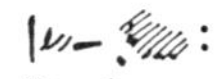: the legs det. before *n-ỉm=w* alone survives. Perhaps restore something like *ỉn-nꜣ-w Mr-ỉb ḥn n-ỉm=w*, 'when Merib approached them'?

ex. 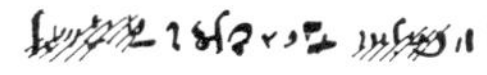: *ỉw Pr-ꜥꜣ ḥms ỉwt nꜣ tp-n-ỉꜣwt* is all certain; the construction is *ỉw*+noun+Stative (cf. Coptic ϩⲙⲟⲟⲥ, Crum, *CD*, 679a), and the sentence is a main sentence, as is shown by the following circumstantial  *r bw-ỉr=w nw r-r=f n-drt.ṯ=w*. *nw* appears certain, and fits the lacuna well. The construction of the sentence seems to be an interesting and early example of the passive periphrasis with agent expressed by *n-drt.ṯ=* (a common Coptic usage with ⲛ̄ⲧⲟⲟⲧ⸗), which seems tautological only because the agent is the 3rd pers. plur. suffix pronoun.

ey. Two complementary sentences seem required: 'Pharaoh spoke to him as he arrived; he recognized Pharaoh when he spoke/said to him . . .'; the high trace at the end of the line would suit *ḏd*, which may have introduced a brief speech in the lacuna, but did not necessarily do so.

ez. : the trace at the beginning of the line is indeterminate; *nw=f r pꜣ mꜣỉ* fits the traces after the lacuna well; the interval should be fractionally less than that shown in the photograph.

fa. : *wšd=f r* and *n-ḥꜣt.ṯ=f* alone are secure. Comparison with x+1/1 suggests strongly that the high trace bending to the left is part of *ḥnwt* 'mistress'; *r tꜣỉ=f ḥnwt* will fit space and traces admirably. The name or epithet of a goddess is clearly required by the det.; the high diagonal trace fits *Ḥwt-Ḥr*, and the final three diagonal strokes, though initially reminiscent of *y*, do not differ greatly from those present in the writing in x+1/20. *tꜣ rpy(t)* fits the traces much less well, and is suspect since it is usually followed by the goddess's name, cf. **2** front, 6/28; note that the interval between the two sides of the column is fractionally too great (n. *ez* above). The stroke over the det.  is doubtless a space filler.

fb. The reading is clear, and the fact that the subject of the sentence worshipped his mistress 'because he had seen the Lady in a dream' is strong evidence that he is Merib and that the reading 'his mistress Hathor' put forward in n. *fa* above is correct. No trace survives after the circumstantial *ỉw=s*.

fc. : the initial trace suits *pḥ* (cf. x+1/30) and *tp-n-ỉꜣwt* is certain (cf. x+1/34); perhaps restore something like *pḥ[=f pꜣ mꜣꜥ n ꜥḥꜥ n nꜣ]* ⌜*tp-n-ỉꜣwt*⌝, 'he reached the place where the beasts were standing'. If so, possibly a short sentence such as 'He rose up' should be restored at the end of x+1/36.

fd. : *mšꜥ=f ỉwt=w bn(-pw)=w pt (n-)ḥꜣ.ṯ=f bn(-pw)=w ẖꜣꜥ* ⌜*n*⌝ *tꜣ mỉt* is all certain; for *ỉwt* cf. x+1/35; for *(n-)ḥꜣ.ṯ=f*, 'in front of him', cf. *DG*, 287. 1, and *(n-)ḥꜣ.ṯ=s* in **2** front, 6/15; for *bn(-pw)=w ẖꜣꜥ tꜣ mỉt* compare *ẖꜣꜥ=w pꜣ myt* in x+1/38, noting the substitution of the masc. *myt* (*DG*, 153. 11) for the fem. *mỉ.t* (*DG*, 152. 3) without apparent change of meaning. The two halves of the column are mounted 0.5 cm. too far apart in the photograph at this point (cf. n. *ez* above).

fe. : *ỉr pꜣ mꜣỉ wꜥ ḫrw*, 'the lion roared' (lit. 'made a voice'), is certain; whether the lion roared to frighten the mountain animals so that they should make way for Merib, or to warn Pharaoh of the approach of the Chamberlain (he already knows of Merib's, cf. x+1/35 where he speaks to him) may be less certain.

ff. : though the traces at the beginning of the line are exiguous in the extreme, comparison with x+1/35, 37 suggests that *nꜣ tp-n-ỉꜣwt* is a quite likely reading. The word preceding *r Pr-ꜥꜣ* was not a verb of motion with the legs det.; the det. is probably the flesh det., followed by *ṯ* or *w*. It seems clear that the animals' fleeing to Pharaoh after their failure to do so on the approach of Merib (x+1/37) is due to the lion's roar.

fg. 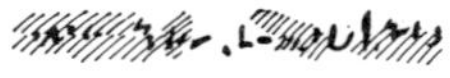: *ẖꜣꜥ=w pꜣ myt n pꜣ mr-ꜥwỉ*; the reading *mr-ꜥwỉ* is assured by comparison with the undamaged writing later in the line. 'They left the way for the Chamberlain' must be contrasted with their behaviour on Merib's approach: 'they did not leave the way to go to the place where Pharaoh was'; whether, however, this discrimination was intentional on the beasts' part, or whether they were panicked into it by the lion's roar, is uncertain, though the latter seems rather more probable. It is also not entirely certain that the lion intends this result; he may have roared to frighten the animals out of Merib's path, and the Chamberlain, following up stealthily, have taken advantage of this.

fh. *sdr=f n=f r-ẖt.ṯ=f*; grammatically the antecedent of *sdr=f* should be the preceding words *pꜣ mr-ꜥwỉ*; that this is so is demonstrated by the fact that Pharaoh immediately addresses him as *pꜣ mr-ꜥwỉ* and also by the fact that Merib has already done obeisance (x+1/36).

fj. 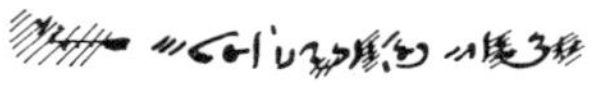: *pꜣ mr-ꜥwỉ* must be vocative because of the following *mtw=k*. The reading of the following sentence is not easy; the participial construction *mtw=k ỉ-ỉr* and the object pronoun *=y* make it clear that the group 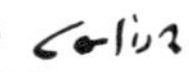 must represent a verb. The dets. should probably represent hieroglyphic ; the form of the first sign is not really correct for *dỉt* in this hand. Much the best reading is probably *ḥk*, 'capture, carry off as booty', of which *DG*, 333. 4 gives writings with these dets., though used separately.

Other demotic writings, it is true, all appear to render as *ḥk* in conformity with hieroglyphic *ḥꜣk* (*Wb.* iii 32. 14 ff.), but this is hardly a cogent objection; more serious is the fact that the writing in **2** front, 6/14 has also been interpreted as a writing of this verb, though *ḥkr*, 'hunger' is also possible (p. 80, *n. cd*), But it has been shown with some probability that this scribe does on occasion write the same root in two different ways (e.g. *dw*, see p. 112, n. *d*). Certainly, 'O steward, you are the one who carried me off . . . . .' makes good sense; the following traces might represent *ỉn.ṭ=y*, '(and) brought me . . .', though other interpretations (e.g. ***n pꜣy*** or ***sḏm***(?)) are possible.

fk. No column number is preserved in the bottom margin (see p. 70).

Translation

BACK (↕)

col. x

1. - - -] it or eat it.[α] O (you) from whom life is requested, the mistress
2. - - -] the whole land. I am in the high(?) mountains [. .
3. - - -] there are no sandals for my feet, ⌜my⌝ [. . . . . .
4. - - -] it. Let me find the way [. . . . . .[β]
5. - - -] words of speech,[γ] a [. . . .] came down [. . . .[δ]
6. - - -] . . . .;[ε] his flesh was fair; ⌜. . . .⌝ [. . . .
7. - - -] him/it instead of bread. He brought [. . . . . .[ζ]
8. - - -] flame. He cooked the . . . [. . . . .[η]
9. - - -] he caused the mountain to echo to his voice[θ] [. . . .
10. - - -] a lion like the . . . . . lion in his possession.[ι] He stopped [. .]
11. - - -] great ⌜of heart⌝ [. . . .] his [. . . .] exceedingly
12. - - -] flesh [. . . . . .
13. *vacat*(?)
14. - - -] . . . . . . [. . . . . .
15. - - -] dream [. . . . . .
16. - - -] to us. [. . . .   .
17. *lost*
18. *lost*
19. *lost*
20. *lost*
21. - - -] . . said [. . . .
22. - - -] thing happened [in the sky
23. *lost*
24. - - -] woke up, saying [. . . .
25. - - -] letter[κ] [. . . .
26. - - -] he reported [. . . .
27. - - -] brought him . . . .
28. - - -] my lord/lady[λ] [. . . .
29. - - -] I hear [. . . .
30. *lost*
31. - - -] ⌜child⌝
32. - - -] letter[κ]

33. *lost*
34. - - -] this girl . . . .
35. - - -] the [. . . .[μ]
36. *lost*
37. *lost*

no surviving trace of last four(?) lines

col. x + 1

1. ['O Hathor] the great, lady of Aphroditopolis, the great goddess, listen . . . ., my sovereign. Have you been accustomed [. . . . .] who pleads before you?[ν] Let Pharaoh Badja(?) know the thing(s) which are [. . . . .][ξ]
2. Who (else) is wont to listen to the voice of the . . . . of Aphroditopolis(?),[ο] in whose heart there is no darkness? Let [me know] the things which have happened to Pharaoh Badja(?), for I have set awe of you in his heart [. . . . . Let][π]
3. me find out what has happened to him before the army/people find him. O [. . . . .] [. . . .] goings(?) [. . . .] your [. . . .].[ρ] They will listen to what I [say,[σ] the Guards]
4. and all the great men of Pharaoh. Are you able to cause [. . . . .] (divine) rage under (the spell of) which Pharaoh Badja(?) is?[τ] Let me know the things which have happened [. . . . .]
5. . . . .] them before the army/people,[υ] for I have set the awe of you in his heart. [. . . . .] with one voice, all of them, saying:[φ] "Merib is the one who has caused [Pharaoh] to perish and be ⌜destroyed⌝".'[χ]
6. [He ended] the words of speech weeping and praying [. . . . .] he [. . . . .] at the sky [. . . . .] is not able [. . . .]
7. . . . . the people] who pray to her; she has been wont to listen to all of them . . . . listen . . . . words heard [. . . . .]
8. . . . [. . . .] He slept, he dreamt a dream[ψ] [. . . . .] . . . . . . [. . . . .] . . . . . ., Lady of . . . . . [. . . . .]
9. as she was [sitting] on a mound of sand, a wave of water pouring [. . . . .] . . . . . . on the bank of the river [. . . . .][ω]
10. The [. . . . . .] she said: '(O) Merib,[αα] do you see this lion, ... [. . . . .], whom I have made?[αβ] I caused him to act as servant of the sword to Pharaoh [. . . . .]
11. who is bound in my hand, since he earlier hearkened to Pharaoh when I had not (yet) ordered it to him.[αγ] Pharaoh cried out [. . . . . .] . . . . . . in the prow of the bark of Preʿ [. . . . .]
12. hostility against him, saying: "I will carry off the one whom you (fem.) have appointed"; his will to attack him grew great. I was enraged against him. I placed a mortal sickness upon him,[αδ] [. . . . . Pharaoh thirsted][αε]
13. and found no water to drink. I brought him sweet water upon the mountain. Pharaoh hungered, and found no bread to eat. He begged from me, and I gave it to him, the ⌜. . . . .⌝ [. . . . .]

14. of flame touched it, she drew it from the altar of/namely Bastet, the great goddess. I caused ⌜the lion to⌝ [. . . . . . .] a . . . .[αζ] I caused the lion to sit opposite the/her [. . . . .]

15. I caused him to bring salt to him, I caused him to act as servant of the sword to him while he was lying upon the mountain. Immediately . . . . flame before him.[αη] I stood upon his upper side, the lion [. . . . .]

16. quaking upon the mountain. They passed on his upper side upon the mountain, they went round (upon) the four . . . . They found him in the condition in which he was. They said to him: "We speak at the instance of [. . . . . We will]

17. rescue/seize you and we will bring you back to Egypt".[αθ] All [these things], it was because of the word that you spoke to me "I have set the awe of you in his heart", that I did them for him. I left him without his saying "I will not listen to . . . . .[αι] [. . . . . ." . . . .]

18. the one who is asking for you from me.[ακ] Go among your army/people; say to it: "Your Master, he is safe". And you shall relate before the Guards these things which I have told you, and you shall say to them: "I will go to the mountain after [. . . . .][αλ]

19. to fetch him back to Egypt". And you shall mount upon a horse. Do not put a rein or bit upon it; do not beat it; do not set a man to walk before it, but leave him with [. . . . . .]'.

20. Merib woke up, and asked what hour it was, and was told: 'It is the first hour [of night][αμ] . . . .' He said: 'I am not going to the *dromos* of Hathor at this hour. I will tell it to the [great men]

21. of Pharaoh: for she is not in her temple; I will not delay in arriving at the [. . . . .'][αν] Merib caused a horse to be brought; he mounted upon it, he did not put a rein or a bit upon it, nor [did he whip it],

22. nor did he set a man to go before it, but the horse went with its [. . . . .].[αξ] When the sixth hour of night happened, he found the Guards [. . . . . . .]

23. Pharaoh;[αο] they had neither drunk nor eaten. They all spoke with one voice, saying: 'Pharaoh [. . . . .] the mountain [according to] your instructions, but we have not found him in any place on earth'.[απ] He said: 'Do not [. . . . . .;]

24. pray, O Guards: for Hathor is accustomed to listen [to those who] ⌜give thought to the offerings⌝ [. . . . .], and she is accustomed to listen to the voice of those who are . . . . of eye when they cense;[αρ] and she will reveal [. . . . .]

25. the wanderings of Pharaoh, and she will give to me every inward quality [. . . . .]. There is no one who knows (about) these wanderings of Pharaoh among you, (but) they are not concealed from me. I will [. . . . .'][ασ]

26. Mer- . . ., the letter-scribe, saying: 'Let us know [. . . . .]. You have spoken, and we have heard those things which you have said. But who is the one who appointed him Pharaoh, except the Chamberlain? [. . . . .]

27. to act as master, as though you had given us a Pharaoh? Is it you who appointed him? Is it you who [. . . . .]? Whom are we to honour if it be not the Chamberlain? It is a Pharaoh other than you whom we honour!'[ατ] [. . . . .] said to them[αυ]

28. every word that he had been told before Isis, all of them. He said 'Behold, those things which [have happened] to Pharaoh, I know [them . . . .] . . . . . [. . . . .] she did not delay. I shall find Pharaoh in her inheritance [in any place] on earth, (while) she [. . . . . .][αφ]

29. I will bring your Master back to you safe'. Every word which the [. . . . .] said, Mer-. . . the letter[-scribe] wrote them down, all of them. It happened that there was in the possession of Neb(et)-ʿonkh a . . . . [. . . . . . .][αχ]

30. the land of Pharaoh. The letter-scribe said: 'O my . . . . , let the children of [. . . . . .] be arrested and let them be imprisoned until Pharaoh arrives, according to the words [. . . . .] which the Chamberlain spoke [. . . . .'][αψ]

31. The Chamberlain said : 'What you have said is good'. The letter-scribe caused the youths [. . . . . .] to be arrested.[αω] When each person looked at his companion among them, they did not allow any one to know [the things which] had happened to them. They placed them in the [. . . . . . .]

32. of the (pleasure)-barge.[βα] After this, Merib mounted upon the horse, he did not place a rein or bit upon it, he did not beat it, he did not set any man to walk in front of it. The horse galloped to the mountain [. . . . . . .]

33. '[. . . . .], without there being anyone who has spoken of them. I will go after him, without any place on earth whither I have [. . . . . . .] being known'.[ββ] The sun rose upon the horse while he was (still) galloping, without his having ceased his mode of galloping [. . . . . . .][βγ]

34. [When] ⌜the sixth hour⌝ came, the Chamberlain saw some mountain beasts, being numerous [. . . . . . .] to heat: giraffe, gazelle, hyena, ⌜wolf⌝, hart and all sorts of beasts [. . . . .][βδ]

35. . . . .] approached them, Pharaoh being seated among the animals without being seen by them.[βε] Pharaoh spoke to him as he arrived. He recognized Pharaoh when he was [. . . . .]

36. [. . . . .] he saw the lion.[βζ] He laid himself down on his belly, and he worshipped ⌜his mistress Hathor⌝ in his heart, because of the fact that he had seen the Mistress in a dream when she was [. . . . . . .][βη]

37. [. . . .] reached [. . . . .] the beasts.[βθ] He walked amongst them; (but) they did not flee before him, nor did they leave the path to go to the place where Pharaoh was. The lion gave a roar [. . . . .]

38. ⌜the beasts⌝, [. . . . .], they . . . . . . to Pharaoh and left the way to the Chamberlain.[βι] He laid himself down upon his belly. Pharaoh said to him: 'O Chamberlain, you are the one who has kept me captive . . . . [. . . . .]'[βκ]

Notes on translation

a. Restore perhaps: '[I have not anything] to eat [or drink]', cf. p. 112, n. *a*.

β. For the possible restoration 'way of life', cf. p. 112, n. *h*.

γ. Probably restore: '[When he had finished] his words of speech', cf. p. 112, n. *j*.

δ. Despite the partial parallel of **2** front 6/18, 'They saw a great beetle coming down from heaven', it seems more likely here that the creature came down from the mountains. The space available is only fractionally less than that occupied by *mꜣi*, 'lion' in x/10; this word might fit the traces, cf. p. 112, n. *j*.

ϵ. Restore perhaps: 'he lay down', cf. p. 112, n. *k*.

ζ. As *i-ir=f in* must be a Second Tense (the relative form is written *r-ir=f* by this scribe, and the antecedent *ʿḳ* is undefined), an emphasized adverbial adjunct should follow, not precede. The translation 'In place of bread he brought . . .' must presumably therefore be rejected. Perhaps restore: 'he brought . . . for him in place of bread, he brought . . . for him in place of water', though these items are placed in the reverse order in x+1/13, where there is probably reference back to the present passage.

η. The nature of the substance cooked is obscure, see p. 113, n. *o*.

θ. This should refer to the lion, cf. x+1/37 *ỉr pꜣ mꜣỉ wꜥ ẖrw*.

ι. If the text were restored on the lines: 'Pharaoh had never seen/known a lion like the young(?) lion in his possession', then only one lion is involved, which seems probable; but possible versions involving two lions cannot be ruled out. On the possible range of meaning of *wꜣḏ*, see p. 113, n. *q*, and p. 138.

κ. Here and in x/32 it is possible that 'the letter-scribe' made his appearance, cf. x+1/26 ff.

λ. Possibly read 'She is my Lady', see p. 113, n. *ab*.

μ. Possibly there is a reference to 'the Guards and the great men of Pharaoh' here, see p. 113, n. *ag*.

ν. Probably restore: 'Have you been accustomed to hear my plea before you?', see p. 114, n. *aj*.

ξ. Perhaps restore 'the things which are happening/will happen', see p. 115, n. *al*, end. The most probable rendering of the Pharaoh's name, *Bꜣ-ḏꜣ*, is used in the translation, see p. 114, n. *al* and p. 136.

o. For the tentative restoration 'the voice of the prophet of the Lady of Aphroditopolis', see p. 115, n. *am*.

π. The restoration *my* seems required at the end of x+1/2 by the following *gm=y*. This leaves space to be filled after *ḥꜣꜥ=y tꜣỉ=t sndyt n-ḥꜣt.ṯ=f*, but no words follow in the repetitions of the phrase in x+1/5, 17. Perhaps supply a vocative.

ρ. If the suggested reading *pꜣỉ=t ḏ(d)tḫ* on p. 115, n. *ap*, be accepted, this further appeal may have read something like: 'O [my mistress, let me find] Pharaoh, let your (fem.) captive go away'. If it is rejected the text may have been very different. See p. 115, n. *ap*.

σ. Note that it is possible to restore [*bn*]-*ỉw=w sdm*, 'they will not hearken', see p. 115, n. *aq*; whether the positive or the negative is correct must depend upon the interpretation of the story, see p. 136, iv.

τ. The substantive *ẖrꜥry* (from the root *ẖꜥr*, 'rage', cf. Černý, *CED*, 251. 3 ϣⲁⲁⲣⲉ) means the rage of a god vented upon a human. Thus the restoration *dỉt rk* followed, perhaps, by a nominal subject: 'Will you be able to cause . . . to remove the divine rage under which Pharaoh Badja(?) is?' seems plausible.

υ. Probably read: 'Let me know the things which have happened [to Pharaoh that I may relate] them before the *mšꜥ*'. Unfortunately, not enough survives of the text for it to be clear whether 'army' or 'people' is the more appropriate translation for *mšꜥ*.

ϕ. For a restoration see p. 116, n. *aw*.

χ. Given the correctness of the restoration at the beginning of l. 6 (cf. p. 116, n. *ay*), this quotation is the climax of Merib's appeal to the goddess, which has probably been occasioned by the accusation against himself of being responsible for Pharaoh's disappearance.

ψ. Reconstruction of the text is hazardous where the traces are so sparse (cf. p. 116, nn. *ay*-*bh*). Perhaps after he had ended his speech weeping and praying Merib arose and looked at the sky. Possibly he saw nothing but heard a voice advising him somewhat as follows: '[Await] tomorrow, no one knows [what the goddess/Hathor will bring]. Those who pray to her, she is wont to listen to all of them. [Do not fear the Guards or the] great [men, but] hearken to [the goddess]'. Then perhaps Merib rejoiced or was comforted at 'the words [which he] had heard' (p. 116, n. *bg*), and, as a result, lay down and slept and dreamt a dream.

ω. The beginning of the dream is mainly in lacuna, and restoration must be conjectural. It is probable that Merib saw the lion, both because of the trace mentioned on p. 116, n. *bj* and because of the goddess's question to him in x+1/10.; whether he also saw Pharaoh or only the goddess depends upon the preceding, very uncertain traces, see p. 116, n. *bj*. For the reading of the traces at the end of x+1/8 as a probable epithet of Hathor, e.g. 'the goddess, Lady of ꜥOn[khtowe]', see p. 116, n. *bk*; the probability that it was Hathor whom Merib saw in his dream is confirmed by his giving thanks to her in x+1/36 (see p. 126, n. *fa*), and his asking whether it was a suitable time to go to the dromos of Hathor in x+1/20 immediately after waking from the dream (see p. 121, n. *cz*). However, the possibility of a connection with the divine or human character Neb(et)-ꜥonkh who appears in x+1/29 cannot be excluded (see p. 137). The circumstantial details of the position in which Merib sees the goddess in his dream are not easy to understand (p. 117, nn. *bl*–*bn*); perhaps 'she being seated upon a mound of sand, with water pouring over her feet(?) (since) the inundation (*pꜣ ym*?) had flowed over the banks of the river' may give the right sort of picture, even if incorrect in detail. If so, there may be a cosmological reference to the 'primeval island'.[1]

aa. For various possible restorations, see p. 117, n. *bo*; 'She said: "O Merib, . . ."' seems simplest and best from the point of view of reconstructing the story.

[1] See A. de Buck, *De egyptische voorstellingen betreffende den oerheuvel*, (thesis) Leiden, 1922

αβ. The passage in lacuna after 'lion' may have contained an epithet, or even the name, of the lion, or have formed a short independent sentence containing the verb 'loved', see p. 117, n. *bp*.

αγ. The long lacuna at the end of x+1/10 renders uncertain the relationship of the clause 'who is bound in my hand' to what goes before, though it seems probable that it refers to the lion, and explains why the goddess was in a position to make it serve Pharaoh.

αδ. The use of pronouns in these sentences causes possible ambiguities (cf. p. 118, nn. *bv-by*). The goddess's rage was clearly against the person who said 'I will carry off the one whom thou hast appointed', and she placed a mortal sickness upon him. As it is Pharaoh who then thirsts and hungers, it is logical to see these sufferings as the results of the sickness inflicted by the goddess. Thus it must be Pharaoh whose threat angers the goddess, and it must be the lion whom she appointed as his servant whom he threatens to carry off—presumably because she has appointed him against Pharaoh's will. This solution accords best also with the fact that in x+1/11 it is Pharaoh who cries out to the goddess while she is in the barque of Preʿ; grammatically therefore it should also be Pharaoh who showed 'hostility against him, saying "I will carry off, etc" '.

αε. The correspondence between the events related in x/1–9 and x+1/13 ff. shows that Pharaoh was in the high mountains when he thirsted and hungered (x/2). Possibly therefore 'I carried him off to the (high) mountains' should be restored at the end of x+1/12, followed by *ꜣby Pr-ꜥꜣ*, 'Pharaoh thirsted' suggested by x+1/13, 'he found no water to drink'.

αζ. If 'I gave it to him' is correct, a new sentence may follow introduced by the words 'The moment that [I gave it]', but the readings are less than certain (p. 119, n. *ca*). For possible interpretations, see p. 119, nn. *cc*, *cd*, e.g. 'I caused the lion [to bring] an oryx'.

αη. The interpretation of this passage is difficult and its role in the story dubious, cf. p. 119, nn. *cb-cg*. The following suggestions may be made:

i. the simplest antecedent for the suffix pronoun in *dmy r-r=f* is Pharaoh, referred to by name and subsequently by suffixes in l. 13.

ii. a clear *n* precedes *sṯy* at the beginning of l. 14, so that it must form part of a genitive nexus, of which the first element may have been either masc. or fem.

iii. As neither good grammar nor good sense can be extracted from the passage by reading *ỉ-ỉr n(=y)*, *ỉ-ỉr=s* *šdy=f* must be read. While it is thus possible that the fem. subject *=s* refers back to *sṯy*, it is at least equally possible that the masc. object suffix *=f* refers back to the nexus . . . . . *n sṯy*.

iv. If the fem. subject suffix *=s* does not refer to *sṯy*, it may either refer back to a female character introduced in l. 13 (cf. p. 119, n. *cb*), or it may refer *forward* to the goddess Bastet; the *n* before *Bꜣstt* would then not be the genitive adjective linking her with *ḫwy* but the particle *n* introducing the postponed subject (Copt. ⲛ̄ϭⲓ). The former involves introducing two new female characters into the narrative at this point, which seems otiose. The latter has the advantage of allowing much the simplest restoration of the lacuna in x+1/15, namely, *n tꜣ wnwt* [*ỉn*]*Bꜣstt* [*tꜣỉ*] *sṯy ỉ-ỉr-ḥr=f*, 'Immediately Bastet brought this flame before him'.

v. The whole passage may then be interpreted consistently as retailing the provision of water, food and a cooked meal for Pharaoh, perhaps somewhat as follows: '[Pharaoh thirsted] and found no water to drink, but I brought him sweet water upon the mountain. Pharaoh hungered, and found no bread to eat; but he begged from me and I gave it to him. The [moment he desired a fire, a spark] of flame came close to him; it was from the altar that she brought it, namely Bastet the great goddess. [I] caused the lion to bring an oryx(?). I caused the lion to sit down opposite to [the place where Pharaoh was]. I caused him to bring him salt, I made him act for him as servant and sword-bearer while he was lying on the mountain. Immediately Bastet [brought] the flame before him . . .'.

αθ. The plural pronouns introduced in x+1/16 (*ỉr=w*, *st ḳdy*, *gm=w-s*) are certainly to be interpreted as a party to the plot, not simply the passive periphrasis with the 3rd pers. plur., since they must correspond to the 1st pers. plur. pronouns in the direct speech which follows (x+1/16 *ḏd=n*, x+1/17 *ỉw=n ỉn.ṯ=k*). As the text now is, these pronouns lack a plural antecedent, which surely would have required to be clearly defined. The persons or creatures concerned pass on the upper side of Pharaoh, go round him on four sides (accepting the restoration proposed on p. 119, n. *ck*) and promise to bring him back to Egypt. When Merib and the Chamberlain reach Pharaoh in x+1/34 ff., he is seated among the mountain beasts but is invisible because of them. It is tempting therefore to identify the plural party in x+1/16 with these mountain beasts, who would then have to be introduced in the lacuna at the end of x+1/15. The space available at the end of the lines can be estimated from the certain restoration [=*f mḫy.ṯ=f*] at the end of x+1/21, so that up to 8/9 groups may be allowed in this line. This would permit at the least a restoration [*ỉr nꜣ tp-n-ỉꜣwt*] *ḫrḫr ḥr pꜣ dw*, 'the wild beasts made a disturbance/quaking upon the mountain'. Were this correct, *pꜣ mꜣỉ* would either have to be read as part of the preceding clause: *tw=y ꜥḥꜥ.k(wi)* [*n*] *tꜣỉ=f rỉt ḥrỉt* [*n*] *pꜣ mꜣỉ*, 'I stood upon the (lit. his) upper side of the lion' (a possible Egyptian construction), or would have to be followed by a very brief complement, e.g. *pꜣ mꜣỉ* [*ḥms.w*], 'the lion being seated', or *pꜣ mꜣỉ* [*ỉr=f ḫrw*]. 'the lion, he roared'. The latter is preferable, both because in the parallel passage in x/9 (the lion) 'caused the mountain to echo to his voice', and because the lion's roaring would account for the panicking of the wild beasts posited above. We suggest the translation: 'Immediately Bastet brought the flame before him, I stood above him, and the lion [gave a roar]. [The wild beasts made] a tumult upon the mountain, they passed on his upper side upon the mountain, they went round on (all) four [sides], they found him in the state in which he was. They spoke as follows: "We have spoken according to the voice [of the goddess Hathor: we will] rescue/seize you and take you back to Egypt" '. If the 'wild beasts' are correctly restored here, it seems probable that it is at Hathor's instance that they speak, because it seems to be her standing above Pharaoh that provokes the lion's roar which precipitates their appearance, and because the beasts' behaviour in x+1/34 ff. may be best explained if they are agents of the goddess.

αι. At this point, the goddess closes her relation of the way in which she has first afflicted, then succoured the king, and turns to Merib to explain her apparently contradictory actions; she has done these things for Pharaoh because Merib has claimed to have put reverence for her in his (Pharaoh's) heart. And by demonstrating that she answers appeals when reverently made she has convinced Pharaoh, for when she left him he did not say, 'I will not hearken . . .'. Whether simply *n=t*, 'to you (fem.)' or something more should be restored at the end of this clause is uncertain.

ακ. The goddess has now informed Merib of 'the things which have happened to Pharaoh' as he had asked (x+1/1–5), and has only to tell him how to find him. It is thus tempting, despite the serious grammatical difficulty involved (cf. p. 120, n. *cr*), to take *pꜣ ỉ-ỉr-dbḥ=k* as a relative form, restoring, for instance: '[I have told you] that which you asked of me; go among your people and tell them "Your Master is safe" '. If the normal rule of orthography in **1** and **2** is observed and *pꜣ ỉ-ỉr-dbḥ=k* is translated as a participle, the passage might perhaps be restored '[Indeed, Pharaoh himself is] the one who has requested you from me', which makes some sense, as the subsequent narrative (x+1/20–38) shows that Pharaoh has good reason to want Merib to rescue him and not the Chamberlain or any member of his party. Whatever is correct, the initial words of the sentence must have stood in x+1/17; probably therefore *n=t* (n. *αι* above) alone closed the preceding speech.

αλ. If *m-sꜣ* be correctly read at the end of l. 18, the most likely restoration appears to be simply *m-sꜣ Pr-ꜥꜣ*, 'I will go to the mountain after [Pharaoh] to bring him back to Egypt'. *Pr-ꜥꜣ ꜥws*, though technically only six groups long, is normally written large enough in this text amply to fill the space available.

αμ. Or, if *gs* be read, 'It is half past the first hour of night', cf. p. 121, n. *cx*. Cf. p. 121, n. *cy* for the following lacuna.

αν. Cf. p. 121, n. *dc*.

αξ. Presumably some phrase like that in x+1/33: 'galloping without ceasing his mode of galloping' is required, though that form of words seems slightly too long for the space.

αο. Perhaps restore: 'who were [in the hall of the palace of Pharaoh]' or the like, cf. p. 121, n. *dg*.

απ. Any restoration of this speech must be speculative. If the readings suggested on p. 122, n. *dj*, are right, perhaps the sense was something like '[Where is] Pharaoh? [We have searched the] mountain according to your advice, but we have not found him in any place on earth'.

αρ. The translation given is based on the rather uncertain readings suggested on p. 122, n. *dm*. At least one word, perhaps a polite jussive parallel with *šn=ṯn*, is probably lost at the end of x+1/23.

ασ. Some noun is probably to be restored at the end of x+1/24, e.g. 'the course of' or 'the secrets of the wandering of Pharaoh' possibly preceded by the dative *n*(=*y*), 'to me'. After *ꜥmy nb*(.*t*) (p. 122, n. *do*) several restorations are feasible; if *ỉw=y* be the correct reading perhaps 'of which I shall have need' seems simplest. At the end of the line 'I will discover him/bring him back' seems required; but see p. 123, n. *dq*.

ατ. Evidently it is Merib's assumption of the right to take upon himself the disposal of affairs of state, properly the province of the Chamberlain, which the letter-scribe derides. The opening sentence of his speech may perhaps have emphasized this, e.g. 'let us know [who has instructed you to search for Pharaoh/ discover the wanderings of Pharaoh]'. For the probable restoration of the end of x+1/26 see p. 123, nn. *dv*, *dw*. Perhaps after 'Is it you who appointed him?' restore something like 'Is it you who have acted for him?'

αv. The arguments for restoring *pꜣ mr-ꜥwi* '[the Chamberlain] said to them' here should perhaps be summarized.

i. The subject of this sentence is necessarily identical with the speaker of the following speech.

ii. It must be this speaker's words that the letter-scribe writes down (x+1/29). There *pꜣ* certainly follows *ḏd*; the only character referred to by a title introduced by the def. article other than the letter-scribe himself is the Chamberlain, and *pꜣ mr-ꜥwi* exactly fits the lacuna.

iii. In x+1/32–8 below, it is clear that Merib and the Chamberlain both discover Pharaoh on the mountain. It is therefore appropriate that the Chamberlain should make this, the second speech claiming knowledge of Pharaoh's whereabouts and giving a promise to find him. Moreover, in x+1/30 the letter-scribe speaks of 'Pharaoh arriving according to the words which [our master] the Chamberlain has spoken', which must surely be a reference back to this speech (cf. p. 124, n. *ej*).

iv. The speaker's informant has been Isis, thus distinguishing him from Merib, whose appeal was to Hathor (cf. p. 123, n. *dz*).

αφ. The Chamberlain being the speaker, Isis must be his informant here on the evidence of the previous sentence, and it is within her inheritance (perhaps simply a flattering term for the world?) that he expects to find Pharaoh. The fem. suffix in *iw=s* must also refer to Isis, perhaps restore 'she giving me her counsel' or the like.

αχ. Cf. p. 124, n. *ee* for the possible reading *ḫtm*, 'seal'. The *wn-m-dr* construction indicating possession (Coptic ⲟⲩⲛⲧⲁ=) shows that *Nb(.t)-ꜥnḫ* must represent the name or epithet of a character in the story, though whether male or female, human or divine, is unfortunately uncertain. The motive for the introduction of the character seems to be to explain why the letter-scribe wishes to have the children of somebody arrested and imprisoned, in which case it is tempting to regard Neb(et)-ꜥonkh as a human character, probably male, possibly even a child of Pharaoh himself if he possesses the royal seal. However, the broken group at the end of x+1/8 may also perhaps be restored in the same way as *Nb(.t)-ꜥnḫ-* . . . . .; there it is in all probability the epithet of a goddess (see p. 116, n. *bk*); and while the identity of the two by no means follows, it cannot be dismissed out of hand.

αψ. Owing to lacunae, it is unclear whose children the letter-scribe wishes the Chamberlain to have arrested and why. Four possibilities exist:

i. They are Pharaoh's children; the motive for arrest would then presumably be that one of them was likely to usurp the throne during the Chamberlain's absence searching for Pharaoh. This has the advantage that Pharaoh's children are most likely to pose a threat to the Chamberlain, and, if Neb(et)-ꜥonkh be one of them, most likely to possess a seal(?) giving authority over the land of Pharaoh.

ii. They are Merib's children; this would fit well with the hostility of the Chamberlain and letter-scribe to Merib. But the precise motive is not clear, unless the character named Neb(et)-ꜥonkh in the previous line who has a seal-ring or other authority in the land of Pharaoh, be one of Merib's children; in that case, he and his siblings might be a danger to the letter-scribe and his colleagues in the Chamberlain's absence.

iii. They are Neb(et)-ꜥonkh's children; the arrest would then be explained by Neb(et)-ꜥonkh's possession of the seal-ring or other authority. But then the abrupt introduction of the whole incident of the arrest at this point where it interrupts the story of Merib and the Chamberlain would seem unnecessary and inconsistent with the general style of demotic narratives.

iv. They are the children of some other unknown character in the tale; to this the objection is the same as to iii.

On balance therefore the argument favours their being the children of Pharaoh, though if so one should probably assume that Merib has left the court by the time the letter-scribe makes his suggestion about their arrest. The slight trace mentioned on p. 124, n. *eg* may be misleading. At the end of l. 30 a short phrase must be restored, e.g. 'which the Chamberlain spoke [before us]' or '[before the great men]'.

αω. Most probably the parentage of the children was again stated in the lacuna, though other restorations are feasible.

βα. Cabin, hold or rowing-pits suggest themselves as possible places of imprisonment on an Egyptian sailing-ship.

ββ. In x+1/34 it is the *Chamberlain* who sees the

mountain beasts which are congregated round Pharaoh. It is therefore necessary for the consecution of the story that he should follow Merib and the horse up to the mountain. This is what the character speaking here says he will do, so the speech must be attributed to the Chamberlain. Whatever the correct restoration of the first words of x+1/33 may be (cf. p. 125, n. *eq*), they presumably belonged to this speech (for restoration cf. p. 125, n. *er*), which must then have been introduced at the end of l. 32.

βγ. See p. 125, n. *es* for a possible restoration.

βδ. See p. 125, nn. *eu–ev* for possible restorations.

βε. In x+1/35–8, there are repetitions or partial repetitions of sections of text: x+1/36, 'he laid himself down on his belly', cf. x+1/38; x+1/37, 'they did not flee before him'; contrast 1/38, 'they fled to Pharaoh'; x+1/37, 'nor did they leave the way'; contrast x+1/38, 'they left the way to the Chamberlain'. These repetitions are best explained if Merib and the Chamberlain successively approached Pharaoh with different results, cf. p. 126, nn. *fb*, *fe*, *fg*.

βζ. As suggested on p. 126, n. *ey* perhaps restore 'He recognized Pharaoh when he spoke'. What should follow is very uncertain; perhaps 'as he walked towards him, he saw the lion'.

βη. For the restoration of the goddess's name cf. p. 126, n. *fa*. For the end of the line there are several possibilities, e.g. 'when she appeared to him' or 'when she was in the form of a woman'.

βθ. For restoration see p. 126, n. *fc*.

βι. Perhaps restore in x+1/37–8: 'The lion gave a roar, and [the beasts were terrified; they ran,] they fled to Pharaoh and left the way (open) to the Chamberlain', see p. 126, nn. *fe*, *ff*, *fh*, and n. *βε* above.

βκ. See p. 126, n. *fj*.

DISCUSSION

1. The characters

i. *Merib*

In the extant portion of the story, Merib is given no court or other title, presumably because he is a central character whose position is already well established. Four facts suggest that he held a high position: *a*. he has been able to persuade Pharaoh to revere Hathor (x+1/2 5, 17); *b*. he can be accused, even if erroneously, of having caused Pharaoh to perish (x+1/5); *c*. he is directly addressed by the Guards, and can address the court of Pharaoh directly in his own right (x+1/22–5); *d*. he can be accused, even if sarcastically, of trying to arrogate to himself authority which, in the absence of Pharaoh, rightfully belongs to the Chamberlain (x+1/26–7). It is not possible on the evidence available to say whether Merib is likely to be related to Pharaoh or not. Presumably he must be adult (see *a–d* above), though he may still be youthful or in early middle age, since he undertakes phenomenally long horse rides (x+1/21–2, 32–4). There appears to be no reason to doubt that Merib is cast in a 'good' role in the story, as he meticulously obeys the instructions of Hathor given in his dream and is instrumental in discovering Pharaoh.

ii. *The Chamberlain*

The Chamberlain (*pꜣ mr-ʿwỉ*) is not given a name in the extant portion of the text. From the speeches of the letter-scribe, it is evident that he is regarded by the Court as having been responsible for Pharaoh's appointment (x+1/26–7), and as being the highest authority in Pharaoh's absence (x+1/29–32). The Chamberlain clearly regards himself as the proper person to find Pharaoh (x+1/28–9), and he claims to have received knowledge of Pharaoh's whereabouts from Isis (x+1/27–8); but as he apparently follows Merib when he rides off to find Pharaoh, this claim may be false. He is anxious that no one should know or be able to follow him whither he is going (x+1/33), and his previous action in approving the arrest of the children (x+1/29–32), though doubtless within his power, is probably to be seen as unscrupulous. This dubious aspect of his character seems to be confirmed when the lion roars, the mountain beasts flee and thus reveal Pharaoh, who immediately accuses the Chamberlain of being responsible for his captivity on the mountain. It is to be inferred thence that the Chamberlain's interests are opposed to those of Merib, and that, with the letter-scribe, he is cast as a 'villain', though whether he is the principal or is being used by the letter-scribe is uncertain in the present state of the text.

iii. *Mer-(. . .), the letter-scribe*

This man is referred to either by his title (*pꜣ sẖ n pꜣ wḫꜣ*) and name (of which the reading is uncertain, cf. x+1/26, 29 and p. 123, n. *dr*), or by his title alone (x+1/30–1). He may perhaps have appeared in broken contexts in x/25, 32. As the personal secretary of the absent Pharaoh he evidently has high influence at Court, since it is he who challenges Merib's authority to take the lead in discovering Pharaoh (x+1/26–7). In this scornful speech he reveals himself as a committed partisan of the Chamberlain. It is the letter-scribe who suggests the arrest of the children to the Chamberlain, who merely assents (x+1/29–32). He also records all that the Chamberlain says (x+1/29). He may thus be viewed on the evidence either as an over-obsequious and officious adherent of the Chamberlain, or as an *éminence grise* who advises the Chamberlain with ill intent and is the true villain of the piece.

iv. *The Guards and the Great men of Pharaoh*

The Guards (*nꜣ sꜣwtî.w*) and the Great men of Pharaoh (*nꜣ rmt.w ꜥꜣ.w n Pr-ꜥꜣ*) first appear in Merib's appeal to Hathor (x+1/3–4), where it is said either that they will, or more probably that they will not, listen to what Merib will say (cf. p. 131, n. *σ*). It is perhaps they who are accusing Merib of destroying Pharaoh (x+1/5, cf. p. 116, n. *aw*). In his dream the goddess advises Merib to recount what she tells him to the Guards (without mention of the Great men) (x+1/18). He therefore rides to where they are, and finds them distraught, complaining that they have been unable to discover Pharaoh; he advises them to pray to Hathor, who listens to the pleas of her worshippers, and tells them that he knows Pharaoh's whereabouts. In general therefore the role of the Guards and the Great men is a relatively passive one, though as members of the court they may be expected to echo the views of the Chamberlain and the letter-scribe.

v. *Pharaoh*

The Pharaoh is named as Pharaoh Badja(?) only in one short passage of the extant text, in which his name appears three times (x+1/1, 2, 4; on the possible readings see p. 114, n. *al*). Nevertheless, all the indications suggest that one and the same Pharaoh is in question throughout. The name is that thought by later Egyptians to have belonged to the first king of the Second Dynasty (see p. 114, n. *al*); it has not previously been found in a literary text. It might be hazardous to see reflections of the fact that Badja was the first king of the Dynasty in the court intrigues which apparently occur in the narrative.

According to the letter-scribe Mer-. . . ., the Chamberlain was responsible for Pharaoh's appointment (x+1/26–7). At the beginning of the extant text, Pharaoh has already been carried off to the high mountain, where he is without food, drink, and sandals (x/1–4). The goddess reveals in Merib's dream that, because of her rage against Pharaoh for rejecting her appointment of the lion to serve him, she has inflicted a mortal disease upon him (x+1/10–12); probably it is this goddess, who no doubt is Hathor, who has caused him to be carried off to the mountains. However, she succours him because Merib has assured her that he has persuaded Pharaoh to revere her (x+1/17), and as a result Pharaoh does not persist in his disobedience to her. When Merib, acting on the goddess's instructions, finds Pharaoh, Pharaoh speaks to him and is recognized by him (x+1/

35–7). When, however, the Chamberlain reaches him, Pharaoh accuses him of responsibility for his captivity (x + 1/38).

Thus, though Pharaoh has been sufficiently deluded to disobey the goddess and has suffered through it, it would seem that he is restored thereby to right thinking, and identifies the Chamberlain as the true agent of his misfortunes.

vi. *Neb(et)-ꜥonkh*

This character, who may be either male or female according to whether the group ʐ should be here read *nb* or *nb.t*, appears with certainty only once in the story (x + 1/29). He/she is in possession of some property, possibly a seal (*ḫtm*; see p. 124, n. *ee*), which pertains to, or affects, the land of Pharaoh; it seems that this fact prompts the suggestion of the letter-scribe to the Chamberlain that certain children should be arrested. Presumably Neb(et)-ꜥonkh, who is given no title, played some part in the court intrigues recorded in the lost part of the story. It seems inherently probable that he/she is related to the children (x + 1/30–1), and may even be one of them; if it was really Pharaoh's seal of which he/she was in possession, the simplest explanation of his/her role may be that he/she was a child of Pharaoh who was still a minor. But this is speculation, for it is uncertain whose children are concerned (p. 134, n. *αψ*).

In x + 1/8 a group *nb(.t)* is followed by a trace which might well, though it need not be, part of *ꜥnḫ*. The context is the beginning of Merib's dream; as the remainder of the dream makes it clear that he sees a goddess, almost certainly Hathor, who addresses him at length, there is every probability that *nb.t ꜥ* . . . should here be read as an epithet of the goddess (see p. 116, n. *bk*). Whether this epithet(?) should be identified with the name in x + 1/29 seems very doubtful, though the possibility cannot be ignored.

vii. *Hathor*

Hathor appears as Lady of Aṭfiḥ (. . . . . *wr.t nb.t Tp-nꜣ-iḥ.w* ⌜*tꜣ ntr.t ꜥꜣ.t*⌝) in x + 1/1 (p. 113, n. *ah*). The goddess who appears in Merib's dream is probably also Hathor, for immediately upon awaking from it Merib asks the time to find out whether it is a suitable hour to visit the *dromos* of Hathor, presumably to thank her (x + 1/20); and it seems to be to her that he gives thanks when his dream is fulfilled (x + 1/36; see p. 126, n. *fa*). However, in the dream she appears to have a different epithet from in x + 1/1; possibly this is *ntr.t* or *ntr.t ꜥꜣ.t nb.t ꜥ*[*nḫ* . . .], which might conceivably be restored *nb.t ꜥnḫ-tꜣ.wy*, 'Lady of ꜥOnkhtowe', the necropolis of Memphis (p. 116, n. *bk*; p. 131, n. *ω*), but many other possibilities exist. In other contexts she is either simply called Hathor (x + 1/20, 24, 36(?)), or addressed by an epithet (e.g. *tꜣ ḥri.t* in x/1, probably something similar in x + 1/3).

Hathor may in one sense be thought of as the principal motivator of the events of the story as preserved in the extant text. It is she who appoints the lion, who is in thrall to her, as Pharaoh's servant and bearer (x + 1/10–11). This action rouses Pharaoh's anger against the lion and provokes his spoken disobedience to the goddess (x + 1/11–12). She therefore punishes him by visiting upon him a mortal sickness, and very probably also by carrying him off to the mountains (though it must be observed that in x + 1/38 Pharaoh blames his captivity on the Chamberlain; this may mean that the Chamberlain actually carried him off, but could also mean that the Chamberlain by bad advice was responsible for Pharaoh's disobedience to the goddess).

When, however, Pharaoh is thirsty and hungry, she provides sweet water and bread, and then arranges for the goddess Bastet to produce fire, and for the lion, as Pharaoh's appointed servant and bearer, to bring him game and salt, and to serve him. And then she stands above Pharaoh on the mountain while certain creatures, probably the mountain beasts, surround him and promise to rescue him (x+1/13–17). It is clearly therefore not Hathor's wish to destroy Pharaoh, but to reduce him to obedience by alternating affliction and succour, giving the latter, however, only when he appeals for it. When she has succeeded in her object, she gives Merib instructions for finding and rescuing Pharaoh (x+1/18–19), and assists him by magic to do so (x+1/21–2, 32–4). It may also be she who is responsible for the lion's roaring and frightening the mountain beasts into flight so that they reveal the Chamberlain to Pharaoh for him to denounce.

Thus Hathor is clearly on the 'good' side; her concern is to bring a deluded and disobedient Pharaoh back to the right path.

viii. *Isis*

Isis appears only in x+1/28, where the Chamberlain tells the court what he has been told 'before Isis' (*m-bꜣḥ ꞽIst*). This could perhaps mean that Isis appeared to him in a dream; but the expression suggests rather that he appeared before her requesting an answer to a prayer or oracle question. He claims (in all probability) that the goddess told him what had happened to Pharaoh, and that he will find him in the goddess's inheritance with her assistance. Thus Isis appears as the divine backer of the Chamberlain, and so presumably as the opponent of Hathor and Merib, unless the Chamberlain's words are entirely deceitful.

ix. *Bastet*

Bastet, the great goddess (*Bꜣstt tꜣ ntr.t ꜥꜣ.t*), appears in x+1/14. Unfortunately, it is not certain whether the goddess herself brings fire to Pharaoh in his affliction on the mountains, as the simplest restoration of x+1/14–15 would suggest (cf. p. 119, nn. *cb–cg*), or whether it is simply from her altar that it is brought. But, either way, Bastet seems here simply to serve as a coadjutor of Hathor in succouring Pharaoh. However, Bastet might just possibly be restored at the end of x+1/8 (see p. 116, n. *bk*) as the goddess whom Merib sees in his dream; but this causes difficulties since she is mentioned in the goddess's speech to Merib (x+1/14).

x. *The lion and the mountain beasts*

The lion (*pꜣ mꜣi*) appears with his name spelt with a divine sign; in x+1/10 it is just possible that a name is given to him (*Mr-* [. . . .] *rn=f*). He probably first appears coming down from the mountain in x/5, and it is said that 'his flesh is goodly'. In the following lines (cf. x+1/10 ff.) he evidently waits on Pharaoh and succours him, and finally 'makes the mountain echo to his voice' (x/9); as a result, someone, possibly Pharaoh, alleges that no lion [has been seen] like *pꜣ mꜣi wꜣḏ* in his possession' (x/10), or, perhaps less convincingly, that 'the lion is not like *pꜣ mꜣi wꜣḏ* in his possession.' Whether *wꜣḏ* here means 'young', 'green', or 'of the papyrus-thicket' is unclear. If the second translation above is right, it could be that Pharaoh unfavourably contrasted the mountain-lion whom the goddess Hathor has sent him with a papyrus-lion already in his possession, but this would complicate matters by implying that there were two lions in the story. Hathor apparently has the lion bound in her possession because he has previously served Pharaoh without her instructions (x+1/10–11); she makes him serve Pharaoh even though Pharaoh objects strongly and is aggressive towards the lion or vice versa. After Pharaoh has been afflicted with mortal disease by the goddess, she continues to make the lion wait upon him (x+1/14–15); and it may be the lion's roar that causes the mountain beasts or other creatures to come round Pharaoh (x+1/16). When Merib and the Chamberlain finally reach Pharaoh, the lion again roars, and it would certainly seem that it is this action that causes the mountain beasts to reveal the Chamberlain to Pharaoh.

Thus throughout the lion acts as an agent of Hathor under her obedience. While his unmammal-like and presumably magical conduct may simply be the result of his association with the goddess, the divine det. after *mꜣi*, and his possible possession of a name may suggest that the lion is really a divine character or a human character who has been magically transformed into a lion by Hathor or Isis for her own ends.

The mountain beasts are specified in x+1/34 as being giraffe, gazelle, hyena, wolf(?), hart, and other sorts of beast; they are also described as 'being numerous . . . heat', a phrase susceptible of various restorations (see p. 125, n. *eu*). Their role in x+1/37–8 is to leave no way open to Pharaoh for Merib, but when the lion roars to flee to Pharaoh and leave the way open to the Chamberlain. Probably they are innocent or unconscious actors in the story, though they may in effect be agents of Hathor. It is at least possible that they first appear in the story as the plural entity in x+1/16–17 (see p. 132, n. $\alpha\theta$), in which case their appearance is probably due to the goddess; but this interpretation is at best dubious.

2. The Story

The extant portion of the story opens with an appeal to a goddess by a male character, who finds himself in high mountains bereft of food, drink, and sandals. The text of x+1/12 ff. shows that this must be the Pharaoh Badja(?) appealing to the goddess Hathor. His appeal is answered by the arrival of the lion, who ministers to Pharaoh's wants, and then makes 'the mountain echo to his voice', bringing the comment that there was 'no lion like the young(?) lion in his possession'.

This paragraph probably ended at x/12. The remainder of the page yields only scraps of text. Somebody dreams a dream, beginning in x/15, and awakes in x/24; the final lines of the page seem to be mainly narrative.

The next page begins with an appeal by Merib to Hathor, Lady of Aṭfiḥ. In it, Merib asks the goddess firstly to inform Pharaoh Badja(?) of his own situation, and secondly to tell him what has happened to Pharaoh before anyone else finds him. Merib's reason why the goddess should answer him is that he has set reverence for her in Pharaoh's heart; the urgency of his finding out what has happened to Pharaoh is that he is being accused of responsibility for Pharaoh's disappearance, probably by the Guards and Great men of Pharaoh. Unless he has information from Hathor and can discover Pharaoh's whereabouts, he fears the Guards and Great men will not believe him.

Merib finishes his speech in an access of weeping, and perhaps looks to heaven for help; apparently the goddess does not appear, but comforting words, assuring him that the goddess always answers the prayers of supplicants, are spoken to him by some unknown person or persons. He sleeps and dreams a dream. In this he sees the lion, and the goddess sitting on a mound of sand, apparently with the waters of the inundation all around her. The goddess is presumably Hathor, but whether in her own person or in human disguise is uncertain. She points out the lion to Merib and tells him its story. She has made the lion sword-bearer to Pharaoh, the lion being in thrall to her because it had earlier served a Pharaoh without her orders. Pharaoh, however, has protested to the goddess and has threatened to carry off the lion and has shown hostility to it, presumably because the goddess has made the lion serve him against his wishes. (Alternatively, Pharaoh may be in thrall, and the lion be hostile to him.) This conduct has enraged the goddess, who has visited Pharaoh with a mortal sickness. Pharaoh is thus thirsty, but the goddess provides him with sweet water; he is hungry and appeals to her, and she gives him bread. In an obscure passage, it would appear that the goddess caused fire to be provided for Pharaoh by the agency of Bastet, and caused the lion to procure game and salt, and to serve a meal before Pharaoh as he lay in captivity on the mountain. (As Pharaoh's predicament may be due to his rejection of the lion as his servant, this manner of succouring him through the lion's agency is clearly intended by the goddess as an object lesson to Pharaoh in obedience.) When Bastet brings the flame before Pharaoh, with the goddess standing above him, the lion roars(?); at this some persons or creatures, possibly the mountain beasts, pass on the upper side of Pharaoh and surround him. When they see his state, they tell him that at the behest of the goddess(?) they will rescue him and take him back to Egypt. This suggests that Pharaoh is held captive outside Egypt, and there is a possibility that the country is named as Emor or Assur (p. 120, n. *cl*).

Here the goddess turns to Merib and tells him that she has only done all these things for Pharaoh because Merib has assured her that he has set reverence for her in Pharaoh's heart. And Pharaoh has been reduced to obedience since, when she left him, he had not said that he would not obey her. So she instructs Merib to go and tell his people that their Master is safe, and to tell the Guards that he will go to the mountain to fetch Pharaoh back to Egypt. He is then to mount a horse, and without guiding or restraining it to let it go as it wills.

On awaking from his dream, Merib decides not to visit the *dromos* of Hathor, since it is the first hour of the night and the goddess will not be there, but to inform the Guards. He obtains a horse, and, riding without use of bridle or whip, reaches the Guards by midnight; he finds them unfed, and distracted by worry at their failure to discover Pharaoh. Merib tries to reassure them that if they pray and carry out the ritual observances Hathor will reveal Pharaoh's whereabouts. These he claims to know and promises to recover Pharaoh. This presumption angers the letter-scribe Mer- . . . , who sarcastically asks whether it was Merib and not the Chamberlain who appointed Pharaoh? And whether he expects them to revere someone other than the Chamberlain? Certainly Merib is not the Pharaoh they acknowledge! The Chamberlain himself then claims that he has knowledge from the goddess Isis of what has happened to Pharaoh, and promises to find him and bring him back safe. The letter-scribe writes down all the Chamberlain says, and, on the grounds that a person named Neb(et)-ʿonkh has a seal-ring or other authority over the land of Pharaoh, advises that some children, possibly those of Pharaoh, should be arrested and imprisoned pending Pharaoh's arrival. The Chamberlain assents, and they are imprisoned on a barge without their having informed anyone.

Merib remounts his horse, which gallops off to the mountain. The Chamberlain decides to follow him, on the grounds that no one yet knows whither to follow him. The horse continues galloping into the morning, and it is not until noon that the Chamberlain sees various species of wild beasts. When Merib approaches, Pharaoh, who is concealed by the beasts, speaks to him; he recognizes Pharaoh and sees the lion. At this, Merib gives thanks to Hathor for her appearance to him in the dream. The mountain beasts, however, do not flee when Merib walks among them, and thus do not reveal the way to reach Pharaoh. But then the lion roars, and the wild beasts flee to Pharaoh, and the way to him is thus left open to the Chamberlain. The Chamberlain does obeisance, but Pharaoh accuses him of being the one who has been responsible for his captivity. Here the text breaks off.

3. The character and relationships of the text

This story is concerned with human intrigues and adventures centring round the court of

Pharaoh Badja(?), resulting from divine intervention in human affairs by the goddesses Hathor and Isis, who employ magical means. These means are exemplified by the lion who is able at the behest of Hathor to act as a servant and bearer to Pharaoh; by Hathor's spiriting away of Pharaoh to the mountain; by her appearance in a dream to Merib; by her magical direction of Merib's horse; and probably by her dictating the conduct of the mountain beasts so that the Chamberlain, not Merib, reaches Pharaoh first. Isis for her part informs and advises the Chamberlain. While divine intervention is thus of the essence of the story, the gods do not appear to take direct action themselves, as sometimes in Homer, but to prompt and make possible action by human beings or creatures on earth.

So far as can be told, no foreign or civil war is likely to have taken place in the text, and the conflict between the good and evil forces was probably worked out entirely through magic and stratagem. The good forces may place themselves in danger by error or disobedience to the gods, and the interest is largely centred on how they are to be extricated from their perilous positions; but no doubt subsists about who is good and who is evil, nor about the eventual triumph of the good.

In these characteristics, the story lies closely within the long tradition of Egyptian story-telling. Within the demotic tradition, it evidently belongs with the Khaʿemwese group rather than the Inaros–Petubastis group of stories. Positive evidence that the text might belong to the Khaʿemwese cycle is confined to the appearance of an adult character named Merib, who could conceivably be the Merib the child, son of Neneferkaptaḥ and Aḥure, of Khaʿemwese I, grown to manhood. Although in 1. Kh. Merib was drowned while still a child, this need not have been so in other stories; or in the present story Merib may appear in a 'reincarnated' form, as does Si-Osiri in 2. Kh. These possibilities exist; but, as in the extant portion of this text Merib's parentage is not given, as neither Setm Khaʿemwese nor any of the other characters of 1. Kh. appear, and as the action is in no way directly related, it is best not to assume any direct relationships between the texts. But the use of the name Merib, perhaps also the use of names derived from the root *mr* for the letter-scribe and possibly for the lion, and the choice of the name Badja(?) for the Pharaoh, do suggest that the setting of the story may be intended to be the times of the Archaic Period–Old Kingdom. In this it would again belong most closely with the Neneferkaptaḥ incident in 1. Kh. It must, however, be borne in mind that, as in 1. Kh. itself, the 'Old Kingdom' incident could have been set in a framework placed later in time, and now lost with the missing pages of the text.

In style, the story combines brief direct narrative passages in the preterite, using deliberately repetitive introductory formulae with extended dialogue sections. Indeed, the narrative serves largely as a frame to the dialogue, which is often used not only to heighten the dramatic effect, but to explain and advance the action itself. In this also, the story stands well within the main classical Egyptian story-telling tradition and compares closely with other demotic stories. There seems little good reason to doubt that the chief art of the story-teller in telling them was in the dramatization of the characters through their speeches.

As has been suggested above, there is no compelling reason in the physical make-up of **2** for believing that the stories on the front and back belong to the same unit. The page numbering is unfortunately lost on the back of the papyrus, and may or may not have been continuous with that of the front. The hands of the texts on back and front seem basically the same; a number of minor variants can be discerned, but these occur as much within each text as between them. No human proper names appear on both sides of the papyrus, while the only divine proper name in common is that of Isis, who is too frequent an actor in stories of partly magical character for this to be of significance. The only other writing which might conceivably indicate a relationship between the texts is that read *nꜣ dw.w* in front, 6/6 and back, x/2; but if the reading be correct, there seems no reason why 'mountains' should not appear independently in separate stories.

When the incidents retailed on the two sides of the papyrus are considered together, it would be difficult to fit them into the body of a single story. An assumption that the 'doomed man' of **2** front is to be identified with the Pharaoh Badja of **2** back fails, not only on the ground that he is not named as Pharaoh on the front, but also because it is Isis, not Hathor, whom he has offended. An identification of the 'doomed man' with Merib encounters not only the objection that he is not named on the front, but also that he addresses Isis as his mother, in which case one would expect Merib to appeal to Isis and not to Hathor. Otherwise, the incidents of the stories are not related, and it is certainly best to regard them as independent.

However, there is clearly a relation between the topic and general subject-matter of these two stories, in that both deal with adventure of a marvellous character, triggered by divine intervention in human affairs through magical means. Thus two possibilities present themselves. Either two or more stories of similar character were written by the scribe on a single papyrus, or a framing story of rather general character may have included two or more long and quite diverse incidents, illustrating, for instance, the importance of not offending the gods, or the marvels that could be wrought by magic (cf. Papyrus Westcar). On the evidence, it is hardly feasible to decide between these possibilities.

3. TJIMOOU AND THE LORD OF THE EAST

Plate 10

71/72-DP79+84 [5765+5770]

Sector 7, West Dump

fr. 1 (DP 79): 10.0 cm. *h.*×7.0 cm. *w.*
fr. 2 (DP 79): 4.0 cm. *h.*×2.5 cm. *w.*
fr. 3 (DP 84): 12.5 cm. *h.*×9.0 cm. *w.*

The papyrus is translucent and of a fine and even texture. Both surfaces have been worn in such a way as to loosen and disturb many of the surface fibres, especially on the front, and there are a number of holes. However, most of the ink is fairly well preserved. The shade of the papyrus is grey upon both surfaces: it is uncertain whether this is due to the erasure of previous writing or to dirt. The horizontal fibres of frs. 1 and 2 clearly correspond, so that, on each of the surfaces, ll. 1–3 of fr. 1 correspond with the three lines preserved upon fr. 2. From the general appearance of the fragments it is probable that fr. 2 belongs (as seen from the front) to the left and (as seen from the back) to the right of fr. 1. They are arranged on the plates in this way. Both the papyrus and the texts suggest that fr. 2 does not join with fr. 1, nor belong very close to it: a gap of at least 1.0 cm., and possibly one much larger, should be left between them. No correspondence of either the horizontal or vertical fibres of fr. 3 with those of frs. 1 or 2 is discernible, although the general appearance of the papyrus and the text suggest that all three fragments do not come from widely separated portions of the original text, and may well have belonged to the same sheet. It is conceivable that the damage that the fragments have suffered has disguised the correspondence of, say, a few fibres at the corners of the fragments. Both surfaces of all the fragments bear remains of a continuous demotic text, which is written the same way up on front and back. The surface with horizontal fibres is here assumed to be the front, although there are no further clues to support this. All three fragments are torn on all sides. In the case of fr. 3, although the bottom edge is quite uneven, the back preserves up to 2.0 cm. of blank papyrus at its foot, which suggests the bottom margin of a column. The front preserves no more than 1 cm. of blank papyrus at its foot, and it is just conceivable that further lines of the same continuous body of text are here lost after l. 9. However, on both the front and the back of fr. 3, the probability is that the last line preserved is the last line of the column. The hand of the texts on each surface of all the fragments is undoubtedly the same. The writing is slightly larger and the spacing of the lines slightly greater on the back than on the front: this feature is consistent on all three fragments.

The fragments are here transcribed and translated simply in the order in which they are arranged in the plates. Frs. 1 and 2 are treated together, in accordance with the suggestions made above. On both front and back surfaces it is uncertain whether the text of fr. 3 should be read before or after the combined texts of frs. 1 and 2. As fr. 3 probably preserves on each side the last lines of a column, there might perhaps be some reason to read the fragments in the order front, fr. 1+fr. 2; then front, fr. 3; then back, fr. 1+fr. 2; and then back, fr. 3, rather than in the order followed below. However, either suggested sequence might be disrupted if in fact the fragments did not belong to the same column of text.

The **hand** is quite large and is rapidly written. Although it is clearly the work of a practised scribe, it has an untidy appearance, which is probably due partly to the present damaged state of the papyrus, and partly to the use of a rather ragged brush. The type of hand stands between that of **1** and **2** in this volume, and **4** and **5**. The hand is rounded, but, in general, the signs are compressed along the line.

Transliteration

FRONT (↔): fr. 1+fr. 2

1. - - - . . . .] . . . . . .[a] [- - - - - - - - - - - - .] *ỉr=f* . . . [- - -
2. . . . . .] ⌜*ỉw*⌝ . . . . .[b] [- - - - - - - - - - - - -] ⌜*pꜣ*⌝ *ḥri-Ỉꜣbt* [
3.] . . .*ḥr n-ỉm=f* ⌜*ḥwy=w*⌝[c] *r-bnr n tꜣ/nꜣ* [- - -] . . .[d] *n/r pꜣ tꜣ* .[
4. *pꜣ*] *ḥri-Ỉꜣbt bn-pw=f ḥrr* [
5. . .] ⌜*ḏd*⌝ *Pr-ꜥꜣ my ỉn=w* ⌜*n(=y)*⌝ [
6. .] . . . *pꜣ ḥri-Ỉ*⌜*ꜣbt*⌝ [
7. . . . .] ⌜*ḫpr ỉw=f*⌝[e] . .[
8. . . . .] .[f][

fr. 3

1. - - - . . . .] ⌜*ḏ*⌝*ḏy ỉn=w n(=y)/-s* [- - -
2. . . . .] . . *mtw=y* . . . *ntỉ* .[g] [
3. . . . .] . . . .[h] [. . .] . . *nꜣ ꜥwỉ.w ḥrr*[j] .[
4. *pꜣ ḥri*]-⌜*Ỉꜣbt*⌝ .[k] *šm=f r ḥwt-nṯr* . .[l] [
5. .] . .[.] . *ỉw r-bnr ẖn* ⌜*ḥwt-nṯr*⌝[m] [
6.] . ⌜*ẖny*⌝[n] *Ṯꜣỉ-n-ỉm=w ỉr=f hrw nfr* ⌜*ỉrm*⌝ [
7.] ⌜*bn*⌝-*pw=f ḥrr r ẖn n tꜣỉ=f* ⌜*st*⌝ [
8.] . . . . . *n pꜣ tꜣ ḫpr grḥ* [
9. . . . .] . . . .[o] ⌜*Ṯꜣỉ-n-ỉm=w*⌝ [

BACK (↕): fr. 3

1. - - -] ⌜*ỉr=f*⌝ [- - -] .*y*. . *h*. .[p] [- - -
2. - - -] . . . *ỉr pꜣ* .[q] [. . . .] . . .[r] [
3.] . . . . . .[s] *ỉw* . . .=*n*[t] *pꜣ* .[
4.] ⌜*dỉ*⌝=*f ỉn=w st r-bnr ḥr*-⌜*ḥꜣt.ṯ=f*⌝ .[
5.] . . . ⌜*dỉ*⌝=*f ꜥš=*⌜*w (n) pꜣ s 3*⌝[u] *m-šs* ⌜*ḏd*⌝ [
6.] *tꜣỉ=s šb(t) bn-ỉw=y šp* . . . .[v] [
7. . .]=⌜*f*⌝ *r (pꜣỉ=f) ꜥwỉ r dỉt* . . . . . .[w] [

up to 2.0 cm of blank papyrus preserved

fr. 2+fr. 1

1. - - -] .⌜=*f*⌝ *šb(t)* .[x] [- - - - - - - - - - - - - -] . . ⌜*ỉ-ỉr*⌝ .[y] [- - -
2.] ⌜*Pꜣ-dỉ-Wsỉr pꜣỉ=*⌝. . .[z] [- - -] . . . . [. .] . . .[aa] [

3.] . . *r-wn* . [- - - - - - - - - - - - - -] *Ṯ꜡i-n-ỉm=w nfr p꜡ ḥm-ntr* . . . [
4. - - -] . . *r ḥwt-ntr n t꜡ wn⸢wt⸣* [
5. . .] *dỉ=y ⸢(n)=n⸣*[ab] . . . . [
6. . .] . [. .] *⸢mn⸣* . . .[ac] [
7. . . . .] . . . [

— — — — — — — — — — — — — — — — —

Notes on transliteration

FRONT

a.].*=f mn* [is a possible reading (i.e. *mn*, 'there is not' etc.).

b. *ỉw*, 'come' (Stative) is probable: cf. front, fr. 3/5 and back, fr. 3/3. In view of the  det. at the end of the following word(s), a personal name may be in question.

c. *ỉwy.w*, 'pledges' (*DG*, 22. 10) would be the most natural reading of the signs out of context, especially because of the det. 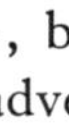, but this would be difficult to parse between the two adverbial phrases *n-ỉm=f* and *r-bnr*. Other possibilities are *dỉt wy=w r-bnr n*, 'cause them to be far off from', and *ḫwy=w r-bnr*, 'cast them forth': cf. the early writings given in *DG*, 78. 2 and 296. 1.

d. *ʿš꜡y* or *ʿš꜡y.t* are conceivable readings: *šm*,  is perhaps possible: cf. *šm=f*, 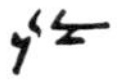, front, fr. 3/4.

e. The reading *ḫpr* is very probable: cf. front, fr. 3/8. Here, probably part of its tail is preserved, and *=k* is not to be read. The following signs are clearly *ỉw*, and probably *ỉw=f*. It is impossible to read *md*.

f. The thick horizontal stroke at the bottom of fr. 1 is probably a supralinear stroke belonging to an eighth line of text. It is unlikely to be the tail of the *ḫpr* in l. 7, or a *=k* under the line: it might conceivably belong to the tail of a previous *ỉr=f*, or to a ruling.

g. *mtw=y rmt nb ntỉ* .[is a possible reading, but *rmt* is dubious, and *mtw=y* is perhaps not certain.

h. Possibly read *hb*, .

j. For the writing of *ḥrr*, cf. front, fr. 1/4 and front, fr. 3/7. For the expression, see ʿOnchsheshonqy, 4/6, 18; 8/9; *Siut*, Vo. 3/16–17; and *Archive of Ḥor*, Text **19**, Vo. 7. The abbreviated writing of *ʿwi.w*,  is remarkable in a literary text.

k. The small trace of ink after the det. of *ỉ꜡bt* may be part of a short word, or the end of the long horizontal stroke of *šm*.

l. The trace after *ḥwt-ntr* is probably not *bnr*: cf. front, fr. 3/5.

m. Cf. front, fr. 3/4.

n. The reading *ḫny* seems certain, although there is no trace of a det. Compare perhaps *DG*, 382. 1, 'to approach', rather than *DG*, 383. 1, 'to row'. The preceding trace may be of *=f*.

o. Traces of a word ending with the det. 

BACK

p. *hyn(.w) hrw*, 'some days', seems the most probable reading, and may have followed *ỉr=f*, 'he spent . . .', directly.

q. Possibly read a title beginning with *mr*, 'overseer'.

r. Uncertain: *t꜡*, 'land', cannot be read.

s. Perhaps read *wb꜡=w*: compare the early writings in *DG*, 84. 13. The group is quite different from the other writings of *ỉ꜡bt*, front, fr. 1/4, 6, and front, fr. 2/2.

t. Between *ỉw*, 'came' (Stative), and , which would most naturally be read as *=n*, there is a short lacuna, perhaps long enough to contain the circumstantial auxiliary *ỉw=* or a suffix pronoun. However, on back, fr. 1/5 there occurs the combination , which might be read as *dỉ=y (n)=n* (see p. 146, n. *ab*). Perhaps simply *ỉw*+suffix+*(n)=n* should be read here, and this would presumably be a prospective form.

u. In the context, the reading *ʿš=w* seems certain. The following signs might be read *r p꜡ 3*, but the sense 'He caused them to cry out against the three very much' is dubious. *n p꜡ s 3* seems the most probable reading, although the form of *s* is attenuated.

v. Possibly read *šp p꜡ ḥ*.[

w. The last traces are indecipherable, and therefore the reading *r dỉt*, unsupported by any context, is uncertain.

x. Before *šb(t)* the tail of an *=f* is clear. The sign after *šb(t)* is not a fem. *.t*, but possibly *p꜡*.

y. *t꜡/n꜡ ỉ-ỉr* is probable.

z. Although in the context of this line the signs  suggest *p꜡ ḥm-ntr*, this is more likely to be the reading of the different group in back, fr. 1/3. Here it is preferable to restore, for example, *pꜣỉ(=y) ỉṯ* or the like, or *pꜣỉ=w*.

aa. The first broken group resembles a det. with a short stroke following, rather than the geographical det. Part of *ỉw*, 'came' (Stative), may follow.

ab. The signs here are clearly , and the first groups are to be read *di=y*. The group might be taken as a 1st plur. object pronoun, but, although this pronoun is naturally rare, only the normal demotic form *ṯ=n* seems to be attested. 'I have placed us . . .' could make sense in an appropriate context, but the following traces here do not support this suggestion. The group might be taken as a writing of (*n*)=*n*, 'to us', for which the normal form in these hands is , 'I have given . . . to us' might yield good sense in context: the phrase might also be restored *r-di=y* (*n*)=*n*, 'that I gave us'. Late-Egyptian writings might suggest the possibility that the group be read *n=w*, 'to them', but the only support for this is the somewhat different form in G. R. Hughes, 'A demotic plea to Thoth in the Library of G. Michaelidis', *JEA* 54 (1968), 176–82, l. 6 of the text.

ac. *mn*, 'remain', etc., seems certain. *ḥr pꜣ* may be suggested for the following signs, but is very uncertain.

Translation

FRONT: fr. 1 + fr. 2

1.] there is not [. . . . . . .] he acted [
2.] came [. . . . .] the Lord of the East[α] [
3.] counsel[β] concerning him to cast them forth from the [. . . . .] on earth [
4.] the Lord of the East. He[γ] did not delay [
5.] Pharaoh said 'Let there be brought to me [
6.] the Lord of the East [
7.] It happened that he [
8.] . . . [

fr. 3

1.] enemy. They brought him/to me [
2.] there belongs to me every man who [
3.] the Houses of Waiting[δ] [
4.] the Lord of the East. He went to the temple [
5.] came out of the temple [
6.] approached Tjimoou.[ε] He spent a holiday with[ζ] [
7.] He did not delay (to go) into his place [
8.] on earth. When night came [
9.] Tjimoou [

BACK: fr. 3

1.] he spent some days [
2.] the overseer [. . . . . .] did [
3.] came to us [
4.] He caused them to bring him out before him [
5.] He caused the three men to cry out together exceedingly, saying: [
6.] in return for it. I will not receive [
7.] he [went] to his house to cause [

fr. 2 + fr. 1

1.] he exchanged [. . . . . . .] that which/who [
2.] Petosiri my [father[η]
3.] there being [. . . . .] Tjimoou. The prophet was favourable[θ] [
4.] to the temple at the [. . . . .] hour[ι] [
5.] I have given . . . . .[κ] [
6.] remain(s) upon the [
7.] . . . . . [

Notes on translation

α. This title, not attested elsewhere, might refer to a foreign potentate, but seems more likely to refer to an Egyptian Governor or Prince, perhaps of the east Delta marches. It recalls the title *pꜣ wr-Ỉꜣbt*, 'the Chief of the East', given in Inaros-texts to Pekrur, ruler of Pi-Soped in the Eastern Delta. Similarly, Volten understood (*pꜣ*) *rmt pr-Ỉꜣbt 2*, '(the) two men of the East', who appear several times in *Ägypter und Amazonen*, always in contexts too broken for certainty, as heroes from Pi-Soped. The Inaros-texts do not use *ḥrỉ* in compound titles, but only in phrases such as *pꜣỉ(=y) ḥrỉ*, 'my lord'.

β. Perhaps restore [*s*]*ẖr n-ỉm=f*.

γ. 'He' may not necessarily refer to 'the Lord of the East', which immediately precedes it. The antecedents of the pronouns on front, fr. 3/4–7 are similarly uncertain.

δ. See p. 145, n. *j*. In ʿOnchsheshonqy the expression 'Houses of Waiting' certainly means a kind of prison, and this is presumably its sense here. However, in the *Archive of Ḥor*, it refers to a place where mummified ibises were stored before their final interment in catacombs, and therefore literally signifies a 'waiting place'. This suggests that 'the Houses of Waiting' refers to a particular kind of prison where offenders against the state were kept during Pharaoh's pleasure prior to trial and sentence, and this sense would suit the context in ʿOnchsheshonqy.

ε. Tjimoou is perhaps the principal character of this text, and he might be the person referred to by the various third person pronouns elsewhere on the front. See n. *θ* below.

ζ. *ỉr hrw nfr* is a common phrase in demotic narratives, meaning 'to spend a holiday', 'to hold a feast', always either explicitly or by implication in company. The kind of context varies considerably, for example, in 1. Kh. 5/18, it is used of the intimate supper between Setna and Tabubu, in 1. Kh. 3/27, of the formal reception of Neneferkaptaḥ and his wife at Coptos, and, at P. Spiegelberg 5/14, of victorious warriors feasting together.

The moral implications of this phrase in Egyptian have received some discussion: see most recently D. Lorton, 'The expression *ỉrỉ hrw nfr*', *JARCE* 12 (1975), 23–31, who mentions the two demotic passages from 1. Kh.

η. 'my father' is no more than a possible restoration here. Another possibility is 'Petosiri, their . . .'. See p. 145, n. *z*.

θ. In view of the simple name Tjimoou in front, fr. 3/6, it is improbable that 'Tjimoounofre the prophet' is to be understood here. *nfr* might be written for *nꜣ-nfr* (as suggested in the translation), or might be Stative, in which case *pꜣ ḥm-nṯr* might begin a new sentence, or be understood, for example, as (*n*) *pꜣ ḥm-nṯr*, 'Tjimoou was good to the prophet'.

ι. A phrase such as 'at the hour of prayer' (cf. **1**, 9/19) or *n tꜣ wnwt n rn=s*, 'in the selfsame hour', 'immediately', might be restored here.

κ. The sense here may be 'I have given to us', but the reading is problematic: see p. 146, n. *ab*.

DISCUSSION

There can be no doubt that parts of the same text are preserved on the front and back surfaces, and it is plainly a narrative. The name of only one character, Tjimoou, occurs upon both the front and the back. Although this hardly amounts to satisfactory proof, it is natural to suppose that he was the principal character of the story.

The technical evidence for the relationship between the three fragments is discussed in the introduction (p. 143). The contents of the text preserved also suggest that all the fragments come from the same portion of the narrative, but it has proved impossible to make out a case for any particular arrangement.

In the episode upon the front, probably both Tjimoou and the Lord of the East appear in audience before Pharaoh. The mention of the prison known as the 'Houses of Waiting' particularly suggests a scene similar to that in the narrative introduction to the wisdom text ʿOnchsheshonqy, where Pharaoh sits in judgement upon conspirators. After this scene, someone visits a temple; a celebration follows; and night falls (probably an incident occurred at night—the obvious possibility is that a character experienced a dream).

On the back, the action in frs. 1 and 2 again concern a temple. A character Petosiri is named. The episode in fr. 3 *may* be subsequent to that of frs. 1 and 2: here it is conceivable that another judicial scene occurs.

The mention of the 'Lord of the East' (see p. 147, n. *a*) might suggest a connection with the Inaros–Petubastis texts, but this could be proved only by the occurrence of well-known names from that cycle. As the episodes preserved here seem to concern audiences before Pharaoh, the prison, and the temple, the story may have been one of intrigue in the manner of the narrative introduction to ʿOnchsheshonqy and **1** and **2** in this volume.

4. THE CAT AND FALCON OF WAX

Plate 11a

71/72-DP161 [5847] 10.0 cm. *h.* × 14.5 cm. *w.*

Sector 7, surface debris

The papyrus is of a considerable thickness: it is opaque and coarse-textured. Its shade is light brown, and slightly grey; but there is no firm evidence that any previous text has been erased. Some of the vertical fibres have been stripped away from the back. The front (↔) surface preserves parts of the first 7 lines of a column of continuous demotic text. The original top edge of the sheet of papyrus is preserved, and an ample margin of 4 cm. stands at the head of the column. The fragment is broken in the middle of the text on all other sides. (Possibly the left-hand edge has been cut rather than torn.) There is no indication of the original extent of the column, or of the papyrus, or of the text. The back (↕) surface is blank.

The **hand** is small, and rapidly, although neatly, written. There is a great variation in the thickness of the strokes. Horizontal strokes are very thick, and sometimes exaggerated in length, while ↗-strokes are thin: ↘-strokes are almost avoided, giving the hand an angular appearance. The hand is similar to that of **5**; and **3** may be compared.

Transliteration

top margin of 4.0 cm.

1. - - -] . . . . . .[a] *⌜mnḥ i-ir⌝-ḥr=f ir=f wꜥt mit mnḥ ir=f wꜥ bik mnḥ ꜥš=f n=w sẖ rsy*[=*w*[b] - - -
2. .] . [. . . . . .] . . .[c] *ḥn=f-s n tꜣ mit mnḥ ḏd pꜣy*[d] *pꜣi*[e] *bik* . [[f]
3. . . . . . .] . . . . . . *m-ir dit gm=w-tn ir=f hy⌜n.w⌝ sẖ r ⌜tm dit⌝*[g] *gm=w* . [[h]
4. . . . . . .] . . . .[j] *pꜣ mtr n pꜣ ꜥwi tꜣ wnw.t rn=s pꜣi=f r-ẖn irm* .[
5. . . . .] . *pꜣ ꜥwi*[k] *irm pꜣ inḥ pꜣ wꜥb r pꜣ itn gm Pꜣ-di-⌜ꜣIst⌝*[l] *pꜣ* . . .[m] *ẖpr ⌜ḏd⌝* [
6. . . . .] *⌜s⌝ḏy=f*[n] *i-ir-ḥr=f n mdt ⌜nbt r-nw⌝*[o] [. .] . [.] . [
7. . . . .] . . . [

— —

Notes on transliteration

a. The first traces resemble *ir=w*: *ḏd=w* is less likely because there is no trace of the long upper stroke that occurs with *ḏd* in l. 2 (cf. l. 5). A possible restoration is *i-ir=w*+verb, although the following distorted traces do not suit the obvious verbs to restore, such as *in* or *tꜣi*. Perhaps *i-ir=w dit šm mnḥ*, 'they sent wax' is just possible.

b. The reading *rsy* is virtually certain, although the det. is lost (*DG*, 253. 5).

c. Perhaps restore *i*]-*ir-ḥr=w*.

d. *pꜣy*, 'to fly', 'to leap'. The same word undoubtedly recurs, undamaged, in l. 4. There, the first sign is : here in l. 2 it is unclear whether it has the shape , or . Therefore, it is uncertain whether the form is merely a slip for the usual uniliteral sign *p*, , found in Roman writings of *pꜣy*, or represents , followed by the expected complement . Against the reading *pꜣy*, it might be argued that the det. resembles rather than the normal . However, it may well in fact represent the flying bird , . This det. is common with *hl*, 'to fly' (*DG*, 327. 2). Therefore, the reading *ptri* that might be suggested because of this det. is here rejected.

e. , with only a dot as the second element, is an acceptable early form of the demonstrative adjective *pꜣi* (*DG*, 128. 2), and, regardless of the context, it seems the only plausible reading of the signs here. The element is less rounded than all the other examples of *pȝ* in this papyrus, perhaps most resembling the *pȝ* of *Pȝ-dỉ-ꜣIst* in l. 5, but it can hardly be correct to try to analyse it into two signs. See p. 151, n. β.

f. The final trace, with its long horizontal stroke, suggests *ḥn*, which occurs earlier in the line. However, other readings, perhaps including *mnḥ*, are possible.

g. Enough remains of the beginning of *tm* and the tail of *dỉt* to justify the reading.

h. r tm dỉt gm=w st is probably to be restored, with *st* written . Despite the appearance of the photograph, the traces are not . *r* is presumably written in the form : cf. 5/5, p. 155, n. *j*.

j. A low trace of ink before *pȝ mtr* may represent *n*. The preceding sign is probably a plur. stroke.

k. The abbreviated writing of *ꜥwỉ* is unexpected in a literary text, especially as a full writing appears above in l. 4. However, no other reading seems plausible, and the abbreviated form also appears in 3 front, fr. 3/3 in this volume. The tall stroke preceding *pȝ ꜥwỉ* has a curled top, and could represent a 3rd plur. suffix (cf. *gm=w*, twice in l. 3).

l. Although the end is damaged, the reading of the proper name *Pȝ-dỉ-ꜣIst* in the common writing seems certain. The possibility should perhaps be mentioned of reading *pȝỉ ỉpd*, , but this is rejected here.

As there are slight uncertainties in the reading of the second half of this line, it should also be pointed out that *gm* is here written a little differently from the two prospective forms occurring in l. 3 (l. 3, , : l. 5,). However, the reading seems secure. 1. Kh. shows a precisely similar alternation between and .

m. The obvious phrase to restore here is *pȝ ỉ-ỉr-ḫpr* 'Petiese discovered what had happened'. The objection to this is that the sign that would read *ỉr* is ligatured to the preceding stroke and is made in one smooth curve, so that the whole writing precisely resembles *pȝỉ=s* (and, although the point is not conclusive, is unlike the *ỉ-ỉr* of *ỉ-ỉr-ḥr* in l. 6). Sense might be made of *pȝỉ=s ḫpr*, although it seems an unparalleled phrase: either 'what had happened to her/it' (normally *pȝ ỉ-ỉr-ḫpr n-ỉm=s*), in which case a fem. antecedent must have stood in the lacuna before l. 5; or 'its occurrence', simply 'what had happened'.

n. The reading *sḏy=f* requires that the tail of the *s* was drawn considerably round to the left, , but seems obviously correct from the context.

o. The upper part of the distinctive first sign of *nw*, , is quite clear.

Translation

1.] They sent (?) wax before him. He made a she-cat of wax. He made a falcon of wax. He read a spell to them. They awoke [[α]
2.] before them (?). He gave orders to the she-cat of wax, saying: Leap (*or* fly) . . . this falcon [[β]
3.] . . . . Do not let yourselves be discovered.' He made some spells to prevent their being discovered [
4.] . . . . . in the middle of the house in the selfsame hour (immediately). He lept (*or* flew) in with [
5.] the house and the courtyard of the priest to the ground.[γ] Petiese[δ] discovered what had happened, that [[ε]
6.] He[ζ] recounted before him everything that . . . . had seen . . . . . [
7. *only traces*

Notes on translation

a. The use of wax images is a well-known feature of Egyptian magical practice, although the body of textual evidence is not large. Examples in magical texts where enemies are meant to be destroyed by the destruction of their images modelled in wax are *Coffin Texts*, i. 157a = Spell 37, final rubric; and P. Bremner Rhind (BM 10188) 23/6–7, 26/3, 26/20, 28/18, and 29/13–14.

Among the documentary texts concerned with the Harem conspiracy against Ramesses III, P. Rollin and P. Lee have long been thought to contain references to the use of wax images by the conspirators (P. Rollin, l. 1; P. Lee 1/4). These passages have most recently been discussed by H. Goedicke, 'Was magic used in the harem conspiracy against Ramesses III?', *JEA* 49

(1963), 71–92, where bibliography may conveniently be found. Goedicke's contention that the texts do not make *any* reference to wax images is not accepted by the present writers.

Wax was widely used as a practical ingredient of prescriptions in Egyptian medical texts (see *Wb. Drog.* 242–6); but also, in the early New Kingdom medical compilation P. Ebers (795 = 94/7–8), an 'ibis of wax' is used for fumigation in one of a series of gynaecological prescriptions. A wax image is mentioned in the demotic P. London–Leiden (recto 11/21) in a magical context, although the passage is damaged, and its punctuation is uncertain.[1]

In Egyptian literary texts, the use of wax images is remarkably consistent. They are employed by famous magicians to carry out tasks that are mechanical but beyond human powers. In P. Westcar (2/21–4/7), the magician Webaoner makes a crocodile of wax to capture his wife's lover. In 1.Kh. (3/28–30; cf. 3/38), Neneferkaptaḥ makes a boat and crew of wax to take him to the hiding place of the magical book written by Thoth. In 2.Kh. (4/15–5/36: see especially 4/15–21 and 5/19–24), the Nubian and Egyptian magicians each make a litter, together with its bearers of wax, to carry off the other's ruler by night. In an unpublished demotic papyrus of Roman date at Copenhagen, of which the late Dr. Volten made a provisional transcription, a magician called Petiese makes a she-cat and a falcon of wax, which he sends to carry out some task, although the damaged state of the papyrus makes its nature uncertain. It is clear that the Copenhagen papyrus and the present Saqqâra fragment do not contain duplicate versions of the identical passage from the same text. It cannot yet be determined if they represent different workings of the same passage, or belong to the same story, or are even less closely related.

It has often been suggested that the 'effective image' mentioned in the *Story of the Eloquent Peasant* (R. 43) refers to an image for use in magic: its material is not stated, nor the way in which it might be used.

Thus, from this limited amount of evidence, at least three distinct uses of wax images may be identified. It is notable that only *wax* images are as yet attested in literary texts, where anonymous figures are set to carry out mechanical tasks. In the case of the kind of magic found in magical texts, where enemies are supposed to be destroyed by the destruction of images specifically identified with them, similar uses of clay images, and of written 'images' upon papyrus, are also found.

The most substantial discussions of wax images in Egyptian magic are A. H. Gardiner, 'Magic (Egyptian)', in *Encyclopaedia of Religion and Ethics*, ed. J. Hastings, vol. 8, see 263 and 266–7; and F. Lexa, *La magie dans l'Égypte antique*, vol. 1, 79 and 105–8. See also the brief mentions by A. Erman, *Die Religion der Ägypter*, 305–8, and H. Bonnet, *Reallexikon der ägyptischen Religionsgeschichte*, 879, under 'Zauber', pp. 875–80.

β. This utterance constitutes a crux. The reading *pꜣy*, 'to fly' or 'to leap' for the verb seems inescapable (see p. 149, n. *d*), and the reading *pꜣi*, perhaps to be understood as the 'strong' form of the definite article, seems the only natural interpretation of the signs that follow (see p. 149, n. *e*). The simplicity of the diction in l. 1 and l. 3 suggests a very obvious interpretation and restoration of l. 2, that gives a straightforwardly balanced pair of commands: 'He gave orders to the she-cat of wax, saying ". . . . . ."; he gave orders to the falcon of wax, saying ". . . . . ."'. It is therefore tempting to read *ḥn* at the end of l. 2, and this would be a very plausible restoration of the traces.

However, this means that the instructions given to the cat were *pꜣy pꜣi bik*, which by itself would most naturally be understood as 'Fly (*or* leap), O falcon'. If this is the sense of the text, several problems arise. The uncertainty (which cannot be discussed at length here) over the precise meaning of the verb *pꜣy*, 'leap' or 'fly', is perhaps not crucial. There is no particular difficulty either in supposing that a falcon might be ordered to 'leap', or that, in a magical context, a cat might be ordered to 'fly'. The occurrences of *pꜣy* in demotic consistently suggest that the sense is 'leap', and no instance of *pꜣy* that *must* be taken in the sense 'fly' seems to be attested; but it cannot be said to be established that the word only has the one sense 'leap'.

The most obvious difficulty is that the cat appears to be addressed as 'falcon'. This might be done for magical reasons, although such an explanation would be more complex than the rest of the text suggests is probable. The problem could be resolved by assuming that the text has muddled the two animals, either by giving to the cat the orders meant for the falcon, or

[1] In 'Magical texts from a bilingual papyrus in the British Museum', ed H. I. Bell, A. D. Nock, and Herbert Thompson in *Proceedings of the British Academy* 17 (London 1933), 9, there is a reference in col. 8, l. 1 to *wʿ twt n Wsir n mnḥ i-ir-k* 'an image of Osiris of wax which you have made', in a receipt to make a woman love you, which was to be buried under the threshold of her house.

by putting the vocative 'O falcon' where 'O cat' should stand.

A further difficulty is that such a brief order, whether it is to be understood as 'fly!', or 'leap!', or 'flee!', or 'pounce!', seems inadequate to make good sense, even if it were in some way explained by the balanced order that followed.

However, it is possible to abandon the attempt to restore two short, balanced orders, and hence also to abandon the reading *ḥn* at the end of l. 2. It is possible that *pꜣi bik mnḥ*, 'this falcon of wax' should be read there. The instructions to the cat might have begun with an explanation, 'This falcon has flown (*or* lept) . . .', or might be restored 'Fly (*or* pounce), (for) this falcon is . . .'.

The brief phrase *pꜣy pꜣi bik* might be explained quite differently, by assuming that a preposition, either *n* or *r*, needed to be supplied before *pꜣi bik*. Thus the sense might be 'Flee from this falcon!', or 'Pounce upon this falcon!' It is plausible to suppose that one of the two creatures was meant to pretend to pursue the other, and such an order, although still rather curt, might make good sense as one of a balanced pair of commands. The phrase *pꜣy n* does not seem to be attested elsewhere: *pꜣy r* and other phrases including *pꜣy* occur several times in P. Krall, of warriors springing to the attack.

γ. It seems equally possible to restore the text so as to give the sense that the house and courtyard were 'razed to the ground' or that they were 'searched thoroughly'. In 1. Kh. 6/16, a house is demolished to discover a tomb long buried beneath it: see especially the phrase *r dit in=w (pꜣi=f) ꜥwi r pꜣ itn*, 'to have his house razed to the ground', 6/14.

δ. The reading of the proper-name Petiese here seems certain (see p. 150, n. *l*). The conceivable reading *gm pꜣi ipd*, 'this bird discovered' is to be rejected and, further, it would be very surprising if *ipd* (in Egyptian often, and perhaps originally, 'duck'; see Faulkner, *JEA* 38 (1952), 128) were used to refer to the falcon (in Coptic, ⲱⲃⲧ is confined to edible birds: Crum, *CD*, 518b).

Petiese is the name of the magician in the unpublished Copenhagen narrative mentioned on p. 151, n. *a*, who manufactures a she-cat and a falcon of wax. This must lend some support to the possibility that in the present fragment 'Petiese' is to be identified with the magician of ll. 1–3, and that here, by contriving the search or the demolition of the priest's house, he has discovered some information that he required. However, it remains a possibility that Petiese was an interested third party, who discovered, perhaps, that the demolition or search had taken place. To judge from the precise wording of l. 5, it is unlikely, although not entirely impossible, that 'the priest' and 'Petiese' could refer to the same person.

ε. It is possible that the text should be read and understood here in such a way as to include a reference to a female character, 'Petiese discovered what had happened to her, that . . .' (see p. 150, n. *m*). It would clearly not be impossible to restore a female antecedent in the lacuna before l. 5.

ζ. It is uncertain who is referred to in this sentence. Possibly the falcon is reporting back to the magician, or Petiese may, for example, be laying new information before the king.

DISCUSSION

In the first three lines of this narrative text, a male character manufactures a wax image of a she-cat and another of a (male) falcon, brings them to life by means of a spell, and sends them to carry out a secret task. This use of wax images is discussed on p. 150 f., n. *a*. Line 4 presumably belongs to the narrative of the cat's and the falcon's mission; it is not so certain, however, if the remaining lines that survive continue this, or if the story has moved on to the consequences of their actions. A male character Petiese is mentioned in l. 5, and it is possible that he is to be identified with the magician of ll. 1–3 (see n. δ above).

Although it is conceivable that an episode of this kind might occur in a narrative of any type, the comparable texts that survive suggest that it belongs to a story devoted specifically to the exploits of a magician or magicians. In each of the two well-known substantial surviving stories about Setm Khaꜥemwese (1. Kh., 2. Kh.), the powers of a great magician of the past, illustrated in a story set within the main narrative, are contrasted with those of the unsuccessful and sometimes ludicrous Setm. It is always possible that fragments of texts concerning magicians other than Setm may preserve parts of such episodes from stories whose central character was nevertheless Setm Khaʿemwese; but it is equally possible that they represent quite separate stories, featuring different magicians.

The various Setm Khaʿemwese texts, and the problems concerning their relationship with other texts and fragments that mention 'High Priests of Ptaḥ' or 'magicians' also arise in connection with **1**: see pp. 46, 62.

5. A NARRATIVE OF EVIL-DOING

Plate 11b

72/73-DP27 [6163] 8.5 cm *h.* × 13 cm. *w.*

Sector 7, South Dump

The papyrus is opaque and coarse-textured. Its shade is light brown, and it has a marked grey tinge: there is no firm evidence to show that the discoloration is due to the erasure of a previous text or texts, rather than to dirt, but this is a possible explanation. Conceivably, a few traces of a previous text can be seen at the ends of the lines of col. 1, see p. 155, n. *h*. The surfaces are worn and rubbed, and there are some holes. The front (↔) surface preserves a substantial part of one column of continuous demotic text and the first few signs of a second column, with a margin of about 1–1.5 cm. between. The edges of the fragment are broken on all sides in the middle of the text, but the top, bottom, and left-hand edges are fairly straight and may well have been cut rather than torn. The back (↕) surface is blank, and there is no evidence to suggest the purpose for which the piece may have been cut. A join between two sheets of papyrus runs vertically about 1 cm. from the left-hand edge of the fragment: the right-hand sheet overlaps the left-hand sheet. The front surface is plainly the original inside of the roll.

It is obvious that the ends of the lines of col. 1 run up to, but not over, the join between the sheets. It is thus extremely likely that the present text was one of those that are arranged so that each column precisely fills a single sheet of papyrus. (The size of the writing suggests each column could not fill two sheets.) As the width of the sheets of papyrus found in the present collection is remarkably consistent at from 14 to 16 cm., it is at least plausible to suggest that restorations of the order of 1–3 cm. are to be expected at the beginnings of ll. 1–3 of col. 1, and of 2–4 cm. for ll. 4–11.

The **hand** is extremely small and cramped, although close examination shows that the signs are made with some precision. There is a marked variation in the thickness of the strokes. The hand is similar to that of **4**; and **3** may be compared. At many points the scribe can clearly be seen to have recharged his brush at the beginning of a clause or sentence.

Transliteration

col. 1

1. - - -] =⌜f⌝ [. . . . .] . . . .[a]
2.] . . .[b] r ỉrt.ṱ=f tḥ n ⌜s⌝nf[c] ḏd wꜣḥ n=k n pꜣ hrw ỉm rsty ỉw=f rwš r t/nꜣi=f
3.] . .=f pꜣ ⌜mn⌝[d] n Gm=w-Ḥp ḏd=y ỉrm ⌜ḥꜣt.ṱ⌝=y ỉnk bn-pw=w ỉr pꜣi gy i-ỉr-ḥr=y
4.] . [.] . . . šm=y n(=y) r-bnr ỉw=y ⌜sny⌝[e] bwt[f] ⌜bn-pw=w⌝ . .⌜y=f⌝[g] šn=y . . .[h]
5. . . . .] sny r-drt=y[j] ḥr tꜣ mꜣy Wsỉr-⌜Ḥp⌝[k] ỉw=f . . . . [. .] . . . .[l] ḏd pꜣ rmt[m]
6. . . . .] ⌜gr=s⌝[n] bn-pw=f šm i-ỉr Bꜣstt . . . .[o] bn-pw=f dỉt . . . . . n ẖrw . . .[p]
7. . . .]. ỉrt.ṱ=f . . btw=f nꜣ-bn . . . .[q] bn-pw=f ỉr=s ꜥn sp-2 ḏd pꜣ ntỉ mtr . . . .[r]
8. . . . .] . . . . .[s] bn ⌜r⌝ . .[t] hwn=f[u] ẖr . . . .[v] ⌜nꜣ⌝-ẖy-ṯꜣi-ḏꜣḏꜣ⌜=f⌝[w]
9. . . . .] . . . =y-s[x] ỉw mn ꜥt.t n-ỉm=f[y] i-ỉr . . . . ntr[z] . . . .[aa]
10. . . . .] ⌜r⌝g[ab] ḥr pꜣ ỉtn bw-ỉr=f mšꜥ ḥr pꜣ myt r bn-pw=f ỉp r
11. . . . .] ntỉ ẖn Kmy . . . ⌜m⌝ḫ⌜y⌝[ac] . . . .[ad]

col. 2

— — — — — —

1. . . [- - -
2. . . . [[a]
3. *ntỉ* . . [
4. . . . . [
5. *pꜣ tꜣ* . . [
6. *r ḏd* . . [
7. . . . . . [
8. *n-ỉm*=[[b]
9. *bn*(-*pw*)=*y* .[
10. . . . . [

— — — — — —

Notes on transliteration

col. 1

a. The long horizontal trace at the beginning of what survives of l. 1 is very probably the tail of a suffix =*f*, as in *ỉr*=*f* etc. (cf. l. 10 below, and another damaged example in l. 4). Nothing can be made of the traces at the end of l. 1.

b. A reading *bnr* (not necessarily *r-bnr*) is possible, but the writing differs from that of *r-bnr* in l. 4 below, which does not end with a dot. Here, the readings *r-r*=*k* or *mtw*=*k* might be considered.

c. The reading of *snf*, 'blood', written with an *s* with a curved tail, , seems certain.

d. The reading of this noun is not certain, although the signs are fairly well preserved. The det., which occurs frequently elsewhere in the text, is clear. The preceding group, , suggests the reading *mn*; perhaps the first two signs should be taken as a phonetic spelling , as it is impossible to read the expected or sign. Such a writing occurs at Insinger 5/23 (*DG*, 160. 3). For the form of the *m* sign, compare *mtr* in l. 7, *mn* in l. 9, and *mšꜥ* in l. 10. For the *n* sign, compare *hwn* in l. 8, although the reading of that word is uncertain. The verb *mn* is common in the sense 'to die' (*DG*, 160. 2), and the noun cited above from Insinger is used for 'death'. Here the meaning 'the death of Gomoapi' is plausible.

e. Comparison with the writing in l. 5 makes the reading *sny* certain.

f. The reading *bwt* of here is quite certain. The writing differs from that of *btw* in l. 7 below, although the only significant difference is in the order of the signs (see p. 156, n. *q*). The form of the *t*, , in *bwt* in l. 4 indicates a pronounced /t/ rather than the fem. .*t* ending. The word should be understood as the masc. noun, 'crime', 'destruction' cf. Černý, *CED*, 28. 3.

g. *bn-pw*=*w* is a possible reading of the signs after *bwt*, but the short stroke below the first sign is difficult to explain, and the shape is perhaps not quite right. For *bn-pw*=*w* see l. 3: *bn-pw*=*f* occurs in ll. 6 (twice), 7, and 10. The signs before *šn*=*y* are perhaps ; however, the word cannot be made out.

h. There are some traces of ink after *šn*=*y*, which cannot be read. They may belong to the end of l. 4 of the text. However, it is also possible that they are traces left when a previous text was washed away. Some traces at the ends of other lines of col. 1 of the text might be explained in the same way, although no example is certain. See p. 156, n. *r* and 157, n. *w*.

j. The writing of *r-drt*=*y* is plain. Other examples of *r* in the form occur in ll. 2 and 8: cf. **4**/3. Certainly no *ṯ* is written before the suffix. The *ṯ* of *ỉrt.ṯ*=*f* in l. 7 is substantial: other examples in the text are too damaged for comparison.

k. The reading of these words *ḥr tꜣ mꜣy Wsỉr-Ḥp* appears satisfactory, and no better interpretation suggests itself. The first sign of *mꜣy*, 'island', is surprisingly made in two parts, and is entirely vertical. However, a similar sign is probably also to be read *m*(*ꜣ*) in **2** back, x+1/25, and an almost vertical example of a *mꜣ* sign, made in one piece, occurs in **1**, 9/7. The sense might perhaps be 'upon the island (of) Osorapis', or 'upon the island (called) Osorapis'. It is difficult to say if either of these interpretations is likely to suit the context.

l. The traces before the lacuna could well be restored as a second occurrence of *mn*, written exactly as in l. 3 above (see p. 155, n. *d*). The word here after *i͗w=f* would presumably be a verb, 'die', and the only doubt over this restoration is whether or not the verb as well as the noun would be written phonetically.

Immediately before *ḏd*, the traces might be interpreted as , and the various readings suggested on p. 155, n. *b* for similar traces occurring in l. 2 might be considered here. However, these readings do not suggest any plausible restoration of the whole phrase.

m. ḏd here is quite plain, and the following signs strongly suggest *pꜣ rmt*. The descending tail of *rmt* almost runs into the line below (the fact that this portion of the tail is not quite in line with what survives of the sign above is probably sufficiently explained by the damaged and distorted state of the papyrus). A reading of the proper-name *Ḏd-ḥr* would not suit the signs here at all well (see n. *p* below).

n. The reading of the signs *gr* seems certain. Although the following sign could conceivably be read *ḥ*, and the last sign might well be  (cf. the writing of *hrw* in l. 2 above), the reading *grḥ*, 'night' is improbable, as a substantial sign  (or the group , or something similar) is expected in this word. The reading *gr=s*, presumably written 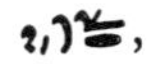, is not, however, certain. Conceivably a place-name, determined by  (cf. the damaged writing of *Kmy*, l. 11 below) might be read.

o. The obvious interpretation of what can be read with certainty here is 'he did not go into the presence of (the goddess) Bastet': however, the last sign before the following *bn-pw=f* is probably  (rather than *=w*), and possibly the reading should contain two proper-names: 'the presence of Bastet-......, son of ....': cf. p. 158, n. *η*.

p. The reading *bn-pw=f dỉt* seems certain. The following signs are . Two possible readings are the proper-name *Ḏd-ḥr*, and *ḥrt*, 'food', etc., which might be written 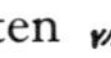 and  respectively.

The last signs appear to be , ignoring a trace which probably belongs to the tail of *rmt* in the line above (see n. *m* above). Probably *ḫrw* is to be read. It seems unlikely that *ḫrw* 'letter' could suit the context. A reading *n ḫrw=w* (= *r ḫrw=w*: cf. *DG*, s.v. 365. 7, on p. 366), 'at their command/disposal' is not perhaps satisfactory. Conceivably a second proper-name could be read, perhaps *Ḏd-ḥr sꜣ Ḫrw-* ....

There are too many difficulties to suggest what kind of restoration is most probable here.

q. Both *btw=f* and *bn* are certain readings, and both are preceded by similar, short, thick, diagonal strokes. The reading *nꜣ-bn* obviously suggests itself, but *nꜣ-bn=f* is not possible. It is difficult to find a different interpretation for the stroke before *btw=f*: it seems too large for *n*, and not substantial enough for *dỉt*. Further, if *btw* is here to be understood as a noun, it is hard to justify the suffix pronoun that follows it. It seems best to suppose that *nꜣ-btw=f* is an adjective verb, apparently otherwise unattested, presumably with the sense 'to be hateful'. If these suggestions are accepted, it might be possible to make sense of the whole passage by restoring *nꜣ-bn rꜣ=f. rꜣ=f* is a far from certain reading, but might suit the damaged traces very well: , Thus the sense might be '... his eye; he is hateful, and his mouth/speech is evil'. However, this solution as a whole is open to the further slight objection that it does not help to solve what may be a related problem in l. 8: see n. *t* below.

r. The sense might be 'He who witnessed ... said ...', but *pꜣ nti mtr pꜣi*, 'That is satisfactory' (cf. 1. Kh. 5/10) might be read, although no substantial tail, as might be expected with the copula, is preserved to the *pꜣi*.

The final word in the line with a long supralinear stroke might be *nꜣy* (not the copula), or conceivably *ky*, 'another'. It does not seem likely that the long horizontal stroke could be a suffix *=k* belonging to the line above, and, despite the difficulties of reading, it seems too substantial to be a trace surviving from an erased text.

s. The first traces might be of *nꜣy* (cf. n. *r* above) and the following word might be *wꜥ* the indef. article: the writing would not be the same as that of *rmt* in l. 5.

t. The signs before *hwn=f*, , present a problem. The first two strokes presumably represent *r* in the form also found in ll. 2 and 5. The last sign does not seem substantial or curved enough for *dỉt* (cf. the form in l. 6 above, and the signs discussed in n. *q* above), and it is obviously implausible to read *nꜣ-hwn=f* as a second unattested adjective-verb (see n. *q* above)—in this case, one for which no likely root or sense can be suggested. Another otherwise unattested adjective-verb, *nꜣ-bḫn=f* appears at ꜥOnchsheshonqy, 3/17, 19.

u. hwn: this word is perfectly clearly written, but there seems no obvious word that could be determined by . Perhaps this is intended as a writing of, or is a mistake for, *hwš*: compare the indeterminate form of *š* in *rwš*, l. 2 above.

v. As no det. can be made out, it cannot be decided which of the many words beginning *ẖr* . . . should be read: e.g. *ẖr* (*.t*), 'food', or *ẖry*, 'down', would suit the traces. The initial *ẖ* sign does not have the same form as the first sign of the word in l. 6 that might possibly be read *ẖrt*, 'food' (see p. 156, n. *p*). Possibly the following word begins with an *s*, and may end with a det. However, there are too many uncertainties to suggest restorations here.

w. *nꜣ*- is the obvious reading of the traces, but is not certain: the other elements all seem clear. It is perhaps arguable whether the whole phrase is to be taken as one proper-name, or two (with the filiation *sꜣ* unwritten, or lost in the horizontal stroke of *ṯꜣỉ*), or even should be understood as a sentence. Although the traces of the tail of a suffix *=f* are quite distinct, it is possible that they survive from a previous text that has been erased.

x. The restoration *gm=y-s* is highly probable in the context.

y. There seems little doubt of the reading here. The det. of *ꜥt.t* is damaged, but the reading seems plausible, and no other interpretation of the sign suggests itself. However, it is difficult to believe that the sense can really be 'I found that there was no limb in him/it'. Possibly *ꜥt.t* has been written here in place of a less common word with a similar writing or pronunciation or both. Conceivably *ꜣt*, 'harm', etc. (*DG*, 13. 1) may be understood. The initial group of *ꜥt.t* is used to write words containing a pronounced /t/: see *DG*, 74. An equally perverse writing of *ꜣt*, 'harm', may occur at *Mythus* 15/17: see *AcOr* 37 (1976), 43, n. *s*.

z. It is difficult to judge to what extent, if at all, the top of the sign following *ỉ-ỉr* bends over to the left. Thus any of the readings *=s*, *-s*, *n*(*=y*), *tꜣ*/*nꜣ*, or *dỉt* might be possible. The next few traces are too badly damaged to suggest a reading, but then the two, tall, fairly well-preserved traces might be read *nṯr*. At a glance the next traces might suggest that the common phrase *pꜣ nṯr ꜥꜣ* be read, but on close inspection this does not seem a possible form of *ꜥꜣ*.

aa. The last signs in the line might read *ꜥꜣ*: the writing is different from the signs that follow *nṯr* earlier in this line. The preceding signs are the dets. of a word for a part of the body associated with the head, but the traces seem to exclude *ḏꜣḏꜣ* (cf. the more plausible writing in l. 8 above), and probably *šn*: no reading is suggested here.

ab. The first trace in l. 10 is probably the tail of an *r* or *l*. The obvious restoration is of the verb *rg*, *lg*, etc., 'to cease' (*DG*, 264. 6), which could suit a wide range of contexts. One other possible reading worth mentioning is *šrg*: cf. *DG*, 520. 5, *šlḳ*. In *Mythus* 12/21 the word may perhaps describe a sand-storm, and a verb of this kind could make sense in the context here.

ac. The reading of an *m* and a *ẖ* is plausible, although not certain. As the following trace may be of a det., possibly *ỉw=f mẖy* might be restored (*mẖy*, 'to fight', *DG*, 176. 3, written).

ad. The clear sign at the end of the line may be the det. , or represent *rsỉ*, 'South', or *nsw*, 'king'. The preceding signs do not suggest that *gy* should be read (cf. the writing in l. 3 above).

col. 2

Only a few signs survive at the beginnings of the lines of col. 2, and only an occasional word can be read. However, there is no indication that col. 2 might not contain more of the same continuous text as that preserved in col. 1.

a. The form of the first group is not at all clear. *gr* (cf. **5**, 1/6) or *w* might be considered, or the reading might conceivably be *ḥb*, 'festival'.

b. Close inspection suggests that, despite the irregularity of the first horizontal stroke, *n-ỉm=* rather than *sdm* should be read here.

Translation

col. 1

— —

1. *only traces*
2.] . . . . . as his eye was weary of bloodshed,[α] saying 'Cease for today. Come tomorrow.' And he cared for his[β]
3.] . . . . . the death of Gomoapi. I spoke with my heart: 'For my part, never has the like been done in my presence'[γ]

4.] . . . . I went off out by myself, and I avoided a crime.[δ] They did not . . . . . it. I asked . . . . .
5.] passed from me on the island of Osorapis[ε] . . . . The man said
6.]. . . . .[ζ] He did not go into the presence of Bastet . . . .[η] He did not put . . . .[θ]
7.] . . his eye; he is hateful, and his speech is evil.[ι] He did not do it ever again, saying 'It is satisfactory . . . . . .[κ]
8.] . . . . evil . . . . Kaijijoief[λ]
9.] I found that there was no limb/harm in him/it[μ] . . . . god . . . .
10.] cease upon the ground. He does not (ever) walk upon the path, as he has not thought of[ν]
11.] which is in Egypt, ... fight . . . *only traces*

— —

col. 2
only traces of the beginnings of ten lines: direct speech occurs in l. 9, 'I did not [. . .'

Notes on translation

α. The sense of this phrase is not certain, especially as no precise parallel is forthcoming. The verb *ṯḥ(r)* ('to become bad': see especially Černý, *CED*, 203. 7) occurs frequently with *ḥꜣt*, 'heart', in expressions meaning 'to grieve'. However, *ỉrt*, 'eye', is a certain reading here (although it might conceivably have been copied in error for *ḥꜣt*, the writing of which is very similar). The word *ỉrt* is not uncommon in demotic literary texts in phrases for emotions outwardly visible, but the only example with *ṯḥ(r)* is *r ỉrt.ṯ=s ṯẖr* at *Mythus* 8/12. Other possible interpretations are 'his eye was evil with blood(-lust)', or 'his eye was ill with blood, bloodshot'.

β. In addition to the problem mentioned in n. *α* above, interpretation of this line is made very difficult by the uncertain nature of the *ỉw=f sdm* verb forms (future, circumstantial, or continuative), and by the impossibility of establishing precisely where any direct speech begins or ends. The contents of the next two lines, however, suggest that the context is either warfare or murderous intrigue.

γ. It is impossible to identify the speaker in this line. The same person is very probably speaking in the following two lines, and probably the remarks he addresses to himself here in l. 3 are a brief expression of revulsion, and he has already resumed his narrative by the beginning of what is preserved in l. 4.

δ. It is natural to assume a metaphorical use of *sny*, 'to pass by', either 'I avoided a crime' or 'I escaped destruction', although the sense 'to pass through, to survive' is possible.

ε. Possibly the phrase 'the island of Osorapis' is simply a place-name, the scene of a previous incident in the story, but this is uncertain. There is no reason to suppose that Osorapis is the name of a character occurring in the story. This phrase with the verb *sny* may refer to the same event as the phrase discussed in n. *δ* above.

ζ. These damaged signs might be restored 'she fell silent'. If this is correct, then either a female character must be supposed to occur in the story, although otherwise unmentioned in what survives, or the reading of the name of the goddess Bastet may be accepted later in this line (see n. *η* below), and she may be supposed to have fallen silent, perhaps after delivering an oracle.

η. It is impossible to be certain that the goddess Bastet is mentioned here, rather than a human being: see p. 156, n. *o*.

θ. The uncertainties earlier in this line make it impossible to suggest which of the readings mentioned on p. 156, n. *p* might be plausible here.

ι. These phrases are problematic: see p. 156, n. *q*.

κ. The phrase translated 'It is satisfactory' might be read 'he who witnessed'.

λ. The readings and restoration of this line is very dubious, and the proper name Kaijijoief is not a certain reading.

μ. On p. 157, n. *y* it is suggested that the sense here may be 'there was no harm in him' or 'in it', although this involves virtually emending the text.

ν. It is tempting to understand this mention of 'walking upon the path' as a metaphor, referring to the path of correct conduct, but this is not certain. In either case the sense of the preceding phrase 'cease (*or conceivably* whirl) upon the ground' is obscure.

DISCUSSION

The nature of this text is not certain. Plainly it is a narrative, but there is no clear indication whether the narrative is a literary story, or concerns real events and forms part of, for instance, a petition or legal report. No example is preserved of any of the commonest formulae of literary narratives. It would be very hazardous to try to assess if any of the metaphorical expressions that occur in this fragment are a sign of a literary style. Unfortunately, only one proper name can be read in the text with anything approaching certainty: Gomoapi in 1/3. This name is not yet known from other stories. It is certainly a plausible name to find in a late-period documentary text from Saqqâra, but there is no reason why it should not occur in a literary text. Much the same might be said of the two names less certainly read, Djeḥo (1/6) and Kaijijoief (1/8), except that Djeḥo does occur in the Inaros texts.

The narrative includes a considerable amount of direct speech. It is plausible to suggest that the whole of the passage preserved belongs to a continuous speech by one person, including short quotations of others' (and his own) remarks. This would plainly suit either literary or documentary style.

If the text is a story, a moralizing tone is maintained almost throughout: but what survives is not closely reminiscent of any published demotic story.

6. A TEXT INCLUDING APPEALS TO GODS

Plate 12a

H5-DP377 [2298] 17.5 cm. *h.* × 13.0 cm. *w.*

Sector 1 (North Courtyard) debris (1966–7)

The papyrus is coarse and uneven-textured, but in parts it is translucent. Its shade is only slightly darker than normal, but towards the bottom of the piece there are a few patches of light-brown stain. The papyrus has many holes, although the front surface has been only a little damaged by rubbing. The edges of the fragment are broken on all sides, except that the bottom edge is fairly straight, and some portions of it appear to be clean-cut; it probably represents the original bottom edge of the roll or sheet. The front (↔) surface, which is presumably the original inside, bears parts of the last 12 lines of a column of continuous demotic text. The beginnings of the last 10 lines are preserved. Up to 2.0 cm. of blank papyrus stands to the right of the column: there is no trace to prove the existence of a previous column. A bottom margin of 3.0 cm. is preserved. In l. 9, a short space, less than 1.0 cm., appears to have been left blank in the middle of the column, between two sentences: it is impossible to tell if this was a general feature of the text. The back (↕) surface is blank.

The **hand** is comparatively large, and is rapidly and skilfully written with a soft brush. The hand of **22** in this volume may be compared, and perhaps also **8**, although it is much smaller and less fluent.

Transliteration

— — — — — — — — — — — — — — — — — —

1. . . . .] ⸢*ḫꜥ*⸣ .[- - -
2. . . .]. *r-r=w dr=w* [
3. ⸢*ḫ*⸣[a] [. .]. ⸢*dỉt*⸣ *mšꜥ g*⸢*r*⸣[
4. *ỉ* ⸢*ʾImn*⸣ [.] ⸢*ntỉ*⸣ *ḫꜣꜥ* . . [. .] . . . . .[
5. . *nḥḥ*[b] *pꜣ nḥm*[c] *nꜣ ẖm.w n* ⸢*ʾImn*⸣[d] [
6. . . . ⸢*pꜣỉ=k*⸣ *pr ỉ ʾImn dỉ=k* .[. .] . .[
7. ⸢*ỉ Sṱ*⸣[e] *sẖm m-ỉr sẖm* [. .] . [
8. . [. . .] . .[f] *pꜣ* . . . . . .[g] . . . *rmt* . .[
9. ⸢*ỉ*⸣ [. .]. *wtn*[h] *n* ⸢*S*⸣*ṱ*[j] vacat *ỉ* . .[.]. . . . .[
10. *wꜥt wnwt pꜣỉ(=y) ꜥḥꜥ*[k] . [.] . . . *n=f*[l] . . . *ḥr* ⸢*rmt*⸣[m] . . . . .[n] [
11. . . . . . *pꜣỉ*⸢*=f*⸣[o] *ꜥḥꜥ* . . . . . .[p] ⸢*r*⸣ *bn-ỉ(w)=k stꜣ.ṱ=k* . . . . .[
12. *šꜥ* . . . .[q] . .[r] ⸢*ỉ*⸣[s] . . . *pꜣỉ(=y)* ⸢*ꜥḥꜥ*⸣ *ỉw=f* . . .[

bottom margin of 3.0 cm.

Notes on transliteration

a. The traces of a large *ḫ*, evidently the first sign in the line, are quite clear. Thus a word beginning with *ḫ* might be read, or the verb *rḫ*, 'to know', etc.

b. The reading is most likely to be *nḥḥ*, 'oil', with a preceding sign, perhaps the def. article *pꜣ*. A more distinctive  or det. is to be expected in writings of *nḥḥ*, 'eternity' (a reading *r nḥḥ*, 'for ever' might be considered), whereas the 'oil' word is frequently written with a nondescript det. (see *DG*, 224). The  sign might well be read *ṯꜣỉ*, but if any of these words are read (*DG*, 663 ff.) it seems impossible to explain the following strokes.

c. The det. of *nḥm* seems rather elaborate (perhaps a combination of  and ) but the word must surely be *nḥm*, *DG*, 223. 2, 'to rescue', etc.

d. *ỉmn* does not have precisely the same form here as in l. 6 below, but no more plausible reading suggests itself in either line.

e. Only the final  det. of the god's name *Sṯ* can be made out for certain here, and the reading depends upon the fact that no other major god's name has this det., and that it is plausible to read the same name again in l. 9 below.

f. The vertical stroke here more resembles the plur. stroke of *dr=w* (l. 2) or of *ẖm.w* (l. 5) than the divine det. of *ỉmn* (l. 6).

g. The signs appropriate to the indef. article *wʿ* seem to occur here, but hardly suit the context or the other traces. Possibly *pꜣỉ(=y) wʿ.ṯ* 'my only one', or something similar should be read.

h. *wtn*, 'drink offerings'; the same det. is to be found in Ryl. 9, col. 10/20. The preceding traces (with the *w* of *wtn*) are . Conceivably *stꜣ.*[*ṯ*]*=k* (cf. l. 11) rather than *ỉ* might be read at the beginning of the line.

j. Both here and in l. 7 above, because of the det. and the context, it seems certain that the name of the god Seth should be read. Here in l. 9 a *ṯ* may be read, but the nature of the preceding signs is uncertain.

k. Both here and in l. 12 below, *pꜣỉ(=y) ʿḥʿ* seems a more probable reading of the traces than *pꜣỉ=f ʿḥʿ*, but this is not certain: cf. the form of *ỉw=f* in l. 12, and of *n=f* in l. 10. An example of *pꜣỉ=f ʿḥʿ* probably occurs in l. 11, written .

l. On close examination, the traces do not support the reading *ḫꜣʿ=w n=f* (cf. l. 4). The trace immediately before *n=f* might be the det. of a verb of motion (cf. *mšʿ* in l. 3) and, if so, a very cramped writing of *šm* might be considered: an obvious restoration of all the traces 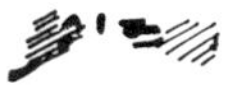 would be *ỉw=f r šm n=f*, 'He/it will go away'.

m. The sign read *rmt* is here assumed to curl to the left at the bottom of its long descending stroke: none of the obvious alternative readings, *=f*, *pꜣỉ*, or *wʿ*, seem possible. Compare the writing of *rmt* in l. 8 above, where damage to the papyrus makes it impossible to tell how far the stroke curves.

n. The trace at the end of l. 10 may be of a large writing of the particle *ỉ*. The preceding trace is likely to be of a suffix *=f*.

o. For *pꜣỉ=f*, see n. *k* above: the preceding sign is presumably the speaking-man det., as occurs in a problematic passage in the next line (n. *q* below).

p. The reading *ḥr pꜣỉ=k* might be considered here: in view of what follows, *pꜣỉ=k* would have to be understood absolutely, 'yours'.

q. For the first signs in l. 12, the reading *šʿ* seems inescapable, and, a little later,  must surely be the sign *ʿn* (see *DG*, 61–2), which here might either stand alone, or be taken together with the preceding signs (conceivably as a writing of the verb *ʿn*, 'to return'). At the beginning of the line, *šʿ-tw* might be read, and this might simply have been written for *šʿ*; but no plausible interpretation of the first half of this line as a whole has suggested itself.

r. Neither *wʿ* nor . . . *rmt* seem satisfactory readings of the traces  here.

s. The particle *ỉ*, rather than *r wʿt*, is probably to be read. Nothing can be made of the slight traces that follow: the word to be restored here must be very short, and there is certainly insufficient room to read *r wʿt wnwt pꜣỉ(=y) ʿḥʿ* (cf. l. 10 above).

Translation

1.] appear [
2.] to all of them [
3.] . . . . . cause . . . . . to walk [
4.] O Amun [. . .] who places . . . . [
5.] the oil, the rescuing from the fevers/wrath of Amun[α] [
6.] . . . your temple. O Amun, may you cause . . . . . [
7.] O Seth, (the) destructive, do not destroy . . . [
8.] . . . . . my only (?) . . . . man . . . [
9.] O . . . drink-offering of/to Seth.[β] (*Space*) O . . . . [

10.] one hour my life$^{\gamma}$ . . . . . to him . . . . . a man . . . . [
11.] . . . . . his life . . . . without your going to return . . . . [
12.] until . . . . O . . . my life . . . . [

Notes on translation

α. The sense of *ẖm*(*m*), the basic meaning of which is 'heat', is not certain here. The word is common, for example in P. Lond.–Leiden, in the sense of 'fever', and this would suit the context here. For the use of the verb *ẖm*(*m*) in the sense 'to be angry', see **2** back, x+1/34 (p. 125, n. *eu*); this meaning, unlike that of 'fever', does not appear to be attested in Coptic (see Crum, *CD*, 677 a–b and Černý, *CED*, 283. 5).

If the reading of *nḥḥ*, 'oil', at the beginning of l. 5 is correct (see p. 160, n. *b*), then the oil is presumably said to prevent or to cure the fevers (or wrath) of Amun. If *r nḥḥ* 'to eternity', were read, then *pꜣ nḥm* etc., 'The rescuing etc.' would no doubt begin a new sentence.

β. The reading of the particle *i͗*, 'O', at the beginning of l. 9 seems probable: however, it is not certain, and no plausible restoration for the very short lacuna that follows, or interpretation of the whole of this surprisingly brief invocation suggests itself. Possibly *i͗* was followed by a wish rather than the name of a god or any similar expression. It is perhaps conceivable that *wtn*, 'drink-offering', was written in error for *wtn*, 'sacred-boat', but this does not make the phrase much more intelligible.

γ. The sense is not clear: possibly 'at one moment (of) my life', or 'my life (is but) an hour'. The recurrence of the phrase in l. 12, and *pꜣi͗=f ʿḥʿ*, 'his life', in l. 11 suggest that the latter is more probable.

DISCUSSION

The nature of this text as a whole is not clear. In ll. 4–9 for certain (and probably down to l. 12, the last line preserved) there occurs a regular sequence of invocations of gods: only the names of Amun (ll. 4–6) and Seth (l. 7; cf. l. 9) are preserved. Other phrases appropriate to prayers addressed to gods can be read in these lines, and it is natural to suppose that one long, continuous series of prayers is in question here. The few words that survive in ll. 1–3 could equally belong in prayers or in simple narrative, and no indication of direct speech is preserved there. The text might therefore be a narrative that included a lengthy prayer, or might be of a religious nature, perhaps most likely magical. Only part of a single column is preserved, and it is impossible to tell if the text originally consisted of one column, perhaps written on a small piece of papyrus cut from a roll (a form in which a short magical text might well be found), or if preceding or succeeding columns are lost.

7. A NARRATIVE MENTIONING ḤAT-BOINU

Plate 12b

H5-DP504 [5964] 10.5 cm. *h.* × 8.0 cm. *w.*

Sector 1 (North Courtyard) debris (1966–7)

The papyrus is of average quality, and translucent. Its shade is a light brown, and it has a grey tint: there is no firm evidence to show that this is due to the erasure of a previous text or texts, rather than to dirt, but it is possible. The surfaces are badly worn, and there are many holes, but the ink has not been badly rubbed. The front (↔) surface preserves the beginnings of 8 lines of a continuous demotic text. The right-hand edge of the fragment is fairly straight and may have been cut. Only about 0.4 cm. of blank papyrus are preserved at the right-hand edge. At the very right-hand edge of the piece a join between two sheets of papyrus is preserved, in which the left-hand sheet overlaps the right-hand sheet: this is the reverse of what is to be expected on the inside of a demotic roll. Up to 2.0 cm. of blank papyrus are preserved at the foot of the fragment. The edges of the fragment other than the right-hand edge are all torn. The back (↕) surface is blank.

Because of the grey tinge, the apparently cut right-hand edge, and the fact that the text appears to be written upside-down on the papyrus, possibly the fragment belonged to a fairly small piece, cut from a used roll to bear a short text.

The **hand** is large and rounded, and is rapidly written with a fairly thick brush. There is no precisely similar hand among the literary texts, although **23** and **25** may be compared. The hands of some Saqqâra letters are more similar.

Transliteration

— — — — — — — — — — —

1. . . . . . .] . . [. . . . .] . . [- - -
2. *r*[a] . . [. .] . *Stḫ*[b] [. . . .] . . [
3. *r-ḥr=y pꜣ ntì* ⌜*ìw=w*⌝ *r ìr=f r* ⌜*ḫꜣꜥ*⌝[c] [
4. *ìw=* . . ⌜*ìr=f*⌝[d] . . [. .] . . . . . . [. . .] . . . [
5. ⌜*ìrm*⌝ *ḥꜣt.ṱ=*. . . . .[e][
6. . . . . . [. .] . . *nꜣ* ⌜*ḥ*⌝*bꜣ.w*[f] . . . *pꜣ* . . . . .[
7. *tꜣ ḫnṱ mḥṱ Ḥwt-Bnw*[g] . . .[h][
8. *mn šr (n) mn*[j] . . .[k] *ḥꜣt.*⌜*ṱ=f*⌝ . .[l][

up to 4.0 cm. of blank papyrus

Notes on transliteration

a. For the form of *r*, see *r-ḥr=y* in l. 3; cf. **5**, 1/5, p. 155, n. *j*.

b. The reading of the name of the god Seth here seems satisfactory, but it is impossible to exclude the possibility that *stì*, *sty*, 'to shoot' (*DG*, 475. 4), might be read.

c. Perhaps restore .

d. The obvious reading is *ìw=y ìr=f*, but the *=y* suffix is not convincing, and *ìr=f* is not written quite as in l. 3: conceivably read *ḏd.ṱ=f*,  ?

e. Although long writings of *ỉrm* are common in the Saqqâra papyri (e.g. **1** front 9/1: cf. the early writings given in *DG*, 39. 9), the form here is surprisingly extended; however, no other restoration suggests itself. *ḥꜣt* is certain: the clear trace below the line, that might suggest *ḥꜣt.ṯ=f*, is much more likely to be part of a  det. of *ḥbꜣ* in l. 6: *ḥꜣt.ṯ=y* might well be read, although the apparent *=y* could be part of the following word.

f. Without adequate context, the first sign in l. 6, , might be taken in several ways (e.g. *wꜥt*, *šr*, *ḥmt*: cf. the same sign in the preceding line; possibly *wꜥt* could be read in both places). *ḥbꜣ.w* (*DG*, 299. 1): restore . Conceivably *mtw=s ḥbꜣ.* might be read.

g. The reading of *mḥṯ*, 'North', written , is certain. Possibly *n mḥṯ* should be read. Preceding this the reading *ḫnṯ* with a divine det. is virtually certain, but it is not clear whether or not this should be understood as a place-name: presumably the first sign in the line can only be the article *tꜣ*. Cf. perhaps *Wb.* iii. 306. 6 ff. or 307. 11 ff.

h. It is plausible that the last signs in ll. 7 and 8 should be read in the same way. *ỉw=s* is a possible reading, but perhaps *ỉn*, beginning two parallel questions, is more probable.

j. The sense here is clearly 'So-and-so, son (or daughter) of So-and-so', but it is impossible to be sure whether *šr* or *ms* should be read. In texts of the Roman period, *šr* is often written with a horizontal line below: the origin of this stroke is obscure, but in practice it serves to distinguish *šr* from other words written with  (cf. n. *f* above): probably the stroke here should be taken as a forerunner of the phenomenon attested later, and neither *šr n* nor *r-ms* should be read.

k. The readings naturally suggested by the traces here, *wꜣḥ* and *ḥr*, etc., are all problematic.

l. See n. *h* above.

Translation

— — — — — — — — — — — — — — —

1. *only traces*
2. . . . .] Seth [
3. . . . . . me. Anything that they will do, to place [
4. I shall do/say it . . . . [
5. with my heart . . . . . [
6. . . . . the griefs . . . . . the . . . . .[
7. Takhent, north of Ḥatboinu[α] . . . . .[
8. So-and-so child of So-and-so[β] . . . . . his heart . . . [

Notes on translation

α. Takhent may plausibly be taken as a place-name, although no name in this form is yet attested in demotic. Because *ḫnt* and other similar forms are frequently found as (or as part of) Egyptian place-names, and because several names *ḥwt-bnw* are attested, it is difficult to identify the places meant here, or to be sure of the interpretation of this line of the text. In particular, it is not clear if ordinary place-names are in question, or the names of shrines etc., appropriate to a magical context.

β. lAthough this phrase is not so far attested in demotic narrative texts, it is probably unnecessary to take it as an indication that the present text is documentary in character. Phrases of this kind occur several times in Mag. Pap. (see Index 365 and 400) to mark where the name of the person upon whom a spell should be supplied. The spells concerned are all erotic prescriptions. The one other non-documentary occurrence of the phrase, in Erichsen, 'Aus einem demotischen Papyrus über Frauenkrankheiten', *Mitteilungen des Instituts für Orientforschung*, 2 (1954), 363–77, l. 20, is in a similar context. However, it is reasonable to suppose that the expression might be found in any magical context.

DISCUSSION

This fragment appears to preserve part of a continuous narrative, although it is impossible to be certain whether it is literary or documentary in character. As indicated in the introduction, the text may have been quite short. The appearance of the fragment and the nature of the hand might suggest that the text was a letter; but these indications are not in themselves compelling, and it would not be easy to explain all the contents as part of a letter. One phrase (see p. 164, n. β) and the mention (not entirely certain) of the god Seth (l. 2) raise the possibility that the text records the formula for a spell or appeal to a god, but this is no more than a possibility.

8. A NARRATIVE MENTIONING ASHSURY AND DARIUS — Plate 12c

H5-DP518 [5978] 8.5 cm. *h.*×4.5 cm. *w.*

Sector 1 (North Courtyard) debris (1966–7)

The papyrus is coarse and uneven-textured, but translucent. It is of a dark-straw shade. The fragment is torn on all sides, and no margins are preserved. The front (↔) surface bears parts of 9 lines of continuous demotic text. The back (↕) surface is blank.

The **hand** is neat and of average size. The lines of the text are well spaced apart. There is a considerable variation in the thickness of the strokes; ↙↗-strokes are very thin, and horizontal strokes are often exaggerated and very thick.

Transliteration

— — — — — — — — —

1. - - -] . [. . .] . . [. .] . . .[a] [- - -
2.].⸢*kr*⸣ . . .[b] *ỉn.ṯ=f* . . .[c] [
3.] *r-ḥr=t pȝỉ=t ṯȝw my wḏȝ=f* . .[
4.] ⸢*ȝ*⸣*šsry*[d] *bn-ỉw=y dỉt* [
5.]. *Ṱrywš* . . .[e] *t/nȝỉ=*⸢*f*⸣.[f] [
6.] *šb tȝỉ=k ḥmt* . . . .[g] [
7.] ⸢*ỉ*⸣*-ỉr=f*[h] *bn(-pw)=f gm mȝʿ*[j] [
8.]*y*[k] *r-dỉ=w*[l] *n=k* .[
9.] *ȝš*⸢*sr*⸣[*y*].[m]

— — — — — — — — —

Notes on transliteration

a. The traces at the end of l. 1 are ; the first sign most probably had the shape , and perhaps *ỉn=w*. might be read (hardly *ỉn.ṯ=.*; cf. *ỉn.ṯ=f* in l. 2).

b. The traces are . The first sign might be restored as *wʿt*. The final det. plainly resembles the det. at the beginning of l. 8 below, where probably the same word should be restored as here, and the obvious reading is of the knife det. In view of this, and of the virtually certain reading of the signs *kr* in l. 2, it is tempting to read *wʿt krṯy*, 'knife' (*DG*, 587. 2, *grṯ*). The signs might be restored .

c. The traces are ; probably *tȝ* or *nȝ* should be read, followed by a word beginning *tr*, or, less probably, *gr*.

d. This is almost certainly the same proper name as in l. 9 below, and the traces can be combined to give the reading *ȝšsry*; it is conceivable that further consonants are lost from the beginning of the name, but the large form of the *ȝ* does not suggest this. Whether or not the name can be regarded as having any connection with *Aššur*, e.g. as a *nisbe*, is problematic.

e. The personal name *Ṱrywš*, Darius, is determined here with the same det. as *ȝšsry* in ll. 4 and 9, and shows no other clear sign of a cartouche; and therefore it seems likely to be the name of a private person. The following signs precisely resemble *y* followed by *=s*, , although clearly no reading along these lines is possible. As the name *Ṱrywš* certainly has no cartouche, *ʿnḫ wḏȝ snb* can hardly be read, and *ḥm-ntr*, which is normally written , and would here have no def. article, will not suit the context. It is perhaps best to assume that this is an idiosyncratic writing of *ỉrm* (a more normal writing might be ; the form of this word certainly varies considerably), which would clearly suit the context.

f. It seems best to read as *tȝỉ=f* or *nȝỉ=f* followed by one trace; although many restorations are possible, one that might be considered is *tꜣi=f ḥmt* (cf. l. 6 below).

g. The traces at the end of l. 6 are ; possibly read *r* followed by a sign such as .

h. The reading *ỉ-ỉr=f* seems inescapable; the 'emphatic' form is not possible at the end of a clause, and, judging by the usage of the other papyri in this volume, this may only be understood as the active participle, the relative form always being correctly written as *r-ỉr=f*. However, for a participle to govern a suffix rather than a 'dependent' pronoun as direct object would be in direct opposition to all normal Egyptian usage. The form is a crux; perhaps this scribe wrote the relative form *ỉ-ỉr=f*, contrary to the regular Memphite practice.

j. As the det. is damaged, a reading of *mꜣꜥ*, 'truth', might be considered as well as of *mꜣꜥ* 'place' (see *DG*, 149–50 for these and other possibilities); however, it is highly probable that this is an example of the phrase common in narrative texts, *bn-pw=f gm mꜣꜥ n pꜣ tꜣ ỉw=f n-ỉm=f*, 'He knew not where on earth he was', expressing a character's horror and amazement at bad news.

k. In view of the traces preserved in l. 2 above (see p. 166, n. *b*), *krṯy* (*grṯ*), 'knife', might be restored here. The traces here in l. 8, considered by themselves, might equally be restored *sfy*, 'sword'.

l. *r-di=w* seems the most probable reading, although *r-dỉ n=k*+nom. subject is perhaps a possibility.

m. A trace of the det. of the name *ꜣšsry* seems to be preserved after the short lacuna, in addition to a trace of the following word. See p. 166, n. *d*.

Translation

— —

1.] . . . . bring (?) [
2.] knife. The . . . . . brought it [
3.] before you (fem. sing.). May your breath (of life) be safe![α] . . . [
4.] Ashsury.[β] I shall not cause [
5.] . . . Darius[γ] with (?) his . . . [
6.] in exchange for your wife. . . . . . [
7.] who had done it. He did not find a place[δ] [
8.] knife (?), that they gave to you . . . [
9.] Ashsury [

— —

Notes on translation

α. This phrase is found in both literary and documentary texts. See, for example, Ryl. 9, 1/4, 20/13, P. Krall 12/13: it may also be read at ꜥOnchsheshonqy 2/9, when fr. *d* is correctly positioned (see *Serapis* 6 (1980), 133). See further **1**, 14/28.

β. This is the name (obviously of foreign origin—possibly Persian or Assyrian, although it has not been positively identified) of a private person.

γ. From the nature of the writing, the name Darius here cannot refer to any of the kings of this name, but must belong to a private person.

δ. This might perhaps be restored as part of a common literary phrase: see n. *j* above.

DISCUSSION

This fragment contains a continuous narrative, incorporating a considerable amount of direct speech. It is uncertain if it is literary or documentary in character. Two well-known phrases seem to occur, of which one is found both in literary texts and in documents, while the other, although distinctively literary, is not sufficiently well preserved to be taken as a secure indication of the nature of the text. Two personal names are preserved that might suggest a documentary text written perhaps late in the period of the First Persian Domination of Egypt. The hand, however, shows no sign of being quite as early as this, and, if the text is later in date, it may perhaps be a little more likely to be a literary narrative.

9. A NARRATIVE CONCERNING ḤARUDJ

Plate 13a

71/72-DP108+116 [5795+5802]
10.0 cm. *h.*×5.0 cm. *w.*

Sector 7, West Dump

The papyrus is coarse and uneven-textured, although much of it is translucent. Its shade is dark straw, with a greyish tinge on both surfaces; it is very difficult to say in each case whether this is due to dirt or the erasure of a previous text—the latter seems more likely, in the case of the front. A join between two sheets of papyrus, right over left, as is to be expected, is preserved at the left-hand edge; it is about 1 cm. wide. The fragment is torn on all sides, and there is no trace of any margin. The front (↔) surface bears parts of 9 lines of continuous demotic text. The back surface is blank.

The **hand** is fairly small and cramped; although it is the work of a practised scribe, he used a relatively coarse brush, and hence the writing has an untidy appearance.

Transliteration

— — — — — — — — — — — —

1. - - - . . . .] . . . [- - -
2. . . . .]*.ry*[a] *n t/nꜣ* . . [
3. . . . .] *Ḥr-wḏꜣ ʿr.ṱ*[b] *ḏd* [
4. . . .] . . *Ḥr-*⌜*wḏꜣ*⌝ . . . *mꜣʿ.*⌜*w*⌝[c] *ʿr* [
5.] . . . *r-ẖ rmt ʿꜣ*[d] *bn-pw Ḥr-wḏꜣ* .[
6.] ⌜*ỉ*⌝*-ỉr ḫpr tꜣ ẖnšỉ sdm-ʿš*[e] [
7.] . . . *ḥꜣt=f*[f] *ḫpr* .[g] *nꜣ ntr.w*[h] .[
8. . .] . . .[j] vacat *ḏd=y* . . . .[k] [
9. . . . . .] . . . . [

— — — — — — — — — — — —

Notes on transliteration

a. The traces are , and *byry*, 'ship' (*DG*, 119. 1), seems a more probable restoration than *y*(*ʿ*)*r*, 'river', *mrt*, 'harbour', or *mr.t*, 'ship' (cf. the phrase *r mr.t* at **1**, 13/24), none of which normally shows a final *y*.

b. The final *ṱ* of *ʿr.ṱ* seems a clear reading, and presumably marks the Stative.

c. *mꜣʿ* here plainly does not have a house det., and so presumably is the verb *mꜣʿ*, 'to be justified' etc., or a related word, rather than *mꜣʿ*, 'place'. The following stroke presumably reads *.w* or *=w*, and *mꜣʿ* might be preceded by *r* or *ntỉ*, but the nature of the construction here is uncertain.

d. The first traces in l. 5 are 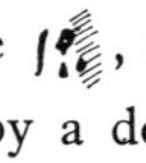, and presumably represent *.w* or *=w*, preceded by a det. or dets. The writing of *rmt ʿꜣ* is . The stroke after *rmt*, although rather short, might suggest the reading *rmt.w*; but, in this case, a normal plur. form of *ʿꜣ* would be expected, as, for example, in **1**, 9/6, or (in a different form) **1**, 14/6.

e. This line recalls the phrase *tꜣy ẖnšṱ.t n ẖl* at I. Kh. 5/6, and perhaps the sense here is 'what had happened (to) the foul servant girl'. The expression is derogatory or abusive, and would no doubt be appropriate only in direct speech.

f. Perhaps read *r-ḥꜣt=f*. No *ṱ* is written before the suffix pronoun.

g. The reading of *ḫpr* seems secure, although the bottom horizontal stroke is not straight, as in the writing in l. 6 above. The short, straight, vertical stroke after *ḫpr* is presumably *.w* or *=w*, but the sense is uncertain.

h. The first signs can hardly leave any doubt of the reading *ntr.w*; presumably the group  represents the normal final  (cf. the alternation of  and  for 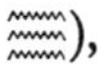), but this is surprising.

j. The traces are .

k. The traces here are . The only clearly identifiable sign after *ḏd=y* is , and this might be read in several ways. Conceivably *n=w* stands immediately after *ḏd=y*.

Translation

— — — — — — — — — — — — — — — — —

1. *only traces*
2.] ship (?) in/of the . . . [
3.] Ḥarudj embarked (?),[α] saying/because [
4.] . . . Ḥarudj . . . . . justified (?) . . . . . embarked (?) [
5.] . . . . . as a great man.[β] Ḥarudj did not [
6.] that happened (to ?) the foul servant girl[γ] [
7.] . . . . . his heart . . . happened . . . the gods . . . [
8.] . . . . . . I said . . . . [
9. *only traces*

— — — — — — — — — — — — — — — — —

Notes to translation

α. The translation 'embarked' is offered here for the verb *ꜥr*, 'to rise, mount up', although the context is not clear, because of the probable mention of 'ship' in l. 1: the verb is often used in such contexts (see, for example, **1**, 13/32).

β. *rmt ꜥꜣ*, literally 'great man', although found in documents, is common in literary texts, used both of courtiers and of great magicians of the past.

γ. For the probable context of this phrase, see p. 168, n. *e*.

DISCUSSION

This text is apparently a continuous narrative. Direct speech occurs at least at one point (see the use of the 1st pers. pronoun in l. 8: for another possible indication of direct speech, see p. 168, n. *e*). A character named Ḥarudj (*Ḥr-wḏꜣ*) is mentioned three times, apparently playing an active role. Ḥarudj, although a common personal name in the Late Period, is also a name that not infrequently occurs in demotic literature. In the case of three Roman period papyri from Tebtunis, he is a, or the, major character of a narrative text (only one of these is so far published, the highly fragmentary P. Tebt. Tait 6, in which a Ḥarudj appears as the chief financial and administrative official of Egypt). The phraseology and all other indications from the contents seem consistent with the idea that the text is a literary narrative, and this is therefore the most probable explanation of its nature.

10. A NARRATIVE MENTIONING A MEETING Plate 13b, c

H5-DP164 [1762] 11.5 cm. *h.* × 8.5 cm. *w.*

Sector 1 (North Courtyard) debris (1966–7)

The papyrus is coarse and uneven-textured, but translucent. Its shade is light brown. The fragment as a whole has suffered much damage, and in particular ll. 1–6 on the back are preserved only upon a thin strip of vertical fibres, from which the horizontal fibres have disappeared, and, in another place, the ends of ll. 2–4 on the front are preserved only upon some horizontal fibres. The front (↔) surface bears parts of 5 lines of continuous demotic text, and the back (↕) surface bears parts of 11 lines of continuous demotic text, written the other way up relative to the text on the front. No trace of any margin is preserved on either surface.

The **hand** is probably, although not certainly, the same on back and front. The writing on the front is slightly smaller than that on the back. The scribe has written rapidly and fairly skilfully with rather a coarse brush, which gives the hand an untidy appearance: despite this, the hand is broadly of the same type as that of **1** and **2** in this volume.

Transliteration

FRONT (↔)

1. - - - . . . .] . . ⸢*h*⸣[a] [- - -
2. . . . . .] *ḫ(r)ʿry r-ḥr=y m-sꜣ ḫpr* [
3.] ⸢*n pꜣ s(s)w n* ⸢*s*⸣*ḫny* ⸢*m-sꜣ=k*⸣ *r-ỉr=y* ⸢*ḫpr*⸣[b] [
4.] . . *tw=y* . . . . ⸢*pꜣỉ=k*⸣ *ʿwỉ* ⸢*ỉw=w*⸣ . .[c] [
5.] . .[d] *šp=w* . . . [

BACK (↕)

1. - - -] . [- - -
2.] . . [
3.] *ḫn*[e] [
4.] . . [
5.]. *ḫn*[f] [
6.] ⸢*nkt*⸣[g] [
7.] . *ʿn* ⸢*sp-2*⸣ [
8.] ⸢*gm.*⸣*ṯ=k mtw=k* . . . . . . [.] . *ỉw* . . .[h] [
9.] . . ⸢*n-ỉm*⸣*=f bn-*[. . .] . . . . . .[j] [
10. . . .] . . . . .[k] [
11. . . . .] . [

Notes on transliteration

a. The traces before the fairly certain reading of *h* might well suit *pꜣi͗=k* etc.

b. The first sign of *sẖny*, written , has a puzzling form, but it is difficult to find an alternative reading; hardly *pꜣ ssw n mḥ 2 ẖny* (= *ẖnn*, 'disorder', *DG*, 385. 1). Conceivably *n-i͗m=k* might be read instead of *m-sꜣ=k*. The reading of *ḫpr* at the end of the line seems virtually certain; cf. the writing of l. 2 above.

c. The precise form of the signs following *tw=y* is uncertain; the traces appear to be 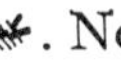. Neither *pꜣ hrw* nor *di͗(=w)* seem possible in the context. The reading *i͗w=w* is uncertain.

d. The traces before *šp=w* are . The traces of ink below l. 5 on the front almost certainly all belong to the writing on the back.

e. Here and in l. 5 below the signs , *ẖn* seem to appear; cf. *sẖny* in front, l. 3, and contrast *ẖr* in front, l. 2.

f. Cf. n. *e* above.

g. The traces are , but *nkt* is not a certain reading.

h. At the beginning of l. 8, *gm* is not assured by the traces, but seems probable. The signs following *mtw=k* can hardly read *gm*; it is not certain that *mtw=k* is the Conjunctive, but the context perhaps suggests this is likely. At the end of the line, *i͗w=y* or *i͗w=f* are possibilities.

j. Towards the end of the line the verb *ẖsy*, 'to suffer', 'to be feeble' (*DG*, 396. 6), might perhaps be read.

k. The traces are 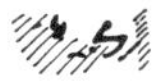; a reading of *r tꜣi͗*, followed by a word beginning *ʿt* might be considered.

Translation

FRONT

— — — — — — — — — — — — — — — — —

1\.] . . . . . [
2\.] wrath against me. Thereafter[a] [
3\.] at the moment of meeting you that I did, it happened [
4\.] . . . I . . . . your house . . . they . . . [
5\.] . . . . . they received . . . . . [

— — — — — — — — — — — — — — — — — — —

BACK

— — — — — — — — — — — — —

lines 1–5, only traces

6\.] possession [
7\.] . . . ever again [
8\.] find you, and you . . . . [
9\.] . . . him . . . . . not . . . . . suffered(?) . . . [

lines 10–11, only traces

— — — — — — — — — — — — —

Note on translation

a. m-sꜣ ḫpr here presumably forms the common conjunction, generally meaning no more than 'then' or 'but'.

DISCUSSION

This text contains several 1st and 2nd pers. pronouns. The contents would suit a private letter, and the fact that the lines on the back are written the other way up relative to those on the front would support the idea that the fragment might come from a letter. However, the contents might be read as belonging to a narrative (or narratives) and the hand, although careless, is not distinctively similar to the common letter hands from Saqqâra. The piece is therefore worth presenting here as possibly literary in character.

11. A NARRATIVE MENTIONING PHARAOH

Plate 14a

H5-DP442 [2363] 11.5 cm. *h.* × 12.0 cm. *w.*

Sector 1 (north Courtyard) debris (1966–7)

The papyrus is of a coarse but consistent texture, and is translucent. Its shade is dark straw. The surfaces are badly worn, especially on the front, where many fibres are loose or missing, although much of the ink remains undisturbed.

The front (↔) surface bears parts of 9 lines of continuous demotic text. The fragment is torn on all sides, and there is no clear sign of any margin. The back surface is blank.

The **hand** is a rapid and skilful one, written with a somewhat coarse brush. It is not greatly different from the general type of the hands of **1** and **2** in this volume, and there are also similarities to those of **4** and **5**.

Transliteration

1. - - - . .] *bꞽn ḏd=f* . .[a] [. .] . . [- - -
2. . .] . . *ꞽ-ꞽr-ḥr=k nꜣ md.wt ḏd=k n(=y) bn-pw=y wn* . . . . . [
3. . .] . . .[b] . . . . *tꜣꞽ*[c] . [.] . *ꞽꞽ* .[d] [. . . .] . *wn* . .[e] [
4. . .] .*=f rḫ tm ḏd* . . .[f] *nꜣ* ⌜*md.wt*⌝ [. . . .] . . . . . [. . . .] . .[g] [
5.] *dꞽ=f ḥwy* . *ẖry*[h] [. . .] *Pr-ꜥꜣ* . [
6. . . .] . . . .[j] *Pr-ꜥꜣ* ⌜*ḥwt-nṯr*⌝ . . . . [
7. . . . . .] . . *wn-nꜣ-w ꜥš* . . . . [. .] . . . . . .[k] [
8. . . . . .] . ⌜*ꞽ*⌝ . . . . *f* . . .[l] [. . . .] . [
9. . . . .] . . . [. . . .] . . . . . [

Notes on transliteration

a. *ḏd=f* [*n*]*=f* is a plausible reading.

b. *ḥr*]*ry*—or *ḥr*]*rꞽ*—might be restored.

c. The virtually certain reading of the copula *tꜣꞽ* suggests a fem. noun might precede. Thus *tꜣꞽ=k wꜥbt* is among possible readings: *=s n-drt* . . . might also be considered.

d. *ꞽw*+suffix is likely before *ꞽꞽ*.

e. *wn-nꜣ-w* is probable at the end of the line.

f. *ḳnbt*, although a dubious reading, is worth considering, as *ḏd ḳnbt*, 'to litigate', is a common phrase.

g. Although the intermediate traces cannot be made out, at the end of the line *Pr-ꜥꜣ*, written exactly as in the following line, is very probable.

h. The presence of *dꞽ=f* presumably establishes that *ḥwy* rather than *dꞽt wy* should be read, but the broken context makes it difficult to decide if the following group should be read *ntꞽ*, *-s*, *n*(*=y*), *tꜣ*, or *nꜣ*. The det. of *ẖry* is too badly damaged for the sense to be clear.

j. Before *Pr-ꜥꜣ*, neither *ḏd n*(*=y*) nor *ḏd n=f* are certain readings.

k. *ḥwt-nṯr* may occur at the end of this line, as in the preceding line.

l. The first substantial trace appears to be of *ꞽ*. A reading *ꞽrm=f* is hardly possible.

Translation

1.] evil. He said . . . . [
2.] . . . before you the words. You said to me: 'I did not open . . . . . [

3.] delay (?). It is your (?) . . . . came . . . . [
4.] he is able not to litigate (?), the matters . . . . [
5.] he caused to throw . . . . Pharaoh [
6.] . . . . . Pharaoh, temple . . . . . [
7.] . . . . . ask/pray . . . . . temple (?) [
8.] . . . . him/his . . . . [

— — — — — — — — — — — — — — — — — —

DISCUSSION

This fragment clearly belongs to a substantial continuous text, containing a narration of some kind. It is possible that it was part of a story; but, if the questionable reading of *ḏd ḳnbt* in l. 4 were correct, it would plainly at least refer to legal matters. Nothing in the form or contents of the text particularly suggests a letter: it may perhaps have belonged to a legal report or other document, but the hand does not in any way rule out the possibility that it was a literary text.

12. A NARRATIVE MENTIONING PETIESE Plate 14b, c

72/73-DP26 [6162] 6.0 cm. *h.* × 8.0 cm. *w.*

Sector 7, South Dump

The papyrus is opaque and coarse-textured, and is of a greyish shade. A join between two sheets of papyrus occurs at the left-hand edge (as is to be expected, the join is right-over-left). The fragment is torn on all sides, and no margins are preserved. The front (↔) surface bears parts of 5 lines of continuous demotic text. The back (↕) surface preserves part of an account arranged in vertical columns. (For convenience, this account is briefly published here: see p. 175.)

The **hand** is bold and carelessly written with a brush that produced considerable differences between thick and thin strokes. It may show some signs of being a relatively early hand, but is difficult to place on the basis of so small a fragment.

Transliteration

(↔)

1. - - - .] . . .[a] *ḥꜣt.ṱ=y tꜣỉ/nꜣỉ=* . [- - -
2. . .] . *Pꜣ-dỉ-ꜣIst* . . . . .[b] *kt*[c] [
3.] . . .[d] *kt* . . . . .[e] *Ḳỉ-ḏꜣḏꜣ*[f] [
4.] . . .[g] *nꜣ mr-mšꜥ.w nꜣ rmt.w ꜥꜣy Pr-ꜥꜣ* [
5. . . . .] . [. . . . .] . [. . . . .] . . [

Notes on transliteration

a. In the torn state of the papyrus, it is not clear if a large writing of *ỉr*, *wn*, or an early form of *ntỉ* occurs here.

b. The det. suggests that a place-name is in question here. *Pꜣ-ḏp* is the obvious reading of the signs, but no identification suggests itself.

c. The group  recurs in the following line, apparently in a similar context. Readings such as *n ỉr*, *ḏd*, and *20* are open to strong objections, and the reading of the fem. form *kt*, 'another', introducing the items of a list, seems less problematic.

d. *ꜥwỉ* is a possible reading here: whether or not this is the case, a place-name might be restored.

e. A personal name might well be read here, but the signs are damaged, and the reading is uncertain.

f. The reading of the personal name *G-ḏꜣḏꜣ*/*Ḳỉ-ḏꜣḏꜣ* seems secure (cf. *DG*, 532 under 531. 7, 569. 9, and 669. 2).

g. It is tempting to restore *nꜣ sꜣwtỉ*].*w* at the beginning of the line, because of its common association with *nꜣ mr-mšꜥ.w nꜣ rmt.w ꜥꜣy*(*.w*) *Pr-ꜥꜣ*, as, for example, in **1**, 9/6.

Translation

1.] . . . my heart . . . . [
2.] . . . (son of) Petiese, of . . . . Another: [
3.] house (?). Another: . . . . (son of) Kidjodj [
4.] . . .[a] and the generals and the great men of Pharaoh [
5. *only traces*

Note on translation

a. Perhaps restore 'the guards and the generals and the great men of Pharaoh' (cf. p. 174, n. *g*).

DISCUSSION

This fragment is worth presenting for consideration here in a volume of literary texts, because of the phrase '. . . the generals and the great men of Pharaoh' in l. 4, which is common in demotic narratives, as they frequently contain scenes set in the royal court. However, there is no reason to suppose the phrase would not be in place in documentary texts, and there is no other hint that the fragment is literary in character. Although there are several uncertainties of reading, it is probable that ll. 2–3 contain a list of persons, giving name, name of father, and place of origin. (This interpretation does not depend upon the dubious reading of the word *kt*, 'another' in ll. 2–3.)

APPENDIX

Fragmentary account on the back surface. This text appears to have no connection with the text on the front.

Transliteration

(↕)

- - -] . . . [- - -			
. . .] *ꜣll ꜥḳ*	*6*	*5*	*ḥḏ* [
. . . .] *ꜥḳ*	*7*	*4*	*ḥḏ* [
. . . . .] *ꜣlly*	*8*	*6.*[a]	*ḥḏ* [
. . . . . . *ꜣ*]*lly*			*ḥḏ*[b] [
. . . .] *ꜥḳ*	*9*	$3\frac{1}{2}$	*ḥḏ* [
. . . . .] . . .			. . [

Notes on transliteration

a. The long tail of a numeral in the hundreds from the lost portion of the papyrus cuts through this figure, rendering the reading of the fraction doubtful.

b. This line shows no figures in the two central columns, and has rather the appearance of having been squeezed in as an afterthought.

DISCUSSION

This appears to be an account of quantities of bread and wine, but in the fragmentary condition of the text it is not possible to determine the functions of the various columns. There is no obvious relationship between the numbers in the two columns of figures; the numerals in the first of these, ascending by steps of one, 6–7–8–9, are perhaps not likely to be quantities of any kind.

13–21. FRAGMENTARY TEXTS IN HANDS BEARING SIMILARITIES TO THOSE OF TEXTS 1 AND 2

13. NARRATIVE Plate 15a

H5-DP524a [5984a] 6.0 cm. *h.* × 3.0 cm. *w.*

Sector 1 (North Courtyard) debris (1966–7)

The papyrus is even-textured and opaque. The front (↔) surface of the fragment preserves small parts of the last three lines of a column, written along the fibres. Below these stands a column numeral, evidently in the bottom margin of the roll. The edges of the piece are torn on all sides (this appears to be the case with the bottom edge, as well as the others, and the original depth of the bottom margin is thus uncertain). The back (↕) surface is blank, although, as the fragment comes from the very foot of the roll, it is not possible to deduce with certainty that the back was not written upon.

The **hand** is difficult to assess from the few signs that are preserved, but it appears to be a small, neat, literary hand, of the same type as those of **1**, **2**, **8**, and **22**, as well as those of the present group of small fragments, **14–21**.

Transliteration

— — — — — — — — —

1. - - - . . .] . . [- - -
2. . . .] . [
3. .]=*y ỉỉ* . . . . [
4.] vacat *mḥ 3* vacat [

2.0 cm of blank papyrus

Translation

ll. 1–2 *only traces* l. 3] I came . . . . . [*set below the column*: '3rd (column)'

DISCUSSION

From the position of the figure at the bottom of this fragment, it is apparent that it belonged to a literary text with numbered columns, such as **1** and **2** (see pp. 1 ff. and 70). It is not possible to establish that this fragment belongs to any of the literary texts in this volume, but it is conceivable that it preserves part of **1**, **2**, or **14–21**.

14. NARRATIVE Plate 15a

H5-DP524b [5984b] 5.0 cm. *h.*×6.5 cm. *w.*

Sector 1 (North Courtyard) debris (1966–7)

The papyrus is fine and even-textured, and is translucent. Its shade is rather dark and greyish. The front (↔) surface preserves parts of 6 lines of continuous text, written along the fibres. The edges of the piece are torn on all sides, and there is no trace of any margin. The back (↕) surface is blank.

The **hand** of this fragment is a small, neat, literary hand, of precisely the same kind as that of **1** and **2** in this volume (which may have been written by one and the same scribe): the ductus and general appearance more closely resemble that of **1**.

The parts of this fragment have become somewhat impacted, and the arrangement shown here is not certain.

Transliteration

1\. - - -] . . . . . [- - -
2\.] . *nti͗ n-drt pꜣi͗=k* . [. .] ⸢*n-i͗m=*⸣ . . [. . .] . [
3\. . .] . . *ꜥḳ* 10 *i͗rm* . . [. .] ⸢*n*⸣ *sṱy r pḥ* . [
4\. . . . . .] . . . *sẖ* [. .] *pr-ḥḏ r-šm n=f n-drt* . . [
5\. . . . .] *šm* ⸢*i͗w*⸣ . .[a] [. . *pꜣ*] ⸢*i͗*⸣*=f pr i͗w=f šny* . [
6\. . . . . . .] . . [. .] . . . . [. . . . .] . .[b] [

Notes on transliteration

a. *i͗w*, the copula, followed by further traces might be read here, but another possible reading would be *i͗w*, 'come'.

b. Possibly the final trace in this line may be of the first sign of *šny*, as in l. 5 above.

Translation

1\. *only traces*
2\.] . . . which is with/from your . . . .[
3\.] . . . 10 loaves together with . . . . in/of fire to reach [
4\.] . . . write/scribe [of the (?)] Treasury to go off by himself, when . . . [
5\.] go . . . . . . [. . . his] House,[a] as he was ill . . [
6\.] . . . . ill (?) [

Note on translation

a. Demotic *pr* is not to be expected as an ordinary word for 'house': unless some special phrase is in question here, it is natural to think in terms of a temple or palace.

DISCUSSION

This fragment appears to be of a continuous narrative text. Direct speech is attested by the 2nd pers. pronoun in l. 2. Although the contents would plainly suit a literary narrative, it is the hand that provides the strongest indication that this piece is literary in character.

15. NARRATIVE

Plate 15a

H5-DP524c [5984c] 12.0 cm. *h.* × 6.5 cm. *w.*

Sector 1 (North Courtyard) debris (1966–7)

The papyrus is fine-textured and translucent. Its shade is rather dark, and it has a slightly greyish tinge. The front (↔) surface preserves parts of 14 lines of continuous text, written along the fibres. The edges of the piece are torn on all sides, and no trace of any margin is preserved. The back (↕) surface is blank.

The **hand** of this fragment is another that very closely resembles those of **1** and **2** (perhaps especially the former), although the size of the writing and the spacing of the lines seem to rule out any possibility that it might belong to either of these texts.

Transliteration

1. - - -] . . . *pꜣ* . [- - -
2. .] . *wꜥ* ⌜*rmt*⌝ . [
3. . .] *r ỉr* . . . . [
4. . .] . . . . . [
5. . . .] . . *=f r-r=w* . . . [
6. . .] . *ḏd Pr-ꜥꜣ my* [
7. .] ⌜*Pr-ꜥꜣ Ḫꜥ=f-Rꜥ*⌝[a] [
8. . . . . . .] *ỉn*[b] [
9. . . . . . .] . . . . [
10. . . . . . .] ⌜*Pr-ꜥꜣ*⌝ [
11. . . . .] . . . . [.] ⌜*Pr-ꜥꜣ*⌝ . . [
12. . . . .] . . . . *r-ḥr=n bn(-pw)*⌜*=n ỉr pꜣ*⌝[c] [
13. . . . .] . . [.] . *nw* [
14. . . . .] . . -*Rꜥ*- .[d] [

Notes on transliteration

a. Although the papyrus is badly damaged, this reading is virtually certain. *Ḫꜥ* will have been written very similarly to the writing at **2** back, x+1/33, . The trace of the tail of the *=f* is quite clear, as are the opening and closing of the cartouche. The traces of *Pr-ꜥꜣ* preceding are also distinctive.

b. *ỉn*: .

c. The 1st pers. plur. suffix after *bn(-pw)* is not certain, as it is ligatured differently from that in *r-ḥr=n* in the same line: however, a reading *ḥrỉ* is not a convincing alternative.

d. This is presumably part of a proper name: certainly not *Ḫꜥ=f-Rꜥ* as written in l. 7 above.

Translation

1.] . . . the . . . [2.] . . . a man . . . [3.] to do . . . . . [4.] *only traces* [5.] he/him . . . to/from them . . . [6.] . . . Pharaoh said 'Let [7.] Pharaoh Khaʿfrēʿ [8.] not (?) [9.] *only traces* [10.] Pharaoh [11.] . . . . Pharaoh . . . [12.] . . . . from us. We (?) did not do the [13.] . . . . . see (?) [14.] . . . . -rēʿ- . . [

DISCUSSION

Despite its fragmentary condition, there can be little doubt that this text belongs to a literary narrative mentioning the Fourth Dynasty king Khaʿfrēʿ, Chephren. Although he was evidently a popular subject of ancient Egyptian story-telling, he has not previously been identified in demotic literature, but see p. 10, n. *h*.

16. NARRATIVE Plate 15a, b

H5-DP524d [5984d] 2.5 cm. *h.* × 3.5 cm. *w.*

Sector 1 (North Courtyard) debris (1966–7)

The papyrus is fine and even-textured, and is translucent. Its shade is rather dark. The edges of the piece are torn on all sides. The front (↔) surface preserves parts of 2 lines of text, written along the fibres: below these there stands up to 1.0 cm. of blank papyrus, but from so small a fragment it is impossible to judge whether this represents the bottom margin or the space between paragraphs of a literary text, or is to be explained in some other way. The back (↕) surface preserves parts of 3 lines of text, written across the fibres, and the other way up to the text on the front. No trace of any margin, or area of blank papyrus, is preserved.

The **hand** of this fragment is small and neat, and, as far as can be judged, is of the same general type as that of **1** and **2** in this volume. It is virtually certain that the hand on the front surface is the same as that upon the back. The damage that the piece has suffered makes detailed comparison with other texts difficult, but it seems to be a little more carelessly written than, for example, **1**, **2**, **14**, and **15**; and it is certainly not possible to state that the hand would be inappropriate for a private letter.

Transliteration

FRONT (↔)

— — — — — — — — — — —

1. - - - - .] . . [. .] . ⸢*bn(-pw)*⸣*=f* . . [- - -
2.] *ḥꜣt.t=f ẖ(r)* . . .[a] [

up to 1.0 cm. of blank papyrus

BACK (↕)

— — — — — — — — — — —

1. - - -] *di͗=f* ⸢*ḥr r*⸣ . [- - -
2.] . *pꜣ nti͗ i͗w* . . . . .[b] [
3. .] . . . ⸢*ẖpr*⸣ . . . ⸢*=f*⸣[c] [

— — — — — — — — — — —

Notes on transliteration

a. The reading of the signs *ẖr* seems certain, but the particle *ẖr* cannot be read, as it is always followed by a det. The traces might suit the verb *ẖ(r)ꜥry*, written , which occurs several times in texts in this volume: see the discussion on p. 24, n. *eu*, on **1**, 10/33.

b. The signs at the end of the line are badly rubbed: possibly read ***nti͗ i͗w pr***:- ***pr***, 'to come forth', *DG*, 134.7.

c. The high trace immediately before the *=f* does not support the obvious restoration *ẖpr n-i͗m=f*: possibly restore *ẖpr ḥn=f*, 'he ordered', or *i͗n=f*, 'he brought'.

Translation

FRONT 1.] . . . he did not . . . [2.] his heart angry(?) [

BACK 1.] he gave his attention to . . . [2.] . . . the one [from(?)] whom there came forth(?)[3.] . . . It happened, that he ordered (?) [

DISCUSSION

The hand and contents make it possible that this fragment might belong to a literary narrative text. The fact that the texts on front and back are written the opposite way up (cf. **10** above) must suggest a letter; but, with no clear indication of this from the contents, and as no other details of the format of the text are forthcoming, the piece seems worth presenting here.

17. NARRATIVE

Plate 15a, b

H5-DP524e [5984e] 4.0 cm. *h.* × 2.5 cm. *w.*

Sector 1 (North Courtyard) debris (1966–7)

As far as can be judged from a small and damaged piece, the papyrus is of rather poor quality. It is virtually opaque, and is of a dark shade. The front (↔) surface preserves parts of 6 lines of continuous text, written along the fibres. The back (↕) surface preserves parts of 6 lines of continuous text, written across the fibres, and the same way up as the text on the front. The edges of the piece are torn on all sides, and there is no trace of any margin on either surface.

The **hand** of this small fragment is particularly difficult to assess, as both surfaces are badly rubbed. It seems very probable that the hand on the front surface is the same as that upon the back. It is a small, fairly neat hand, apparently a literary hand of a type similar to that of **1** and **2** in this volume.

Transliteration

FRONT (↔)

— — — — — — — — —

1. - - -] . . . . [- - -
2.] . . . . . ⸢*dỉt*⸣ *ỉw*[a] [
3. . .] . . . . . *bw-ỉr* [
4.] . . . . . *m-ỉr* . [
5. . . . . . .] . . [
6. . . . .] . [

— — — — — — — — —

BACK (↕)

— — — — — — — — —

1. - - - . . . .] . [- - -
2. .] . . . . ⸢*ntỉ ỉw=k*⸣ . . . [
3.] . . . *mw* . . . . [
4.] *ẖn* ⸢*wtn*⸣ . [
5. ⸣ . . [
6. ⸣ . . [

— — — — — — — — —

Note on transliteration

a. The reading of the distinctive signs of *ỉw*, 'come', seems certain, and the preceding sign might well be read *dỉt*: conceivably] . . . *pꜣ ntỉ dỉt ỉw* might be read, but this is very uncertain.

Translation

FRONT

1.] *only traces* [2.] . . . . . caused to come [3.] . . . . does not [4.] . . . . . Do not [5–6. *only traces*

BACK

1.] *only traces* [2.] . . . which you . . . [3.] . . . water . . . . [4.] in (a) divine barque [5–6. *only traces*

DISCUSSION

The hand and layout suggest this text might be a literary narrative, and what little survives of the contents could at least be said to be consistent with this. The word *wtn*, '(divine) barque', in back, l. 4, is not a completely certain reading, but might indicate a literary text.

18. NARRATIVE

Plate 15a, b

H5-DP524f [5984f] 2.0 cm. *h.* × 1.5 cm. *w.*

Sector 1 (North Courtyard) debris (1966–7)

This very small fragment appears to consist of fine and even-textured papyrus, and it is translucent. Its shade is rather dark, and both surfaces are badly rubbed. The front (↔) surface preserves a few signs from 3 lines of text, written along the fibres, and the back (↕) surface preserves a few signs from 2 lines of text, written across the fibres, and the same way up as the text on the front. The edges of the piece are torn on all sides, and there is no sign of any margin.

Although only a few signs are preserved, the **hand** appears to be a small, neat, literary hand, in every way similar to that of **1** and **2** in this volume. The hand on the front seems to be the same as that on the back.

Transliteration

FRONT (↔)

— — — — — —

1. - - - - . . .] . [- - -
2.] . . . . . [
3. .] . . . [

— — — — — —

BACK (↕)

— — — — — —

1. - - - *ḥ*]⌜*wn*⌝*y*[a] [- - -
2.] . ⌜*šr*⌝ [. .] . [

— — — — — —

Note on transliteration

a. It seems certain that the surviving signs are to be restored , which strongly suggests that *ḥwny*, 'youth' (*DG*, 296. 4), should be read.

DISCUSSION

This minute fragment is included here because the hand suggests that it may well belong to **1** or **2** in this volume, although it has not proved possible to join it to either text, nor are there good grounds for deciding to which text it is more likely to belong.

19. NARRATIVE

Plate 15a, b

H5-DP524g [5984g] 2.5 cm. *h.* × 2.0 cm. *w.*

Sector 1 (North Courtyard) debris (1966–7)

This small fragment is badly worn: the papyrus appears to be translucent, and its shade is rather dark. The front (↔) surface preserves parts of 4 lines of text, written along the fibres, and the back (↕) surface preserves parts of 4 lines of text, written across the fibres, and the same way up as the text on the front. The edges of the piece are torn on all sides. A small blank space is preserved at the end of back, l. 3, but it is impossible to judge its significance: apart from this there is no sign of any margin.

As far as can be judged, the **hand** of this fragment is a small, neat, literary hand resembling that of **1** and **2** in this volume. The hand on the front seems to be the same as that on the back.

Transliteration

FRONT (↔)

— — — — — — —

- - - . .] . [- - -

.] . . . . [

] . *ḏd=y* . . [

] . . . . [

— — — — — — —

BACK (↕)

— — — — — — —

- - - .] . . . . . [- - -

] . . . . . . [

] . . *=s n=w* vacat [

] . . . . . . [

— — — — — — —

DISCUSSION

This small fragment is included here because the hand suggests that it might possibly belong to **1** or **2** in this volume, or to a similar text. However, it has not proved possible to assign it to any particular text.

20. NARRATIVE Plate 15a

H5-DP524h [5984h] 2.0 cm. *h.* × 2.0 cm. *w.*

Sector 1 (North Courtyard) debris (1966–7)

The papyrus of this small fragment is opaque, and its shade is greyish. The front (↔) surface preserves traces of 2 lines of text, written along the fibres, and the back surface is blank. The edges of the piece are torn on all sides, and there is no trace of any margin.

The **hand** appears to be a small, neat, literary hand, similar to that of **1** and **2** in this volume

Transliteration

— — — — — —
1. - - -] . . . . . [- - -
2.] . *pꜣ i-ỉr* . [
— — — — — —

DISCUSSION

This small fragment is included here because its hand suggests that it may belong to **1** or **2**, or a similar literary text, although it has not been possible to assign it to any one text in this volume.

21. NARRATIVE

Plate 15a, b

H5-DP524j [5984j] 5.0 cm. *h.* × 4.0 cm. *w.*

Sector 1 (North Courtyard) debris (1966–7)

The papyrus of this fragment is even-textured, thin, and translucent. Its shade is light brown. The front (↔) surface preserves parts of 7 lines of continuous text, written along the fibres, and the back (↕) surface preserves parts of 8 lines of continuous text, written across the fibres, and the same way up as the text on the front. The edges of the piece are torn on all sides, and no trace of any margin is preserved.

Although the back (↕) surface of this fragment is badly worn, it seems clear that the **hand** on each surface is one and the same. It is a small, neat, literary hand, closely resembling that of **1** and **2** in this volume, although a little smaller and more careless than most of what is preserved of either. The orthography of two words, *ỉrm* and *n=s*, differs significantly from that found in **1** and **2**.

Transliteration

FRONT (↔)

1. - - - . . . . . .] . . . . [- - -
2.] . . . . . . *wꜥb=s pꜣ* .[a] [
3.] . . .[b] *i-ỉr-ḥr pꜣỉ* (*=y*) *ỉt ỉrm* . [
4.] ⸢*ỉw*⸣*=y ỉỉ.k r-bnr ỉrm* [
5. .] ⸢*tḥ*⸣*r ḏd=f n=s* [. . . .] . . [
6.] . . . *ṱ* . . . .[c] ⸢*ḏd=f n=s*⸣ [
7.] . . . . [

BACK (↕)

1. - - - . . .] . . [- - -
2. . . .] . . *ṯꜣỉ=w* . . . . . [
3.] .*=s rk ỉw=s* . . . . [
4.] . . . . *gp g*(*r*)*ty*[d] . . . . [
5. . . .] . . . *=f ḏd* . . . . . [
6.] . . . [. . .] . . . . [
7.] . . . . ⸢*ḏd n=s*⸣ . . . ⸢*ỉw=f ḏd*⸣ [
8. . . . .] . . [

Notes on transliteration

a. In view of the apparent following def. article, and the lack of any alternative interpretation of this line, *wꜥb* must presumably be taken as a verb with pronoun following.

b. Presumably a subject or object pronoun must be read before *i-ỉr-ḥr*.

c. Probably [*ꜥꜣ*]*y.ṱ n ms*. . . . . might be read: cf. **1a**, l. 20.

d. The dets. of the last legible word are certainly . It might therefore be read *g*(*r*)*ty*, 'knife' (unless *pty*, 'bow' might as a weapon be written with these dets.). This being so, *gp*, 'to grasp', is a preferable reading of the preceding word, rather than *sgp* etc.

Translation

FRONT

1.] *only traces* [
2.] . . . . . she/it was pure; the . . . [
3.] . . . . . before my father with . . . [
4.] I came out with . . . . . [
5.] grief. He said to her . . . . [
6.] older (?) . . . . . He said to her [
7.] *only traces* [

BACK

1.] *only traces* [
2.] . . . they took . . . . . [
3.] . . . . . turn, she . . . . [
4.] . . . . . seize (a) knife . . . . . [
5.] . . . said . . . . . [
6.] *only traces* [
7.] . . . said to her . . . . . he said [
8.] *only traces* [

DISCUSSION

All the indications of hand and layout, together with the short phrases that can be understood of the contents, suggest this fragment belonged to a literary narrative. It is most unlikely that it could belong to **1** or **2**, and there is no reason to link it with any other text in this volume.

22. A NARRATIVE MENTIONING DJEḤO, SON OF NEKHTANEBOF(?)

Plate 15c

H5-17A [661A] 7.0 cm. *h.* × 7.0 cm. *w.*

Sector 1, debris (1965–6)

The papyrus is even-textured and translucent. Its shade is a little darker than average, and there is a patch of light-brown stain. The edges of the piece are torn on all sides, and a small portion is torn and missing from the middle. The front surface preserves parts of 6 lines of continuous text, written along the fibres. No trace of any margin is preserved. The back surface preserves traces of the ends of 3 lines of demotic, written the same way up as the text on the front: no attempt is made to transcribe the verso traces here.

The **hand** is fairly small, and is neatly and skilfully written. It is of a similar type to that of **1** and **2** in this volume.

Transliteration

— — — — — — — — — — — — — — — —

1. - - - . . . .] . [. . . .] . [- - -
2. . . . .] . . . . .[a] *tꜣ pšt* . . . . .[b] [
3.] . . . *=f*[c] *m-šs šm Pr-ꜥꜣ r pr*[d] [
4.] . *bꜣk.w n Ḏd* .[e] [. .] *Nḫt-nb=f*[f] [
5.] . . .[g] *r-ẖ(t) pꜣ ntỉ ỉw=w ỉr=f n* . . . *Prs*[h] [
6.] *Nḫt-nb=f dỉ* . . . [. . . .] . [

— — — — — — — — — — — — — — — —

Notes on transliteration

a. Before *tꜣ pšt*, a det. followed by suffix *=w* are possible readings, perhaps preceded by *ḳ*.

b. The reading *tꜣ pšt* seems certain. At the end of the line, the signs suit *ḏꜣḏꜣ* much better than *ỉꜣbt*, and *pšt* is hardly likely to have as a geographical det.: perhaps *tꜣ pšt ḥnꜥ ḏꜣḏꜣ*, in which *ḏꜣḏꜣ* might have the sense of 'capital'? However, the context is quite uncertain.

c. Although the signs are damaged, a det. seems possible before *=f*. The phrase *m-šs* usually follows circumstantial expressions or adjectives. However, the verb *mkḥ* (*mḳḥ*), 'to be sad, in pain', is found in a *sdm=f* form with *n-m-šs* following at 2. Kh. 5/34: another possibility might be to restore (*ỉw*) *nꜣ-bỉn=f*.

d. Almost certainly *šm Pr-ꜥꜣ r pr-Pr-ꜥꜣ* is to be restored here: cf. **1**, 13/24, and 14/10.

e. The reading of *ḏd* seems certain, and none of the signs that follow can be tall. In the context, with *bꜣk.w n* preceding (most probably *bꜣk* in the sense 'servant', being written with no det., rather than 'tax' or 'document'), it seems impossible to understand *ḏd* as the verb, 'to say'. The most probable restoration is *Ḏd-ḥr sꜣ Nḫt-nb=f*.

f. Clearly the same personal name is to be read here as in l. 6 below. Here in l. 4, traces of the final *=f* are plainly visible. In l. 6, the *=f* and personal-name det. are completely preserved. The first signs of the name are almost certainly to be read *nḫt*, and therefore there seems no alternative to reading the name as *Nḫt-nb=f*, although the form of the *nb* element is surprising. Although they are damaged, none of the writings of the names in ll. 4–6 appear to have the form of royal names.

g. The traces at the beginning of l. 5 might be of the proper name *Ḏd-ḥr* (cf. n. *e* above).

h. *Prs*, 'Persian', written , seems a certain reading. In view of the very small space for any restoration before *Prs*, the reading *n* ⌜*nꜣ rmt*⌝*.w Prs* (cf. Canopus 3:12) seems plausible.

Translation

— — — — — — — — — — — — — —

1. *only traces*
2.] . . . . the share . . . . [
3.] . . . . . very much. Pharaoh went to the palace of Pharaoh [
4.] . . servants of Dje[ḥo, son of] Nekhtanebof [
5.] . . . in accordance with that which is done . . . . . Persian[a] [
6.] Nekhtanebof . . . . . . gave/caused . . . .[

— — — — — — — — — — — — — —

Note on translation

a. Perhaps the sense is 'in accordance with that which is done for (*or* to) the men of Persia, the Persians'.

DISCUSSION

This fragment certainly belongs to a continuous narrative text, although whether it was of a literary or documentary character is hard to decide. The stock phrase 'Pharaoh went to the palace of Pharaoh' in l. 3 certainly has literary parallels. The reading of l. 2 is very uncertain, but the one extremely tentative suggestion made on p. 188, n. *b* has a documentary tone.

The principal interest of the text is the probable mention of a private individual named Djeḥo son of Nekhtanebof in connection with 'that which is done for (*or* to) the men of Persia'. The possibility must be considered that the man referred to is the Pharaoh Djeḥo (generally called in modern works 'Tachos') son of Nekhtanebof (i.e. the earlier of the two kings Nectanebo), perhaps after he had fled to the Persian Court upon the collapse of the Egyptian advance into Syria in 360 BC. The form of the names cannot settle this point. Whether or not the persons named are royal would do little to determine if the text is literary or documentary. It should also be pointed out that, if the text can be seen as literary, then the occurrence of this kind of name is of interest, even if entirely private individuals are in question.

23. A NARRATIVE MENTIONING A JOURNEY

Plate 15d

H5-17B [661 B] 8.0 cm. *h.* × 7.5 cm. *w.*

Sector 1, debris (1965–6)

The papyrus is of mediocre quality, but quite thin and translucent. The front surface preserves parts of 9 lines of continuous text, written along the fibres. The left-hand edge of the piece is torn and irregular, but the right-hand edge and the top and bottom edges are straight, and appear to have been cut. The back surface preserves traces of a demotic account, written the other way up to the text on the front. Although it is damaged, it may have been complete in 5 lines: it is plausible that both the top and bottom edges, which interrupt the text on the front, were cut when a small piece of papyrus was being prepared for this account. On the front, a margin of 1.0 cm. is preserved between the beginnings of the lines of text and the right-hand edge of the piece, and it is uncertain at what stage this edge was cut: a margin of 1.5 cm. stands before the beginnings of the lines of the text on the back.

The **hand** is fairly large and rounded, and is very rapidly written. It is an informal hand, and most resembles some of the letter hands from Saqqâra.

Transliteration

— — — — — — — — — — — —

1. [. . . . . . .] . . . [- - -
2. *n pꜣ dmỉ bn(-pw)=y md* . . .[a] [
3. *n-ỉm=w*[b] *ḫpr dwy n* . . .[c] [
4. *ḫd*⌜*y*⌝ . . . .[d] [
5. *pḥ=y pꜣ sbṯ n* [
6. *=y*[e] *n nꜣ mdwt ntỉ ḫpr n pꜣ* .[f] [
7. *nꜣ mdwt ntỉ ḫpr n-ỉm=*⌜*w*⌝[g] [
8. *stby*[h] *ỉr=y* [
9. . .[j] *rsty* . . . [

— — — — — — — — — — — —

Notes on transliteration

a. The traces at the end of l. 2 suggest the reading of the negative word *ỉn*, but all the evidence of other Saqqâra papyri indicates that the preceding negative  should be read *bn(-pw)=y*, and therefore the traces here must be interpreted in some other way. The first sign has every appearance of being a distinctive *ỉ*. The context makes it unlikely, but not impossible, that one of the other *ỉn* words is in question.

b. Most probably *n-ỉm=w* is to be read here, written : compare the writing  in l. 7 below, which is not precisely identical. Some Roman literary demotic texts appear to employ a writing of ***n-ỉm=w*** that ends with a -sign, as an alternative to the normal writings, and it is probable that such writings are specifically used for ***n-ỉm=w*** in the sense of 'there', in other words, **ⲙⲙⲁⲩ** rather than **ⲙⲙⲟⲟⲩ**. The present text may similarly employ two distinct writings, and the sense 'there' may be to be understood in l. 3, and 'to them' in l. 7.

c. The traces at the end of the line suggest that a

month and day date might be restored, *tpy* . . .: after the initial vertical stroke, only very slight traces are preserved.

d. The traces following *ḫdy* are . The first sign seems more likely to read *pꜣỉ* than *pꜣ* (cf. writings of *pꜣ* in ll. 2, 5, and 6(?)), unless part of the following sign has run into it. It does not seem possible to read *pꜣỉ=k*.

e. The reading of a suffix *=y* belonging to a word in the previous line seems inescapable. This phenomenon is found in demotic letters, but is also known in literary texts, at any rate from the Roman period.

f. The reading *n pꜣ* seems more likely than a more rounded form of *n-ỉm=* (see p. 190, n. *b*), which should contain one more stroke.

g. Probably read *n-ỉm=w*, in the sense 'the things that had happened to them': cf. n. *b* above.

h. *stby*, determined with , can hardly represent *stb* 'evil', from the old *sḏb* (*DG*, 476. 4); but the word for 'implement', 'weapon' is normally written *stbḥ* or *stbḥ=f* (*DG*, 476. 5: Coptic ⲥⲧⲉⲃⲁⲉⲓϩ, Crum, *CD*, 363b or ⲥⲟⲧⲃⲉϥ, ibid.). In view of this, and as no definite or indefinite article is preserved, *stby* might be taken as a writing of the verb *sbt*, 'to prepare' (*DG*, 424. 1).

j. Reading uncertain: *pꜣ rsty* or *pꜣỉ=f rsty* seems possible.

Translation

— — — — — — — — — — — — — —

1.] *only traces* [
2. in the city. I did not speak . . . [
3. there. There came the morning of . . . . . [
4. northwards . . . . [
5. I reached the wall/fortress of [
6. I [told/heard?] the things that had happened in/to the [
7. the things that had happened there/to them [
8. prepare(?). I made [
9. . . . . . next day . . . . . [

— — — — — — — — — — — — — —

DISCUSSION

This fragment preserves part of a narrative, frequently employing the first person, and probably entirely couched in direct speech. It might belong to a story, or to a letter, report or petition. The hand of the text, and, to a lesser extent, the shape of the fragment, give some support to the possibility that it belongs to a letter. However, no obvious restorations to provide the very short line lengths that would be expected in a letter in the upright format suggest themselves. The contents might be entirely appropriate in a literary story, but no distinctive phrases are preserved to establish if the text is literary or documentary.

APPENDIX

It does not seem possible to decide whether the account on the back is or is not in the same hand as the text on the front; it does not exhibit any clear connection with it, and therefore is simply transliterated separately here: 1. *250 gr 300* [2. *mḥ=w n ḥꜣt-sp 3.t ꜣbd 3* . . [3. [. . .]. . . . . . [4. . . . . *3.t* . . . . [5. . . . .[

TEXT 24

24. A NARRATIVE MENTIONING THE GREAT MEN OF PHARAOH — Plate 16a

H5-DP204 [1802] 16.5 cm. *h.* × 15.5 cm. *w.*

Sector 1 (North Courtyard) debris (1966–7)

The papyrus is fairly coarse-textured, but is thin and translucent. The front surface of the fragment is discoloured by an even grey wash, which is presumably due to the erasure of a previous text. Parts of 6 lines of continuous text are preserved, written along the fibres. 2.5 cm. of blank papyrus are preserved at the foot of the fragment; but, although all the edges are roughly straight, the piece has probably been torn on all sides. Evidently it originally belonged to a roll. A normal join between two sheets of papyrus is preserved 2.0 cm. from the right-hand edge. The back (↕) surface is blank.

The text is written in a large, bold, and formal **hand**, of a kind commonly found in legal instruments. The hand shows every sign of being early, both in its general appearance, and in various details: the form of *pꜣỉ=* in l. 2, 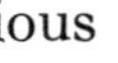, may be noted, and the long, flat top of *ntỉ* in l. 3, and the det.  in l. 6. The hand is probably Saïte in date, and certainly no comparable hand is preserved from after the first Persian period.

Transliteration

— — — — — — — — — — — — — — — —

1. - - - - . .] . . [. . .] . . . . [- - -
2. . .] . .[a] *ḏd nꜣ rmtw ꜥꜣyw Pr-ꜥꜣ pꜣỉ⸢=n⸣*[b] [
3.] . *hp*[c] *ntỉ ỉw tꜣ kny*[d] *Pr-ꜥꜣ* . [
4.] *m-bꜣḥ Pr-ꜥꜣ tꜣỉ nꜣ mdwt* . . . .[e] [
5.] ⸢*hp*⸣ *ḏd=w n(=y) mtw=k rmt-rḫ ỉw=k rḫ ỉr* ⸢*hp*⸣ [
6.] . . .[f] *ḏd Pr-ꜥꜣ ỉ-ỉr* ⸢*hp*⸣ [

2.5 cm. of blank papyrus

Notes on transliteration

a. The trace preserved at the beginning of the line is probably of the det. : cf. n. *f* below.

b. Probably restore *pꜣỉ=n* [*nb ꜥꜣ ỉ Pr-ꜥꜣ*.

c. As it seems impossible to read *pꜣ hp*, or *pꜣỉ hp*, presumably *hp* is not by itself the antecedent of *ntỉ ỉw*: it is conceivable that *pꜣỉ=s hp*, 'her judgement', etc., might be restored, but there appears to be no parallel for such a phrase.

d. The writing of *kny* is 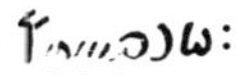: the dets. strongly suggest that the word should be identified with *ḳnḥ*, 'shrine' (*DG*, 541. 3), although the omission of the *ḥ* is a problem: possibly it may be connected with the existence of a Coptic Bohairic form ⲕⲉϩⲛⲓ (see Crum, *CD*, 113a, ⲕⲛϩⲉ). Conceivably the word might be a fem. form of the word for 'carrying-chair': cf. *ḳny*, *DG*, 540. 1 (masc.) and *ḳnj.t*, *Wb*. v. 52. 1 ff.

e. If *tꜣỉ*, the copula, ends a sentence, it might be possible to read the beginning of the next sentence *nꜣ mdwt r-ḏd* . . . [. Presumably *nꜣ mdwt* is to be read here, as, in l. 3, *tꜣ* has the form .

f. The signs at the beginning of l. 6, , might well be restored as part of *ḳn*, 'brave', 'strong' (*DG*, 539. 2).

Translation

— —

1.] *only traces* [
2.] . . . . . The great men of Pharaoh said: 'Our [great lord,
3.] . . judgement, which the chapel of Pharaoh . . .[α] [
4.] in the presence of Pharaoh. The words that [. . . .] spoke [
5.] judgement. They said to me: 'You are a wise man, who is able to execute judgement.[β] [
6.] . . . . . Pharaoh said: 'Execute judgement [

Notes on translation

α. Two kinds of restoration seem possible here. 1. 'the . . . of judgement which is in (resides in?) the chapel of Pharaoh', understanding *ntỉ ỉw (n) tꜣ kny*; 2. 'the . . . of judgement, that the chapel of Pharaoh (for example) ordered'.

The term here translated 'chapel' presents a lexicographic problem (see p. 192, n. *d*). The writing, however, indicates that a building (or at least some kind of structure) of religious significance should be in question. Even if the translation 'chapel' is secure, close parallels for the subject-matter are needed to clarify the context.

β. For a survey of the uses of *hp* in legal and other contexts, see C. F. Nims, 'The term *hp*, 'law, right', in demotic', *JNES* 7 (1948), 243–60. A translation 'act justly' does not seem likely.

DISCUSSION

This fragment plainly concerns judicial matters, and presumably a case heard before Pharaoh. It might well be a documentary report; but there is nothing to suggest that it could not belong to a story: the phrases in l. 2 are common in narratives, and the comparatively well-preserved sentence in l. 5 clearly could occur in a story.

25. A NARRATIVE INCLUDING AN OATH BEFORE PHARAOH

Plate 16b

71/72-DP134 [5820] 12.5 cm. *h.* × 10.5 cm. *w.*

Sector 7, West Dump

The papyrus is opaque and coarse-textured. The front surface has a marked grey tinge, which is probably due to the erasure of a previous text or texts. The back surface is free of this grey discoloration, and is of a dark-straw shade. The edges of the fragment are torn on all sides. The front (↔) surface preserves parts of 9 lines of continuous demotic text, written along the fibres: no part of any margin survives. This text is that edited here. The back (↕) surface preserves part of a text written across the fibres and the other way up to the text on the front.

The **hand** of the text on the front is large, and is rapidly written with a brush that permits an untidy variation in the thickness of the strokes. The hand is rounded, and signs are sometimes ligatured together with rounded movements of the brush. A writing of *ꜥšꜣ*, 'many', that is typical of early papyri occurs in l. 7 (see p. 195, n. *k*). Although the readings are not certain, *nb* and the following groups in l. 8 are plainly of an early form. The hand does not resemble any of the formal literary hands from Saqqâra, nor the report hands. Its informality makes it difficult to compare with other material, but it seems likely to be an early hand, perhaps of the First Persian Period, although no precision is possible concerning its date.

Transliteration

— — — — — — — — — — — — — —

1. - - - . .] . . . .⌜*ỉw*⌝=*w h* . [.] . .[a] [- - -
2.] *Pr-ꜥꜣ ỉẖ*[b] *pꜣ tꜣ ỉw=f* . . .[c] [
3. . .] *mdwt ỉw=w pḥ r pꜣ ntr nꜣ-w* ⌜*bw*⌝-[*ỉr*[d]
4. . .] . . *mn*[e] *m-bꜣḥ Pr-ꜥꜣ* [
5. .] . . . .[f] *rmt nb ꜥnẖ ḥr=k ꜥnẖ nꜣỉ=k ntrw* . [
6.] *nꜣ rmt.w ntỉ ẖꜣꜥ pꜣ hp mtw=w ḏd ỉw mn* .[g] [
7.] . .[h] *ẖpr šꜥ{-tw}*[j] *rnpt ꜥšꜣ.w*[k] *ỉ-ỉr=w*[l]. . . [
8.] ⌜*Pr-ꜥꜣ*⌝ . . . . . *ḏt*[m] *ỉ-*⌜*ỉr=y*⌝ . . . [
9. . .] . . . *y*[n] [. . . .] . . . . [

— — — — — — — — — — — — — —

Notes on transliteration

a. The restoration of l. 1 is not certain. In the middle of the line, *ỉw=w* seems the only natural reading of the signs ſȷı, and the preceding traces seem to exclude the reading *pꜣỉ=w*. Following *ỉw=w*, *h* is certain. The possibility must be considered that this and the following traces belong to *hp*, written, as in l. 6, with the final vertical stroke well spaced from the first signs of the word. However, the second sign is not entirely convincing as *p*, even when allowance is made for the fibres displaced at its top; and a verb is required after *ỉw=w*. Possibly *hn* might be read, or conceivably *hp* as a writing of the verb 'to hide' (*DG*, 275.1 →302. 2). The final traces in the line might read *rmt nb*: cf. l. 5 below.

b. The reading of *ỉẖ*, 'what', here seems certain: contrast the writings of *ꜥnẖ* in l. 5 below.

c. The restoration *ỉw=f wš* is plausible, *wš* being written : *ỉw=f k* . . [might possibly be read.

d. The final signs in l. 3 are plainly . At the beginning of a sentence the restoration of *bw-ỉr* is overwhelmingly probable.

e. The apparent presence of the group suggests the verb *mn* in an unexpected writing (the pen has made the initial *m*-sign in two detached strokes, but, even if the reading *mn* is rejected, it is difficult to interpret this sign other than as *m*). The verb might be *mn*, 'to remain', but the final det. perhaps suggests *mn*, 'to land', in the sense 'to die'. Cf. a similarly problematic writing in text no. **5**, 1/3.

f. The group here is likely to be a det. similar to that of *hp* in l. 6, and probably *i-ỉr-ḥr rmt nb* cannot be read. The restoration *smy rmt nb*, 'Everyone cried . . .', might be considered.

g. The slight traces would suit the restoration *ỉw mn mtw* very well.

The context does not suggest how the problematic *ỉw* before *mn* should be explained here.

h. At the beginning of l. 7, the restoration *i-ỉr ḫpr* would suit the traces: perhaps *pꜣ i-ỉr ḫpr*, 'that which had happened'.

j. The form *šʿ-tw* (the writing proper to the suffix conjugation, Coptic ϣⲁ(ⲛ)ⲧ(ⲉ)=) is presumably written for the preposition *šʿ* in this common phrase.

k. The writing of *ʿšꜣ(w)* here is a notably early form: cf. Ryl., iii. 337.

l. The reading *i-ỉr=w* seems certain. The extra stroke at the foot of the first stroke may be a smudge, or possibly the sign is intended to be of the form : *bw-ỉr* would certainly be written with a more substantial first sign (cf. l. 3 above).

m. The reading of *Pr-ʿꜣ* is certain (cf. l. 2 above), and so is that of *ḏt*, written, as often, . Possibly should be understood as an almost hieratic writing of the common phrase *ʿnḫ ḏt*, and the traces immediately following *Pr-ʿꜣ* might be restored , *nb*. It is dubious if *nb=y*, 'my Lord', is a possibility, but one of the many phrases 'Lord, possessor of . . .' might be restored, perhaps in abbreviated writing.

n. Perhaps restore *ḳy*, 'high' (*DG*, 531. 7), written] ///.

Translation

1.] . . . . as they . . . . [
2.] Pharaoh: 'What on earth does he lack (?) [
3.] They are matters that affect/come to the attention of the God. [. . . . . . .] do not [
4.] . . . die (?) in the presence of Pharaoh' [
5.] everyone [shouted (?)]: 'As your highness lives,[α] as your Gods live,' [
6.] the men who abandon the law, and they say: 'We (?) have no' [
7.] that had happened, for many years. They . . [
8.] Pharaoh, Lord (?) . . . , may he live for ever, I . . .[β] [
9.] high (?) [

Notes on translation

α. This is the form of the royal oath used in Pharaoh's presence, literally 'as your face lives'. See for example ʿOnchsheshonqy, 4/2.

β. It is not possible to be certain if these phrases belong to words spoken directly to Pharaoh.

DISCUSSION

This fragment plainly narrates part of a debate, possibly a judicial case, before Pharaoh. It is quite impossible to judge from the contents whether the text is a documentary report of an actual case, or represents an episode from a story. The ungainly, informal hand, and the fact that the papyrus has been reused, does nothing to settle the question.

26. A NARRATIVE MENTIONING KHAʿḤAPE (?) Plate 16c

71/72-DP156 [5842] 8.5 cm. *h.* × 7.0 cm. *w.*

Sector 7, surface debris

The papyrus is just translucent, and is of mediocre quality. Both surfaces have a marked grey tinge, which is probably due to the erasure of previous texts. This discoloration is of a darker shade upon the back of the piece. In some places on both surfaces it has been removed by the wear that the fragment has suffered. The text is written along the fibres: parts of 6 lines of continuous text are preserved. The edges of the fragment are torn on all sides, and no part of any margin survives. The back (↕) surface is blank (apart from the discoloration mentioned above).

The **hand** is fairly large, and is rapidly written with a brush that in places seems rather ragged. It is angular, and a number of strokes markedly slope to the right. The poor state of preservation of the fragment makes its appearance difficult to judge, but the hand seems quite skilled, and to resemble some of the literary hands in this volume: it is most similar to the hands of **4** and **5**.

Transliteration

— — — — — — — — — — — — — —

1. - - - . . . .] . . . .[a] [- - -
2. . .] . . . . . *pꜣ nti rwš i pꜣi(=y)* .[b] [
3.]. . . *bn(-pw)=f gm-ṯ=s* ⸢*ḥꜣt*⸣[c] *ḏd n=f* ⸢*ntr*⸣[d] [
4.] *m-ir dit ir* . .[e] . . . . .[f] *ḫpr iw=y* . [
5.] . . . . .[g] *pꜣ ntr* . *pꜣi=f* . . .[h] *n ḥꜣt* [
6.] . . . . ⸢*s-ḥmt 2.t*⸣[j] . . . . [

— — — — — — — — — — — — — —

Notes on transliteration

a. Possibly read] . . . *=f ʿn tw=y* . . . [.

b. The most probable restoration is *pꜣi(=y) nb* [*ʿꜣ*], *nb* being written in the early form .

c. *gm-ṯ=s* is an obvious reading, and the following signs can be plausibly explained only as *(n-)ḥꜣt*, 'formerly', : presumably a blot of ink has distorted the top of the sign.

d. The reading *ntr* seems very probable: the fact that *ntr* is generally, except in certain circumstances, preceded by an article suggests here the restoration *ntr nb*.

e. Because of the det., it seems unlikely that the verb *gm* can be read here, even although l. 3 might suggest that *m-ir dit gm-ṯ=s* ⸢*Ḫʿ-Ḥp*⸣ would be appropriate. Perhaps *m-ir dit ir-st* ⸢*Ḫʿ-Ḥp*⸣ is the most probable reading (a form *ir.ṯ=s* with a *ṯ* is not to be expected).

f. A proper name, possibly *Ḫʿ-Ḥp*, might be read here: the signs appear to be .

g. A word ending . . .*y*, with a double det., the second of which is , seems likely here. This may be a verb: an *=s* suffix might follow, or a reflexive object-pronoun *-s* (which would imply that *pꜣ ntr* was the subject).

h. The readings in this line are far from certain: *pꜣi=f wʿb* seems a likely reading, in which case *pꜣ ntr n pꜣi=f wʿb n ḥꜣt* [would be the natural restoration, even though it may be tempting to understand *wʿb n ḥꜣt* as 'pure in heart'. The phrase 'his priest' virtually demands that a god be the antecedent of 'his'.

j. The readings here are dubious, and the context obscure.

Translation

— — — — — — — — — — — — — —

1.] . . . . . him/it again. I(?) . . . . . [
2.] . . . . . . the one who cared. 'O my [great lord (?)[α]
3.] . . . . he had not found her/it previously. [Every] god said to him [
4.] 'Do not permit Khaʿḥape (?)[β] to do it.' It happened that I [
5.] . . . . the god to/from his priest in the heart [
6.] . . . . two women (?) . . . . . [

— — — — — — — — — — — — — —

Notes on translation

α. This phrase, which, it must be noted, is very largely restored, might suggest that the king is being addressed here.

β. The reading of the personal name Khaʿḥape is by no means certain: if it is correct, then it may be said that it is not a name hitherto known from demotic literature, and would not be out of place in a documentary text. But it does not offer strong grounds for arguing that the text is not literary.

DISCUSSION

The nature of this text is quite uncertain. It contains some direct speech, and, in fact, it is conceivable that all that survives is direct speech. The fragment might belong to a story, or to a report, petition, or letter.

27. COPYBOOK, INCLUDING NAMES OF BIRDS, TREES, AND PLACES

Plate 17

71/72-DP111+129+133 [5797+5815+5819]
Overall: 35.0 cm. *h.*×17.0 cm. *w.*

Sector 7, West Dump

The papyrus is opaque and coarse-textured. The three fragments joined together clearly represent almost the full height of the original sheet, although the top edge is torn and uneven, and the bottom edge is not perfectly clean cut. The front (↔) surface preserves part of 21 lines of continuous text. This is divided into two sections where the nature of the contents of the text appears to change between ll. 14 and 15: either a space equivalent to one line of writing has been left blank between these two lines, or the first section ended with a short line, nothing of which is preserved, and the second was begun at the start of a fresh line (i.e. l. 15). The column height is 31.0 cm. It is quite impossible to judge from external features the original length of the lines (the maximum line length preserved is 14.5 cm.: any plausible restoration of ll. 2–4 would demand a line length at least a little longer than this minimum), or whether the surviving column originally stood alone or formed part of a roll. The bottom margin varies from 1.5 to 2.0 cm., and up to 2.0 cm. of the top margin are preserved.

Towards the bottom of the column, there is a horizontal band of grey discoloration, almost certainly due to the washing-off of writing. (This band occupies the area that lies between 17.5 and 6.0 cm. from the bottom of the sheet; in the plate, its extent is disguised by the difference of shade between the two lower fragments.) A possible explanation is that a roll or portion of a roll bearing a contract, written in the common format of a single broad column only a few lines deep, has been reused for the present copybook text: the contract has been washed off and the front surface of the papyrus has been reused, the other way up.

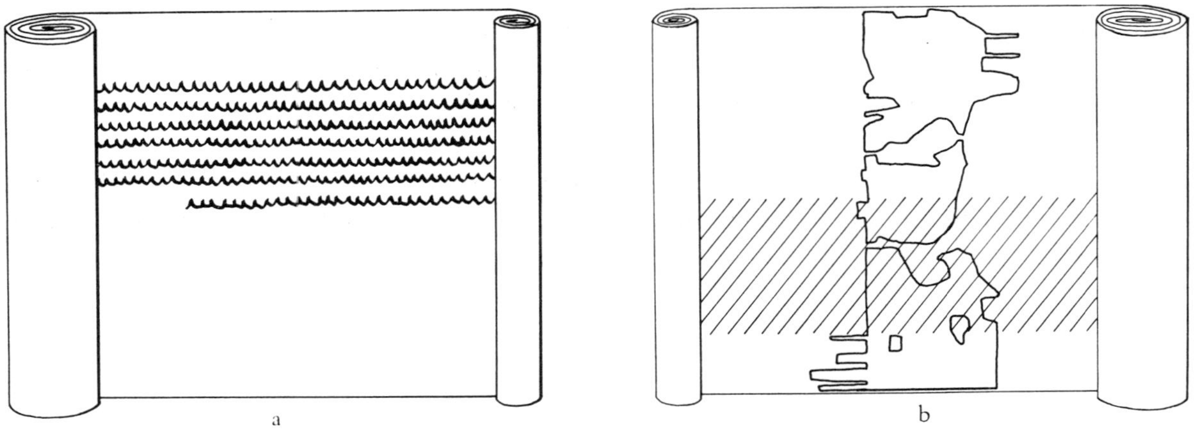

FIG. 3 Text **27**: a. hypothetical reconstruction of roll bearing original documentary text; b. diagram showing relation of extant fragments to roll.

On close examination, an explanation of this kind is more plausible than to suppose that a portion of the present text has been erased and rewritten. If the papyrus has indeed been reused the wrong way up, then this might suggest that it is more likely that a sheet cut from a roll, rather than a complete roll, has been employed. However, this line of speculation cannot rule out the possibility that the text may have been an extensive one.

The back (↕) surface is blank.

The **hand** is large, and, although the text is rapidly and carelessly written, it seems to be the work of a practised scribe. It might therefore be mistaken to try to explain the numerous anomalies and obscurities in the text, especially those involving matters of orthography, as due merely to the blunders of a beginner. The hand does not closely resemble any of the other hands in this volume.

A mark of punctuation in the form of a short diagonal stroke is often, but not consistently, used: those examples that are well preserved and beyond doubt are indicated by a colon (:) in the transliteration. There are traces of a number of corrections. For example, in l. 2 a few signs have been roughly sponged away, and the text rewritten (see p. 200, n. *h*); in l. 5 a correction appears to have been made without any attempt to erase the faulty text (see p. 203, n. *v*). In the last two lines, the writing is very careless, and some signs, either through haste or because of corrections, appear to overlap one another. In two places (ll. 12 and 13) the preposition *r* is omitted, although written out in parallel phrases in the preceding lines. The name of the *mnw*-bird occurs in a slightly different writing in l. 4 from that in l. 9, *H̱ry* seems to be written with a different shape of *ẖ* in l. 1 from that in l. 21, and two forms of *p* and two forms of *š* occur (see pp. 200–7, nn. *c*, *w*, *x*, *be*).

Transliteration

up to 2.0 cm. of blank papyrus

1. ---] . . . . .[a] [. .] . . . .[b] *.rgy Yb*[c] *tꜣ/nꜣ H̱ry*[d] *r* . .[e] [- - -
2. .] . [. . . . .] *pꜣ hb*[f] *ḥr pꜣ hbyn*[g] *pꜣ rd*[h] *ḥr pꜣ rr.*[j] [
3.] . . [. . .] . . ⌈*r pꜣ*⌉ *wy*[k] *ḥr pꜣ wrṯ*[l] *r pꜣ smn*[m] *ḥr pꜣ sry*[[n]
4.] . . . *ḥr pꜣ* ⌈*ẖt*⌉*-ršꜥ*[o]: *r*[p] *pꜣ mnw*[q] *ḥr pꜣ mn(w)*[r] : *r pꜣ ky*⌈*my*⌉[s] [
5. . . . . . .] .[t] *ḥr pꜣ ḏpḥ*[u] ⌈: *r pꜣ*⌉[v] *pꜥry*[w] ⌈*ḥr*⌉ [*pꜣ*] ⌈*p*⌉[.] . [[x]
6. . . . .] . . . . . . [*r*] ⌈*pꜣ ẖ*⌉. . .[y] *ḥr pꜣ ẖ*⌈*dỉ*[z] *r pꜣ dr*⌉[[aa]
7. . . . .] ⌈*r*⌉ *pꜣ* [. . . . . . . *r*] *pꜣ ḳsnw*[ab] *ḥr pꜣ* . . . . .[ac] [
8. . . . . . .] *gy* ⌈*ntỉ-ỉw*⌉[ad] [. . . . .] . . . [
9. . . . .] . . *b*⌈*y*⌉ . . .[ae] *šm n=f mnw*[af] *r M*. . .[ag] [
10. . . . .] . . . *r Rb*⌈*ỉ*⌉[ah] *šm n=f bnw*[aj] *r B*⌈*b*⌉[*l*[ak]
11. . . . .] . . .[al] *šm n=f nry*[am] *r* . . . .[an] [
12. . . . .] . *Prs*[ao] *šm n=f* . . *nỉnỉ*[ap] . .[aq] [
13. . . . .] . . .[ar] *šm n=f drỉ*[as] *Dry*[at] [
14. . . . . .] . . . . . . *šm* [. .] . . . . [. .] . . . .[au] [

2.5 cm. of blank papyrus

15.]⌈*brṯ*⌉[av] . . . .[aw] *brwš*[ax] *ỉw=s grg*[ay] *ỉw=y rwd ỉw=s* .[az] [
16. . . .] . . . *r rk=f ỉw=s ꜥḥꜥ ḥr-rꜣ pꜣ ẖyṯ ẖr* . . . [
17.]. *r pꜣ ẖr* . [. . .] . . *ẖr* . . . . .*=y*[ba] *n ḥs* : . . . *ḥr ꜣs*[[bb]
18.]. *nꜣỉ=s mdw(t)* : *ẖr wẖꜣ=s r pꜣ swr pꜣ wnm* ⌈*pꜣ*⌉ . . . . [
19.] . . *nw pꜣ mšꜥ pꜣ tꜣ dr=f r-r=w ḏd=w* . . . . *nw*[bc] . . . . [
20.] *tꜣ gmy*[bd] *gy hbyn* . . . *tꜣ* ⌈*pš*⌉*ry*[be] *gy* [
21.].[bf] *ḳb*⌈*ꜣ*⌉[bg] *wꜥb tꜣ/nꜣ H̱ry gy kry*[bh] *wr* : [bj] vacat [

bottom margin of 2 cm.

Notes on transliteration[1]

a. Slight traces of ink are preserved on a narrow strip of horizontal fibres at the beginning of l. 1. Traces of one sign are similarly preserved in l. 2.

b. The sign preceding might be read *rmt*, as far as its form is concerned, but it is more probable that is the end of a plant-name (. . . *ṯm*, or . . . *ṯš*?). For the form of the det., cf. *ršꜥ* in l. 4, and other examples in ll. 15 and 20. The traces would not suit a reading [*p*]*ꜣi=s rmt*. Possibly see *Wb*. ii. 469. 2 (*rdm.t*); cf. *DG*, 265. 3 (*ltm*) and *Wb*. ii. 378. 2 ff. (*nḏm*).

c. The reading *yb* (with a det.: cf. various writings given in *DG*, 49. 7–9) is certain. The natural assumption is that this is a writing of the town-name *Yb*, 'Elephantine', with the place-name det. (cf. the writing of *Rbỉ* in l. 10). However, it is possible that the word is followed by the punctuation mark that occurs at several points in the text, and *yb*, 'ivory' might be understood.

The preceding sign is presumably to be understood as a det. of a word (written) that has every appearance of reading *mrgy*. The form of the initial sign is precisely correct for *m* (cf. *mnw* and *mn* in l. 4, and *mꜣꜥ* in l. 9). However, as would be the case in many hands, it is not possible to rule out *š*, which is generally made with a heavier, flatter top (cf. *brwš* in l. 15, and *pšry* in l. 20: it is not surprising that a more elaborate form of *š* appears to occur in *ršꜥ*(?) in l. 4). A reading *ẖ* (cf. *Ḫry* in l. 1, and *ḥyṯ* in l. 16) is most unlikely. None of these three readings suggests any attested demotic word. A further possibility is that the sign is a simplified form, as found in some hands, of the used to write initial *g* (also *gr*). If *grgy* is read, then there are several possible identifications of the word (see *inter alia DG*, 586; Crum, *CD*, 830 ff.; Westendorf, *KH*, 467 ff.; and Černý, *CED*, 336 ff.) of which *grg*, 'to found', etc., *DG*, 586. 4 is perhaps the most plausible. It is debatable if the occurrence of a *grg* in the writing in l. 15 supports or casts doubt on this reading. The two different writings of *Ḫry* in this text provide a good parallel for the use of two different forms of the initial sign. In a text of this kind it is of course conceivable that the word is a rare or foreign one. It may be most promising to suggest a connection with the words listed as *mgꜣ*, *mgꜣ.t* at *Wb*. ii. 164. 5–11: a Nubian plant may be in question.

d. The reading of *Ḫry* here, with the det., is certain; but it is not clear whether the preceding article should be read *tꜣ* or *nꜣ*, nor whether the country Syria or its inhabitant(s) are meant. The sense is obscure in l. 1, but the word recurs in l. 21, where the context hardly suggests that the meaning is 'the Syrian woman' (see p. 207, n. *bf*). As there is no good reason to suppose that *Ḫr*, the country, can be fem., the reading *nꜣ Ḫry*, 'the Syrians', seems preferable in both cases.

e. Although it is impossible to be sure that the apparent at the end of l. 1 should not be understood as parts of more than one sign, *r Mn-nfr* and *r-ỉn* are among possible readings. The former would provide a plausible contrast with *Yb* earlier in this line.

f. *hb*, 'ibis': *Wb*. ii. 487. 1 (*hbj*); *DG*, 272. 1; Crum, *CD*, 655b (ϩⲓⲃⲱⲓ); Westendorf, *KH*, 354; Černý, *CED*, 274. 7.

The context, the clear def. article *pꜣ* preceding, and the assonance with *hbyn* make the reading *hb* certain, although the writing is not quite as expected (cf. *DG*, 272. 1). The *b* is written very small, as often in writings of *hb*, 'to send', in Saqqâra papyri. It is difficult to say if the following sign is the expected divine det., or the expected vertical stroke accompanying the *b*. The final sign, for the form of which there is no precise parallel, is perhaps intended to be a specific det. (hieratic), as distinct from the general det. used for all the other surviving bird-names in the text. No other reading of this portion of l. 2 seems plausible. For the possibility that the ibis occupies a special position in this text, see pp. 212–13.

g. *hbyn*, 'ebony': *Wb*. ii. 487. 7 ff. (*hbnj*); *DG*, 273. 3; not found in Coptic.

Ebony does not occur where expected in Coptic versions of Ezekiel 27:15, presumably because the relevant phrase is lacking in the Septuagint.

Ebony is listed among other woods in the demotic list of omens drawn from minerals and other substances at P. Berlin 8769 B, col. 2, l. 5.

h. *rd*, an unidentified bird: *Wb*. ii. 463. 12; apparently not otherwise attested in Demotic or Coptic. The Egyptian examples (E. Naville, *The Festival-hall of*

[1] Because of the particular nature and lexicographic interest of the text, brief references to the chief dictionaries are given in the notes on each of the key words in ll. 2–13, but no attempt is made to discuss the words or their etymologies, except as far as is necessary for the basic understanding of the text.

Osorkon II in the Great Temple of Bubastis (London, 1892), pl. 22, frs. 3 and 4; F. L. Griffith and W. M. F. Petrie, *Two Hieroglyphic Papyri from Tanis* (London, 1889), pl. 10, fr. 18) give some idea of the nature of this bird, as the dets. show a little individual character: a long-legged bird, resembling a heron or crane?

From the examples preserved in ll. 3–7, it is clear that ll. 2–7 consist of parallel phrases, all circumstantial in form: *r pꜣ* (bird name) *ḥr pꜣ* (tree name). It may be noted that the circumstantial is not employed in ll. 9–13. However, there is definitely no trace of the expected *r* before *pꜣ rd* in l. 2: it is not omitted in any other surviving example (although for other peculiarities see p. 202, n. *p* and p. 203, n. *v*.) A short portion of the text here (its precise extent is uncertain) has been roughly sponged away and re-written, leaving a distinctive grey stain on the papyrus, and it is possible that the *r* was accidentally omitted in the course of this correction.

j. rr, 'vine': *Wb.* i. 32. 12 ff. (*ỉꜣrr.t*); *DG*, 7. 16 (*ꜣllj*); Crum, *CD*, 54b (ⲉⲗⲟⲟⲗⲉ); Westendorf, *KH*, 34; Černý, *CED*, 34. 1.

The final trace in l. 2 is probably part of a or det. of *rr*: the det. appears less likely.

The form *rr* presents two problems in the present context, even though in both respects the writing is not unparalleled in demotic: i. the lack of initial *ꜣ* (cf. for example, Mag. Pap. Demotic glossary nos. 7, 520, and 524); ii. the use of two *r*s (cf., for example, the writings in P. Vindob. D 6257) in a word generally reckoned always to have been pronounced with two *l* sounds. It would perhaps be perverse to suggest that the assonance in question here is anything other than of *r*: the writing may have been intended specifically to emphasize this.

k. wy, an unidentified bird: probably *Wb.* i. 272. 6 (*wjꜣ.t*); apparently not otherwise attested in Demotic or Coptic.

The traces before *wy* would suit the reading *r pꜣ*, but do not compel it. The immediately preceding sign seems certain to be the det. of the name of a tree, (almost certainly not), and so it will belong to the preceding phrase. This makes the reading *r pꜣ wy* inescapable.

A bird with the name *wrt* occurs, together with a *kymy* (cf. l. 4 of the present text), at Krugt. A/5 and 9 (cf. *wrd*, *Wb.* i. 336. 17 f.), but it plainly cannot be read here.

Although only the fem. form *wiꜣt* is attested in Egyptian, it is possible that the *wy*-bird of the present text was originally the source of the 𓅱 hieroglyph, which is often accepted to be a representation of a quail-chick. However, such an identification must present problems in the present context. One might expect adult birds of distinct species to be listed, and *pꜥry*, 'quail', occurs in l. 5 of the text. The usual identification of the hieroglyph may well not be correct, or may not be correct for all periods. Further, the hieroglyph will not serve to prove that any corresponding word must refer specifically to the young of the species.

l. wrṯ, 'rose': not in *Wb.*, and apparently not attested in Egyptian; *DG*, 95. 6 (fem.); Crum, *CD*, 490a (ⲟⲩⲣⲧ, generally masc.); Westendorf, *KH*, 276; Černý, *CED*, 215. 4.

There appears to be no evidence for any kind of rose in Egypt before the Ptolemaic period (for this point see, for example, L. Keimer, *La Rose égyptienne* (Botanica, 1), *Études d'égyptologie*, 5 (Le Caire, 1943), esp. 19 ff.).

m. smn, 'Nile-goose': *Wb.* iv. 136. 2 ff. (*śmn*); *DG*, 433. 6; Crum, *CD*, 339a ⲥⲙⲟⲩⲛⲉ); Westendorf, *KH*, 187; Černý, *CED*, 153. 2.

Before the det. of *smn*, there stands the group . A similar group, sometimes more distinctly written, occurs in *mnw*, ll. 4 and 9, and in *bnw*, l. 10, and probably also in *ḳsnw*, l. 7 (see p. 203, n. *ab*). From these examples it is clear that the group is a virtually hieratic writing of . This group might be expected in a hieratic writing of the words, but does not normally occur in the demotic script (the only exception in the case of these particular words is the writing of *smn* in Mag. Pap. 27/9). One problem, however, remains: the same group undoubtedly occurs in *ḏr(w)*, l. 13, where it must be supposed to be a mistake (see p. 206, n. *as*).

n. sry[, presumably a tree-name: no certain identification.

The reading *sry* is certain, but there is no trace of the following sign, and it is therefore impossible to judge whether the name is simply *sry*, or a longer word. It is difficult to assess the likelihood of a connection with the *sry* of Duemichen, *Geographische Inschriften*, 2, pl. 88, col. 25 (*Wb.* iv. 192. 12, *śrj(.t)*), occurring in a series of tree descriptions. Other possibilities all appear open to serious objections: *sry-bn(y)* might be read, and might be understood (*a*) as the equivalent of Coptic ⲥⲣⲃⲛⲛⲉ, 'palm-thorn', Crum, *CD*, 40b and 354b (where other compounds of ⲥⲟⲩⲣⲉ, not attested earlier, are listed), or (*b*) as *šn-bn(y)*, 'palm-fibre',

DG, 518. 3 and 513. 1; Coptic ϣⲛⲃⲛⲛⲉ Crum, *CD*, 40b, with possible confusion with *ẖt*, 'tree', and *šn*, 'tree'; also *srpt*, 'lotus', *DG*, 442. 8, and the plant-name *sl*, *sꜣl*, *sꜥl* (cf. *DG*, 444. 3–4).

o. *ẖt-ršꜥ*, reading and identification uncertain.

At the beginning of the line, the end of a bird-name with det. is clear, followed by *ẖr pꜣ*. Therefore, is presumably a tree- or plant-name. The det. is , and not : it is difficult to know if this is significant, indicating, for example, that a shrub or plant rather than a tree is in question, or that the tree was remarkable for its foliage (cf. the specific det. of *wrṯ* in l. 3, doubtless used because the rose was employed for garlands in the Graeco-Roman period).

Although the first signs are damaged, it seems very likely that the name is compounded with *ẖt*, 'tree', 'wood', of which is a standard writing (for these common compounds, see, for example, Crum, *CD*, 546b, under ϣⲉ, 546a, and Westendorf, *KH*, 301; cf. *Wb*. iii, 340. 6 ff.; 341. 7 ff.; 342. 9 ff.), or at least that the scribe thought he was writing a compound of this type.

The obvious reading is therefore *ẖt-ršꜥ*, although it is perhaps conceivable that the apparent *r* is to be understood as a det. of *ẖt* (the det. is attested, for example, with *ꜣlly*, 'vine', and *kꜣm*, 'garden', but not apparently with *ẖt*, although the particular plant in question might have prompted its use).

The possibilities that follow all assume mistakes on the part of the scribe, or at least peculiarities of orthography. A connection with *ẖrš*, 'bundle' (*DG*, 367. 3; *Wb*. iii. 330. 12) seems unlikely. The name might be analysed as *ẖ(t)-tršꜥ* = *ẖt dšr* (the Coptic form of *dšr* is ⲧⲱⲣϣ; cf. *Wb*. iii. 340. 7; v. 491. 1 ff.). Another possibility is the *ẖr-šꜣ.t* of Duemichen, *Geographische Inschriften*, 2, pl. 88, col. 22 (*Wb*. iii. 330. 14; iv. 401. 10). The final ꜥ is problematic for all these possibilities; conceivably is the preposition *šꜥ*, used as a kind of group.

The reading must remain doubtful, but it is still probable that the name began with *ẖt*, ϣⲉ, and the obvious assumption is that the assonance with the accompanying bird-name was with this element of the word.

p. The signs following *ẖt-ršꜥ* might plausibly be read *ỉw pꜣ*, on the assumption that the Circumstantial Preformative, elsewhere in this passage written *r*, had in this single case been written *ỉw*. However, in several other places in the text a stroke is employed as a mark of punctuation, and it seems likely that here one of these marks should be read, followed by the expected *r*.

q. *mnw*, 'dove': *Wb*. ii. 79. 3–5 (*mnw.t*, *mnw*); *DG*, 161. 5 (*mn.ṯ*); apparently not found in Coptic, which uses ϭⲣⲟⲟⲙⲡⲉ, also the commoner word in Demotic (*grmp*, *DG*, 585. 3).

It seems unlikely that the word is to be identified as the word for swallow: *Wb*. ii. 68. 2 ff. (*mn.t*); *DG*, 117. 3 (*bnj*); Crum, *CD*, 40a (ⲃⲏⲛⲉ); Westendorf, *KH*, 24; Černý, *CED*, 24. 1. This, although not common, apparently occurs in Demotic always with a *b*: the use of the *nw*-group here (see p. 201, n. *m*) also favours *mnw*, 'dove'.

r. *mn(w)*, 'fruit-tree(?)': *Wb*. ii. 71. 13 ff. (*mnw*); apparently not otherwise attested in Demotic or Coptic.

Although it is questionable if the sign in this word should be transliterated *nw*, certainly its use is appropriate to a word written *mnw* in Egyptian.

In view of the possibility, rejected in n. *q* above, of identifying the *mnw*-bird of this text with *bny*, 'swallow', it should be said here that it seems improbable in the extreme that the *mnw*-tree should be identified with *bny*, 'date-palm' (Egyptian *bnr.t*, Coptic ⲃⲛⲛⲉ).

Although Egyptian *mnw* may be used as a vague term, it is clearly plausible to understand many of its occurrences as referring to fruit-trees; it is also found referring to resin-bearing trees. The basic sense may be of orchard trees or cultivated trees, or trees grown for a product, or, of course, trees of a certain size and form. The term may even, at root, have been more precise than this: at any rate, it need not be seen as surprising to find it in the present list.

s. *kymy*, 'hen': this late word for hen is not in *Wb*., and apparently not attested in Egyptian; *DG*, 560. 5; Crum, *CD*, 818a (ϭⲁⲓⲙⲉ); Westendorf, *KH*, 448; Černý, *CED*, 331. 1.

Černý accepts, and Westendorf mentions with a note of query, the suggestion that *kymy* derives ultimately from the Egyptian name for the black ibis, *Wb*. v. 166. 5 (*gm.t*): this word was presumably the source of the *gm* hieroglyph, and the word (whether or not in the form *kymy* it had retained the sense of black ibis) might have been included in the present text for this particular reason.

t. The usual bird det. is clear at the beginning of l. 5, but nothing more survives of the bird-name here.

u. *ḏpḥ*, 'apple-tree': *Wb*. v. 568. 10 (*ḏpḥ*), cf. v.

296. 12 (*tpḥ*); *DG*, 677. 8 (*ḏpḥ*), 680. 5 (*dmpḥ*); Crum, *CD*, 771b (ϫ(ⲉ)ⲙⲡⲉϩ); Westendorf, *KH*, 423; Černý, *CED*, 314. 8.

v. The signs between *ḏpḥ* and *pꜥry* are cramped and confused. Most probably the expected mark of punctuation and *r pꜣ* should be read: . Possibly *r pꜣ* was at first omitted, and was then squeezed into the available space.

w. pꜥry, 'quail': *Wb.* i. 504. 14 (*pꜥr.t*); not in *DG*, but unpublished examples are given in Černý, *CED*; Crum, *CD*, 267a (ⲡⲏⲣⲉ); Westendorf, *KH*, 150; Černý, *CED*, 127. 3.

Despite the damage, the writing is certainly 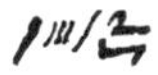.

x. The traces of the top of a *p* in the form 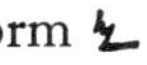 (as in *ḏpḥ*, also here in l. 5) are distinctive. From the position of the *p* after the clear traces of *ḥr*, it is plainly the first sign of a plant-name, as is to be expected after *pꜥry*: it also appears to be positioned rather high, and presumably another sign was written below it.

A problematic plant-name *pšry* seems to occur in l. 20 below, and it is conceivable that the word is there repeated from the present passage, although the writing in l. 20 would not suit the apparent high position of the *p* in l. 5.

As other plausible restorations do not seem to be forthcoming, it is worth mentioning here the *pḳr*-tree, which might well be written *pky*, , and would suit the traces very well: not in *Wb.* as such, but see i. 561. 6–9 and i. 561. 10 (*pḳr*); *DG*, 141. 4 (*pk* in dem Ausdruck *w(wꜥ)-pk*); Crum, *CD*, 286b (ⲟⲩⲡⲱⲕⲉ, under ⲡⲱϭⲉ), cf. ibid. ⲡⲟϭⲗⲉ; Westendorf *KH*, 159 (ⲡⲱϭⲉ and ⲡⲟϭⲗⲉ); Černý, *CED*, 133. 1–2 (ⲡⲱϭⲉ and ⲡⲟϭⲗⲉ), and 356. 2 ⲟⲩⲡⲱⲕⲉ). See also V. Loret, 'Le Kuphi', *Journal asiatique*, 8e sér., tome 10 (1887), 125–6; id., *La flore pharaonique* . . . (2e ed. Paris, 1892), 80–1; H. Schäfer, 'Das Osirisgrab von Abydos und der Baum *pḳr*', *ZÄS* 41 (1904), 107–10; A. M. Blackman, 'The funerary papyrus of ꜥEnkhefenkhons', *JEA* 4 (1917), 123 n. 2; L. Keimer, *Die Gartenpflanzen im alten Ägypten*. I (Hamburg, 1924), 153–4.

y. ḫ . . . , a bird-name: reading and identification uncertain.

It is probable that both the bird- and the plant-name at this point in the text begin with , *ḫ*.

The traces at the beginning of l. 6 are badly damaged. It is plausible to see the end of a tree-name, with  det., although nothing of the name can be read. Just the correct space follows for *r pꜣ* to be restored (there is a slight trace of the top of the *pꜣ*). The traces of the bird-name would therefore be , and *ḫ* is the natural restoration of the first sign. No reading particularly recommends itself. *Wb.* iii. 257. 1 (*ḫbś*) and *Wb.* iii. 355. 20 (*ḫdw*) might be considered: the latter might better suit the traces (?). The bird-name read *ḫnms* at Orakel e/6 (*DG*, 362. 9), whether or not this is the correct reading, could not suit the traces here.

z. ḫdi, a tree-name: reading and identification uncertain.

The *ḫ* seems a certain reading in the case of the tree here. The writing appears to be , *ḫdi*. (For the second sign, the *d*, the less natural readings *b*, *s*, *ḳ*, or *d* might be considered, if any likely restoration suggested itself.) It is improbable that *ḫt*, 'tree', 'wood', would be written out in this way. However, it is perhaps worth mentioning the possibility that the tree of *Wb.* iii. 342. 9–12 (cf. 13) might be read *ḫdi* (cf. the verb *ḫtj*, *Wb.* iii. 347. 16 ff.): if this possibility were admitted, the orthography and palaeography of the demotic would present no problems, but the *Wb. Drog.* (pp. 405–7) is no doubt correct to understand all the Egyptian writings as *ḫt-ds*, and it would be necessary to suppose that a misunderstanding of the writing lay behind the form in the present demotic text. A reading of *ḫdn*, 'garlic' (*DG*, 373. 2), which might be written 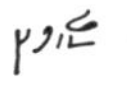 or 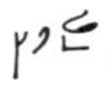, does not suit the precise form of the signs, and the det., almost certainly  and not , strongly suggests a tree rather than a vegetable.

aa. Probably at the end of l. 6 the bird-name *dr*, which occurs in l. 13 below, should be restored: for the name see p. 206, n. *as*.

ab. ḳsnw, 'sparrow': *Wb.* v. 69. 6 (*ḳśn.w*); apparently not otherwise attested in Demotic or Coptic. (The root *ḳsn* survives in Demotic (*DG*, 550. 3); a connection with *ḳns* (*DG*, 541. 5) and Coptic ϭⲟⲛⲥ is questionable: see Westendorf, *KH*, 459.)

This bird-name is apparently written 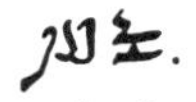. The only natural reading of the first two signs is *ḳs*, and the following group could reasonably be taken as a further occurrence of the *nw*-group (see p. 201, n. *m*), although the first sign is here made in one stroke, rather than the two strokes shown by all the other examples.

It may be noted that, as *Wb.* states, *ḳsnw* is presumably the name of the bird represented by the  hieroglyph (Gardiner, *Egyptian Grammar*, Sign-list, G37).

ac. The writing of what presumably constitutes the beginning of the tree- or plant-name accompanying *ḳsnw* is . There is no obvious way of reading a word beginning *ḳ* (or *k*) to match *ḳsnw*. Nor is any reading readily forthcoming, even if this question of assonance is set aside.

It is possible that the tree-name was a compound expression, the second part of which (now lost) began with *ḳ* (neither *ḫt*, *DG*, 370. 2 nor *šn*, *DG*, 513. 2 seem likely readings). Another possibility is that the name began with *i͗*, and that this syllable was disregarded for the assonance with *ḳsnw* (cf. a different problem with *rr* for *ꜣrr* in l. 2): *i͗* would be a plausible reading of the first vertical stroke of the word. In this case one might consider the Egyptian words *Wb.* i. 34. 1 f. (*i͗ꜣḳ.t*, 'leek'); *Wb.* i. 138. 5 (*i͗ḳrw*, a tree); and in Demotic *DG*, 1. 11 (*ꜣjḳj*, 'reed': cf. Westendorf, *KH*, 140 for a possible connection with ⲟⲉⲓⲕ); *DG*, 12. 7 (*ꜣkj*, 'sesame': cf. Westendorf, *KH*, 140, ⲟⲕⲉ). V. Loret, 'Le champ des souchets', *Rec. trav.* 13 (1890), 200, identified *Wb.* i, 22. 8 (*ꜣg*) with ⲟⲉⲓⲕ (but also with Egyptian *i͗ꜣk* and Coptic ⲁⲕⲉ = ⲟⲕⲉ), as a word for reed. Finally, some forms of the *ḳd*-sign found in hieratic might suggest that the vertical stroke here be read *ḳd*, although there is no good parallel in Demotic: if so, then the *ḳdt*-tree, *Wb.* v. 79. 9 ff. (*ḳd.t*) and *DG*, 552. 2 (*ḳt.t*), is an obvious possibility.

ad. The regular sequence of birds and trees has presumably come to an end by l. 8, as there seems no way of interpreting what can be read here to match the phrases of ll. 2–7. Possibly there stands here a sentence introducing and explaining the following section (simply by way of example *tw-s nꜣ mꜣꜥ.w n pꜣi͗=w gy nti͗ i͗w nꜣ ꜣpd.w/mꜣḥy.w n rn=w šm r-r=w* might be restored), or conceivably a sentence summarizing in much the same way the preceding section. The restoration of *nti͗ i͗w* is not certain.

ae. The signs here are apparently . The det. is almost certainly (which occurs several times in ll. 2–6, and is appropriate to words for trees, wood, various manufactured articles, etc.); the shape is wrong for  (appropriate to words for plants), and such a reading makes the preceding strokes more difficult to interpret. After *by* and before the det., a group  or  is likely: either *byn* should be read, or this group may represent a  or  found in a hieratic writing (cf. the similar group discussed in p. 206, n. *as*). A writing of *hbyn* (cf. l. 2) can hardly be in question. The top of the sign before *by* may or may not be damaged. If  can be restored, and is read as *w* (see two examples in l. 3), then *šwby*, 'persea tree' is the obvious restoration *Wb.* iv. 435. 10 ff. (*šwb*); *DG*, 496. 3 (*šwb*); Crum, *CD*, 603a (ϣⲟⲩⲏ(ⲏ)ⲃ: note the forms ϣⲟⲩⲉⲃⲉ and ϣⲃⲉ). An initial *i͗* is a possible reading (cf. n. *ac* above, although it does not seem possible to reconcile the signs here with the traces at the end of l. 7), in which case the tree *i͗b*, *Wb.* i. 60. 17 f. might be considered: other possibilities are *i͗b*, *Wb.* i. 61. 17 (*sic*); *i͗bw*, *Wb.* i. 62. 3 f.; *i͗bšꜣ*, *Wb.* i. 64. 15 ff.

The word here shows no sign of being a place-name. Possibly the second half of a compound place-name may be in question, or the list of birds and places may begin with the *mnw*-bird immediately following.

af. *mnw* (see p. 202, n. *q*) is here written slightly differently from the form in l. 4, as it lacks the initial 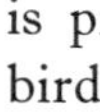, but is plainly the same word. In l. 4 the *mnw*-bird is preceded by an absolute minimum of six pairs of birds and trees. It is difficult to see how, on any interpretation or restoration, the *mnw*-bird here in l. 9 could possibly occupy the same position in the second series, that of bird- and place-names, which is unlikely yet to have begun at the beginning of what survives in l. 8, and may in fact begin here with *mnw* (see n. *ae* above): for the general question of the order of the items in the text, and the particular expectation that the ibis would stand first, see p. 212 f.

ag. *M* . . . [, presumably a place-name.

The form of the  sign would suit a reading *mꜣꜥ* very well, but the following signs are then difficult to explain, and no plausible restoration of a compound place-name seems to be forthcoming. A reading of *Mḥw*, 'Lower Egypt', *DG*, 174. 7, would suit all the signs (there are parallels for dets. ). As several other place-names in ll. 10–13 seem to be of foreign towns and countries, it is questionable if Lower Egypt is to be expected here; but this reading receives considerable support if *Šmꜥ*, 'Upper Egypt' is read in l. 12.

ah. *Rbi͗*, a place-name: reading and identification uncertain.

The det. appears to be the geographical det. proper to Egyptian town-names (although examples with foreign place-names are not rare). Before the det., the two strokes are most naturally read as the group  (in demotic transliteration, it is simply a matter of convention whether this ending is represented by *i͗* or *i͗w*). If the reading *Rbi͗(w)* is accepted, then three interpretations might be considered: (i) in view of the other well-known Late Period names of countries that are preserved, Babylon and Persia, the obvious possibility is *Rbw*, 'Libya', Gauthier, *DNG*, 3. 117, *r(a)bou*, *rabou*; *Wb*. ii. 414. 2 ff.; see Gardiner, *Onomastica*, 1, 121* ff. (ii) The *Rbiw*, *Rbiꜣ* of Gauthier, *DNG*, 3. 116 (*rabaâou*, *rabaâa*), in or near Palestine: this identification would perhaps assume that the name in the present list derived from the traditional lists of Asiatic place-names, going back to the Eighteenth Dynasty; so, for the actual location of *Rbiw*, the geographical realities of the Late Period may not be very relevant. In any case, several possibilities must be considered, among them, two cities famous in later history: Rabbath Ammon, Philadephia, city of the Decapolis; and Rabbath Moab, Areopolis, in Moab. However, at least two other cities, found in the Old Testament, also come into consideration, the *hā-Rabbāh* of Josh. 15: 60, in Judah, and the *hā-Rabbīth* of Josh. 19: 20, further north in the tribe of Issachar: it may or may not be possible to identify the first of these two with the *Robbō* of Eusebius, *Onomasticon*, identified with *Khirbat Rabbā* by G. Beyer, 'Das Stadtgebiet von Eleutheropolis . . .', *Zeitschrift des Deutschen Palästina-Vereins*, 54 (1931), 217. (iii) *ꜣrby*, Arabia', *DG*, 6. 10: cf. Gauthier, *DNG*, 1. 5, *arbinou* etc. See p. 201, n. *j* on (*ꜣ*)*rr*, although there seems to be no parallel for such a writing of *ꜣrby*.

If the two strokes before the det. could be taken as the *nw*-group (see p. 201, n. *m*), which seems much less probable than *i*(*w*), then several place-names might be considered (references to Gauthier, *DNG*): *rboun*, 3. 135; *rabana*[1], 3. 116; *rabana*[2], 3. 116; *rabouna*?, 3. 118. Of these, clearly the first Rabana, for which see Gardiner, *Onomastica*, 2. 115* (391), would suit the apparent Egyptian town det.

aj. *bnw*, 'the *Benu*-bird': *Wb*. i. 458. 3 ff.; *DG*, 117. 5 (*bnw*), 112. 2 (*bjn*); apparently not attested in any form in Coptic.

The writing here does not have a divine det., nor is the det. in any way distinctive. It seems, however, most unlikely that *bny*, 'swallow', should be understood (see p. 202, n. *q*).

It may be noted that naturally the  hieroglyph (Gardiner, *Egyptian Grammar*, Sign-list, G31) is proper to the word *bnw*, although in Egyptian writing in general such a precise distinction is meaningless, and it is difficult to know if it is better to say that the *Benu*-hieroglyph is used for 'herons' of all kinds, or a heron is used for the *Benu*-bird.

For the problems of the *Benu*-bird, see, for example, the articles 'Phönix' in Bonnet, *Reallexikon der ägyptischen Religionsgeschichte*, and in the *Lexikon der Ägyptologie*, and, for the latest contribution to discussion of the ornithological origin of the *Benu*-bird, see E. Hoch, 'Reflections on prehistoric life at Umm an-Nar, Trucial Oman . . .' in *South Asian Archaeology 1977: papers from the Fourth International Conference of South Asian Archaeologists in Europe* (Naples, Istituto Universitario Orientale, Seminario di Studi Asiatici, 1979), 589–638.

ak. *Bb*[*l*], 'Babylon', i.e. the Mesopotamian Babylon: Gauthier, *DNG*, 2. 20 (*bbr*)—see Gardiner, *Onomastica*, 1. 192*; 2. 324; *DG*, 115. 4 (*bbl*).

The two *b*s seem a certain reading, and, in view of the other names that can be read, *Bbl* is a natural restoration: there is, however, another possibility, the *babaoui* of Gauthier, *DNG*, 2. 3, which is probably the same as *bbâ*, ibid. 2. 20.

al. Nothing can be read of the place-name here, but the det. could plausibly be restored as the  proper but not exclusive to Egyptian place-names (cf. p. 204, n. *ah*).

am. *nry*, 'vulture'; *Wb*. ii. 277. 1 ff. (*nr.t*); *DG*, 221. 1 (*nr*); Crum, *CD*, 228b (ⲛⲟⲩⲣⲉ); Westendorf, *KH*, 125; Černý, *CED*, 110. 4.

It may be noted that the *nrt* is the bird depicted by the  hieroglyph (Gardiner, *Egyptian Grammar*, Sign-list, G14).

an. The traces of the beginning of the place-name accompanying *nry* are , and they appear to be at least partly damaged.

No convincing restoration is offered here. The possibility might be considered of *Nḫb*, 'Elkāb', *DG*, 226. 1. The appropriateness of a major city of Upper Egypt in this context is questionable; on the other hand, Elkāb had as its principal deity the vulture-goddess *Nḫbt*, which may have made it particularly fitting as the destination of the *nry*-vulture.

ao. *Prs*, 'Persia' or 'Persian': Gauthier, *DNG*, 2, 144 (*pers*); *DG*, 136. 5.

The writing is , and the reading appears secure. *Prs* will presumably correspond to the *pꜥry*-bird, which occurs in l. 5 above. The det. is that regularly used for foreign personal names: it may be used here, as often, with a place-name, or a compound expression for 'the land of Persia(ns)' may be in question. For the form of the det., compare *Ḫry* in l. 1 above and l. 21 below.

ap. . . *nini*, a bird-name: reading and identification uncertain.

The writing appears to be  The natural reading of the end of the word is *-nìnì*, and it is extremely probable that the name is the same as the that occurs in Orakel e/11, where the first sign is badly damaged. Here the first sign appears to be undamaged, but it is obscure how it might be read: all the possibilities mentioned below must suppose that the sign was made in a form different from that which would naturally be expected. For the bird at Orakel e/11, Spiegelberg suggested the reading *gnìnì*, comparing the *gn.w* bird (see *Wb.* v. 174. 2 ff.). From hieroglyphic sources, the *ꜣbnn*-bird of *Wb.* i. 8. 6 written : see Gardiner *Onomastica*, 2. 256*) best matches the ending *-nìnì* in the present text. The possibility might also be considered of *ẖnn*, *Wb.* iii. 288. 4 ff. (*ẖnn.t*); conceivably this word might have been able to serve as the name of a specific bird (see Gardiner's remarks, *Onomastica*, 2. 256*–7*).

aq. Presumably a place-name immediately follows . . *nìnì*: as with *Dry* in the next line, no preposition *r* is written, but there is no special reason to suggest the reading of a compound bird-name. The traces are . In this fragmentary text the necessary palaeographic comparisons are not to hand, but two readings seem particularly to suit the initial sign: *Šmꜥ*, 'Upper Egypt' (which would receive some support if *Mḥw*, 'Lower Egypt', is read in l. 9); and *Ꞽwnw*, 'Heliopolis' and a number of other place-names written with , including some outside Egypt.

ar. The det. proper but not exclusive to Egyptian place-names seems certain here: before the det., the word *ḥꜥ*, *DG*, 350. 3, is a possibility.

as. drì, 'kite': *Wb.* v. 596. 2 ff. (*ḏr.t*), cf. v. 596. 1 (*ḏr.w*): *DG*, 647. 1 (*tr.t*); Crum, *CD*, 429b (ⲧⲣⲉ); Westendorf, *KH*, 241; Černý, *CED*, 194. 1.

This bird-name, which may also occur in l. 6 (see p. 203, n. *aa*), is written , and plainly begins with the sign. There can be little doubt that the name should be identified with *ḏr.t*/ⲧⲣⲉ, a word found at all stages of the language. Although only fem. forms are attested in Egyptian, the word is masc. or fem. in Coptic, and a single masc. example appears to occur at *Mythus* 12/6, *pꜣ drꜣ*. However, the demotic writing in the present text includes an unmistakable example of the *nw*-group that occurs in several other bird-names in the text (see p. 201, n. *m*). In all the other cases the presence of the group is perfectly appropriate, but here it is inexplicable. Possibly the scribe merely thought that the group was a flourish that could be used at will before the det. of bird-names; but it is much more probable that the writing here is, or derives from, a mechanical miscopying of a hieratic writing , a mistake that might easily arise in many late hieratic hands.

at. Dry, 'Dōr': Gauthier, *DNG*, 6. 87, (*dir*), cf. 6. 97 (*dr*(?)).

Presumably *Dry* here is to be identified with the well-known Dōr, Dora, on the coast, south of Mt. Carmel.

au. It is probable, but not certain, that the list of birds and places is continued in l. 14. Comparison with the overall length of the preceding list of birds and trees suggests this is likely.

The first traces in the line are probably the end of a place-name: they might be restored , and perhaps be read]*gyꜣ*. The following signs might tentatively be restored *šm* [*n=f*] *ḳsnw* [*r*] *Pr-* . . . . . [. The *ḳsnw*-bird similarly occurs towards the end of the preceding list (l. 7), but the traces here do not set the reading beyond doubt. *Pr-* seems a very probable reading for the beginning of the place-name: this prefix was no doubt disregarded for the assonance. The trace immediately following *Pr-* might plausibly be explained as the dot or short stroke found in this text under various signs, including *k* and *g*. It is not certain whether or not such a dot could be used under a *ḳ* sign. Special factors may apply in this text, but a consideration of phonetics in general would suggest that written *ḳ* or *k* or *g* might, in appropriate words, be found representing the same sound as the *ḳ* of *ḳsnw*. Therefore there is every reason to suppose that a place-name could be read here to match *ḳsnw*.

av. The traces at the beginning of the line are plainly of a plant-name: seems a plausible restoration, although it is uncertain whether *brṯ* is the complete name, or further signs are lost before them. No identification is suggested here. A reading *ꜥrṯ* is less convincing: *ꜥrṯ.t* at *DG*, 67. 3 might provide a parallel, but is itself a lexicographic puzzle.

If *brṯ* is the correct reading, it cannot be accidental that the first consonants match those of *brwš* later in the same line. It remains uncertain if this has come about simply under the influence of the preceding lists, or the names derive from an elaborate catalogue of plants.

aw. The signs here present a problem. It is natural to read as *tꜣ*(*y*), presumably the copula, and hence presumably terminating a phrase. In that case the  that follows can only be the def. article *tꜣ*, and it then seems impossible to make any kind of continuous sense of the rest of the line. The text would be reasonably intelligible if 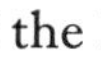 could be read *gm=s*. The difficulty with this reading is that there seems to be no evidence that this kind of writing of *gm* occurs before the Roman period, and there is no such writing in any of the other Saqqâra papyri. It receives slight support from the very similar sign 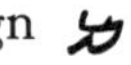 in l. 17 below, where a verb is expected after *ḫr*, but the sense there is not sufficiently clear to settle the question.

ax. The plant-name *brwš* might conceivably be a form of ⲃⲣⲉϣⲏⲩ, 'coriander', Crum, *CD*, 44a (masc.). However, the generally accepted and doubtless correct etymology, deriving the word from *prt-šꜣw*, 'seed of the *šꜣw* plant', can hardly be said to support the identification here: see Crum, *CD*, 44a; Černý, *CED*, 26. 9; Westendorf, *KH*, 27; cf. *Wb. Drog.* 475. The plant det. would not necessarily rule out the sense 'coriander-seed', but the orthography would otherwise be surprising.

ay. If *ỉw=s grg* here qualifies *brwš*, it might have the sense 'established', 'planted'. The small vertical stroke immediately before *ỉw=s* might be an accidental mark, or belong to the previous erased text: otherwise it must be taken as a mark of punctuation (cf. p. 202, n. *p*), although this would not necessarily imply that *ỉw=s grg* could not qualify *brwš*.

az. The nature of the contents of l. 15 is uncertain: ll. 16–19 appear to be a section of narrative, or, at the least, to contain sentences of a narrative character, but it is not so easy to see anything of this kind in l. 15. The chief problem is to make continuous sense of the alternation *ỉw=s* . . . *ỉw=y* . . . *ỉw=s*. Possibly these are isolated phrases, written down as an exercise. The difficulty would partly be removed if *ỉw=y-rwd* were understood as a plant-name: for a name including a 1st pers. pronoun, cf. Mag. Pap. verso 2/3, *mn-pꜣ-nfr-r-ḥr=y*. This would provide two plants, each qualified by a 'Circumstantial' phrase: however, the problems mentioned in p. 206, n. *aw* would remain. Perhaps the sense may be 'coriander, which is planted when I flourish, and which [ripens/wilts(?) when I . . . .]'.

ba. The restoration of *ḫr*, written as in l. 16 (there is also a damaged writing in l. 18), seems certain. It is therefore to be expected that a verb+subject would follow to provide a 'habitual' verb form. If the dubious reading *gm*, suggested on p. 206, n. *aw*, is accepted for the following sign , it might be possible to read *ḫr gm=⌜w⌝-ṯ=y*, or *ḫr gm=s-ṯ=y*.

bb. The sign  here is rather different from the two signs for which the reading *gm* was suggested as a possibility on p. 206, n. *aw* and n. *ba* above: here a reading *gm=s-ṯ(=y) ꜣs*[would be a very dubious possibility.

bc. Immediately after *ḏd=w*, there stands the group , with apparently a small space following. Hardly read *m-bꜣḥ*: a form of *mtw* (*mtw=k*?), or *wꜣḥ*, might be considered. After this, the traces are  : *gy n nw* might be read, but *g* appears elsewhere in the text to be formed , rather than , and there seems little room for the det. (but see the cramped writing in l. 21 below). Possibly *dỉ=y nw* might be read.

bd. In the last two lines of the column, probably three similar explanations or glosses of words are preserved. The first is perhaps to be understood as 'The *gmy*, a kind of ebony tree'. No reading is suggested here for the word following *hbyn*, possibly an adjective (or similar phrase) qualifying *hbyn*, or possibly belonging to the next phrase. The precise identification of *gmy* is problematic, and the probable context of a gloss on a rare word increases the uncertainty: see *Wb.* v. 37. 14 ff. (*ḳmꜣ*); v. 170. 5 (*gmj*); v. 170. 6 (*gmj*): cf. the word for gum, Wb. v, 39. 3 ff. (*ḳmj.t*): see *DG*, 537. 3 (*ḳm*: note the det. , as in the present text), and 537. 6 (*ḳmꜣ*). A name derived from the word for gum seems a possibility.

be. *pšry*, a plant-name: the traces of the *p* are faint but distinctive. The *š* might be read *m*: possibly compare *Wb.* ii. 108. 14–109. 2 (*mrw*, *mrj*).

bf. The obvious interpretation of l. 21 is that it contains a gloss upon the phrase 'the sacred *ḳbꜣ*-vessel of the Syrians': however, it seems impossible to restore the traces at the very beginning of the line to read as the required def. article, either *pꜣ* or *tꜣ* (see n. *bg* below). These traces would suit the det. of *gy* very well: possibly the sense is that '. . . is a kind of sacred *ḳbꜣ*-vessel; and the "Syrian" is a kind of great pot', where *Ḫry* would be used as the name of a kind of vessel. However, it is also possible that the phrase glossed by *gy kry wr* was a longer one, and other restorations might be made at the beginning of the line. See in general Comte [M. É. L. R.] Du Mesnil du Buisson, *Les Noms et signes égyptiens désignant des vases ou objets similaires* (Paris, 1935). Conceivably the mention of vessels in l. 21 may concern the *hbnt*-vessel, *Wb.* ii. 487. 13 ff., and have been prompted by the occurrence of *hbyn*, 'ebony', in l. 20 (cf. l. 2).

bg. *ḳbꜣ* is written . It is not obvious whether *ḳbḥ* or *ḳbꜣ* should be read here: however, the latter is well attested throughout Egyptian as the name of a vessel, *Wb*. v. 25. 2 ff. (*ḳbj*, masc. and fem.); *DG*, 534. 2 (*ḳb.t*); Crum, *CD*, 99b (ⲕⲏⲃⲓ, fem.), and is perhaps more likely here. Its gender in the present text might be masc. or fem.

bh. In view of the det., *kry* here is presumably Coptic ⲕⲗⲉ, Crum, *CD*, 102a, 'vessel for liquids', a Semitic loan-word, and this would match the occurrence of *ḳbꜣ* earlier in this line. The possibility should perhaps be mentioned of understanding Coptic ⲕⲣⲓ, ⲕⲗⲓ, Crum, *CD*, 115a, to which the jar det. would not be inappropriate; cf. Westendorf, *KH*, 60 (ⲕⲗⲓ), with a reference to P. E. Kahle, *Bala'izah: Coptic Texts from Deir el-Bala'izah in Upper Egypt* (Oxford, 1954), I, 466 (text 48, l. 28).

bj. Clearly the last signs in l. 21 are the divine det. belonging to *wr*, and a mark of punctuation (see p. 202, n. *p*), and a place-name det. (see p. 205, n. *al*) is not in question. Although the papyrus is damaged, sufficient of the surface is preserved to show that an empty space stood after *wr*. This at least makes it possible that the text came to an end at this point.

Translation

1.] . . . . Elephantine, Syrians . . . . . [
2.] . . . . . the ibis[α] (was) upon the ebony-tree; the *rd*-bird (was) upon the vine [
3.] . . . . . the *wy*-bird was upon the rose; the Nile-goose was upon the *sry*[
4.] . . . was upon the *ḫt-ršʿ*; the dove was upon the fruit(?)[β] tree; the cock[γ] [
5.] . . . was upon the apple-tree; the quail was upon the *p* . . . . . [
6.] . . . . ; the *ḫ* . . . was upon the *ḫ* . . . ; the kite (?) [
7.] the [. . . . .] the sparrow was upon the . . . . [
8.] kind/fashion that (?)[δ] [. . . . .] . . . . . [
9.] . . . . ; the dove went away to Lower Egypt (?) [
10.] . . . . . to *Rbi*;[ε] the Benu-bird went away to Babylon [
11.] . . . . . the vulture went away to . . . . . [
12.] . . . Persia; the . . . *nini*-bird went away to Upper Egypt (?) [
13.] . . . . . ; the kite went away to Dōr[ζ] [
14.] . . . . went . . . . [

space

15.] . . . . coriander (?) . . . . [
16.] . . . to cease (it?), as she stood at the entrance. . . . . . [
17.] . . . . . the street . . . . sing/praise . . . . [
18.] . . . her business/words. She wished for drink and food and (?) . . . . [
19.] . . . The host of the entire land looked at them. They said . . . . [
20.] the *gmy*, a kind of ebony . . . . . ; the *pšry*, a kind [
21.] . . . sacred *ḳbꜣ*-vessel of the Syrians, a kind of great jar. *space*

Notes on translation

Most of the names, particularly those of birds, plants, and places, have required comment in the notes to the transliteration above. The notes here are therefore designed merely to assist the reading of the translation. For comment on the structure of the text, see the discussion below, especially pp. 209–10.

α. Specifically the sacred ibis, the bird of the god Thoth.

β. Possibly the tree-name here may signify a particular species of tree.

γ. This appears to be the word for 'hen, cock', but

this late-period term may derive from the old name for the black ibis, and possibly in this context 'black ibis' might be meant.

δ. A possible restoration here, mentioned on p. 204, n. *ad*, is 'The places after their fashion that the aforesaid birds went off to'; but many other kinds of restoration are as likely.

ε. Perhaps 'Libya', but there are several other possibilities (see p. 204, n. *ah*).

ζ. On the coast of Palestine.

DISCUSSION

The understanding of this text as a whole is hampered by a number of problems, which arise partly from the nature of its contents, and partly from its fragmentary state of preservation: not one line survives intact.[1]

The best starting-point will be to provide a brief description of the central and most substantial portion of the text, ll. 2–14. Two successive lists occur here. In the first of these (ll. 2–7), various birds are said to be 'upon' various trees or plants. Each phrase follows the pattern (to cite the first example in l. 2) [*r*] *pꜣ hb ḥr pꜣ hbyn*, 'the ibis was upon the ebony-tree'. In each case where the text is well preserved, it is evident that the initial sound of the bird-name and the initial sound of the plant-name are the same. The second list (ll. 9–14) consists of a series of phrases in which various birds are said to 'go away' to various places. For example, (in l. 10) *šm n=f bnw r Bb*[*l*], 'the *Benu*-bird went off to Baby[lon]'. Only in one single case is it certain that a bird-name found in the first list recurs in the second, but two other examples can be restored with some degree of confidence, and it is a reasonable working hypothesis that the scribe's intention was to repeat the first list of birds, although the contents cannot have been arranged in precisely the same order. As in the first list, so also in the second, several indubitable instances can be seen where the bird-name and place-name that are paired together begin with the same sound.

Before discussing the questions raised by these two lists, an account may be given of the other portions of the text.

The first line of the column, although it contains problematic readings, clearly can form no part of the list of birds and plants; in fact, there is good reason (see p. 212 f.) to suppose that this list may begin precisely with the sacred ibis which stands at the beginning of what is preserved of l. 2. The nature of the sentence-structure, if any, in l. 1 is not obvious. The apparent mention of 'Elephantine', at the southern border of Egypt, and of 'the Syrians' might have a connection with the foreign place-names of ll. 9–14. However, l. 1 may contain disconnected glosses of the kind seen at the very end of the column: it may be relevant that l. 1 and l. 21 both seem to mention *nꜣ Ḫry*, 'the Syrians'. The first line shows no sign of containing a title or explanatory phrase, either introducing the lists of ll. 2–14, or providing a heading to the text as a whole.

Line 8 lies between the two lists of birds: although very little is preserved, it does not seem possible to interpret it as forming part of either list. It may perhaps be a preface to the second list, or a postscript to the first (see p. 204, n. *ad* and n. δ above).

After the second list of birds, a space has been left. When the text resumes in ll. 15–21, nothing of the same kind can be recognized. Phrases and sentences that would be appropriate in a story occur in ll. 16–19: some problems of reading and interpretation remain unresolved, but it is perfectly likely that this is a passage of continuous narrative. No proper names can be made out, but at least one female character and 'the people (*or* army) of the entire land' are involved. The contents of l. 15 are obscure:

[1] We are deeply indebted to Professor J. R. Harris of Durham University for fruitful comment upon this text and upon parallels to it elsewhere in Egyptian literature.

conceivably it may belong to the narrative passage that follows, but more probably it consists of disconnected phrases or words. At the end of the column, the obvious interpretation of l. 20 is as containing glosses upon plant-names, and l. 21 appears to deal similarly with names of vessels.

Thus the nature of the text as a whole is far from certain. The way in which the papyrus seems to have been reused (see p. 198), and, less cogently, the fact that a space has been left at the end of l. 21 (see p. 208, n. *bj*), are slight indications that the text may have been written upon a sheet of papyrus cut from a discarded roll, and may have occupied only a single column. It is perhaps most plausible to suppose that the text was a writing-exercise which included the lists of birds, an extract from a narrative, and explanations of rare words, strung together with no pretence of continuity. Yet the possibility cannot entirely be excluded that the lists and glosses were incorporated, however inconsequentially, into a narrative text or a text cast in the form of a letter.

The two lists of birds with plants and places raise a number of questions. There appears to be no exact parallel in Egyptian or demotic texts for the way in which they are arranged with the same sound occurring at the beginning of each of the words that are paired together. In some examples the same demotic sign begins each of the two words concerned. In one case (*rr*, l. 2), it is conceivable that an unusual writing has been used deliberately to achieve this; in another (*mnw*), the word occurs twice, each time matching a word that begins with the sign , but in one instance *mnw* also has this initial sign (l. 4), in the other it is lacking (l. 9). All these examples where the initial sign is the same involve uniconsonantal signs (, , , , , ; probably ; *p* appears in two forms, and). Although the uniconsonantal signs are frequent (, , and also occur as initial signs), they cannot be said to be accorded any special status in this text, over and above their usual prevalence in the demotic script, and especially in writings of foreign words. Apart from the form of *mnw* found in l. 9, a clear illustration is *drỉ* in l. 13, beginning with the group , although demotic writings with a uniconsonantal sign are attested in other texts, and could surely have been used here, had the scribe so wished.

In some cases the matching of the sounds of the two words goes beyond what we would regard as the first sound (*hb*/*hbyn*, *mnw*/*mnw*, *drỉ*/*Dry* are examples: in some respects, of course, a group like or was for the Egyptians indivisible), but this is not true in other examples. The possibility that the vowels, largely unrepresented in the script, might in some way have matched is, for a number of reasons, difficult to assess, but there does not seem to be any likely instance of this.

Had the text been better preserved, it might have been possible to comment on phonetic aspects of the lists, and on what stage in the development of the language it represents. However, as it is impossible to be sure what did *not* occur in the lists, only trivial conclusions can be drawn from what survives. It is also difficult to speculate on the dialect: the written *ḫ* (l. 6) might represent the same sound as *š*, or a guttural; written *l* does not occur, and *rr* (l. 2) and *Rbỉ* present problems in this very respect.

The lists are plainly evidence of an interest in the individual sounds of language, beyond the mere use of assonance as a literary device. Several questions therefore arise: to what extent is the text systematic, does it show that the Egyptians had a recognized list of the sounds of their language, and, if so, did this list have an accepted order?

Although neither point can be proved, it appears reasonable to assume that the same bird-names occur in the two lists, and to assume that no sound occurs more than once in each list. On this basis, despite the fragmentary state of the text, some observations can be made on the probable number of items the lists included.

If the absolute minimum restorations demanded by the traces and the layout of the text are made in a consistent fashion in ll. 2–7, the number of items in the first list is 15. This may be illustrated by the following scheme

h r [ ] *w s* ? *m k ḏ p* [ ] *ḫ d* [ ] *ḳ*

[ ] represents a single item lost, and ? represents the uncertain case of the *ḫt-ršʿ*(?) in l. 4. It is not absolutely certain that no item preceded *h*, or that no item followed *ḳ*.

A similar reconstruction of the second list produces the following scheme

m [ ] *r b* [ ] *n* [ ] *p* ? [ ], *d*, [ ] *ḳ*

? represents the problem of the ... *nỉnỉ*-bird etc. in l. 12. It is not absolutely certain that no item followed the *ḳ*, and there is real doubt whether or not an item or items preceded the *m*, and thus whether or not the second list is defective.

At the end of the lists, the order could well be the same in each. Towards the beginning, no ingenuity of reading or interpretation seems likely to be able to reconcile them.

The alternatives to this reconstruction are to restore an extra item in each line of the text, raising the total in the first list to 20 or 21, or to restore two items (it is difficult to be sure that exactly two would be required in every line), raising the total to approximately 25, which happens to be the size of the Egyptian alphabet according to Plutarch, *De Iside*, 56.

The initial consonants that can be identified with some confidence are, in the conventional order adopted by modern scholars:

w b p m n r h ḫ s ḳ k d ḏ

The most obvious gaps in this list are *y* and *f*: it is possible that the *ḫ* represents the same sound as *š*. Thus, if the list were restored to contain 15 or 16 items, it could represent much the same range as the consonants employed in the Coptic alphabet(s), ignoring those essentially used for foreign words, and probably also omitting *l*. Such speculations cannot be pursued any further here, but, if the state of preservation of the text makes minimum restorations along these lines possible, that must also to some degree suggest they are probable. On the other hand, it would not be difficult to draw up a list of 20 or 21 consonants that matched rather better the conventions of the demotic script.

Although the present text has no close parallel in Egyptian or Demotic, texts are known in which words beginning with the same sound are grouped together. These are probably best divided into two types. First, there are lists of titles of gods or of personal names. Such lists are preserved both from the Late Period and from earlier, and probably are simply an elaboration of the long Egyptian tradition of compiling names and titles, and may be no evidence for any established list of consonants. Note, for example, the ostraca discussed by G. Posener in Annexe 1: 'Deux ostraca littéraires d'un type particulier et le livre Kmj.t', in *La Transmission des textes littéraires égyptiens*, [by] B. van de Walle (Bruxelles, 1948), 41 ff.; the material discussed by H. Grapow and W. Westendorf in *Literatur*. 2., verbesserte und erweitete Aufl., mit Beiträgen von H. Altenmüller [and others],[1] *Handbuch der Orientalistik*, 1. Abt., 1. Bd., 2. Abschnitt. (Leiden, 1970), 224; P. Cairo 31169 verso; and W. Spiegelberg, *Demotica 2. Sitzungsberichte der Bayerischen Akademie der Wissenschaften, Philosophisch-philologische und historische Klasse*, Jahrgang 1928, 2. Abh., no. 30, 44–9. Secondly, there

[1] Cf. A. Mariette, 'Note sur l'utilité des allitérations pour le déchiffrement des hiéroglyphes', *Revue archéologique*, 8e NS, 15 (1867), 290–6; also B. Watterson, 'The use of alliteration in ptolemaic', *Orbis aegyptiorum speculum: glimpses of ancient Egypt: studies in honour of H. W. Fairman* (Warminster, 1979), 167–9.

are more systematic texts, known only from the Late Period. Their whole organization, and perhaps purpose, concern their arrangement with initial sounds matching, and they are thus closer to the present Saqqâra text. Note in hieratic P. Carlsberg 7, edited by E. Iversen as 'Fragments of a hieroglyphic dictionary'; and P. Carlsberg 12 verso, edited by A. Volten as 'An "alphabetical" dictionary and grammar in demotic'. Smaller fragments which may be of the same kind may be found in W. Spiegelberg, *Demotica 1. Sitzungsberichte der Bayerischen Akademie der Wissenschaften, Philosophisch-philologische und historische Klasse*, Jahrgang 1925, 6. Abh., no. 7, 22–5; and E. Bresciani, *Testi demotici nella collezione Michaelidis, Orientis antiqui collectio*, 2 (Roma, 1963), 15–16 [= *Oriens antiquus*, 2 (1963), 15–16].

It is difficult to say if the order of the consonants in the first list of the present text is likely to have been a fixed and generally recognized order. The discrepancies in the second list do little to encourage this belief, but if the text were better preserved a simple explanation for them might be apparent. The place-names listed are probably names in common use in the Late Period, and the same may well be true of the plant- and tree-names. The bird-names, however, include several that, as far as our evidence goes, seem obscure or even obsolete. In a number of cases the orthography might hint that the name had been copied from a hieratic source. In several cases the bird-name seems to be that of the particular bird depicted by a common hieroglyph. These points may suggest only that the bird-names had been drawn from an onomasticon or other earlier source. On the other hand, it may be that the list of birds is fundamental to the list of consonants, and perhaps that this was the way in which Egyptians learned their consonants, as in England children learn 'A is for apple' and so forth.[1]

It may be noted that P. Carlsberg 7 appears to begin with the sacred ibis, *hby*, as probably does the first list in the present text. This was linked by Iversen (p. 8) with Plutarch's statement (*Quaest. conviv.* 9. 3. 2 [738E]) that the Egyptian alphabet began with the Ibis.[2] It had previously been usual to regard this merely as a mistaken corollary to Plutarch's supposed other opinion, that the Egyptian alphabet began with *'aleph* (see, for example, K. Sethe, *Der Ursprung des Alphabets, Königliche Gesellschaft der Wissenschaften in Göttingen: Nachrichten, Geschaftliche Mitteilungen*, 1916 [also repr. Berlin, 1926], Exkurse 17.

In his edition of P. Carlsberg 12, Volten mentioned (p. 507, n. 5) an unpublished Copenhagen papyrus in which he stated that *m* preceded *ḫ*, and *w* preceded *s*: detailed re-examination of this text has established that it is not arranged on any phonetic principle, but the small fragment from which Volten deduced that *w* preceded *s* does not belong to the same text, and may remain slight evidence for this order. In fact l. 3 of the present Saqqâra text shows *w* preceding *s*.[3]

Many uncertainties remain, but the possibility may be left for consideration that the bird-lists in this text may derive in some way from a systematic text such as P. Carlsberg 7, in which words and hieroglyphs were arranged according to their first consonants, and/or from a tradition that identified the consonants of the Egyptian language by the names of birds; and, however corrupt the text may be, it may give some indication of the regular order in which the

[1] A useful survey of some comparable material in other languages may be found in R. Marcus, 'Alphabetic acrostics in the Hellenistic and Roman periods', *Journal of Near Eastern studies*, 6 (1947), 109–15; but this subject, together with the question whether or not the Saqqâra text might show any foreign influences cannot be discussed here. See also G. R. Driver, *Semitic Writing from Pictograph to Alphabet* (*The Schweich Lectures of the British Academy*, 1944, newly revised 3rd edn., London, 1976), 179–85.

[2] For the particular problem of the Ethiopic alphabet, where *h* also appears as the initial letter, see A. M. Honeyman, 'The letter-order of the Semitic alphabets in Africa and the Near East', in *Africa*, 22 (1952), 136–47.

[3] See now *JEA* 68 (1982), 210–27.

Egyptians remembered their consonants. If this were accepted, it would then be no surprise to find the sacred ibis at the head of such a list: as Iversen (p. 8) has pointed out, Plutarch was no doubt correct in attributing this to the Egyptian scribe's special reverence for the god Thoth. Why, however, the list was one of *birds*, and on what principle its order, if there was a fixed order, was determined, are questions that remain.

THE INDEXES

Six indexes are provided: A. Demotic words; B. Demotic titles and epithets; C. Demotic personal names; D. Demotic divine names; E. Demotic place names; F. Coptic words quoted. In the demotic indexes, entries are made in transliteration. References are quoted by the serial number of the text in this publication in **bold** type, followed by 'front' or 'back' (where necessary) and the column number in normal type, followed by the line number or numbers. In all instances, the line numbers quoted follow the oblique stroke /. In texts **1** and **2**, because of the complexities of the order and numbering of the columns, numbers in the form x, x+1, etc. have been used where the original column or line number is unknown. In other fragmentary texts the surviving columns and lines have simply been numbered 1, 2, etc. Because of the fragmentary state of the texts, all doubtful readings, partial restorations, and editorial conjectures are included in the indexes, but are marked with a question-mark. In all such instances, and in many others which require comment, references are given to the notes to the passages in question in the form (n. *ab*). Readers are advised to refer to such notes when making use of the indexes.

In Index A all verbs, substantives, adjectives, adverbs, conjunctions, and the less frequent prepositions and particles are indexed. Pronouns, demonstratives, articles, verbal auxiliaries and tense preformatives, and the commonest prepositions and particles are in general omitted on practical grounds. For certain other very common words (e.g. the verbs *ỉr*, *ḫpr*, *ḏd*) only exceptional usages are noted. For ease of identification, the part of speech is indicated and a translation given, but these are often doubtful, and reference should be made by users to the notes *ad locos*. In Indexes B–E every item, however doubtful, that may be relevant has been included.

The Coptic index (F) is deliberately eclectic, for many of the references to Coptic words in the text of the volume are made merely for the purpose of identifying a demotic word. Wherever a quotation of possible interest for lexicographical or etymological purposes is made, it is indexed.

These procedures, somewhat arbitrary in principle, are adopted in the interests of economy, clarity, and what we hope will prove the reader's convenience.

INDEX A: DEMOTIC WORDS

ꜣyr (subst.) 'hart', **2** back, x+1/34 (n. *ev*)
ꜣyṯy (subst.) 'want', **1**, 9/1 ? (n. *c*)
ꜣ(w)ỉ (subst.) 'bull', **2** front, 6/31 ? (n. *fn*)
ꜣby (vb.) 'be thirsty', **1**, 9/24 ? (n. *br*)
ꜣbd (subst.) 'month', **1a**/24 ? (n. *z*), 24 *bis* ? (n. *aa*); **23** back/2
ꜣpwṯ (subst.) 'messenger', **2** front, 6/26 ? (n. *ew*)
ꜣll(y) (subst.) 'vine', **12** back/2, 4, 5; see also *rr*
ꜣs[..](?) '. . . ?', **27**/17 ? (n. *bb*)
ꜣsḳ (vb.) 'tarry', **2** front, 6/18, 24
ꜣḳ (vb.) 'perish', **2** back, x+1/5
ꜣkm (vb.) 'be dark', **1**, 9/1 ? (n. *c*); **2** front, 6/2 (n. *q*)
ꜣt (subst.) 'back', **1**, 9/28 (n. *bz*)
ḥr ꜣt.ṯ (prep.) 'upon', **1**, 14/24, 29; **2** front, 6/5
ꜣṯḥ (vb.) 'pour', **2** back, x+1/9 ? (n. *bm*)

ỉ (particle) 'O!', **1**, 14/8 *ter*; **2** back, x/1 (n. *b*), 15 ? (n. *v*); x+1/3 ? (n. *ap*), 10 ? (n. *bo*); **6**/4, 6, 7, 9 *bis*, 10 ? (n. *n*), 12 ? (n. *s*); **24**/2 ? (n. *b*); **26**/2 (n. *b*)
ỉꜣw (vb. imp.) 'give!', **1**, 10/34 ? (n. *ex*)
ỉꜣw[.] (vb. or subst.) 'be old, old age', **2** front, 6/23 (n. *eg*)
ỉꜣwt (subst.) 'cattle', see *tp-n-ỉꜣwt*
ỉꜣbṯ (subst. or adj.) 'east', **2** front, 6/30 ? (n. *fh*); **3** front, frag. 1+2/2, 4, 6 (in title *ḥrỉ-ỉꜣbt*)
ỉỉ, *ỉw* (vb.) 'come', **1**, 9/14, 18, 19, 23, 29, 35; 10/34; 13/17, 29; 14/9, 31; **2** front, 6/10, 18, 22, 23, 27, 30; 7/2; **2** back, x/5; x+1/35; **3** front, frag. 1+2/2, frag. 3/5; **3** back, frag. 3/3, frag. 2+1/2 ? (n. *aa*); **11**/3; **13**/3; **14**/5 ? (n. *a*); **17** front/2; **21** front/4
ỉ-ỉr (prep.) 'before', **5**, 1/6 (n. *o*)
ỉ-ỉr-n (prep.) 'before', **2** front, 6/9 ? (n. *at*)
ỉ-ỉr-ḥr (prep.) 'before', **1**, 7/x+4; 10/5, frag. 4/x+4; 14/6, 35; **2** front, 6/1, 18; **2** back, x+1/5, 15, 18 ? (n. *ct*); **4**/6; **5**, 1/3; **11**/2; **21** front/3
ỉ-ỉr-ḏꜣḏꜣ (prep.) 'upon', **2** front, 6/4 (n. *y*)
ỉynm (subst.) 'skin', **2** front, 6/3 ? (n. *s*)
ỉwꜣy (subst.) 'wrong', **1**, 9/6 (n. *r*); 13/4
ỉwỉw (subst.) 'dog', **2** front, 6/13 (n. *bx*)
ỉwf (subst.) 'flesh', **2** front, 6/17, 19; **2** back, x/6, 12
ỉwn (subst.) 'colour', **2** front, 6/20 ? (n. *dm*)
ỉwt (prep.) 'among', **1**, 10/25 ? (n. *eb*); **2** back, x+1/18, 35, 37
ỉb (subst.) 'heart', see *ḥrỉ-ỉb*
ỉp (vb.) 'think', **5**, 1/10
ỉpy (subst.) 'quantity', **1**, 9/35 ? (n. *cu*)
ỉpy-nsw (subst.) 'royal harem', **1**, 13/27, 28; 14/20 ? (n. *dn*)
ỉfd (subst.) 'block', **2** front, 6/19
ỉm (vb. imp.) 'come!', **5**, 1/2
ỉn (vb.) 'bring', **1**, 10/24, 36, 37; 13/32; 14/5; 16/x+5, x+6; **1a**/19, 21; **2** front, 6/14, 17; **2** back, x/7, 27 ? (n. *aa*); x+1/15, 17, 21 ? (n. *dd*), 29; **3** front, frag. 1+2/5; frag. 3/1; **3** back, frag. 3/4; **4**/5 (n. *γ*); **8**/1 ? (n. *a*), 2
ỉn (post-negative particle) **1**, 9/5, 29; 10/27; 13/9; 14/4; **2** front, 6/7; **2** back, x+1/20, 21, 25; **15**/8
ỉn (interrogative particle) **1a**/15; **2** front, 6/20 *bis*, 22, 28, 29 *bis;* **2** back, x+1/1, 4 ?, 10; **7**/7 ?, 8 ? (n. *h*)
ỉn (conj.) 'if, when', **2** back, x+1/4 ?
ỉny (subst.) 'stone', **2** front, 6/2, 19
ỉn-mwt (subst.) 'ghost', **2** front, 6/12 ? (n. *bu*), 24 ? (n. *ek*)
ỉn-nꜣ-w (conj.) 'if, when', **1**, 9/23; **2** back, x+1/22 ? (n. *df*), 34 ? (n. *et*)
ỉnḥ (subst.) 'courtyard', **4**/5
ỉn-ḳdy (vb.) 'sleep', **1**, 7/x+6 ? (n. *k*); **1a**, x/4, 22; **2** back, x/7 ? (n. *n*); x+1/8
ỉnk (pronoun) 'I', **1**, 14/28; **2** front, 6/11; **5**, 1/3
ỉr (vb.) 'do', **1** front, frag. 2/x+2 *et passim;* in Stative, **1**, 10/2 (n. *cz*)
ỉrt.ṯ= (subst.) 'eye', **2** front, 6/19, 30; **5**, 1/2 (n. *α*), 7 (n. *q*)
ỉrỉ (subst.) 'companion', **1**, 9/12; 10/18; 13/22, 30, 31, 32; 14/3, 8; **2** front, 6/16; **2** back, x+1/31
ỉrp (subst.) 'wine', **1**, 9/2; 14/6

ỉrm (prep.) 'together with', **1**, 7/x+4 *et passim*
ỉḫ, ỉẖ (interrogative pronoun) 'what?', **1**, 9/21; **1a**/6; **2** front, 6/26, 29; **25**/2
ỉs (*n-sw*) (adj.) 'belonging to', **1**, 14/4 (n. *ce*)
ỉt (subst.) 'father', **1**, 13/16 (n. *z*); 14/8, 12; **3** back, frag. 2+1/2? (n. *z*); **21** front/3
ỉtn (subst.) 'ground', **2** front, 6/25; **4**/5; **5**, 1/10

yꜥby (vb.) 'be sick', **1a**/6
yꜥby (subst.) 'sickness, trouble', **1**, 9/9, 23; 10/9; 13/18
yb (subst.) 'ivory', **27**/1? (n. *c*); cf. **2** front, 6/3? (n. *t*)
ym (subst.) 'sea, lake', **2** front, 6/13? (n. *by*); **2** back, x+1/9? (n. *bn*)
yr (subst.) 'river', **2** back, x+1/9? (n. *bn*); **9**/2? (n. *a*)
ys (vb.) 'hasten', **2** front, 6/26? (n. *ew*)

ꜥꜣ (adj.) 'great', **1**, 9/4, 6 *bis*, 30; 13, frag. 5/x+3; 13/4, 15, 16, 28; **1a**/16, 20; **2** front, 6/6? (n. *ah*), 18; **2** back, x+1/1? (n. *ah*), 9? (n. *bn*), 14; **5**, 1/9? (n. *aa*); **12** front/4; **21** front/6? (n. *c*); **24**/2, 2 *bis*? (n. *b*); **26**/2? (n. *b*)
ꜥꜣy, ꜥw (vb.) 'be great', **1**, 10/29 (n. *ek*); **2** front, 6/9? (n. *at*); **2** back, x/11
ꜥꜣpy (subst.) 'winged beetle', **2** front, 6/18
ꜥꜥn (vb.?) '. . . . ?', **2** front, 6/1? (n. *g*)
ꜥwỉ (subst.) 'hands', **2** front, 6/11 (n. *bm*)
ꜥwỉ (subst.) 'house', **1**, 9/5, 7, 20, 22, 26, 29, 31; 10/11, 26? (n. *ed*), 28; 13/32; 14/11, 13; **2** front, 6/10? (n. *ba*), 18? (n. *dd*); **2** back, x+1/23? (n. *dj*), 28? (n. *ec*); **3** back, frag. 3/7; **4**/4, 5; **10** front/4; **12** front/3? (n. *d*); see also the title *mr-ꜥwỉ*
ꜥwỉ.w n ḥrr (subst.) 'Houses of Delay', a prison, **1**, 13/19 (n. *ae*); **3** front, frag. 3/3 (n. *j*)
ꜥwỉ-n-drt (subst.) 'utmost', **1**, 7/x+4 (n. *g*); 9/3; 10/35 (n. *fb*)
ꜥb (subst.) 'libation', **2** back, x+1/24? (n. *dm*)
ꜥm(ỉ) (vb.) 'know', **1**, 14/14 (written *mỉ*, n. *cw*); **2** front, 6/15 (n. *cj*)
ꜥmy (subst.) 'character', **2** back, x+1/25? (n. *do*)
ꜥn (adj.) 'beautiful', **1**, 9/22; **2** front, 6/9? (n. *au*)
ꜥn (advb.) 'again', **1**, 9/21; 13/10, 24, 26; 14/9; **1a**/13; **2** front, 6/7; **5**, 1/7; **6**/12? (n. q); **10** back/7; **26**/1? (n. *a*)
ꜥn-smy (vb.) 'report', **1**, 13/23? (n. *am*); 14/7; **2** back, x/26? (n. *z*)
ꜥnḫ (vb.) 'live', **1**, 7/x+5? (n. *h*); 9/1, 29; 10/26; 14/4; **25**/5 *bis*, 8 (n. *m*)
ꜥnḫ (subst.) 'life', **2** front, 6/24; **2** back, x/1, 4? (n. *h*)
ꜥnḫ (subst.) 'oath', **1**, 7/x+5 (n. *h*); 13/31
ꜥr (vb.) 'mount, embark', **1**, 13/24, 32; **2** front, 6/5 (n. *ab*), 11 (n. *bl*); **2** back, x+1/19, 21, 32; **9**/3 (n. *b*), 4
ꜥry (subst.) 'thistle', **1**, 9/34 (n. *cs*)
ꜥḥꜥ (vb.) 'stand', **1**, 10/1; 13, frag. 4/x+4; 13/6, 29; **2** front, 6/10, 16, 24; **2** back, x+1/15? (n. *ch*); **27**/16
ꜥḥꜥ (subst.) 'life-time', **1**, 13/2; **6**/10, 11, 12
ꜥẖ (subst.) 'brazier', **1**, 14/3, 4, 36
ꜥẖy (vb.) 'hang', **1**, 9/32 (n. *cm*)
ꜥs (particle) 'behold!', **2** front, 6/12? (n. *bn*), 23 (n. *ef*)
ꜥš (vb.) 'summon, read', **1**, 9/18, 19; 10/3; 14/32; **1a**/7; **2** front, 6/1? (n. *f*), 6, 14? (n. *ce*), 31; **2** back, x+1/7, 11; **3** back, frag. 3/5; **4**/1; **11**/7; see also the title *sdm-ꜥš*
ꜥš-sḫn (subst.) 'circumstances', **1**, 9/16
ꜥšꜣ (vb.) 'be numerous', **2** back, x+1/12, 34
ꜥšꜣ (adj.) 'many', **3** front, frag. 1+2/3? (n. *d*); **25**/7
ꜥḳ (subst.) 'bread', **2** back, x/7; x+1/13? (n. *bz*); **12** back/2, 3, 6; **14**/3
ꜥḳr (subst.) 'reed', **1**, 13/7 (n. *j*)
ꜥt.t (subst.) 'limb', **5**, 1/9? (n. *y*); **10** back/10? (n. *k*)
ꜥḏb (vb.) 'freeze', **2** front, 6/9

wꜣy (vb.) 'be far off', **1**, 9/21 *bis*; 13/21 (n. *ah*); 14/12; **2** front, 6/1? (n. *l*), 7, 13? (n. *bz*); **2** back, x/12? (n. *s*)
wꜣḥ (vb.) 'alight, stay', **2** front, 6/18; **5**, 1/2; **7**/8? (n. *k*)
wꜣḏ (adj.?) 'young', **2** back, x/10 (n. *q*)
wy (subst.) 'species of bird', **27**/3 (n. *k*)
wꜥ (subst.) 'curse', **2** front, 6/27 (n. *ez*), 28
wꜥ (adj., indef. art.) 'one, a', **1**, 9/2 *et passim*; see also numeral *1*
wꜥ.ṯ (adj.) 'alone', **6**/8? (n. *g*)
wꜥb (vb.) 'be pure', **21** front/2
wꜥb (adj.) 'pure', **27**/21 (n. *bf*)
wꜥb.t (subst.) 'wash-slab?', **1**, 9/32 (n. *cl*)
wꜥb.t (subst.) 'purification-place?', **2** front, 6/8? (n. *aq*); **11**/3? (n. *c*)
wbꜣ (prep.) 'for, towards', **1**, 10/24; **2** front, 6/9 (n. *av*); **2** back, x+1/14 (n. *cd*); **3** back, frag. 3/3? (n. *s*)
wbn (subst.) 'radiance', **2** front, 6/12 (n. *bo*)
wpy (vb.) 'open, judge', **2** front, 6/16 (n. *cq*), 26
wpy (subst.) 'judgement', **2** front, 6/7? (n. *ao*), 16 (n. *cq*), both in *ỉr-wpy*
wn (vb.) 'exist', **1a**/15; **2** back, x+1/29 in *wn m-dr*; as auxiliary *passim*
wn (vb.) 'open', **2** back, x+1/24? (n. *dn*); **11**/2
wnwt (subst.) 'hour', **1**, 9/14, 35; 13/17; 14/36; **1a**/18; **2** front, 6/17 (n. *cw*), 25; **2** back, x+1/13? (n. *ca*), 15? (n. *cg*), 22? (n. *df*), 34? (n. *et*); **3** back, frag. 2+1/4; **4**/4; **6**/10
wnm (vb.) 'eat', **1**, 13/3; **2** front, 6/11; **2** back, x/1; x+1/13, 23; **27**/18
wn[ḥ] (vb.) 'reveal', **2** back, x+1/24? (n. *dn*)
wnš (subst.) 'wolf', **2** back, x+1/34? (n. *ev*)
wr (adj.) 'great', **2** back, x+1/1 (n. *ah*), 8? (n. *bk*), 30? (n. *ej*); **27**/21 (n. *bj*)
wrs (subst.) 'head-rest', **2** front, 6/4
wrṯ (subst.) 'rose', **27**/3 (n. *l*)
wḥm (vb., advb.) 'repeat, repeatedly', **1**, 9/23? (n. *bo*); **2** front, 6/28 *bis* (n. *fa*)
wḫꜣ (vb.) 'desire', **1**, 9/29; **2** front, 6/29, 30; **2** back, x/1; x+1/33? (n. *er*); **27**/18
wḫꜣ (subst.) 'letter', **2** back, x/25? (n. *y*), 32? (n. *ae*); x+1/26, 29? (n. *ed*), 30, 31 (all in the title *sẖ n pꜣ wḫꜣ*)
wsḫy (subst.) 'hall', **2** front, 7/6
wsṯn (vb.) 'overween', **2** front, 6/28; **2** back, x+1/5? (n. *aw*)
wš (subst., vb.) 'failure, fail', **1**, 16/x+5 (*ỉr-wš*); **25**/2? (n. *c*)
wšd (vb.) 'address, worship', **2** front, 6/18; **2** back, x+1/27 *bis*, 36
wṯy (subst.) 'inheritance', **2** back, x+1/28 (n. *ec*)
wtn (subst.) 'barque', **2** back, x+1/11; **17** back/4
wtn (subst.) 'libation', **1**, 14/6; **6**/9 (n. *h*)
wdb (subst.) 'turner?', **2** front, 6/13 (n. *cb*)
wḏꜣ (vb.) 'be safe', **1**, 10/23 (n. *dx*); 14/28; **2** back, x+1/18, 29; **8**/3

bꜣḥ in *m-bꜣḥ* (prep.) 'before', **1**, 13, frag. 4/x+2? (n. *b*); 13/27; 14/7; **2** front, 6/5; **2** back, x+1/1? (n. *aj*), 28; **24**/4; **25**/4
bꜣk (subst.) 'servant', **2** front, 6/26; **22**/4
bỉn (adj.) 'evil', **1**, 9/4; **5**, 1/8? (nn. *s, t*); **11**/1
nꜣ-bỉn (vb.) 'be evil', **5**, 1/7? (n. *q*); **22**/3? (n. *c*)
bỉk (subst.) 'falcon', **2** front, 6/9 (n. *au*); **4**/1, 2
byry (subst.) 'ship', **1**, 13/21? (n. *ag*), 32; **2** front, 6/10? (n. *az*); **9**/2? (n. *a*)
bw (subst.) 'place', in *r-bw-nꜣy* (advb.) 'hither', **1**, 14/31 *bis*
bwt (subst.) 'crime', **5**, 1/4 (n. *f*)
bny (subst.) 'date-palm', **1**, 9/35 (n. *ct*)
bnw (subst.) 'phoenix', **27**/10 (n. *aj*)
bnr (advb.) 'outside' in compound advbs.
n-bnr 'outside', **1**, 9/27

r-bnr 'out, outwards', **1**, 9/3, 14, 19, 27, 35; 10, frag. 4/x+3; 13/17, 27, 28; 14/18, 22; **2** front, 6/18? (n. *dc*); **3** front, frag. 1+2/3; frag. 3/5; **3** back, frag. 3/4; **5**, 1/4; **21** front/4
(*n*) *pꜣ bnr* 'outside', **1**, 9/17
brwš (subst.) 'coriander', **27**/15 (n. *ax*)
brṯ (subst.) name of plant or tree, **27**/15 (n. *av*)
btw in adj. vb. *nꜣ-btw=f*? 'be sinful', **5**, 1/7 (n. *q*)

p.t (subst.) 'sky', **2** front, 6/14, 18; **2** back, x/5? (n. *j*) 22? (n. *w*); x+1/6
pꜣy (vb.) 'fly', **4**/2 (n. *d*), 4
pꜥꜥry (subst.) 'quail', **27**/5 (n. *w*)
pr (vb.) 'come forth', **16** back/2? (n. *b*)
pr (subst.) 'house, temple', **2** front, 6/8? (n. *aq*); **2** back, x+1/21; **6**/6; **14**/5 (n. *α*)
pr-ỉꜣbt 'the east', **2** front, 6/30 (or *pr-ỉmnṭ*, n. *fh*)
pr-ỉpy-nsw 'royal harem', **1**, 13/27, 28; 14/20? (n. *dn*)
pr-ꜥnḫ 'House of Life', **2** front, 6/1? (n. *h*)
pr-Pr-ꜥꜣ 'royal palace', **1**, 13/24; 14/10; **22**/3? (n. *d*)
pr-nfr 'embalming-place', **2** front, 7/5 (nn. *fu*, *ασ*)
pr-ḥtp 'burial-place?' **1**, 14/23 (perhaps incomplete, n. *du*)
pr-ḥḏ 'treasury', **1a**/12; **14**/4
pry (vb.) 'see (a vision)', **2** back, x+1/8 (n. *bh*)
pḥ (vb.) 'reach', **1**, 9/7, 18, 20; 14/7, 31; **2** back, x+1/30, 33? (n. *eq*), 37? (n. *fc*); **14**/3; **23** front/5; **25**/3
psy (vb.) 'cook', **2** back, x/8
pš.t (subst.) 'share', **22**/2? (n. *b*)
pšn (vb.) 'share', **1**, 16/x+4
pšry (subst.), name of plant or tree, **27**/20 (n. *be*)
pky (subst.), name of plant or tree, **27**/5? (n. *x*)
pgy (subst.) 'mourning-linen', **1**, 9/15 (n. *as*); 14/32
pt (vb.) 'flee', **1**, 14/18? (n. *de*), 22; **2** back, x+1/32, 37
pty (subst.) 'bow', **21** back/4? (n. *d*)

fꜣy (subst.) 'income', **1a**/9? (n. *h*); **2** front, 7/3 (n. *ft*); **2** back, x/14? (n. *u*, perhaps vb.)
fꜣy (subst.) 'bearer', in the title *sdm-ꜥš fꜣy* (q.v.), **2** back, x+1/10 (n. *br*), 15 (reading rejected)
fꜥi (subst.) 'hair', **2** front, 6/4? (n. *y*)
fty (vb.) 'wipe', **2** back, x+1/14? (n. *cb*, rejected)

mꜣi (subst.) 'lion', **2** back, x/10 *bis*; x+1/8? (n. *bj*), 10, 14? (n. *cc*), 15, 36, 37
mꜣy (adj.) 'new', **1**, 9/7
mꜣy (subst.) 'island', **5**, 1/5 (n. *k*)
mꜣꜥ (vb.) 'be justified', **9**/4 (n. *c*)
mꜣꜥ (subst.) 'place', **2** back, x+1/33, 37; **8**/7 (n. *j*)
mi (vb.) 'know', **1**, 14/14 (n. *cw*); for *ꜥmi*, q.v.
my (vb. imp.) 'give, let!', **1**, 10/5 *et passim*
my-ḥṯ (subst.) 'oryx?', **2** back, x+1/14? (n. *cc*)
mi.t (subst.) 'cat', **4**/1, 2
mi.t (subst.) 'road', **2** back, x/4; x+1/37
myt (subst.) 'road', **2** front, 6/17, 24; **2** back, x+1/38 (n. *fd*); **5**, 1/10
mw (subst.) 'water', **1**, 9/32, 33; **2** back, x+1/9, 13 *bis*, 15? (n. *cg*); **17** back/3
mw.t (subst.) 'mother', **1**, 13/10? (n. *n*, perhaps divine name); **2** front, 6/6 (n. *ah*), 15, 29; **2** back, x+1/8? (n. *bk*)
mwy (vb.) 'think', **2** back, x+1/24 (n. *dm*)
mwt (vb.) 'die', **1a**/23; **2** front, 5/x+3? (or subst.?; n. *b*); 6/9? (n. *ay*), 15, 15 bis? (n. *ck*), 29 (n. *ff*); 7/4
mwt (subst.) 'death', **2** front, 6/17, 23, 25 (n. *eq*); 7/9; **2** back, x+1/12 (n. *by*); see also *in-mwt*
mwt.ṯ (subst.) 'dying man', **2** front, 6/9 (n. *ax*)
mfky (subst.) 'turquoise', **2** front, 6/3? (n. *u*)
mm (subst.) 'giraffe', **2** back, x+1/34
mn (vb.) 'remain', **3** back, frag. 2+1/6? (n. *ac*)
mn (vb.) 'is not', **1**, 13/31; 14/14; **2** front, 6/15, 23; 7/7; **2** back, x/3; x+1/2, 25 (n. *dp*), 33; **3** front, frag. 1+2/1? (n. *a*); **5**, 1/9
mn-mtw= 'has not', **1**, 9/11; **25**/6? (n. *g*)
mn (vb.) 'moor, die', **5**, 1/5? (n. *l*); **25**/4 (n. *e*)
mn (subst.) 'death', **5**, 1/3
mn (subst.) 'so-and-so', **7**/8 *bis* (n. *j*)
mn.t (subst.) 'day-time', in *m-mn.t* (advb.) 'daily', **1**, 9/24; 14/19
mnw (subst.) 'dove', **27**/4 (n. *q*), 9
mn(w) (subst.) 'fruit-tree', **27**/4 (n. *r*)
mnḥ (subst.) 'wax', **4**/1 *ter*, 2, 2 *bis*? (n. *f*)
mnḫy (subst.) 'clothes', **1**, 14/1; also written *mnš.w*, **2** front, 6/11
mnḳ (vb.) 'complete', **2** front, 6/20, 25; **2** back, x/5? (n. *j*); x+1/6? (n. *ay*), 7? (nn. *bf–bg*)
mr (vb.) 'love', **2** back, x+1/10? (n. *bp*)
mr (vb.) 'bind', **1**, 9/31 (n. *ch*)
mr.t (subst.) in *r-mr.t* (advb.) 'on board', **1**, 13/24; **9**/2? (n. *a*)
[*m*]*rgy* (subst.), name of a plant or tree, **27**/1? (n. *c*)
mrṯ (subst.) 'manner', **2** back, x+1/16? (n. *cl*)
mhwꜣ (subst.) 'family', **1**, 13/22, 30; 14/3
mḥ (vb.) 'fill', **1**, 9/32; **23** back/2? (or *mḥ* 'seize')
mḥ (prefix of ordinal numbers) **1**, 7/x+8 (*mḥ*-7); 14/37 (*mḥ*-14); 16/x+8 (*mḥ*-16); **2** front, 6/28 (*mḥ*-2), 32 (*mḥ*-6); **2** back, x+1/20 (*mḥ*-1½?, n. *cx*); **13**/4 (*mḥ*-3)
mḥ, *mḥṯ* (vb.) 'seize', **1**, 13/11? (n. *r*); 14/13, 23 (n. *dt*); **2** front, 6/1? (n. *j*); **2** back, x+1/30 (n. *eg*), 31; **23** back/2? (or *mḥ* 'fill')
mḥṯ (adj.) 'north', **7**/7 (n. *g*)
mḥw (subst.) 'tomb', **1a**/23 (n. *y*)
mḫy (vb.) 'beat', **2** back, x/2? (n. *e*); x+1/19, 21 (n. *dd*), 32; **5**, 1/11 (n. *ac*)
ms (vb.) 'give birth', **1a**/20; **2** front, 6/10 (n. *bd*); **21** front/6 (n. *c*)
ms (subst.) 'calf', **2** front, 6/31 (n. *fn*)
msty (vb.) 'hate', **1**, 9/22
mšꜥ (vb.) 'proceed', **1**, 9/7, 17; 13/33; **1a**/27; **2** back, x+1/3? (n. *ap*), 19, 22 *bis*, 32, 37; **5**, 1/10; **6**/3
mšꜥ.w (subst., pl.) 'wanderings', **2** back, x+1/25 *bis*
mšꜥ (subst.) 'army, people', **1**, 13/32; 14/1, 2; **2** front, 6/1; **2** back, x+1/3, 5, 18; **27**/19
mky (vb.) 'protect', **1**, 10/23? (n. *dv*)
mkḥ (vb.) 'be in pain', **22**/3? (n. *c*)
mkṯr (subst.) 'tower', **1**, 10/10; 13/14, 33
mtꜥṯ (subst.) 'bridle', **2** back, x+1/19 (n. *cv*), 21, 32
mtw= (prep.) 'belonging to, from', **1**, 9/11, 21; 10/24 *bis* (n. *ea*); 13/2, 26; 14/16? (nn. *cz*, *da*); **2** front, 6/15, 23; **2** back, x/1 (n. *c*); x+1/13, 18 (n. *cr*); **3** front, frag. 3/2? (n. *g*); **25**/6 (n. *g*)
mtr (vb.) 'be suitable', **5**, 1/7 (n. *r*)
mtr (subst.) in ⌜*n*⌝ *pꜣ mtr* (advb.) 'in the middle', **4**/4 (n. *j*)
md (vb.) 'speak', **1**, 9/8; 10/31, 32; **2** front, 6/10, 22? (n. *eb*), 26; **2** back, x/9; x+1/23, 35; **23** front/2
mdt (subst.) 'word, thing', **1**, 9/3, 25 *bis*; 10/22, 27, 29, 31, frag. 4/x+2; 13/12, 16, 25, 26; 14/14, 30, 35; 16/x+3, frag. 1/x+2; **2** front, 6/21, 25; **2** back, x/5, 22? (n. *w*); x+1/6, 17, 28, 29, 30; **4**/6; **11**/2, 4?; **23** front/6, 7; **24**/4; **25**/3; **27**/18
mdt bin.t 'misfortune', **1**, 9/4; 13/11
mdt nfr.t 'favour', **1**, 10, frag. 4/x+4; 14/32? (n. *el*)

mḏꜥ(y) (vb.) 'grieve', **1**, 9/1? (n. *c*, ? metathesis of *ḏmꜥy*)

n-ỉm, *n-ỉm=w* (advb.) 'there', **1**, 9/16 (n. *av*); 14/16? (nn. *cy*, *cz*); **2** front, 6/30; **23** front/3 (n. *b*)
nꜥm.w (subst., pl.) 'drapes', **2** front, 6/3 (metathesis for *nmꜥ.w*)
nꜥš (vb.) 'be victorious', **2** front, 6/7? (n. *an*), 22 *bis* (n. *ec*)
nw (vb.) 'see', **1**, 9/27 *bis*, 28, 31; 10/13; 13/14, 15; **2** front, 6/18 *bis*, 19 *bis*, 25; 7/1, 8; **2** back, x+1/10, 31, 34, 35, 36? (n. *ez*), 36 *bis*; **4**/6; **15**/13; **27**/19, 19 *bis* (n. *bc*)
nw (subst.) 'sight', **2** front, 6/19 *bis* (nn. *dg*, *dk*)
nw (subst.) 'hour', **1**, 9/5, 19; 13/18; **2** back, x+1/20 *bis*
-nw (suffix of ordinal numbers) **1**, 16/x+3, x+5 (4-*nw*); **2** front, 6/13? (n. *bx*); **2** back, x+1/16? (4-*nw*, n. *ck*)
nwy (subst.) 'lance, standard?', **2** front, 6/11 (n. *bl*)
nb (subst.) 'gold', **1**, 14/5 (n. *ck*)
nb (adj.) 'all, every', **1**, 9/3 *et passim*; see also *rmt nb*
nb.t (subst.) 'flame', **2** front, 6/31 (n. *fq*)
nbỉ, *nby* (vb.) 'be evil', **2** front, 6/7? (n. *al*), 8
nfr (adj.) 'good', **1a**/15; **2** back, x+1/13
nꜣ-nfr (vb.) 'be good', **1**, 10/30; **2** back, x/6; x+1/31
nm (interrogative pronoun) 'who?', **1**, 14/17; **1a**/22; **2** back, x+1/2 (n. *am*), 26, 27
nmḥ (adj.) 'free', **2** front, 6/6? (n. *ah*)
nry (subst.) 'vulture', **27**/11 (n. *am*)
nhpy (vb.) 'mourn', **1**, 14/20, 27
nhr (subst.) 'monster?', **2** front, 6/14 (n. *cc*)
nhs (vb.) 'awake', **2** front, 6/19; **2** back, x/24? (n. *x*); x+1/20
nḥy (vb.) 'trust', **1**, 9/16
nḥm (vb.) 'seize, rescue', **1**, 10/33 (n. *ev*); **2** front, 6/20; **2** back, x+1/17; **6**/5 (n. *c*)
nḥḥ (subst.) 'oil', **6**/5 (n. *b*)
nḫy (subst.) 'mourning', **1**, 13/28
nkt (subst.) 'things', **1**, 16/x+5; **2** front, 6/4, 21; **10** back/6
ntỉ (relative adj.) 'who', **1**, 7/x+5, *et passim*
ntr (subst.) 'god', **1**, 9/22, 25; 10/33; 13/25? (n. *at*); **2** front, 6/7, 22, 23, 26, 27, 30; **5**, 1/9; **25**/3; **26**/3 (n. *d*), 5; see also *dwꜣ-ntr*
ntr.t 'goddess', **1**, 9/29? (n. *cb*); **2** back, x+1/1? (n. *ah*), 8 (n. *bk*), 14;
ntr.w 'gods', **1**, 9/20; **2** front, 6/12, 16, 16 *bis*? (n. *cr*); **9**/7; **25**/5
ntr.. 'divine . . . . .?', **2** front, 6/11 *bis* (n. *bj*)
nḏm (adj.) 'sweet', **2** front, 6/6? (n. *ah*)

rꜣ (subst.) 'mouth, door', **1a**/7; **2** front, 6/26; **2** back, x+1/23 (n. *dh*); **5**, 1/7? (n. *q*)
n-rꜣ (prep.) 'from the door of', **1**, 13/17
r-rꜣ (prep.) 'to the door of', **1**, 9/20? (n. *bf*); 14/9
ḥr-rꜣ (prep.) 'at the door of', **1**, 14/36; **27**/16
rỉt (subst.) 'chamber', **1**, 9/8; **2** front, 6/10
rỉt ḥrỉ.t 'upper part, upper side', **1**, 13/33; **1a**/27; **2** back, x+1/15 (n. *ch*), 16
rỉt ẖrỉ.t 'lower part', **2** back, x+1/15? (n. *ch*)
rwš (vb.) 'care for', **1**, 14/8? (n. *cn*); **2** back, x+1/23? (n. dk); **5**, 1/2; **26**/2
rwd (vb.) 'grow?', 'be strong?', **27**/15? (n. *az*)
rmy (vb.) 'weep', **1**, 9/15, 19 *bis*, 21, 25; 10/24; 13/6; 14/8; **2** front, 6/10; **2** back, x+1/6, 23? (n. *dk*)
rmt (subst.) 'man', **1**, 7/x+2 (n. *b*); 9/10, 35; 13/2, 28, 31; 14/4; **2** front, 6/12; **2** back, x+1/19, 22, 31, 32; **5**, 1/5; **6**/8, 10; **15**/2; **22**/5? (n. *h*); **25**/6
rmt(.t) 'woman', **1**, 9/22, 29, 30
rmt ꜥꜣ 'great man', **1**, 9/4, 6, 30; 13, frag. 5/x+3; 13/15; 14/1, 6, 7, 27; 16/x+6; **2** back, x/35? (n. *ag*); x+1/4? (n. *ar*), 5? (n. *aw*), 7? (n. *be*); **9**/5; **12** front/4; **24**/2; see p. 48.
rmt n pꜣ tꜣ 'anybody', **1**, 14/14; **2** back, x+1/31 (n. *el*)
rmt nb 'everybody', **3** front, frag. 3/2? (n. *g*); **25**/5
rmt rḫ 'wise man', **24**/5
rmt ḫm 'humble man', **2** front, 6/12 (n. *br*)
rn (subst.) 'name', **1**, 14/27; **4**/4
rnpt (subst.) 'year', **1**, 9/1; 13/9; 14/19; **25**/7
rr (subst.) 'vine', **27**/2 (n. *j*); see also *ꜣll(y)*
rhy (subst.) 'evening', **1**, 9/23
rḫ (vb.) 'know', **1**, 9/6; 14/21; **2** front, 6/7, 12, 22, 29 (n. *fd*); **2** back, x+1/1, 4, 25? (n. *dp*), 26, 31, 33; **6**/3? (n. *a*)
rḫ (vb.) 'be able to', **1**, 9/3; 10/27; 13/26; **2** front, 6/1? (n. *l*), 29 *bis* (n. *fd*); **2** back, x+1/4 (n. *as*), 6; **11**/4; **24**/5
rḫ (subst.) 'knowledge', **2** front, 6/15
rḫ (subst.) 'acquaintance, initiate', **2** front, 6/22
rḫ (vb.) 'wash', **1**, 9/32? (n. *cj*)
rsỉ (adj.) 'south', **1**, 9/13 (n. *an*); 16/x+2; **2** front, 6/3? (n. *t*); **5**, 1/11? (n. *ad*)
rsy (vb.) 'awake', **4**/1 (n. *b*)
rswy (subst.) 'dream', **2** back, x/15? (n. *v*); x+1/8, 36
rsṯ, *rsty* (subst., advb.) 'tomorrow', **2** back, x+1/6? (n. *bb*); **5**, 1/2; **23**/9
ršꜣ (vb.?) 'rejoice', **2** front, 6/3 (n. *t*)
ršꜥ (subst.), in *ḫt-ršꜥ*, name of a plant or tree, **27**/4 (n. *o*)
rk (vb.) 'turn', **2** front, 6/9 (n. *av*), 19 (n. *dk*); see also *rk* 'cease'
rk (vb.) 'cease', **1**, 10/35 (n. *ez*); 13/33; **2** front, 6/7? (n. *ap*); **2** back, x/10 (n. *q*); x+1/4? (n. *τ*); **5**, 1/10? (n. *ab*); **21** back/3; **27**/16; see also *rk* 'turn', written in same way
rd (subst.), a species of bird, **27**/2 (n. *h*)
rdwỉ (subst.) 'feet', **2** back, x/3, 11? (n. *r*)
n-rdwỉ.ṯ= (prep.) 'at the feet of', **1**, 14/33
rd.ty (subst.) 'way, manner', **2** back, x+1/27 (n. *dv*)

lwl (subst.) 'child', **1**, 13/23 (n. *ao*)
lh[b] (subst.) 'vapour', **1**, 9/35? (n. *cw*)
lg (vb.) 'hide', **1**, 9/28? (n. *by*)
ltm (subst.), name of plant or tree, **27**/1? (n. *b*)

hy (subst.) 'expense', **1**, 7/x+7? (n. *m*)
hyꜣ(t) (subst.) porch', **1**, 9/7 (n. *v*), 20? (n. *bf*); 13/10; 14/19; see also *ẖyṯ*
hyn.w (adj., pl.) 'some', **1**, 7/x+7? (n. *m*); 9/10, 34 *bis*; 10/33, 34; **2** back, x+1/34; **4**/3
hwn (adj. vb.?) '. . . .?', **5**, 1/8? (n. *u*, reading *r nꜣ-hwn=f* and comparing *hwš*)
hwš (vb.) 'be humiliated', **1a**/9; **2** front, 6/31; see also *hwn*
hb (vb.) 'send, write', **1**, 13/26; **2** front, 7/2
hb (subst.) 'ibis', **27**/2 (n. *f*)
hbyn, *hbny* (subst.) 'ebony', **2** front, 6/3? (n. *t*); **27**/2 (n. *g*), 20
hbr (subst.) 'affliction?', **1**, 10/34 (n. *ey*)
hp (subst.) 'law', **24**/3 (n. *c*), 5 *bis*, 6; **25**/6
hmy (particle) 'would that', **2** front, 6/27, 28
hmhm (vb.) 'tread?', **1**, 10/1? (n. *cy*)
hn (vb.) 'agree', **1**, 10/1? (n. *cy*); **25**/1? (n. *a*)
hnw (subst.) 'jubilation', **2** front, 6/6? (n. *ag*)
hrw (subst.) 'day', **1**, 9/4; 10/18; 14/15; **2** front, 6/25 (n. *eq*); **3** back, frag. 3/1? (n. *p*)
pꜣ (hrw) 'today', **1**, 9/21; 13/5 (n. *f*); 14/34; **5**, 1/2
hrw nfr 'holiday', **3** front, frag. 3/6 (n. ζ)

ḥꜣ (prep.) 'behind', **1**, 9/28 (n. *ca*); **2** front, 6/4 (n. *z*), 17 (n. *cw*)
ḥꜣ.t (subst.) 'front, forehead', **2** front, 6/9? (n. *au*), 20? (n. *dm*)
ḥꜣ.t (subst.) 'prow', **2** back, x+1/11

(n-)ḥꜣ(.t) (advb.) 'before, formerly', **2** front, 6/27 (n. *ez*), 28 (n. *fb*); **2** back, x+1/11 (n. *bu*); **26**/3 (n. *c*)

(n-)ḥꜣ(.t), *(n)ḥꜣ.ṯ=* (prep.) 'before, in front of', **2** front, 6/15 (n. *cg*), 25 (n. *eq*); **2** back, x+1/19, 22, 32, 37

r-ḥꜣ(.t), *r-ḥꜣ.ṯ=* (prep.) 'in front of', **1**, 13/10 (n. *n*); 14/16 (n. *cy*); **9**/7 (n. *f*)

ḥꜣt-sp (subst.) 'year . . .', **23** back/2

ḥꜣt.ṯ= (subst.) 'heart, mind', **1**, 9/3? (n. *f*); **2** front, 6/23, 24? (n. *em*); **2** back, x/11; x+1/12; **5**, 1/3; **7**/5; **12**/1

n-ḥꜣt.ṯ= (prep.) 'in, in the heart of', **1**, 9/5; 10/35; **2** front, 6/21 (n. *dw*), 22? (n. *eb*); **2** back, x+1/2 *bis*, 5? (n. *au*), 17, 36; **16**/2?; **26**/5 (n. *h*)

ḥr-ḥꜣt.ṯ= (prep.) 'upon the heart of', **3** back, frag. 3/4; **7**/8? (n. *k*)

ḥyṯy (subst.) 'hyena', **2** back, x+1/34

ḥw (subst.) 'excess', **1**, 13/31 (n. *bl*)

ḥwt (subst.) 'palace', **1**, 14/9 (n. *cp*), 10, 36 (n. *et*)

ḥwt-ntr 'temple', **1**, 9/18, 19; 10/29; **3** front, frag. 3/4, 5; **3** back, frag. 2+1/4; **11**/6, 7 (n. *k*)

ḥwt- . . . 'temple of fire?', **2** front, 6/31 (n. *fo*)

ḥwꜣy (subst.) 'wickedness', **1**, 9/6? (n. *r*); 13/4?

ḥwy (vb.) 'strike, cast', **2** front, 6/11 (n. *bm*); **3** front, frag. 1+2/3 (n. *c*); **11**/5 (n. *h*)

[ḥ]wny (subst.) 'youth', **18** back/1? (n. *a*)

ḥwrꜥ (vb.) 'rob', **2** back, x+1/12

ḥb (subst.) 'festival', **2** front, 6/11? (n. *bl*), 27, 28 *bis* (n. *fc*); **5**, 2/2? (n. *a*)

ḥbꜣ.w (subst.) 'griefs', **7**/6 (n. *f*)

ḥbs (subst.) 'garment', **1**, 9/2, 15, 31; 10/27? (n. *ef*); 14/24; see also *ṯꜣỉ-ḥbs*

ḥp (vb.) 'be concealed', **1**, 9/8 (n. *y*); **2** back, x+1/25 (n. *dq*)

ḥm (subst.) 'craft', 'craftsman', **2** front, 6/4 (n. *aa*)

ḥm.t (subst.) 'wife', **1**, 9/7, 30, 33; 10/12, 28? (n. *eh*); 13/3; 14/28; **8**/5? (n. *f*), 6; see also *s-ḥmt*

ḥmꜣ (subst.) 'salt', **2** back, x+1/15

ḥmꜣr (subst.) 'death-bird', **2** front, 6/8 (n. *as*), 23, 30

ḥms (vb.) 'sit', **1**, 9/1, 26, 27; **2** front, 6/19; **2** back, x+1/35

ḥmt (subst.) 'copper', **1**, 9/32 (pl. 'copper utensils?', n. *cn*); **2** front, 6/2 (*ḥmt ꜣkm*, perhaps bronze or niello, n. *β*)

ḥn (vb.) 'order', **1**, 9/6; 13/4, 27; 14/3, 13; **4**/2, 2 *bis*? (n. *f*); **16** back/3? (n. *c*)

ḥn (subst.) 'pot', **1**, 9/32

ḥny (subst.) 'canal', **2** front, 6/13 (n. *bz*)

ḥny (subst.) 'incense', **2** front, 6/5

ḥnꜥ (prep.) 'with', **22**/2? (n. *b*)

ḥnw.wt (subst.) 'coffins', **1**, 14/2 (n. *by*)

ḥnḳt (subst.) 'beer', **1**, 9/2, 10; 16/x+4

ḥr (subst.) 'face', **1**, 10, frag. 4/x−5; 14/22; **2** front, 6/4, 20 (n. *dr*), 26; **16** back/1; **25**/5

ḥr nb 'everybody', **2** front, 6/17

ḥr, *ḥr-ꜣt.ṯ=* (prep.) 'upon', **1**, 14/24, 29, 30; **2** front, 6/5; **2** back, x+1/13, 14, 15; **5**, 1/10 *bis*; **27**/2–7 *passim*, 17?

n-ḥr= (prep.) 'upon', **2** back, x−1/19, 21, 32

r-ḥr (prep.) 'before', **1**, 9/2, 19, 23, 30; 13/9; 14/32; **1a**/9? (n. *h*), 24; **2** front, 6/10; **2** back, x+1/20, 25; **7**/3; **8**/3; **10** front/2; **15**/12

ḥrỉ (adj.) 'upper', see *rỉt-ḥrỉ.t*, also titles (index B)

ḥrỉ-ỉb (subst.) 'centre', **1**, 14/12 (n. *cu*)

r-ḥrỉ (advb.) 'upwards', **1**, 13/32; **2** front, 6/5, 13? (n. *cb*), 18? (n. *dc*)

ḥrr, *ḥrry* (vb.) 'delay', **1**, 13/19, 23, 24; 14/6; **2** back, x+1/21, 28? (n. *eb*); **3** front, frag. 1+2/4; frag. 3/7; **11**/3? (n. *b*)

ḥrḥ (vb.) 'beware of', **1**, 9/30? (n. *cf*); **1a**/4? (n. *c*); see also *ḥrṯ*

ḥrṯ (vb.) 'beware of', **1**, 9/30? (n. *cf*); see also *ḥrḥ*

ḥs (vb.) 'sing, praise', **2** front, 6/11; **27**/17

ḥs.w (subst.) 'chants', **2** front, 6/6 (n. *aj*), 27 (n. *ey*)

ḥsy (adj.) 'wild', **2** front, 6/31? (n. *fn*)

ḥḳ (vb.) 'hunger?', 'capture?', **2** front, 6/14 (n. *cd*); see also *ḥḳr*, *ḥk*

ḥḳr (vb.) 'hunger', **2** back, x+1/13; see also *ḥḳ*

ḥk (vb.) 'capture', **2** back, x+1/38? (n. *fj*); see also *ḥḳ*

ḥty (subst.) 'fear', **2** front, 6/27

ḥṯy (subst.) 'instant' in *n tꜣỉ ḥṯy* (advb.) 'instantly', **1**, 13/8; 14/33; **2** front, 6/15? (n. *co*)

ḥtp (vb.) 'rest', **1**, 14/2

ḥtrỉ (subst.) 'horse', **2** back, x+1/19 (n. *cv*), 21 (n. *dd*), 22, 32 *bis*, 33

ḥḏ (subst.) 'money', **1**, 9/7; 10/34; **2** front, 6/2? (n. *r*), 21? (n. *dx*); **12** back/2, 3, 4, 5, 6; see also *pr-ḥḏ*

ḫꜣ (subst.) 'flame', **1**, 14/5 (n. *cj*; or 'offering-stand'?)

ḫꜣꜥ (vb.) 'place, leave', **1**, 9/14, 18, 31, 32 *bis* (n. *ck*); 10/23? (n. *dy*); 13/4; 14/13; **2** front, 6/9, 17, 29? (n. *fe*); **2** back, x+1/2, 5, 17, 17 bis? (n. *cq*), 19, 31, 33, 37, 38; **6**/4; **7**/3; **25**/6

ḫꜣst (subst.) 'necropolis', **1**, 14/15, 30

ḫy (adj. vb.) 'be high', **2** back, x/2? (n. *e*); **5**, 1/8 (n. *w*; in proper name *Nꜣ-ḫy-ṯꜣỉ-ḏꜣḏꜣ=f*?, q.v.)

ḫyṯ (subst.) 'doom', **2** front, 6/17

ḫꜥ (vb.) 'rise', **2** front, 6/13; **2** back, x+1/33; **6**/1

ḫwy (subst.) 'altar', **2** front, 6/5? (n. *ad*); **2** back, x+1/14

ḫpr (vb.) 'become', **1**, 7/x+2; 9/4 *ter*, *et passim*; possibly a subst. use in **4**/5 *pꜣỉ=s ḫpr* (n. *m*)

ḫf (vb.) 'be laid waste', **1**, 9/17

ḫfṯ-ḥr (subst.) 'dromos' of temple, **2** back, x+1/20

ḫm (adj.) 'small, lowly', **2** front, 6/12 (*rmt ḫm*); (subst.) 'little one', **1a**/15 (n. *q*); **2** front, 6/26

ḫm-ẖr (subst.) 'child', **1**, 13/22

ḫm-ẖr(.t) (subst.) 'girl-child', **1**, 9/4, 7, 9 *bis*

ḫmꜥ (subst.) 'rubble?', **1**, 13/33 (n. *bp*)

ḫny (subst.) 'disorder', **10** front/3? (n. *b*)

ḫnm (vb.) 'cense?', **2** back, x+1/24? (n. *dm*)

ḫnšỉ (subst.) 'stench', **9**/6 (n. *e*)

ḫnṯ (adj.) 'foremost', **2** front, 6/4 (n. *aa*)

ḫnṯ (subst.) '. . .?', **7**/7 (n. *g*), perhaps in place name *tꜣ ḫnṯ*, q.v.

ḫnty (subst.) 'thorn-tree', **1**, 9/34? (n. *cq*); 10/20 (n. *ds*)

ḫr= (vb.) 'said', **2** front, 6/20

ḫr (particle), **2** back, x/6; x+1/1, 2? (n. *am*), 7, 24 *bis*? (n. *dm*); **27**/16, 17, 18

ḫryr (subst.) 'rage, carnage', **1**, 10/33 (n. *eu*); 14/5 (n. *ch*); see also *ḫrꜥry*

ḫrꜥry (vb.) 'rage', **1**, 9/2? (n. *d*); **2** back, x+1/4 (n. *at*), 12? (n. *bx*); **10** front/2; **16** front/2 (n. *a*)

ḫrꜥry (subst.) 'rage', **2** front, 6/31 (n. *fp*)

ḫrw (subst.) 'voice', **1**, 9/10; **2** front, 6/28; **2** back, x/9? (n. *p*); x+1/2, 5, 16? (n. *cm*), 24, 37; **5**, 1/6 (n. *p*)

ḫrr (subst.) 'rein', **2** back, x+1/19 (n. *cv*), 21, 32

ḫrḫr (vb.) 'quake, destroy', **2** back, x+1/16

ḫtm (vb.) 'shut', **1a**/7; **2** back, x+1/24? (n. *dm*)

ḫtm (subst.) 'seal-ring', **2** back, x+1/29? (n. *ee*)

⌜*ḫt*⌝*-ršꜥ* (subst.) '. . . . .-tree', **27**/4 (n. *o*)

ḫdỉ (subst.), name of a plant or tree, **27**/6 (n. *z*)

ḫ[dw?] (subst.), name of a bird, **27**/6 (n. *y*)

ẖ(.t) (subst.) 'belly', **1**, 13/4 (*ḫꜣꜥ ẖt.ṯ=s*) (n. *e*); **2** front, 6/20; **2** back, x+1/36, 38

r-ẖṯ (prep.) 'in presence of?', **1**, 13/1 (n. *a*, status uncertain)

ẖ(t) n (prep.) 'within, throughout?', **1**, 13/28 (n. *bb*)

ẖ(.t) (subst.) 'type, species', **2** back, x+1/34 (n. *ev*)

r-ẖ(.t) (prep.) 'according to, as if', **1**, 9/8, 31; **2** front, 7/8; **2** back, x/10; x+1/30; **9**/5; **22**/5

ẖ-th.ṯ? (subst.) 'disaster', see *sn-th.ṯ*

ẖyṯ (subst.) 'porch', **27**/16; see also *hyꜣ* and note *v* on **1**, 9/7.
ẖm (vb.) 'be hot, heat', **1**, 9/33? (n. *co*); **2** back, x+1/34 (n. *eu*)
ẖm.w (subst.) 'fevers?', **6**/5 (n. *a*)
ẖn (prep.) 'in, within', **1**, 9/10; 13/31; 14/2; **2** front, 6/8, 18? (n. *dd*), 24; **2** back, x/2; x+1/21; **3** front, frag. 3/5 ('from within'); **5**, 1/11; **17** back/4
  r-ẖn (advb.) 'within', **1**, 9/30; **3** front, frag. 3/7; **4**/4
ẖny (vb.) 'approach?', **1**, 10/1? (n. *cy*); **2** back, x+1/35? (n. *ew*); **3** front, frag. 3/6? (n. *n*)
ẖr (subst.) 'street', **27**/17
ẖr (subst.) 'boy', **2** front, 6/31, 31 *bis*? (n. *fq*); **2** back, x+1/31 (n. *ek*); see also *ḫm-ẖr*
  ẖr.t (subst.) 'girl', **1**, 9/26; 10/3, 24, 27, 36, 37; 13/1, 7; 14/18; **2** front, 6/24, 26, 27; see also *ḫm-ẖr(.t)*
ẖrỉ (subst.) 'food', **1**, 14/19; **5**, 1/6? (n. *p*)
ẖry (adj.) 'lower', **2** back, x+1/15 (n. *ch*, possibly restore *rỉt ẖry.t*)
  r-ẖry (advb.) 'downwards', **1**, 9/18 (n. *az*), 31; **2** front, 6/18; **2** back, x/5; **5**, 1/8? (n. *v*)
ẖry (?) '. . . ?', **11**/5 (n. *h*, uncertain)
ẖrd (subst.) 'child', **1**, 13/25 (n. *at*, part of proper name *H̱rd-pꜣ-ntr*?), 26; **2** back, x+1/30
ẖsy (vb.) 'be feeble', **10** back/9? (n. *j*)
ẖdy (vb.) 'travel downstream', **23** front/4
ẖdb (vb.) 'kill', **1**, 7/x+3, x+3 *bis*? (n. *e*); 13, frag. 4/x+3? (n. *c*); 13/2, 8; **1a**/19; **2** front, 6/12, 13, 21

s (subst.) 'man', **3** back, frag. 3/5 (n. *u*)
  s-ḥmt (subst.) 'woman', **1**, 14/20; **2** front, 6/11? (n. *bg*); **26**/6? (n. *j*); see also *ḥm.t*
st (subst.) 'place', **2** front, 6/10? (n. *ba*), 18? (n. *dd*); **3** front, frag. 3/7
  st-dbꜣ 'place of punishment', **2** front, 6/24
sꜣ (subst.) 'back', in
  m-sꜣ (prep.) 'after, behind, except', **1**, 7/x+6; 9/11, 14? (n. *ap*), 25, 28; 10/34; 13/23; 14/5; **1a**/7; **2** front, 6/23, 24, 27, 29 *bis*; 7/2; **2** back, x+1/18, 26, 27 *bis*, 32, 33; **10** front/2, 3? (n. *b*)
sꜣb (vb.) 'be rebellious', **2** back, x+1/12 (metathesis for *sbꜣ*, q.v.)
sỉ (vb.) 'sate', **2** front, 6/13 (n. *bv*)
sʿ? (subst.), in title *ḥrỉ-sʿ*?, **2** front, 6/14 (n. *cc*, meaning uncertain), q.v.
sʿḥʿ (subst.) 'accusation', **2** front, 6/15
swn (vb.) 'recognize', **2** back, x+1/35
swr (vb.) 'drink', **1**, 9/2, 10; 10/35? (n. *fc*); 13/3; 16/x+4; **2** front, 6/11; **2** back, x/1? (n. *a*); x+1/8? (n. *bg*), 13, 23; **27**/18
sbꜣ (vb.) 'be rebellious', **2** front, 6/7? (n. *al*); see also *sꜣb*
sbꜣ.w (subst.) 'doors', **2** front, 6/2 (nn. *o*, *p*)
sbt (subst.) 'mound', **2** back, x+1/9
sbṯ (subst.) 'wall', **23** front/5
sp (subst.) 'time', in
  sp-2 (advb.) 'again', **2** front, 6/11? (n. *bl*); **5**, 1/7; **10** back/7
  n pꜣ sp mḥ-2 (advb.) 'for the second time', **2** front, 6/28 (n. *fa*)
  ḥꜣt-sp (subst.) 'year', **23** back/2
sp (subst.) 'remainder', **1**, 13/28 (in *ỉr-sp*, n. *bc*)
spr? (vb.) 'petition', **2** front, 6/11? (n. *bh*)
spṯ (subst.) 'shore', **2** back, x+1/9
sf (subst.), in advb. *n sf* 'yesterday', **1**, 14/26; 16/x+1? (n. *a*)
sfy (subst.) 'sword', **2** back, x+1/10, 15 (n. *br*)
sm (vb.) 'greet', **2** front, 6/14? (n. *ce*)
  sm.w (subst.) 'greetings', **1**, 13/29
smꜣ (vb.) 'unite', **2** front, 6/3? (n. *t*)
smy (vb.) 'report', **2** back, x+1/18? (n. *ct*); **25**/5? (n. *f*); see also *ʿn-smy*
smn (subst.) 'Nile goose', **27**/3 (n. *m*)
smt (subst.) 'likeness', **1**, 9/24; 14/9; 16/x+1; **2** front, 6/19, 21 *bis*
sn (subst.) 'brother', **1**, 7/x+4; 13/10; 14/8, 36; **2** front, 6/6? (n. *af*)
sn-th.ṯ? (subst.) 'disaster', **2** front, 6/14 (n. *cc*, perhaps to be read *ẖ-th.ṯ*)
sny (vb.) 'pass by', **1**, 13/18; **2** front, 7/4; **5**, 1/4 (n. *e*), 5
snf (subst.) 'blood', **5**, 1/2 (n. *c*)
snḥ (vb.) 'bind', **2** front, 6/14? (n. *cc*); **2** back, x+1/11
snd (vb.) 'fear', **1**, 9/27
  sndy.t (subst.) 'fear, awe', **1**, 14/26; **2** back, x+1/2, 5, 17
sr (subst. or adj.) 'prophecy, prophetic', **2** front, 6/15
sry (subst.) 'thorn-tree?', **27**/3 (n. *n*)
sh (subst.?) '. . . .?', **1**, 7/x+5? (in *Sh-Rʿ*, possibly a proper name, q.v.; n. *h*, or read *Ḫʿ-Rʿ*)
shrꜣ (subst.) 'barge', **2** back, x+1/32 (n. *en*)
sḥn (vb.) 'order', **1**, 9/25; 13/12; **2** back, x+1/11, 12, 26 (n. *du*), 27? (n. *dw*)
sḥn (subst.) 'order', **2** back, x+1/23; see also *ʿš-sḥn*
sḫ (subst.) 'blow, reproach', **1**, 13/21 (n. *ah*)
sḫy (subst.) 'power', **1**, 10/35 (n. *fa*, restore *ỉr-sḫy*?)
sḫn (vb.) 'be covered, be clad', **2** front, 6/2
sḫny (vb.) 'meet', **10** front/3
[s]ḫr (vb.) 'counsel', **3** front, frag. 1+2/3? (n. *β*)
sẖ (vb.) 'write', **2** back, x+1/29; **14**/4 (or 'scribe')
sẖ (subst.) 'document', 'spell', **4**/1, 3
sẖ (subst.) 'scribe', see titles, Index B
sẖm (vb.) 'destroy', **6**/7 *bis*
ssw (subst.) 'time', **10** front/3
sšm (subst.) 'image', **2** front, 6/16 *bis* (nn. *cs*, *ct*), 17, 31 (n. *fm*)
sšn (subst.) 'lotus', **1**, 14/24, 29
sḳ (vb.) 'collect', **1**, 16, frag. 1/x+3? (n. *a*)
sḳrḳr (vb.) 'be rolled', **2** front, 6/3 (n. *w*)
skr (vb.) 'travel', **1**, 9/33; 14/34
sgn (subst.) 'balm', **2** front, 6/13 (n. *ca*)
stꜣ.ṯ (vb.) 'withdraw, turn', **1**, 9/28 (n. *ca*); 10/10; **2** front, 6/5, 10? (n. *ba*), 19? (n. *dj*); **2** back, x+1/19; **6**/9? (n. *h*), 11
sṯy (subst.) 'flame', **2** back, x/8? (n. *o*); x+1/14, 15; **14**/3
stby (vb.?) 'prepare', **23** front/8 (n. *h*)
sṯny (subst.) 'counsel', **2** front, 6/15
sdm (vb.) 'hear', **1**, 9/3 (n. *g*), 10; 14/2; **1a**/13; **2** front, 6/6? (n. *ak*), 10; **2** back, x/29; x+1/1? (n. *ah*), 1 *bis*? (n. *aj*), 2, 3, 7 *ter*? (n. *bf*), 11 (n. *bu*), 17, 24 *bis*, 26
sdr 'lie down, prostrate self', **1**, 9/8 (n. *w*); **2** front, 6/20; **2** back, x/6? (n. *k*); x+1/8? (n. *bg*), 15, 36, 38
sḏy (vb.) 'relate', **1**, 14/35; 16/x+3; **2** front, 6/14? (n. *ce*), 16 (*ỉrỉ n sḏy*), 25; **4**/6
sḏy (subst.) 'utterance', **2** front, 6/15

šyš.w (subst.) '. . . .?', **1**, 10/6 (n. *df*)
šʿ (subst.) 'sand', **2** back, x+1/9
šʿ (prep.) 'to, until', **1**, 10/31; 13/22 (n. *aj*); 14/23; **6**/12 (n. *q*); **25**/7 (n. *j*, *šʿ-tw* written for *šʿ*?)
  šʿ-r (conj.) 'until', **2** front, 6/23 (n. *eh*), 29 (n. *ff*)
šw (subst.) 'profit, value', **1**, 10/30 (n. *el*), 31, 32
  r-šw (advb.) (post-negative) 'at all', **1**, 9/2
šwby (subst.) 'persea-tree', **27**/9? (n. *ae*)
šb(t) (subst.) 'exchange', **1**, 14/12; **2** back, x/7; **3** back, frag. 3/6; frag. 2+1/1; **8**/6
šbw (subst.) 'filth?', **1**, 9/8 (n. *z*); 10/2, 4
šp (vb.) 'receive', **3** back, frag. 3/6; **10** front/5
šfꜣ (subst.) 'splendour?', 'fable?', **2** front, 6/13 (n. *bx*, perhaps part of proper name *Pꜣ-n-tꜣ-šfꜣ*, q.v.)
šm (vb.) 'go', **1**, 9/3, 5, 15, 16, 22, 27; 13/23, 24, 27; 14/10, 11, 12, 15, 20; **1a**/3, 7, 8; **2** front, 6/8, 10 *bis*, 17? (n. *cz*); **2**

back, x+1/18 *bis*, 20, 33, 37; **3** front, frag. 1+2/3? (n. *d*), frag. 3/4; **4**/1? (n. *a*); **5**, 1/4, 6; **6**/10? (n. *l*); **14**/4, 5?; **22**/3; **27**/9–14 *passim*

šn (vb.) 'pray', **1**, 9/23; 10/29 (n. *ej*); 13/26; 14/29; **1a**/20? (n. *v*), 21; **2** front, 6/23? (n. *ed*), 30? (n. *fj*); **2** back, x+1/20, 24; **5**, 1/4

šn (subst.) 'prayer', **2** front, 6/6? (n. *af*)

šny (vb.) 'be sick, be in trouble', **2** front, 5/x+1? (n. *a*); 6/6? (n. *af*), 20; **14**/5, 6? (n. *b*)

  šn (subst.) 'sickness', **2** back, x+1/12 (n. *by*)

šn(y) (subst.) 'hair', **2** front, 6/4? (n. *y*)

šr (subst.) 'son', **1**, 9/11; 10/24; **1a**/24? (n. *z*), 25 (n. *ab*); **2** front, 6/7? (n. *ap*), 12? (n. *bq*); **2** back, x/1? (n. *b*); **18** back/2

  šr.t (subst.) 'daughter', **1**, 13/11; **2** front, 6/7? (n. *ap*), 11? (n. *bg*); **2** back, x/34? (n. *af*)

šrf (vb.) 'shame', **1**, 14/16 (n. *cz*); **2** front, 6/12

šrr (vb.) 'pray', **2** back, x+1/6 (n. *az*)

šrg (vb.) 'whirl?', **5**, 1/10? (n. *ab*)

šs (subst.) in advb.

  m-šs 'exceedingly', **1**, 9/6; 13/4, 13; 14/10, 11; **2** front, 6/10? (n. *bb*); **2** back, x/11; **3** back, frag. 3/5; **22**/3

šs-nsw (subst.) 'royal linen', **1**, 9/2

šs-tp(y)? (subst.) 'fine linen', **2** front, 6/20? (n. *dr*)

ššt (subst.) 'window', **2** front, 6/2

šky (vb.) 'dig', **1**, 13/34

šdy (vb.) 'withdraw, take', **2** back, x+1/14? (n. *cb*)

ḳy (adj.) 'high', **2** front, 6/31 (n. *fp*); **25**/9? (n. *n*)

ḳbꜣ (subst.) a vessel, **27**/21 (n. *bg*)

ḳbꜥ (subst.) 'vengeance', **2** front, 6/12 (n. *bs*), 12 bis? (n. *bu*)

ḳp (vb.) 'hide', **2** front, 6/19? (n. *dg*), 19 *bis* (n. *dk*); see *kp*

ḳmꜣ (subst.) 'creation, form', **2** front, 6/1 (n. *e*)

ḳn (adj.) 'valiant', **2** front, 6/7, 13, 22

ḳnb.t (subst.) 'agreement', **2** front, 6/7? (n. *ao*); **11**/4? (n. *f*)

ḳnm (vb.) 'be blind', **2** front, 6/20? (n. *dm*); see also *knm*

ḳnḥy (subst.) 'chapel', **2** front, 6/1, 8? (n. *aq*); see also *kny*

ḳ(n)s (vb.) 'do violence to, slay', **2** front, 6/13 (n. *bw*), 20? (n. *dm*)

ḳns (subst.), in advb. *n ḳns* 'by force', **1**, 10, frag. 4/x+3?

ḳnṱ (vb.) 'be angry', **2** front, 6/20? (n. *dm*)

ḳry.w (subst.) 'door-bolts', **2** front, 6/2

ḳḥ (subst.) 'corner, side', **2** back, x+1/16? (n. *ck*)

ḳsnw (subst.) 'sparrow?', **27**/7 (n. *ab*); see also *ksn*

ḳd (subst.) 'building', **2** front, 6/2? (n. *n*)

ḳdt (subst.) '*kite*', a weight, **1**, 9/7

ḳdy (vb.) 'go round', **1a**/10; **2** back, x+1/16

  m-ḳdy (prep.) 'like', **1**, 7/x+6?; **2** front, 6/31

kꜣ (subst.) 'shrine?', **2** front, 6/10 (n. *bc*), 18? (n. *da*)

ky (adj.) 'other', **5**, 1/7? (n. *r*)

  k.t, fem., **2** front, 6/21; **12** front/2 (n. *c*), 3

kymy (subst.), species of bird, **27**/4 (n. *s*)

kp (vb.) 'hide, cover', **2** back, x+1/24? (n. *dm*); see *ḳp*

km (vb.) 'complete', **1**, 14/1 (n. *bv*)

km (subst.) 'garden', **1**, 9/17, 24; 14/18

kny (subst.) 'litter?', **24**/3 (*tꜣ kny Pr-ꜥꜣ*, n. *d*, perhaps for *ḳnḥy* 'chapel', q.v.)

knm (vb.) 'be blind', **2** back, x+1/24? (n. *dm*); see *ḳnm*

kry (subst.), a vessel for liquids, **27**/21 (n. *bh*)

krp (vb.) 'be revealed', **2** front, 6/12

krṱy (subst.) 'knife', 8/2 (n. *b*), 8? (n. *k*); see also *g(r)ṱy*

khy (subst.) 'land', **2** back, x+1/30

kḥs (subst.) 'gazelle', **2** back, x+1/34

ksn (vb.) 'be weak', 'be small', **2** back, x+1/24? (n. *dm*); see also *ḳsnw*

kky (subst.) 'darkness, wickedness', **2** back, x+1/2

gꜣ? (adj.) 'ugly', **2** front, 6/20? (n. *dr*)

gy (subst.) 'manner', **1**, 9/28, 30; **2** back, x+1/33; **5**, 1/3; **27**/8 (n. *ad*), 19? (n. *bc*), 20 *bis*, 21 (nn. *bd*, *bf*)

gy (subst.), name of a plant or tree, **1**, 9/34 (n. *cr*)

gp (vb.) 'grasp', **21** back/4? (n. *d*)

gm (vb.) 'find', **1**, 9/26 (n. *bu*); 10/8; 14/25, 30, 34; **1a**/22; **2** front, 6/16; **2** back, x/4; x+1/3 *bis*, 13, 13 bis? (n. *bz*), 16, 22, 23, 28? (n. *ec*); **4**/3 *bis*, 5; **5**, 1/9? (n. *x*); **8**/7 (n. *j*); **10** back/8; **26**/3; **27**/15? (n. *aw*), 17? (n. *ba*), 17 *bis*? (n. *bb*)

gm (subst.) 'power', **1**, 13/30 (n. *bh*)

gmy (subst.), name of a plant or tree, **27**/20 (n. *bd*)

gmꜥ (vb.) 'sin', **1**, 13/25

gr (vb.) 'be silent, cease', **2** front, 6/27; **5**, 1/6? (n. *n*)

gr (particle) 'also', **2** front, 6/29; **2** back, x+1/2? (n. *am*)

grr (subst.) 'burnt-offering', **1**, 14/6, 10

grr (subst.), name of a plant or tree, **1**, 9/34 (n. *cq*); 10/20

grḥ (subst.) 'night', **1**, 9/17; **1a**/18; **2** back, x+1/22 (n. *df*); **3** front, frag. 3/8

gr-šr.w (subst.) 'soldiers', **1**, 13/6 (n. g)

grg (vb.) 'found, plant', **27**/15 (n. *ay*)

grg (subst.) 'bed', **2** front, 6/3? (n. *t*)

g(r)ṱy (subst.) 'knife', **21** back/4 (n. *d*); see also *krṱy*

  g⌈r⌉ . . (subst.?) '. . . .?', **6**/3; see also **8**/2? (n. *c*)

gs (subst.) 'half', **2** back, x+1/20? (n. *cx*); as numeral, **12** back/6

tꜣ (subst.) 'land', **1**, 9/13 (*tꜣ rsỉ* n. *an*); 13/18; **2** front, 6/14; **2** back, x/2; **5**, 2/5; **27**/19

  tꜣ.wy 'the Two Lands', **2** front, 6/11 (n. *bf*, in title *nbt-tꜣ.wy*, q.v.)

  n pꜣ tꜣ (advb.) 'on earth, at all', **1**, 9/11; 14/14; **2** back, x+1/23, 28 (n. *ec*), 31? (n. *el*), 33; **3** front, frag. 3/8; **25**/2

tꜣỉ (dem. pronoun, fem.) 'this', in

  r-tꜣỉ (advb.) 'till now', **1**, 13/9; 14/19

tw-s (particle) 'behold', **2** front 6/23; **2** back, x+1/28

ṱwy (subst.) 'sandals', **2** back, x/3

twn (vb.) 'raise', **1**, 9/33? (n. *cp*)

twt (subst.) 'statue', **2** front, 6/13 (n. *bv*); 7/5

ṱp (subst.) '. . . .?', **2** front, 6/3? (n. *s*)

tp(y) adj.) 'first (quality)', **2** front, 6/20? (n. *dr*); **23**/3? (n. *c*)

tp-n-ỉꜣwt (subst.) 'beasts', **2** back, x+1/34, 35, 37 (n. *fc*), 38? (n. *ff*)

tm (neg. vb.) 'not to be', **1**, 9/3; 13, frag. 4/x+4; **2** front, 6/23; **11**/4

tn (vb.) 'be exalted', **2** front, 6/3? (n. *v*)

tn (adj.) 'noble?', 'distinguished?', **2** front, 6/9? (n. *au*)

tn (interrogative advb.) 'where?', **1**, 9/15; 14/23; **2** front, 6/9? (n. *au*), 30; **2** back, x+1/23 (n. *dj*)

tr . . (subst.?) '. . . .?', 8/2? (n. *c*)

th.ṱ (subst.) 'transgression' in compound *sn-th.ṱ* (*ẖ-th.ṱ*?), q.v.

th, *thr* (adj. vb.) 'be weary, be sad', **2** front, 6/24? (n. *em*); **5**, 1/2 (n. *a*); **21** front/5

ṱhb (vb.) 'dip', **1**, 14/24 (n. *dv*), 29? (n. *ef*)

ṱkn (vb.) 'approach, attack', **2** back, x+1/12.

tkr (vb.) 'hasten', **1**, 9/33? (n. *cp*)

tgs (subst.) 'boat', **1**, 13/21?; 14/5

ṯꜣỉ (vb.) 'take', **1**, 9/2, 9; 13/25; 14/5 *bis*, 21; 16/x+2; **1a**/11; **2** front, 6/12 *bis* (*ṯꜣỉ ḳbꜥ*, n. *bu*), 23, 26, 29; **5**, 1/8; **21** back/2

ṯꜣỉ (prep.) 'since', **1**, 13/9; 14/19, 35

ṯꜣỉ-ḥbs (subst.) 'suit of clothes', **1**, 9/2

ṯꜣw (subst.) 'breath', **1**, 10/23? (n. *dx*); 14/5; **2** front, 6/15, 29; **8**/3

ḏꜣỉ (advb.) 'here', **1**, 9/1 (n. *a*)
dỉ, dỉt (vb.) 'give, cause, place', **1**, 7/x+2 *et passim*
dw (subst.) 'mountain', **2** front, 6/6 (n. *ah*); **2** back, x/2 (n. *d*), 9 (n. *p*); x+1/13, 15, 16, 18? (n. *cu*), 23? (n. *dj*), 32? (n. *ep*), 34, 34 *bis*? (n. *ev*)
dwꜣ, dwy (subst.) 'morning', **2** front, 6/26; **23**/3
(*n*) *dwy* (advb.) 'in the morning', **1**, 9/26
dwꜣt (subst.) 'the underworld', **2** front, 6/14
dwꜣ-nṯr (vb.) 'worship, give thanks', **2** front, 6/24
dw(*n*) (subst.) 'bosom' in
ḥr-dw= (prep.) 'beside', **2** front, 6/21? (n. *dy*)
dbꜣ (vb.) 'retaliate, punish', in subst. *st-dbꜣ* 'place of punishment', **2** front, 6/24
r-dbꜣ (prep.) 'because of', **1**, 9/21; 10, frag. 5/x+3; 14/16 (n. *da*), 17; **2** front, 6/12, 21, 26? (n. *eu*), 30; **2** back, x+1/17, 36
dbḥ (vb.) 'request', **2** back, x+1/13, 18 (n. *cr*)
dbḥ, dbḥy (subst.) 'request', **2** front, 6/23; **2** back, x+1/1? (n. *aj*)
dpy? (subst.) 'crocodile', **2** front, 6/20? (n. *dr*)
dmỉ (subst.) 'city', **1**, 9/17, 20; 10/26; **23** front/2
dmy (vb.) 'touch', **2** back, x+1/14
dny (subst.) 'cry', **1**, 14/32
dr (subst.) 'limit', in adj. phrase
r dr= 'all of', **1**, 9/6; 10/25 (n. *ec*); 13/20, 31; **2** back, x/2; x+1/4, 5, 7, 17, 23, 28, 29; **6**/2; **27**/19
drt.ṯ= (subst.) 'hand', **2** front, 6/20; **2** back, x+1/11
m-dr(*t*) (prep.) 'by, in the possession of', **1**, 9/5; **2** back, x+1/29
n-drt (conj.) 'when', **1**, 9/27; 14/22; **2** front, 6/27; **2** back, x+1/11; **14**/4
n-drt.ṯ= (prep.) 'in the hand of, by', **1**, 10/33; 14/16; **2** front, 6/22; **2** back, x/10; x+1/35 (n. *ex*); **14**/2
ḥr-drt (prep.) 'from', **1**, 9/35 (n. *cv*)
drỉ (subst.), species of bird, 'kite', **27**/6 (n. *aa*), 13 (n. *as*)
d[*gy*]? (subst.) 'fruit', **2** back, x/8? (n. *o*)
d[. . .] (subst.) '. . . . ?', **2** back, x/8 (n. *o*, something cooked)

ḏꜣ (subst.) 'loss, mischance', **1**, 9/11 (n. *ag*)
ḏꜣ? (subst.) 'fire-drill', **2** front, 7/7? (n. *fw*)
ḏꜣḏꜣ (subst.) 'head, capital', **5**, 1/8 (n. *w*, in proper name *Nꜣ-ḥy-ṯꜣỉ-ḏꜣḏꜣ=f*?), 9? (n. *aa*); **22**/2? (n. *b*)
ỉ-ỉr-ḏꜣḏꜣ (prep.) 'upon', **2** front, 6/4
ḏpḥ (subst.) 'apple-tree', **27**/5 (n. *u*)
ḏḥm (vb.) 'be defiled', **1**, 9/31
ḏkm (vb.) 'wash', **1**, 9/9 *bis*, 33
ḏt (subst.) 'eternity', in advb. 'for ever', **25**/8 (n. *m*)
ḏ(*d*)*tḥ* (vb.) 'imprison', **2** back, x+1/3? (n. *ap*), 30 (n. *eh*)
ḏd (vb.) 'say', **1**, 7/x+3 *et passim*; imp. *ỉḏdy*, **2** back, x+1/18 (n. *cs*); relative form *nꜣ-w-ḏd=k*, **2** back, x+1/31; substantival uses, **2** front, 6/21, 25, 28; **2** back, x/5
ḏdy (vb.) 'run, gallop', **2** back, x+1/33 *bis*
ḏdy (subst.) 'enemy', **3** front, frag. 3/1

Uncertain

[.]*nỉnỉ* (subst.), species of bird, **27**/12 (n. *ap*; *ꜣbnỉnỉ*, *ḫnỉnỉ*, and *gnỉnỉ* suggested as possible readings)

Numerals

1 **1**, 9/7; **2** back, x+1/20; see also *wꜥ*
2 **2** front, 6/28; **5**, 1/7; **10** back/7; **26**/6? (n. *j*)
3 **3** back, frag. 3/5 (n. *u*); **12** back/6; **13**/4; **23** back/2 *bis*, 4
4 **1**, 16/x+3, x+5; **2** back, x+1/16? (n. *ck*); **12** back/3
5 **2** front, 6/16 *bis*? (nn. *cp*, *cr*); **12** back/2
6 **1**, 13/9; 14/19; **1a**/18 (n. *t*); **2** front, 6/32; **2** back, x+1/22, 34? (n. *et*); **12** back/2, 4
7 **1**, 7/x+8; **12** back/3
8 **12** back/4
9 **12** back/6
11 **1**, 13/17
14 **1**, 14/37
16 **1**, 16/x+8
100 **1**, 9/1
250 **23** back/1
300 **23** back/1

Fractions

½ **12** back/6; see also *gs*, **2** back, x+1/20 (*mḥ-1.t gs*? n. *cx*)

INDEX B: DEMOTIC TITLES AND EPITHETS

wꜥb 'priest', **1**, 9/12, 14; 13/22, 29, 30, 31; 14/30; **4**/5; **26**/5? (n. *h*)
wn 'shrine-opener', **1**, 9/20, 26, 30, 31, 33; 10/12, 25, 28 (n. *eh*)
wḥm-nsw 'royal herald', **1a**/12

Pr-ꜥꜣ 'Pharaoh', **1**, 9/5, 6; 13, frag. 4/x+2?, x+3?; 13/17, 19, 20, 24 *ter*, 27; 14/3, 7, 10, 11 *bis*, 13, 20, 29? (n. *eh*); **1a**, 17, 21, 22, 25; **2** back, x+1/1 (n. *al*), 2, 4, 10? (n. *bs*), 11, 17? (n. *cr*), 21, 23 *bis*, 25 *bis*, 26? (n. *ds*), 26 *bis*, 27 *bis*, 28 *bis*, 30 *bis*, 35 *ter*, 37, 38 *bis*; **3** front, frag. 1+2/5; **11**/4? (n. *g*), 5, 6; **12** front/4; **15**/6, 7, 10, 11; **22**/3; **24**/2, 2 *bis*? (n. *b*), 3, 4, 6; **25**/2, 4, 8

fꜣỉ 'bearer', in *sdm-*[*ꜥš*]*fꜣỉ*, **2** back, x+1/10 (n. *br*, rejected), 15

mr-ꜣḥ.w? 'overseer of fields', **1**, 9/6? (n. *p*, rejected reading)
mr-ꜥwỉ 'steward', **2** back, x+1/26, 27, 29? (n. *ed*), 30, 31, 32? (n. *eq*), 34, 38 *bis*
mr-pr-ỉpy-nsw 'steward of the royal harem', **1**, 13/27, 28 (n. *ba*)
mr-pr-nsw 'royal steward', **1**, 13, frag. 4/x+4
mr-mšꜥ 'general', **1**, 9/6 (n. *p*); 14/1; 16/x+6; **12** front/4
mr-sẖ 'chief scribe', **1**, 9/12? (n. *aj*); 13/30

nꜣ-w ꜥwỉ.w . . . . 'those of the houses of . . . . ?', **1**, 13/32 (n. *bo*)
nb 'lord', in epithets *nb ꜥꜣ*, **1**, 13/16? (n. *r*); **1a**/16; **24**/2? (n. *b*); **26**/2? (n. *b*); *nbššm*, **2** front, 6/16 (n. *cs*), 31? (n. *fm*); *nb* . . . ., **25**/8 (n. *m*)
nb.t 'lady', **2** back, x/28; in epithets *nb.t-ꜥnḫ*, **2** back, x+1/29 (n. *ee*, perhaps proper name); *nb*(*.t*)*-ꜥ*. . ., **2** back, x+1/8? (n. *bk*); *nb.t-tꜣ.wy*, **2** front, 6/11 (of Isis, n. *bf*); *nb.t Tp-nꜣ-ỉḥ.w*, **2** back, x+1/1 of Ḥatḥor (n. *ah*), 2? (n. *am*)
nsw 'king', **2** front, 6/3? (n. *t*); **5**, 1/11? (n. *ad*); in epithet *nsw* . . . ., **2** front, 6/22 (of Osiris?, n. *ea*, perhaps *nsw nḥḥ*); see also *wḥm-nsw*, *pr-*[*ỉpy*]*-nsw*, *mr-pr-ỉpy-nsw*, *mr-pr-nsw*, *ḥm.t-nsw*

rpy(*t*) 'Lady', as epithet of Isis, **2** front, 6/10, 27, 28
rpꜥṯ? 'princess', **1a**/14? (n. *p*)

ḥm 'craftsman', **2** front, 6/4 (n. *aa*, perhaps part of a compound title)
ḥm-nṯr 'prophet', **1**, 9/11, 12, 13; 13/1, 7, 29? (n. *bd*); 14/4 (these references all to *ḥm-nṯr Ḥr-nb-Sḫm*); 16/x+3, x+5 (both to *pꜣ ḥm-nṯr 4-nw*); **1a**/9 (*ḥm-nṯr Ḏḥwt*? n. *h*); **2** back, x+1/2? (*pꜣ* [*ḥm-nṯr nb.t*] *Tp-ỉḥ.w*? n. *am*); **3** back, frag. 2+1/3 (*pꜣ ḥm-nṯr . . . . .*)
ḥm.t-nsw 'queen', **1**, 14/9
ḥnw.t 'mistress', as epithet of Ḥatḥor, **2** back, x+1/1 (n. *ah*), 36? (n. *fa*)
ḥrỉ 'master', **1**, 9/8; **2** front, 6/20 (with reference to Imḥotep); **2** back, x+1/18, 27, 29 (all with reference to Pharaoh)
ḥrỉ.t 'mistress', **2** back, x/1; x+1/36 (both probably with reference to Ḥatḥor)
ḥrỉ-ỉꜣbt 'lord of the east', **3** front, frag. 1+2/2, 4, 6; frag. 3/4?
ḥrỉ n pꜣ pr-ḥḏ 'master of the treasury', **1a**/12 (n. *n*)
ḥrỉ-sꜥ? 'master of the . . .?', **2** front, 6/14? (n. *cc*)
ḥrỉ-tp 'magician', **1a**/7? (n. *f*)

sꜣwtỉ 'guard', **1**, 9/6; **2** back, x/35? (n. *ag*); x+1/18 (n. *ct*), 22, 24; **12** front/4? (n. *g*)
swnw 'physician', **1a**/7? (n. *f*)
smꜣ-tꜣ.wy? 'uniter of the Two Lands', **2** front, 6/22 (n. *ea*, rejected reading)
sḫ 'scribe', **14**/4?; see also *mr-sḫ* 'chief scribe'
sḫ n pꜣ wḥꜣ 'letter-scribe', **2** back, x+1/26, 29 (n. *ed*), 30, 31
stm '*setm*-priest', **1**, 7/x+3; 14/20, 21
sdm-[*ꜥš*] 'servant', **1**, 9/5; 14/11; **2** back, x+1/10 (n. *br*), 15 (both *sdm-*[*ꜥš*] *fꜣỉ/sfy*); **9**/6 (n. *e*)

INDEX C: DEMOTIC PERSONAL NAMES

ꜣššry **8**/4 (n. *d*), 9 (n. *m*)

Bꜣ- . . . **2** back, x+1/1 (n. *al*), 2, 4

Pꜣ-(n-)tꜣ-šfꜣ? **2** front, 6/13? (n. *bx*)
Pꜣ-dỉ-ꜣIst **4**/5; **12** front/2
Pꜣ-dỉ-Wsir **3** back, frag. 2+1/2
Ptḥ-ḥtp **1**, 14/20, 21

Mr-ỉb **2** back, x/31? (n. *ad*); x+1/5, 10? (n. *bo*), 20, 21, 32, 35? (n. *ew*)
Mr- . . . **2** back, x+1/26 (n. *dr*, perhaps read *Mry*), 29
Mr- . . .] **2** back, x+1/10? (n. *bp*, perhaps name of the lion?)

Nb(.t)-ꜥnḫ **2** back, x+1/29? (n. *ee*; cf. also n. *bk* on x+1/8)
Nꜣ-nfr-Sḫmt **1**, 13/25? (n. *as*); 14/31; **1a**/11, 16, 23
Nꜣ-ḥy-tꜣỉ-ḏꜣḏꜣ=f? **5**, 1/8? (n. *w*)
Nḫṯ-nb=f **22**/4 (n. *f*), 6

Ḥr-wḏꜣ **9**/3, 4, 5

Ḥr-mꜣꜥ-ḫrw **1**, 13/31, 33; 14/2, 14, 15; 16/x+4, x+5
Ḥr-[. . . .] **1a**/6 (n. *e*), 27 (n. *ac*; perhaps *Ḥr-mꜣꜥ-ḫrw*)

Ḥꜥ=f-Rꜥ **15**/7 (n. *a*); see **1**, 7/x+5 (n. *h*; read *Ḥꜥ–Rꜥ*?)
Ḥꜥ-Ḥp **26**/4 (n. *f*)

Ḫrd-pꜣ-nṯr? **1**, 13/25? (n. *at*)

Sh-Rꜥ? **1**, 7/x+5? (n. *h*; or read *Ḥꜥ–Rꜥ*?)

Ḳỉ-ḏꜣḏꜣ **12** front/3 (n. *f*)

Gm=w-Ḥp **5**, 1/3

Ṯrywš **8**/5 (n. *e*)

Ṯꜣỉ-n-ỉm=w **3** front, frag. 3/6, 9; **3** back, frag. 2+1/3

Ḏd-ḥr **5**, 1/6? (n. *p*); **22**/4? (nn. *e*, *f*), 5? (n. *g*)
Ḏd(t)-sšp **1**, 9/11 (n. *af*), 13; 10/6–7; 14/27, 28

[. . . .]*-Rꜥ* **15**/14? (n. *d*)

INDEX D: DEMOTIC DIVINE NAMES

ꜣIỉ-m-ḥtp **2** front, 6/19, 20 (n. *dq*)
ꜣImn **6**/4, 5 (n. *d*), 6
[*ꜣImn*]*-Rꜥ* **2** front, 6/22? (n. *ea*, reading rejected)
ꜣIst **1**, 10/14? (n. *dn*); **2** front, 6/9, 10, 12? (n. *bt*), 15, 16, 17 *ter*, 20, 22, 27, 27 bis? (n. *ez*), 28, 30; **2** back, x+1/28

Wsir **2** front, 6/22? (n. *ea*), 30
Wsir-Ḥp **5**, 1/5

Bꜣstt **2** back, x+1/14, 15? (n. *cg*); **5**, 1/6 (n. *o*, perhaps part of personal name)
Bs **2** front, 6/4? (n. *x*)

pꜣ-Rꜥ **1**, 7/x+5; **2** back, x+1/11 (n. *bv*), 33

Mwt **1**, 13/10? (n. *n*)

Nfr-ḥr **2** front, 6/22 (n. *dz*; as epithet of Imḥotep)

Ḥwt-Ḥr **2** back, x+1/1? (n. *ah*), 20, 24, 36? (n. *fa*)
Ḥr **2** front, 6/22
Ḥr-wr **1**, 10/33
Ḥr-nb-Sḫm **1**, 9/11, 12, 13, 20; 10/25; 13/1, 7, 22?, 29; 14/4

Sḫmt **2** front, 6/31 (n. *fp*)
Skr **2** front, 6/27, 28, 28 bis? (n. *fc*)
St, *Stḫ* **6**/7? (n. *e*), 9; **7**/2 (n. *b*)

Ḏḥwt **1a**/9? (n. *h*); **2** front, 6/22

. . . .? unread divine name, **2** front, 7/1 (n. *fr*)

INDEX E: DEMOTIC PLACE-NAMES

ꜣIwnw? 'Heliopolis?', **27**/12 (n. *aq*, perhaps read *Šmꜥ*)
ꜣImnt.t, *ꜣImnṯ* 'the West, the Underworld', **2** front, 6/9? (n. *at*), 21 (n. *dv*); see also *pr-ỉꜣbt/ỉmnṯ*? **2** front, 6/30 (n. *fh*)
ꜣImrṯ 'Amor', **2** back, x+1/16? (n. *cl*)
ꜣIšrṯ 'Ashur', **2** back, x+1/16? (n. *cl*)
Yb 'Elephantine', **2** front, 6/3 (n. *t*); **27**/1? (n. *c*)
ꜥnḫ-tꜣ.wy 'ꜥOnkhtowe', **2** back, x+1/8? (n. *bk*)

INDEX F: COPTIC WORDS QUOTED

ϣⲟⲣϣⲣ (vb.) 'destroy', **2** back, x+1/16 (n. *cj*)
ϣⲏⲩⲉ (subst.) 'altar', **1**, 14/5 (n. *cj*); cf. **2** front, 6/5 (n. *ad*); **2** back, x+1/14
ϣⲁϣ^{B} (subst.) 'part of building', **1**, 10/6 (n. *df*)
ϣⲱϥ (vb.) 'be laid waste', **1**, 9/17 (n. *ax*)

ϩⲁⲉ (subst.) 'end', **2** front, 6/15 (n. *cg*)
ϩⲓⲃⲱⲓ (subst.) 'ibis', **27**/2 (n. *f*)
ϩⲁ(ⲉ)ⲓⲃⲉⲥ^{S}, ϧⲏⲓⲃⲓ^{B} (subst.) 'shade', **1**, 9/8 (n. *z*)
ϩⲃⲟⲥ (subst.) in ϭⲓϩⲃⲟⲥ (subst.) 'clothing', **1**, 9/2 (n. *e*)
ϩⲁⲙⲟⲩⲗⲁϩϫ^{S} (subst.), of uncertain meaning, **2** front, 6/8, 23, 30 (n. *as*; see *JEA* 61 (1975), 198–200)
ϩⲱⲣ^{S}, ϩⲁⲣⲉϩ (vb.) 'guard against', **1**, 9/30 (n. *cf*)
ϩⲁⲉⲓⲧ^{S} (subst.) 'gateway', **1**, 9/7 (n. *v*)
ϩⲟ(ⲉ)ⲓⲧⲉ^{S} (subst.) 'hyena', **2** back, x+1/34 (n. *ev*)
ϩⲟⲟⲩ (vb.) in ⲡⲉⲑⲟⲟⲩ (subst.) 'evil', **1**, 9/6 (n. *r*)

ϫ(ⲉ)ⲙⲡⲉϩ (subst.) 'apple', **27**/5 (n. *u*)

ϭⲏ^{B} (subst.) 'quince', **1**, 9/34 (n. *cr*)
ϭⲓⲗ̅ⲗ̅^{S} (subst.), of uncertain meaning, **1**, 9/34 (n. *cq*)
ϭⲁⲓⲙⲉ^{S} (subst.) 'hen', **27**/4 (n. *s*)
ϭⲣⲟⲟⲙⲡⲉ (subst.) 'dove', **27**/4 (n. *q*)
ϭⲏⲟⲩ^{B} (subst.) 'coriander-plant', **1**, 9/34 (n. *cr*)
ϭϩⲟⲥ^{S}, ϭⲁϩⲥⲉ^{S} (subst.) 'gazelle', **2** back, x+1/34 (n. *ev*)

CONCORDANCES OF NUMBERS

A. BY TEXT

Text no.	*Excavator's no.*	*Antiquities Service Register no.*	*Plate*
1	H5-DP1+2+2A	1598+1599+1600	1–3
1a	H5-DP523	5983	3
2	H5-DP153(A+B) +357+376	1751 (A+B)+ 2278+2297	4–9
3	71/72-DP79+84	5765+5770	10
4	71/72-DP161	5847	11
5	72/73-DP27	6163	11
6	H5-DP377	2298	12
7	H5-DP504	5964	12
8	H5-DP518	5978	12
9	71/72-DP108+ 116	5795+5802	13
10	H5-DP164	1762	13
11	H5-DP442	2363	14
12	72/73-DP26	6162	14
13	H5-DP524a	5984a	15
14	H5-DP524b	5984b	15
15	H5-DP524c	5984c	15
16	H5-DP524d	5984d	15
17	H5-DP524e	5984e	15
18	H5-DP524f	5984f	15
19	H5-DP524g	5984g	15
20	H5-DP524h	5984h	15
21	H5-DP524j	5984j	15
22	H5-17A[1]	661A	15
23	H5-17B[1]	661B	15
24	H5-DP204	1802	16
25	71/72-DP134	5820	16
26	71/72-DP156	5842	16
27	71/72-DP111+ 129+133	5797+5815+5819	17

B. BY ANTIQUITIES SERVICE REGISTER NO.

Antiquities Service Register no.	*Excavator's no.*	*Text no.*	*Plate*
661A	H5-17A[1]	**22**	15
661B	H5-17B[1]	**23**	15
1598	H5-DP1	**1**	1, 2
1599	H5-DP2	**1**	1, 2
1600	H5-DP2A	**1**	3
1751 (A+B)	H5-DP153 (A+B)	**2**	4, 6
1762	H5-DP164	**10**	13
1802	H5-DP204	**24**	16
2278	H5-DP357	**2**	4, 6
2297	H5-DP376	**2**	4, 6
2298	H5-DP377	**6**	12
2363	H5-DP442	**11**	14
5765	71/72-DP79	**3**	10
5770	71/72-DP84	**3**	10
5795	71/72-DP108	**9**	13
5797	71/72-DP111	**27**	17
5802	71/72-DP116	**9**	13
5815	71/72-DP129	**27**	17
5819	71/72-DP133	**27**	17
5820	71/72-DP134	**25**	16
5842	71/72-DP156	**26**	16
5847	71/72-DP161	**4**	11
5964	H5-DP504	**7**	12
5978	H5-DP518	**8**	12
5983	H5-DP523	**1a**	3
5984a–j	H5-DP524a–j	**13–21**	15
6162	72/73-DP26	**12**	14
6163	72/73-DP27	**5**	11

[1]These two papyri were registered under object numbers before the papyrus registration numbers were started in 1966/7.

PLATES

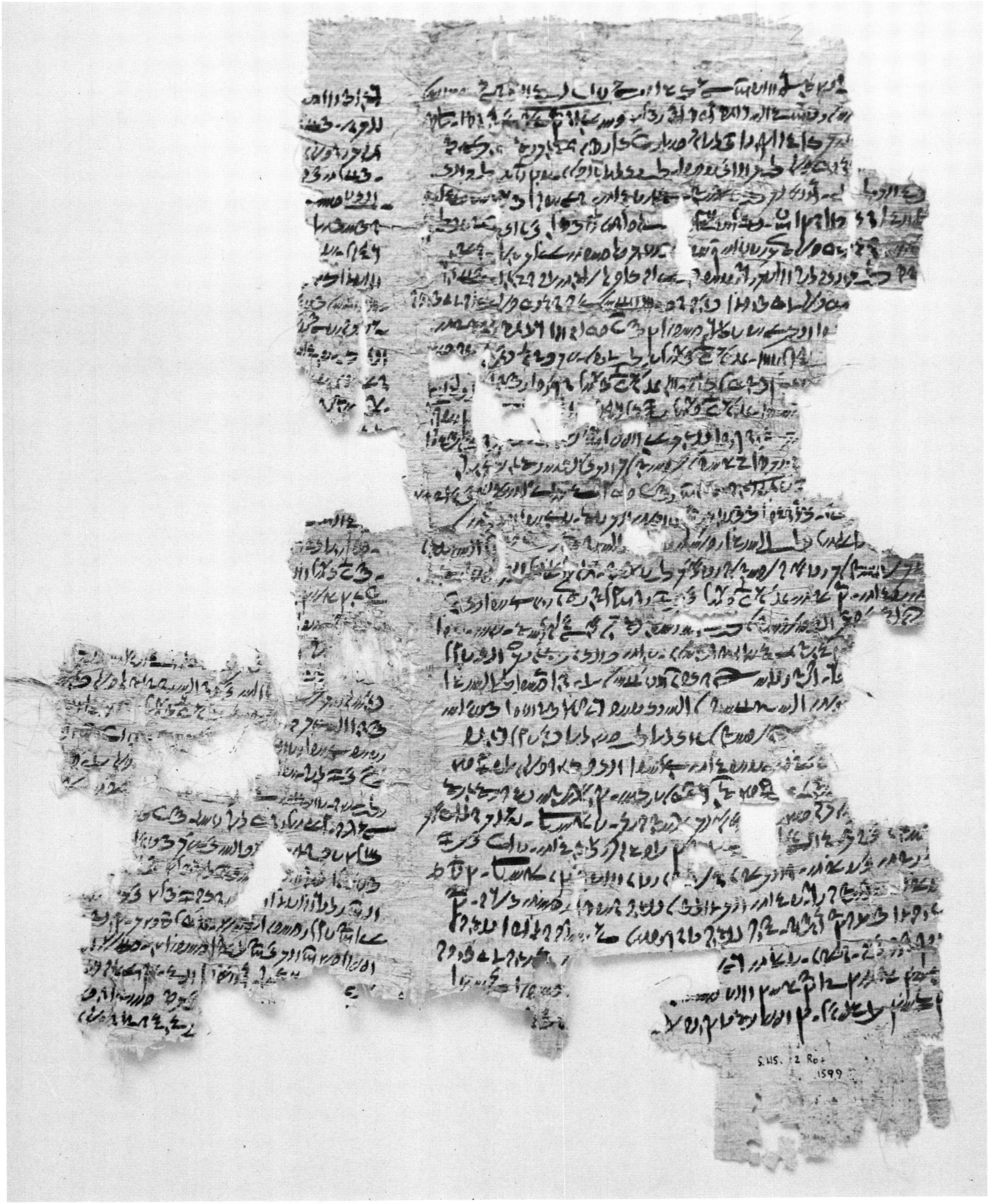

Text 1, front: fr. 3 (cols. 9–10)

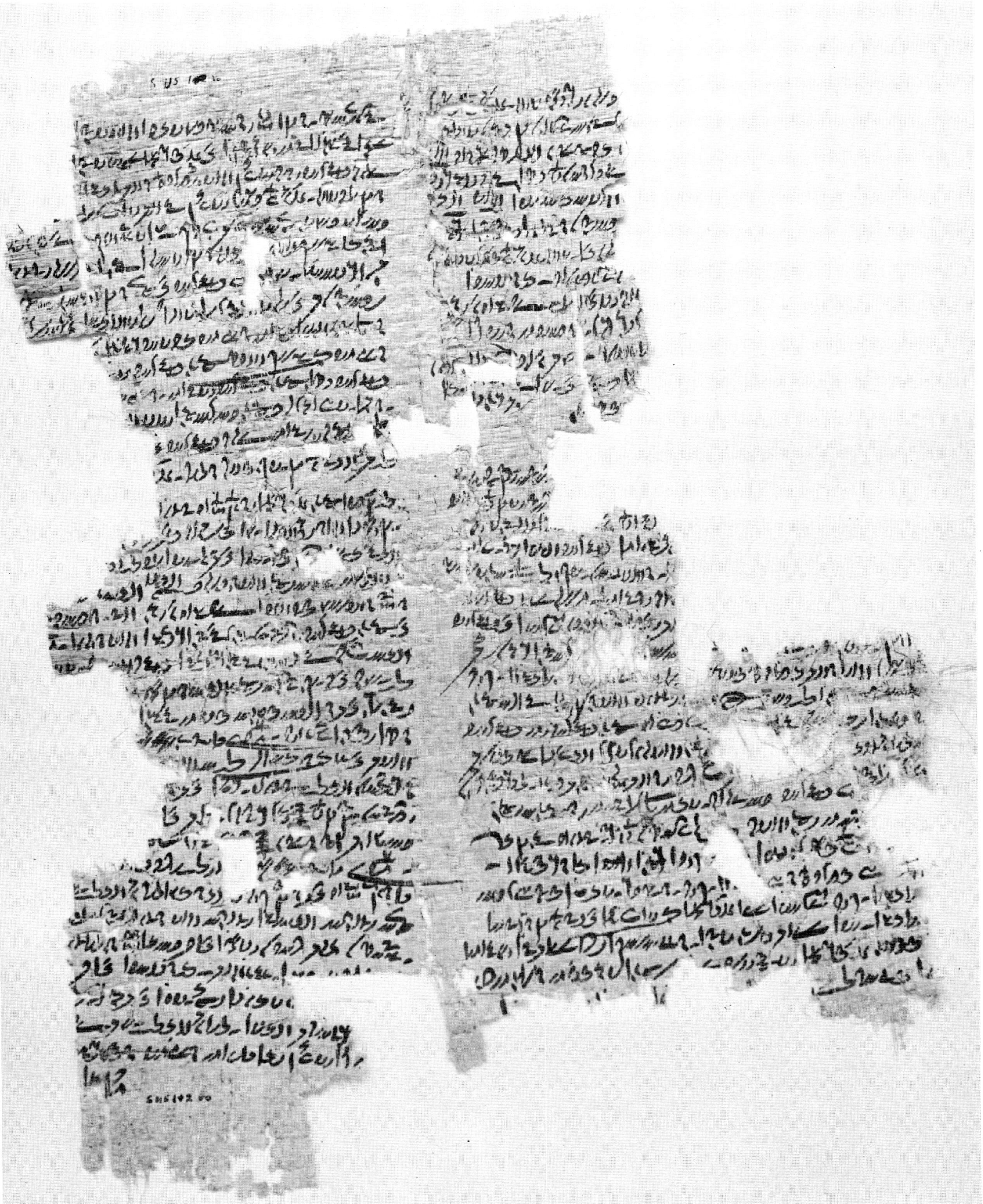

Text 1, back: fr. 3 (cols. 13–14)

a. Text **1**, front: frs. 1–2, 4–5

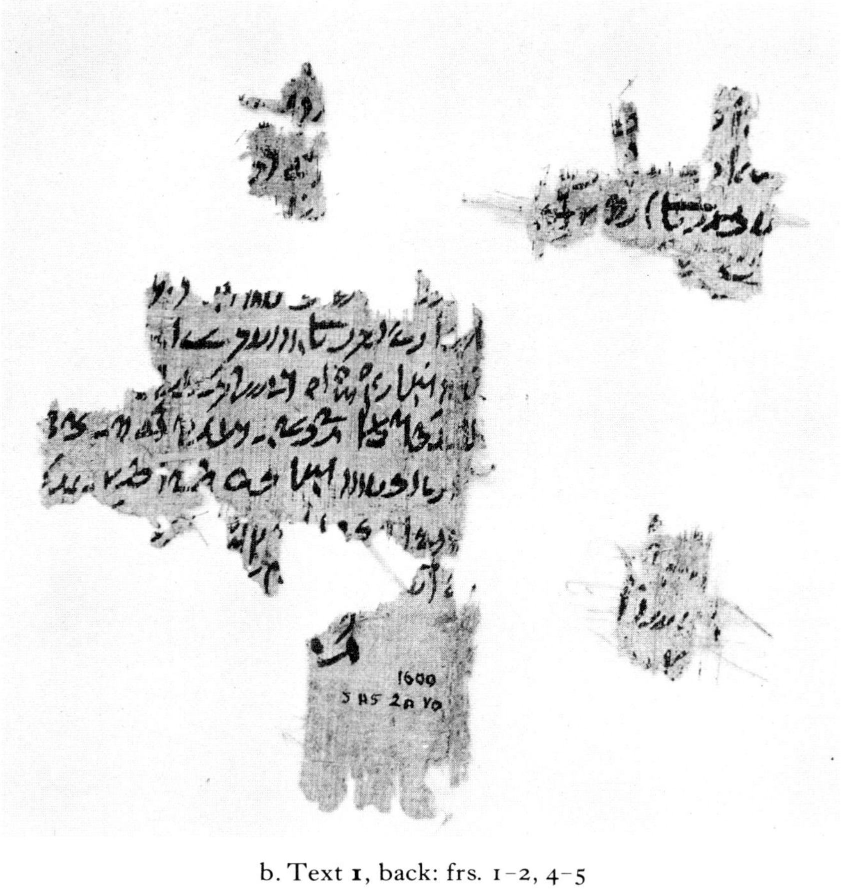

b. Text **1**, back: frs. 1–2, 4–5

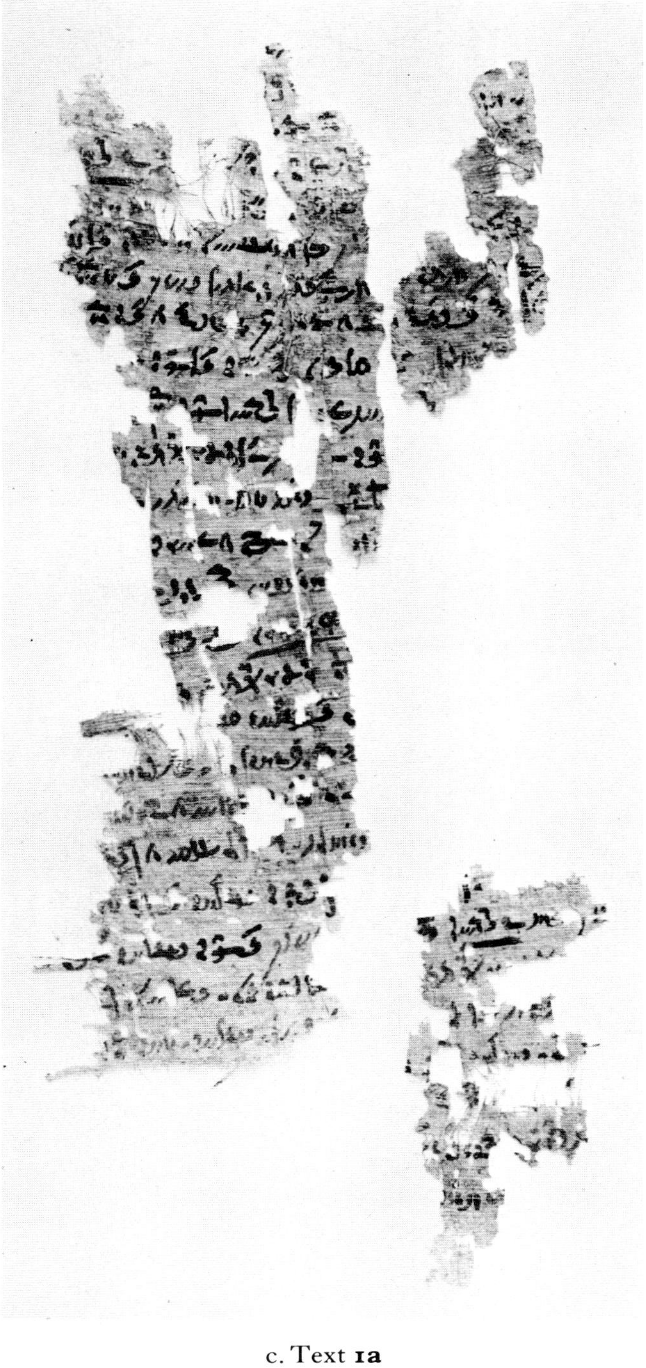

c. Text **1a**

Text **2**, front

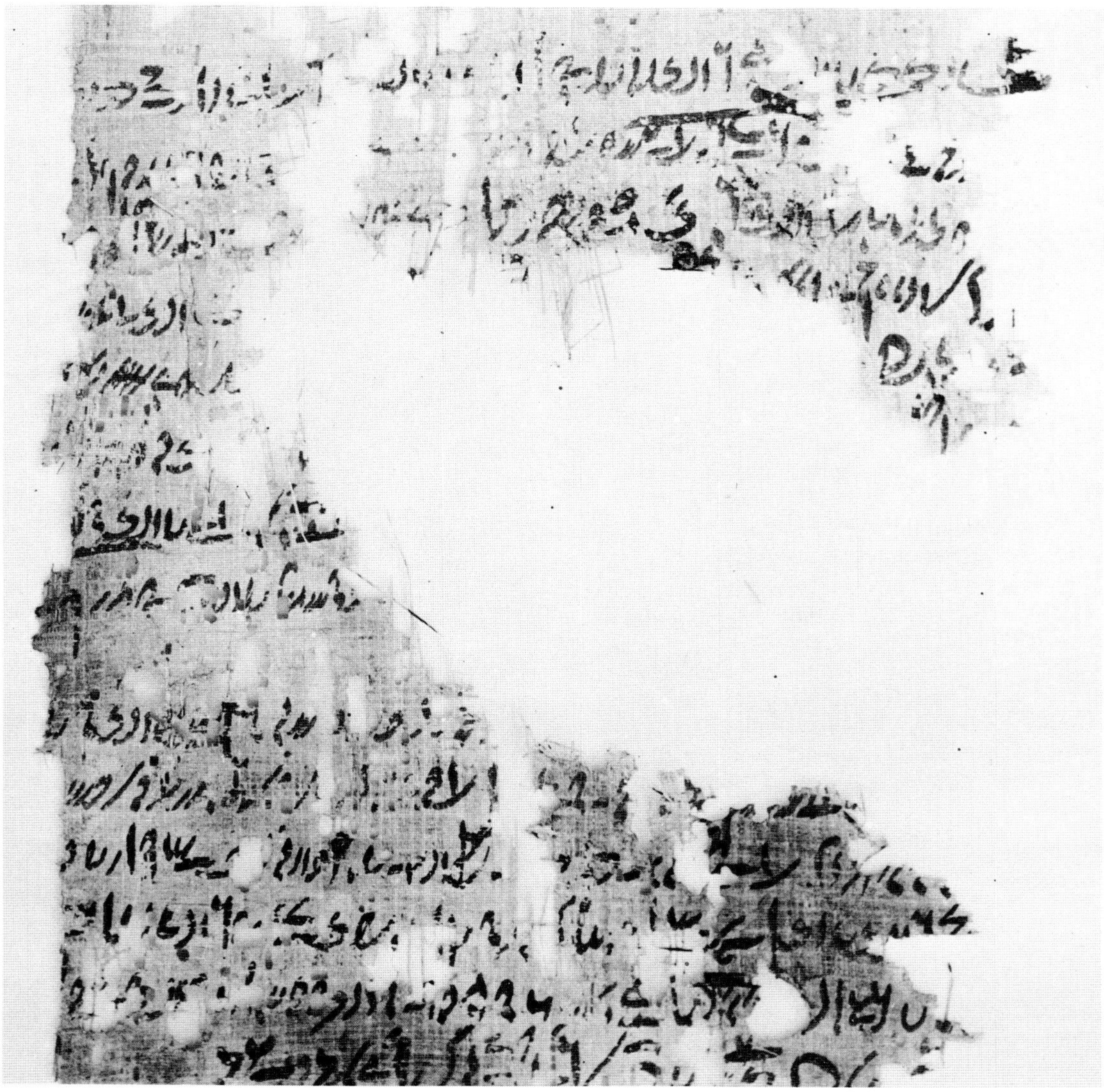

a. Text 2, front, detail

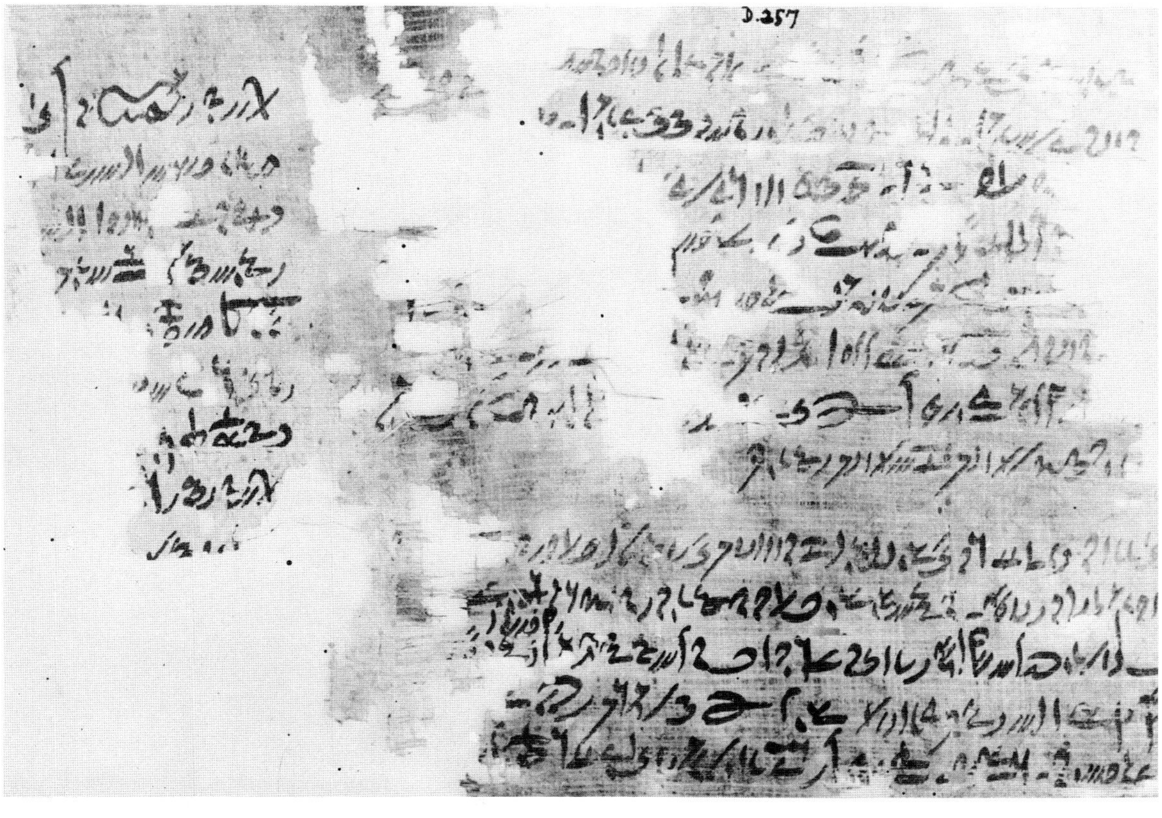

b. Text 2, front, detail

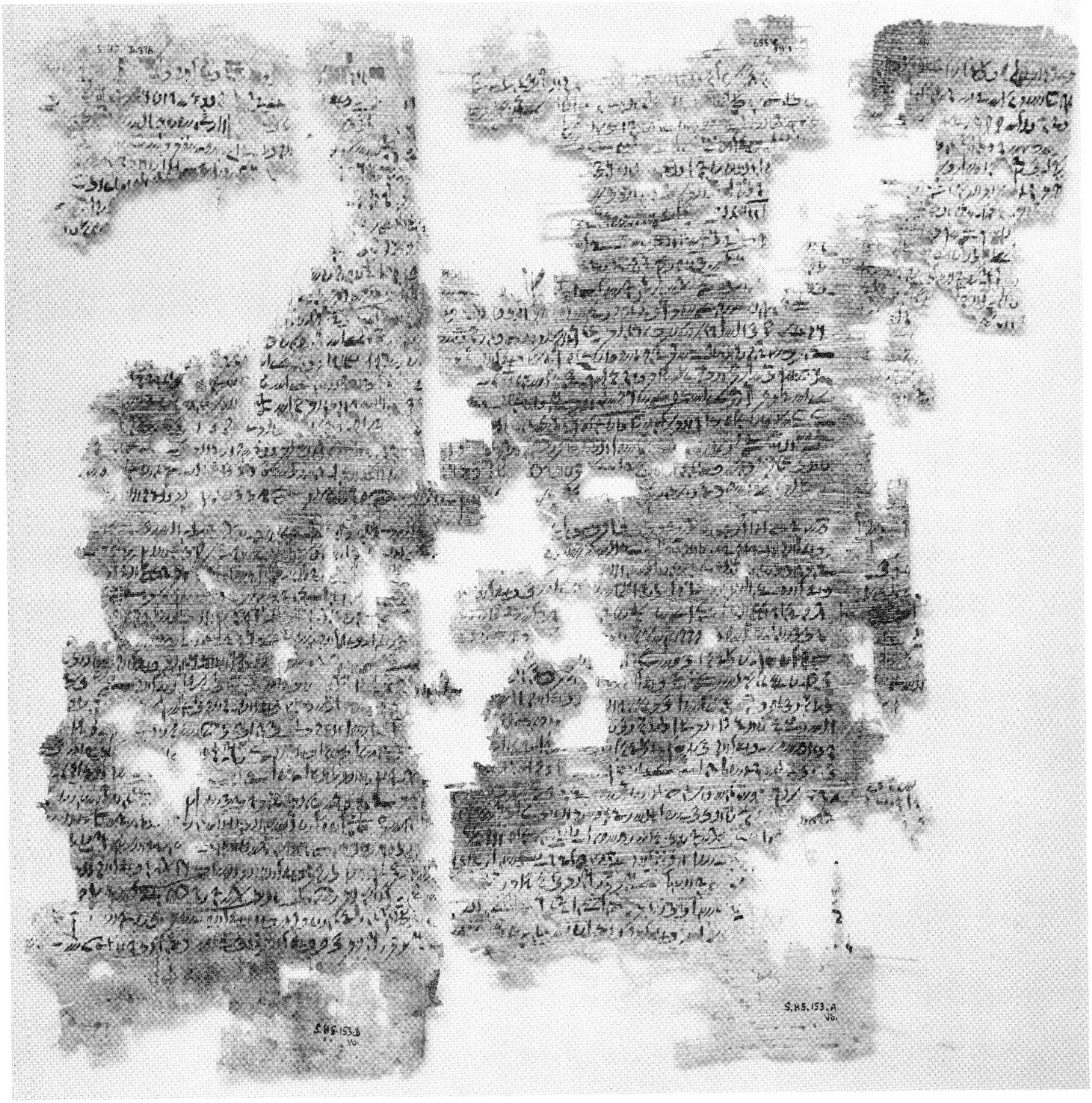

Text **2**, back

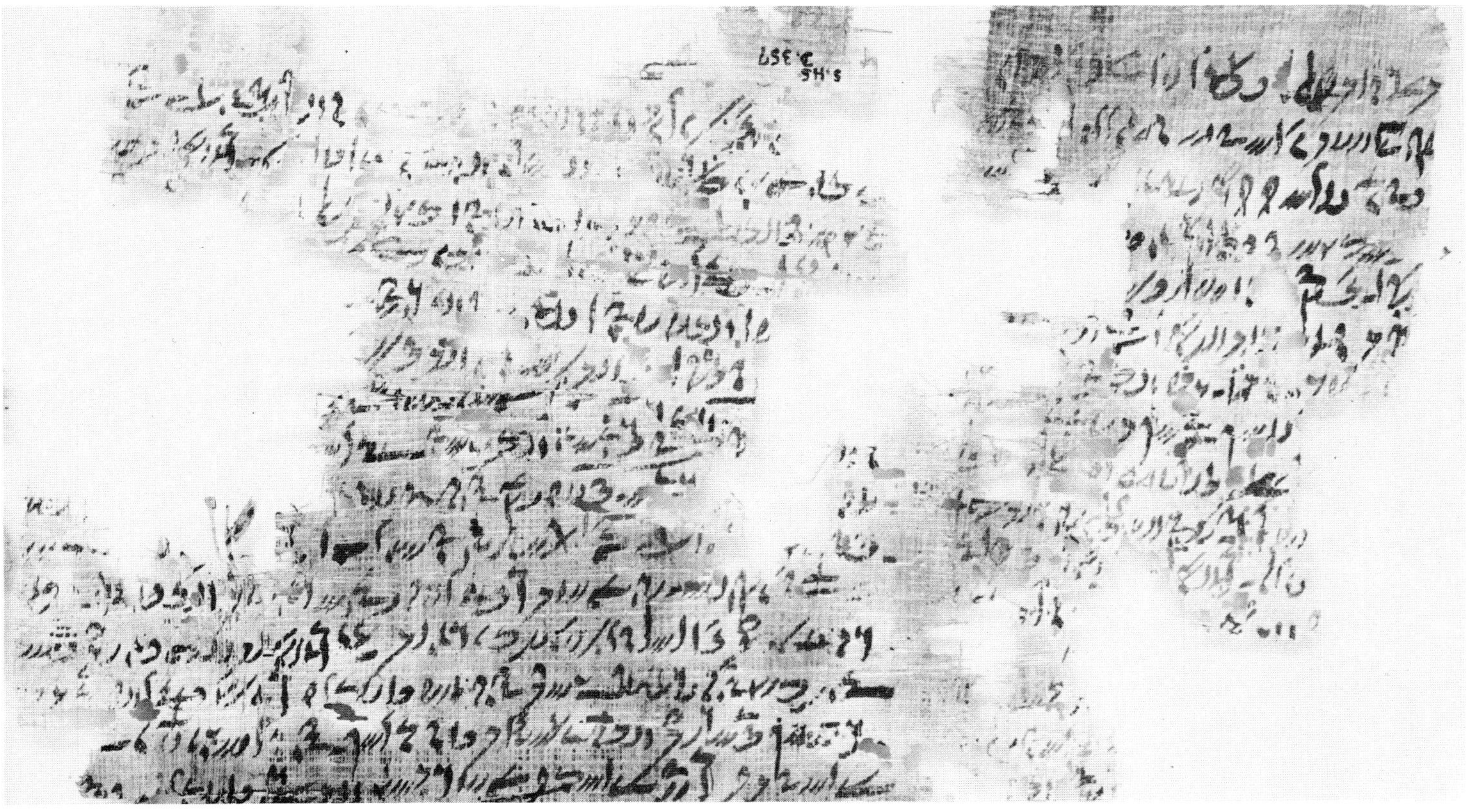

a. Text **2**, back, detail

b. Text **2**, back, detail

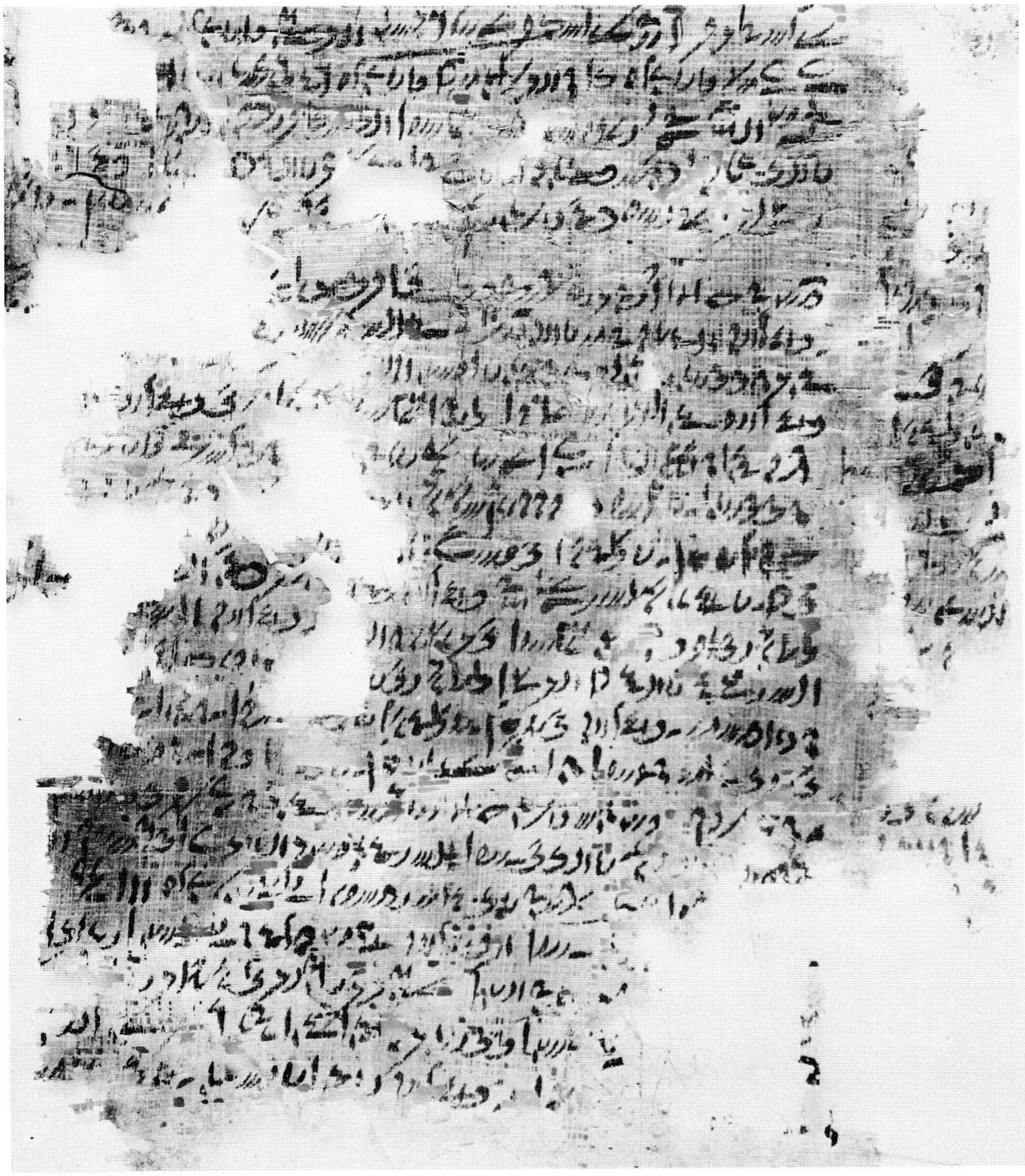

Text **2**, back, detail

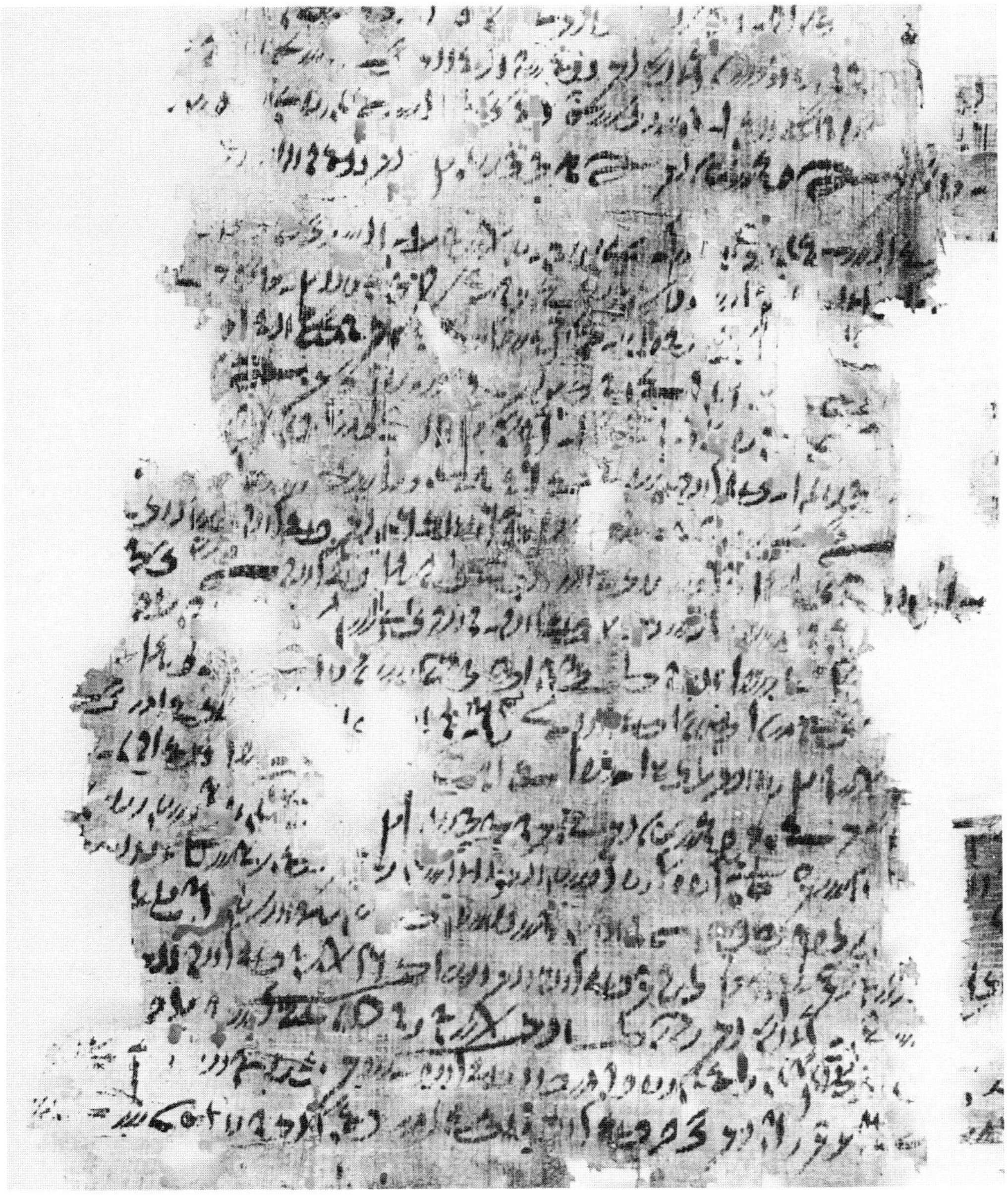

Text **2**, back, detail

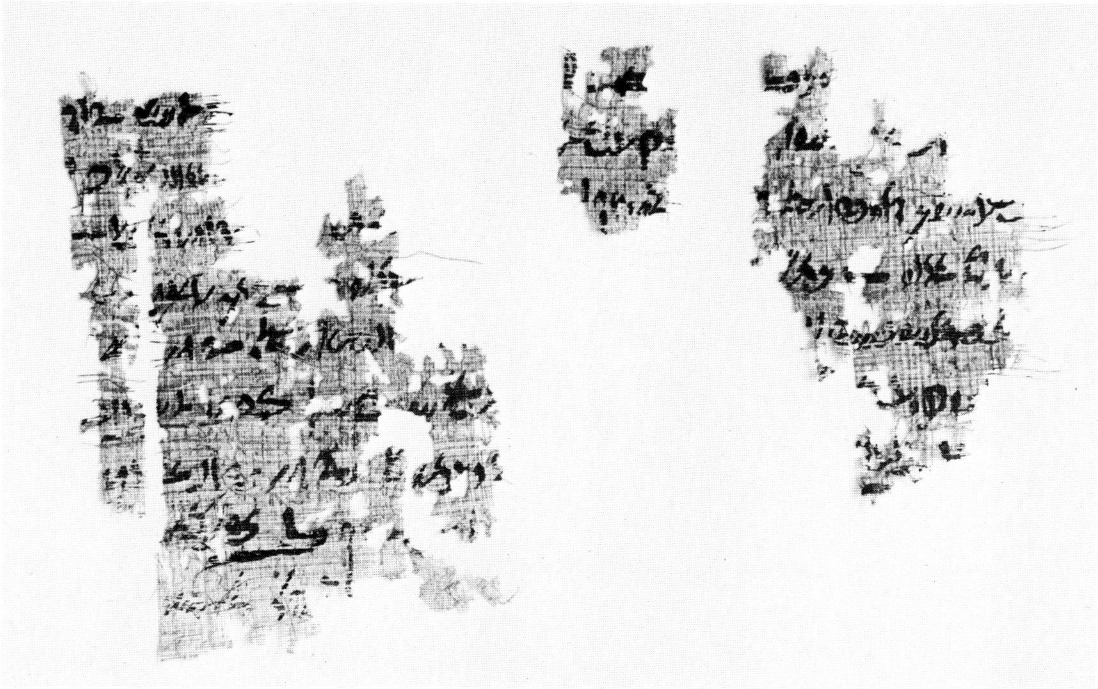

a. Text **3**, front

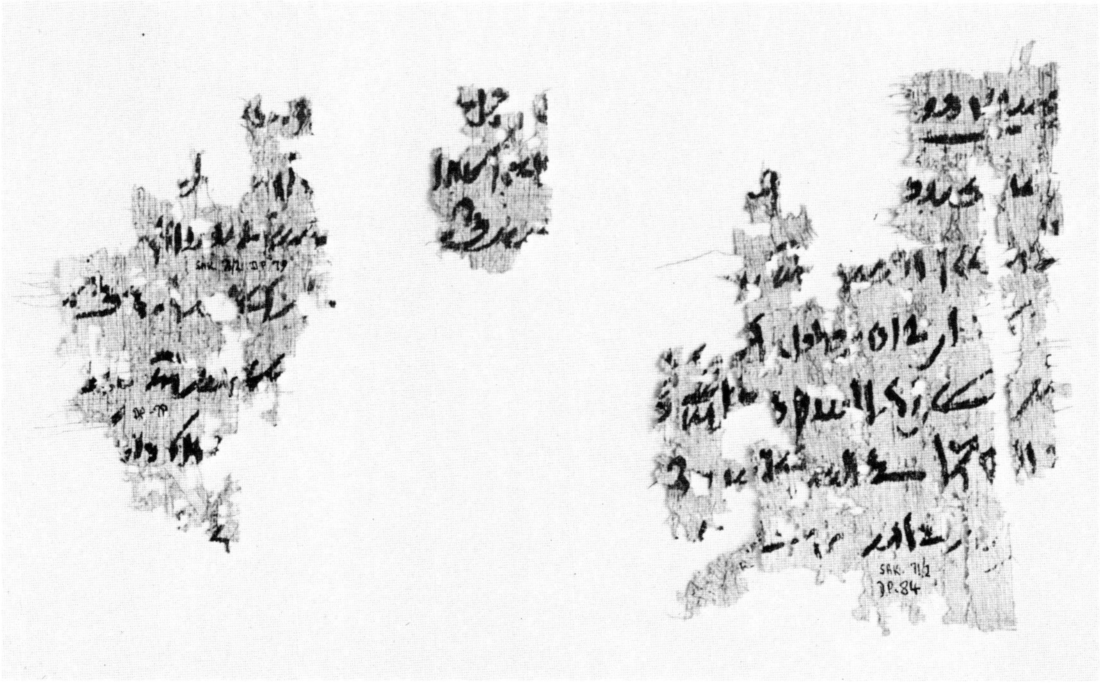

b. Text **3**, back

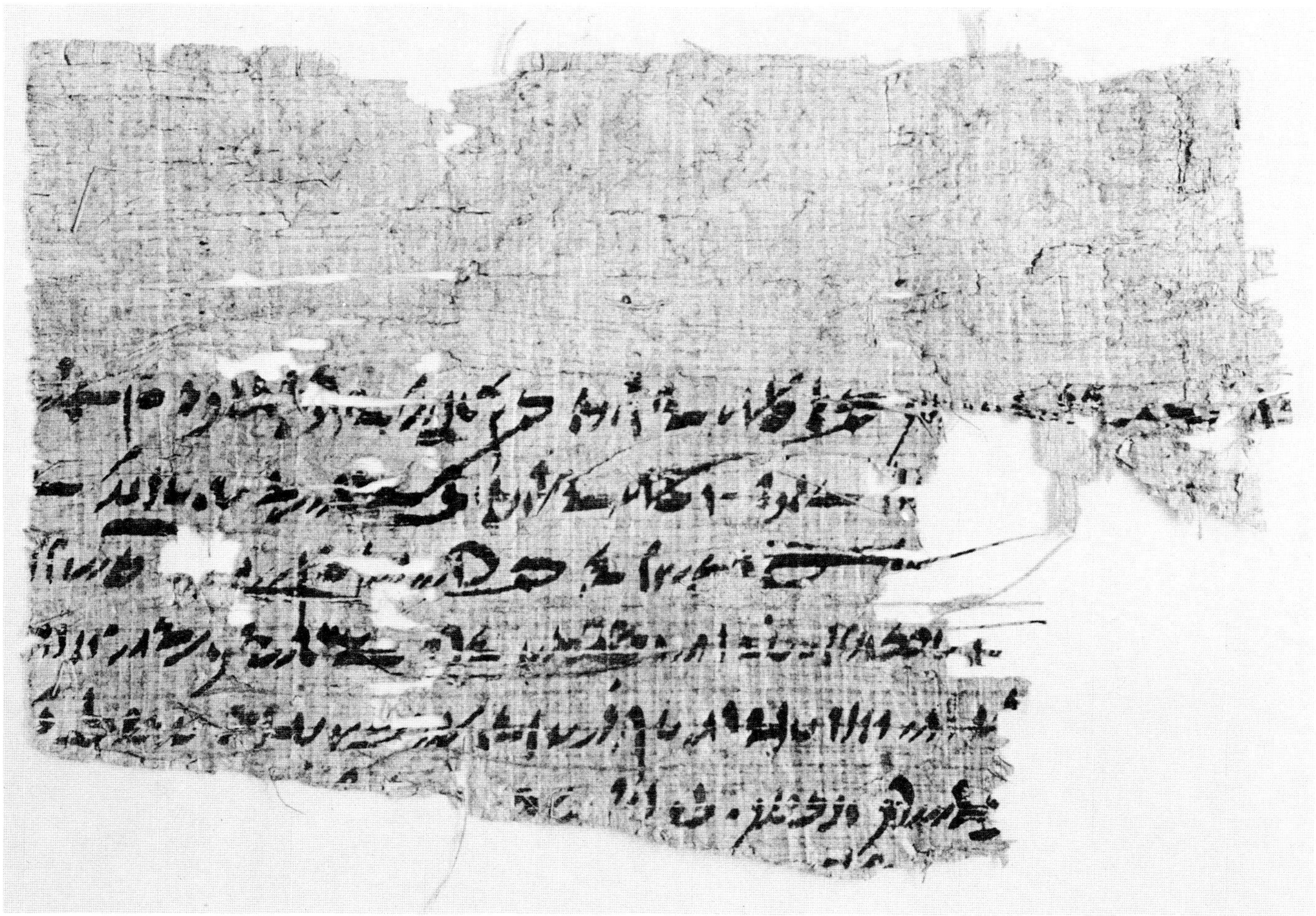

a. Text **4**

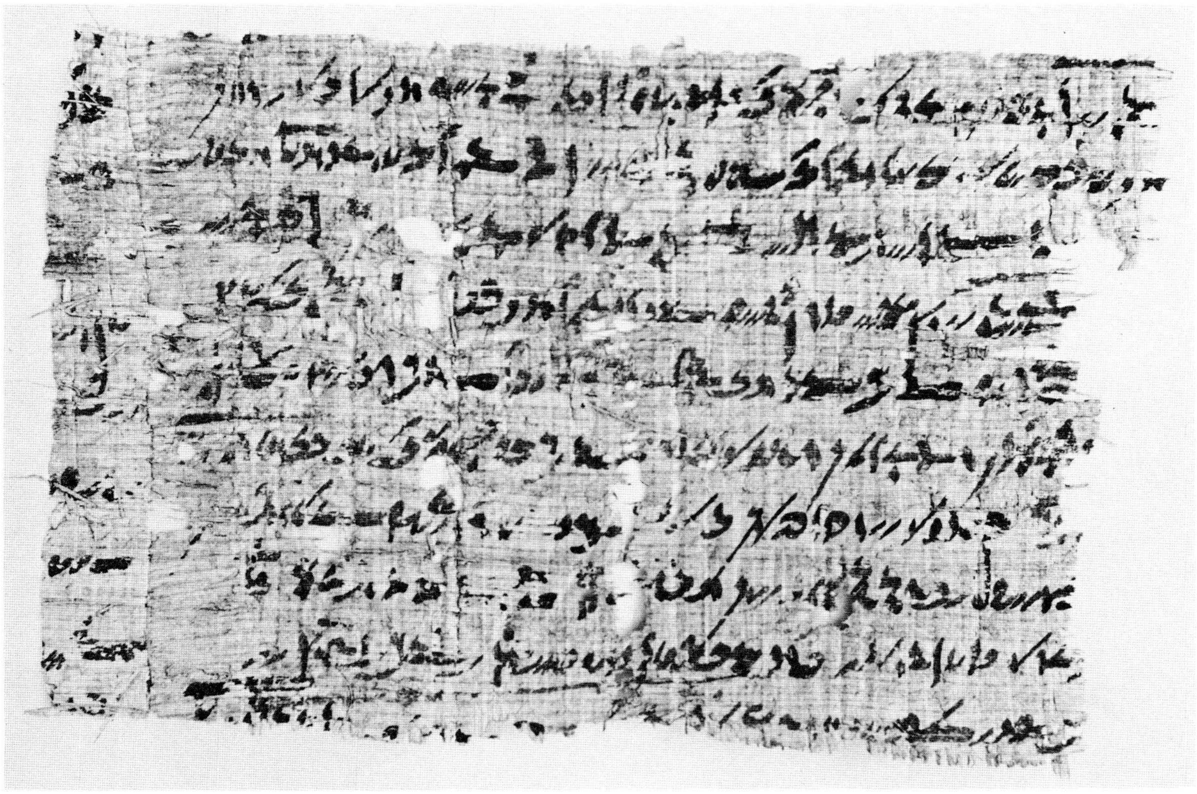

b. Text **5**

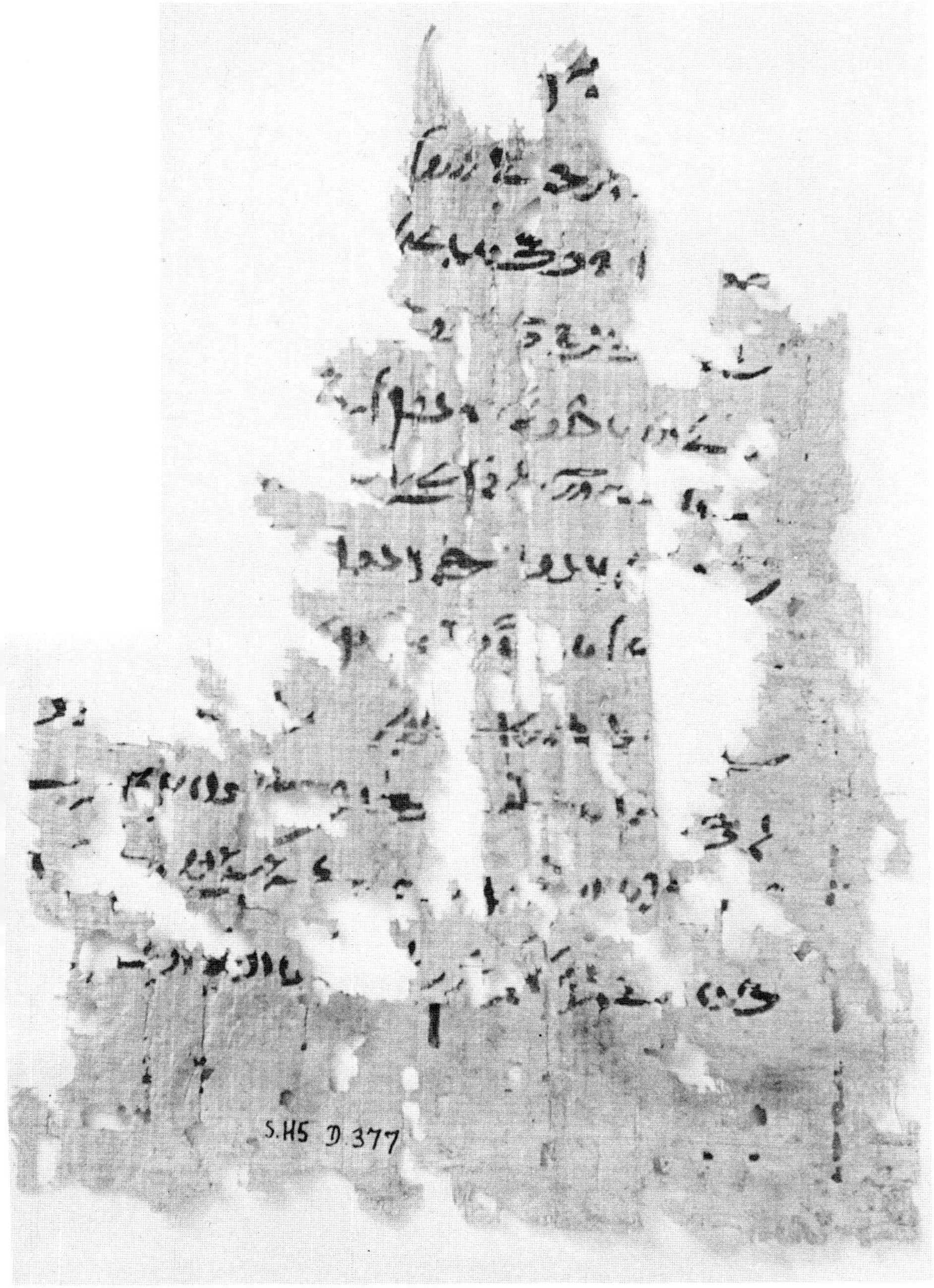

a. Text **6**

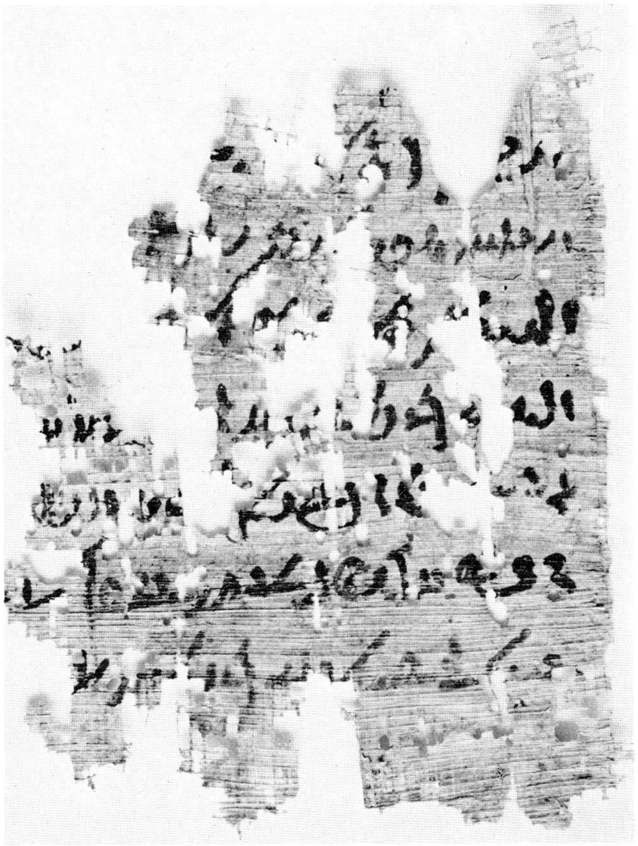

b. Text **7**

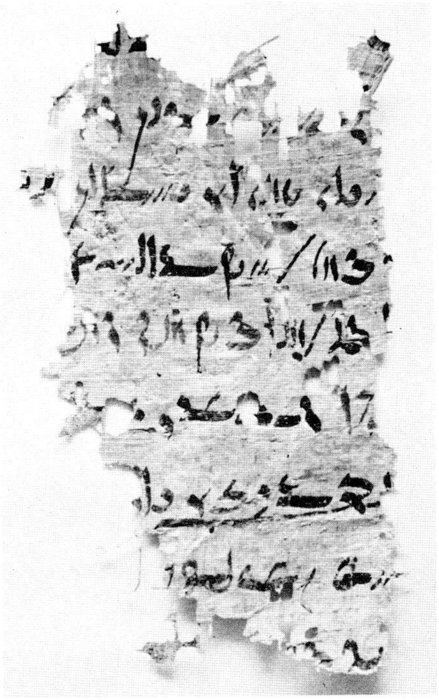

c. Text **8**

b. Text **10**, front

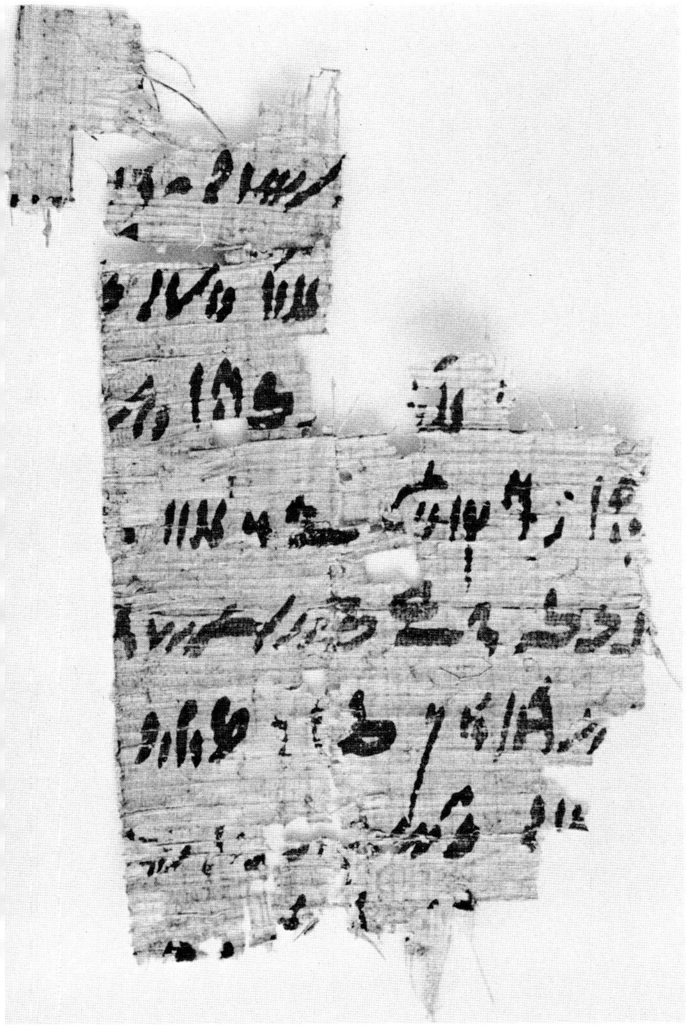

a. Text **9**

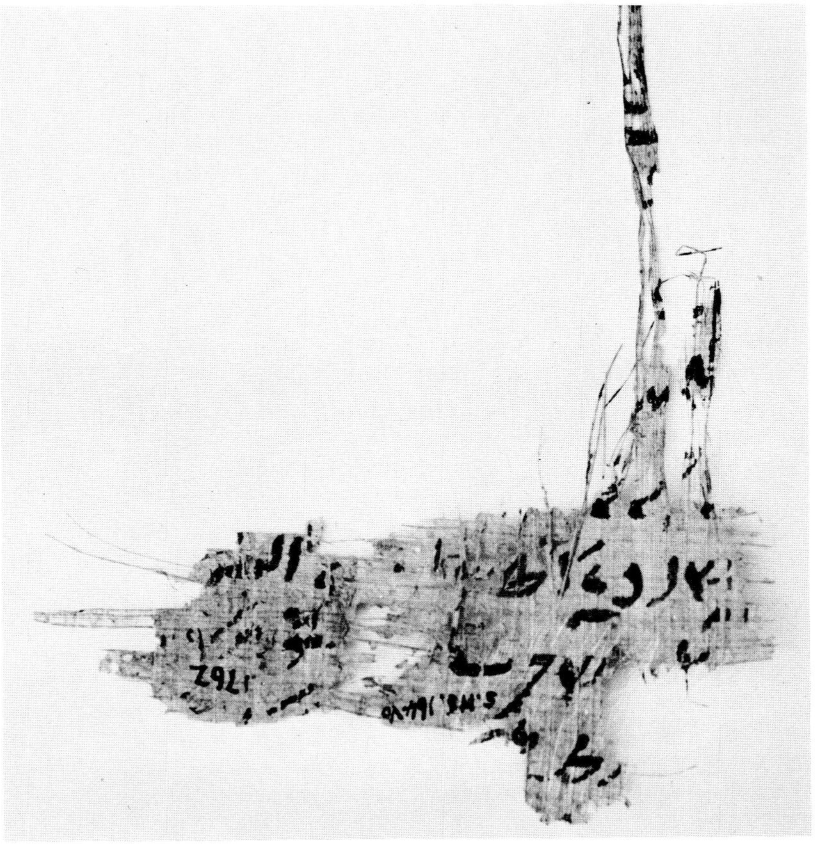

c. Text **10**, back

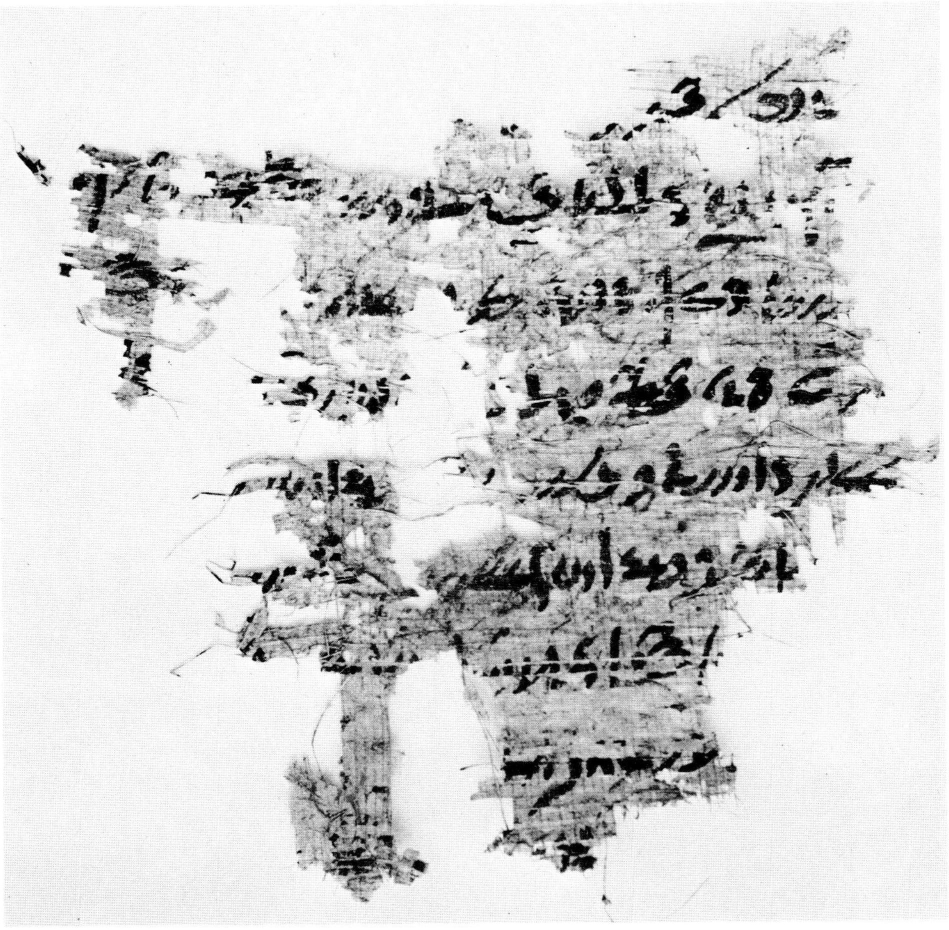

a. Text **11**

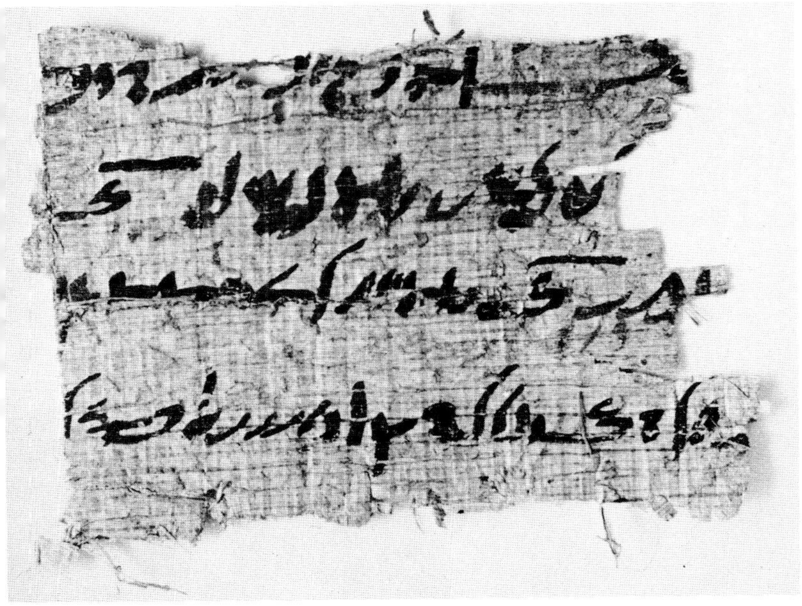

b. Text **12**, front

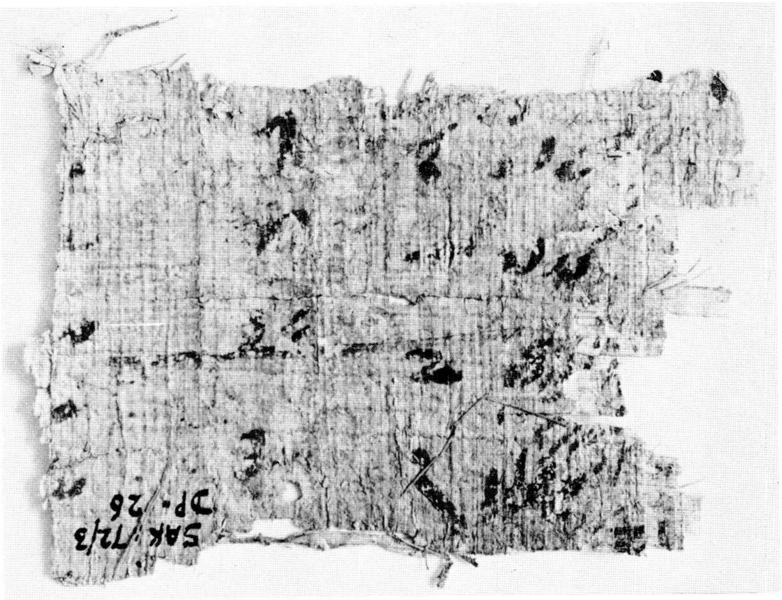

c. Text **12**, back

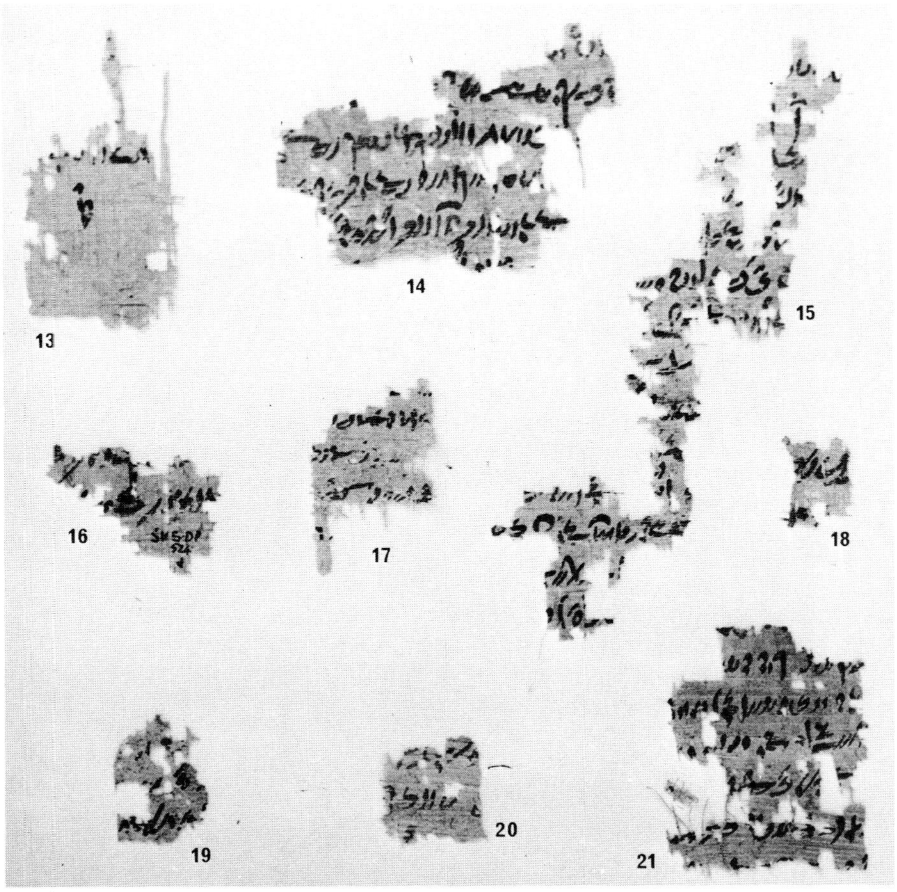

a. Texts **13–21**, front

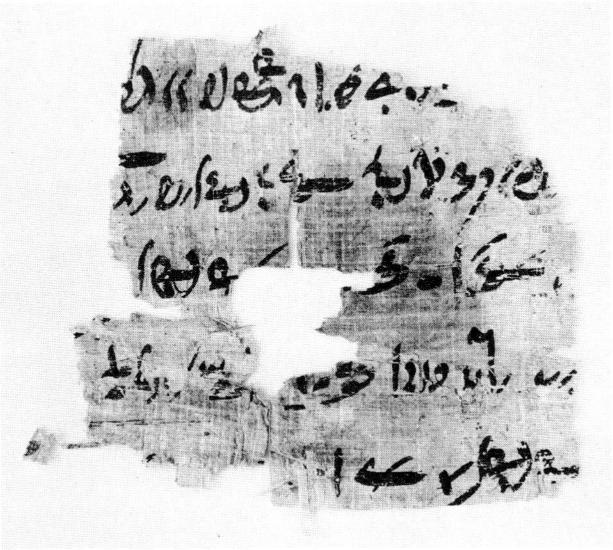

c. Text **22**

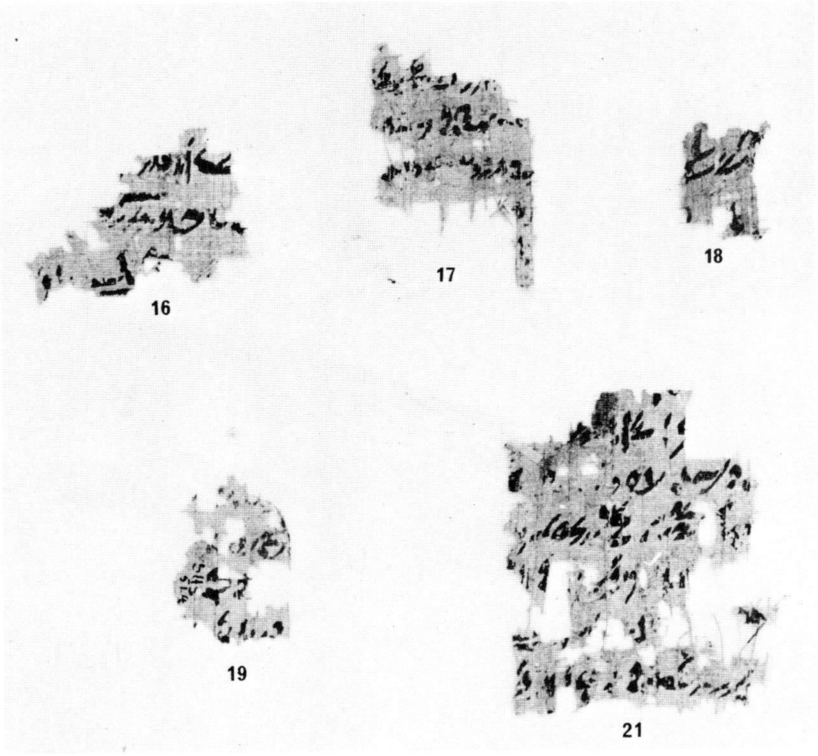

b. Texts **16–19**, **21**, back

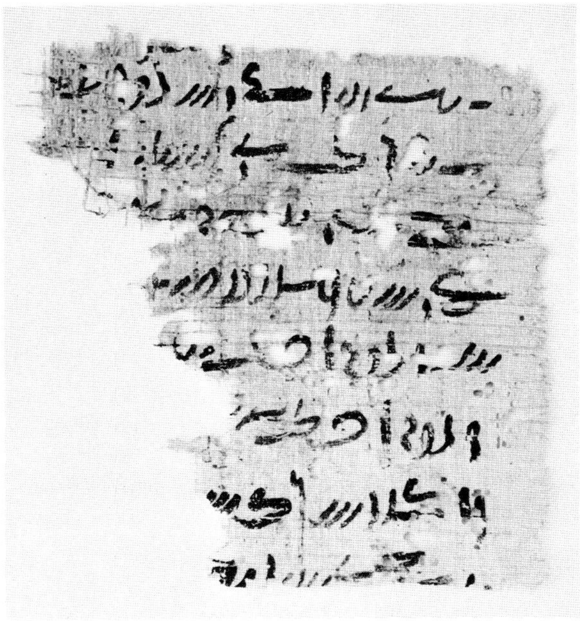

d. Text **23**

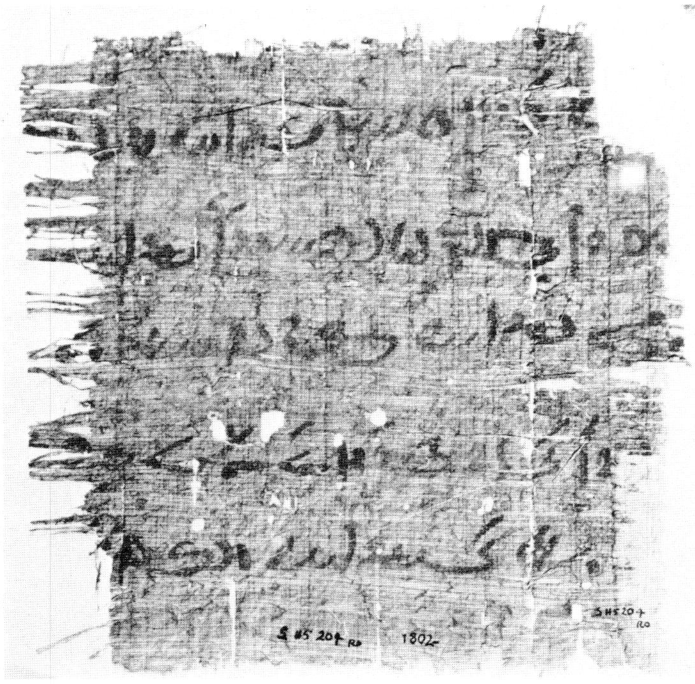

a. Text **24**

c. Text **26**

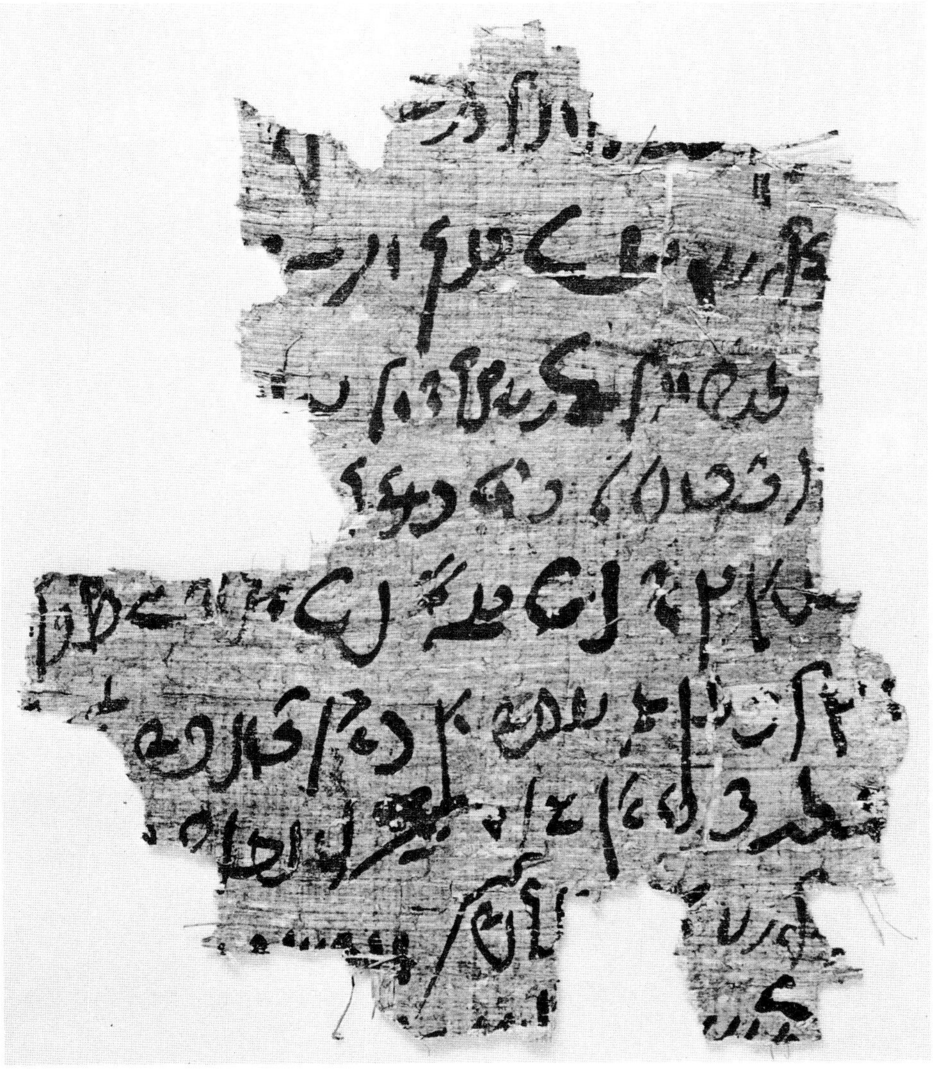

b. Text **25**

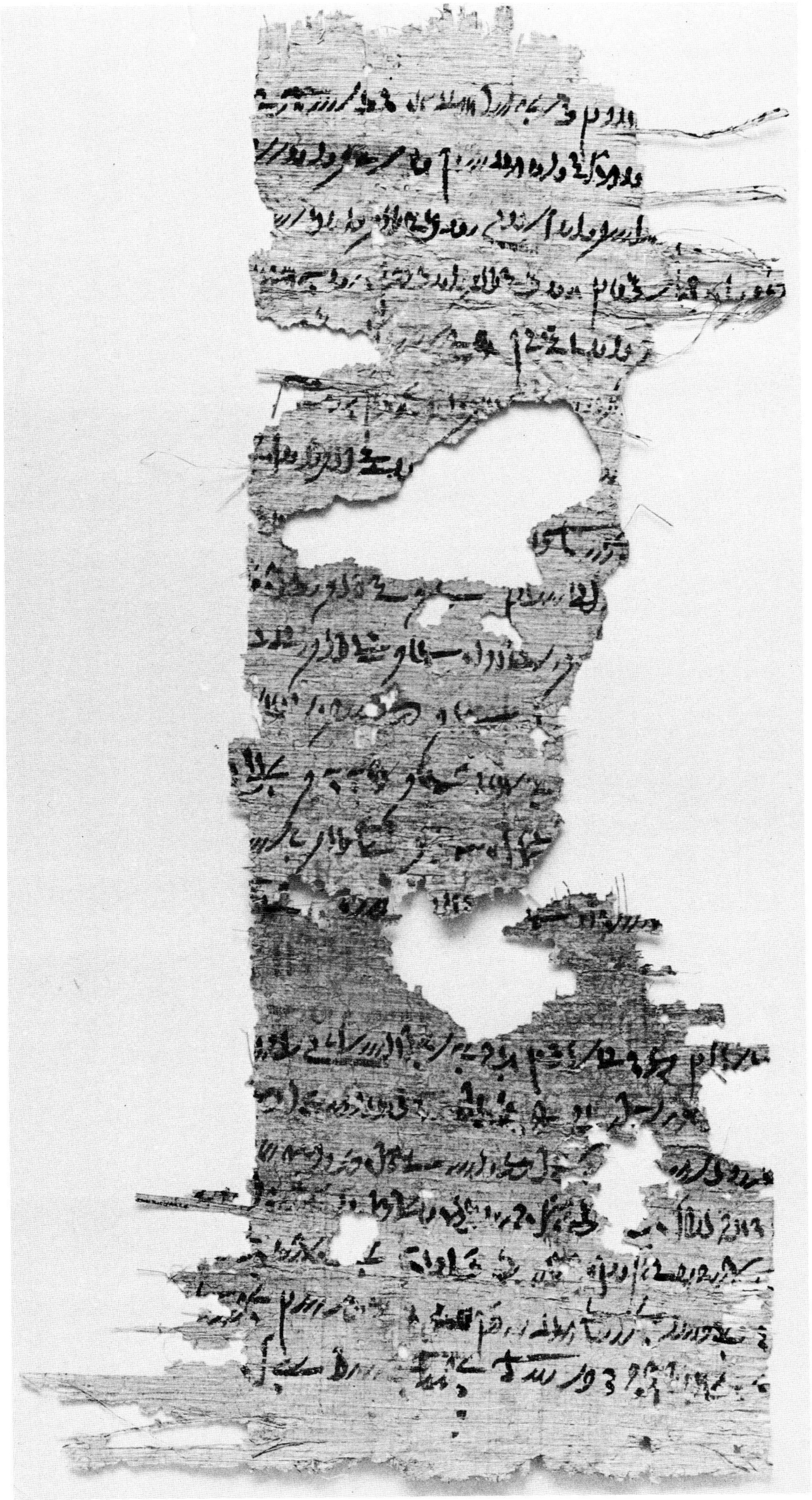

Text **27**